THE DYNAMIC FIRM

THE DYNAMIC FIRM

The Role of Technology, Strategy, Organization, and Regions

Edited by

ALFRED D. CHANDLER, JR., PETER
HAGSTRÖM and ÖRJAN SÖLVELL

OXFORD
UNIVERSITY PRESS

OXFORD

UNIVERSITY PRESS

Great Clarendon Street, Oxford OX2 6DP

Oxford University Press is a department of the University of Oxford.
It furthers the University's objective of excellence in research, scholarship,
and education by publishing worldwide in

Oxford New York

Athens Auckland Bangkok Bogotá Buenos Aires Calcutta
Cape Town Chennai Dar es Salaam Delhi Florence Hong Kong Istanbul
Karachi Kuala Lumpur Madrid Melbourne Mexico City Mumbai
Nairobi Paris São Paulo Singapore Taipei Tokyo Toronto Warsaw
with associated companies in Berlin Ibadan

Published in the United States
by Oxford University Press Inc., New York

First published in paperback 1999

British Library Cataloguing in Publication Data
Data available

Library of Congress Cataloging in Publication Data
Data available

ISBN 0-19-829052-7 (hbk.)
ISBN 0-19-829604-5 (pbk.)

3 5 7 9 10 8 6 4 2

Printed in Great Britain
on acid-free paper by
Biddles Ltd, Guildford
and King's Lynn

This book is dedicated to the memory of
Gunnar Hedlund

PREFACE

This is an edited volume of the revised papers that originally were presented at the Third Prince Bertil Symposium on the Dynamic Firm in Stockholm, June 1994. The symposium was organized by Professors Alfred D. Chandler, Jr., Peter Hagström and Michael E. Porter of the Harvard Business School, Paul Krugman of the Massachusetts Institute of Technology, and Gunnar Hedlund and Örjan Sölvell of the Institute of International Business, IIB. The practical arrangements were assumed by IIB at the Stockholm School of Economics.

A small number of scholars drawn from different disciplines were invited to present their thoughts on different approaches on the evolution of the firm. The main thrust of the symposium was to approach the firm from either a technological, strategic/organizational or geographical vantage point. The objective was to stimulate a creative discussion in order to take the first steps towards bridging these perspectives. The concluding session on the Dynamic Firm with Professors Alfred Chandler, Paul Krugman, Richard Nelson, Michael Porter and Nathan Rosenberg as panelists was particularly provocative, generating new insights on and ideas for an emerging research agenda.

The structure of the book reflects the three themes of the symposium, and the included papers have benefited from the input from designated reviewers and the ensuing exceedingly lively debate. Contrary to tradition, each paper was presented by the discussant and the author's role was relegated to that of participant, but with the right of first reply to the presentations.

We hope that this book will trigger challenging new cross-disciplinary research regarding dynamic aspects of the firm: a topic hitherto under-researched and not well understood. The ambition to foster "transdisciplinary" research fits well with IIB's overall aim and scope, and owes much to Gunnar Hedlund who, very sadly, passed away in April 1997.

Editorial and practical assistance by Ms Vanja Ekberg and Mr Niclas Lilja, both of IIB, and by Mr John Callow, are gratefully acknowledged.

Finally, we would like to thank the Prince Bertil Foundation for providing financial support for the symposium.

Stockholm and Boston   Alfred D. Chandler, Jr.
April 1997   Peter Hagström
                                                                              Örjan Sölvell

ACKNOWLEDGEMENTS

Allen J. Scott, "The Geographic Foundations of Industrial Performance", *Competition and Change*, 1: 51–66. Reprinted by permission of Harwood Academic Publishers.

Reprinted from *Information Economics and Policy*, Vol. 6, Cristiano Antonelli, "Localized Technological Change and the Evolution of Standards as Economic Institutions", pp. 195–216, 1995 with kind permission from Elsevier Science-NL, Sara Burgerhartstraat 25, 1055 KV Amsterdam, The Netherlands.

Ikujiro Nonaka and Hirotaka Takeuchi, "A Theory of the Firm's Knowledge-Creation Dynamics", from *The Knowledge-Creating Company* by Ikujiro Nonaka and Hirotaka Takeuchi. Copyright © 1995 by Oxford University Press. Used by permission of Oxford University Press, Inc.

John Cantwell, "The Gobalization of Technology: What Remains of the Product-Cycle Model?", *Cambridge Journal of Economics*, 19:155–74, 1995. Used by permission of Oxford University Press.

CONTENTS

LIST OF FIGURES

LIST OF TABLES

LIST OF CONTRIBUTORS

Cristiano Antonelli, Professor, Dipartimento di Economia, Università Degli Studi di Torino

John Cantwell, Professor, Department of Economics, University of Reading

Alfred D. Chandler, Jr., Professor, Harvard Business School

Benjamin Coriat, Professor, U.F.R. de Sciènces Economiques et de Gestion, Université Paris-Nord

Giovanni Dosi, Professor, Dipartimento di Scienze Economiche, Università Degli Studi di Roma "La Sapienza"

John H. Dunning, Professor, Graduate School of Management, Rutgers University

Michael J. Enright, Professor, Harvard Business School

Takahiro Fujimoto, Professor, Faculty of Economics, University of Tokyo

Masahisa Fujita, Professor, Department of Economics, University of Pennsylvania, Philadelphia

Peter Hagström, Professor, Institute of International Business, Stockholm School of Economics

Gunnar Hedlund, Professor, Institute of International Business, Stockholm School of Economics

Ryoichi Ishii, Professor, Department of Economics, University of Pennsylvania, Philadelphia

Lars-Gunnar Mattsson, Professor, Centre for Marketing, Distribution and Industry Dynamics, Stockholm School of Economics

Richard Nelson, Professor, School of International and Public Affairs, Columbia University

Ikujiro Nonaka, Professor, Institute of Business Research, Hitotsubashi University, Tokyo

Pari Patel, Professor, Science Policy Research Unit, University of Sussex

Keith Pavitt, Professor, Science Policy Research Unit, University of Sussex

Michael E. Porter, Professor, Harvard Business School

Nathan Rosenberg, Professor, Stanford University

Allen J. Scott, Professor, University of California, Los Angeles

J.-C. Spender, Professor, Rutgers University

Örjan Sölvell, Professor, Institute of International Business, Stockholm School of Economics

Hirotaka Takeuchi, Professor, Institute of Business Research, Hitotsubashi University, Tokyo

David J. Teece, Professor, University of California, Berkeley

Eric Von Hippel, Professor, Alfred P. Sloan School of Management, Massachusetts Institute of Technology

Ivo Zander, Professor, Institute of International Business, Stockholm School of Economics

1

Perspectives on Firm Dynamics

PETER HAGSTRÖM
WITH
ALFRED D. CHANDLER, JR.

Partial theories of the underlying long-run competitiveness of firms abound. However, more complete theories of explaining the functioning of, and change in, firms in an ever more internationalized environment still seem elusive. Perhaps we have reached the limit of approaches firmly anchored in one of the various subdisciplines when it comes to the question of understanding the firm as it evolves over time.

However, this is not to say that different academic fields are not approaching the area of dynamic firm behavior. Economists are to a larger extent aware of the economic significance of discretionary firm differences. Voluntarism is now more commonly emphasized at the expense of determinism. The unique firm is receiving more attention. On the other hand, recent research in the fields of strategy and organization brings in deterministic elements to an increasing degree. We have here the contours of an emerging field where researchers are seeking to understand dynamism within constraints; constraints which are found in the external environment as well as within the organization. There is also a rejuvenated interest in the large and complex—often global—firm, and in its internal efficiency; again downplaying the role of the external environment and deterministic adaptation.

These developments notwithstanding, one way to break free from traditional academic demarcations, and to stimulate new thinking, is to make available, and to juxtapose, different approaches to a single topic. Here, the topic is the dynamic firm, and the perspectives offered are those that take their point of departure in seeing the firm fundamentally as being characterized by the technology it employs, in deriving firm behavior primarily from the strategy employed and the organization in place, and in concentrating on the firm's geographical embeddedness and its role in regional economies. Of course, there are overlaps (and also some conflicting arguments), but they are indeed to be welcomed as they indicate both inquisitiveness and vitality.

1. TECHNOLOGY

Our understanding of what technology really is and how technological change processes come about has grown significantly in the last years, not least as a result of advances within the industrial organization field and of the arrival of new growth economics. Technology is no longer seen as a simple residual, but a concept involving many facets. Moreover, the technology field has moved our view of technological shifts from being seen only as exogenous shocks to an enhanced understanding of endogenous elements in the creation of new technology and in the stimulation of growth. Gone is the firm that perfectly and seamlessly adapted to changes in the external environment.

A one-dimensional view of technology has been replaced by an appreciation of technology as more complex, embodying different elements that go beyond the traditional ones of high and low technology, and of product and process technology. In addition, the broader concept of knowledge and the creation of knowledge have cast doubt over the traditional information-processing view of technology. Technology is now more often defined as an interplay between hardware, software, "organization-ware", "human-ware" and other types of invisible assets.

Firm-level technological change is increasingly understood as a growth process, in turn primarily driven by endogenous processes within firms (e.g. firm trajectories, organizational routines, searching zones) as well as within regional settings (e.g. industrial districts, clusters, development blocks, national trajectories). The evolutionary process involves a search for and adoption of new technologies (for instance, from the scientific community), exploitation (voluntary dissemination) and imitation (involuntary dissemination). Pressures from competition, other new technologies and from visionary challenges posed by management seem to add impetus to the innovation process.

The dynamics inherent in technology translates into dissemination and transfer of technology, and into combination of different technologies. A new literature is emerging, bringing inertia and trajectories to the forefront, thus limiting the impact of strategic choice. Moreover, the sometimes advanced perception that these trajectories to some extent are embedded in the environment connects them to regions and geographical districts.

Similarly, the now classical product life-cycle view, based on initial creation combined with dominant designs, is undergoing changes. The process of creation followed by a period of exploitation is questioned by the arrival of the idea of continuous innovation. Hence, technological change also links back to traditionally deterministic forces found in competition and other environmental pressures.

Takahiro Fujimoto's contribution to this volume in Chapter 2 tackles firm evolutionary capabilities head-on using the car industry in general, and

Toyota in particular, as an example. He extends the resource view of the firm to look in detail at how capabilities change over time, attempting to explain interregional and interfirm differences. Instead of applying the concepts of resource-based or capability theories on the firm as a unit, Fujimoto brings the analysis to the operational level. This approach has merit in that it serves to make the rather abstract notion of capabilities of the firm much more concrete. In the process, Fujimoto makes a compelling argument for not only interpreting capabilities as something directly affecting the level of competitive performance and the improvements of performance, but also as the accumulation of these static and improvement capabilities. In other words, successful firms are not only competitive and know how to improve to stay competitive, they also know how to sustain these skills over time; a concept not too dissimilar in spirit from double-loop learning or "learning how to learn." The chapter goes on to explore in some depth this novel interpretation of evolutionary capability as a firm-specific ability to acquire both static and improvement capabilities. This concept of second-order dynamic capabilities still awaits application at the strategic level of the firm.

While Fujimoto drew on microlevel observations, Chapter 3 instead approaches the firm from the perspective of its critical role in contributing to overall economic growth. *Richard Nelson* and *Nathan Rosenberg* address the broad question of technological advance and how it comes about. The famed and elusive "technological residual" in economists' growth models has traditionally been treated as exogenous and has only in the last decade or so come to be incorporated as endogenous, as a function of firms' investment in research and development. Nelson and Rosenberg elaborate on this theme by focusing on the neglected role of science in technological advance and on the inherent uncertainty associated with such advance, while also backing their case with concrete examples. The very important contribution of private firms that do invest consciously in creating new or improved technology and appropriate the benefits thereof is given its due. However, there is much more to the story. Applied science, typically performed at universities, and research and development carried out by firms feed off each other. This interdependence stems from externalities, but also from less obvious linkages such as private laboratories and the like providing a labor market for university-trained researchers, and from applied university research rapidly responding to the need for scientific explanations of technological advances made by private firms. The fundamental uncertainty often associated with technological breakthroughs further complicates this picture. Far from being simply risky and thus probabilistic, Nelson and Rosenberg intriguingly argue that there is commonly true surprise involved in the discovery of new technology. In addition, the point that in fact "old" science often lies behind these breakthroughs is made. Nelson and Rosenberg close by acknowledging that incorporating the interdependence of public and private R&D, and the uncertainty regarding technological advance, into mainstream formal growth models may be difficult however realistic it is. The suggested avenue to pursue is to follow an evolutionary approach to technological change.

Eric von Hippel highlights the problem of *"sticky" information*; the fact that information needed for technical problem-solving tends to be costly to acquire, transfer, and put to use in a new location. When the requisite sticky information resides at only one location, problem-solving tends to take place at that location. When more sites collectively serve as a repository of the demanded sticky information, problem-solving is iterated between these sites or the problem will be broken down so as to simulate the first case. The final avenue is to make investments that reduce the stickiness, and thus costs, of applying such information at other sites. The findings have significant implications for more general issues like patterns in the diffusion of information, the specialization of firms and the locus of innovation.

Cristiano Antonelli takes up the last point in particular in Chapter 5. He argues that localized technological change cannot be seen in isolation from national systems of innovation and the firm itself. Antonelli shows how the often misunderstood role of standards plays an important part in the dynamics of technological change. Far from being only something of a public good, the adoption of standards poses a dilemma for individual firms: should it stick to the local, monopolistic position built on proprietary knowledge or should it adhere to standards for better dissemination? There is also a cost for the firm associated with adopting standards. Antonelli incorporates the emergence of standards into a formal model which then yield incentives for cooperative behavior among firms for the adoption of standards.

2. STRATEGY/ORGANIZATION

Previously, strategy and organization have been seen as two fairly distinct areas of inquiry within the broader fields of business administration and microeconomics. By treating them as one, one recognizes the increased difficulty experienced by scholars in maintaining the earlier distinction. Newer attempts at prying open the proverbial "black box" that is the firm more often than not come to deal with management and individual firms than with the traditional "decide what to do and subsequently find a way how to carry it through," on the one hand, and with the old preoccupation with industries and relative positioning in oligopoly games, on the other.

For one thing, technology tends to leave artifacts in that the more or less perfect voluntarism in strategic-choice models is being circumvented by the notions of technological trajectories and organizational routines. More recent catchwords are competencies, knowledge and learning. Rather than just monitoring or controlling the execution of decisions, management takes on a flair of knowledge management with a more complex view of the set of resources available (or potentially available) to a firm at any given time. Balancing the restrictions of routines against the need for creativity and entrepreneurship has come to attract more attention. In other words, Schumpeter has stepped into the "black box."

In parallel, unique aspects of strategy are more readily identified, but to the detriment of the well-known generic strategies and homogenization at the industry level. In terms of the firms' organization, the efficacy of stand-ard structural forms has come to be questioned, and *a fortiori* so regarding large firms. Instead, there is greater concern with the flexibility of small firms and networks of firms, and with possibilities for large firms to emulate that dynamism internally.

Configuration of firms and of groups of firms, and the subsequent need for coordination, are more recent "black box" issues. The scope for innova-tion appears to be considerable in terms of choice both of organizational structure(s) and of coordination mechanisms. Scale and scope may be prov-ing to be more malleable than was previously recognized. Likewise, changes in communications and transport pose new challenges and offer new op-portunities, forcing a "rethink" of time and space as constraints for firms, particularly small ones.

The contribution by *Benjamin Coriat* and *Giovanni Dosi* in Chapter 6 brings us back to perspective of the individual firm. It highlights the specificity of organizational competencies and their routinized, inertial and conflictual properties. Persistent and distinctive variation among firms, it is argued, can best be understood by taking these properties into account, but only after also taking account of the pervasive influence of institutions in different countries. Otherwise, superior firm characteristics should, of course, easily disseminate. Coriat and Dosi take on the daunting task of untangling the role of organizational routines in explaining firm differences. With firms' critical competencies embodied in the operational routines, they are difficult to copy and their evolution is constrained by both charac-teristics of the firm itself and the environment of the firm. Coriat and Dosi call this *competence specificity*. But competencies are not only seen as involving problem-solving and learning skills, they also include skills and rules governing firm internal relationships. Hence, we actually also have a dual role of organizational routines; as problem-solving procedures, and as governance devices or mechanisms for coordination. The firm is then inter-preted as a behavioral entity that must compromise between several dif-ferent functions and activities. Consequently, this complex picture is not reducible to viewing a firm simply as a nexus of contracts. Instead, we are offered a richer and intriguing story, where competencies—and routines—co-evolve with the environment in which they are embedded. Inertia is thus "built into" this concept of the firm. In prying open this "organizational black box," Coriat and Dosi also indicate several avenues for future research.

In the following chapter, *David Teece* also addresses the wider issue of linkage between organizational variables and the application of new technology. In particular, Teece focuses on innovation at the level of the firm and on the choice of organizational firms that go best with different types of innovation. In the process, we are served a comprehensive analysis of the underlying properties of technological innovation *per se*, and a set of archetypal governance modes for firms. The thrust of the argument is the need to take a broader view of innovation, looking not only at market structure but relating it to organizational structure and firm boundaries as well. Both the formal and the informal structures of the firm, and the network of external linkages that they have, substantially influence innovative activity in firms. Teece goes on to suggest that the complex and increasingly common inter-firm arrangements that exploit complementarities and often are linked to the development of technology in fact constitute an organizational innovation of great importance.

Chapter 8 stays inside the firm pointing to the limits of hierarchy and suggesting an explanation to why the concept of a simple hierarchy has been so readily accepted and seemingly successful. *Peter Hagström* and *Gunnar Hedlund* argue that the historically successful hierarchy actually has hidden a different, underlying structure that only now is being revealed. Hierarchy ensures relative efficiency in a known, stable situation. Hagström and Hedlund find that those are hardly the salient characteristics of the present competitive environment. Indeed, firms are found to experiment with ways to deal with these new pressures; experiments ranging from *ad hoc* measures to radical structural transformations. The fundamental tradeoff here is one of (flexible) efficiency today and of positioning for tomorrow. One-dimensional hierarchy could achieve that yesterday. The authors conclude that, in effect, there are, and always have been, three structural dimensions at play, namely *position, action and knowledge*. These dimensions have coincided—or misalignments have not been apparent—but that is seen to be less and less the case nowadays. And nowhere is this more apparent than in the modern multinational corporation. Hagström and Hedlund then "try out" their theoretically and historically derived model on an illustrative case firm.

Pari Patel and *Keith Pavitt* bring the story back to the specificities of firm competencies. They use data on more than 400 of the largest firms in the world to demonstrate that these firms are characterized by being "multi-technology" and increasingly so; and that they are both stable and differentiated, with the firms' main products strongly influencing their technology profile and direction of localized search. Together with home-country conditions, the main products are also found to play an important role for the rate of search. Any determinism is, however, modified, since when looking at levels and rates of increase in technological activities, unexplained variance does suggest that there is considerable scope for managerial choice. The extensive empirical data are argued to support several challenging conclusions such as large firms being heavily constrained in their technology choices and that a technology strategy really cannot be outsourced; that large firms are immune to a surprising extent to radical technological breakthroughs; and that they are less than "focused" in their technology strategy. Patel's and Pavitt's contribution hence complements Teece's earlier one in interesting ways.

In Chapter 10, *Ikujiro Nonaka* and *Hirotaka Takeuchi* explore the thesis that the apparent success of Japanese firms rests on their ability for organizational knowledge creation. The Japanese experience is taken as a launching pad for a proposed more general theory of how knowledge is, and can be, created in organizations. Two simultaneous *knowledge spirals* are identified as evolving over time. First, knowledge is created and expanded through the social interaction between tacit and explicit forms of knowledge. Nonaka and Takeuchi call this process *knowledge conversion*, and trace its different modes—as well as the requisite enabling conditions—that maintain this knowledge spiral. Second, another spiral describes how knowledge created at the individual level is transformed into knowledge at the organizational level through a phased process. As the spirals interact over time, innovation is seen to emerge. Clearly, there is a certain normative bent to Nonaka and Takeuchi's proposition. Their view of knowledge creation implies that some important lessons for non-Japanese firms are contained therein.

Lars-Gunnar Mattsson stresses the embeddedness of the individual firm in the network of firms with which it necessarily has ties. This *markets-as-networks* approach interprets the generic governance structure for production systems to be multidimensional exchange relationships between actors, typically firms. A key notion here is one of coordination and interdependence in these long term—but by no means static—relationships. In turn, it is argued, there are dynamic, indirect and direct interactions between such relationships. In a fundamental way, the relationships determine the constraints and opportunities that the firm operates under. The approach is thus designed to incorporate both change and stability. The issue of different types of overlap between networks is singled out for scrutiny, especially as it relates to the international context. Applying these constructs, *Mattsson* finds the approach to be especially well suited to improve our understanding of dynamic interaction between the international firm, and the international markets and industries.

3. REGIONS

The direction of current research regarding geographical aspects of the firm is more unclear. Spatial perspectives on the firm have received far less attention than either technology-oriented or strategy and organization-oriented views of the firm.

In economics, regional economics has, however, offered an avenue for more dynamic conceptions of the firm. More empirically grounded research points in the direction of the role of "natural" regions—as opposed to politically determined such—for firm growth and survival. The blurred distinction between external and internal trade is one example of this, as is the greater propensity to actually name "country A" and "region B" even outside the realms of policy research. Dynamic and shifting economies of scale, which have spatial impacts, have been found to add to our under-standing of the uneven distribution of economic activity.

Economic geography can be said to have been "rediscovered" by other disciplines, thereby ending its relative isolation and opening new possibili-ties for interdisciplinary dialogue. Agglomeration advantages and external linkages, or clustering effects, have come to receive greater attention, par-ticularly as regards their relative stability or instability over time. One could talk of "spatial trajectories" and "the multidimensionality of locational advantages" influencing firm behavior.

There seems to be a shift away from what could perhaps best be seen as a more traditional preoccupation with (regional) planning, the collective behavior of firms, the manufacturing sector, description, and with adap-tation to given locational conditions to more of a concern with *de facto* variable spatial behavior of individual firms; firms also outside manufactur-ing and also allowing for the multifunctionality and multinationality of firms. On the last point, the internal workings of the firm have come to command more attention. Ambitions in terms of explanation have more of a tendency not to shy away from individual firms' possibilities to more actively influence their local environment(s). Firms are also more com-monly seen to be able to select, rather than only be selected by, particular sites.

The third and last section of the book makes spatial aspects of firm behavior explicit. *John Cantwell* fires the first shots by calling into question two of the central hypotheses associated with earlier versions of the product life-cycle model. Based on one hundred years of US Patent Office data on the patents granted to large European and American industrial firms, Cantwell rejects the hypothesis that innovations almost always originate in the home country of the parent company. Internationalization of industrial research is found to be neither insignificant nor a new phenomenon. The second hypothesis, that international investment is led by technology lead-ers, fares better. It is consistent with the data, but Cantwell makes an extended interpretation in order to take account of more recent trends toward a much wider range of firms being engaged in internationalization. Instead, Cantwell suggests that technology leaders now are ahead in the globalization of technology. These firms would be most competent in exploiting the locationally differentiated potential of foreign centers of technological excellence. Technology leadership can then be said to manifest itself in superior management of internal international networks with multiple locations for innovation, rather than just in a wider geographical dispersion of investments.

In Chapter 13, *John Dunning* moves the analysis to a higher level of abstraction. He takes issue with the all too persistent notions of only locationally immobile assets and arm's-length transactions determining the international division of labor and competitive advantages of firms and nations. Dunning prefers to stress the important roles of created assets; how they are created and deployed; and that of multinational enterprises in the international economy. Painting with broad brush strokes, Dunning traces the historical roots of inadequate explanations before turning to more recent developments in the theory of spatial specialization of economic activity. The role of firms in coordinating activities and in governing transactions is explored in some depth, and the place of government in this scheme of things introduced. None of the main modalities of organizing economic activity (markets, hierarchies, interfirm alliances and governments) is argued to escape the profound effects of globalization. From largely having been regarded as alternatives, it is now more realistic to view these modalities as having complementary roles in the organization of resources and capabilities. Dunning follows through many of the implications of his personal odyssey through the effects of globalization, and enters a strong plea for a more systemic approach by academics in addressing the issues raised. Research on these current, either macro or micro, organizational and management issues seems to call for crossing traditional disciplinary demarcation lines.

In the following chapter, *Michael Enright* shifts the focus to clearly defined regional clusters and how the characteristics of those help shape the strategy of individual firms. An extensive review leads to the conclusion that this link has largely been ignored in the mainstream literature on the subjects of clusters and of firm strategy, respectively. Enright observes that critical resources and capabilities are more often found to be spatially determined than simply existing within any single firm. Moreover, activities are shared across firms, which, consequently, spells interdependence among firms in a given cluster. Apart from strategic interdependence, the tendency for rapid information flows and a unique mix of competition and cooperation existing within clusters have important implications for firm strategy and the study thereof. Enright demonstrates how events in clusters highlight significant issues like the scope of the firm, levels of cooperation and competition, and external sources of firm advantage.

Masahisa Fujita and *Ryoichi Ishii* begin Chapter 15 by drawing our attention to the frequently overlooked fact that only a relatively limited number of firms actually survive over time. Building on the experience of (surviving) Japanese electronics firms after World War II, they look at the explanatory contribution of selective factor disadvantages operating at the country level, and of local rivalry. Stressing the spatial influence on firm strategy the kinship of their argument with that of Enright is close. Since Fujita and Ishii look at the global operations of their nine selected firms, they can also bring the geographical dispersal and local spatially determined dynamics as they impact firm strategy to the fore. Their detailed analysis shows globalization of the chosen firms to be a function of the desire to remain competitive. However, fundamental problems are seen to have arisen for the Japanese electronics industry as well as for the Japanese economy. They are identified as primarily institutional and competitive in kind.

Allen Scott takes a broader and more conceptual approach than Fujita and Ishii when concentrating on the local environment of firms. In fact, the firm subsides in his treatment to a player in regional production systems in line with the avowed objective of explaining the collective performance of these regional systems. Dovetailing the argument of the previous contribution, Scott finds that geographic space has become more, not less, important in terms of its economic effects in today's global economy. However, Scott raises a more fundamental point in that the observed patterns of locational differentiation and specialization, and of interregional trade in effect have become more finely grained. Spatial characteristics are argued to underpin much of industrial performance. Localized clusters of economic activity have appeared historically and continue to do so. They are identified as being transactions-intensive, feeding off increasing returns and agglomeration economies. Scott goes on to develop the notion of path-dependency of clusters over time, and the dangers that may hold, before proposing a generic policy agenda that boosts the critical system of formal and informal collective order found in clusters.

Spatial path-dependence stays with us in Chapter 17 by Örjan Sölvell and Ivo Zander. The overriding issue here is one of the international diffusion of knowledge or, rather, the isolating mechanisms that may retard such diffusion. In view of earlier contributions to this volume, Sölvell and Zander provocatively argue that multinational corporations are *not* particularly well-equipped to transfer knowledge between local innovation systems. The observed difficulty of transferring tacit knowledge and process technology, and the localized nature of knowledge creation, are used to establish the importance of local systems. The authors also believe that there are isolating mechanisms operating at the national level. In addition to identifying problems with knowledge transfer within the multinational corporation, Sölvell and Zander point out that the multinational firm is likely to neglect its own subsidiaries in its endeavor to become an insider in the local innovation cluster. Rather closely echoing Scott's view, but from a slightly different vantage point, Sölvell and Zander suggest that the international competitive advantage of firms in fact is more intimately linked with dynamism within discrete local systems than commonly recognized.

In Chapter 18, *J.-C. Spender* continues the established line of argument by sketching a consistent knowledge-based theory of the firm and where geography matters. Consequently, organizational knowledge must then also have a spatial dimension. Spender advances the idea that it does. He differentiates the types of knowledge by employing the dichotomies of explicit/implicit, and individual/social knowledge. The argument that rents arising from knowledge differences, rather than from efficiency differences, is at the heart of competitive advantage allows Spender to associate each type of knowledge with a particular type of rent. Now, all firms are said to contain all four types of knowledge, although the principal reason for the existence of firms is said to be the rents that accrue from activity-based learning. That neatly identifies implicit and social knowledge, called *collective knowledge*, as the key type for firms. It follows that this type of knowledge best can be created in dense, cluster-like environments with ample opportunity for direct interaction. Successful, new industrial districts are offered as good illustrations of this argument. Other types of knowledge have other geographical implications for firms.

Michael Porter and *Örjan Sölvell* return with a final chapter with their view of how to link geography, innovation and firm competitive advantage. Porter and Sölvell span many of the themes raised above, and they highlight several of the more contentious issues as seen from their vantage point. The stress is on the geographical dimension and its importance for technological development in a broad sense, and, by implication, for sustainable firm competitive advantage. The dense, localized clusters reappear, as does the geographical embeddedness of firm activities and knowledge. Among other things, Porter and Sölvell devote considerable space to the interesting things that go on outside the legal boundaries of the firm in this environment. In particular, extra-firm innovative activities and their determinants are explored at some length.

The contributions to this volume collectively offer a rich menu of approaches, both theoretically and empirically grounded, to dealing with dynamics and to arriving at a more realistic understanding of the firm in this context. The reader looking for a research agenda will find ample food for thought. More questions are perhaps left unanswered than get an unambiguous resolution and some differences of opinion remain. Finally, it is in the nature of emerging areas of inquiry to introduce possible extensions to existing theory, be it old or new theory, and to suggest innovative concepts. Here, the reader is also well rewarded.

It may be no coincidence that dynamic aspects of the firm are receiving increased attention at this juncture. The contemporary pressures on the firm of themselves seem to generate an implicit demand for new explanations of firm behavior. Indeed, one may hypothesize that the variance in the population of surviving firms actually has increased, and that observed firm behavior lately, in fact, has become more complex and difficult to comprehend. Increased structural diversity among firms, and a concomitant erosion in the efficacy of formal means of control and coordination, could be one explanation for the greater emphasis firms seem to be putting on using informal means for managing the organization.

Bringing different perspectives to bear on a single, overriding issue is one way to try to improve our understanding of observed phenomena, however complex they may be. That is the very purpose of this volume on *The Dynamic Firm.*

PART I

TECHNOLOGY IN THE FIRM

2

Reinterpreting the Resource-Capability View of the Firm: A Case of the Development-Production Systems of the Japanese Auto-Makers[1]

TAKAHIRO FUJIMOTO

1. INTRODUCTION

Resource-based or capability theories of the firm have attracted much attention among business academics and practitioners in recent years. They portray a business firm as a collection of firm-specific resources, organizational routines, capabilities and competencies which may explain interfirm differences in competitiveness, as well as intertemporal dynamics (i.e. evolution) of business-enterprise systems.[2]

On the other hand, the competitive strength of some of the Japanese auto-makers, such as Toyota, became a hot issue during the 1980s, as the global market share of Japanese cars continued to increase and the Japanese assemblers and parts-makers started up their local transplants in the USA and Europe. Empirical researches on productivity, manufacturing quality and product-development performance revealed the competitive advantages of the Japanese auto-makers over average Western makers in this period,[3] and practices and techniques of competitive Japanese auto-makers, as well as philosophies behind them, were introduced to Western readers.[4] By the end of the decade, the view that the source of their competitiveness was not so much certain individual techniques or technologies as the overall pattern of the total manufacturing-development system prevailed among researchers and practitioners in this field. Some parts of the system were in fact introduced in Western countries in the 1980s and 1990s through the local Japanese transplants and interfirm collaboration, and bench-marking studies by Western makers, which all contributed to the catch-up by some American and European auto-makers during the same period.

Given the basic facts that interfirm and interregional differences in the overall patterns of manufacturing- and product-development systems resulted in significant performance differences across the firms, and that the patterns of the competitive Japanese auto companies emerged during the postwar period, it seems natural to predict that the resource-capability theories of the firm can be effectively applied to the case of the Japanese auto-makers. Thus, the present paper tries to examine the applicability of the resource-capability approach to the production and development systems in a single international industry.

For the above purpose, however, the existing framework of the resource-capability approach needs some modification and reinterpretation. While most of the existing resource-capability literature, found in the fields of strategic management, applied economics or business history, analyze the dynamics of the overall systems of multiproduct firms, they are not designed for detailed competitive analyses of a production and product-development system at a single plant or project level, which researches in technology and operations management often focus on.[5]

For a better match between the resource-capability approach and the detailed competitive analyses of manufacturing systems, there are at least two steps to be undertaken: first, we have to prepare an analytical framework that can describe detailed routines of production, procurement and product-development operations, as well as their performance in a consistent manner, and apply it to current empirical studies. Second, based on the first "static" analyses, we need to prepare a dynamic framework that can analyze evolution of the routines at the operational level, and apply it to historical studies.

For the first task, the author proposes a reinterpretation of such basic concepts as firms, products, resources, activities, competitive performance and capabilities consistently from the information's point of view by describing the product-development and production processes and their outputs as assets, creation and transmission of value-carrying information that is ultimately embodied in the product (Fujimoto 1994*b*). Due to limits of space, however, this chapter will skip the first task and concentrate mostly on the second: proposing a dynamic framework for analyzing development-production systems, and applying it to the historical case of the evolution of Toyota-style system. Section 2 will propose an evolutionary framework; Section 3 will present historical cases.

2. A FRAMEWORK FOR THE EVOLUTIONARY CAPABILITY OF MANUFACTURING FIRMS

2.1 Three Levels of Development-Production Capabilities

We can redefine capability in production and product development as follows: *Development-production capability* of a firm refers to certain firm-specific patterns of productive resources and activities (i.e. information stocks and their creation and transmission) that result in competitive advantages over its rivals. Assuming that both competitive performance and capabilities change over time, we have to distinguish at least three levels of a firm's capability: (1) *static capability*, which affects the level of competitive performance; (2) *improvement capability*, which affects the pace of performance improvements; and (3) *evolutionary capability*, which is related to the accumulation of the above capabilities themselves (Table 2.1). The latter two can be regarded as the first-order and second-order dynamic capabilities respectively.

Static capability   The capability of consistently achieving a high *level* of competitive performance. Several aspects of development-production capability affect the levels of product competitiveness: design quality, conformance quality, factor productivity, throughput time and flexibility. As the author points out in other papers, static capabilities in production and product development can be consistently described and analyzed in terms of accuracy, efficiency, and speed of information creation and transmission between productive resources (i.e. information assets), as well as information content and redundancy of the resources themselves (Fujimoto 1989, 1994*b*).

Improvement capability   This refers to the ability of the development-production system for consistently and quickly achieving *improvement* in

TABLE 2.1. Three levels of production-development capability

	Basic nature	Influence on:	Components
Static capability	Static and routine	Level of competitive performance	Productivity = efficiency of information transmission Throughput time = efficiency of information reception Quality = accuracy of information transmission Flexibility = redundancy of information stock
Improvement capability	Dynamic and routine	Change in competitive performance	Problem finding Problem solving Retention of solutions
Evolutionary capability	Dynamic and non-routine	Change in capability	Pre-trial capability: *ex ante* rationality entrepreneurial visions Post-trial capability: *ex post* rationality retention and institutionalization

competitive performance such as quality and productivity. As this is essentially capability of repetitive problem solving and learning, it consists of the following sub-capabilities:[6]

- Problem finding: Ability of the system to reveal and visualize problems, diffuse problem information to problem solvers, keep consciousness of problems, willingness of organizational members to accept higher performance goals, and so on.
- Problem solving: consistency between knowledge, skills, responsibility and authority for solving problems; levels and diffusions of tools for problem solving; knowledge sharing on alternative action plans and their effects, and so on.
- Retention of solutions: Ability to quickly and accurately formalize and routinize new solutions in standard operating procedures; stability of organizational members who internalize the solutions, and so on.

Evolutionary capability   This refers to the organizational ability of acquiring the static and improvement capabilities (i.e. capability of capability building). It is, in a sense, "metacapability." While improvement capability is routine in that it facilitates repetitive problem solving in a regular situation, evolutionary capability is non-routine, as acquisition of new capabilities is rather irregular and rare.

Evolutionary capability (i.e. the firm-specific ability of capability building) plays only a partial role in the overall evolutionary process of development-production systems, though. When a company changes its static or improvement capabilities to a new system, the firm-specific evolutionary capability may contribute to this "system-emergence" process, but other factors such as environmental imperatives and pure luck may also have significant influences on the change. After all, the evolutionary process of system emergence is a complex interaction between the firms and their environments.

Capability building can be regarded, in a broad sense, as a process of organizational learning and problem solving, as in the case of improvement capability. The problem is how to increase the firm's long-term competitiveness, and the solutions are a new set of development-production capabilities that the firm acquires. Unlike the case of improvement capability, though, the problem-solving process here is much less streamlined, and the firms have much less control on the entire problem-solving cycle. The problems and solutions are often disjointed. The regular sequence from problems to solutions to retention may not exist, as trials of solutions precede problem recognition in many cases.[7] Solutions to certain non-competitive problems may subsequently and inadvertently become solutions for competitive problems. Thus, the standard model of problem-solving cycles does not seem to be relevant to the case of evolutionary capability. This is one of the reasons why we should analyze improvement capability and evolutionary capability separately.

Of the three levels of development-production capabilities described above, the current chapter will focus on the third level: evolutionary capability of a manufacturing firm. Let us now examine further the process of system emergence.

2.2 System Emergence and Evolutionary Capability

Logic of system emergence   Generally speaking, a new system of production and development gradually emerges as a result of a complex interactions of firms and environments, in which firm-specific evolutionary capability may play only a partial role. Thus, we have to analyze the evolutionary capability of the firms in the broader context of system emergence in general.

There are at least several alternative logical ways of explaining emergence of a new pattern of systems or capabilities (Fig. 2.1).[8]

- *Random trials:* This logic assumes that it is a matter of pure chance for an organization to choose a particular trial. A lucky one gets a better system, while an unlucky one gets a poor one.
- *Rational calculation:* An organization deliberately chooses a new course of action that satisfies or maximizes its objective function by examining a feasible set of alternatives based on its understandings of environmental constraints and limits of capabilities.[9] In other words, this is the case of rational problem solving.
- *Environmental constraints:* An organization detects certain constraints imposed by objective or perceived environments, and voluntarily prohibits certain sets of actions. The constraints may be objective (e.g. laws and regulations), or it may be self-restraints based on its perception of the environments.
- *Entrepreneurial vision*: A desirable set of activities is directly chosen by entrepreneurs of the organizations based on their visions, philosophies or intuitions without much analysis of their capabilities and constraints.
- *Knowledge transfer:* A certain pattern is transferred from another organization to the one in question. The transfer may happen within the industry (competitor, supplier, customer, etc.) or across the industries. Also, the transfer may be a *pull* type, where the adopter-imitator of the system takes an initiative, or it may be a *push* type, where the driving force of the transfer exists on the side of the source organizations.

A combination of different "logics" would be normally needed for explaining a particular system emergence. In any case, it should be noted that neither rational problem solving alone nor firm-specific dynamic capability seem to fully explain the evolutionary process of new system emergence.

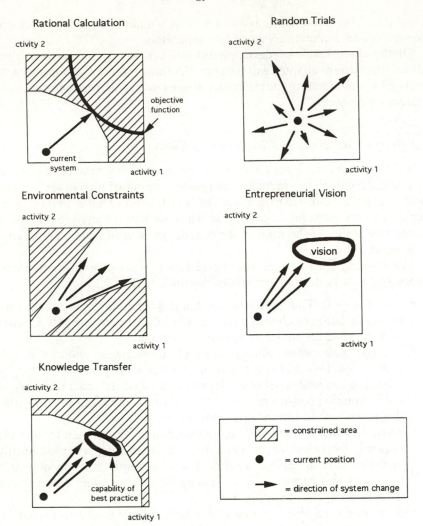

Fɪɢ. 2.1. Some generic hypotheses of system emergence

Source: Adapted from Fujimoto and Takahiro (1994), "The Origin and Evolution of the 'Black Box Parts' Practice in the Japanese Auto Industry," Tokyo University Faculty of Economics, Discussion Paper 94-F-1.

Evolutionary capability versus historical imperatives   Suppose that we have observed universally prevalent, region-specific and firm-specific patterns of a certain development-production capability at the same time: a situation that researchers of a single international industry often encounter. How can we explain the evolution of such a pattern by the above logic of system emergence?

(1) *Universally prevalent* patterns of practice may emerge when rational problem solvers share identical objectives and constraints worldwide (a neoclassical situation), when the universally best practice has transferred to everyone, when severe selection environments allow only a particular pattern to survive, etc.

(2) *Region-specific* patterns of capabilities may emerge when the firms face region-specific environmental constraints or objectives, when knowledge transfers occur only within each region, etc.

(3) *Firm-specific* patterns may emerge when each company is allowed to take "random walks" in changing its systems, when each company faces different environmental constraints, when each company is led by different entrepreneurial visions, when firms have different levels of problem-solving capabilities, when knowledge transfers between firms are limited, etc.

Thus, although pure chances and historical imperatives often play important roles in the system-emergence and capability-building process, a company may still be able to build certain development-production capabilities faster and more effectively than its competitors by exercising certain evolutionary capabilities.

For example, certain historical imperatives may explain why the Japanese makers in general acquired certain region-specific capabilities, but it does not explain why certain Japanese makers have had better capabilities than other Japanese. To the extent that firm-specific patterns of performance and capability are observed, differences in each firm's evolutionary capability may matter.

It is also important to distinguish the following two types of evolutionary capabilities:

(1) *Pre-trial capability:* A firm's ability to find and make trials or experiments for new capability acquisition earlier and more effectively than competitors. This category may include the ability of rational calculations for identifying potentially effective trials (*ex ante* rationality); entrepreneurial visions for intuitively finding effective trials.

(2) *Post-trial capability:* It often happens that trials for new capability are made inadvertently, and they turn out to be effective in competition. In this case, a firm can still create firm-specific advantages through post-trial capabilities, including the ability of grasping the potential competitive consequences of the trials (*ex post* rationality), and the ability of routinizing and retaining the trials.

Thus, even when the competing companies do not differ in pre-trial capabilities or the level of *ex ante* rationality, a firm may still be able to outperform the others by possessing better *ex post* capabilities than the others.

Having proposed an evolutionary framework of the resource-capability view for analyses of development-production systems of manufacturing firms, the next section will apply it to the historical case of Toyota, the most effective Japanese auto-maker of the 1980s. The following analyses will demonstrate that Toyota's distinctive competencies in production and product development include not only static and improvement capabilities, which much of the existing literature points out, but also evolutionary capabilities.

3. CAPABILITY BUILDING IN TOYOTA-STYLE DEVELOPMENT-PRODUCTION SYSTEMS

This section presents some cases of system evolution or emergence and reinterprets them. Our main focus is Toyota Motor Company, known as one of the most competitive auto-makers of the 1980s. Before analyzing the patterns of historical evolution, let us first summarize some seemingly "stylized" facts based on the empirical work conducted through the early 1990s.

(1) *Evolutionary process:* The so-called Toyota-style system was not developed all at once by rational strategic decision-making, but gradually evolved during the postwar period (or even since the 1930s).[10]

(2) *Regional specificity:* During the 1980s, the Japanese auto-makers tended to cluster in terms of competitive performance and practices in many cases, and outperformed the US and European firms on average.[11]

(3) *Individual firm specificity:* Despite the regional effect, there were significant differences in performance and practices among the Japanese auto-makers in many other aspects. Thus, region-specific patterns and firm-specific patterns in production-development capabilities and performance coexisted during the 1980s.[12]

(4) *Hybridization:* The Toyota-style system has not been a totally unique and original production system that challenges the traditional Ford system, despite the sharp contrasts between the two systems since the 1980s. The Toyota system has adopted various elements of the Ford system and hybridized them with their own indigenous system and original ideas. There is an obvious continuity between the two systems.[13]

Thus, it can be predicted at this point that neither rational-strategic decisions nor environmental determinism alone would be able to explain the overall evolutionary process of this system of development-production capabilities. Based on the above argument, the rest of this section explores the historical evolution of various elements of what is known as Toyota's static/improvement capability, such as "Just-in-Time", mechanisms for productivity improvement, multitasking, flexible production, Total Quality Control (TQC), suppliers' design capability and heavyweight product-manager system.

3.1 Capability building for "Just-in-Time"

The origin of the "Just-in-Time" (JIT) system is a complex combination of entrepreneurial visions, knowledge transfer from other firms and industries, environmental constraints and rational behaviors.

Entrepreneurial vision   The idea and slogan of "Just-in-Time" was created and advocated by Toyota's founder-entrepreneur Kiichiro Toyoda during the 1930s. Although concrete methods (e.g. the "supermarket" system, and the "Kanban" system) did not exist, Kiichiro had strongly insisted that the downstream should order only the quantity that it needed. When Kiichiro started the automobile business, he first posted the words "Just in Time" on the walls, and told his subordinates to receive just twenty engine-blocks in the morning and no more if only twenty were needed that day. Kiichiro was frequently walking about the factory and threw away anything above what was needed.[14]

Knowledge transfer from Ford   Toyota's "Just-in-Time" and the Ford system of the early days (the era of Highland Park experiments) had much in common in that both pursued synchronization of upstream and down-stream processes.[15] The Ford system synchronized work-stations by physically linking them by continuous conveyors; the "Just-in-Time" system created pressures for synchronization by eliminating buffer stocks between the stations (thus forming an invisible conveyor line). Although it was after World War II that Toyota introduced conveyor systems on a large scale, it is likely that Kiichiro had the Ford system in mind when he advocated the "Just-in-Time" concept.

Knowledge transfers from the textile industry   Another important source of the Toyota Production System seems to be the production experiences of Toyoda Spinning and Weaving, which were transferred by Taiichi Ohno, the actual inventor of JIT. When Ohno was working as supervisor at the spinning factory of this textile company, he realized that its rival, Nichibo (Japan Spinning) was outperforming Toyoda in productivity through a bench-marking study. Further studies revealed that the production system of Nichibo was very different from that of Toyoda Spinning and Weaving. Toyoda had separate buildings for process steps; Nichibo had adopted the line layout along the process flow. Toyoda moved yarns in large lots; Nichibo conveyed them in small lots. Toyoda had emphasized skills of reworking (yarn tying) at the downstream step; Nichibo had emphasized making good yarns at the upstream and eliminating reworking at the down-stream. In this way, Ohno obtained some of the key ideas of Toyota Produc-tion System, including product-focused layout, small-lot production and "doing things right the first time", through the bench-marking study of the textile industry. When Ohno moved to Toyota Motor Manufacturing in 1943, his first impression was that it would be easy to raise productivity of the automobile business by three to five times by simply introducing the production system adopted by Toyoda Spinning and Weaving.[16]

Historical imperatives—the 1950 crisis   Although productivity increased rapidly, Toyota faced a crisis during the 1948–9 recession. With many finished goods and inventories piling up, Toyota was on the verge of bank-ruptcy. It also fired 2,000 employees, which triggered a series of strikes by the labor union.[17] Two lessons that Toyota was forced to learn from this crisis, among others, were "limited volume production" (*genryo seisan*) and human resource management with long-term stabilization of employment.

The lesson learned from the crisis was that productivity increase and cost reduction had to be accompanied by "limited volume production", which meant that production had to be limited to just *enough* that could be sold and just *when* it could be sold. It was learned that productivity increase for the sake of itself was no good, and that producers should not simply imitate the American-style mass production.[18]

Diffusion of the Kanban system   Although the concept of "Just-in-Time" was created by Kiichiro Toyoda in the 1930s, the Kanban system, a formal mechanism that originated the idea, started in the late 1950s under the leadership of Taiichi Ohno.[19] The system was originally called the "super-market system", in that the downstream station had to come to the up-stream to pick up just enough parts, whereas the latter had to produce just enough to replenish what was taken by the former.[20] The system, which linked the upstream and the downstream by standardized returnable con-tainers and reusable slips called *kanban*, had already been articulated around 1949, according to Ohno, but the Tax Office did not allow this arrangement until the mid-1950s on the grounds that the system did not document accounting records for each transaction.

Unlike TQC, diffusion of JIT was rather slow, as it started as Ohno's informal experiments, as opposed to a company-wide movement. Initial experiments were made only where Ohno directly supervised. He intro-duced the Kanban system first in the body-welding line, in which small lot production was the key. Ohno told the shop-floor people, "Kanban is like money: if you take out parts without Kanban, you are stealing the parts." The Kanban system was then introduced to the upstream press operations, and then to such components as engine-oil pans and tappet covers. It was also installed at the Motomachi assembly plant upon its completion in 1959. In the early 1960s, when Ohno became the main plant manager he introduced Kanban to casting, forging and heat treatment, the most difficult processes for small lot production.[21] In 1962, Kanban was authorized and adopted at the company-wide level. In 1965, Toyota formally started diffusion of the system to the suppliers.

3.2 Capability building for productivity improvement and multitasking

Kiichiro's vision and bench-marking In September 1945, soon after the end of World War II, GHQ (General Headquarters) approved Toyota's production of trucks. Relying mostly on old equipment dating back to the 1930s, Toyota's production activity was severely limited by financial and capacity constraints. Its annual production finally surpassed the prewar peak (about 16,000 units) in 1953.[22] It is remarkable that, in this desperate situation, Kiichiro Toyoda already had future competition with the Western auto-makers in mind. According to Taiichi Ohno, Kiichiro launched an ambitious goal of catching up with the productivity level of the American auto-makers within three years.[23] Ohno estimated the productivity level of the American makers to be ten times as high as that of Toyota right after the war.[24] Although Kiichiro's goal was too ambitious, Toyota did increase productivity by ten times between 1945 and 1955 in some of the core operations, according to Ohno. When Ohno visited Ford and GM engine plants in 1956, he found that the American plants had not improved productivity since the 1930s, and that productivity at Toyota's engine plant at that time was already higher than them in gross terms (i.e. unadjusted for product and process characteristics).

It is important to note that GM and Ford, establishing their knockdown assembly plants in the mid-1920s, virtually dominated the Japanese motor-vehicle makers around 1930 with a combined market share of over 90 per cent until the Japanese government enforced a protectionistic law in 1936. It is likely that the memory of the dominance of the American mass producers made Kiichiro and other Toyota managers continue bench-marking and set high operational targets to compete with their imaginary rivals in America, even with a fully protected domestic market between the 1930s and 1950s.[25]

Adoption and modification of Taylorism The traditional craft system persisted in Toyota's production processes during the 1930s and 1940s.[26] Foremen-craftsmen led teams of workers as masters and were responsible for production volume and quality. They told their subordinates, "Steal the way in which others are doing," "Learn for yourself by your skin feeling." Workers machined a variety of parts using general-purpose equipment, while sharpening their own cutting tools. Process flows were often disturbed, work-in-process inventories piled up, and lack of balance in machine utilization occurred.

These kinds of craft-production environments remained even after World War II, but they were gradually replaced by standardization of operations, product-focused layouts, and multiskilled workers handling more than one standard job. Taiichi Ohno, the champion of the "Just-in-Time" system, recalls the situation when he was assigned to be section head of Toyota's machine shop in 1946.[27]

The first thing that I did was standardization of jobs. The shop-floor of those days was controlled by foremen-craftsmen. Division managers and section managers could not control the shop-floor, and they were always making excuses for production delay. So we first made manuals of standard operation procedures and posted them above the work-stations so that supervisors could see if the workers were following the standard operations at a glance. Also, I told the shop-floor people to revise the standard operating procedures continuously, saying, "You are stealing money from the company if you do not change the standard for a month."

In this way, the shift from craft production to Taylor-type standardization made progress in the late 1940s at least in Toyota's machine shops, despite some resistance from traditional crafts people. It should be noted, however, that the seemingly Tayloristic movement of work standardization at Toyota was accompanied by continuous improvements of the standards themselves. Thus, unlike the Ford system in America, in which work standardization tended to mean freezing of standard operations and vertical separation between single-skilled workers and élite industrial engineers, standardization under Ohno's leadership emphasized continuous improvements at the shop-floor.[28] Also, in Ohno's machine shops, work standardization and training of multiskilled workers were carried out in parallel. In other words, decomposition of craft jobs into standardized tasks and recombination of the tasks to multiskilled jobs occurred at the same time. Unlike American Taylorism-Fordism that essentially created single-skilled workers, Toyota in the late 1940s replaced traditional craft jobs with multiskilled jobs. Overall, Ohno claims that Toyota increased productivity by 5–6 times by 1950 while relying mostly on old machines of the 1930s.[29]

Transfers from the textile industry It is obvious that Ohno, with his experience in spinning operations, applied the concept of multimachine work assignment to the automobile industry:[30]

Improvement of productivity from 1945 to 1950 was relatively easy. For example, there were three or four workers around one machine, particularly when it was an important one, prior to the war. So simply assigning one worker to one machine increased productivity by three, four times. Workers with craftsmen's mentality resisted such measures, but labor saving was relatively easy as turnover ratio was very high at that time.

Historical imperatives—forced growth The introduction of work standardization, centralization of tool maintenance and productivity improvement with low production growth created tensions between the craft-type foremen and machinists. Researchers point out that the militant craftsmen-foremen played a central role in Toyota's labor conflicts in 1950.

Although Toyota increased production capacity in response to special orders of trucks for the US Army (APA) during the Korean War, it carefully avoided adding employees for the expansion, as the memory of the labor crisis was still fresh. Toyota also had to expand the capacity while using the old machines. It is likely that Toyota was predicting fluctuation of production volume following the business cycles, and was trying to minimize the number of the permanent work-force in order to avoid further dismissals and strikes.

This prediction turned out to be generally wrong, however. Production started to grow rapidly in the 1950s, and it continued to grow without large recessions until 1990. Toyota, however, maintained a conservative recruitment policy. Productivity increased almost automatically by expanding the scale of production while minimizing the increase in the number of workers. Thus the pattern of production expansion without adding employees, and the reduction of finished goods inventory (i.e. limited volume production) was installed at Toyota through its experience of the crisis and the subsequent growth. During the high-growth era of the 1960 and 1970s, Toyota absorbed the workload required for the growth by hiring temporary workers, subcontracting out subassembly jobs, prolonging overtime work, and improving labor productivity, but it tended to keep a conservative recruitment policy as far as permanent workers were concerned.

3.3 Capability building for flexible production equipment

Visions of a modified Ford system Kiichiro Toyoda of Toyoda Automatic Loom started engine research and prototyping on a small corner of its facility around 1931, five years before the protectionist law was launched. Ford and GM were dominating the domestic automobile market then. Kiichiro's business concept at this early stage was as follows:

(1) Develop a 3,000-cc-class automobile and compete directly with the American models both in price and performance.
(2) Although Toyota would learn from the American system of mass production, it would take into account situations of the Japanese market that would limit the production volume to only several hundred units per month, and would modify the system accordingly.[31]

Kiichiro's vision of competing directly with Ford and GM was a quite ambitious (even reckless) one considering that it was made when the American knockdown vehicles were still dominating the market. His vision apparently ignored the principle of economy of scale and cost curves. On the other hand, Kiichiro did not try to introduce the Ford system directly but to adapt it to the Japanese conditions (small market, bad roads, etc.) both in product and process technology. Kiichiro's vision, although unrealistic at that time, functioned as driving force for Toyota's dramatic productivity improvement in the late 1940s and early 1950s. This seems to demonstrate Kiichiro's "capability of business conceptualization" at this early stage of business development.[32]

Forced flexibility of machines   When Toyoda's Kariya Assembly Plant was completed in 1936; its capacity (150 units per month) was quite small compared with standard American plants.[33] Based on Kiichiro's vision to "match Toyoda's unit cost of producing several hundred units per year with that of Americans producing 20,000–30,000 units per year"[34] Toyoda had to modify the Ford system for small volume production. For example, it replaced a part of body-stamping processes with manual jobs in order to save fixed cost for tooling. The size of the Koromo plant, established in 1938, was still much smaller than that of average American factories (2,000 units per month, 5,000 employees). Thus, Toyota continued to select production technologies deliberately, considering the limits of production scale.[35] For example, it purchased only a few press machines for the door-panel process, where American makers would have installed several dozens. Toyota also kept its machining operations somewhat flexible by introducing multispindle balling and horning machines that were adjustable to design changes, unlike standard Detroit-type machines. It also made the machine-shop flat so that its process layout could be changed easily. In this way, the small scale of Toyota's production forced the company to chose flexible production systems deliberately.

Learning from Ford   Soon after the end of the 1950 labor crisis, Eiji Toyoda and Shoichi Saito, who eventually became leaders of Toyota, went to America and visited Ford's River Rouge factory and other facilities. Their study of the American automobile factories was intensive and lasted for three months; these visits were obviously motivated by Toyota's plan to modernize its production facilities. Soon after their return, Eiji and Saito launched a five-year plan for modernization of production equipment (1951–5). The goal of the plan was to replace old equipment with new, introduce conveyors and automation and to expand the monthly production scale to 3,000 units. Although Toyota was suffering from a severe shortage of cash, Toyota managed to carry out 4.6 billion yen investment between 1951 and 1955. The equipment introduced during this period included continuous casting lines for engine-blocks, 2,000-ton press machines, and multiple-spot welders. Eiji was particularly impressed by the conveyor system at the River Rouge factory, and told his staff to adopt conveyors extensively on his return from America. He also gave orders to standardize pallets and containers, which may have facilitated introduction of the Kanban system subsequently.

Transfer machines, a typical Detroit-type automation that links a series of single-purpose machine tools by automated transfer devices, was introduced to a part of the engine-machining process in the late 1950s. The first machine, developed jointly by Toyota and Toyoda Machine Tools, was installed in 1956. Although it is likely that Toyota studied the transfer machines in Detroit, the machines themselves were developed and built by the Japanese companies including Toyota itself.

Historical imperatives—shortage of investment funds In the first five years of the postwar restoration, Toyota was forced to increase productivity and achieve the goal of producing 1,000 trucks per month without sufficient funds and equipment. Therefore, the improvements of Toyota's production system during this period tended to rely on such "soft" methods as work standardization, changes in layout and job assignment as well as investments on relatively inexpensive jigs.

Taiichi Ohno took charge of the Koromo assembly-plant in 1945. He stressed factors other than machines as he had observed a large productivity gap between Toyota and the Western makers although they were using similar equipment. Here we can detect certain philosophies of the subsequent Toyota Production System that emphasize mechanisms which reveal problems purposefully, as well as total system improvements other than mechanization. This may be partly ascribed to insights of Toyota managers, but it is also likely that the historical imperatives of capital shortage forced the company to de-emphasize mechanization solutions. The concept of low-cost automation and semi-automation for cost effectiveness is still prevalent at Toyota.[36]

Product-focused layout Although the engine-machining factory had already adopted product-focused machine layout (i.e. installing machine tools according to process sequence for a particular product group), transmission and suspension factories had been organized by types of machines (e.g. balling, lathe, milling, grinding).[37] The level of in-process inventories was high. It took Ohno and his staff two years to convert the layout to a product-focused one. As the number of machines increased, the machine utilization ratio decreased, but Ohno told his people to disregard this apparent loss.[38] The number of workers was not much increased, however, as Toyota trained multiskilled workers, who operated multiple machines, often with U-shape layouts, along the process flow (i.e. *takotei mochi*).[39]

In a sense, however, the product-focused layout may be regarded as an incomplete version of Detroit-type automation with fully automated material handling and product-focused machine layout (e.g. transfer machines).

While diffusion of transfer machines at Ford was rather limited to high-volume items, the diffusion of process-focused layout at Toyota was wide-spread.[40] Thus, simply speaking, the patterns of diffusion of mechanization at Ford and Toyota may be contrasted as "incomplete diffusion of complete automation" versus "complete diffusion of incomplete automation." It is likely that the latter approach had more significant positive effects on cost reduction and productivity improvement.[41]

3.4 Capability building for Kaizen and Total Quality Control

Adoption of suggestion system and TWI from the USA   Another system of Ford's that impressed them was the suggestion system (i.e. workers making suggestions for improvements on various technical and organizational issues). Soon after they came back to Japan, Eiji and Saito started the "Idea Suggestion System" (*soi kufu teian seido*) in 1951, which subsequently became a core element of Toyota's TQC (Total Quality Control) and Kaizen (Continuous Improvement) systems. Toyota recognized the suggestion system as a competitive weapon from the beginning: "In order to survive in competition with foreign automobiles in future, we have to reduce manufacturing costs by making use of our suggestions" (comment by Saito, 1951).[42]

Another important system that Toyota introduced from America around this time was formal training of "scientific management" for supervisors, called Training Within Industry (TWI).[43] TWI, introduced to Toyota in 1951, was applied to general foremen (*kakari-cho*) and managers above them. Among other features, TWI included training of improvement activities by supervisors. Supervisors subsequently played a leading role in Kaizen activities at Toyota, whereas the role of supervisors in Kaizen was very limited at Ford after it established the mass-production system. According to Nemoto (1992), Kaizen activity was formally incorporated into the responsibility of shop-floor supervisors (*shoku-cho* and *kumi-cho*) around 1955.[44]

The introduction of TWI for training of shop-floor supervisors may be closely related to the replacement of traditional foremen-craftsmen with modern supervisors in the early postwar era. Facing the shortage of talent for the new job, Ohno had to convert plant staff and engineers to carry out the supervising jobs as a temporary measure. Toyota thus needed a formal training program for the new supervising jobs. It is likely that TWI was used for filling the shortage of the craft-style foremen.

From SQC to TQC   The automobile industry did not play an active role when the Total Quality Control concept emerged in Japan in the 1950s. After both Nissan and Toyota dispatched their staff to the seminars of the US Statistical Quality Control (SQC) in 1949 and adopted it, both companies were emphasizing capability of inspection, but the TQC concept was not prevalent.[45] In the late 1950s, Nissan moved one step ahead of Toyota and won the Deming Prize in 1960, and outperformed Toyota in domestic car-market share and exports in the early 1960s. Toyota's low quality level was criticized by the US military forces (APA). Import liberalization was forthcoming.

Against this background, Toyota introduced Total Quality Control (TQC) in 1961. Unlike JIT, TQC was introduced to the company in a top-down manner, and its diffusion was quick. Eiji Toyota explained the reasons for TQC as follows:

Improvements in quality did not progress as fast as improvements in efficiency. Also, the problems of newly recruited workers, insufficient education programs, lack of managers' capabilities and skills, and poor coordination across functions surfaced. At the same time, competition of quality against the rival auto makers intensified.[46]

In 1963, the model changeover of Corana (a small passenger car) was chosen as a company-wide theme for TQC. In 1965, Toyota received the Deming Implementation Prize.

Unlike Nissan, whose top managers tended to regard TQC as a campaign for winning the prize, Toyota's managers were more committed to the continuation of TQC. In 1965, Toyota created a procurement administration department (*kobai kanri bu*) and started to introduce both JIT and TQC to the suppliers.[47] Toyota won the Japan Quality Control Award in 1970, when Toyota had outperformed Nissan in the rapidly growing domestic market.

3.5 Emergence of the black box parts system[48]

The black box parts system refers to a certain pattern of transactions in which a parts supplier conducts detailed engineering of a component that it makes for an automobile-maker based on the latter's specification requirements and basic designs.[49]

The system probably originated with either the locomotive or aircraft industry of the prewar era, since the earliest adopters of this practice included prominent suppliers in these industries.

The American auto industry was not the source of this practice, however. Historical evidence makes us suppose that the transactions between Toyota and Nippondenso in 1949 was probably another origin of the black box parts practice. Historical imperatives, or technological constraints, seem to have played an important role here: first, before the war, Toyota could not find good quality electric parts suppliers in Japan, so it was almost forced to design and make such parts in-house; second, after the war, Toyota had to separate the electric parts factory for its own survival; third, when

Nippondenso was created in 1949 as a result of the separation, Toyota found that it had to rely on the engineering capability of Nippondenso, as virtually all the electrical engineers had moved to the separated company. In this way, the historical imperative that Toyota lacked the technological capability for electric parts appears to have forced Toyota to apply the approved drawing (i.e. black box parts) system to its transactions with Nippondenso from the beginning.

The diffusion of the black box practice peaked much later—in the late 1960s, which coincides with the period of rapid model proliferation during the motorization period. This fact makes one infer that another historical imperative of high growth with limited resource inputs in the product engineering area of the auto companies created constant pressures to sub-contract detailed component engineering wherever possible: the diffusion of the black box practice.

From the suppliers' point of view, the black box arrangement meant a great opportunity to develop its own design capability, build up a techno-logical entry barrier against the auto-makers' efforts to make the parts in-house, and survive as a first-tier parts supplier. Competitive pressures from the rival suppliers also accelerated their efforts to build up design and engineering capability in order to match up with their competitors' efforts.

It should be noted, however, that the content of the black box parts practice was in fact very different between Toyota and Nissan, that the former exploited the potential benefits of the practice in terms of cost reduction much more effectively, and that Nissan adopted Toyota's system during the 1980s after it realized the difference between the two compa-nies.[50] This indicates that, although both companies had to respond to similar historical pressures from the environment toward black box parts, their evolutionary capabilities were significantly different, which created a significant difference in effectiveness of the black box parts system at the two companies.

3.6 Evolution of the heavyweight product manager

Transfer from the Aircraft Industry   The heavyweight product-manager system is one of the core capabilities of effective product-development organization. Historical evidence indicates that the origin of this powerful project-leader system is the "chief designer" organization in the prewar aircraft industry (Hasegawa 1993; Maema 1993). Because of the nature of the aircraft, which required a high system integrity, its development project inherently needed a strong product manager, an aircraft engineer, who played a role of strong system-concept creator and project coordinator at the same time. When the Japanese aircraft industry disappeared after the war, a large number of talented aircraft engineers were forced to find jobs in other industries, including automobiles. The massive inflow of the aircraft engineers dramatically enhanced the technological capability of the postwar auto-makers.

Toyota as pioneer   Although all of the postwar auto-makers benefited from the technological capabilities that the ex-aircraft engineers brought with them, including body structural analysis and aerodynamics, Toyota was virtually the only company that directly adopted the institutional aspect of the aircraft development system: the heavyweight product managers (or what Toyota called *shusa*) system. Tatsuo Hasegawa, once a young chief designer of Tachikawa Aircraft, recalls that he had a clear intention to introduce the chief designers system to Toyota when he came to Toyota.[51] Toyota formally adopted the product-manager system in the 1950s, far ahead of the other Japanese auto-makers. Hasegawa led some projects as product manager during the 1960s, including the first generation of the Corolla.

Diffusion process   Diffusion of the heavyweight organization occurred much later, though. Honda introduced a strong project-leader system in the early 1970s after Soichiro Honda, the one-man chief engineer, retired. All the other auto firms moved to heavyweight product-manager organizations between the late 1970s and the 1980s. The sizable time lag between the origin of the heavyweight system (1950s) and its diffusion (1970s and 1980s) indicates that the real competitive advantage of the system became obvious when the market started to emphasize "product integrity," or coherence of the total vehicle design.[52] During the 1980s and the early 1990s, the heavyweight product-manager system was adopted by many of the Western auto-makers.

4. SYSTEM EMERGENCE AND EVOLUTIONARY CAPABILITIES: A SUMMARY

4.1 Summary of historical analysis

The above historical analysis of the successful development-production systems in postwar Japan seems to be consistent with the predictions mentioned at the beginning of Section 3. That is:

- Many of the capabilities were gradually acquired by the competing firms throughout the postwar period, particularly between the 1950s and 1970s, although some of the practices dated back to the prewar era. There were apparently *no grand strategies* for the sequence of capability acquisition. It was rather a long-term *evolutionary* process.
- Some aspects of the capabilities of the effective development-production systems were found in the Japanese firms in general. There

were obviously region-specific factors (i.e. the Japan effect) in the evolutionary process.

- Some other aspects of the capabilities were found only in certain manufacturers known for their high competitive performance, typically Toyota. Thus, interfirm differences in capability building was observed even within the group of Japanese auto-makers. In other words, firm-specific factors (i.e. the Toyota effect) coexisted with the region-specific patterns during the 1980s.

- Still other aspects of the system were generic, or common with automobile mass producers worldwide, in that they all introduced some elements of the standard Ford system directly or indirectly (i.e. the Ford effect). It is a myth that the Toyota system is a totally unique antithesis of the Ford system. It was rather a product of continuous *hybridization*.

To sum up, the historical findings were generally consistent with the prediction mentioned earlier that the Toyota-style system we have observed during the 1980s was a combination of (1) universally adopted practices (Ford effect), (2) region-specific capabilities (Japan effect) and (3) firm-specific capabilities (Toyota effect).

Also, the foregoing cases of system emergence and capability building seem to indicate that the development-production capability of the effective Japanese auto-makers gradually emerged as a result of complex interactions of entrepreneurial visions, historical imperatives, interfirm and interindustrial transfer of resources and practices and pure chance, as well as the firms' own evolutionary capability (Fig. 2.1). Table 2.2 indicates the complexity of the dynamics in the selected cases.

Let us now try to classify these explanations roughly into universal, region-specific and firm-specific effects in the capability-building processes:

(1) Factors affecting universally adopted capabilities

Perceived pressures of international competition   Toyota's capability building was consistently motivated, since the 1930s, by perceived competitive pressures from the US mass producers, particularly Ford. Even with a strongly protected domestic market between the 1930s and 1950s, Toyota's consciousness of the imaginary competitive pressures persisted.

Direct and indirect adoption of the Ford system   Motivated partly by the above consciousness of international competition, Toyota adopted many elements of the Ford system and the American mass-production system, mostly indirectly, including moving conveyors, transfer machines, product and component designs, the Taylor system, supervisor training programs and statistical quality control. Pure dichotomy between the Ford system and the Toyota system as the post-Ford paradigm is therefore misleading.

(2) Factors affecting region-specific capabilities

Benefits of historical imperatives by forced growth Some of the region-specific imperatives that all the Japanese firms faced during the postwar era almost "forced" them to make certain responses, some of which turned out to be contributing to competitive advantages of those firms. Many of such responses were not recognized as competitive weapons when the firms first adopted them. For example, *the imperative of forced growth*, both in production and product development, with limited supply of production inputs and the fear of labor conflicts, turned out to facilitate capability building for productivity improvements through avoidance of intrafirm overspecialization, division of labor between assemblers and suppliers as well as avoidance of excessive use of high-tech equipment on the shop-floor.

Benefits of historical imperatives by forced flexibility Likewise, the *imperative of forced flexibility* in the fragmented market also benefited the Japanese firms. This is partly because of the region-specific patterns of industrial growth: a rapid production growth accompanied by rapid product proliferation. The flexibility that the firms acquired tended to be recognized as a necessary evil to cope with the fragmented market, rather than a measure for international competition, when the capabilities were first instituted. It should also be noted that, as is obvious from the comparison of the Japanese and UK production systems, that fragmented markets do not automatically create effective flexibility.

Benefits of historical imperatives by lack of technology While excessive use of high-tech automation equipment often even became obstacles to productivity improvement, the effective Japanese firms apparently avoided such problems. This may be partly because they consciously rejected the temptation for overspecialization, but it also seems to be partly because high technology was not there in the first place. To the extent that this was caused by certain region-specific technology gaps, the lack of technology may bring about unintended competitive benefits to firms of a region.

Region-specific knowledge transfer Region-specific patterns of capabilities may also emerge when intraregional knowledge transfers are more dense and frequent than interregional ones. The suppliers network shared by the Japanese firms was one of such transfer instruments. Intense competition between domestic manufacturers during the 1960s and 1970s may also have facilitated their efforts for learning from the domestic competitors.

Benefits of unintended transfer As in the case of engineers from the prewar aircraft industry, the "push-type" knowledge transfer, which the receivers did not intend to make, brought about rapid increase in automobile

TABLE 2.2. Summary of evolution of selected production-development capabilities

	"Just-in-Time"	Multitasking with product-focus layout	"Jidoka" and flexible equipment	"Kaizen" and TQC	Black box parts	Heavyweight product manager
Competitive effect rationality	Pressure for productivity improvement Throughput time Inventory cost	Productivity improvement	Pressures for quality improvement Flexibility	Quality improvement Productivity improvement	Cost reduction by manufacturability Development lead time and productivity	High product integrity Development lead time and productivity
Entrepreneurial vision	Kiichiro Toyoda, 1930s ("Just in Time" slogan) Taiichi Ohno, 1940s–1950s	Kiichiro Toyoda, 1945 (productivity catch-up)	Kiichiro Toyoda, 1931	Top-down introduction of TQC (Eiji Toyoda)	Kiichiro Toyoda's "parts specialists" vision?	
Transfer from other industry	Textile (benchmarking of Nichibo) Aircraft	Textile industry: multimachine operation in spinning (through Ohno)	Textile industry: Sakichi Toyoda's automatic loom	TQC was established in other industries (e.g. process industry)	Prewar locomotive or aircraft parts supplier	Prewar aircraft industry (chief designer system) Forced transfer (collapse of aircraft industry)

Transfer from Ford system	The synchronization idea from Ford (invisible conveyor line)	Productivity bench-marking with Ford Modified Taylorism	Adoption of Detroit-type automation wherever possible	Suggestion system from Ford Training Within Industry Statistical Quality Control	High production growth and model proliferation created pressures for subcontracting, subassembly and design
Constraints: growth with resource shortage		Limit of permanent work force after the 1950 strikes "Forced" productivity increase	Shortage of investment fund: low-cost automation had to be pursued	Shortage of supervisors replacing craftsmen-foremen = needs for TWI	
Constraints: shortage of technology	Lack of computer technology in the 1950s and 1960s		Lack of adaptive control automation: "Jidoka" needs human intervention		Lack of electric parts technology at Toyota in 1949 (separation of Nippondenso)
Constraints: small and fragmented market			"Forced" flexibility of equipment due to small volume		

technologies and product development systems of the postwar automobile industry in Japan.

Benefit of incomplete knowledge transfer Although the Japanese auto firms tried to adopt many of the practices and techniques from the US mass producers (i.e. the Ford system), some of them were incomplete due to the historical imperatives mentioned above and the lack of absorption capacities by the firms. In this sense, the Kanban system may be regarded as an incomplete version of the conveyor system, U-shape machine layouts as incomplete transfer machines, and "jidoka" as incomplete adaptive automation. The very incompleteness of a transfer may have facilitated its subsequent diffusion to the entire system. For example, the case of the Kanban system may be regarded as *complete diffusion of incomplete synchronization technology*.

(3) Factors Affecting Firm-specific Capabilities

Benefits of self-fulfilling visions Firm-specific entrepreneurial visions sometimes played an important role in building distinctive development-production capability. This was particularly the case when apparently unrealistic visions that went against common sense triggered self-fulfilling efforts to achieve bold objectives. Kiichiro Toyoda in the 1930s and 1940s played a pivotal role in this sense in advocating cost reduction without economy of scale, catch-up with Ford and "Just-in-Time" philosophy. Nissan of those days did not have his counterpart.

Linkage to other industries Some of the linkages to other industries, which were technologically advanced in the past, may be firm-specific. For example, Toyota's inherent connection with the textile industry may have facilitated knowledge transfer from it (particularly through Taiichi Ohno) and created its competitive advantages in production-control techniques.

Advantages by post-trial capability Even when no firms recognized the potential competitive advantage of the new system when they first tried it, some firms could still create firm-specific competitive advantages by exercising *post-trial capability:* by recognizing the potential competitive advantage of the new system, modifying it to exploit the potential, institutionalizing it and retaining it until the advantages were realized. For example, even though all the Japanese auto-makers faced similar environmental pressures for adopting the black box parts system in the 1960s, only Toyota appears to have created a system that could fully exploit the potential advantages of this practice. Although all the Japanese auto-makers accepted aircraft engineers after the war, Toyota was the only company that institutionalized the heavyweight product-manager system that was prevalent in the aircraft industry. Thus, even when all the Japanese firms faced certain historical imperatives that facilitated new practices, only some of them may have exploited this potential luck by employing firm-specific evolutionary capability.

In summary, a combination of the logic of system emergence, including historical imperatives, knowledge transfers, entrepreneurial visions and post-trial capabilities, seems to be able to explain why firm-specific, region-specific and universally adopted capabilities coexisted, as well as how they emerged, in the effective product development and production systems in the Japanese auto industry of the 1980s.

The present chapter tries to demonstrate that the resource-capability view of the firm may be applied effectively to the historical case of development-production systems in a single business situation, where both interregional and interfirm differences in competitive performance are consistently observed. As for Toyota, this chapter has argued that the strength of this company comes not only from static or improvement capabilities, but also evolutionary capabilities, which existing literature does not seem to have explicitly analyzed. Such small-scale studies at the operational level, in turn, may serve as building blocks for higher levels of strategic analyses of multiproduct, multidivisional manufacturing firms.

NOTES

1. This chapter is basically an abridged version of Fujimoto (1994*b*), which was presented at the Prince Bertil Symposium in Stockholm in June 1994.
2. For the concepts of resource, organizational routine, capability and competence, see for example, Penrose (1959), Nelson and Winter (1982), Chandler (1990, 1992), Prahalad and Hamel (1990), Grant (1991), Leonard-Barton (1992), Teece, Pisano and Shuen (1992), and Teece, Rumelt, Dosi and Winter (1994). For evolutionary aspects of the firm and its strategies and technologies, see also Dosi (1982), Nonaka (1985).
3. See for example, Harbour (1980), Abernathy, Clark and Kantrow (1981, 1983), Womack, Jones and Roos (1990), Fuss and Waverman (1990), Clark and Fujimoto (1991, 1992) and Cusumano and Takeishi (1991).
4. For example, Ohno (1978), Shingo (1980), Monden (1983/1994), Schonberger (1982), Toyota Motor Corporation (1987), Coriat (1991).
5. Such recent literature as Chandler (1990), Prahalad and Hamel (1990) and Teece, Rumelt, Dosi and Winter (1994) mainly analyze the multiproduct or multiindustry situations.
6. A standard linear model of problem solving is used here for simplicity (e.g. Simon 1945, 1969; March and Simon 1958). Problem-solving activities in real

situations may be less structured, less streamlined and less continuous. See, for
example March and Olsen (1976) and March (1988). See, also von Hippel and
Tyre (1993).

7. See also the "garbage can" model in March and Olsen (1976) and March (1988).
8. See also Fujimoto (1994, 1995).
9. The neoclassical decisions further assume that the economic actors are equally
   capable and face the identical environment.
10. See for example, Fujimoto and Tidd (1993).
11. See, for example Womack, Jones and Roos (1990) and Clark and Fujimoto
    (1991).
12. See, for example Cusumano (1985), and Clark and Fujimoto (1991).
13. See, for example Ohno (1978), Abernathy, Clark and Kantrow (1983),
    Shimokawa (1991) and Fujimoto and Tidd (1993).
14. Toyota Motor Corporation (1978: 64).
15. See Shimokawa (1991).
16. Wada (1995) also points out that there was another source of the synchronized
    production idea from the prewar aircraft industry.
17. For labor movements at this stage, see for example Cusumano (1985, ch. 3).
18. Interview with Ohno by Shimokawa and Fujimoto, 16 July 1984.
19. See Ohno (1978).
20. The term "Kanban" was coined as a catchy word when Toyota challenged the
    Deming Award in 1965.
21. Interview with Ohno by Shimokawa and Fujimoto, 16 July 1984.
22. Cusumano (1985: 61 and 75).
23. Interview with Ohno by Shimokawa and Fujimoto, 16 July 1984.
24. This was based on his estimation around 1935 that US productivity in spinning
    operations would have been nine times higher than that of the Japanese.
25. See Fujimoto and Tidd (1993) for details of the UK—Japan comparison in this
    regard.
26. Toyota Motor Corporation (1978: 92–5).
27. Interview with Taiichi Ohno, 16 July 1984, at the headquarters of Toyota Gosei.
    Interviewers, Professor Koichi Shimokawa of Hosei University and the author.
28. On the transformation of the Ford system from that of dynamic experimenta-
    tion to a static system of fragmented jobs, see for example Abernathy, Clark and
    Kantrow (1983, ch. 6) and Shimokawa (1991).
29. Interview with Ohno by Shimokawa and Fujimoto, 16 July 1984.
30. Interview with Taiichi Ohno, 16 July 1984, at the headquarters of Toyota Gosei.
    Interviewers, Professor Koichi Shimokawa of Hosei University and the author.
31. Toyota Motor Corporation (1978: 41).
32. See Okouchi (1979).
33. According to Abernathy (1978: 138), capacity of a standard Ford assembly plant
    was about 400 to 500 units per 8 hours, or about one minute cycle time, since the
    mid-1910s.
34. Toyota Motor Corporation (1978: 60).
35. Toyota Motor Corporation (1978: 85).
36. See for example Fujimoto (1993*b*).
37. As for the change of machine layout in the early Ford system, see for example
    Hounshell (1984: 221–2). Wada (1995) points out that the prewar aircraft indus-

try may be another source of the product-focused layout and semiflow production system.

38. For example, the number of balling machines increased from 50 to 200. Interview with Ohno by Shimokawa and Fujimoto, 16 July 1984.
39. It should be noted, here, that multiskilled workers are different from traditional crafts people: the former did a series of standardized tasks along the process flow; the latter were all-round players who did everything related to their trade regardless of process flow or work standards.
40. For the development and diffusion of Detroit-type automation, see Hounshell (1994).
41. Due to limitations of space, a discussion of *jidoka* ("autonomation") is omitted. See Fujimoto (1994*b*).
42. Toyota Motor Corporation (1978: 181).
43. See Robinson and Schroeder (1993) for detailed illustration of TWI.
44. See Nemoto (1992).
45. See for example Udagawa (1993) and Nonaka (1994).
46. Toyota Motor Corporation (1978: 251).
47. Masao Nemoto, the first head of Purchasing Administration Department, as well as Taiichi Ohno, played a central role in this diffusion process.
48. For capability building in the Japanese supplier system in general, see for example Fujimoto (1994*b*)
49. For further details, see Fujimoto (1995).
50. See Fujimoto (1994*a*).
51. Hasegawa (1993). See also Maema (1993).
52. For the concept of product integrity, see Clark and Fujimoto (1990, 1991).

REFERENCES

Abernathy, W. J. (1978), *The Productivity Dilemma* (Baltimore: Johns Hopkins Press).
——Clark, K. B. and Kantrow, A. M. (1981), "The New Industrial Competition," *Harvard Business Review*, Sept.–Oct., 68–81.
————(1983), *Industrial Renaissance*: *Producing a Competitive Future for America* (New York: Basic Books).
Chandler, A. D. (1990), *Scale and Scope* (Cambridge, Mass.: Harvard University Press).
——(1992), "What Is a Firm?" *European Economic Review,* 36: 483–92.
Clark, K. B. and Fujimoto, T. (1990), "The Power of Product Integrity," *Harvard Business Review*, Nov.–Dec., 107–18.
————(1991), *Product Development Performance*: *Strategy, Organization and Management in the World Auto Industry* (Boston, Mass.: Harvard Business School Press).
————(1992), "Product Development and Competitiveness," *Journal of the*

Japanese and International Economies, 6: 101–43.

Coriat, B. (1991), *Penser a l'Envers* (Paris: Christian Bourgois Editeur) (in French).

Cusumano, M. A. (1985), *The Japanese Automobile Industry* (Cambridge, Mass.: Harvard University Press).

——and Takeishi, A. (1991), "Supplier Relations and Management: A Survey of Japanese-Transplant, and U.S. Auto Plants," *Strategic Management Journal*, 12: 563–88.

Dosi, G. (1982), "Technological Paradigms and Technological Trajectories," *Research Policy,* 11: 147–62.

Fujimoto, T. (1989), "Organizations for Effective Product Development: The Case of the Global Automobile Industry," Harvard University, D.B.A. diss.

——(1993), "Strategies for Assembly Automation in the Automobile Industry," Tokyo University Faculty of Economics Discussion Paper 93-F-13.

——(1994), "Iwayuru Toyota teki jidosha seisan kaihatsu system no kigento shinkani tsuite" (On the Origin and Evolution of So-called Toyota-style Production-Development System), presented at Tokyo Center of Economic Research Conference, Mar., Tokyo University Faculty of Economics Discussion Paper 94-J-12 (in Japanese).

——(1995), "A Note on the Origin of the 'Black Box Parts' Practice in the Japanese Auto Industry," in H. Shiomi and K. Wada (eds.), (Oxford: Oxford University Press).

——and Tidd, J. (1993), "The U.K. and Japanese Auto Industry: Adoption and Adaptation of Fordism," Imperial College Working Paper, presented at Entrepreneurial Activities and Corporate Systems Conference, Jan., Tokyo University. The Japanese version: "Ford system no donyu to genchi tekio: Nichi-ei jidosha sangyo no hikaku kenkyu," *Kikan keizaigaku ronshu* (The Journal of Economics, Tokyo University), 59/2: 36–50, and 59/3: 34–56.

Fuss, M. and Waverman, L. (1990), "The Extent and Sources of Cost and Efficiency Differences between U.S. and Japanese Motor Vehicle Producers," *Journal of the Japanese and International Economies*, 4: 219–56.

Grant, R. (1991), "The Resource-Based Theory of Competitive Advantage: Implications for Strategy Formulation," *California Management Review*, June, 114–35.

Harbour, J. (1980), "Comparison and Analysis of Manufacturing Productivity," Final Consulting Report, Harbour and Associates, Dearborn Heights, Mich.

Hasegawa, T. (1993), "Nihon ni okeru jidoshagijutsu no okori to tenkai: watakushino keiken" (Origin and development of Automobile Technologies in Japan: From My Experience), Kagaku Gijutsu Seisaku Kenkyusho (NISTEP) Research Material, Seminar Note 43 (in Japanese).

Hounshell, D. A. (1984), *From the American System to Mass Production 1800–1932: The Development of Manufacturing Technology in the U.S.* (Baltimore: Johns Hopkins Press).

——(1994), "Planning and Executing 'Automation' at Ford Motor Company, 1945–1960: The Cleveland Engine Plant and its Consequences," presented at 21st Fuji Conference, Jan.

Leonard-Barton, D. (1992), "Core Capabilities and Core Rigidities: A Paradox in Managing New Product Development," *Strategic Management Journal,* 13: 111–25.

Maema, T. (1993), *Man-Machine no Showa densetsu* (The Legend of Man-Machine in the Showa Era], i and ii (Tokyo: Koden-sha) (in Japanese).

March, J. G. (1988), *Decisions and Organizations* (Oxford: Blackwell).

——and Simon, H. A. (1958), *Organizations* (New York: Wiley).

——and Olsen, J. P. (1976), *Ambiguity and Choice in Organizations* (Bergen, Norway: Universitetsforlaget).

Monden, Y. (1983), *Toyota Production System: Practical Approach to Production Management* (Noreross, ga.: Industrial Engineering and Management Press).

——(1994), *Toyota Production System: An Integrated Approach to Just-in-Time* London: Chapman & Hall).

Nemoto, M. (1992), *TQC seiko no hiketsu 30-kajo* (30 Secrets of Successful TQC) (Tokyo: Nichikagiren) (in Japanese).

Nelson, R. R. and Winter, S. G. (1982), *An Evolutionary Theory of Economic Change* (Cambridge, Mass.: Belknap, Harvard University Press).

Nishiguchi, T. (1993), *Strategic Industrial Sourcing* (New York: Oxford University Press); (also, 1989, "Strategic Dualism," unpubl. Ph.D. diss., Oxford University).

Nonaka, Ikujiro (1985), *Kigyo shinkaron* (The Theory of Corporate Evolution) (Tokyo: Nihon Keizai Shinbunsha) (in Japanese).

Nonaka, Izumi (1994), "The Development of Company-Wide Quality Control and Quality Circles at Toyota Motor Corporation and Nissan Motor Co. Ltd," presented at the 21st Fuji Conference, Jan.

Ohno, T. (1978), *Toyota seisan hoshiki* (Toyota Production System) (Tokyo: Diamond) (in Japanese).

Okouchi, A. (1979), *Keiei kosoryoku* (Entrepreneurial Imagination) (Tokyo: Shuppankai Tokyo University) (in Japanese).

Oshiima, T. (1987) (ed.), *Gendai nihon no jidosha buhin kogyo* (The Automobile Parts Industry in Modern Japan) (Tokyo: Nihon keizai hyoronsha) (in Japanese).

Penrose, E. T. (1959), *The Theory of the Growth of the Firm* (Oxford: Blackwell).

Prahalad, C. K. and Hamel, G. (1990), "The Core Competence of the Corporation," *Harvard Business Review*, May–June, 79–91.

Robinson, A. G. and Schroeder, D. M. (1993), "Training, Continuous Improvement, and Human Relations: The U.S. TWI Programs and the Japanese Management Style," *California Management Review*, Winter, 35–57.

Sato, Y. (1980) (ed.), *Teiseichoka ni okeru gaichu shitauke kanri* (Outsourcing and Subcontracting Management in a Low-Growth Period) (Tokyo: Chuo kezai sha) (in Japanese).

Schonberger, R. J. (1982), *Japanese Manufacturing Techniques*. (New York: Free Press).

Shimokawa, K. (1991), "Ford system kara Just-in-Time system e" (From the Ford system to the Just-in-Time system), in K. Nakagawa (ed.), *Kigyo keiei no rekishiteki kenkyu* (A Historical Study of Corporate Management) (Tokyo: Iwanami-Shoten) (in Japanese).

Shingo, S. (1980), *Toyota seisan houshiki no IE teki kosatsu* (An Industrial Engineering Analysis of Toyota Production System) (Tokyo: Nikkan Kogyo Shinbunsha) (in Japanese).

Simon, H. (1945), *Administrative Behavior*, 3rd edn. (New York: Macmillan).

——(1969), *The Science of the Artificial* (Cambridge, Mass.: MIT Press).

Teece, J. T., Pisano, G. and Shuen, A. (1992), "Dynamic Capabilities and Strategic Management", University of California Berkeley, Working Paper.
——Rumelt, R., Dosi, G. and Winter, S. (1994), "Understanding Corporate Coherence: Theory and Evidence", *Journal of Economic Behavior and Organization*, 23: 1–30.
Toyota Motor Corporation (1978), *Toyota no ayumi* (History of Toyota) (Toyota City, Aichi) (in Japanese).
——(1987), *An Introduction to the Toyota Production System* (Toyota City Aichi).
Udagawa, M. (1993), "Nihon jidosha sangyo ni okeru hinshitsu kanri katsudo-Nissan to Toyota" (Quality Control Activities in the Japanese Automobile Industry: Nissan and Toyota), Hosei University Center for Business and Industrial Research, Working Paper No. 36 (in Japanese).
von Hippel, E. and Tyre, M. (1993), "How 'Learning by Doing' is Done: Problem Identification in Novel Process Equipment," MIT Sloan School, Working Paper.
Wada, K. (1991), "The Development of Tiered Inter-Firm Relationships in the Automobile Industry: A Case Study of the Toyota Motor Corporation", *Japanese Yearbook on Business History*, 8: 23–47.
——(1995), "The Emergence of 'Flow Production' Methods in Japan," in H. Shiomi and K. Wada (eds.), *Fordism Transformed* (Oxford: Oxford University Press).
Womack, J., Jones, D. T. and Roos, D. (1990), *The Machine that Changed the World* (New York: Rawson Associates).

3

Science, Technological Advance and Economic Growth

RICHARD R. NELSON AND
NATHAN ROSENBERG

1. INTRODUCTION

Economists studying economic growth have long understood that technological advance was the principal driving force. During the 1950s a number
of economists made estimates, using the newly available time series on
National Product, of the percentage of measured growth that was accounted for by technological advance. All such studies showed the fraction
to be large (Abramovitz 1956; Fabricant 1954; Kendrick 1956; Solow 1957).
But this empirical evidence came, not so much as surprising news, but
rather as quantitative support for understandings that had already been
shared among economists for some time. Thus, Abramovitz had stressed
the key role of technological advance in his 1952 survey article on the
"Economics of Growth" (Abramovitz 1952). And indeed there is a sense in
which technological advance was center stage in Adam Smith's analysis in
The Wealth of Nations.

While there is no serious dispute about the importance of technological
advance in economic growth, a far more difficult issue has been the complex
question of just how technological advance comes about. In the early
growth models, such advance was treated as "exogenous" and as a "public
good." But of course, even long before Schumpeter, economists had well
understood that much of the work that leads to technological advance was
undertaken by business firms. And firms would not engage in R&D unless
the technology that they created was, at least to some extent, proprietary.

Spurred on by the studies showing the economic importance of technological advance, and by the limited understanding of how such advance
comes about, a number of economists, historians and other social scientists
have researched that question over the last thirty years. Moreover, the last
half-dozen years have seen the development of a number of new growth
models in which technological advance is treated as endogenous—the result
of investment in R&D by private firms. In these models the new technology
created by firms is treated as proprietary, but with spillovers (Grossman and
Helpman 1991; Romer 1990; Verspagen 1991). These new models go some

distance toward capturing some of the understandings about technological advance that have been won over the years by economists and other scholars who have studied the subject empirically. However, in this essay we wish to highlight two aspects of technological advance that these models miss.

One of these is the role of science in technological advance. Most of the new formal growth theory is mute about this. In some models there is an endogenous force that, in effect, renews technological opportunities as they are mined out by applied R&D, and this force might metaphorically be considered to be the advance of science. But there is no explicit treatment of what science is, and who does science, and why.

The second aspect of technological advance that we believe has not been treated adequately is the uncertainties that such advance inevitably involves. Some of the new growth models have treated the arrival of new technology as probabilistic, but the assumption built into these models is that the events that occur have all been explicitly foreseen as possibilities. However, the advent and development of the transistor, the laser, or recombinant DNA technology, have all involved elements of real surprise. The treatment of uncertainty in the new models represses this.

The discussion which follows fills out and elaborates these two points. The concluding section explores their challenges for growth theory.

2. THE RELATIONSHIPS BETWEEN SCIENCE AND TECHNOLOGY

In our view, understanding of the relationships between science and technology has been hindered by a tendency of those who have not studied the subject closely to see "science" as an activity that defines its own puzzles, and accepts or rejects proposed solutions in terms of its own criteria. According to such a view, the contribution of scientific advance to the promotion of technology is basically a byproduct of the scientific enterprise. By creating new knowledge, science almost inadvertently sheds light on certain technological problems, and spotlights certain technological opportunities that had not been seen before.

Such a perspective, however, misses much of what science is all about. While a few fields of modern science are "self-contained" in the sense suggested above, most are not. Modern chemistry grew out of ancient alchemy—the search for riches through manipulation of chemical reactions. Much of modern biology grew up as a search for understanding what lay behind human, animal and plant diseases. As fundamental a field of physics as thermodynamics came into being as a result of puzzles raised by the operation of the steam engine.

Put more generally, the growing contribution of science to the development of new technology in the course of the twentieth century has taken place, in large measure, because particular disciplines have been put into place expressly for that purpose. It is a telling feature of a number of these disciplines that they are difficult to classify and that, in fact, their designation or classification has frequently changed over time. Thus metallurgy, which was once "mining engineering," has been merged into a more capacious "materials science," research on computers has been labelled "computer science," but this particular "science" is usually located in schools of engineering, and the engineering disciplines themselves are now frequently labeled "engineering sciences." MIT at present has a "Department of Materials Science and Engineering." At many universities the borderline between the department housing the scientific discipline that is called "applied physics" and the Department of Electrical Engineering is decidedly porous. The difficulty in drawing boundary lines is totally understandable. It is reflective of a complex expansion, overlapping and increasing intertwining of the separate disciplines that make up the realms of science and technology.

This intertwining has become further complicated as technology itself has become more sophisticated. That is to say, technologies, or the problems and needs that technologies address, have themselves become the subject matter of scientific research. To an increasing degree, especially but by no means only in industrial research laboratories, the research agenda of trained scientists has been determined by the need to improve the performance characteristics of a technology which, in turn, involves understanding the technology in terms of underlying scientific principles. Thus, important new technological developments such as the transistor, the integrated circuit, the laser, the computer or beta-blocking drugs, become the subject matter of scientific inquiry, so that performance might eventually be improved. For such research to be effective, the "scientist" must become intimately familiar with the technology.

The development of modern science-based technologies, a process that perceptibly accelerated in the last quarter of the nineteenth century, depended directly on the parallel growth of two primary institutions, and soon led to the development of others. The rise, initially in Germany, of the modern organic chemical-products industries, and the new industries organized around technologies based upon electricity and magnetism, required university-trained scientists and engineers. Universities had to establish academic programs in these fields and to develop curricula that would equip students with the intellectual skills that would enhance their usefulness to private industry.

On the industry side, it soon became apparent that, to be effective, innovation in these new industries required that firms establish their own research laboratories, staffed by these university-trained scientists and engineers, and sharply focused upon the particularities of the firm's technological needs and the needs dictated by its competitive environment. The interdependence between emerging industrial research labs, on the one hand, and the new and augmented university curricula in fields such as chemistry, physics and engineering on the other, is apparent. Without industrial laboratories there was no prospective market for the increasing number of university graduates. On the other hand, without such an augmented supply of university-trained scientists and engineers, it was impossible to institutionalize research and development activities at the level of the individual firm (Mowery 1981).

It is extremely curious how little attention, even to this day, has been devoted to examining the factors behind the growing demand for technically trained personnel. Historically, the dimension of the American experience that seems to have been so distinctive by comparison with most other industrialized countries was the roughly simultaneous growth of the applied disciplines in its universities along with the industrial laboratories that created a demand for the graduates of such educational programs. Even in the extensive recent literature on LDCs and how appropriate policy changes might convert them into NICS, this factor is largely ignored. Great emphasis is placed on the importance of expanding the supply of young people with appropriate scientific and engineering training. At the same time, the factors that will determine the demand—the employment opportunities for such personnel—have been totally neglected. More often than not the resulting mismatch in LDCs has led to unemployment, underemployment and emigration of the small pool of educated youths.

The growing links between universities and industry made sense only to the extent that the growth of knowledge could be made to assume a form and a content that would be of direct assistance to the changing needs of various industrial sectors. The discipline of metallurgy may be said to have emerged in the last third of the nineteenth century to meet the requirements of a rapidly expanding steel industry. Electrical and chemical engineering emerged around the turn of the century to meet the needs of the new industries producing electrical equipment and chemical products. But the distinctive requirements of these new industries, in turn, created an entirely new set of demands for metals and alloys with new combinations of performance characteristics.

The American higher educational system was particularly notable for the speed with which it responded to industrial needs. MIT introduced its first course in electrical engineering in 1882, the same year in which Edison's Pearl Street station, the first in the United States, went into operation. Cornell University introduced a course in electrical engineering in 1883 and managed to award the first doctorate in the subject as early as 1885 (Rosenberg and Nelson 1994). At the same time it should be stressed that American universities were by no means more advanced in the underlying discipline of physics. Indeed, American teaching and research in this field were qualitatively far behind many European countries, especially Germany. Right through the decade of the 1920s it was common for the cream of young American scientists to pursue their advanced training in Europe, particularly in Germany. Evidently the economic contributions of universities did not depend upon their leadership in the performance of "frontier" scientific research.

But the new applied disciplines did not just define new educational programs. They also served as focal points for more practical research activities that advanced the stock of useful knowledge in subjects of evident commercial value to innovating firms. Moreover, they formed the basis for new scientific and technologically based professional societies that brought together people from both universities and industry. The new professional organizations were concerned with the body of knowledge and technique relevant to the practice of their fields, and they were dedicated to the exchange and spread of such knowledge among the professional community. It should be noticed that the activities of members of these associations cannot be readily accommodated by simple models of individual firm profit maximization, but rather need to be understood in terms of voluntary collective action. The focus was on certain common interests and goals that often transcended the specific needs of the individual firms. Such goals included safety which, it often turned out, required research whose findings far transcended safety alone. The setting of standards was another common goal. One organization which, in fact, combined the separate concerns of safety and standards was the American Society for Testing Materials, established in 1902. Moreover, members of professional associations typically committed themselves to certain ethical standards and modes of behavior— including the free exchange of useful knowledge itself—that were not necessarily consistent with the maximizing behavior of a firm in a competitive situation.

Finally, the government was an institutional actor that might assume a wide variety of roles of direct relevance to technological innovation. As early as the Civil War, the United States federal as well as state governments became the patrons of the new agricultural research system that was located primarily at universities. In the course of the twentieth century the growing concern with issues of public health led to government support of research on relevant topics and in relevant disciplines, with that research centered both in university medical schools and in public hospitals. Governments quickly came to understand the importance of certain technologies, such as electrical and electronic-based technologies, to national security needs, and began to act also as patrons for selected categories of research.

It is obviously not possible, in a single paper, to examine the operation of each of these new useful disciplines that constitute the focal point of our own research agenda. Indeed, it is central to our own understanding that, precisely because the growth of useful knowledge has become predicated upon highly specialized disciplines, that these disciplines typically have distinct methodologies, research strategies, priorities and specific goals that set them apart from one another. Chemical engineers and aeronautical engineers are necessarily products of very different kinds of professional training, and both these engineers operate in environments that are distinctly different from that of medical pathologists or oncologists. We propose, therefore, to illustrate some of these distinctive features. We will also, before we are done, attempt to establish certain common denominators of trained professionals as producers as well as purveyors of useful knowledge.

We begin with the broad question of the relationship between science and technology. Even where scientific findings have profoundly influenced technological activities, it is essential not to conclude that these findings were derived from recent research at the scientific frontier. In fact, many points of contention over the economic importance of science really derive from the fact that the science that was essential to some technological breakthrough was simply *old* science. Indeed, often this science was so old that it was no longer considered by some to be science. This confusion is accentuated by the fact that spokesmen for the economic importance of science are anxious to make a case for larger research budgets and, in making this case, are wont to emphasize the benefits that may be derived from what goes on at the research frontier.

The fact is that technology draws upon scientific knowledge and methodology in highly unpredictable ways—ways where we are likely to cover up our ignorance by evoking such shameless tautologies as "when the time is ripe." The body of knowledge that is called "science" consists of an immense pool to which small annual increments are made at the "frontier." However, the true significance of science is diminished, rather than enhanced, by extreme emphasis upon the importance of the most recent *increments* to that pool. The lags may be very long indeed, often because much essential complementary technology needs to be put in place before it can truly be said that "the time is ripe" for some particular invention. Consequently, the perspective of the economist needs to be distinctly different from the perspective of the historian of science or that of contemporary advocates of larger science budgets in the public sector.

3. THE FUNDAMENTAL UNCERTAINTIES INVOLVED IN TECHNOLOGICAL ADVANCE

Scientific knowledge and its advance helps technologists to understand the artifacts and processes with which they work better, and to improve them and tailor them to new purposes. That this is the case is not surprising. As we have stressed, this is exactly the purpose of much of "science." But one of the striking characteristics of technological advance is that attempts to "invent" almost always reach beyond what is well known. It is as if advances in science cannot reduce significantly uncertainties at the frontiers of technology, at least not durably, because new knowledge induces inventors to reach further.

Also, the dynamics of technological advance takes directions of its own. Technology builds from technology as much as it builds from science. And the problems, uncertainties, and procedures for dealing with uncertainties in efforts to advance technology have special characteristics in their own right.

Consider the laser. The first lasers were developed around 1960, and lasers have expanded into a remarkably diverse range of uses in the past thirty years—including telecommunications, reproduction of high-quality music, research in chemistry, delicate surgery and, not least, the Hewlett-Packard printer that produced the manuscript of the present paper. Yet the "pure" science underlying the laser, as an historian of science might well point out, had been formulated by Einstein as long ago as 1916. That underlying science involves an understanding of the energy levels of molecules and solids, and the specific principle was formulated in Einstein's work on stimulated emission (Whinnery 1987). An historian of science might say that everything of real interest had been completed by 1916, and the rest was "just" engineering and product development. At the same time, what is relatively uninteresting to the historian of science may be the most essential part of the story from the point of view of technological innovation and economic impact. It is difficult to imagine laser technology developing when it did without the technological developments during World War II underlying microwave radar—microwave detectors, magnetron and klystron sources, waveguide networks, etc.

Amid this specialization of interests it is essential to retain the point that there may be lags of many decades between a given increment to science and the useful applications that may one day flow from it. This long separation in time between a fundamental breakthrough in science and its commercial application is one important reason—but only one—why the commercial benefits of basic research need not be captured by firms in the country where the basic research was performed. Perhaps equally important and equally neglected, the development of sophisticated, high-performance technologies, such as lasers and other complex instrumentation, has in turn given rise to much new basic scientific research in order to provide the intellectual basis for generating improvements in the performance of the technology. This is a central aspect of the point made earlier of the increasing intertwining of science and technology.

This brings us to a second major source of disjunction between an advance in science, and its eventual influence upon technology and the economy, that has received little attention. The problem is that, even when scientific research opens up an entirely new field of technological possibilities, this "opening up" is usually a multistage process. The reason is that it is hardly ever possible to proceed directly from new scientific knowledge into production, even when that new knowledge is actually knowledge of a specific final product—a new chemical entity, for example—as opposed to the discovery of some new piece of information about the natural universe that may serve as an *input* in the eventual development of a new final product. In fact, the emergence of the two powerful disciplines of electrical and chemical engineering, beginning in the late nineteenth century, occurred for precisely this reason. It was not possible to move directly from the enlarged understanding of the electromagnetic and synthetic organic chemical realms into the production of goods that incorporated this new scientific knowledge. The reason here was simple. *The necessary technologies could in no way be deduced from or derived from the scientific knowledge alone.* On the contrary, distinctly different bodies of knowledge had to be drawn upon, or created *de novo*, before production could begin. Sometimes, as in the cases of electrical and chemical engineering, this required the development of entirely new disciplines.

The essential point is that the design and construction of plants devoted to, say, large-scale chemical processing activities involves an entirely different set of activities and capabilities than those that generated the new chemical entities. To begin with, the problems of mixing, heating and contaminant control, which can be performed with great precision in the lab, are immensely more difficult to handle in large-scale operations, especially if high degrees of precision and quality control are required. Moreover, economic considerations play a much larger role in the design of chemical process equipment, since cost considerations come to play a decisive role in an industrial context.

Thus, the discovery of a new chemical entity has commonly posed an entirely new question, one that is remote from the scientific context of the laboratory: how does one go about producing it? A chemical process plant is far from a merely scaled-up version of the original laboratory equipment. Experimental equipment may have been made of glass or porcelain. A manufacturing plant will almost certainly have to be constructed of different materials. Moreover, efficient manufacturing is, inherently, something drastically different from a simple, multiple enlargement of small-scale experimental equipment. This indeed is what accounts for the unique importance of the pilot plant, which may be thought of as a device for translating the findings of laboratory research into a production process that is not only technically feasible but also economically efficient. The pilot plant, which is intermediate in size between the equipment in the laboratory and the projected full-size production plant, is a way of confirming whether the scaling-up predictions provided by a simplified theory are in fact working with reasonable accuracy. The pilot plant is, thus, not so much a technological innovation as a technology *of* innovation.

Pilot plants have in the past been essential not only for the purpose of the reduction of uncertainties with respect to scale. They also provided other sources of knowledge that were essential to successful economic performance, knowledge that, in recent years, is being partially generated by computers. Until a pilot plant was built the precise characteristics of the output could not be determined. Test marketing could not proceed without the availability of reliable samples. Other essential features of the production process could not possibly be derived from scientific knowledge alone. Consider the recycle problem. Very few chemical reactions are complete in the reaction stage. Therefore products of the reaction stage will include not only desired end products but also intermediates, unreacted feed, and trace impurities—some measurable and some unmeasurable. In particular, impurities are identified by the operation of the pilot plant and methods of removing them devised in order to achieve a steady-state condition on a continuing basis.

It has been true of many of the most important new materials that have been introduced in the twentieth century that a gap of several, or even many years, has separated their discovery under laboratory conditions from the industrial capability of manufacturing them on a commercial basis. This was true of the first polymers that W. H. Carothers had produced with his glass equipment at the du Pont laboratories. It was also true of polyethylene and terephthalic acid, an essential material in the production of terylene, a major synthetic fiber. In the case of polyethylene, one of the most useful of plastics, it could be produced under experimental conditions for nearly thirty years before methods were finally developed for producing it on a commercial scale.

Beginning early in the twentieth century an entirely new methodology, totally distinct from the science of chemistry, had to be devised in order to manage the transition from test tubes to large-scale manufacture. This new methodology involved exploiting the central concept of unit operations. The term, coined by Arthur D. Little at MIT in 1915, provided the essential basis for a rigorous, quantitative approach to large-scale chemical manufacturing, and thus may be taken to mark the emergence of chemical engineering as a unique discipline, a discipline not reducible to "applied chemistry."

It is time that we made explicit a point that has been only implicit in the discussion so far. The point is central to the question of just what it is that engineers do. Much successful innovation is not so much a matter of invention, as a patent examiner would define a patentable invention. Rather, the common denominator of engineering activity is a matter of design, i.e. undertaking to devise a product or process that will achieve a desirable cluster of performance characteristics subject to certain cost constraints. This design activity is a large part of what the D of R&D is all about—and one must remember that most of R&D is in fact D. These activities involve engineering design activities that are very sophisticated and therefore extremely costly. (Not long ago McDonnell Douglas estimated that the mere redesign of the wing for a new wide-bodied jet that would be a successor to the DC-10 would be likely to cost a billion dollars.) It is important to note, moreover, that determining where "design" ends and "research" begins is a matter of some real difficulty as soon as one deals with relationships that cannot be optimized by referring to codified data in engineering handbooks. Here again, science and technology are deeply intertwined.

What has been said about the design of chemical process plants has parallels throughout the engineering disciplines. Science and technology are intertwined, but at the same time there is a strict limit to what can be delivered by science alone. Optimizing a design with respect to several variables and determining the appropriate tradeoffs are not activities for which science can provide guidance. This is particularly the case, of course, when the tradeoffs need to be determined with respect to economic considerations.

A further point. Not only can one not deduce optimal design from any set of scientific principles. Usually it is necessary to resort to experiment in order to generate optimal design data. Even more strongly, optimal design from an engineering viewpoint is the outcome of a frequent interplay between research and observed practice—including the outcome of experiment and testing. A major design advance almost always carries with it significant uncertainties about how well the design will work, uncertainties that are not resolved until the design is actually tested.

Again, this designing activity is a far cry from laboratory research in the sense that it cannot be deduced from the findings of that research. In this sense, wind tunnel tests with small aircraft models, and subsequent aircraft prototypes—such as the new Boeing 777 that is about to be tested and the development costs for which, Boeing claims, amounted to $4 billion—bear close similarities to the pilot plant in the chemical processing industries. In both cases there are large uncertainties attached to technical designs that incorporate significant elements of novelty. The technical uncertainties readily translate into huge financial losses if new designs fail or if they are introduced prematurely into practice. It is worth recalling that Rolls-Royce was driven into bankruptcy by the poor performance of the new composite material, Hyfil, that the firm attempted to introduce into the blades of the new jet engines for the ill-fated Lockheed L-1011—and Lockheed was, in turn, driven out of the commercial aircraft industry largely as a result of its late entry into the wide-bodied market. Testing of aircraft models and prototypes and chemical pilot plants are specialized modalities for determining optimal new product design or, alternatively, for the reduction of technological uncertainties in innovation. In both cases there is also the question of the reliability of design data as they relate to the scale of the experiments that generate the data. The smaller the scale of the pilot plant and the smaller the size of the airplane model and wind tunnel, the less reliable the design information generated by early experiments.

Through such vehicles as building and testing pilot plants and prototypes, and testing experimental new drugs, the activities aimed to advance technology generate new knowledge as well as new products and processes. Here again it is not uncommon for new scientific understanding to follow rather than lead, as when the science of aerodynamics created theoretical understanding of the factors determining lift and drag, *after* the first flying machines had been built and flown, or when William Shockley developed a theory of holes and electrons in semiconductors in order to explain how and why the transistor, that had *already* been invented, actually worked, or when the earliest working lasers demonstrated their powerful potential and thus stimulated a huge increased commitment of resources to the science of optics. Once again the new device or process that works, *but not terribly well*, initiates scientific research directed at refinement, improvement and variegation.

The Wright Brothers' 1903 machine was scarcely more than a large, ungainly bicycle with a primitive engine and attached wings. (The resemblance to the bicycle was no coincidence, since the Wright Brothers had previously been designers as well as manufacturers of bicycles.) Their airplane's parts were secured by baling wire and glue, and its total flight was a mere couple of hundred yards. Not until the 1930s did aircraft shed their struts and external bracing wire, the non-load-carrying skin involving the use of doped fabrics, and assume their stressed-skin monocoque construction form. Only with the design and development of the DC-3 did the airplane finally become a reliable means of transportation on commercial routes.

But the performance gap that separates the DC-3 of fifty years ago from today's wide-bodied aircraft, equipped with powerful jet engines, swept-back wings, sophisticated electronics, and a capability for flying over most weather turbulence, is also immense. It almost has to be said of the airplane that everything of economic significance is attributable to the subsequent improvements, since 1903, that have been made within the original, crude framework of the Wright brothers' flying machine (Hallion 1977; Miller and Sawers 1969).

The point made here with respect to performance improvement of aircraft is, in fact, a point of broad generality that is commonly lost in the literature on the economics of innovation. Most industrial R&D expenditures are upon products that have been in existence for a long time— aircraft, automobiles, cameras (which have been in existence fully 150 years), etc. It is these existing products that serve to define the framework within which improvements can be identified and undertaken. Even the transistor, which has so drastically transformed the world in the second half of the twentieth century, has been around now for more than forty years. Its introduction in the late 1940s laid the groundwork for what has turned out to be a continuing microelectronics revolution. Yet the original transistor was a fragile, unreliable and expensive piece of apparatus. It was only the subsequent improvements in that original, primitive device that made the later microelectronics revolution possible.

The larger point here is that technical advance appears to be characterized by a high degree of continuity and a great many cross connections between the separate lines of development. New or improved technologies hardly ever emerge from a clean slate. Today's developments draw on what was learned and created yesterday and the day before, and they in turn influence what is feasible and what may happen tomorrow. But at the same time developments in one scientific field, or one field of technology, strongly influence what is feasible and what is interesting in adjacent fields of science and technology (Rosenberg 1994).

In the discussion above, the role of universities, that was highlighted at the start of this section, has almost faded from view. We want to conclude this section by bringing universities back in. The so-called "Yale Survey" provides a convenient vehicle for discussing the role of universities in modern technological advance (Levin, Klevorick, Nelson and Winter 1987).

The Yale survey asked a set of questions of industrial R&D executives. One block of questions asked the respondents to assess the importance of various fields of science to technological advance in their industry. Every field where such advance was rapid rated one, or usually several, fields of science as very important. However, only a significantly smaller number rated *university research* as important to technological advance in their own line of business.

A variety of informal follow-up inquiries gives us confidence in the following interpretation. In many industries where technological advance is an important vehicle of competition, and where, therefore, an effective industrial R&D operation is essential to the company's success in an industry, industrial R&D draws both extensively and intensively on modern science. To be effective, industrial researchers need strong training in the relevant fields of science, and that is what universities provide them. However, by and large, the science that is being tapped in industrial R&D is, as we suggested above, not particularly "recent" science. On the other hand, as science progresses, the pool of knowledge and techniques on which industrial R&D can draw, progresses as well. University research contributes to that pool.

The Yale questionnaire also asked the respondents to identify the particular fields of university research that were contributing most to technological advance in their line of business. It is very interesting, and strongly supportive of the case that we have been making, that the most frequently cited fields were applications-oriented sciences, like material science or computer science, or medical science, and the engineering disciplines.

We also want to note that the industries generally regarded as experiencing the most rapid rates of technological advance did tend to rate university research as important to technological advance in their industries. Included here are industries such as pharmaceuticals, computers and semiconductors. Our interpretation is that these industries were indeed drawing extensively on "recent science" and that a good portion of that recent science was being done at universities. However, again, the fields of university research that were most cited by these industries tended to be the applications-oriented sciences and the engineering disciplines.

4. IMPLICATIONS FOR MODELING OF TECHNOLOGICAL ADVANCE AND ECONOMIC GROWTH

We want now to lay out what we see as the major implications of our analysis for formal theorizing about the relationships between technological advance and economic growth. We have three major points.

First, we believe that the treatment of technological change in recent growth models has got some matters basically right. Technological advance is, to a considerable extent, the result of investments consciously made to achieve new or improved technology, and private for-profit business firms are, to a considerable extent, the locus and funders of such research. Such investments are profitable for them because a portion of what emerges from industrial R&D is proprietary. On the other hand, there are certainly significant externalities from private industrial R&D. Firms do learn from and draw from the successful experiences of their competitors. In addition, new technology created by private firms also yields externalities by feeding back to influence research in the engineering disciplines and applied sciences, which may go on in universities.

This leads us to our second point. It is that, in addition to firms that perform R&D and incorporate the results in their own production, growth models should incorporate other actors that also do research, but whose findings are placed in the public domain. That is to say, we believe that theory ought to explicitly incorporate entities such as universities. Public funding ought to be included in such models as well and, as a first approximation, all of that funding can be presumed to go to universities.

We understand full well that the essence of artful formal modeling is strategic parsimony. Models cannot include everything that empirical research identifies as important. However, we would argue that, in this case, there are compelling reasons for incorporating universities, with public funding, into the model. The principal reason is that, under natural forms of modeling, diminishing returns are encountered as an aggregate variable such as total cumulated business R&D expenditures increases. One can look to offsets to such diminishing returns through various devices that yield economies of scale. In fact, a very strong case can be made, based on empirical observations, that one of the major factors offsetting diminishing returns to business sector R&D is a flow of new or improved understandings coming from publicly funded R&D, principally publicly funded university R&D. Thus, building in university–public R&D provides a natural way of enabling models to explain sustained economic growth, a way that is an alternative to or complement for various forms of increasing returns.

Such a treatment would build in science at least in a metaphorical way. It would not explore the endogenous nature of many sciences, or their close and designed links with technologies. Modeling that would remain a challenge. But we believe that building science in, even in the simple way that we propose, would at least get the challenge into view.

The third issue suggested by our analysis is that uncertainty with respect to the treatment of technological advance needs to be built into formal growth models in a fundamental way. Some of the recent models do in fact treat the generation of new technology resulting from R&D spending as being stochastic, but these models assume that the actors are in possession of full knowledge of the relevant probability distributions. Thus in these models, while "unlikely" events may occur, nothing happens that is not foreseen as a possibility. Yet time and again in the history of technological change, new technologies emerge with properties that no one had really reflected upon before, and in many cases new uses for new technologies have been completely unforeseen. Put another way, the world of economic growth is full of what Frank Knight called real "uncertainties," and which he contrasted sharply with what he called "risk." In the world of risk, learning basically amounts to the modifying of subjective probability distributions based on the acquisition of new information. Nothing occurs that had never been seriously entertained before, and revised subjective probability distributions cannot potentially involve introduction of possible states of the world that had not even been considered before. Yet this is precisely what frequently happens in the real world of technological advance.

We believe that encompassing this kind of learning in a formal growth model will require adoption of an essentially evolutionary approach to the role of technological change. But this is not the place to pursue that argument.

REFERENCES

Abramovitz, M. (1952), "Economics of growth", in Bernard Haley (ed.), *A Survey of Contemporary Economics* (Homewood, Ill.: Irwin), i. 132–78.

——(1956), "Resource and Output Trends in the United States since 1870," *American Economic Review Papers and Proceedings*, May.

Fabricant, S. (1954), "Economic Progress and Economic Change," NBER, 34th Annual Report, pt. I, May.

Grossman, G., and Helpman, E. (1991), *Innovation and Growth in the Global Economy*. (Boston: MIT Press).

Hallion, R. (1977), *Legacy of Flight* (Seattle: University of Washington Press).

Kendrick, J. K. (1956), "Productivity Trends: Capital and Labor," NBER Occasional Paper 53.

Levin, R. C., Klevorick, A. K., Nelson, Richard R. and Winter, Sidney W. (1987), "Appropriating the Returns from Industrial Research and Development," Brookings Papers 3.

Miller, R. and Sawers, D. (1969), *The Technical Development of Modern Aviation* (New York: Praeger).

Mowery, D. (1981), "The Emergence and Growth of Industrial Research in American Manufacturing, 1899–1945," Ph.D. thesis, Stanford University.

Romer, P. (1990), "Endogenous Technological Change," *Journal of Political Economy*, Oct.

Rosenberg, N. (1994), "Critical Issues in Science Policy Research," in *Exploring the Black Box* (ch. 8) (New York: Cambridge University Press).

——and Nelson, R. (1994), "American Universities and Technical Advance in Industry," *Research Policy*, 23/3 (May), 323–48.

Solow, R. (1957), "Technical Change and the Aggregate Production Function," *Review of Economic and Statistics*, Aug.

Verspagen, B. (1991), "A New Empirical Approach to Catching Up or Falling Behind," *Structural Change and Economic Dynamics*, Dec.

Whinnery, J. (1987), "Interactions Between the Science and Technology of Lasers," in J. Ausubel and D. Langford (eds.), *Lasers* (Washington, DC: National Academy Press).

4

*"Sticky Information" and the Locus of Problem Solving: Implications for Innovation**

ERIC VON HIPPEL

1. INTRODUCTION

To solve a problem, needed information and problem-solving capabilities must be brought together—physically or "virtually"—at a single locus. The need to transfer information from its point of origin to a specified problem-solving site will not affect the locus of problem-solving activity when that information can be shifted at no or little cost. However, when information is costly to acquire, transfer and use—is, in our terms, "sticky"—we find that patterns in the distribution of problem solving can be affected in several significant ways. In this paper we explore this general matter within the specific context of technical, innovation-related problem solving.

It has not always been clear that technical information used by innovators in the course of their problem-solving work might be costly to transfer from place to place. Indeed, the central tendency in economic theorizing has been to view information as costlessly transferable, and much of the research on the special character of markets for information has been based precisely on this characteristic. Thus, Arrow observes that "the cost of transmitting a given body of information is frequently very low. . . . In the absence of special legal protection, the owner cannot, however, simply sell information on the open market. Any one purchaser can destroy the monopoly, since he can reproduce the information at little or no cost" (1962: 614–5). However, a number of scholars with an empirical as well as theoretical interest in the economics and diffusion of technological information have long argued, and to some extent shown, that the costs of information transfer in technical projects can vary significantly (Nelson 1959, 1982; Rosenberg 1982; Griliches 1957; Mansfield 1968; Pavitt 1987; and Teece 1977).

In this paper we first review and draw on the work of these scholars to provide a reasoned basis for our assumption that information used by

* I am very grateful to my colleagues Anne Carter, Bradley Field, Dietmar Harhoff, Zvi Griliches, Ralph Katz, Richard Nelson, Nathan Rosenberg, Stephan Schrader, Stefan Thomke, Marcie Tyre and Jessie von Hippel for their contributions to the ideas explored in this paper. I thank the Sloan Foundation for funding the research reported on in this paper.

technical problem solvers is in fact often "sticky" (Section 2). We then explore four patterns in the locus of innovation-related problem solving that appear related to information stickiness. First, when information needed for innovation-related problem solving is held at one locus as sticky information, the locus of problem-solving activity will tend to take place at that site (Section 3). Second, when more than one locus of sticky information is called upon by problem solvers, the locus of problem-solving activity may move iteratively among such sites as innovation development work proceeds (Section 4). Third, when the costs of such iteration are high, problem-solving activities that draw upon multiple sites of sticky information will sometimes be "task partitioned" into subproblems that each draw on only one such locus (Section 5). Fourth, when the costs of iteration are high, efforts will sometimes be directed toward investing in "unsticking" or reducing the stickiness of information held at some sites (Section 6).

Finally, we will conclude the paper with a discussion of the likely impact of information stickiness on a number of issues of interest to innovation researchers and practitioners. For example, we will reason that the incentives to invest in reducing the stickiness of given information are affected by how frequently that information is a candidate for transfer. Such a pattern would, in turn, offer an economic explanation for a general shift of innovation-related problem solving toward users, as in the current trend in which the producers of software and other products seek to "empower" users by offering them tools that reduce the cost of problem solving and innovation carried out at user sites (Section 7).

2. "STICKY" INFORMATION

As an aid to exploring patterns in the locus of innovation-related problem solving as a function of information transfer costs, we coin the term "sticky" information. We define the stickiness of a given unit of information in a given instance as the incremental expenditure required to transfer that unit of information to a specified locus in a form usable by a given information seeker. When this cost is low, information stickiness is low; when it is high, stickiness is high. Note that in our definition, information stickiness involves not only attributes of the information itself, but attributes of and choices made by information seekers and information providers. For example, if a particular information seeker is inefficient or less able in acquiring information unit x (e.g. because of lack of certain tools or complementary information), or if a particular information provider decides to charge for access to unit x, the stickiness of unit x will be higher than it might be under other conditions. The purpose of being inclusive with respect to causes of information stickiness in this definition is to allow us to focus on the impact of information stickiness independent of cause.

As noted earlier, a number of reasons have been advanced, and explored as to why information might be sticky. Some reasons have to do with the nature of the information itself, some with the amount of information that must be transferred, and some with attributes of the seekers and providers of the information.

With respect to the impact of the nature of the information to be transferred on variations in information stickiness, consider that some information is encoded in explicit terms, while some is "tacit." Polanyi has pointed out that many human skills, and much human expertise, both extensively employed in technical problem solving, are of the latter sort. He observes that "the aim of a skilful performance is achieved by the observance of a set of rules which are not known as such to the person following them" (Polanyi 1958: 49, italicized in original). For example, swimmers are probably not aware of the rules they employ to keep afloat (e.g. in exhaling, they do not completely empty their lungs), nor are medical experts generally aware of the rules they follow in order to reach a diagnosis of various symptoms. "Indeed," Polanyi says, "even in modern industries the indefinable knowledge is still an essential part of technology." And, he reasons, "an art which cannot be specified in detail cannot be transmitted by prescription, since no prescription for it exists. It can be passed on only by example from master to apprentice . . ."—a relatively costly mode of transfer (Polanyi 1958: 52–3).

Rosenberg (1982) argues that drawing on technologically useful information involves not just dealing with theoretical knowledge derived from science, but requires breaking open and examining what transpires "inside the black box" of technological phenomena. Indeed, much technological knowledge is costly, difficult, and slow to diffuse since it deals with "the specific and the particular," consists of "innumerable small increments," and may well be tacit (Rosenberg 1976: 78). Nelson argues that technological knowledge is "partly a private good and partly a public one," that is (1) "a set of specific designs and practices," and (2) "a body of generic knowledge that surrounds these and provides understanding of how things work" (Nelson 1990: 1, 8, 13). The former is often relatively costly and difficult to acquire, learn to use, and diffuse (Nelson 1982), and thus can be private to its creators in certain respects (Nelson and Winter 1982, ch. 4). In contrast, "generic knowledge not only tends to be germane to a wide variety of uses and users. Such knowledge is the stock in trade of professionals in a field, and there tends to grow up a systematic way of describing and communicating such knowledge, so that when new generic knowledge is created anywhere, it is relatively costless to communicate to other professionals" (Nelson 1990: 11–12).

The cost of transferring information sufficient to solve a given innovation-related problem can also vary according to the amount of information called for by a technical problem solver. Sometimes stickiness is high because a great deal of information with a nonzero transfer cost per unit is drawn upon to complete innovation development work. Thus, successful anticipation and avoidance of all field problems that might affect a new aeroplane (Rosenberg 1982, ch. 6), or a new process machine (von Hippel and Tyre 1994) or a new type of laser (Collins 1974/1982) would require that a very large amount of information about the use environment be transferred to the development lab—because one does not know in advance which subset of that information will be relevant to anticipating potential failures. Scientists trying to build a successful copy of a research apparatus often face great difficulties for the same reason. "It's very difficult to make a carbon copy [of a gravity wave detector]. You can make a near one, but if it turns out that what's critical is the way he glued his transducers, and he forgets to tell you that the technician always puts a copy of *Physical Review* on top of them for weight, well, it could make all the difference" (interviewee in Collins 1975: 213).

Information stickiness can also be high because organizations must typically have or acquire related information and skills to be able to use the new knowledge that may be transferred to them. (For example, artists seeking to generate computer art using the mathematics of fractals will not typically be aided by receipt of a software program designed for mathematicians. They must either get the information they seek in "user friendly" form (which in practice means that the transmitter must understand what the recipients already know or can easily learn and must adapt access to the new information accordingly) and/or the recipients must learn the additional complementary information needed to use the existing math program.) Thus, Pavitt points out that "even borrowers of technology must have their own skills, and make their own expenditures on development and production engineering; they cannot treat technology developed elsewhere as a free, or even very cheap, good" (Pavitt 1987: 186). Similarly, Cohen and Levinthal argue that a firm's learning or absorptive capacity with respect to new, outside technical information is "largely a function of the firm's prior related knowledge." This stock of knowledge includes not only "basic skills or even a shared language" but also knowledge generated in the course of a firm's own R&D, marketing and manufacturing operations, and technical training programs (Cohen and Levinthal 1990: 128–9). And, again similarly, Evenson and Kislev find in studies of the economic impact of scientific research on agricultural productivity that "little knowledge is borrowed if no indigenous research takes place" (Evenson and Kislev 1975: 1314).

Information stickiness can also vary due to other attributes of an information transmitter and receiver. For example, it has been shown that specialized personnel such as "technological gatekeepers" (Allen 1977; Katz and Allen 1982; Katz, Allen and Tushman 1980) and specialized organizational structures such as transfer groups (Katz and Allen 1988) can significantly affect the cost of transferring a given unit of information between organizations. And, of course, the decisions of information possessors as to the pricing of access to proprietary information also directly affect the stickiness of that information.

Evidence on the costs of transferring technical information from place to place during innovation-related problem solving also supports the view that technical information can be sticky. A number of empirical studies have been carried out on the costs of transferring a product or process technology from one firm or location to another with full cooperation on both sides. These show that the costs of information transfer do vary and can be significant. For example, Teece (1977) studied twenty-six international technology transfer projects and examined the costs of transmitting and absorbing all the relevant unembodied technological knowledge (i.e. information on methods of organization and operations, quality control, manufacturing procedures, and associated information, but not the knowledge embodied in capital goods, blueprints or technical specifications). He found that transfer costs varied widely for the projects in his sample, ranging from 2 per cent to 59 per cent of total project costs, and averaging 19 per cent— a considerable fraction (Teece 1977: 245, 247).

In sum then, it does appear likely that information sought by technical problem solvers will often be sticky. Therefore it will be useful to examine the effects that information stickiness might have on the locus of innovation-related problem solving. In the following sections we identify four such effects.

3. STICKY INFORMATION AND THE LOCUS OF INNOVATION-RELATED PROBLEM SOLVING

When information transfer costs are a significant component of the costs of the planned problem-solving work, it is reasonable that there will be a tendency to carry out innovation-related problem-solving activity at the locus of sticky information, other things being equal—just as, in the case of production, it is reasonable that a firm will seek to locate its factory at a location that will minimize transportation costs, other things being equal.

Evidence bearing on this matter can be found in a number of places. Thus, Rosenberg (1982, ch. 6) describes "learning by using", which involves problem solving carried out in use environments by, typically, product users. For example, after a given jet engine had been in use for a decade, the cost of maintenance declined to only 30 per cent of the initial level because users had learned to perform this task better (Rosenberg 1982: 131). Rosenberg argues that such learning by using must be carried out at the user locus because that is the site of the information drawn upon by problem solvers. Similarly, agricultural researchers seeking to develop new plant varieties that will flourish under given local conditions often find it efficient to shift problem solving to sites where such conditions exist. Griliches (1957), for example, observed that the complex, innovative process of developing hybrid corn seed was carried out separately by local agricultural experiment stations and private seed companies in order to incorporate unique location-specific factors (such as soil type, topography, length of growing season, fertilizer requirements, rainfall, and insect and disease resistance) required in a hybrid for that specific locality.

Finally, Mowery and Rosenberg (1989, ch. 4) proposed that independent research contractors are most likely to supply research services that exploit little or no firm-specific knowledge because such knowledge is, in our terminology, sticky. To test their hypothesis, they examined the content of all projects carried out by three major independent R&D contracting firms (the Mellon Institute, the Battelle Memorial Institute, and Arthur D. Little, Inc.) between 1900 and 1940. They found that the bulk of the projects carried out by the independent R&D contractors were of a nature that required a relatively small amount of firm-specific knowledge, and reasoned that the projects requiring large amounts of such knowledge had been carried out in client firms' internal labs. This finding is what we would expect if the locus of problem solving is affected by the locus of sticky information.

4. STICKY INFORMATION AND "ITERATION"

When the solving of a given problem requires access to sticky information located at two or more sites, we propose that problem-solving activity will sometimes move iteratively among these sites. We base this proposal on the finding that problem solving in general (Baron 1988: 43–7) and technical problem solving in particular (Marples 1961; Allen 1966) has trial and error as a prominent feature. If and as each cycle of a trial-and-error process requires access to sticky information located at more than one site, it seems reasonable that iterative shiftings of problem-solving activity among sticky information sites will occur as problem solving proceeds (von Hippel 1990*a*).

Iteration of the predicted type can often be observed in the problem solving involved in new product and service development. In these arenas two information bases located—at least, initially—in physically different places are typically important for successful problem solving. The first is information on need, located initially with the user. The second is information on solution technologies, located initially at the site of the manufacturer. If need information is sticky at the site of the potential product user, and if solution information is sticky at the site of the product developer, we may see a pattern in which problem-solving activity shuttles back and forth between these two sites.

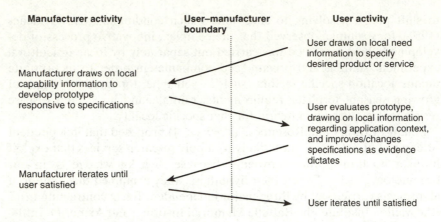

FIG. 4.1. Iterative problem-solving pattern often encountered in new product
and service development

Thus, as shown schematically in Figure 4.1, a problem solver may first draw on user-need information to generate some attributes for a desired new product or service. Then, manufacturer information may be drawn upon in order to develop a prototype that appears responsive to the specification. The prototype is next tested within its proposed use context to verify function and the accuracy of the initially stated need. If the two do not match satisfactorily—and they often do not—the loci of need and/or capability information must be revisited in search of a closer match. This cycle may be repeated few or many times until an acceptable match is found.

This pattern of iterative shifting of innovation development activity from site to site will be less costly than the transfer of sticky information to a single problem-solving locus given a key condition. The intermediate outputs of problem solving conducted at each locus that *are* transferred between sites must be less sticky than the information operated upon to produce the outputs. Intuitively it seems reasonable that this will often be the case. Such an intermediate output may be in the form of nonembodied information transferable at low cost, or it may be in the form of a prototype that can be economically transferred. For example, an artist may not be able to transfer all information involved in the creative process that brings him or her to specify to a supplier, "I need a green paint of precisely X hue and luminance." However, that (nonembodied) need specification is very simple and precise, and it can be transferred at very low cost. Similarly, the responding paint manufacturer may be able to create and transfer the requested shade of green to the artist (embodied in a prototype or final

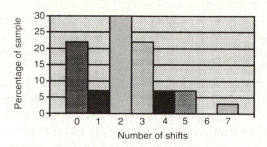

FIG. 4.2. Number of shifts between plant and lab during problem solving
Source: Tyre and von Hippel 1993.

product), but not be able to transfer the complex knowledge drawn on by that firm's chemists to achieve the feat.

Recent empirical studies report the iterative problem-solving pattern described in Figure 4.1. Tyre and von Hippel (1993) explored the innovation-related problem solving involved in identifying and diagnosing twenty-seven field failures in process equipment used to automatically assemble complex circuit boards. They observed repeated shifts in the locus of technical problem-solving activity occurring during this work, with the number of shifts found ranging from 0 to 7, and averaging about 2.3 times per problem identified and diagnosed (Figure 4.2). These shifts involved engineers traveling back and forth between development lab and plant (two to three hours by car), carrying out technical problem-solving activities at each site, and carrying intermediate findings back and forth in their minds and/or computer data disks. For example, to begin the diagnosis of a machine that was failing in the field, the designers of that particular machine would often visit the plant where it was being used in order to observe the malfunction in context and run diagnostic tests. Then they would return to the development lab (the site of specialized lab equipment, relevant expertise, and other types of information) to examine the test results and continue their diagnostic work. Often this work would lead to the need for a second trip to the field for more data collection, and so forth.

In this study, the cost of the iterative shifting of innovation-related problem-solving activity observed did appear to be less than the cost of transferring all information needed by technical problem solvers to a single locus—say, the development lab. While no particular item of information found useful for diagnosing a particular process-machine malfunction was very costly to transfer from the plant to the development lab, the specific items needed by the lab could not be identified without problem-solving and trial-and-error activities conducted in the plant. As a consequence, shifting all information needed to diagnose field problems from plant to lab would have meant shifting a great deal of information—effectively the entire use environment—from plant to lab (von Hippel and Tyre 1994). Carrying out such a massive information transfer would have been much more costly than the iterative transfer of problem-solving activity between plant and lab that was found to have taken place.

In studying product innovation in the Danish food industry Kristensen (1992) observed a similar iterative pattern. Here, information is passed back and forth between Danish food producers and customers located in culturally, linguistically and geographically distant markets. Often, prototypes are used as the medium for information transfer because, as Kristensen points out, "prototypes are not only inexpensive and fast to produce in the food products industry; they are also small and inexpensive to transport." When, for example, a Danish bakery firm was asked to develop a new frozen unbaked cake by a British retail food chain, the bakery's production department responded by developing several prototypes of the proposed cake and sending them to the customer to bake, taste and smell, and to evaluate on the basis of "local tastes and the situation they were meant for—a type of social gathering not practised in Denmark." Comments on the baked cakes were sent back to the producer, who adjusted the recipes accordingly, "using his familiarity with baking and with local raw materials." In total, "five successive revised generations were sent during the course of three months before the Danish producer and the United Kingdom retail chain's test kitchen reached the generation of satisfactory variations." Kristensen reports that over 40 per cent of the 103 Danish food producers he studies had developed one or more products within the previous two years via such iterative interactions with customers (Kristensen 1992: 204–5, 210).

The likely ubiquity of the iteration pattern we describe is suggested by the recent emergence of product-development procedures specially designed to implement such a pattern. For example "rapid prototyping" is a method of software development explicitly designed to shuttle repeatedly between manufacturer and users, replacing the traditional, specification-driven ("waterfall") method of software development. In that traditional method, systems analysts meet with users at the start of a project to determine user needs and agree on a written product-requirements specification, and they then work isolated from further user contact until the completed product is delivered (in six to eight months or up to two years or more), all too often "late, over-budget and not what the customer wanted" (Zelkowitz 1980: 1037). In the rapid prototyping method, manufacturers respond to initial user need inputs by quickly developing and delivering to users (usually within weeks) an inexpensive, easy to modify, working model that simulates a lot of the functionality of the proposed new software. Users then learn by using the prototype in their own setting on their own data and clarify their needs, in part by drawing on their tacit knowledge and experience (Gronbaek 1989: 114–16). Users then relay requests for changes or new features to the software developers, who respond by drawing on their own sticky information and tools to make modifications to the prototype. Some of these modifications are minor, such as altering report formats, and some are major, such as implementing a new feature or modifying the basic structure of the prototype (Feld 1990: 14). A revised prototype is then sent to the user, and this process of iteration between developer and user is repeated until an acceptable fit between need and solution is found. A number of individual case studies and experiments have shown that rapid prototyping methods are not only less costly than traditional, noniterative methods but are able to "better satisfy true user requirements and produce information and functionality that is more complete, more accurate, and more meaningful" (Connell and Shafer 1989: 15; Boehm *et al.* 1984; Gomaa 1983).

5. STICKY INFORMATION AND "TASK PARTITIONING"

When more than one locus of sticky information must be drawn upon to solve a problem, common experience suggests that even iteration can sometimes be very costly with respect to time and effort. For example, no patient likes the shuffling back and forth and time lags involved when a medical condition involves even routine diagnostic tests by and coordinated problem solving among several physicians in different specialities. And, similarly, no designer likes the cost in time and money and frustration involved in repeated redesign of a finished product or service as a result of new information uncovered in the course of test marketing conducted at user sites.

As a consequence, we reason that when the information transfer costs of iteration are high, innovation-related problem-solving activities that require access to multiple loci of sticky information will sometimes be "task partitioned" into subproblems that each draw on only one such locus of sticky information. Because there are many different ways to partition a given innovation project, the selection of a particular partitioning can have a very strong effect on how much information from one task must be drawn upon to solve another as the technical problem-solving work progresses (von Hippel 1990*b*). As a schematic illustration, consider alternative ways of partitioning the project of designing a new aeroplane:

Firm X is responsible for the design of the aircraft body, and firm Y is responsible for the design of the engine, and

Firm X is responsible for designing the front half of both the aircraft body and engine, and firm Y is responsible for designing the back half of both.

Taken together, each of these proposed task partitionings has the same project outcome—a complete aircraft design. But the two differ greatly with respect to the level of information exchange and/or iterative relocation of problem-solving activities. Clearly, information transfer costs would be much higher in the second alternative than in the first: many design decisions affecting the shape of the "front half" of an aircraft body would force related changes on the designers of the "back half" of the body, and vice versa, because the two halves cannot be considered independently with respect to aerodynamics.

As a real-world example of the task partitioning of an innovation project, consider the problem-solving work involved in designing a silicon-integrated circuit on a semiconductor chip for a custom application. In this design problem, two sticky data bases are central to the problem-solving work: (1) information at the circuit-user locus involving a rich and complex understanding of both the overall application in which the custom integrated circuit will play a role and the specific function required of that circuit; (2) information at the circuit manufacturer locus involving a rich and complex understanding of the constraints and possibilities of the silicon fabrication process that the manufacturer uses to produce integrated circuits.

Traditionally, custom-integrated circuits were developed in an iterative Figure 4.1-like process between a circuit user possessing sticky need information and an integrated circuit manufacturer possessing sticky information about designing and producing silicon-integrated circuits. The process would begin with a user specifying the functions that the custom chip was to perform to a circuit design specialist employed by the integrated circuit manufacturer. The chip would then be designed at the manufacturer locus, and an (expensive) prototype would be produced and sent to the user. Testing by the user would typically reveal faults in the chip and/or the initial specification, responsive changes would be made, a new prototype built, and so forth.

More recently, the Application Specific Integrated Circuit (ASIC) method of making custom-integrated circuits has come into wide practice. In the ASIC method, the overall problem of designing custom-circuits is partitioned into subproblems that each draw on only one locus of sticky information, thereby eliminating the need to iterate between two such sites in the design process. The manufacturer of ASICs draws on its own sticky information to develop and improve the fabrication processes in its manufacturing plant, a "silicon foundry". The manufacturer also draws on its own sticky information to design "standard" silicon wafers that contain an array of unconnected circuit elements such as logic gates. These standard circuit elements arrays are designed by the manufacturer to be interconnectable into working integrated circuits by the later addition of custom interconnection layers designed in accordance with the needs of specific users. To facilitate this user task, the manufacturer provides custom-circuit users with a user-friendly Computer-Aided Design (CAD) software package that enables them to design a custom interconnection layer that will meet their specific application needs and yet stay within the production capabilities of the manufacturer's silicon foundry. This CAD software also allows the user to simulate the function of the custom circuit under design, and to conduct trial-and-error experiments. Taken together, these capabilities allow the user to both design a circuit, and to refine need specifications and the desired circuit function through an iterative process that draws only on sticky information located at the user site. In sum, by partitioning the overall circuit design task somewhat differently than is done in the traditional method, the ASIC method of designing custom-integrated circuits reduces the need for the iterative shifting of the locus of innovation-related problem solving between user and manufacturer.

6. STICKY INFORMATION AND INVESTING IN "UNSTICKING" INFORMATION

The stickiness of a given body of information is not immutable. Thus, when the costs of iteration are considered to be high, efforts will sometimes be directed toward investing in "unsticking" or reducing the stickiness of some of the information. For example, firms may reduce the stickiness of a critical form of technical expertise by investing in converting some of that expertise from tacit knowledge to the more explicit and easily transferable form of a software "expert system" (Davis 1986). Or they may invest in reducing the stickiness of information of interest to users by converting it into a remotely accessible and user-friendly computer data base. This is what the travel industry did, for example, when it invested substantial sums to put its various data bases for airline schedules, hotel reservations, and car rentals "on-line" in a user-accessible form.

However, incentives to unstick information can vary. For example, suppose that to solve a particular problem, two units of equally sticky information are required, one from a user and one from a manufacturer. In that case, there will be an equal incentive operating to unstick either of these units of information in order to reduce the cost of transfer, other things (such as the cost of unsticking) being equal. But now suppose that there is reason to expect that one of the units of information, say the manufacturer's, will be a candidate for transfer n times in the future, while the user's unit of information will be of interest to problem solvers only once. For example, suppose that a manufacturer expects to have the same technical information called on repeatedly to solve n user product-application problems and each problem involves unique user information. In that case, the total incentive to unstick the manufacturer's information across the entire series of user problems is n times higher than the incentive for an individual user to unstick its problem-related information. And, as an important consequence, it is reasonable that the locus of problem-solving activity will tend to shift to the locus of the less frequently called-upon information—in the case of our example, to the user.

As illustration, recall the shift from the traditional iterative method of designing custom integrated circuits to the ASIC task-partitioning method that we described earlier. During the problem-solving work of circuit design, each circuit designer requires access to the same information about the constraints of the circuit-manufacturing process, but requires different information about the specific application being designed for. As a consequence, the ASIC manufacturer found it economic to unstick the repeatedly called-upon production process information by investing in encoding it in a user-friendly CAD package. And, as a further consequence, the problem-solving activity of custom-circuit design was shifted to the locus of sticky information regarding each unique application—the user.

The particular pattern just described will often hold in real-world problem solving, we suggest, because it offers a way for manufacturers to seek economies of scale by producing standard products, while at the same time enabling users to carry out the problem solving needed to adapt these to specific local needs and conditions. Consider, for example, the current trend in software (Feld 1990) toward "empowering users." To empower users, manufacturers invest in unsticking some of their programming expertise and information by offering user-friendly programming languages such as Object Oriented Programming (OOPs), and user-tailorable application programs or tool boxes. This has the effect of shifting the problem-solving activity involved in tailoring software to local conditions to the locus of sticky information regarding those local conditions—the user.

7. DISCUSSION AND SUGGESTIONS FOR FURTHER RESEARCH

In this paper we have begun to explore the impact of sticky information on the locus of innovation-related problem solving, and we propose that further study of information stickiness can be of significant value and interest to both innovation researchers and innovation practitioners.

In the course of our initial work we have observed and discussed four patterns in the distribution of innovation-related problem solving associated with efforts made by technical problem solvers to reduce information transfer costs. First, when technical information that is costly to acquire, transfer, and use is held in one locus of sticky information, innovation-related problem-solving activities will tend to move to that locus; second, when more than one locus of sticky information is called upon to solve a problem, the locus of problem-solving activity will tend to iterate among these sticky information sites as innovation development work proceeds; third, when the costs of such iteration are high, innovation-related problem-solving activities that require access to multiple loci of sticky information will sometimes be "task partitioned" into subproblems that each draw on only one such locus of sticky information; and fourth, when the costs of iteration are high, investments may be made toward investing in "unsticking" or reducing the stickiness of information held at some sites.

This short list is not intended to be exhaustive, and further work may identify additional patterns as well as usefully elaborate on the four already identified. For example, in the present paper we have not examined patterns in the distribution of innovation-related problem solving that will be visible when a problem *can* be solved using only technical information that can be acquired, transferred and used without cost or nearly so. We speculate that, in such cases, the locus of problem-solving activities will depend on the costs associated with locating the noninformation components necessary to the technical problem-solving work. Problems appropriate for problem solvers who "telecommute" can fall into this category because the data inputs and outputs called upon can be sent nearly anywhere at low cost over telecommunication networks. Therefore, telecommuters can locate themselves wherever they and their employers find it most cost-effective and convenient to carry out their problem-solving work.

Innovation practitioners may wish to use the information transfer patterns we have discussed in this paper to consciously manage their information transfer costs. The value of doing this in any particular circumstance will depend on these strategies not adversely affecting other innovation cost factors or an innovator's abilities to appropriate innovation-related benefit. We think this can often be the case even though, on the face of it, the latter condition seems problematic. After all, patents and trade secrecy and lead time can all be important to an innovator's ability to profit from an innovation (von Hippel 1988, ch. 5), and these all depend on an innovator's maintaining at least some secrecy at least for a while. But how can one expect an innovating firm to keep secrets if it conducts problem solving not on the innovator's premises but at sites of sticky information? For example, would not a firm that wants to keep a chemical formula a trade secret be ill-advised to conduct some of the technical development work at a customer site?

Often, however, conducting innovation-related problem solving at remote sites need not compromise an innovator's ability to protect commercially important secrets. First, consider that firms can come to some legal arrangement that will maintain secrecy for problem solving done at another locus. Second, consider that firms routinely do locate some of this type of problem solving off their premises without taking legal precautions, and with no apparent impact on their ability to appropriate benefit from their innovations. In some instances, this is explicable because the innovation development task undertaken outside the firm is just a piece of the whole, and revealing a part does not reveal the whole to would-be imitators. Thus, firms routinely ask outside suppliers to develop components of an innovative product, engage in market research and product testing on customer sites, and so forth. In other instances, an innovation being worked upon without benefit of secrecy is nonetheless protected because it is tied in some way to a product or service or process that is protected. Thus, a supplier of a proprietary computer program may benefit from nonproprietary improvements to it, because the improvements will only operate in conjunction with the proprietary program.

The concept of information stickiness can also enable us to understand more about patterns of specialization among individuals and firms. Since an organizational boundary can add to the costs of information transfer, it seems likely that firms seeking to economize with respect to the transfer of sticky information will seek to align their organizational boundaries—and their specializations—with the partitionings dictated by the types of innovation-related problem-solving tasks that are important to them. For similar reasons, consideration of the impact of sticky information may be useful in studying the various collaborative innovation patterns that are being practised by firms today (e.g. Gemunden 1980). We also propose that studies of sticky information can increase our understanding of how firms protect, sell, trade, diffuse and appropriate benefit from information. Thus, stickiness can help the possessors of valuable information to prevent unintentional diffusion to competitors, but that same property may make it more costly to diffuse the information intentionally.

Studies that use information stickiness as a variable can also help researchers to explore patterns in the *nature* of problems selected by technical problem solvers. It seems reasonable that problems that involve low information transfer costs would tend to be selected preferentially. Thus, a firm may elect to develop new products that draw on local information in preference to those that require costly information transfers from suppliers or users or others. Similarly, responses to information transfer costs, such as a decision to partition problem-solving tasks in a different way, or to unstick certain information, can affect the kind of solutions that technical problem solvers may develop to a given problem. For example, the development of single-site "desktop publishing" (which removed the need for iterative problem solving among author, graphic designer and printer) may well enable author/"publishers" to create very different documents as well as less expensive ones. And the development of home medical diagnosis kits (which reduce the need for information transfers among patient, doctor and medical laboratory) may bring about qualitative and quantitative changes in the type of medical care that is demanded and the way it is delivered.

Finally, it is interesting to speculate among the patterns in the locus of innovation-related problem solving that will emerge as the computerization of problem-solving activities continues to make information even more accessible via computer networks and increasingly portable, inexpensive and user-friendly computer equipment and software. Taken together, these trends can certainly facilitate "anywhere" problem solving when all of the information drawn upon to solve a technical problem is nonsticky, as in the instance of telecommuting discussed above. When information transfer costs vary and at least some of the needed information is sticky, however, these same trends can make the patterns discussed in this paper even more salient. Thus, researchers equipped with computers and network access will be free to transfer their work to and among field sites containing sticky information, managers will be free to move decision-making to the sites of critical tasks, and product designers will be free to design products working directly with users at user sites. It will be an interesting world to develop and explore!

REFERENCES

Allen, Thomas J. (1966), "Studies of the Problem-Solving Process in Engineering Design," *IEEE Transactions on Engineering Management*, EM-13, 72–83.
——(1977), *Managing the Flow of Technology: Technology Transfer and the Dissemination of Technological Information Within the R&D Organization* (Cambridge, Mass.: MIT Press).
Arrow, Kenneth J. (1962), "Economic Welfare and the Allocation of Resources of Invention," in Richard R. Nelson (ed.), *The Rate and Direction of Inventive Activity: Economic and Social Factors*, a Report of the National Bureau of Economic Research (Princeton: Princeton University Press), 609–25.
Baron, Jonathan (1988), *Thinking and Deciding* (New York: Cambridge University Press).
Boehm, Barry W., Gray, Terence E. and Seewaldt, Thomas (1984), "Prototyping Versus Specifying: A Multiproject Experiment," *IEEE Transactions on Software Engineering*, SE, 290–303.
Cohen, Wesley M. and Levinthal, Daniel A. (1990), "Absorptive Capacity: A New Perspective on Learning and Innovation," *Administrative Science Quarterly*, 35/1: 128–52.
Collins, H. M. (1974/1982), "Tacit Knowledge and Scientific Networks," in Barry Barnes and David Edge (eds.), *Science in Context: Readings in the Sociology of Science* (Cambridge, Mass.: MIT Press), 44–64.
——(1975), "The Seven Sexes: A Study in the Sociology of a Phenomenon, or the Replication of Experiments in Physics," *Sociology*, 9: 205–24.
Connell, John L. and Shafer, Linda Brice (1989), *Structured Rapid Prototyping: An Evolutionary Approach to Software Development* (Englewood Cliffs, NJ: Prentice-Hall).
Davis, Randall (1986), "Knowledge-Based Systems", *Science*, 231/4741: 957–63.
Evenson, Robert E. and Kislev, Yoav (1975), *Agricultural Research and Productivity* (New Haven: Yale University Press).

Feld, Bradley A. (1990), "The Changing Role of the User in the Development of Application Software," Working Paper no. BPS 3152-90, Sloan School of Management, MIT, Cambridge, Mass.

Gemunden, Hans Georg (1980), "Efficient Interaction Strategies in Marketing of Capital Goods" (in English), Working Paper, Institut für Angewandte Betriebswirtschaftslehre und Unternehmensführung, University of Karlsruhe, Karlsruhe, Germany, n.d., pub. as "Effiziente Interaktionsstrategien im Investitionsgutermarketing," *Marketing ZFP*.

Gomaa, Hassan (1983), "The Impact of Rapid Prototyping on Specifying User Requirements", *ACM Sigsoft Software Engineering Notes*, 8: 17–28.

Griliches, Zvi (1957), "Hybrid Corn: An Exploration in the Economics of Technical Change," *Econometrica*, 25: 501–22.

Gronbaek, Kaj (1989), "Rapid Prototyping with Fourth Generation Systems: An Empirical Study," *Office: Technology and People*, 5: 105–25.

Katz, Ralph and Allen, Thomas J. (1982), "Investigating the Not Invented Here (NIH) Syndrome: A Look at the Performance, Tenure, and Communication Patterns of 50 R&D Project Groups," *R&D Management*, 12: 7–19.

——— (1988), "Organizational Issues in the Introduction of New Technologies," in Ralph Katz (ed.), *Managing Professionals in Innovative Organizations* (Cambridge, Mass.: Ballinger). 442–56.

——— and Tushman, Michael L. (1980), "External Communication and Project Performance: An Investigation into the Role of Gatekeepers," *Management Science*, 26: 1071–85.

Kristensen, Preben Sander (1992), "Flying Prototypes: Production Departments' Direct Interaction with External Customs," *International Journal of Operations and Production Management*, 12/7, 8: 195–211.

Mansfield, Edwin (1968), *Industrial Research and Technological Innovation: An Econometric Analysis* (New York: W. W. Norton).

Marples, David L. (1961), "The Decisions of Engineering Design," *IRE Transactions on Engineering Management*, June, 55–71.

Mowery, David C. and Rosenberg, Nathan (1989), *Technology and the Pursuit of Economic Growth* (New York: Cambridge University Press).

Nelson, Richard R. (1959), "The Simple Economics of Basic Scientific Research", *Journal of Political Economy*, 67: 297–306.

——— (1982), "The Role of Knowledge in R&D Efficiency," *Quarterly Journal of Economics*, 97: 453–70.

——— (1990), "What is Public and What is Private About Technology?", Consortium on Competitiveness and Cooperation, Working Paper no. 90-9, Center for Research in Management, University of California at Berkeley.

——— and Winter, Sidney G. (1982), *An Evolutionary Theory of Economic Change* (Cambridge, Mass.: Harvard University Press).

Pavitt, Keith (1987), "The Objectives of Technology Policy," *Science and Public Policy*, 14: 182–8.

Polyani, Michael (1958), *Personal Knowledge: Towards a Post-Critical Philosophy* (Chicago: University of Chicago Press).

Rosenberg, Nathan (1976), *Perspectives on Technology* (New York: Cambridge University Press).

——(1982), *Inside the Black Box: Technology and Economics* (New York: Cambridge University Press).

Teece, David J. (1977), "Technology Transfer by Multinational Firms: The Resource Cost of Transferring Technological Know-How," *Economic Journal*, 87: 242–61.

Tyre, Marcie J. and von Hippel, Eric (1993), "Locating Adaptive Learning: The Situated Nature of Adaptive Learning in Organizations," Working Paper no. BPS 3568-93, Sloan School of Management, MIT, Cambridge, Mass.

von Hippel, Eric (1988), *The Sources of Innovation* (New York: Oxford University Press).

——(1990*a*, rev. 1991), "The Impact of 'Sticky Information' on Innovation and Problem-Solving," Working Paper no. BPS 3147-90, Sloan School of Management, MIT, Cambridge, Mass.

——(1990*b*), "Task Partitioning: An Innovation Process Variable," *Research Policy*, 19: 407–18.

——and Tyre, Marcie J. (1994), "How 'Learning by Doing' is Done: Problem Identification in Novel Process Equipment," *Research Policy* (forthcoming).

Zelkowitz, Marvin V. (1980), "A Case Study in Rapid Prototyping," *Software—Practice and Experience*, 10: 1037–42.

5

Localized Technological Change and the Evolution of Standards as Economic Institutions[1]

CRISTIANO ANTONELLI

1. INTRODUCTION

Economic analysis has recently made much progress in appreciating the key role of standards as institutions that shape both markets and organizations. This large and still growing literature has focused on the emergence of standards as a process mainly driven by demand-side forces: firms adhere to standards because of the incentives generated by network externalities and the consequent larger demand for their products. Less attention has been paid to the analysis of the role of standards on the supply side of firms, both with respect to the relationship between standards and technological change and to the supply conditions of standards themselves. This paper attempts to provide an integrated approach: one which takes advantage of the many advances made on the demand-side analysis on the role of network externalities and user inertia, and also elaborates on the supply conditions of standards. More specifically, it focuses on standards as specifications of new technologies and on the role of the switching costs that are necessary for firms to adhere to a standard. The costs of switching from own product specifications and to adhering to a common standard are in fact relevant and all the more important the more localized the process of technological change in the specific, idiosyncratic features of the environment of each firm. The costs of standardization are then matched with its benefits so as to provide a general rationale for understanding the features of the emergence of standards in an economic environment featuring technological change, technological variety, asymmetries among firms and selection processes.

Section 2 reviews the main contributions to the economic literature on standards and sets the basic conditions of the analysis. Section 3 presents a simple modeling of the emergence of standards as the outcome of the cooperative behavior of firms in a context of monopolistic competition with both switching costs and network externalities. The general features of the evolution of standards as economic institutions are presented in the conclusions.

2. STANDARDS AS ECONOMIC INSTITUTIONS

The variety of standards has been explored and a rich taxonomy has been elaborated. A first distinction stresses the difference between product standards, document standards and compatibility standards: the former concern products, the second refer to information codes, the latter refer to processes (Farrell and Saloner 1987; Besen 1990). In turn such processes can refer to both production and consumption. According to the process that leads to standardization and the role of agents in it, more specific categories of standards have been further elaborated. A first classification distinguishes between mandatory standards and voluntary standards: mandatory standards are mandated by public authorities, voluntary standards emerge in the market process. De facto standards emerge *ex post* in the market process as the result of the interaction of agents and can be either unsponsored or sponsored standards according to the role of sponsoring entities. De jure standards are elaborated *ex ante* either by committees and agreements or mandated by standard setting authorities (David 1987; David and Greenstein, 1990). In functional terms a further distinction has been drawn between standards that perform a reference function and consequently reduce transaction costs, and standards that perform a compatibility function and consequently enhance or make possible technical coordination among different components of a technological system.

Elaborating upon the large literature, standards can be defined as institutions and more specifically non-pure private goods that: (a) are vectors of technical, commercial and procedural information; (b) emerge in the process of selection and diffusion of technological and organizational changes as the result of the interactive cooperative behaviour of learning agents within clubs; (c) change the extent and context of the market and shape the competition process and (d) affect radically the division of labor and the organizational setup of firms.

This definition has many implications. It concerns the following:

  (i) role of information costs;
  (ii) scope of economic action of agents;
 (iii) notion of non-pure private and quasi-public goods;
 (iv) effects of standards on transaction costs;
  (v) effects of standards on demand;
 (vi) effects of standards on market structure and competition;
 (vii) relationship between standardization and regulation;
(viii) role of standards as carriers of knowledge and externalities; and
 (ix) interplay between standards and technological change.

(i) The role of information costs

A standard is a set of technical, commercial and procedural specifications
that define the functions and the composition of an economic artifact: hence
standards perform the basic role of carriers of technical information about
the way to use and to manufacture an economic artifact. As David and
Steinmueller (1994) make clear

> the economics of standards . . . belongs to the domain of information economics.
> The establishment of standards has the greatest significance when economic agents
> cannot assimilate without substantial costs all the relevant information about the
> commodities that may be exchanged with other agents; and about the processes by
> means of which those goods and services can be produced. In a very broad sense,
> then, to ask about the effects of standards upon economic competition simply is to
> inquire into the ways in which competitive processes may be affected by the creation
> and distribution of information. (p. 3)

If we accept the proposition that both knowledge and the computational
capability of the decision-maker are severely limited,[2] information costs
play a major role in defining the economic environment in which firms and
economic agents behave. Hence standards are institutions that "provide
the structure for exchange that (together with the technology employed)
determines the costs of transacting and the costs of transformation." (North
1991: 34).

From an information economics point of view standardization is an important aspect of the process of technological change: new technologies in
fact command higher levels of information costs for the higher levels of
uncertainty and ignorance about the specifications of new products, new
processes and new organizations they bring about. Moreover standards
perform an important unintended role as carriers and converters of tacit
knowledge: standards in fact codify the characteristics of new products and
new processes that command market recognition and make explicit a
number of technical specifications that become actual instructions for
standards adopters (Winter 1993).

(ii) The nature of economic action

In the neoclassical theory, firms and more generally, economic agents can
adjust either prices or quantities to market signals within a given set of
structural or environmental features such as technology, consumers preferences and primary resources. Within the received theory, firms in fact
cannot change intentionally and purposely the characteristics of the economic environment: such changes take place exogenously. In this theory,
institutions such as property rights and standards belong to the same class
of environmental features. Hence firms are not expected to play a role in
the emergence of standards (North 1991). In our approach the scope of

agents' interactive behaviour is not limited to traditional price–output combinations, but embraces the search and actual action intentionally directed towards the introduction of changes in the economic environment that make it less restrictive for each agent (Phillips 1970). Second and most important, we do not assume that firms and more generally agents are in equilibrium when the search process takes place. In fact the notion of behavior itself implies that agents are placed in a dynamic environment, receive some feedbacks and have some objectives, but are far from optimal solutions (David 1987; North 1991).

Here the economics of clubs provide important insights to grasp the essence of cooperative behavior when it does not concern the traditional price/quantities variables. Standardization is in fact the outcome of a cooperative process, that takes place both *ex ante* and *ex post*, intentionally and unintentionally, but responds to the basic tradeoff of club membership as analyzed by Buchanan (1965). Besen's (1990) careful analysis of the organization and working procedures of ETSI (European Telecommunications Standards Institute) provides clear evidence on the structure and the functions of a typical standardization institute as a club where membership, roles and powers of members are subject to a severe scrutiny.

(iii) Standards as non-pure private goods

Standards here are defined as non-pure private goods rather than public goods in order to stress their quasi-public character. Kindleberger (1983) argues that standards "clearly fall within Samuelson's (1954) definition of public goods in that they are available for use by all and that use by any one economic actor does not reduce the amount available to others" (p. 377). Yet the standardization of each agent's products entails two distinct classes of costs: (i) adoption costs when standards are given; (ii) elaboration costs for standards not yet established.

Irrespective of the character of the standard—whether mandatory or voluntary, and the role of each firm in its elaboration—whether active or passive—the adoption of a given standard by each economic agent is by no means free: in fact, each producer has its own highly specific production features that affect the product (Berg 1989). The adoption of a given standard, that is a set of product characteristics, that differ from the type of product that each agent would manufacture and deliver, entails a variety of costs that can be summarized as switching costs. In order to share a given standard, a firm must change the character of its localized production process, the features of the intermediate inputs that are available in its enviroment, the know-how and the experience accumulated in its own specific localized learning process. Hence it should be clear that the more localized the technological change, the larger the switching costs for firms to adhere to a common standard. Conversely, the more firms rely upon generic, explicit knowledge based upon common technological and scientific principles, the lower the costs to adhere to a common product specification (Antonelli 1994*b*).

When a standard is voluntary and the firm participates in its elaboration, sponsoring costs of new standards add to adoption costs and interact with them. Sponsoring costs consist of the resources that are necessary to participate in committees and other clubs whose function is drawing a standard out of the variety of technical specifications of a given class of products performing similar functions that are offered by each producer and required by each user.

The important role of adoption costs and sponsoring costs for firms adhering to a standard suggests that in fact the notion of non-pure private goods recently elaborated by Romer (1990) can apply. Standards, like "a design for a new good can be used as many times and in as many different production processes as desired." As non-pure private goods, standards have three important properties. They are:

(a) a non-rival input;
(b) productive; and
(c) excludable to some extent.

As carriers of technical and commercial information, standards are productive in that they make it possible to take advantage of the benefits of technological and network externalities. Moreover, the disclosure of technical and commercial information can be properly articulated so as to partially exclude some firms.

Voluntary standards can be thought of as non-pure private goods that are generated and made available to the members of a club that decide to share various technical and commercial information and, consequently, a market demand for their products and the use of the same pool of intermediate and primary inputs. Within the club technical information is shared, its use is non-rival and it is productive because it gives access to more efficient production processes and higher levels of demand. Finally and most important, membership in the club gives each firm the power to influence the final specification of the standard so as to minimize the technical distance between the standard itself and the present technical specifications of each firm's current products and processes. Outsiders however may face considerable disadvantages when adhering to a standard: hence, standards are partially excludable (Steedman 1987; Parrinello 1993).

(iv) Standards and transaction costs

Institutions provide the structure for exchange and make possible specialization. Standards, as institutions that are carriers of technical and commercial information, reduce transaction costs in a variety of ways: they reduce the variety of asset specifications because they make wider the range of possible users and consumers for a given set of standardized products so as to reduce bilateral dependence; they increase the frequency of transactions and reduce market uncertainty; and they make it possible to increase the number of parties involved in the market place. Consequently they help reduce the extent to which market exchanges are personalized and the scope for moral hazard, shirking and opportunistic behavior (Williamson 1985 and 1993). Standards make it possible to reduce transaction costs with given levels of governance costs. They make it possible to reduce the size of governance structures and consequently to shrink the optimum size of firms. By the same token, standards make it possible to increase the division of labor among firms. Standards can be thought of as substitutes for organizations (Demsetz, 1993). With low levels of standardization firms find it more profitable to internalize exchanges and diversify in a variety of related activities so as to economize on transaction costs. Without standards and with constant average production costs, the costs of internal bureaucratic coordination of exchanges between complementary production processes are lower than the costs of arm's-length transacting in the market place.

Empirical evidence shows that the introduction of document standards as by EDIFACT makes possible the division of labor within large technological systems such as the automobile components industries. Historically one can trace the effects of the diffusion of procedural standards such as bar codes on the vertical separation of retailing from manufacturing in many mass industries where the dynamics of scale and scope have pushed manufacturing firms to integrate downstream into distribution (Chandler 1990). In fact the relationship between communication and organization is much more complex: Brousseau (1994) explores the interactions between the standardization of communications procedures and the standardization of the organization of firms.

(v) Standards and demand

The demand for standardized products may be higher because of relevant network externalities. Demand may be more elastic because of lower inertia determined by switching costs for consumers and users of previous units of durable products. The demand for standardized products may also be higher because of the important revenue effects generated by lower transaction costs for acquiring information on the characteristics of the products and their performances (Farrell and Saloner 1987; Saloner 1990).

When demand analysis is focused on new products, standards play an even larger role in enhancing demand. Standards in fact reduce the risks for users to be locked into previous vintages of durable products. Consequently standards help to reduce adoption lags of new products.

Empirical analysis confirms that standards enhance diffusion rates both among competitors and consumers (Link and Tassey 1987).

(vi) Standards, market structure and the competitive process

Standards affect both demand and supply conditions of firms. Hence they shape market structure in many ways. With larger and more elastic demand curves, and increasing returns in production, both for economies of scale and learning economies, equilibrium unit costs for standardized products are likely to be lower. Independent of production costs, mandatory standards lower market prices: mandatory standards in fact provide the basic function of spreading information, reduce monopoly power of innovators and consequently reduce barriers to entry and extraprofits. Mandatory standards in fact make it possible to reduce the amount of tacit knowledge that it is necessary to command in order to manufacture a new product and consequently make it easier to enter new markets.

Standards help to reduce information asymmetries for members of the same standardization club. Hence they can help in fitting a small monopolistic niche into a larger oligopolistic market. (See Section 3.)

Voluntary standards can play a basic role in building multiple barriers to entry. Voluntary standards that are the outcome of standardization clubs in fact can make entry more difficult on both demand and supply sides for potential competitors and rival suppliers in differentiated markets. Within a given aggregate demand for a family of new products, performing similar functions but fragmented into a variety of niches, the demand for standardized products is likely to grow faster and attract consumers from the adjacent market niches because of the powerful effects of network externalities. At the same time switching costs and elaboration costs on the supply side make entry more difficult for potential competitors (Ronnen 1991).

Innovating firms that operate in the markets for durable goods with repeated purchases may be reluctant to adhere to industry standards because of the possible decay of the advantages provided to firstcomers by inertia among users of durable products. Lack of standards in fact provide firstcomers with a protection of their markets shares that is equal to the switching costs for buyers to buy incompatible products supplied by rivals. In this context, public standard-setting institutions may play a major role. The analysis of Swann and Shurmer (1994) shows that the pre-announcement of institutional standards by a standard-setting authority has important and positive effects on the dynamics of the competitive process.

(vii) Standards and regulation

Standards can substitute for regulatory interventions directed towards price–output combinations when the introduction of standards is likely to lower market prices and overall costs of manufacturing firms. From this viewpoint standards can substitute for regulation. Mandatory standards can be designed so that firms are obliged to leave their small market niches and enter into competition in larger markets. Mandatory standards can be especially effective when the markets have not been able to provide the correct amount of voluntary standards for the lack of active participation in standardization clubs, which in turn may be determined by locking-in effects of monopolistic rents provided to singular innovators by their small fragmented demand niches.

The introduction of GSM standards in the European mobile telephone industry, for example, has favored competition in telecommunications services because of the international roaming that the Pan-European standard makes possible. In addition the GSM standard has almost swept away the typical bilateral monopoly market structure in the telecommunications equipment industry where one or a few large buyers usually confronted one or a few suppliers: now all the European mobile service providers can procure standardized equipment from a variety of competitive suppliers (Hawkins 1993).

(viii) Standards and the spillover of externalities

Standards play a major role in making explicit the tacit and localized knowledge on which new products and manufacturing processes are based. The elaboration of voluntary standards within standardization clubs makes possible the cooperation of firms in the definition of common technical specifications where each member of the club shares the information and know-how that are specific to their own production processes and localized learning procedures. From this point of view standards not only are carriers of tacit knowledge, but also and most importantly converters of tacit, localized knowledge into generic, explicit technological and organizational knowledge. By the same token, the diffusion of new products is enhanced by the definition of standards: newcomers in fact can enter the new markets imitating stardardized products (Winter 1993).

It is clear then that standardization makes possible the spreading of relevant technological externalities into the economic system. Moreover, because standardization makes it possible to take advantage of increasing returns in production as determined by the economies of scale and the learning economies, it generates important pecuniary externalities for downstream users.

Hence standardization appears to be an essential part of the process of virtuous, cumulative growth to which Young (1928) refers:

Every important advance in the organization of production regardless of whether it is based upon anything which in a narrow or technical sense, would be called a new "invention" or involves a fresh application of the fruits of scientific progress to industry, alters the conditions of industrial activity and initiates responses elsewhere in the industrial structure which in turn have a further unsettling effect. Thus change becomes progressive and propagates itself in a cumulative way. (p. 533)

(ix) Standards and technological change

The innovation capability of firms rests upon varying combinations of localized and generic knowledge. The former consists of tacit knowledge acquired by means of learning processes embedded in the specific features of the production process and the market for product and for inputs in which each firm operates. The latter consists of explicit and codified knowledge that is elaborated and communicated by means of common procedures.

Technological changes based upon localized knowledge lead consequently to a variety of product and process specifications. Each firm, building upon its own learning process and the innovative stimuli provided by their economic environment, attempts to introduce innovations. Hence at any point in time a variety of rival product innovations are generated and introduced in the market place. Each product innovation is partially rival with the others in that it performs similar functions and addresses similar needs of potential users and consumers (Antonelli 1994*a*).

Standardization is an aspect of the process of diffusion, selection and adoption of technological changes. According to Utterback (1994) product standardization takes place when a dominant design is selected out of the variety of product innovations. In fact when product standards are defined as that product specification "which is accepted for current use through authority, custom, or general consent" (Utterback 1994: 29) the concepts of standards and dominant design overlap. The overlapping of standards and dominant design provides important insights about the relationship between product standards, compatibility standards and procedure standards (Abernathy and Clark 1985; Clark 1985). After the emergence of a dominant design, the flow of rival product innovations shrinks and the competition among firms shifts to the new battleground of process innovations. Compatibility standards emerge as a result of a selection process of the rival alternative production technologies in the market place.

From all this it is clear that standards are viewed as the outcome of a process of technical and economic selection that reduces variety to a common dominant design (Metcalfe and Gibbons 1989; Metcalfe 1992). The original variety of rival technological innovations consists in a plurality of alternative specifications of new products that are introduced by each firm according to its own localized innovation processes, built upon the specific character of their learning processes. Market selection and incremental innovations induce each firm to converge towards the dominant standard and less adaptive firms are pushed out of the market. As Metcalfe and Miles (1994) show, standardization can be thought of as one aspect of a possible, and yet not deterministic, process of technological convergence and selection that follows the generation of innovations and parallels the adoption of innovations. Adoption of innovations is enhanced by standardization and its driving forces such as the reduction in costs stemming from increasing returns, the reduction in market prices stemming from the fall of barriers to entry and the new competition brought in by imitators. Standards favor diffusion especially when they help turn small monopolies into larger oligopolies and increase the value for users by means of network externalities.

The outcome of standardization processes consequently is deeply intertwined with the dynamics of market selection. Hence it is influenced by the amount of initial variety and diversity among the original designs, the extent to which the positive feedbacks of increasing returns and network externalities feed the convergence, and the extent to which switching costs as determined by localized learning and sunk costs on the supply side and inertia on the demand side slow the process. The timing of standardization reflects the balance between the incentives to converge and give way to standards and the resistance to them.

3. A SIMPLE MODEL OF A STANDARDIZATION CLUB WITH BOTH SWITCHING COSTS AND NETWORK EXTERNALITIES

In this section we shall try to model the emergence of de facto standards on the supply side as the result of cooperative coordination among rival innovators[3]; and as part of the process of introduction, diffusion and selection of new technologies. The economics of standards and the economics of technological change seems in fact to be so intertwined that it can not be separated.

De facto standards are the outcome of the emergence of standardization clubs: membership in standardization clubs entails both gains and costs for firms and can be both passive and active. Active membership consists in dedicated efforts to specify new standards; passive membership consists in the efforts that are necessary to adopt the specific requirements of standards that have been designed by active members. In both cases the emergence of standards and their specifications emerge out of a balanced decision process of each firm whether to adhere to the standardization club or remain out of it. Such decision in turn depends on a variety of factors that this simple model of club membership should help clarify.

According to our approach to localized technological change, we model the aggregate market for new similar products as a collection of niches, each with its own negatively sloped market demand where each innovator is a local monopolist (Greenstein 1990). Let us assume that two identical firms have introduced at the same time two rival product innovations that perform similar functions in two independent market niches. The two firms, as innovators, enjoy the advantages of lead times and barriers to entry and are transient monopolists in their respective niche markets. Their identical costs functions and demand functions are respectively:

$$CT_1 = A + b(Q_1) \tag{1}$$

$$CT_2 = A + b(Q_2) \tag{2}$$

$$P_1 = B - d(Q_1) \tag{3}$$

$$P_2 = B - d(Q_2) \tag{4}$$

Their total profits will be determined, according to the usual maximization procedures, by the price–output combination where marginal costs equal the marginal revenue:

$$dCT_i = dRT_i (i = 1, 2) \tag{5}$$

The decision to standardize consists in assessing the effects of four different sets of changes:

(1) the effects on the total costs of each monopolist of the switching costs that are necessary to meet the changes, with respect to their "natural" design, to manufacture and deliver a new product based upon a common standard;

(2) the amount of sponsoring costs that are necessary to elaborate and establish the technical specifications of a standard;

(3) the effects on the demand for the new standardized product for each firm with respect to the two independent demand curves; and

(4) whether these changes are symmetric for the two firms or induce asymmetric costs and demand share conditions.

In order to assess these issues we can explore the product space into which the firms are localized.

The simplest product space can be thought to be linear: firms are distributed along a segment. Their products reflect the specifications of their production processes, of their primary and intermediate inputs, of the localized character of their learning processes. The distance of each firm from the others measures the extent to which each firm has to modify this set of production specifications in order to manufacture and deliver a product that respects the standards: consequently the distance of each firm from the others also measures the amount of switching costs that each firm has to expend in order to assimilate the technical specifications of its products to those of the others (von Weizsacker 1984).

The adoption of a standard implies some switching costs: the more localized the production process and the innovation capabilities of each firm in a narrow area of the product space, the larger the switching costs. Such switching costs can be thought to be both the actual and the perspective ones: a firm that adopts a standard not only changes the product specifications that are closer to its own know-how, but also loses the opportunity to enhance its learning capability and hence its capacity to generate eventually higher productivity levels and new product innovations (Antonelli 1994*a*).

Switching costs (SW) for each firm can be modeled as a function of the technological distance between the vector of technological characteristics of the standard (a) and the vector of the characteristics of the localized technology (b):

$$SW_i = s(a - b) \qquad (6)$$

The technological distance (a − b) between the standardized technology and the localized technology in turn can be characterized as the geometric distance between the technical point which represents the standard (a) and the technical point that represents the localized technology (b) in a simple technique space with two technical characteristics (X, Y):

$$d(a - b) = \left((X_a - X_b)^2 + (Y_a - Y_b)^2 \right)^{1/2} \qquad (7)$$

In such a context the relative localization of the proposed standard with respect to the boundaries of the original product space plays a major role: the closer the standard to the specifications of each firm the lower the switching costs for that firm.

Sponsoring costs matter when the firms are actively involved in the definition of the technical specifications of the standards: a firm that only adopts a standard has no elaboration costs. A firm that is not participating in the definition of a standard, however, has little opportunity to influence it: consequently the emerging standard is likely to be much more "distant" from its "natural" design. A first result of our analysis consists in making clear the alternatives between passive and active membership in a standardization club. A tradeoff emerges: a firm that adopts a de facto standard has no sponsoring costs but higher switching costs and vice versa.

On the demand side we can assume that the introduction of a voluntary standard makes it possible for potential users to take advantage of: (a) lower transactions costs; (b) larger choice sets; (c) network externalities.

Users of a standardized product have lower transaction costs in assessing their quality and product characteristics so they can devote their revenue exclusively to actually purchasing the products: without product standards an important share of consumers' revenue would be expended in assessing the characteristics of the products. A standardized product has lower search costs. Compatibility standards are especially relevant for products that are part of broader technological systems. Compatibility increases the number of systems that can be operated with a given component and the number of components that can be used with a given system. Compatibility standards consequently increase both component variety and system variety (Matutes and Regibeau 1987).

The value for consumers of products that are compatible because of standards, is finally enhanced by the effects of network externalities when each user has larger opportunities to interface its products with other complementary products. In this case the stock and the aggregate demand for the compatible product enters the utility function of each consumer and the demands of the consumers are interdependent (Rohlfs 1974; Allen 1988).

The final demand of households as well as the derived demand of firms for products that are standardized both with respect to their qualities and performances and are compatible with other complementary products is likely to be much larger and more elastic. Such a larger demand is an important incentive for a firm to decide to adhere to a standard.

We can now consider the effects of standardization for the two innovating monopolists on both cost curves and demand curves:

(1) their cost curves will be higher both because of sponsoring costs and switching costs: symmetrically if the standard is equidistant from each of them and the two firms share the sponsoring costs;

(2) their cost curves can be steeper because of the competition in the same markets for intermediate inputs and skilled manpower of the two firms that originally purchased their own specific inputs in two distinct markets;

(3) the new demand curve is now larger than the sum of the two previous demand curves, but it will be shared by the two firms.

The distribution of demand shares, purchasing costs, sponsoring costs and switching costs among the two firms plays a major role in determining the outcome of the standardization process.

Let us analyze the perfectly symmetric case with two identical firms that:

(A) elaborate a standard that is perfectly equidistant from the two original product specifications so that the two firms will face the same levels of purchasing costs and switching costs in order to adhere to the standard and the same amount of sponsoring costs in order to establish the technical specifications of the standard itself;

(B) are able to collude perfectly and share symmetrically the outcome of the standardization process.

The new costs curves will be:

$$CT_1 = SC_1 + SW_1 + A + b'(Q) \tag{8}$$

$$CT_2 = SC_2 + SW_2 + A + b'(Q) \qquad (9)$$

where SC are the sponsoring costs; SW are the switching costs and b' are augmented purchasing costs for intermediary inputs in intermediate markets where supply curves have a positive slope.

Because of network externalities and revenue effects determined by lower information and transaction costs the new demand for the two firms is now expressed by one larger curve with a larger price elasticity[4]:

$$P = W - w(Q) \qquad (11)$$

with respect to the demand curves (3) and (4) we assume here that $W > (2B)$ and $w < (2d)$.

If the two firms decide to share symmetrically the new demand they will collude and operate on the market place as a cartel. Hence the standardization club opens the way to a combination formed to regulate production, pricing and marketing of goods. Now the profits will be defined as the outcome of the maximization of revenues stemming from the combined cost curves of the two firms with the given common demand curve:

$$dCTT = dRT \qquad (12)$$

where CTT are the total costs of the cartel.

It is clear that total profits of the cartel may be higher than the sum of the profits of the two independent monopolists, *but may not be: the effects in the changes of price–output combinations within a monopolistic market structure are in fact highly unpredictable.* Cartel profits will be larger not only if the new demand curve is sufficiently larger to offset the increase in costs, but also and most important if the new equilibrium point on average costs is farther from price.

Another result has been obtained: standardization will take place only when the profitability of the new market structure will be larger than the profitability of two separated market niches. Standardization is likely to take place when:

(i)   sponsoring and switching costs are lower than the incremental revenue stemming from standardization. This amounts to saying that the lower the technological variety of firms the greater the chances that standardization takes place;

(ii) the effects on the slope of marginal costs generated by augmented competition on intermediary markets is smaller than the reduction in the slope of the aggregate demand;

(iii) the manufacturing cost curves of the producers are influenced by economies of scale and learning economies so that the positive slope of the new aggregate supply curve in the equilibrium quantity is smaller than each of the supply curves of the two firms;

(iv)   the new aggregate demand curve is not only higher but also more elastic than the previous ones;

(v)   the aggregation of the two demand curves has no effects on the monopolistic control of the cartel on the new market;

(vi)   the two firms participating in the standardization club are able to transform it into a cartel so as to maximize their joint profits.

The relevance of increasing returns in production as a major source of incentives to join a standardization club reveals an important additional condition:

(vii) when increasing returns are determined by learning economies that shape the long-term cost curve as an L, that is affect strongly the slope of average costs only in the early stages of production, the timing of standardization becomes relevant. The window for establishing standards is in fact reduced to the time span along which learning economies display their effects. After that window, the incentive to join the standardization club, declines.

The collusive and monopolistic behavior of the standardization club is an important condition that requires additional thought: if the two firms are not able to transform the standardization club into a cartel, the risks that the standardization does not take place are higher. Such a possibility is further enhanced when we relax the simplifying assumption that only two firms enter the club first and then cartelize. It is clear that the larger the number of firms involved the lower the chances that such a cartel can be contrasted by regulatory interventions or impeded by the opportunistic behavior of each member. This makes it possible to grasp one more condition:

(viii) the chances that standardization takes place are larger the smaller the number of members in the standardization club. These chances are lower the more different are the cost and demand functions of the firms; the more different the more likely an explicit profit-sharing agreement will be required (Fellner 1949; Phillips 1962).

This leads us to explore a more realistic hypothesis: the firms are able to agree upon the definition of standards but are unable or impeded in transforming the standardization club into a cartel. Now the firms will operate in the new market place as oligopolists and the essence of their behavior can be retained by means of the traditional Cournot model.

In a Cournot model of duopoly the equilibrium price will be lower the larger the number of firms and the profits (P) will be accordingly lower. Now in fact the equilibrium conditions imply that:

$$\left(dP_1/dQ_1 = dR_1/dQ_1 - dC_1/dQ_1 = 0 \right.$$
$$\left(\right. \tag{13}$$
$$\left(dP_2/dQ_2 = dR_2/dQ_2 - dC_2/dQ_2 = 0 \right.$$

The Cournot equilibrium conditions for firms in an oligopolistic market make it possible to take into account the effects of:

(a) asymmetries in the original conditions of the firms that can now differ in terms of size and efficiency;

(b) asymmetries among firms in terms of economies of scale and learning economies;

(c) asymmetric effects of the standardization on the two firms in terms of differentiated purchasing costs, switching costs and sponsoring costs; and

(d) asymmetric effects of different cross-demand elasticities.[5]

The character of the distribution of localized innovators in the product space plays here a major role. While a homogeneous distribution has no effects in the creation of asymmetries, it is clear that any two players that happen to be co-localized in the same product space have also lower switching costs in adhering to a common standard and lower sponsoring costs because the two products are already very close. Co-localized players are likely to become quickly core members of any standardization club. This makes it possible to state a further result of our analysis:

(ix) the larger the extent to which firms rely on tacit and localized knowledge in introducing innovations the larger the switching costs, hence the larger the role of generic knowledge the larger the chances that standards are rapidly introduced in an industrial system.

Each firm will still join the standardization club only if the expected profits in the new oligopolistic market are larger than those reaped in its smaller monopolistic niche. Because of the asymmetries that now are allowed, however, some firms will be earning more profits than before and others less: the extent of the larger profits for the former however will depend on the membership decision of the latter. The slope and position of the demand curve is in fact determined by the membership of all the firms. In such conditions we have two new cases for standardization clubs to emerge:

(x) the room for side-payments from core members of the club to marginal potential members as an incentive to marginal ones to join the club. Such side-payments can take a variety of forms such as reduction in sponsoring costs or elaboration of standards that reduce the amount of switching costs for marginal members and privileged conditions in their access to input markets.

(xi) the incentive structure for core players to allow marginal potential members to join actively the standardization club and consequently to allow them to interfere with the definition of standards so that their switching costs are lower, or to relegate them to a passive role where marginal members can only adopt but not influence a standard.

The full appreciation of cost asymmetries among firms as determined by switching costs makes it possible to appreciate the dynamics of the emergence of de facto standards.

(xii) De facto standards can emerge in the market place when imitators decide to enter the market place adopting the standard introduced by innovators: in this case innovators however do not bear the costs of switching from their own original design. In such conditions switching costs, as sunk costs, become a source of barriers to entry and limit pricing for innovators. Former monopolistic innovators in fact can react to entry, fixing the market price for their products where the demand equals the long-term average costs for new competitors that however include switching costs. Formally we see that:

$$P_L = P_C(1+E) \qquad\qquad (14)$$
$$CT_m = A + SW_m + b(Q)$$
$$CT_i = A + b(Q)$$
$$P_Q = Z - z(Q)$$
$$E = (CT_m - CT_i)/Q_e$$

where P_L = limit price; P_C = competitive price; E = premium for the established firm; CT_i = cost curve of the innovator; CT_m = cost curve of the imitator; SW_m = switching costs for imitators; P_Q = demand curve for the standardized product; Q_e = equilibrium demand with limit price.

From equation (14) it is clear that the larger the levels of switching costs that imitators have to bear and the larger the equilibrium demand—and the smaller the slope of the demand curve—the larger the profits for innovators. When production exhibits increasing returns, demand increases over diffusion curves and it features network elasticity, and entry takes place sequentially. The emergence of de facto standards is however convenient for both innovators and early imitators. The shift of the demand curve towards the right, augmented by network externality, in fact makes it possible, for the innovator and the first imitators, to take advantage of larger markets even with a larger price elasticity. Limit prices in fact remain at a higher level that takes into account the larger production costs of *late* imitators. Clearly incumbents, as early innovators, have a strong incentive to select highly idiosyncratic dominant designs for their products that are likely to become eventually de facto standards, to maximize the switching costs for their potential and actual competitors and hence their barriers to entry, and to limit prices and profits.

Thus standards that emerge in the market place are likely to be strongly influenced by a path-dependent market process, one where standards are the idiosyncratic dominant designs of early innovators, and are specified under the influence of product rivalry in conditions that are far away from competitive equilibria.

Finally the results of the analysis of the conditions that lead to the emergence of standardization clubs in an oligopolistic market suggest that:

(xiii) the intervention of public authorities that are able to reduce the sponsoring costs and to establish mandatory standards are likely to be beneficial only to the extent that standardization was impeded by the effects of sponsoring costs. Mandatory standards—especially at the international level—that oblige firms to adhere to a common standard can generate relevant switching costs and a reduction of welfare even if they lead to reductions of market prices[6].

(xiv) mandatory standards in intermediate markets however are likely to generate a large welfare net gain if the effects of reduction in price in upstream markets are likely to generate important positive technological externalities that favor the diffusion of innovations in that industry, and pecuniary externalities in downstream industries that use that standardized input for their own production processes.

4. CONCLUSIONS

Because the emergence of standards is embedded in the circumstances of cooperation among rivals, technological change and monopolistic competition where behavior is necessarily out of equilibrium, standardization, even without increasing returns, is a highly path-dependent process. The final outcome of standardization processes, both in terms of the distribution of standards across the original variety of products and production processes, and the technical features of the emerging standards, if any, depend upon the sequence of events as they take place, the original characters of the technological system considered, the amount of resources that are necessary to achieve standardization, the nature of market structures, the specific and highly idiosyncratic combinations of elasticities of monopolistic supply and demand curves in a context characterized by transient monopolistic market power and monopolistic behavior where the notion of long-term competitive equilibria makes little sense (David 1992 and 1993).

Each standard consequently is by no means necessarily the best possible technical specification sorted out of a given set of technical and economic alternatives, but rather reflects the complexity of the environment and the behavior of agents in the ability of players to decipher and order the environment and the balance of forces among players (North 1991).

In such an approach, standards are viewed as part of a more general process of institutional and technological change where the behavior of firms is influenced by market structure and the more general characteristics of the economic environment, but it is not limited to price–output adjustments. It embraces a much wider scope of action which consists of technological innovations, organizational changes and the elaboration of new institutions. Hence standardization can be viewed as a process of recursive structural change where firms on one hand adjust to a given set of structural features with traditional price output changes, and, on the other, react with a range of structural actions (Phillips 1970).

The outcome of the standardization process is strongly influenced by the specific set of productive and technological characteristics on the supply side such as:

(i) the technological diversity of firms;
(ii) the localized character of the innovation processes and consequently the extent to which firms rely on localized rather than generic knowledge;
(iii) the distribution of the firms in the product space in terms of relative density of firms localized in the product space;
(iv) the role of increasing returns in production as determined by economies of scale and learning economies;
(v) the ability of core members of potential standardization clubs credibly to fund side-payments in order to induce marginal members to join the club or to exclude potential members whose contribution is not viewed as positive;
(vi) the actual number of innovating firms that have introduced products that are likely to be standardized;
(vii) the timing of the standardization efforts;
(viii) the active role of public authorities that establish mandatory standards or help standardization committes to work by lowering the levels of sponsoring costs; and
(ix) the magnitude of internalized gains from externalities effects.

If we take into account the long-term effects of standards in terms of lower levels of transaction costs, higher levels of specialization and more effective division of labor among firms and higher rates of diffusion, such a set of specific characteristics appear to be one of the distinctive features of national systems of innovation (Nelson 1993) and a major ingredient in explaining the differentiated capability of countries to achieve higher levels of productivity.

The retreat of firms into small monopolistic niches, determined by the prevailing role of localized knowledge, impedes firms adhering to standards, but also prevents firms from taking advantage of the larger opportunities to generate further technological innovations offered by generic knowledge. Conversely, the initial push exerted by positive feedbacks of the standardization processes may prevent firms from being locked into the specific limits of their localized knowledge. A positive feedback between standards and access to generic knowledge is likely to further emphasize the eventual positive role of a successful standardization process: the Schumpeterian tradeoff between static and dynamic efficiency displays its effects once more.

NOTES

1. The comments of Almarin Phillips, Eric Brousseau, Stan Metcalfe, Godefroy Dang N'Guyen and Don Lamberton to previous versions of this paper as well as the financial support of local and national funds of Ministero dell'Università e della Ricerca Scientifica e Tecnologica are acknowledged.
2. See Simon (1986: S210–1), quoted by North (1991: 23), Lamberton (1971) and Langlois (1986).
3. See Foray (1994) for a parallel analysis of the emergence of standards on the demand side.
4. When the utility function is affected by network externalities and it is specified as follows:

$$U = x^{aZ} y^b \qquad (10)$$

where Z is the level of aggregate demand for compatible products, x is a standardized product, y a vector of other products; a and b are other conventional parameters; it is easily shown that both the intercept and the price elasticities of the demand for standardized products are larger.
5. The demand functions here are interdependent.
6. Ronnen (1991) in fact claims that standards lead to higher welfare, but he makes no provision for switching costs.

REFERENCES

Abernathy, W. J. and Clark, K. B. (1985), "Innovation: Mapping the Winds of Creative Destruction," *Research Policy*, 1/14: 3–22.
Allen, D. (1988), "New Telecommunications Services: Network Externalities and Critical Mass," *Telecommunications Policy*, 3/12: 257–71.
Antonelli, C. (1994*a*), "Increasing Returns: Networks Versus Natural Mono- poly: The Case of Telecommunications," in G. Pogorel (ed.), *Global Telecom-*

munications Strategies and Technological Change (Amsterdam: Elsevier Science Publishers).

Antonelli, C. (1994*b*), *The Economics of Localized Technological Change and Industrial Change* (Boston: Kluwer Academic Publishers).

Berg, S. V. (1989), "The Production of Compatibility: Technical Standards as Collective Goods," *Kyklos*, 3/42: 361–83.

Besen, S. M. (1990), "The European Telecommunications Standards Institute," *Telecommunications Policy*, 4/14: 521–30.

Brousseau, E. (1994), "EDI and Inter-Firm Relationships: Toward a Standardization of Coordination Process?" *Information Economics and Policy*, 3–4/6: 319–48.

Buchanan, J. M. (1965), "An Economic Theory of Clubs," *Economica*, 1/32: 1–14.

Chandler, A. D., Jr. (1990), *The Dynamics of Scale and Scope: The Dynamics of Industrial Capitalism* (Cambridge, Mass.: Harvard University Press).

Clark, K. B. (1985), "The Interaction of Design Hierarchies and Market Concepts in Technological Evolution," *Research Policy*, 5/14: 235–51.

David, P. A. (1987), "New Standards for the Economics of Standardization," in P. Dasgupta and P. Stoneman (eds.), *Economic Policy and Technological Performance* (Cambridge: Cambridge University Press).

——(1992), "Why are Institutions the 'carriers of history'? Notes on Path-Dependence and the Evolution of Conventions, Organizations and Institutions," paper prepared for presentation in the Stanford Institute for Theoretical Economics Summer Program on "Irreversibilities."

——(1993), "Path-Dependence and Predictability in Dynamic Systems with Local Network Externalities: A Paradigm for Historical Events," in D. Foray and C. Freeman (eds.), *Technology and the Wealth of Nations* (London: Pinter).

——and Greenstein, S. (1990), "The Economics of Compatibility Standards: An Introduction to Recent Research," *Economics of Innovation and New Technology*, 1–2/1: 3–42.

——and Steinmueller, E. (1994), "Economics of Compatibility Standards and Competition in Telecommunication Networks," *Information Economics and Policy*, 3–4/6: 217–42.

Demsetz, H. (1993), "The Theory of the Firm Revisited," in O. E. Williamson and S. G. Winter (eds.), *The Nature of the Firm* (Oxford: Oxford University Press).

Farrell, J. and Saloner, G. (1987), "Competition Compatibility and Standards: The Economics of Horses, Penguins and Lemmings," in L. H. Gabel (ed.), *Product Standardization and Competitive Strategy* (Amsterdam: Elsevier Science Publishers).

Fellner, W. J. (1949), *Competition Among the Few* (New York: Knopf).

Foray, D. (1994), "Coalition and Committees: How Users Get Involved in Information Technology Standardization: Technologies and Networks as Methods of Coordination," *Information Economics and Policy*, 3–4/6: 269–94.

Greenstein, S. (1990), "Creating Economic Advantage by Setting Compatibility Standards: Can 'Physical Tie-ins' Extend Monopoly Power?" *Economics of Innovation and New Technology*, 1–2/1: 43–62.

Hawkins, R. W. (1993), "Changing Expectations: Voluntary Standards and the Regulation of European Telecommunications," *Communications and Strategies*, 11: 53–85.

Kindleberger, C. P. (1983), "Standards as Public Collective and Private Goods," *Kyklos*, 3/36: 377–96.

Lamberton, D. M. (1971) (ed.), *Economics of Information and Knowledge* (Harmondsworth, UK: Penguin).

Langlois, R. N. (1986) (ed.), *Economics as a Process* (Cambridge: Cambridge University Press).

Link, A. N. and Tassey, G. (1987), The Impact of Standards on Technology-Based Industries: The Case of Numerically Controlled Machine Tools in Automated Batch Manufacturing," in L. H. Gabel (ed.), *Product Standardization and Competitive Strategy*.

Matutes, C. and Regibeau, P. (1987), "Standardization in Multi-Component Industries," in L. H. Gabel (ed.), *Product Standardization and Competitive Strategy*.

Metcalfe, J. S. (1992), "Variety Structure and Change: An Evolutionary Perspective on the Competitive Process," *Revue d'Economie Industrielle*, 59: 46–61.

——Gibbons, M., Rosenbloom, R. S. and Burgelman, R. A. (1989) (eds.), "Technology, Variety and Organization," *Research on Technological Innovation Management and Policy* (Greenwich, Conn. and London: JAI Press), iv. 153–93.

——and Miles, I. (1994), "Standards Selection and Variety: An Evolutionary Approach," *Information Economics and Policy*, 3–4/6: 243–68.

Nelson, R. R. (1993) (ed.), *National Systems of Innovation* (Oxford: Oxford University Press).

North, D. C. (1991), *Institutions, Institutional Change and Economic Performance* (Cambridge: Cambridge University Press).

Parrinello, S. (1993), "Non-Pure Private Goods in the Economics of Production Processes," *Metroeconomica*, 3/44: 195–214.

Phillips, A. (1962), *Market Structure Organization and Performance* (Cambridge, Mass.: Harvard University Press).

——(1970), "Structure Conduct Performance and Performance Conduct Structure," in J. W. Markham and G. F. Papanek (eds.), *Industrial Organization and Economic Development*, in honor of E. S. Mason (Boston: Houghton Mifflin).

Rohlfs, J. (1974), "A Theory of Interdependent Demand for a Communications Service," *Bell Journal of Economics and Management*, 1/5: 16–37.

Romer, P. M. (1990), "Endogeneous Technological Change," *Journal of Political Economy*, 5.2/98: S71–102.

Ronnen, U. (1991), "Minimum Quality Standard Fixed Costs and Competition," *Rand Journal of Economics*, 4/22: 490–504.

Saloner, G. (1990), "Economic Issues in Computer Interface Standardization," *Economics of Innovation and New Technology*, 1–2/1: 135–56.

Samuelson, P. (1954), "The Pure Theory of Public Expenditure," *Review of Economics and Statistics*, 36 (Nove.): 387–9.

Simon, H. A. (1986), "Rationality in Psychology and Economics," in R. M. Hogarth and M. W. Reder (eds.), "The Behavioral Foundations of Economic Theory," *Journal of Business*, 59/4: S209–24.

Steedman, I. (1987), "Free Goods," in J. Eatwell, M. Milgate and P. Newman (eds.), *The New Palgrave: A Dictionary of Economics* (London: Macmillan).

Swann, P. and Shurmer, M. (1994), "The Emergence of Standards in PC Software: Who Would Benefit from Institutional Intervention?" *Information Economics and Policy*, 3–4/6: 295–318.

Utterback, J. (1994), *Mastering the Dynamics of Innovation* (Boston: Harvard Business School Press).

von Weizsacker, C. C. (1984), "The Costs of Substitution," *Econometrica*, 4/52: 1085–116.

Weiss, B. H. and Sirbu, M. (1990), "Technological Choice in Voluntary Standards Committees: An Empirical Analysis," *Economics of Innovation and New Technology*, 1–2/1: 111–34.

Williamson, O. E. (1985), *The Economic Institutions of Capitalism* (New York: Free Press).

——(1993), The Logic of Economic Organization," in O. E. Williamson and S. G. Winter (eds.), *The Nature of the Firm*.

Winter, S. G. (1993), "On Coase Competence and the Corporation," in O. E. Williamson and S. G. Winter (eds.), *The Nature of the Firm*.

Young, A. (1928), "Increasing Returns and Economic Progress," *Economic Journal*, 38: 527–42.

PART II

STRATEGY/ORGANIZATION

6

Learning how to Govern and Learning how to Solve Problems: On the Co-Evolution of Competences, Conflicts and Organizational Routines*

BENJAMIN CORIAT AND GIOVANNI DOSI

1. INTRODUCTION

This work is meant as an exploration of the origins and roles of different organizational routines which sustain diverse corporate structures and reproduce over time different "strategies" and performances.

There is indeed quite robust evidence that firms—despite obvious regularities—persistently differ in their characteristics, behaviors and revealed performances. For example, they clearly differ in their sizes, their forms of internal organization, their degrees of vertical integration and intersectoral diversification, etc. But they also differ in their revealed performances—in terms, for example, of innovative success, speed of adoption of new technologies, inputs productivities and profitabilities. Relatedly, a major puzzle concerns the reasons of persistence of these asymmetries. Why apparently "superior" organizational forms diffuse very slowly, if at all, within industries and, even more so, across national borders?

A good part of the answer, in our view, certainly rests upon the specificities of organizational competences. In fact, the first building block in our argument, directly developing on evolutionary theories, is that firms are crucial (although not exclusive) repositories of knowledge, to a large extent embodied in their operational routines, and modified through time by their "higher level" rules of behavior and strategies (such as their "metarules" for innovative search, diversification, etc.). In this view, competences are the collective property of the routines of an organization, and—due to their partial tacitness—are often hard to transfer or copy.

* We gratefully acknowledge support of this research by the French Ministry for Foreign Affairs, the Italian Ministry of University and Research, the Italian National Research Council (CNR, Progetto Strategico) and the International Institute of Applied System Analysis (IIASA, Laxenburg, Austria). The draft has benefited from conversations with Sidney Winter, and from the comments of several participants at the Prince Bertil Symposium (Stockholm, June 1994) and in particular of Nathan Rosenberg.

Competence specificity leads straightforwardly to an easy possibility of "lock-in" and thus also to persistent diversity at firm-level and, moreover, to specificities at the level of "national trajectories."[1]

In this work we shall focus primarily on the non-random distribution of competences across countries (and, relatedly, on the differences in the national patterns of organizational evolution).

In order to interpret these international (or, also, interregional) differences, one must account, first, for the properties of the networks in which firms are embedded: these linkages with other firms—within and outside their primary sectors of activity—and with other organizations (such as public agencies) shape and constrain the opportunities facing each firm to improve its problem-solving capabilities. Second, "national systems" of production and innovation entail also a broader notion of embeddedness of microeconomic behaviors into a set of social relationships, rules and institutional constraints (Granovetter 1985). In turn, these embeddedness properties contribute to determine the evolution of organizational structures and, together, competences and strategies.

There are, however, two complementary aspects of this embeddedness argument (as well as to the earlier "lock-in" one). These two aspects also correspond to two perspectives on the nature and function of business firms themselves.

The first one—which has been highly emphasized in the evolutionary literature—concerns the *coordination* and *problem-solving* nature of organizational routines. Hence, their specificities are shown to be related to the "cognitive" features of the operational or search tasks at hand.

Indeed, one of the authors in earlier works has claimed that, in a first approximation, one could start with the assumption that a "weak incentive compatibility" among individual agents could be taken for granted, and directly analyze the collective problem-solving features of particular ensembles of routines composing the repertoire of each organization (Dosi and Marengo 1994).[2] It is proving to be a fruitful investigative strategy. However, it neglects the second major role of organization and organizational routines, namely their being a *locus of conflict, governance, and a way of codifying microeconomic incentives and constraints*—as often emphasized by the other author (Coriat 1979 and 1990).

In this work we begin an exploration of this double—"cognitive" and "governance"—role of organizational routines.

Just to mention a few archetypal examples, the "Chandlerian" (primarily American) modern large corporation embodies the development of novel competences of managerial problem solving, as recently Teece (1993) and Chandler (1992) himself have convincingly argued. At the same time, however, that organizational form embodies equally specific forms of internal governance of conflicts and incentives, which, in a shorthand, can be identified with "Taylorism" and "Fordism."

Conversely, in an archetypal "Japanese" corporation (Aoki 1988 and 1990; Coriat 1991*b*), the patterns of competence accumulation are nested in quite different forms of governance and conflict management. Many other historical examples could be cited, from Germany to Italy to Britain.

Of course, governance mechanisms are today a quite familiar domain of economic analysis, but, most often, elegant equilibrium rationalizations have assumed away the crucial problem-solving tasks associated with the development of routinized, inertial and conflictual behaviors. Here, we take a rather different route, and move some steps toward an appreciation of the co-evolution of (highly imperfect) *mechanisms of governance*, on the one hand, and *"what a firm is able to do and to discover,"* on the other.

In this preliminary work, we aim to identify the properties, in both the "cognitive" and "governance" domains, of some distinctive set of routines—or *protocols*—of different organizational forms, and suggest a coevolutionary story regarding their origins.

The embeddedness argument clearly comes out enhanced. Particular patterns of conflict, "truces" and mechanisms of incentive governance present an intrinsic collective nature, grounded in the institutions of each country. Together with the cumulative nature of learning processes, they contribute to explain the persistence of national specificities in organizational setups and corporate routines.

2. SOME BACKGROUND FINDINGS AND HYPOTHESES ON LEARNING, CORPORATE ORGANIZATIONS AND GROWTH

Let us start by placing the discussion that follows concerning the relationships between processes of learning and mechanisms of organizational governance in the perspective of a broader set of questions and findings regarding the linkages between technological change, specificities in the institutional organization of economic activities and growth.

A useful point of departure are a few findings that evolutionary-inclined practitioners in economics, but also many economists of other intellectual origins, economic historians and organizational theorists would consider robust stylized facts (although of course this is a theory-ridden and by no means uncontroversial evaluation).

For our purposes, the preliminaries of our argument are: (a) even within commonly shared organizational patterns, the persistent heterogeneity across firms—and, even more so, across countries—in their abilities to develop, imitate, adopt technological innovations; (b) roughly similar persistent differences across countries in their input productivities and incomes; (c) the long-term correlation between the two sets of phenomena (which, indeed, a few economists would theoretically interpret in causal manners, in terms of co-evolutionary processes).

Many more details on the evidence and the causality linkages have been discussed elsewhere (cf. Dosi, Pavitt and Soete 1990). For example, there is an emerging evolutionary view on the microeconomics of technological innovation, grounded in the specificities of the learning processes which characterize particular classes of problem-solving activities. In turn, this view naturally leads to predictions of intersectoral heterogeneity in innovative patterns, asymmetries in innovative performance across firms, possible path-dependency and "lock-ins."[3]

At a more aggregate level, a few scholars have attempted to show—both at theoretical and empirical levels—that growth can be viewed as a process fueled by heterogeneous efforts of innovation checked by some market selection.[4] One is also able to show that these same processes in multieconomy settings may yield convergence but also (and more often) divergence, forging ahead and falling behind in relative per capita income.[5] Complementary empirical findings highlight the crucial importance of technological change as apparent determinant of trade patterns and growth.[6]

As annoying as it might be for economists of other entrenched beliefs, here we shall take these phenomena for granted while investigating their microeconomic foundations and some implications for "national trajectories" and possible lock-in phenomena.

Indeed, a few implications are prima facie observationally indistinguishable from those derived from other modeling assumptions. For example, "new growth" and "evolutionary" theories at least in a first approximation overlap in their prediction of, first, innovation-driven self-sustained growth, and, second, long-term differentiation in growth patterns across countries.[7] Most likely, one encounters here a generic property of learning: technological learning, no matter how roughly represented, tends to imply the possibility of international differentiation, even when embedded into equilibrium dynamics and scarcity constraints on underlying endowments (e.g. in the labor force, skills, capital, etc.). It is, indeed, an important theoretical result, already implicit in the pioneering work of Arrow (1974) on the peculiar nature of "information"—even when neglecting those differences between "information" and agent-specific "knowledge" emphasized by evolutionary theorists (Pavitt 1984; Winter 1981 and 1987; Dosi and Egidi 1991).

As argued at greater length elsewhere,[8] a distinctive feature of evolutionary models is the attempt to represent the possible emergence of relatively ordered and differentiated economic systems as self-organizing processes floating in a world where "endowments" and "available technological blueprints" are seldom functionally binding constraints. Rather, technological learning within a notionally unlimited space of opportunities, at the levels of both individual firms and whole industries and countries, determines economic performances. "Endowments" are seldom binding because one can continuously improve their quality and efficiency, while one can hardly separate the contribution of individual factors to growth, because of a rich structure of positive feedbacks. In this respect the evidence on the microeconomics of innovation (cf. Dosi 1988), shows a highly variegated pattern of search and development of new products and production processes, which nonetheless manifest a general inseparability between what firms do to allocate their resources to production and the processes through which they learn how to do better what they already do, or how to do new things.

First, learning is to a good extent a sort of joint production with manufacturing activities themselves. Obviously, this includes phenomena of learning by doing, but it is also likely that search activities, such as R&D, will occur within firms and industries in fields related to what they are currently good at doing. Second, part of the technological knowledge is often tacit, specific to particular problem-solving activities, somewhat idiosyncratic, embodied in people and organizations, cumulative in its developments. Third, there are sorts of general knowledge inputs (often related to "dominant" and pervasive technologies, such as mechanical engineering, electricity and more recently microelectronics) which enter most manufacturing activities, irrespectively of one country's specializations, so that the rates at which these general competences grow influence the overall efficiency of each country.

As a consequence, current allocative processes influence future opportunities of learning in ways that, to a good extent, are not and *cannot* be signaled and traded through the market.

The coupled dynamics between learning and resource allocations may entail "virtuous circles" of sustained learning and efficient allocation of resources, or conversely, in "vicious circles," whereby, irrespective of the efficiency by which available resources are used, the system generates relatively low rates of innovation and, thus, also relatively low rates of increase in input efficiencies. This conjecture, already expressed in a quite confused fashion by some Continental European writers on trade of the nineteenth century (e.g. Ferrier, List, etc.), is quite akin to the Kaldor–Myrdal idea of "circular causation." A contemporary, more rigorous formalization is in terms of path-dependent processes wherein "localized" learning and dynamic increasing returns amplify microfluctuations and may "lock" the system-dynamics into trajectories that may well be "inferior" from a normative point of view, but still be stable over time (cf. Arthur 1988; Arthur, Ermoliev and Kaniovski 1987; David 1975 and 1985). One can also see intuitively how international trade may reinforce polarization among countries and lock-in into particular patterns of growth: competition on the world market and specialization influence the rates and direction of innovative learning by firms and countries, which in turn affect international competitiveness and specialization.

Both the evolutionary story and the "equilibrium story" on endogenous technical change, trade and growth, it has already been mentioned, easily generate international differentiation in income levels and rates of growth. In addition, in our view, the former is capable of generating a richer variety of dynamic patterns (albeit trading it off against lower formal elegance), and also mapping them into the underlying characteristics of technological learning (e.g. its features of cumulativeness, partial tacitness, appropriability, etc.). However, this is not the issue we want to discuss here. Rather, let us consider the nature and importance of alternative microeconomic assumptions.

As is obvious, in the standard aggregate-production-function story on growth, organizational specificities of firms and countries are entirely absent. The most natural way of interpreting its microfoundations is in terms of an underlying General Equilibrium. In several of the "new trade" and "new growth" models there is indeed an explicit microfoundation, based on imperfectly competitive equilibria. However, precisely because of the equilibrium assumption, it is hard to account for any influence of particular forms of corporate and industrial organization upon competitiveness and growth. Putting it another way, one senses a striking conflict between any equilibrium account of trade and growth and, say, Porter's analysis of the specific organizational and technological features underlying, for example, the Italian competitiveness in ceramic tiles or the British failures in mechanical engineering (cf. Porter 1990), or, even more so, the stories that business economists usually tell about painstakingly discovered "superior" competitive strategies.

Empirically, corporate organizations embody specific innovative search heuristics, modes of internal management, production rules, strategies for dealing with suppliers and customers (e.g. vertical integration, arm's-length relationships, collaborative agreements, reliance on the markets, etc.), patterns of labor-relations, strategies toward multinational investment, etc., but do these differences affect *aggregate* competitiveness and growth?

One hypothesis could be, of course, that the microeconomic links between organizational forms and competitiveness identified by business economists are local disequilibrium phenomena which cancel out in the aggregate.

An alternative hypothesis to the same effect is to assume that, in general, organizational specificities are only epiphenomena without any long-lasting consequences on performance.[9]

Conversely, we build here on the ideas that specific problem-solving competences deeply affect the ability of both individual firms and whole countries to generate and adopt new technologies and that these competences are not orthogonal to the forms of corporate organization. Indeed, an emerging view on firm-specific "dynamic capabilities" supports this view (cf. Teece *et al.* 1992 and 1994), naturally overlapping with a much longer tradition of business studies pointing at the two-way causality between corporate strategies and structures, and their effects on performances. A *locus classicus* here is Chandler's interpretation of the emergence of the modern multidivisional corporation in the United States and the specificities of its development in other countries (Chandler 1962, 1990 and 1992). And, as forcefully emphasized by Teece 1993, a major distinguishing feature of the Chandlerian corporation rested in its ability to accumulate specific managerial competences in the domains of innovative search, production coordination and marketing.

At a microeconomic level, all this implies also that given any set of technological competences and techniques of production which a firm can master, particular organizational structures and strategies affect both the actual efficiency that a firm displays and the rates and direction of accumulation of innovative knowledge (and, relatedly, the patterns of competitiveness over time).

A growing empirical evidence corroborates this view. For example, Patel and Pavitt (1994) find that "a firm's existing product mix and associated competences strongly constrain the directions in which it seeks to exploit technological opportunities and acquire competences"; and that ". . . the firm's home country will influence its rate of technological accumulation" (p. 20). (See also Cantwell 1989; Nelson 1994; Porter 1990.)

At an aggregate level, the argument implies that the international distribution of organizational structures and strategies is not random but reflects some country-specific characteristics which display persistence over time. In open economies, this means also that, given the patterns of technological and cost-related advantages/disadvantages of any one country, the degree to which these advantages are exploited in terms of international competitiveness[10] depends also on the organization forms and strategies of the domestic firms. Size, degrees of diversification and vertical integration, propensity to invest abroad, etc. are obviously indicators, but at least equally important are the attitudes toward growth, profitability, market shares, uncertainty, innovation, the nature of internal hierarchies, the relationship between industry and finance, the ways conflict is managed, etc.

Finally, this implies that country-specific organizational characteristics may reproduce over time despite the selective pressures of international competition.

The general interpretative perspective, as discussed in Dosi (1992), might be summarized in four general propositions:

Proposition 1

In contemporary economies, *a good deal of knowledge about technology and exchange governance is embodied in organizations (primarily business firms), which reproduce and augment it via institutionalized procedures and "routines"* that are only limitedly subject to strategic decision at each point in time.

Another way of saying the same is that a lot of what is commonly considered as part of the "control variables" of corporate decision-makers is in fact part of the "state variables" of individual business units—possibly modifiable only in the long term (more on this in Winter 1987).

Proposition 2

Since the prevalent forms of market interaction are generally quite different from pure competition, agents plausibly engage in objectively strategic interdependences. However, *the environments are complex and non-stationary, so that the high-dimensionality of the state—and control—spaces renders strategic behavior quite "opaque."* The mapping between information, actions and outcomes is, at best, imprecise—often undertaken on the grounds of roughly calibrated heuristics and sheer untested beliefs. Hence, *behavioral discretionality is very high.* In general, neither "backward inductive" rationality nor environmental selective pressures and adaptive learning are able to render behaviors uniform. Putting it another way, neither learning nor selection are likely to induce anything resembling symmetric Nash equilibria, or, for that matter, equilibrium behavior of any sort.

Proposition 3

Technological and organizational learning within each firm is to a good extent local and path-dependent. Agents learn, building upon previous knowledge and are often also "blind" vis-à-vis other learning trajectories. They are rather good at solving particular classes of problems but not others, irrespectively of the economic incentives that an ideal external analyst would be able to identify.[11]

The model of the firm telegraphically hinted here suggests that a firm is a behavioral entity (we borrow the definition from Kreps 1990) embodying highly idiosyncratic, specific and inertial compromises between different functions, namely: (i) resource allocation; (ii) information processing; (iii) incentives to individual performance; (iv) control and power exercise; (v) learning. Remarkably, most breeds of economic theories focus primarily upon one single function, often trying to "explain" it on the grounds of the usual maximization cum equilibrium assumptions (for an impressionistic map, see Table 6.1). In the picture of the firm proposed here, on the contrary, we broaden the analysis of its evolutionary features accounting also for fundamental tradeoffs between the functions mentioned above.

To illustrate them in a somewhat caricatural way, think of the possible tradeoffs between performance control and learning. While the former is

TABLE 6.1. Representations of the firm in economic theories

Functions	Theories
Allocations of resources.	Marshallian firms.
Information processing. Incentives to individual performance	Team theories, principal/agent, cooperative games, transaction costs.
Control and power exercise.	"Radical" (Anglosaxon) theories.
Learning and problem solving.	Evolutionary theories.

French theories of "Regulation" and "Conventions" (bracketing Team theories, principal/agent, cooperative games, transaction costs; and "Radical" (Anglosaxon) theories.)

likely to imply rigid task specifications, the latter generally involves a lot of experimentation, trial-and-error, "deviant" behaviors. (More on this below.) In fact, it is easy to imagine a lot of different organizational arrangements on an ideal continuum between the Prussian army and a university department full of crazy scientists. Indeed, some of these functional tradeoffs are discussed at length in, for example, the microanalytic part of Nelson and Winter (1982), or, from a diverse angle, in the works of Simon, Cyert and March. Moreover, the organizational and management literature is rich with taxonomies describing the specificities of the sociological and "cultural" architecture of firms and the way they affect internal relations, behaviors toward the external environment and performances.

One of the points of this paper is precisely to expand on the notion of "competence" and suggest that it also involves specific patterns of governance of the functions hinted earlier. That is, competences do not only involve problem-solving skills concerning the relationship between the firm and the outside environment, but also skills and rules governing internal relationships. The two are not disjoint: the rates and direction of learning are shaped by the internal structure and the internal norms of behaviour of individual organizations. In this respect Aoki's suggestive comparison between two "ideal types"—the "Japanese firm" and the "American firm"— is a good case in point: different internal governance structures affect learning and performance, even in the presence of identical economic opportunities (Aoki 1988).

More generally, this leads us to our last proposition.

Proposition 4

Firms are behavioural entities embodying specific and relatively inertial competences, decision rules and internal governance structures *which, in the longer term, co-evolve with the environment in which they are embedded.*

The strength of norms, routines, "corporate cultures" resides precisely in their persistence and reproduction over time. As sociologists and organizational theorists tell us, such an inertiality provides some degree of consistency among individual behaviors and motivations to action even if incentive compatibilities are much weaker than those prescribed by economic theory, and even if information about a changing and complex world borders pure ignorance. But precisely that same inertiality makes organizational arrangements quite differentiated, and, often highly suboptimal in their ability to seize technological and market opportunities. (A more detailed discussion is in Dosi and Marengo 1994.)

All four propositions, taken together, imply that, certainly, learning and environmental selection tend to reduce the variety of both technological and organizational innovations that continuously emerge. However, the "locality" of learning, the "opaqueness" of the environment and the positive feedbacks linking particular directions of technological learning with particular organizational setups all imply persistence of different forms of corporate and industrial organization, even when *ex post* they yield different competitive performances. In a jargon nearer to economists: as one can easily generate multiple equilibria stemming from non-convexities and increasing returns in the technology space, so one can easily conjecture multiple "organizational trajectories" stemming, in a loose analogy, from organizational learning about norms, competences, corporate structures.

Moreover, if these propositions are correct, one can identify a possible bridge between (evolutionary) modeling of growth and the rich and variegated account of the patterns of industrialization and growth provided by historians and industrial sociologists alike. Just to give some hints: Ronald Dore's fascinating anatomy of the Japanese industrial system (Dore 1973), Albert Hirschman's analyses of the emergence and role of markets (Hirschman 1977 and 1982), Lazonick's account of the relationship between industrial relations and patterns of industrial development (Lazonick 1993), all appear indeed compatible in principle with an evolutionary "explanation" of growth embedded in the dynamics of changing behavioral entities (firms, but also other social actors, for example banks, workers, public agencies, etc.) and in a technological dynamics with path-dependent learning and widespread increasing returns.[12]

In this respect, we share Zysman's view that collective social entities—such as nations—grounded in specific institutions and commonly shared norms of behavior, shape the patterns of opportunities and constraints facing micro agents and, as a consequence, also the aggregate paths of economic change (Zysman 1994).

However, while a lot of promising investigations have focused on technologies and firms as units of analysis, much less attention has been devoted so far in this perspective to the detailed anatomy of corporate organizations, the ways this links up with economy-wide institutions, and, ultimately their effect on economic performances.

3. COMPETENCES AND FORMS OF ORGANIZATIONAL GOVERNANCE: A PRELIMINARY LOOK INTO THE ORGANIZATIONAL BLACKBOX

As already mentioned, evolutionary economists and business analysts alike most often share the inclination to look at the repertoire of behavioral norms and practices—or routines—within each organization in order to identify "what a firm is good at," how it differs from other firms and also its proximate domains of future change.

Indeed, there are good reasons for the widespread presence of routinized behaviors which we do not need to repeat here:[13] suffice to say that they appear to be robust forms of adaptive learning in complex and changing environments.[14] Moreover, as Nelson and Winter (1982) thoroughly argue, the ensemble of organizational routines, to a large extent, stores and reproduces the problem-solving knowledge of the organization itself. Together with the hypothesis on the widespread emergence of routinized behaviors, a common feature of most evolutionary analyses is the emphasis on their problem-solving properties. This is indeed a major distinguishing building-block of this perspective—and of the earlier pioneering contributions of Herbert Simon—as compared to more orthodox interpretations of organizational arrangements, primarily focused upon the relationships between distribution of information, incentives and resulting equilibrium outcomes. Putting it in a somewhat extremist way, "evolutionists" tend to assume that some, rather rough, incentive compatibility is sufficient to motivate individual efforts and then get down to the analysis of how the set of particular individual actions painstakingly combine in order to solve some equally specific problems, say, building cars and, moreover, doing it at competitive costs, search for better varieties of them, etc. Conversely, e.g. a "principal/agent" theorist would more easily assume that everyone is naturally able to build the "optimal" car—whatever that means—conditional on the available information, and then point at the details of sophisticated self-seeking interactions which could be undertaken by the members of the organization on the grounds of asymmetric access to information. Elsewhere (Dosi and Marengo 1994), one argues at greater length that the former approach is indeed a much more promising first approximation to organizational behaviors.

Relatedly, a growing effort has gone also into formal representations of processes of search, recombination, reinforcement of sequences of elementary operations yielding particular problem-solving procedures. (See Marengo 1992.) However, routines emerge and are implemented in organizations composed of a plurality of individuals who might have diverging interests. Certainly, a "firm can be understood in terms of hierarchy of practiced organizational routines, which define lower order organizational skills and how these skills are coordinated, and higher-order decision procedures for choosing what is to be done at lower level" (Nelson 1994: 234–5). This hierarchy, however, also entails a mechanism of exercise of authority and governance of the admissible behaviors by which individual members can pursue their interests. This is indeed acknowledged by Nelson and Winter (1982) who suggest that routines can be seen also as "truces" amongst potentially conflicting interests, but this complementary nature of routines has been so far relatively neglected in that literature which explicitly builds upon evolutionary ideas.[15] The double nature of routines as problem-solving skills and as mechanisms of governance appears with particular clarity when analyzing the emergence and establishment of new principles of management and work practices.

Here, we shall consider two archetypal examples, namely "Taylorism" and "Fordism" on the one hand and "Ohnism" and "Toyotism," on the other.

4. TAYLORISM, "SCIENTIFIC MANAGEMENT" AND ROUTINES

Much has been written about Taylor's "Scientific Management" principles based on the systematic subdivision of organizational tasks and grounded in so-called "Time and Motion Studies" (Taylor 1911/1967 and 1971): however, except for the work of a few historians, largely unknown to economists, the implications of that approach to management has been largely underestimated in organization theory, let alone economics.

That underestimation appears also in the pioneering work of March and Simon (1958). While they acknowledge Taylor's as one of the classic contributions to organizational theory (and practice)[16] they primarily emphasize, ". . . the use of men as adjuncts of machines in the performance of routine productive tasks . . . ," aimed to ". . . the goal (of using) the rather inefficient human organism in the productive process in the best way possible" (March and Simon 1993).[17] On the contrary, we shall argue that, first, Taylor had the pioneering understanding that questions of organization of production are essentially questions of know-how and competence; and second, that the distribution of knowledge is intimately connected with the distribution of power. Third, the establishment of Tayloristic practices is a paradigmatic example of coevolution between forms of incentive governance, routines, competences, under circumstances of acute interest conflict.

In all this, it is certainly true that one of Taylor's major contributions to management practices have been Time and Motion Studies (TMS), but the latter have been the precondition of an epochal wave of codification of previously tacit knowledge of working operatives in a set of elementary procedures and acts. In turn, such a codification was a prerequisite for a changing control upon such knowledge itself, previously embodied in its "aggregate" form into the specific experience of skilled workers, whose abilities to bargain on the condition of its use had been a major obstacle to productivity growth in the nineteenth century.

Some historical examples and some references to Taylor's own analysis might help in illustrating these points.

At the beginning of the twentieth century a prevalent form of production organization was still the system of "inside contractors/helpers."[18] Under that practice, the owner of a firm would entrust production to a set of skilled workers, operating on its premises, who acted as "inside contractors", hiring in turn their own "helpers." The contractors directly supervised and rewarded the helpers, either with a fixed salary or in proportion to their own gains.

Under the system, the possibility of control of the owner upon the contractors was quite limited: only the latter knew the methods of production, and times and rates of remuneration had to be painstakingly negotiated. Hiring directly the skilled workers as waged employees did not improve very much the outcome, since worker-specific, and tacit, knowledge allowed workers to master the pace of work. "Soldiering" (nowadays one would say "shirking") was a normal pattern of behavior:

Underworking, that is deliberately working slowly so as to avoid doing a full day's work, "soldiering" as it is called in this country, "hanging it out" as it is called in England, "ca'canny" as it is called in Scotland is almost universal in industrial establishments and prevails to a large extent in the building trades; and . . . this constitutes the greatest evil by which the working people of both England and America are now affected. (Taylor 1911/1967: 13–14)

And moreover,

So universal is soldiering . . . that hardly a competent workman can be found in a large establishment, whether he works by the day or on piecework, contract work, or under any of the ordinary system, who does not devote a considerable part of his time to studying just how slow he can work and still convince his employer that he is going at a good pace. (ibid. 20)

Taylor's description of the phenomenon in terms of "initiative and incentives" is surprisingly near the current parlance of principal/agent theorists, although he does not at all share with the latter the faith in the existence of some incentive-compatible equilibrium contract, irrespectively of the chosen reward system. The diagnosis is that

. . . as the cause for soldiering—the relations which exist between employers and employees under almost all systems of management which are in common use—it is impossible to make clear to one not familiar with this problem why it is the ignorance of employers as to the proper time in which work of various kind should be done—makes it the interest of the workman to "soldier." (ibid. 18)

   In turn, this ignorance concerns the tacit knowledge associated with each trade.[19]

   Incidentally note that—unlike most current representations of incentive-compatibility issues—one finds here an explicit emphasis on problem-solving knowledge as distinguished from sheer information,[20] and also an implicit assumption that particular social groups (e.g. skilled workers), independently of the fine tuning of incentive mechanisms, share particular forms of collective behaviors (in this case, rendering de facto collusion easier).

   Rather than attempting to adjust the incentive structure, the general Tayloristic programme involves a major redefinition of the nature of productive knowledge and a novel distribution of it within the organization. Time and Motion Studies aim precisely at the control of the knowledge of working operatives themselves, yielding the development of detailed operational protocols, that were to become the elementary production routines of modern corporations.

   This transformation required also a major organizational transformation, namely the establishment of a specific corporate function, the Department of Planning—as repository of the general "production intelligence" of the factory. The Department analyzes the elementary tasks, allocates them to the individual workers and establishes the coordinating procedures. A major transfer of knowledge occurs, from individual workers to the management; a good deal of tacit knowledge is decomposed, codified and made easily transmissible via operational protocols.

   The end result has been that the tasks of the Tayloristic organization, "first are repetitive; second, these tasks do not require complex problem-solving activity by the workers who handle them . . ." (March and Simon 1993: 32). But this is so precisely because the overall problem-solving and coordinating activity had been taken in charge by a specific managerial institution, the Department of Planning. Indeed, the story of "Scientific Management"—and, at its core, TMS procedures—is precisely the story of the transformation of individual skills into organizational competences codified into hierarchies of routines.

   This transformation, we suggest, had the same importance for the emergence of the modern (archetypal "American") corporation as the Chandlerian emergence of the managerial divisionalized organization. In fact, the two can be seen, to a large extent, as different levels of descriptions of the same major organizational innovation. The "Tayloristic revolution" describes at the level of production routines a process which co-evolves with the reshaping of the organizational structure of the firm, entrusting the general knowledge on coordination and strategies upon professional managers—as described by Chandler.[21]

Later on, we shall also argue that the rates and modes of international adaptation of such "American" (Chandlerian and Tayloristic) corporations have deeply affected for a long period the growth patterns of each country.

First, however, let us focus on the nature of the emerging Tayloristic routines and their birthmarks stemming from the conflict that they triggered.

At a social level, the introduction of Scientific Management has been accompanied by the *open-shop campaign*, in the effort by the managers to hire non-unionized workers. Here is another element of the co-evolutionary dynamics between transformation of the knowledge bases and transformation of the collective institutions—*in primis*, the labor market—in which firms are embedded. The organizational transfer of tasks from skilled workers to "specialized" ones has been painfully accompanied by the formation of new rules of hiring, firing and labor mobility which sustained the implementation of the new working procedures inside the organizations.

Not surprisingly, the process was ridden with conflict. The case of the Watertown Arsenal (documented by Aitken 1985) is only one of the many examples of the resistance of the labor movement to the diffusion of Scientific Management.[22]

Tayloristic routines as they finally emerged fully displayed their double nature as sets of problem-solving protocols and as devices of social control. TMS methods defined a new "economy of time" together with a new "economy of control." This implied also a new production paradigm whose implicit but fundamental assumption was that the productivity of any industrial unit is a positive direct function of the productivity of the individual worker considered at his work station; and "productivity" itself is measured by the number of elementary units of work performed by the individual worker during a given unit of time (e.g. the hour or the working-day). This production paradigm performed also for a long time as a "focusing device"—in Nathan Rosenberg's terminology—shaping the direction of routine improvement and competence accumulation.

As argued at greater length elsewhere (Coriat 1979/1994, 1992, 1993*a*), this led to a very specific trajectory of production learning, whereby an increasing fragmentation of tasks proved to be conducive to efficient manufacturing of high volume, standardized, low-cost products but is likely to be less suitable for differentiated high-quality products.

It is important to notice that this particular paradigm of organization of collective competence and of social control embodies also a specific mechanism of incentive governance. The approach Taylor suggested was twofold: on the one hand, he designed a new pay system (the so-called "differential piece-rate system"); on the other hand, incentives had to be matched by direct visual control upon work practices by foremen.

Patterns of problem solving and patterns of governance and control turned out to be intimately linked within a structure of organizational routines which constrained also the patterns of learning (the "trajectory" of technological and organizational change).

In order to highlight the specificities of these routines and their internal consistency requirements between problem solving and governance, let us compare "Taylorism" with another organizational archetype, namely "Ohnism" and "Toyotism"—as the new Japanese production practices are often called.

5. "OHNISM" AND JAPANESE PRODUCTION ROUTINES

As it is handy to identify an archetype of labour management practices with Taylor's original vision and normative programme—notwithstanding the obvious nuances in the fulfillment of such a model—so it is easy to point at T. Ohno for the general statement of an alternative set of "Japanese" production practices (cf. Ohno 1988).

The two major specificities of "Ohnism" might be identified with (a) "Just-in-time" organization of production flows, and (b) production routines based on the principle of "auto-activation" (for more on this see Coriat 1991a). Briefly, just-in-time coordination methods consist of just producing what can actually be sold, catering for orders insofar as they appear, rather than producing and stocking on the grounds of expectations of future sales.[23] "Auto-activation" or "autonomation" (*jidoka*) is a complementary organizing criterion for production tasks based on the idea that each worker has the time needed to complete his assignments and pass on a flawless product to his partner at the next stage of production. Moreover, "autonomation" entails the possibility—and, indeed the duty—to apply "local intelligence," identify anomalies, and, in case, stop the entire production flow. In turn, "autonomation" implies (i) a multiplicity of skills of each worker; (ii) some discretionality and autonomy in decision making; and (iii) patterns of coordination between production tasks smoothly flowing in temporal sequences from inputs to outputs.[24]

A casual observer, and especially an economist, might consider all this as belonging to the domain of diverse and ephemeral managerial practices. On the contrary, one of us has argued elsewhere (Coriat 1991a) that these two basic principles of production entail organizational forms significantly different from the "Tayloristic" (or "American") archetype sketched above, and with that, also different patterns of organization of knowledge.

The "seeding" of the evolutionary process which yielded these organizational outcomes, can be identified—as in the earlier Tayloristic example—into complementary problem-solving and incentive-compatibility dilemmas, most likely embedded in broader, more inertial institutions and cultures. Japan, in its industrializing and reconstruction efforts, especially after World War II, was forced to find ways of achieving productivity gains other than classic "Fordist" methods based on the exploitation of economies of scale. To a good extent, it shared also the requirement, felt earlier so acutely by the Tayloristic philosophy, to place operatives' knowledge under management control (a lag most likely due also to the previous authoritarian regime which tended to surrogate for incentive incompatibility with loyalty and force). In any case, the crux of the matter was, as in other modernizing countries, to reshape the distribution of knowledge away from variegated groups of highly skilled workers. And on the conflict-of-interest side, social polarization, in the decade following World War II, was certainly at a rather critical level. The course that labor relations and working organization actually took—by no means the only notional one[25]—was a specific and original way of work rationalization which did not stop at the Tayloristic breakdown of complex workers skills, but recomposed the tasks for multifunctional workers, with flexible working standards.[26] A major consequence of this organizational innovation was that it implied a production engineering approach (concerning design and layout of production lines, programming principles, etc.) radically different from that which has prevailed in America amid the numerous Ford-inspired recommendations.[27]

For our purposes, we want to emphasize that the combination of "just-in-time" with "auto-activation" has given rise to a novel series of routines, both at the level of intra- and inter-organization practices.

A first crucial difference from the "American" theory and practice can be sketched as follows. Whereas the Tayloristic approach has been aimed to separate the functions of production, maintenance, quality control, planning, etc. and to fragment the tasks required by each function, the Japanese way on the contrary has been to create work stations where the different tasks are to different degrees reaggregated.[28] Thus, one can observe that the fundamental significance of the Japanese approach consists of a reconstitution at shop-floor level of something like a general and reaggregated function of manufacturing, the main characteristic of which is that it puts together again tasks which Taylor's approach recommended be carefully and systematically kept apart.[29] On this basis, one observes the introduction of specific protocols entailing permanent manipulation of *kanban* and used either to command or to deliver "just-in-time" the internal flows of semi-finished products.

One can wonder how it is possible to reaggregate general functions in manufacturing without losing control of productivity, i.e. can the Taylorian legacy be so deeply abandoned?

The answer to this question (crucial for the understanding of the "control" dimension of the Japanese routines) is twofold.

First, TMS is not abandoned at all. As has been pointed out by a very attentive and pertinent commentator, TMS has been "regained" (see Adler

1993), i.e. the idea of fragmenting tasks is maintained but, the jobs are now broken down into basic "transferable work components." Such a component is defined as: "the smallest practical combination of acts that can be transferred from one worker to another." Thus flexible work standards and reaggregation of elementary tasks are made compatible with the objective of maintaining workers' knowledge and work standards under control.[30] Second, the Japanese methods embed specific practices of controlling workers' tasks and activities, one of the most important being what is termed "management by eyes," elaborated and designed by T. Ohno himself. This principle is indeed very simple and consists in organizing the workshops, and the work on the lines, in such a way that everything can be very easily (physically) visible. For example, any worker has the right (and in fact more than the right, the duty) to stop the line any time he thinks it necessary to guarantee the quality of his performance; at the same time, each stop is signaled by a red light appearing on an electronic panel hanging above the line (It is the so-called "andon" system).

More generally, Ohno explains the principle of "managing by eyes" as follows:

In order to allow "autoactivation" to detect anomalies, one needs that anything "abnormal" appears immediately to the naked eye. The principle ought to apply to quality (every faulted product should immediately surface) as well as to quantity (progress of work vis-à-vis previous plans should be effortlessly measured at the very work place). This should not only apply to the machines but also to the methods of production, the circulation of kanbans, the levels of stocks, etc. (Ohno 1988)

Note again the learning side of this set of routines—as well as those associated with "just-in-time": far from being simple devices to minimize faulty pieces of output or inventories, they fulfill primarily the task of immediately highlighting the presence of a problem and allowing or forcing operatives to handle it.

6. MICROROUTINES, INCENTIVES AND INSTITUTIONAL EMBEDDEDNESS

More generally, a crucial implication of each distinct pattern of organization of production is that it involves a specific set of problem-solving routines *and equally specific, and broadly consistent, forms of incentive governance and control*. In a telegraphic summary, Taylorism introduces also a new reward mechanism based on a piece-wage system, made of a fixed part—corresponding to a minimum number of pieces per day, and a variable part—triggered by above minimum output and pushing upward the whole per-piece wage rates (also, on the part below, the minimum threshold).[31]

"Fordism" further modifies the reward mechanism, introducing the famous "five-dollar day" wage (well above the current wage at the time), but, *together*, eliminates workers' discretionality in the choice of working pace by incorporating it into the predetermined speed of conveyors along the assembly line. Finally, it introduces systematic screening and testing of workers themselves, in terms of their social attitudes, their loyalty and obedience. This task is delegated to a special institution: the so-called "Sociological Department."[32]

Conversely, "Ohnism" implies a complex reward structure involving (a) a base salary; b) individual bonuses; and c) collective performance bonuses.

As M. Aoki has forcefully shown on several occasions, the two stylized and archetypal organizational forms, called the "American" and the "Japanese" enterprises, differing in the internal architecture with respect to both information-processing and incentive-governance, are likely to yield also systematically different performances.[33] Our argument indeed strengthens the point. The set of "Japanese" (or "Ohnist") production routines does not only embody different channels of information processing but also distributes knowledge within the organization in ways remarkably different from the "Tayloristic"/"Chandlerian" enterprise. And at the same time, on the governance side, individual incentives to efficiently perform and learn are sustained by company-specific rank—hierarchies, delinked from functional assignments (Aoki 1990).

The collective "embeddedness" dimension is equally important. We mentioned earlier that the establishment of "Tayloristic" organizational routines coevolved with the development of what one could shorthandedly call the "American labor market." Symmetrically, radically different institutional norms (such as life-time employment, etc.) became established with respect to large Japanese corporations. Yet at another level, different corporate strategies (with respect to investment growth, diversification, R&D, etc.) appear to taxonomically match specific institutional relationships between financial and industrial actors.[34]

At a much finer level of detail, these modal patterns of relationship between diverse economic agents, again, are entangled into identifiable sets of behavioral routines. For example in Coriat (1994), one tries to identify typical protocols of interfirm transactions, conditional on the internal modes of governance and problem solving.

A revealing illustration is the relationship between "core" companies and their suppliers. Under the Japanese system of organizational routines, Asanuma (1987 and 1989) sharply illustrates the protocols for information-flows, competition/cooperation—"relational rent-sharing" as Aoki (1988) would phrase it. Among this specific set of routines, those concerning quality selection are clearly of crucial importance. Producing almost without inventories (of either inputs or outputs) implies that product quality of the semi-finished products either ordered or received by core companies

must be very high. As a consequence, the process of selection of subcon-
tractors implies very detailed protocols (in the case of the French auto
industry they are discussed in Coriat 1994).[35]

Similar exercises could fruitfully be done (and, indeed, ought to be done)
with respect to other types of interactive procedures (e.g. with respect to the
labor market, financial investors, etc.) Just to mention an example, it seems
to us that Lorenz' argument on the importance of trust (or rather the lack
of it) in British production practices belongs precisely to this domain of
analysis: the "truces" that emerged codified in particular sets of routines
tended to foster conservatism, and hinder the diffusion of technological and
organizational innovation (Lorenz 1994). In any case, for the little we know
about the behaviors of enterprises with respect to their external environment, the evidence seems to corroborate our conjectures (i) that somewhat
typical and rather inertial behavioral patterns tend to emerge, (ii) that these
patterns can be roughly mapped into distinctive internal hierarchies of
routines within the organization; (iii) that broader collective institutions—
e.g. on the labor or financial markets—constrain and shape the sustainable
routines; and (iv) that also in the relationships amongst legally independent
actors, interactive routines enfold problem-solving complementarities and
asymmetric mechanisms of control.[36]

"Taylorism," the Chandlerian M-form organization, "Fordism" or for
that matter, "Ohnism" and "Toyotism" represent major organizational innovations, with—in principle—a universal character. And, indeed,
at least the former three spread internationally, well beyond the countries where they were originally introduced, spurring deep modifications
in industrial structures and shaping long-term productivity growth (on
"Taylorism" and the M-form, see Kogut 1992, and Chandler 1990). It
is possibly too early to evaluate the international diffusion of Japanese
practices, but rich case-study evidence already suggests their widespread
impact.

However, the rates and patterns of diffusion of all these major organizational paradigms have been shaped by the institutional context of each
country, which implied also some inevitable "hybridization." This, in some
cases, also yielded major modifications further down the road. In this respect, Japanese practices may indeed be considered as a profound organizational innovation originally grounded in the local adaptation of Taylorism
and Fordism, which eventually led to a distinct archetype of organizational
routines for problem solving and governance of industrial relations.

One can see here a good example of the notions of embeddedness,
(limited) lock-in, and potential invadability. Embeddedness implies that
earlier patterns of industrial organization, labour practices, etc. carry their
influence over the ways new forms are introduced: it applies to the original
adaptations of Taylorism and Fordism to Japan or Sweden, as well as to that

of the M-form corporation in e.g. the UK, Germany or Japan. Lock-in entails the prediction of progressive dominance of some specific patterns of governance and problem solving and their rather inertial reproduction over time. However, each "national system" remains potentially "invadable"—to use the jargon of current evolutionary games: it might be unable to generate internally radically new organizational experiments, but is not immune to the progressive adoption of organizational innovations developed elsewhere.

7. FROM CORPORATE ROUTINES TO PATTERNS OF DEVELOPMENT: PRELIMINARY CONCLUSIONS AND MANY RESEARCH ITEMS ON LEARNING, INCENTIVES AND PATTERNS OF CHANGE

We began this work by presenting what we consider to be a few "stylized facts" on the relationship between technical change and growth, together with some microeconomic evidence on innovative activities. In turn, many of these "facts" entail challenging puzzles for the theory. Old ones like "why levels and growth rates of income differ" demand—it is increasingly acknowledged—the dissection of the black box of technological change, as Nathan Rosenberg urged us quite a while ago. Investigations in this perspective have recently increased momentum and, in our view, are significantly adding novel insights into the processes by which knowledge is augmented, to a good extent also as a result of exploratory endeavors of profit-motivated agents, together with those of other institutions. While one progresses in opening up the "technological black box," however, there is yet another black box—the organizational one—whose anatomy is plausibly quite important also for every macro economist who does not consider the specificities of corporate organizations simply as veils covering deeper and invariant economic mechanisms.

The proposition that organizational structures matter in terms of performances, in fact, can be quite easily supported even in term of otherwise quite orthodox theories, whenever one abandons the most restrictive assumptions on perfect information, complete markets, etc. (see, within an enormous literature, Aoki 1990; Sah and Stiglitz 1985; Radner 1992). Even more so, if one accounts for the endemic occurrence of transaction costs as Oliver Williamson (1985*a,b*) emphasizes.

Of course, the learning dimension that evolutionary and organizational economists add to the picture further reinforces the point. The path-dependent, often organization-embodied, nature of knowledge makes corporate structures the prime carriers of diverse problem-solving skills, to a good extent stored and reproduced via organizational routines.

However, routines do not only represent problem-solving procedures but are at the same time control and governance devices. In this work we have analyzed precisely this double nature of theirs. Moreover, we have argued, specific sets of routines often bear the mark of the conflicts which accompanied their emergence and establishment.

The two archetypal sets of routines which we have outlined in this work namely "Tayloristic" and "Ohnistic" (loosely speaking, "Japanese") production methods vividly illustrate these points. More precisely, we have tried to show that the explanation of particular sets of routines can be traced back to the coevolution between corporate patterns of knowledge distribution and mechanisms of coordination and governance.

All this, most likely, reinforces phenomena of path-dependence and international differentiation, generally sustained by mutually shared conventions, norms and implicit or legally enforced institutions.

There are several rather general implications of the perspective outlined in this work, which can only be sketched out in this paper.

As we have emphasized above, the multiple facets of organizational arrangements and the forms of their institutional embeddedness are, in our view, an integral part of the explanation of the diversity of development patterns that one observes: in fact, we suggest they are among the core elements of those diverse "social capabilities" identified by Abramovitz (1989) as "deeper causes" of contemporary growth.

Other, more theoretical implications, have only been briefly mentioned. For example, the foregoing interpretation of the nature of organizational routines encompasses the tasks of incentive governance analyzed by, for example, principal agent models. But it radically departs from the latter in that it considers "what the agents believe to be their interests," the ways they pursue them and the knowledge that they possess to be the evolutionary outcome of search, conflict and mutual adjustment sanctioned thereafter by rather inertial rules and organizational structures. Corollaries of this view are also the predictions that (a) it might be generally misleading to reduce whatever pattern of intra- or interorganizational relations to a set of "contracts" (whether optimal or not); b) given the organizational routines, individual performances are likely to be rather insensitive to any fine tuning of incentives; and c) path-dependency phenomena will tend frequently to carry over the reproduction of particular organizational arrangements well beyond the time of their possible usefulness.

Other implications—nearer the concerns of the economics of innovation—regard the effect of established sets of routines upon the "trajectories" of technical progress (and here is also where the economics of innovation can meet analyses from other disciplinary camps which have emphasized the aspects of "social construction" of technical change).

Indeed, we see ahead a promising research agenda.

NOTES

1. Cf. Coriat (1994*b*), Lazonick (1990; 1993), Zysman (1994).
2. This assumption is in the same spirit as Nelson and Winter (1992).
3. Within a rapidly growing literature, see Freeman (1982); Nelson and Winter (1982); Pavitt (1984); Rosenberg (1985); Dosi (1988); Dosi *et al.* (1988); David (1985); Arthur (1988); Saviotti and Metcalfe (1992).
4. See the pioneering work of Nelson and Winter (1982), and, among others, Silverberg *et al.* (1988); Eliasson (1986); Chiaromonte, Dosi and Orsenigo (1993); Silverberg and Verspagen (1994).
5. Dosi *et al.* (1994*a*).
6. Cf. Dosi, Pavitt and Soete (1990), Fagerberg (1987; 1988), Soete and Verspagen (1993), and the broad discussion in Abramovitz (1989).
7. Cf. Romer (1986, 1990*a,b*); Helpman and Krugman (1989); Grossman and Helpman (1991); Aghion and Howitt (1992).
8. Dosi and Orsenigo (1988); Dosi (1992).
9. Indeed, the irrelevance of organizational forms can be argued from quite different theoretical points of view. Take, for example, an extreme version of a transaction-cost model of corporate organization. The model would suggest that observed institutional setups (e.g. within and between firms) are the organizational response to a requirement of efficient governance of exchanges. Hence, any observed international difference in the typical modes of organizing transactions would be primarily attributed to lags and leads in diffusion of more efficient forms of organization (if transaction costs do not dramatically differ across countries, which is likely to apply to developed economies, although it might not to comparisons among countries at different stages of development). In the long term, an extreme version of a transaction-cost theory of organization would suggest that one should observe *convergence in institutional setups*, driven by the differential efficiency of various organizational modes.

    At the symmetric opposite, consider an extreme version of the Marglin–Piore–Sabel interpretation of industrial organization (more faithful and sophisticated arguments along these lines are in Marglin (1974), Piore and Sabel (1984); needless to say, we are purposefully overemphasizing in order to clarify the point). Here, in a first approximation, the cross-sectional and intertemporal differences in the modes of organization of firms and industries would be simply responses to power criteria, and reproduce with the inertia that institutions generally entail. The set of *equally efficient* organizational regimes, this interpretation would suggest, is wide, and the observed variety results from a selection within such a set, driven primarily by considerations of social control and income distribution. Hence, again, national specificities in corporate and industrial organization would not be among the fundamental variables explaining "why levels and growth rates of income differ across countries."
10. On this notion of "competitiveness" cf. Dosi, Pavitt and Soete (1990).
11. Promising explorations of the idea are in Levinthal (1992), and Levinthal and March (1994). See also Dosi and Lovallo (1994).

12. And, at a more aggregate level of description, this interpretation is highly complementary with a "Regulationist" view—in the French institutionalist sense of the patterns of "socio-economic tuning" characterizing particular countries and phases of development (Boyer 1988*a,b*; Boyer and Coriat 1986).

13. Cf. Nelson and Winter (1982); March (1994); Dosi and Egidi (1991); Dosi and Marengo (1994); Dosi *et al.* (1994); Cohen (1987).

14. Like Nelson and Winter (1982), Dosi *et al.* (1994) and Teece *et al.* (1994), we include under the broad heading of "routines" relatively invariant norms of behavior which are context-dependent and approximately event-independent (in the sense that they are rather insensitive to the information on changes in the states of the world, given a particular context). Moreover, routines might be straightforwardly stationary rules (such as ". . . close the door of the factory every day at 7 p.m. . . .") or higher-level "dynamic rules" (such as ". . . search for new techniques in such and such directions . . ."; ". . . when something goes wrong do *x* and send a message to *y* . . .", etc.).

15. Important exceptions are Postrel and Rumelt (1992) and Kogut (1992).

16. The other being that by Guklick and Urwick, concerned with "the grand organizational problems of departmental division of work and coordination."

17. Hence they characterize the approach as "physiological organization theory," because it encompasses primarily physiological variables (p. 32) and add "Traditional Time and Motion Study Methods have avoided problem-solving tasks, and thus have not dealt with the aspects of human behaviour that will concern us throughout most of this volume" (p. 33).

18. Cf. Montgomery (1979); Hounshell (1984); S. Meyer, III (1982).

19. "The managers recognize frankly the fact that the 500 to 1,000 workmen included in the twenty or thirty trades who are under them, possess this mass of traditional knowledge, a large part of which is not in the possession of the management." "This mass of rules of thumb or traditional knowledge may be said to be the principle asset or possession of every tradesman" (ibid. 32).

20. That distinction is of course a major building block of the analyses of production and innovation of Nelson and Winter (1982); Winter (1981); Dosi (1988) and Pavitt (1984).

21. On the importance of routines and competences underlying the Chandlerian corporation, see Chandler himself (1992) and Teece (1993).

22. Taylor himself had also to justify his practices before a Special Committee of the House of Representatives, cf. Taylor (1971).

23. The so-called *Kanban* approach, originally named after a procedure of dropping paper orders of components "upstream" of the production chain, has been a well-known implementation.

24. Note that this does not apply to "Taylorist"/"Fordist" patterns of organization of production whereby each elementary "shop" (e.g. "the drilling shop," "the boring shop," etc.) produces for a buffer stock of intermediate goods.

25. To make a more general theoretical point: as with path-dependent models with multiple attainable limit states, conditional on the initial setups, we are far from claiming that the Japanese initial conditions telegraphically sketched here "determined" in any strong sense the observed outcome. Rather we just suggest that they contributed to select the feasible evolutionary path, together with

broader social circumstances, analyzed from different perspectives by Aoki (1988); Dore (1973); Gerlach (1993), among others.

26. Cf. Monden (1983). The linearization of the production processes hinted above is associated with these more flexible production standards and also permits switching from some predetermined production time to a "shared" time: cf. Monden (1983) and Coriat (1991).

27. Broadening the field of observation from the shop-floor level to the enterprise as a whole, the same principle of relative despecialization can be observed, particularly with the establishment of horizontal lines of communications between marketing, R&D and manufacturing. These flexible interdepartmental communications make it possible to get closer to the market as regards quality trends and at the same time to reduce lead times (cf. Clark and Fujimoto 1989, for example).

28. In more detail, this process of despecialization and reaggregation of tasks affects four domains. The first of these reaggregations concerns the reassociation of tasks within direct manufacturing itself: "versatility" and multispecialization are the norm and stand in opposition to the principles of compartmentalization and repetitivity featured by American Tayloristic patterns. The second consists of the reacquisition by direct operatives of the tasks of diagnostics, repair and light maintenance; self-management and self-inspection make sense and prove effective only if the front-line operatives are also in charge of the routine maintenance of the plant and machinery. The third is the reintroduction of quality control at the work stations. Here again, the be-all and end-all of the principle of self-management and self-inspection is to tackle product quality at the work stations themselves. Lastly, there is also a reaggregation of programming and manufacturing tasks, which constitutes the necessary condition of the *Kanban* method (Coriat 1991*a*, 1992).

29. In its spirit and in its practical details, the method appears as the implementation of principles of despecialization, not only in terms of the employee's work, but in a more global perspective as a despecialization of the "general work of the enterprise," reaggregating on the shop floor the tasks (production, programming or quality control, etc.) systematically kept apart by Taylorism.

30. For a number of very convincing illustrations of this kind of practices in Japanese transplants in the USA see Parker and Slaughter (1988).

31. So for example, suppose that the minimum output is 200 pieces per day corresponding to wages of $2 (i.e. 1 cent per piece): output up to 10% higher would entail, says, a 10% upward adjustment of the whole wage; a 20% higher output a wage 40% higher, etc. Incidentally, note that the principle appears in violation of "marginal productivity" criteria but seems more akin to a modified version of an "efficiency wage" principle.

32. The "Sociological Department" goes as far as checking on the workers' families, their social habits, etc. On the story of the Five-Dollar Day, and the role attributed to the "sociological department," see S. Meyer, III (1992).

33. Aoki (1988; 1990).

34. For example, "market-based" and "bank-based" forms of finance of investment and interfirm selection: cf. Zysman (1994), Aoki (1988), Dosi (1990). A tentative combinatorial exercise among the viable forms of governance among

    internal routines, labor-market interactions, modes of finance and innovative strategies is presented in Aoki and Dosi (1992).

35. Briefly, they typically show a five-stage procedure of selection and relationship construction, going from the "assessment of quality aptitude"; to tentative efforts of knowledge transfer to the contractors; evaluation of the preliminary outcomes; acceptance into the core company "product quality assurance circle"; and, finally, permanent "real time" assessment of deliveries.

36. For example, with respect to this latter point, in Coriat (1994) we argue that networking routines, while being certainly a mechanism of collective learning, generally imply also persistent asymmetries and interfirm hierarchies. The embeddedness argument is formulated, in quite general terms in Granovetter (1985), and more specifically with regards to corporate strategies of production and innovation, in Lazonick (1990 and 1993), Soskice (1993) and Zysman (1994). See also Boyer (1988a) and Dosi, Pavitt and Soete (1990).

REFERENCES

Abramovitz, M. (1989), *Thinking About Growth* (Cambridge: Cambridge University Press).

Adler, P. (1993), "Time-and-Motion Study Regained," *Harvard Business Review*, Jan.–Feb., no. 93101.

Aghion, P. and Howitt, P. (1992), "A Model of Growth Through Creative Destinction," in Foray and Freeman (eds.), *Technology and the Wealth of Nations*.

Aitken, H. G. J. (1985), *Scientific Management in Action: Taylorism at Watertown Arsenal, 1908–1915* (Princeton: Princeton University Press).

Aoki, M. (1988), *Information, Incentives, and Bargaining Structure in the Japanese Economy* (Cambridge: Cambridge University Press).

——(1990), "Towards an Economic Theory of the Japanese Firm," *Journal of Economic Literature*, 26/1.

——and Dosi, G. (1992), "Corporate Organization, Finance and Innovation," in V. Zamagni (ed.), *Finance and the Enterprise* (New York: Academic Press).

Arrow, K. (1974), *The Limits of Organizations* (New York: Norton).

Arthur, B. (1988), "Competing Technologies," in Dosi *et al.* (eds.), *Technical Change and Economic Theory*.

——Ermoliev, Y. and Kaniovski, Y. (1987), "Path-dependent Processes and the Emergence of Macro Structures," *European Journal of Operational Research*, 30/3 (June), 294–303.

Asanuma, B. (1987), "Transactional Structure of Parts Supply in the Japanese Automobile and Electric Machinery Industries: A Comparative Analysis," Working Paper, Kyoto University.

——(1989), "Manufacturer-Supplier Relationships in Japan and the Concept of Relation Specific Skill," *Journal of the Japanese and International Economies*, 3/1: 1–30.

Berggren, C. (1988), "The Swedish Experience with 'New Work Concepts' in Assembly Operations," in B. Dunkbaar, U. Jurgens and T. Munch, *Die Zukunft der Arbeit in der Automobilindustrie* (Berlin: Ed. Sigma).

Boyer, R. (1988*a*), "Technical Change and the Theory of Regulation," in Dosi *et al.* (eds.), *Technical Change and Economic Theory*.

——(1988*b*), "Formalizing Growth Regimes," in Dosi *et al.*, *Technical Change*.

——(1989), "New Directions in Management Practices and Work Trajectories," paper presented for the OECD Conference on "Technical Change as a Social Progress," Helsinki, 11–13. Dec.

——and Coriat, B. (1986), "Technical Flexibility and Macro Stabilisation," *Ricerche Economiche*, 40/4 (Oct.–Dec.), 771–835.

Cantwell, J. (1989), *Technological Change and Multinational Corporations* (Oxford Blackwell).

Chandler, A. D. (1962), *Strategy and Structure* (Cambridge, Mass.: MIT Press).

——(1990), *Scale and Scope* (Cambridge, Mass.: The Belknap Press of Harvard University Press).

——(1992), "Organizational Capabilities and the Economic History of the Industrial Enterprise," *Journal of Economic Perspectives*, 6: 79–100.

Chiaromonte, F., Dosi, G. and Orsenigo, L. (1993), "Innovative Learning and Institutions in the Process of Development: On the Microfoundations of Growth Regimes," in Thomson (ed.), *Learning and Technological Change*.

Clark, K. B. and Fujimoto, T. (1989), "Product Development and Competitiveness," paper presented to the International Seminar on Science, Technology and Growth, OECD, Paris, April.

Cohen, M. (1987), "Adaptation and Organizational Routines," Working Paper, Ann Arbor, Michigan Institute of Public Policy Studies.

Cole, R. E (1989), *Strategies for Learning* (Berkeley: University of California Press).

Coriat, B. (1979), *L'Atelier et le Chronomètre: Essai sur le Taylorisme, le Fordisme et la Production de Masse*, 1st edn. (Paris: Christian Bourgois), paperback edn. 1994 (Paris: Collection Bourgois/Choix).

——(1990), *L'Atelier et le Robot: Essai sur le Fordisme et la Production de Masse à l'Age de l'Electronique*, 1st edn. (Paris: Christian Bourgois) paperback edn. 1994 (Paris: Collection Bourgois/Choix).

——(1991*a*), *Penser à l'Envers, Travail et Organisation dans l'Entreprise Japonaise* (Paris: Édition C. Bourgois).

——(1991*b*), "Technical Flexibility and Mass Production: Flexible Specialization and Dynamic Flexibility," in G. Benko and M. Dunford (eds.), *Industrial Change and Regional Development* (London: Belhaven Press).

——(1992), "The Revitalization of Mass Production in the Computer Age," in M. Torper and J. Scott (eds.), *Pathways to Industrialization in Regional Development* (London: Routledge).

——(1993*a*), "Incentives, Bargaining and Trust: Alternatives Scenarii for the Future of Work," Communication to the Conference on "Maastricht Revisited" (MERIT: Limburg University).

——(1993*b*), "Globalisation, Variety and Networks: The metamorphosis of the Fordist Firms," paper presented at the Conference "Hierarchies, Markets, Power in the Economy: Theories and Lessons from History," Fifth International Week on the History of the Enterprise, Castellanza, 15–17 Dec.

Coriat, B. (1994), "Taylor, Ford et Ohno: Nouveaux développements dans l'analyse du Ohnisme," *Japon in Extenso Revue.* 31 (Mar.–Apr.), 7–23.

Cremer, J. (1993), "Corporate Culture and Shared Knowledge," *Industrial and Corporate Change*, 2/3: 351–86.

David, P. A. (1975), *Technical Choice, Innovation and Economic Growth* (Cambridge: Cambridge University Press).

——(1985), "Clio and the Economics of QWERTY," *American Economic Review, Papers and Proceedings*, 75/2 (May), 332–7.

Dertouzos, M. L., Lester, R. K. and Solow, R. M. (1989), *Made in America* (Cambridge, Mass.: MIT Press).

Dore, R. (1973), *British Factory, Japanese Factory* (London: Allen & Unwin).

Dosi, G. (1988), "Sources, Procedures and Microeconomic Effects of Innovation," *Journal of Economic Literature*, 26/3 (Sept.), 1120–71.

——(1992), "Industrial Organization, Competitiveness and Growth," *Revue d'Economie Industrielle*, 59 (Jan.–Mar.), 27–45.

——and Egidi, M. (1991), "Substantive and Procedural Uncertainty," *Journal of Evolutionary Economics* 1/1: 145–68.

——and Lovallo, D. (1994), "Rational Entrepreneurs of Optimistic Martyrs? Some Considerations on Technological Regimes, Corporate Entries and the Evolutionary Role of Decision Biases," paper presented at the Conference on Technological Foresights and Oversights, Stern Business School, New York University, Mar. 1994.

——and Marengo, L. (1994), "Some Elements of an Evolutionary Theory of Corporate Competences," in R. W. England (ed.), *Evolutionary Concepts in Contemporary Economics* (Ann Arbor: University of Michigan Press).

——and Orsenigo, L. (1988), "Coordination and Transformation: An Overview of Structures, Behaviours and Change in Evolutionary Environments," in Dosi *et al* (eds.), *Technical Change and Economic Theory*.

——Freeman, C. and Fabiani, S. (1994), "The Process of Economic Development: Introducing Some Stylized Facts and Theories on Technologies, Firms and Institutions," *Industrial and Corporate Change*, 3/1: 1–46.

——Pavitt, K. and Soete, L. (1990), *The Economies of Technological Change and International Trade* (Brighton: Wheatsheaf/Harvester, and New York: New York University Press).

——Fabiani, S., Aversi, R. and Meacci, M. (1994), "The Dynamics of International Differentiation: A Multi-Country Evolutionary Model," *Industrial and Corporate Change*, 3/1: 225–42.

——Marengo, L., Bassanini, A. and Valente, M. (1994), "Norms as Emergent Properties of Adaptive Learning: The Case of Economic Routines," CCC Working Paper, Center for Research in Management, Graduate Business School, U. C. Berkeley.

——Marsili, O., Orsenigo, L. and Salvatore, R. (1993), "Learning, Market Selection and the Evolution of Industrial Structures," CCC Working Paper, CRM, Grodmate Business School, U. C. Berkeley, 93–3.

——Freeman, C., Nelson, R., Silverberg, G. and Soete, L. (1988), (eds.), *Technical Change and Economic Theory* (London: Pinter, and New York: Columbia University Press).

Eliasson, G. (1986), "Microheterogeneity of Firms and the Stability of Industrial

Growth," in R. Day and G. Eliasson (eds.), *The Dynamics of Market Economies* (Amsterdam and Oxford: North Holland with the Industrial Institute for Economic and Social Research, Stockholm; distributed in USA and Canada by Elsevier Science, New York), 79–104.

Fagerberg, I. (1987), "A Technology Gap Approach to Why Growth Rates Differ," *Research Policy*, 16/2–4 (Ang.), 87–99.

——(1988), "Why Growth Rates Differ," in Dosi *et al.* (eds.), *Technical Change and Economic Theory*.

Foray, D. and Freeman, C. (1992), (eds.), *Technology and the Wealth of Nations* (London: Pinter).

Freeman, C. (1982), *The Economics of Industrial Innovation*, 2nd edn. (London: Pinter).

Gerlach (1993), *Alliance Capitalism* (Berkeley: California University Press).

Granovetter, M. (1995), "Economic Action and Social Structure: A Theory of embeddedness," *American Journal of Sociology*, 19: 481–510.

Grossman, G. M. and Helpman, E. (1991), *Innovation and Growth* (Cambridge, Mass.: MIT Press).

Helpman, E. and Krugman, P. (1989), *Trade Policy and Market Structure* (Cambridge, Mass.: MIT Press).

Hirschman, A. (1977), *The Passion and the Interest* (Princeton, Princeton University Press).

——(1982), "Rival Interpretations of Market Societies: Civilizing, Destructive or Feeble?" *Journal of Economic Literature*, 20/4 (Dec.), 1463–84.

Hounshell, D. A. (1984), *The Development of Manufacturing Technology in the United States* (Baltimore: The Johns Hopkins University Press).

Kogut, B. (1992), "National Organizing Principles of Work and the Erstwhile Dominance of the American Multinational Corporation," *Industrial and Corporate Change*, 1: 285–317.

——(1993) (ed.), *Country Competitiveness* (Oxford: Oxford University Press).

Koike, K. (1988), *Understanding Industrial Relations in Modern Japan* (London: Macmillan).

Kreps, K. W. (1990), *A Course in Microeconomic Theory* (Princeton: Princeton University Press).

Lazonick, W. (1990), *Competitive Advantage on the Shopfloor* (Cambridge, Mass.: Harvard University Press).

——(1993), "Industry Clusters in Global Webs: Organizational Capabilities in the American Economy", *Industrial and Corporate Change*, 2: 1–24.

Levinthal, D. A. (1992), "Surviving Schumpeterian Environments: An Evolutionary Perspective," *Industrial and Corporate Change*, 1: 427–43.

——and March, J. G. (1994), "The Myopia of Learning," *Strategic Management Journal* (forthcoming).

Lorenz, E. (1994), "Organizational Inertia and Competitive Decline: The British Cotton, Shipbuilding and Car Industries, 1945–1975," *Industrial and Corporate Change*, 3/2: 379–404.

March, J. G. (1994), *A Primer on Decision-Making* (New York: Free Press) (forthcoming).

——and Simon, H. (1958), *Organization* (New York: John Wiley).

————(1993), *Organization*, 2nd edn. (Oxford: Blackwell).

Marengo, L. (1992), "Coordination and Organizational Learning in the Firm," *Journal of Evolutionary Economics*, 2/4 (Dec.), 313–26.

Marglin, S. (1974), "What do Bosses Do? The Origins and Functions of Hierarchies in Capitalist Production," *Review of Radical Political Economy*, 6/2 (Summer), 60–112.

Meyer, S., III (1992), *The Five-Dollar Day* (Princeton: Princeton University Press).

Monden, Y. (1983), "Toyota Production System," (Atlanta: Institute of Industrial Engineers,).

Montgomery, D. (1979), *Worker's Control in America* (London: Cambridge University Press).

Nelson, R. (1993), *National Innovation Systems* (Oxford: Oxford University Press).

——(1994), "The Role of Firm Differences in an Evolutionary Theory of Technical Advance," in L. Magnusson (ed.), *Evolutionary and Neo-Schumpeterian Approaches to Economics* (Boston: Kluwer).

——and Winter, S. (1982), *An Evolutionary Theory of Economic Change* (Cambridge, Mass.: The Belknap Press of Harvard University Press).

Nomura, M. (1993), "Farewell to Toyotism," Working Paper no. 17, Cahiers du GERPISA, Paris.

Ohno, T. (1988), *L'Esprit Toyota* (Paris: Ed Masson).

——and Mito (1993), *Présent et avenir du Toyotisme* (Paris: Ed Masson).

Parker, M. and Slaughter, J. (1988), *Choosing Sides: Union and the Team Concept, A Labor Note-Book* (South End Press).

Patel, P. and Pavitt, K. (1994), "Technological Competences in the World's Largest Firms: Characteristics, Constraints and Scope for Managerial Choice," Working Paper, SPRU, University of Sussex.

Pavitt, K. (1984), "Sectoral Patterns of Innovation: Toward a Taxonomy and a Theory," *Research Policy*, 13/6: 343–73.

Piore, M. and Sabel, C. (1984), *The Second Industrial Divide* (New York: Basic Books).

Porter, M. E. (1990), *The Competitive Advantage of Nations* (London: Macmillan).

Postrel, S. and Rumelt, R. P. (1992), "Incentives, Routines and Self-Command," *Industrial and Corporate Change*, 1: 397–425.

Radner, R. (1992), "Hierarchy: The Economics of Managing," *Journal of Economic Literature*, 30: 1382–415.

Romer, P. (1986), "Increasing Returns and Long-Run Growth," *Journal of Political Economy*, 91: 1001–37.

——(1990*a*), "Are Non-Convexities Important for Understanding Growth?" *American Economic Review*, 80: 97–103.

——(1990*b*), "Endogenous Technological Change," *Journal of Political Economy*, 98: 71–102.

Rosenberg, N. (1985), *Inside the Blackbox* (Cambridge: Cambridge University Press).

Sah, R. K. and Stiglitz, J. (1985), "Human Fallibility and Economic Organization," *American Economic Review, Papers and Proceedings*.

Sandberg, Ä. *et al.* (1993), *Technical Change and Co-Determination in Sweden* (Philadelphia: Temple University Press).

Saviotti, P. and Metcalfe, S. (1992), (eds.), *Evolutionary Theories of Economic and Technological Change* (Reading: Harwood Publishers).

Silverberg, G. and Verspagen, B. (1994), "Learning, Innovation and Economic Growth: A Long-run Model of Industrial Dynamics," *Industrial and Corporate Change*, 3/1: 199–224.

——Dosi, G. and Orsenigo, L. (1988), "Innovation, Diversity and Diffusion: A Self-Organization Model," *Economic Journal*, 98/393 (Dec.), 1032–54.

Soete, L. and Verspagen, B. (1993), *Technology and Growth: The Complex Dynamics of Catching Up, Falling Behind and Taking Over*, (MERIT: University of Limburg).

Soskice, D. (1993), "Innovation Strategies of Companies: A Comparative Institutional Explanation of Cross Country Differences," Berlin, WZB, mimeo.

Taddei, D. and Coriat, B. (1993). "Made in France: L'Industrie française dans la compétition mondiale," éd. du Livre de Poche (Paris: Hachette).

Taylor, F. W. (1911), *The Principles of Scientific Management*, Norton Library, (New York: Harper and Row), Ist edn. 1911, paperback edn. 1967.

——(1971), "Testimony Before the Special Comittee, House of Representatives," in F. W. Taylor, *Scientific Management* (New York: Greenwood).

Teece, D. (1993), "The Dynamics of Industrial Capitalism: Perspectives on Alfred Chandler's *Scale and Scope*," *Journal of Economic Literature*, 31: 199–225.

——Pisano, G. and Shunen, A. (1992), "Dynamic Capabilities and Strategies Management," CCC Working Paper, CRM, Graduate Business School, U.C., Berkeley, Calif.

——Rumelt, R., Dosi, G. and Winter, S. (1994), "Understanding Corporate Coherence: Theory and Evidence," *Journal of Economic Behavior and Organization*, 23/1 (Jan.), 1–30.

Thomson, R. (1992), (ed.), *Learning and Technological Change* (London: Macmillan).

Williamson, O. (1985a), *Markets and Hierarchies* (New York: Free Press).

——(1985b), *The Economic Institutions of Capitalism* (New York: Free Press).

Winter, S. (1981), "An Essay on the Theory of Production," in S. Hymans (ed.), *The Economy and the World Around it* (Ann Arbor: University of Michigan Press).

——(1987), "Knowledge and Competences as Strategic Assets," In D. Teece (ed.), *The Competitive Challenge* (Cambridge, Mass.: Ballinger).

Womack, J., Jones, D. and Roos, D. (1991), *The Machine that Changed the World* (Cambridge, Mass.: MIT Press).

Zysman, J. (1994), "How Institutions Create Historically Rooted Trajectories of Growth," *Industrial and Corporate Change*, 3/1: 243–83.

7

Design Issues for Innovative Firms: Bureaucracy, Incentives and Industrial Structure*

DAVID J. TEECE

1. INTRODUCTION

It is increasingly recognized that the dynamism of a competitive private enterprise system flows from the development and application of new technology and the adoption of new organizational forms. As a result, attention is being focused on trying to develop a better understanding of the institutional environment in which these activities take place. The business firm is clearly the leading player in the development and commercialization of new products and processes.[1] However, much of the literature in economics proceeds as if the identity of the firm in which innovation is taking place is of little moment. Moreover, the links between firm structure and strategy and the innovation process are poorly understood.[2]

In this paper, it is suggested that the formal and informal structures of the firm, as well as the network of external linkages that they possess, have an important bearing on the strength as well as the kind of innovative activity conducted by private enterprise economies.[3] Frameworks are presented to indicate how firm structure and the nature of innovation are linked. The approach adopted eschews optimality and embraces comparative analysis, in the spirit of Williamson (1975, 1985),[4] whereby alternatives are compared to each other rather than to hypothetical ideals. Institutional context is also considered. In particular, the role of capital markets is at least addressed, and the legal infrastructure is not assumed away completely. Indeed, various aspects of the legal system, and in particular intellectual property law, are explicitly considered.

The general approach adopted involves (1) identifying the fundamental characteristics of technological development, (2) determining the factors that affect innovation at the level of the firm, (3) identifying distinctive archetypes or governance modes for firms, and (4) choosing from available alternatives the organizational forms better suited to deal with various

* I am grateful for helpful comments from Glenn Carroll, Richard Nelson, Nathan Rosenberg, Oliver Williamson and two anonymous referees.

types of innovation. It is hoped that analyzing innovation in this manner will help broaden the agenda for industrial organization economists and organization theorists as they begin to grapple with understanding one of the most distinctive features of modern corporations.

2. FUNDAMENTAL CHARACTERISTICS OF TECHNOLOGICAL DEVELOPMENT

It is impossible to identify the organizational requirements of the innovation process without first specifying underlying properties of technological innovation. Fortunately, there appears to be an emerging consensus among scholars who study the innovation process with respect to the stylized facts. In the main, these appear to characterize innovation independent of the organizational context in which it takes place.

2.1 Uncertainty

Innovation is a quest into the unknown. It involves searching and the probing and reprobing of technological as well as market opportunities. With hindsight, much effort is spent traveling down blind alleys. Serendipity and luck play an important role. There are various types of uncertainty. Tjalling Koopmans (1957) has made a useful distinction between primary and secondary uncertainty. Both are critical in the context of innovation. Secondary uncertainty arises "from lack of communication, that is, from one decision-maker having no way of finding out the concurrent decisions and plans made by others." Primary uncertainty arises from "random acts of nature and unpredictable changes in concurrent preferences" (1957: 162–3). Williamson recognizes a third kind of uncertainty, what he calls behavioral uncertainty, attributable to opportunism. Such uncertainty can lead to *ex post* surprises.[5] It is important to note that secondary uncertainty can be affected by changing the boundaries of the organization. As G. B. H. Richardson (1990) and Oliver Williamson (1975) have explained, vertical integration can facilitate the coordination of complementary investments through the sharing of investment plans. Secondary uncertainty is thus a function of organizational form.

2.2 Path Dependency

Technology often evolves in certain path-dependent ways, contoured and channeled by what might be thought of as technological paradigms (Dosi 1982). A technological paradigm is a pattern of solutions to selected technical problems which derives from certain engineering relationships. A paradigm identifies the problems that have to be solved and the way to inquire about them; within a paradigm, research efforts become channeled along certain trajectories.[6] Relatedly, new product and process developments for a particular organization are likely to lie in the technological neighborhood of previous successes.

2.3 Cumulative Nature

Technology development, particularly inside a particular paradigm, proceeds cumulatively along the path defined by the paradigm. The fact that technological progress builds on what went before, and that much of it is tacit and proprietary, means that it usually has significant organization-specific dimensions. Moreover, an organization's technical capabilities are likely to be "close in" to previous technological accomplishments.[7]

2.4 Irreversibilities

Technological progress exhibits strong irreversibilities. This follows not just because innovation typically requires specialized investments, but because the evolution of technologies along certain trajectories eliminates the possibility of competition from older technologies, even if relative prices change significantly. Thus mechanical calculators are unlikely to ever replace electronic ones, even if the relative prices of silicon and steel were to switch by a factor of 1,000[8] in favor of steel.

2.5 Technological Interrelatedness

Innovation is characterized by technological interrelatedness between various subsystems. Linkages to other technologies, to complementary assets, and to users must be maintained if innovation is to be successful. If recognizable organizational subunits such as R&D, manufacturing and marketing exist, they must be in close and continuous communication and engage in mutual adaptation if innovation in commercially relevant products and processes is to have a chance of succeeding. Moreover, successful commercial innovation usually requires quick decision making and close coupling and coordination among research, development, manufacturing, sales and service. Put differently, organizational capacities must exist to enable these activities to occur with dispatch.

2.6 Tacitness

The knowledge developed by organizations is often highly tacit. That is, it is difficult if not impossible to articulate and codify (Polanyi 1962; Winter 1987). A corollary is that technology transfer is often difficult without the transfer of key individuals. This simultaneously explains why imitation is often costly, and why the diffusion of new technology often depends on the mobility of engineers and scientists (Teece 1977; Nelson and Winter 1982). Relatedly, an organization's technology ought not be thought of as residing in some hypothetical book of blueprints, or with some hypothetical chief engineer, but in an organization's system and habits of coordinating and managing tasks. These systems and habits have been referred to as organizational routines (Nelson and Winter 1982). It is the performance of these routines that is at the essence of an organization's technological capacity.

2.7 Inappropriability

Under many legal systems, the ownership rights associated with technical know-how are often ambiguous, do not always permit rewards that match contribution,[9] vary in the degree of exclusion they permit (often according to the innate patentability or copyrightability of the object or subject matter) and are temporary. Accordingly, investment in innovative activity may not necessarily yield property which can be reserved for the exclusive use of the innovator. But the activity may nevertheless still be valuable enough to attract some investment, depending in part on other institutional arrangements to be examined later. The degree to which new products and processes are protectable under intellectual property law will henceforth be referred to as the intellectual property regime. For expositional simplicity, regimes will be classified as strong if patents and copyrights are effective, and weak otherwise. Clearly, the industrial world does not readily bifurcate, and there exists a continuum of appropriability regimes, as data assembled by Levin *et al.* (1987) make apparent. Relatedly, the absence of good legal protection presents what Arrow has referred to as the "fundamental paradox of information." In order to provide full information to the buyer, the seller of know-how may have to disclose the object of the exchange, but in so doing the basis for the exchange evaporates, or at least erodes, as the potential buyer might now have in its possession that which he was seeking to acquire. Hence, transactions in the market for know-how must thus proceed under conditions of ignorance. Accordingly, at least until reputations become established, exchange is likely to be exposed to hazards. Optimal resource allocation is unlikely to result.

3. ORGANIZATIONAL AND MARKET DETERMINANTS OF THE RATE AND DIRECTION OF INNOVATION

While our understanding of innovation has been enriched in recent years, the basic framework employed in policy debates about innovation, technology policy and competition policy are often remarkably naïve and highly incomplete. Even basic considerations such as those identified in 2. above are frequently neglected. In economics, for instance, it is not uncommon to find debate about innovation policy collapsing to a rather outmoded discussion of the relative virtues of competition and monopoly, as if they were the key determinants of innovation. Clearly there is much more at work. In this section, various classes of variables—some economic, some organizational—are identified that impact the rate and direction of innovation. Subsequent sections will identify distinct types of organizations based on various organizational attributes. A final section will then endeavor to match these organizations to different types and levels of innovation.

3.1 Monopoly Power and the Financing of Innovation

One reason why our understanding of innovation has not proceeded faster in the last half century is that many researchers, particularly economists, have overly focused on just one variable: the degree of market power that a firm or firms may have. The evidence is unequivocal that competition and rivalry is important for innovation; but few believe that the world of perfect competition in which firms compete in highly fragmented markets using identical nonproprietary technologies is an organizational arrangement that any advanced economy would aspire to emulate. Nevertheless, many policy debates proceed on the assumption that fragmented markets assist innovation. Clearly rivalry and competition are important to innovation, but belief in the virtues of perfectly competitive systems is lore, reflecting casual empiricism and prejudice and not careful theorizing and empirical study. Likewise for monopoly.

Schumpeter was among the first to declare that perfect competition was incompatible with innovation. He noted, "The introduction of new methods of production and new commodities is hardly conceivable with perfect—and perfectly prompt—competition from the start. And this means that the bulk of what we call economic progress is incompatible with it."[10] The Schumpeterian notion that small entrepreneurial firms lack financial resources adequate to perform innovation is an organizational failure hypothesis which has never been exposed to significant comparative institutional analysis.

The consensual "Schumpeterian" position, as advanced by Kamien and Schwartz (1982), is that innovation is greater in monopolistic industries than in competitive ones because innovators with monopoly power can use this power to exclude imitators, and the resulting higher profits can be used to finance R&D.[11] Scholars have been slow to question the organizational assumptions embedded in this position. Briefly, the assumptions appear to include the following. First, imitation is relentless—imitators swarm around the rent opportunities created by new products and processes. While commonly correct, it should also be recognized that intellectual property law can sometimes keep imitators at bay for considerable periods of time, without creating monopoly power. In such circumstances, the necessity for market power to exclude imitators fades, because the legal system provides the necessary barrier. Second, it is assumed that monopolistic industries will generate innovation simply by virtue of the access provided to free cash flows.

However, there are an enormous number of variables that can potentially intervene between the generation of monopolistic rents and the allocation of resources to the development of new products and processes. Consider, first, single-product firms. The notion that innovation requires the cash flow generated by the exercise of monopoly power assumes both that (1) capital markets are inefficient, and (2) that monopolistic levels of internal cash flows are adequate to fund the requisite R&D programs. If capital markets are operating according to what Fama (1970) has called strong form efficiency, then cash flow is unimportant because firms with high-yield projects will be able to signal their profit opportunities to the capital market and the requisite financing will come forth on competitive terms. Thus if there is strong form efficiency and zero transaction costs (its corollary), cash will get matched to projects whether or not the cash is internally generated.

Of course, the world cannot be characterized by zero transaction costs, but that does not mean that the availability of internal cash flows from monopoly (as to competitive) product-market positions is what makes the difference between being able to fund a project and not being able to fund it. Significant innovative efforts involve expenditures in a particular year which may be many times available cash flows. So the availability of marginally higher cash flows occasioned by monopoly power are unlikely to grossly change the financial picture, except in unusual circumstances.

Furthermore, even in the absence of adequate internal cash flow, firms need not go to the capital market to find the requisite financing. The Schumpeterian view of the innovation processes appears to be one that involves full integration, from research, development, manufacturing and marketing. But the financial requirements associated with developing and commercializing new products and processes can be accomplished with myriad organizational arrangements including research joint ventures, coproduction, and comarketing arrangements. With such arrangements, there is the possibility that the capital requirements associated with a new project could be drastically reduced for the innovator. Economies of scale and scope can often be captured through interfirm arrangements.

The link between market power and innovation in specific markets is further undone if the multidivisional multiproduct firm is admitted into the scene.[12] The basic function and purpose of the multiproduct structure is to allocate cash generated everywhere to high-yield purposes anywhere. If a multidivisional multiproduct firm does operate this way, and there is plenty of evidence to suggest that they can and do, then the link between market power in a particular market and the funding of innovation in that market is undone. In a multiproduct firm selling products in markets A through Z, the cash generated by virtue of power in market A can indeed fund innovation relevant to market A, but it can equally well fund innovative activity in market Z. The fungibility of cash inside the multiproduct firm thus unlocks the relationship between market structure and innovation proposed by Schumpeter.

When firms do go into the capital market they generally have multiple sources of funding available. Generically, these can be split into debt and equity. The various types of debt and equity can on the one hand be thought of as financial instruments or, as Williamson suggests, as different "governance structures" (Williamson 1988). Williamson explains that the decision by firms to use debt or equity to support individual investment projects is likely to be linked to the asset specificity of the underlying investment. If assets are not particularly specific and can be redeployed with little loss in value, debt instruments are suitable. Debt holders have little need to monitor management because they are protected by marketable collateral. Since debt owners do not expect to be residual claimants, they do not need to closely monitor management. Attention is instead on the payment of interest and repayment of principal. Debt financing will be progressively more expensive, possibly marketable only in a package with other instruments like warrants, as asset specificity deepens. In order to fully utilize debt financing, innovating firms either adjust their investments to make them more redeployable, and hence amenable to debt financing, or they issue equity instead.[13]

Since new product development programs commonly involve investment in assets that are substantially irreversible (like R&D) and/or non-redeployable (like specialized equipment), debt is only of limited value in financing innovation, unless a firm has collateral and is under-leveraged to begin with. Accordingly, the fund sources generally available to support new product development are internal cash flow and new equity. In instances when a firm does not already have substantial cash flows, then equity is the major source of new funds. The properties of each are now briefly explored.

The role of equity is made distinct if it is considered in the context of "start-up" firms which do not already have free cash flows. Investors have obvious problems in evaluating the prospects for new products and processes, and the best investees have problems, though less serious, in identifying the best investors. The investors' problems are rather obvious. The investor has the difficult challenge of calibrating investment prospects in an environment where there is usually high market uncertainty, high technical uncertainty and bountiful opportunism and optimism. Several kinds of opportunism are possible. One is simply that the technology can be misrepresented. This tendency however can be checked if the investor hires technical consultants to validate the entrepreneurs' claims. Another is that the tenacity and veracity of the entrepreneur are difficult to calibrate, with consequences much more unfortunate for the investor than for the entrepreneur. Ascertaining whether the entrepreneurs' optimism is honest yet misplaced is perhaps even more difficult. There is "much evidence that in the context of planning and action most people are prone to extreme optimism in their forecasts of outcomes, and often fail to appreciate the chances of an unfavorable outcome"[14] (Kahneman and Lovallo 1990: 2). Decision-makers often take risks because they deny their existence or underestimate their extent (March and Shapira 1987).

Now consider internally generated cash flow. Even in the United States where there is a vibrant venture capital market, internal "free" cash flow is the major source of private financing for innovation. These funds can be readily allocated by management and are not typically constrained by covenants. It is in effect equity financing, without the transaction costs of going to financial markets external to the firm. Management is ultimately responsible to the stockholders for the way free cash flows are allocated.

Over the last half decade, a controversial body of literature has emerged which in essence argues that free cash flows must be distributed to shareholders, rather than being invested internally in discretionary projects, if firms are to operate efficiently (Jensen 1989). The basic idea is that the discipline of debt is needed to cause capital to be channeled to high-yield uses in the economy, as well as in the firm. There are severe problems with this thesis, not least of which is that debt holders are loss averse and not at all business-opportunity driven. While it may indeed be the case that free cash flows do sometimes get misallocated by managers, to delimit them in the manner proposed by advocates of the free cash flow hypothesis is to force the firm into equity markets to finance innovation. For reasons explained earlier, this is not always desirable because the new issues markets, both public and private, have disabilities with respect to recognizing and funding new opportunities.

To summarize, innovation clearly requires access to capital. The necessary capital can come from cash flows or from equity. At least with respect to early stage activity, debt financing is unlikely to be viable, unless the firm has other assets to pledge. However, certain downstream investments needed to commercialize innovation can be debt-financed if they are redeployable. The point, however, is that all of this has little to do with firm size and the presence or absence of market power.

3.2 Hierarchy

Hierarchy arose to help in the administration of military, religious and governmental activities.[15] While hierarchies are old, deep hierarchies are relatively new. Anthropologists point out that most tribes, clans and agricultural enterprises have rather flat hierarchies. The Roman Catholic Church, for instance, has only four levels. Centralizing and decentralizing are not genuine alternatives for organization; the key issue is to decide the mix. Hierarchies can accomplish complex organizational tasks, but they are often associated with organizational properties inimical to innovation, such as slow (bureaucratic) decision making and weak incentives.

Bureaucratic decision making   Decision-making processes in hierarchical organizations almost always involve bureaucratic features. In particular, a formal expenditure process involving submissions and approvals is characteristic. Decision making is likely to have a committee structure, with top management requiring reports and written justifications for significant decisions. Moreover, approvals may need to be sought from outside the organizational unit in which the expenditure is to take place. While this may ensure a matching up of expenditures to opportunities across a wider range of economic activity, it unquestionably slows decision making and tends to reinforce the status quo.

The latter characteristic follows from committee decision-making structures, which almost always tend toward balancing and compromise. But innovation is often ill-served by such structures, as the new and the radical will almost always appear threatening to some constituents. Put differently, representative structures, bureaucratic or political, often tend to endorse the status quo. Strong leaders can often overcome such tendencies, but such leaders are not always present and their capacities are often thwarted by the organization.[16]

One consequence is what Williamson (1975) has referred to as a "program persistence bias," and its corollary the "anti-innovation bias." Program persistence refers to funding of programs beyond what can be sustained on the merits, and follows from the presence or influence of program advocates in the resources allocation process. This proclivity almost automatically has the countervailing effect of reducing funds available to new programs, which are unlikely to be represented as well in the decision-making process. As Anthony Downs (1967) points out, "the increasing size of the bureau leads to a gradual ossification of operations—since each proposed action must receive multiple approvals, the probability of its being rejected is quite high—its cumbersome machinery cannot produce results fast enough, and its anti-novelty bias may block the necessary innovation" (p. 160).

The sharpening of global competition, and diversification (organizationally and geographically) in the sources of new knowledge compels firms to make decisions faster, and to reduce time to market in order to capture value from technological innovation. It seems clear that to accomplish such responsiveness, organizations need new structures and different decision-making protocols to facilitate entrepreneurial and innovative behavior. Burgelman (1984) identifies a menu of such arrangements which include: special business units, micro new ventures department, new venture division and independent business unit. Clearly, all of these designs imply smaller, flatter and more specialized structures within which to conduct activities where speed and responsiveness are critical. In the limit, the spinoff or spinout of a new division signifies that the enterprise's (or at least the individuals associated with it) chances of success are greater outside rather than inside an established hierarchy. In addition to the creation of semi-autonomous units, firms can attempt to "delayer" by stripping out layers of middle management. But flattening organizations need not fundamentally redefine the relationships between people and functions in the organizations. Functions may still work sequentially, with decisions being made from fragmented perspectives.

In essence, the organizational challenge appears to be that activities are not as decomposable as they used to be, and that cross-functional interaction must take place concurrently, rather than sequentially, if firms are to cut time-to-market for new products and processes. Cross-functional and cross-departmental networks must be strengthened without causing information overload. Computer network infrastructures can assist cross-functional interaction by project teams, concurrent engineering teams, network teams, task forces and the like. If such activity becomes completely unstructured, it augments rather than displaces bureaucracy. Instead of random ad hoc approaches, what is needed are well-defined cross-functional teams, which can be redefined as needed. With organizational subunits cross-linked in this way, authority occurs as much from knowledge as position in the organizational hierarchy. The challenge is to develop a culture which supports the establishment of cross-functional teams which draw on the requisite knowledge, wherever it may be located.

Low-powered incentives   As they grow, organizations often become characterized by what Williamson (1985: 153) calls "low-powered incentives." Low-powered incentives can be defined as those where the covariance of employee compensation with business unit performance is low. One reason is that compensation structures inside large organizations need to be sensitive to relative as well as absolute levels of compensation. If the compensation structure itself has value through the relativities it establishes, then the enterprise will be reluctant to disturb the structure to support innovation. Another reason is that stock options cannot be granted at the divisional level if, as is almost always the case, the division's shares are nontradable in public markets. The absence of a public equity market for business unit shares thus deprives the firm of the opportunity to provide an objective capital market-based augmentation to compensation.[17] If the employee is rewarded instead through stock in the total enterprise, the impact of divisional, departmental, and individual performance is likely to be severely diluted.

Principal-agent distortions   Business firms of great size are rarely owner-managed. Inasmuch as managers (agents) tradeoff enterprise performance for their own welfare, innovation is likely to be impaired. This is because the interests of managers are sometimes at odds with what innovation requires, because the tenure of top management is usually much shorter than the gestation period for major innovations. Moreover, principals must invest in costly information collection and monitoring activities in order to check up on the performance of agents. These costs can be considerable. Moreover, principals may insist on certain expenditure controls which themselves slow decision making and thwart innovation.

Myopia   Organizations can become closed to changes in the market and business environment and to new sources of technology. Individuals in organizations, including chief executive officers, can fall into the trap of adopting a citadel mentality. The availability of free cash flows can help sustain that mentality and behavior for considerable periods of time. Closed systems may be able to hone the routine, but they will lose the capacity to engage the new. Organizations can become closed through administrative arrangements (as when the firm's boundaries are delimited by its organization chart), through legalistic (rather than relational) contracting with suppliers and customers, and through social and cultural norms which stress the importance of inside rather than outside considerations.

3.3 Scope

The scope of product-market activities may impact the innovative performance of firms in at least three ways. One has just been discussed in the context of finance: the multidivisional multiproduct firm is in a position to reallocate cash from businesses that have positive cash flow to new businesses with negative cash flow. A second hypothesis, put forward at various times by Schumpeter, Richard Nelson and others, is that the product-market portfolios of multiproduct firms will increase the payoff to uncertain R&D by increasing the probability that new products and processes resulting from corporate R&D can be commercialized inside the firm. Neither of these will be the main focus here.

Instead, it is suggested that multiproduct firms can more readily develop and commercialize "fusion" technologies which involve the melding of technological capacities relevant to disparate lines of business. This fusion—as with mechanics and electronics (what Kodama (1986) calls "mechatronics")—by no means occurs automatically and requires internal structures which are flexible and permeable.[18] Indeed, there appears to be less diversity in firms' products than in their technologies (Pavitt, *et al.* 1989). Nevertheless, the multiproduct firm does afford opportunities for economies of scope based on transferring technologies across product lines and melding them to create new products (Teece 1980, 1982). Despite the path-dependent nature of technological change, the diversity of application areas for a given technology are often quite large, and it is often feasible and sometimes efficient to apply the firm's capabilities to different market opportunities.

Suppose application areas outside of the core business do in fact open up. The question arises as to whether potential scope economies deriving from the application of proprietary know-how in new markets add more to the innovating firm's value if they are served through licensing and related contractual arrangements to unaffiliated firms who then serve the new product markets in question, or by direct investment, either *de novo* or by merger/acquisition. This is an important question, the answer to which ought to help shape a positive theory of the scope of the firm's activities.

Whether the firm integrates or not is likely to depend critically on four sets of factors: (1) whether the technology can be transferred to an unaffiliated entity at higher or lower cost than it can be transferred to an affiliated entity; (2) the degree of intellectual property protection afforded to the technology in question by the relevant statutes and laws; (3) whether a contract can be crafted which will regulate the sale of technology with greater or less efficiency and effectiveness than department-to-department or division-to-division sales can be regulated by internal administrative procedures; and (4) whether the set of complementary competences possessed by the potential licensee can be assessed by the licensor at a cost lower than alternatives. If they are lower, the available returns from the market will be higher, and the opportunity for a satisfactory royalty or profit-sharing arrangement accordingly greater.

These matters are explored in more detail elsewhere (Teece 1980, 1982, 1986). Suffice to say that contractual mechanisms are often less satisfactory than the alternative. Proprietary considerations are more often than not served by integration, and technology transfer is difficult both to unaffiliated and affiliated partners, with the consequences that integration (or multiproduct diversification) is the more attractive alternative, except where incumbents are already competitively established in downstream activities, and are in a position to render *de novo* entry by the technology-based firms unattractive because of the excess capacity it would generate. Hence, multiproduct firms can be expected to appear as efficient responses to contractual, proprietary and technology transfer problems in an important set of circumstances. Mixed modes, such as joint ventures and complex forms of profit-sharing collaboration, will also be common according to how the set of transactions in question stacks up against the criteria identified above.

3.4 Vertical Integration

The characteristics of technological development identified earlier also have important implications for the vertical structure of the firm, and vice versa. Economic historians have long suggested that there may be links between vertical structures and the rate and direction of innovation. For instance, Frankel (1955) has argued that the slow rate of diffusion of innovations in the British textile and iron and steel industries around the turn of the century was due to the absence of vertically integrated firms. Kindleberger (1964) has gone so far as to suggest that the reason why West Germany and Japan have overtaken Britain may be due to "the organization of [British] industry into Separate Firms dealing with each other at arm's length." This "may have impeded technological change because of the possibility that part of the benefits of that change would have been external to the separate firms" (pp. 146–7). General Motors' early dominance in the diesel-electric locomotive industry has also been attributed to the fact that it was integrated into electrical supply while its competitors were not (Marx 1976). A systematic exploration of the relationship between technological innovation and enterprise boundaries is needed.

For present purposes, it is useful to distinguish between two types of innovation: autonomous (or "stand-alone") and systemic. An autonomous innovation is one which can be introduced without modifying other components or items of equipment. The component or device in that sense "stands alone." A systemic innovation, on the other hand, requires significant readjustment to other parts of the system. The major distinction relates to the amount of design coordination which development and commercialization are likely to require. An example of a systemic innovation would be electronic funds transfer, instant photography (it required redesign of the camera and the film), front-wheel drive, and the jet airliner (it required new stress-resistant airframes).

This is not so with systemic innovation, where internal organization (integration) can often assist the workings of the market. Integration facilitates systemic innovations by facilitating information flows, and the coordination of investments plans. It also removes institutional barriers to innovation where the innovation in question requires allocating costs and benefits, or placing specialized investments into several parts of an industry.

Comprehensive evidence with respect to these propositions has yet to be assembled. The only statistical test performed to date relates to the petroleum industry (Armour and Teece 1978). These findings indicated that firm and R&D expenditures for basic and applied research in the US petroleum industry, 1951–75, were statistically related to the level of vertical integration which the enterprise possessed.[19] Anecdotal historical evidence also exists. According to Frankel (1955: 312–13), the lack of vertical integration in the British iron and steel industry hindered the introduction of technical innovation in the latter part of the century because the innovations in question displayed interrelatedness. Frankel (pp. 313–14) argues further that the failure of the British to put the automatic loom into place in the cotton industry was due to the lack of vertical integration. Other historians share this perspective. Kindleberger has studied the reasons for the failure of the British railroads to abandon the 10-ton coal wagon in favor of the more efficient 20-ton wagon. Kindleberger (1964) concludes that the reason for the slow rate of diffusion was institutional and not technical. In short, it stemmed from the absence of vertical integration.[20]

3.5 Organizational Culture and Values

Market power is an element of industrial structure; scale, scope, integration and hierarchy can be thought of as elements of the formal structure of an organization. Of equal if not greater importance is the informal structure of an organization. Culture is the essence of an organization's informal structure. It is "the pattern of beliefs and expectations shared by the organization's members. These beliefs and expectations produce norms that powerfully shape the behavior of individuals and groups" (Schwartz and Davis 1981: 33).

Culture can be thought of as the "central norms that may characterize an organization" (O'Reilly 1989: 305). A strong culture is a system of informal rules that spells out how people are to behave most of the time. By knowing what is expected of them, employees will waste little time deciding how to act in a given situation (Deal and Kennedy 1982). There need not be consensus within an organization with respect to these beliefs, as the guiding beliefs or vision held by top management and by individuals lower down in the organization may not be congruent. It is the latter, however, which define an organization's culture (O'Reilly 1989: 305).

There seems to be an emerging consensus (Deal and Kennedy 1982; Peters and Waterman 1982; O'Reilly 1989) that the following set of norms assists the development and commercialization of new products and processes. With respect to development, these include: the autonomy to try and fail; the right of employees to challenge the status quo; open communication to customers, to external sources of technology and within the firm itself. With respect to commercialization or implementation, teamwork, flexibility, trust and hard work are considered to be critically important. The right culture is not just an important asset to assist in technological development; it may be a requirement.

Economists have given almost no attention, and little sympathy, to the topic of culture.[21] Occasionally, economists may speak of the importance of trust and consciousness. Thus Arrow (1974: 28) notes that "social demands may be expressed through formal rules and authorities, or they may be expressed through internalized demands of conscience. Looked at collectively, these demands may be compromises which are needed to increase the efficacy of all."[22] If Arrow is right in his claim that values can increase efficiency, it is unfortunate that the topic has been left to organizational sociologists and psychologists, and that economic science ignores what appears to be an important set of variables in the understanding of organizational performance.

One way for economists to begin grappling with culture is to see it as control on the cheap, of which reduction in shirking is just one element.[23] If individuals can be motivated and directed without pecuniary incentives and the exercise of authority, tremendous resource savings can ensue, and innovation processes can avoid the burdens of bureaucracy. Conversely, if a firm's culture and strategy do not align, it is likely to be unable to implement its strategy, especially strategies which involve innovation. For instance, a declaration by top management of a firm that the firm is now going to be more open to external sources of technological ideas will not ensure that the strategy will be successful if there is a well entrenched "not invented here" culture inside the organization. The failure to develop new norms supportive of a particular strategy "means that changes will persist only where they are closely monitored and directly rewarded" (O'Reilly, 1989: 310).

3.6 External Linkages

Economists, as well as many organization theorists, have traditionally thought of firms as islands of hierarchical control embedded in a market structure and interacting with each other through the price mechanism. Indeed, Coase (1937) has referred to firms as "islands of conscious power." Coase's metaphor needs to be transformed from islands to archipelagoes to capture important elements of business organization. This is because firms commonly need to form strategic alliances, vertically (both upstream and downstream), laterally, and sometimes horizontally in order to develop and commercialize new technologies.[24] Compared to arm's-length market contracts, such arrangements have more structure, involve constant interaction among the parts, more open information channels, greater trust, rely on voice rather than exit, and put less emphasis on price. Compared to hierarchies, such alliances or networks among firms call for negotiation rather than authority and put great emphasis on boundary-spanning roles. Although firms connected through alliances have a high degree of autonomy, the relationship may well be anchored by a minority equity position. These arrangements can be used to provide some of the benefits of integration while avoiding some of the costs. This undoubtedly helps explain the proliferation of alliances in recent decades.

The variety of such arrangements to link organizations is almost unlimited, and the resultant forms quite diverse. A constellation of licensing, manufacturing and marketing agreements will typically characterize many interorganizational arrangements. R&D joint ventures, manufacturing joint ventures, co-marketing arrangements and consortia are just a few of the resultant forms. Some of these arrangements constitute extremely complex open systems, and some may be unstable. The managerial functions in these interorganizational networks are quite different from the authority relationship which commonly exists in hierarchies. Managers have to perform boundary-spanning roles, and learn to manage in circumstances that involve mutual dependency.

3.7 Assessment

The above discussion of the variables which impact firm-level innovation suggests that economic and organizational research needs a richer framework if the innovation process is to be better understood. Economic research needs to pay greater attention to organizational structure, both formal and informal, and organizational research needs to recognize the importance of market structure, internal structure and the business environment. Figure 7.1 is a diagrammatic presentation of the various classes of variables that have been identified, as well as considerations deemed to be important but assumed away in this analysis. For instance, the firm's human

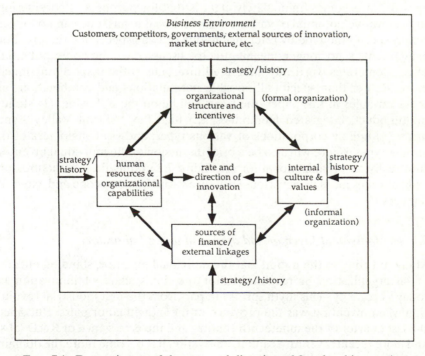

FIG. 7.1. Determinants of the rate and direction of firm-level innovation

resources/capital and the mechanism by which firms attract, train and hold first-rate people has not been deeply analyzed. Nor has the role of government in the support of the scientific and technological infrastructure been analyzed. Another major omission has been the strategy by which firms identify what projects to engage and what assets to build or buy in order to commercialize technology.

In Sections 4. and 5. consideration is given to identifying particular organizational forms that have distinct implications for certain types of innovation. The treatment is illustrative and not comprehensive. It suggests that there are a variety of organizational modes that can support innovation, but that there are important differences amongst organizations in the types of innovation they can support.

4. DISTINCTIVE GOVERNANCE MODES (ARCHETYPES)

In the previous section, various organizational characteristics were identified. Distinctive governance modes arise when these characteristics are represented to greater or lesser degrees. The specification of governance mode requires attention to at least four classes of variables: firm boundaries, internal formal structure, internal informal structure and external linkages. What becomes immediately clear is that for purposes of considering the innovative potential of various organizational forms, one can no longer simply specify the type by reference to one or two aspects of structure. For example, it is no longer meaningful to discuss the innovative potential of conglomerates, vertically integrated firms, etc. without specifying much more. Rather than specify all possible permutations and combinations of these variables in this paper, the focus will be on the following: (1) stolid, multiproduct, integrated hierarchies; (2) high flex "Silicon Valley"-type firms; (3) hollow corporations of various types; and (4) conglomerates of various types. There will also be a brief discussion of the individual inventor (not really an organizational form). Figure 7.2 graphs these structures on ordinal scales measuring various structure variables plus scope and external linkages.

4.1 The Individual Inventor and the Stand-alone Laboratory

Many still cling to the notion that the individual inventor, standing outside of an organization, is responsible for the lion's share of innovation in today's economy. This myth springs in part from the first industrial revolution when invention was the province of the individual or pairs. But since the last quarter of the nineteenth century and the emergence of R&D labs, and more recently venture capital, innovation has become more the domain of organizations, not individuals.

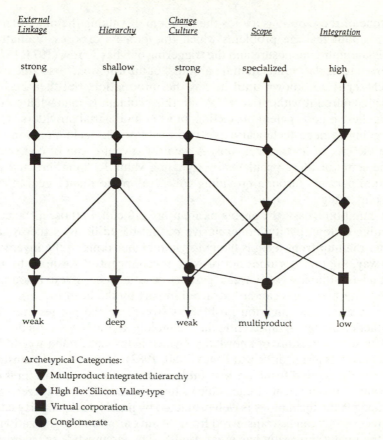

FIG. 7.2. Identifying archetypical firms by scope, structure and integration

The problems that the inventor-entrepreneurs have in extracting value from new technology are considerable. However, when an inventor (or an enterprise) can rely on the instruments of intellectual property protection to protect invention from imitation, theory suggests that the inventor can appropriate a substantial fraction of the invention's market value. When property rights are weak (the normal case), the inventors' ability to capture value are dramatically circumvented (Teece 1986). In the case where the individual inventor has a patent but little else, then the patent-holder's options include: (i) licensing the technology to incumbent firms who already have the necessary complementary assets in place; (ii) using the patent as collateral to raise debt funds to help develop an organization to exploit the technology; (iii) exchanging the patent for equity in a start-up, equity-funded firm; (iv) exchanging the patent for equity in an established firm.

None of these options avoids the problem of valuing the patent and the concomitant leakage problems which this process exposes. Valuation is likely to require disclosure and the triggering of what Arrow (1974: 152) has referred to as the "fundamental paradox" of information: "Its value for the purchaser is not known until he has the information, but then he has in effect acquired it without cost." While this problem is somewhat softened when there is good patent protection, most nonindustrial providers of funds are going to need technical experts to evaluate the technology, in which case the risk of leakage remains. A wealthy inventor can of course overcome some of these problems by signaling value to financiers and joint-venture partners through providing collateral, performance guarantees or by coinvesting.

If imitation is easy, the problems are more difficult. In those instances the granting of low royalty, nonexclusive output-based licenses (i.e. royalties rather than up-front fees) is likely to yield higher rents to the inventor. In this way, the inventor does not provide much incentive for firms to invent around (in the case of a weak patent) or otherwise invest resources in imitation; these costs can be extracted in part by the licensor.

Even when the valuation problem is overcome the parties must meet another challenge—transferring the technology to the buyers. As discussed earlier, the tacit nature of knowledge (which helps make imitation difficult) also makes transfer difficult (Teece 1980, 1982). Hence the circumstances where imitation is difficult are also the circumstances where transfer is often difficult. The only clear circumstance where the inventor can succeed alone is when (1) the technology is well protected by intellectual property law, (2) the technology can be transferred from the inventor to an organization, and (3) the inventor already has great wealth. The circumstances where these factors occur together is likely to be relatively rare.

The stand-alone research laboratory faces many of the same challenges as the individual inventor. The main difference is that the laboratory can bring multiple organizational skills to bear on the R&D process, and the probabilities of fusing multiple technologies is likely to be enhanced from the bringing together of multiple-research disciplines. Moreover, if scale economies exist in R&D, the laboratory is better able to capture these than the individual. But the framework would suggest that stand-alone laboratories cannot be viable, unless they happened to work in areas where strong intellectual property protection is assured.[25]

4.2 Hierarchical, Multiproduct, Integrated Firms

It is not uncommon to find such enterprises on the industrial scene. N.V. Phillips and IBM in the 1980s and 1990s are good examples. Hierarchical is meant to signal the presence of bureaucratic decisions, absence of a powerful change culture, and high-powered incentives. Such enterprises are also likely to be internally focused. As a consequence, external changes in the market as well as in the science and technology establishment are unlikely to get recognized in a timely fashion. Decision making is slow and ponderous.

However, if such organizations are able to achieve what Downs (1967: 160) calls "breakout"—which a new organization, possibly a new venture division, is set up for a special task—it may be able to overcome the anti-innovation bias, at least temporarily. Burgelman (1983) has argued that "autonomous strategic behavior" can take place inside large firms, if management sets up the appropriate internal structures. However, such firms will need to establish what has been referred to as "breakout" structures— entities separate from current operations which we used to incubate new projects. The range of such enabling structures is quite large and includes venture teams' "skunkworks," new venture divisions and the like. The suitability of these various structures depends on a variety of technological, market and organizational factors which will not be explored here.

Nevertheless, integrated firms overcome some basic problems associated with relying on an economy of Lilliputian firms' response to market-failure problems. Integrated firms can readily support systemic innovation as discussed earlier. Integrated firms can also adapt to uncertainty (Williamson 1975) in a sequential fashion as events unfold. (Managerial hierarchies are often better at adjudicating disputes inside the firm than courts are at adjudicating disputes between and among firms.) Large multiproduct, multidivisional integrated firms will have greater volumetric requirements than small venture-capital-funded firms. Accordingly, indivisibilities are likely to be less frequent. If it is a process technology which is at issue, the vertically integrated firm is capable of using the technology in-house and taking profits not by selling the technology directly, but through selling products that embody or use the process. Thus inasmuch as this type of firm does not have to utilize the market for know-how to capture value from the technology, the appropriability problem is solved. Inasmuch as contracting is internal, specialized assets are protected and recontracting hazards are not a concern. The technology transfer process is likely to be internal, so the tacitness problem is eased considerably, as the redeployment of personnel internally raises far fewer default issues than does external redeployment.

Such firms are likely to need alliance structures in order to tap into external sources of new knowledge. If large integrated firms are able to successfully team up with other firms[26] that have the entrepreneurial structures in place to promote creativity, then such firms are likely to be able to access a pipeline of new product and process concepts. The benefits here are a corollary to the benefits associated with strategic alliances.[27] However, the absence of a change culture and an outward orientation mean that such relationships may not be sought.

4.3 High Flex "Silicon Valley"-Type Firms

The distinguishing features of such firms are that they will possess a change culture upon which there is great consensus. They will have shallow hierarchies and significant local autonomy. Such firms will resist the hierarchical accouterments of seniority and rank found in category (4.2) above, and they will resist functional specialization which restricts the flow of ideas and destroys the sense of commonality of purpose. Examples of such firms are Intel, Hewlett Packard, Motorola, Raychem, Genentech and 3M.

Decision making in these firms is usually simple and informal. Communication and coordination among functions is relatively quick and open. One or two key individuals, typically the founders, make the key decisions. In the early stages, these firms, however, typically do not have a steady stream of internally generated cash with which to fund new opportunities. Hence, connections to the venture capital community or to other firms with cash available are important. These firms are likely to be highly innovative. But they are also likely to be severely cash constrained. Those that are not are likely to do very well.

The highly specialized nature of such firms and the absence of good intellectual property protection create strategic risks. Such firms will be active in the market for know-how, which is riddled with imperfections. The ability to capture the rents from innovation is by no means assured. But if such firms are able to develop and manage these external relationships without losing their distinct culture and responsive structures, then many of the problems stemming from uncertainty,[28] indivisibilities,[29] inappropriability,[30] asset specificity[31] and tacitness[32] can be overcome, while

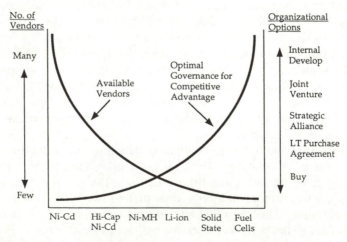

FIG. 7.3. Available sources and organizational options for Motorola in battery-cell technology

organizational failure issues are held at a distance because organization is accomplished by markets. By providing considerable autonomy and strong incentives, this organizational form is likely to be able to support many different types of innovation.

4.4 Virtual Corporations

The term "virtual corporation" has been used in business parlance in the 1980s and 1990s to refer to business enterprises that subcontract anything and everything. A key question is whether the innovative capacities of such companies are impaired by the absence of manufacturing and other capabilities in-house. Virtual corporations are of course smaller than they might otherwise be (by virtue of the absence of vertical integration) and thus generally have shallow hierarchies. They might well have innovative cultures and external linkages to competent manufacturers.

Defined this way, virtuals have the capacity to be very creative and to excel at early-stage innovation activities. If they do indeed establish a strong alliance with a competent manufacturer, they may also have the capacity to be first to market, despite the absence of the requisite internal capabilities.

The hazards associated with "virtual" structures are not unlike the hazards facing the individual inventor. The problem is that unless the firm is operating in a regime of tight appropriability, the innovator may not be able to capture value from the innovation, and the manufacturer, by integrating into research and distribution, is likely to become the firm's competitor (Teece 1986). Accordingly, the virtual corporation is not seen to be a viable long-run organizational form, except in limited circumstances.

4.5 Conglomerates

In the framework developed here, the conglomerate is not an especially distinctive organizational form. It is likely to be decentralized, and this favors the innovation process. It can also use the internal capital market to fund the development of new technologies. However, the importance of this is likely to be reduced the more (i) access to capital, including venture capital, is available for new stand-alone businesses, and (ii) headquarters management acts much like external capital market agents. Accordingly, on grounds of access to capital and diversity of activities, one would not expect the conglomerate to look too different from a portfolio of stand-alone firms with respect to its innovative capacity.[33]

However, there are two ways in which one might expect the conglomerate to underperform a portfolio of stand-alone firms with respect to innovation. One is that it is difficult for conglomerates to develop distinctive company-wide corporate cultures. Accordingly, it may be quite difficult to build a strong internal change culture at the corporate level. Furthermore, the existence of subunits inside a larger structure is likely to thwart the establishment of strong divisional cultures. Certainly, as compared to a stand-alone firm, getting across to employees the notion that the unit must ultimately "stand on its own bottom" will be quite a challenge. As a consequence, free riding may well be accentuated. Likewise, the design of high-powered incentives for top management and employees will be hindered by the absence of a security geared to divisional performance. As a consequence, the conglomerate does not appear to be a viable form in environments characterized by rapid technological change.

4.6 Alliances

We define an alliance enterprise as a virtual that has developed strong commitments to other enterprises, usually through equity-based links to affiliated enterprises lying upstream, downstream, horizontal and lateral from its core business. Such structures include consortia (e.g. Airbus, SEMATECH) as well as semipermanent teaming arrangements that transcend particular projects. Many new biotech firms in the United States are heavily alliance-dependent to fund their R&D and move drugs to the market.

The viability and desirability of alliances and other external linkage arrangements depends importantly not just on the efficacy of this form of contract, but also on the resources/capabilities which can be accessed in this fashion. These alliances are essential in the 1980s and 1990s to the pharmaceutical industry as a mechanism to tap into the drug development capabilities of new biotech firms. Because the biotechnology revolution has occurred outside the organizational gambit of the established pharmaceutical industry, alliances have been embued with virtues they might not otherwise possess. Put differently, the value of a contract can easily be confused with what it enables one to access. The comparative institutional approach used here imputes to the alliance only that which it can uniquely access as compared to other arrangements.

5. MATCHING INNOVATION AND ORGANIZATIONAL ARCHETYPES

The diversity of organizational forms observed is semipermanent and not a transitional feature of modern industrial economies. This in and of itself suggests that different organizational arrangements are suited to different types of competitive environments and differing types of innovation. One cannot possibly expect to be comprehensive in developing a taxonomy of innovations and organizational archetypes. However, an important illustration is developed below: the matching of autonomous and systemic innovation to different organizational structures.

An autonomous innovation is one that can be introduced to the market without massive modification of related products and processes. Power steering, for instance, did not initially require any significant alternatives to the design of cars or engines. Turbocharging requires minor modification to engines, not their complete redesign. Likewise with electronic ignition and disc brakes. By contrast, the move to front-wheel drive required the complete redesign of many automobiles in the 1980s. Such a change is a systemic innovation. Other examples are "lean production" (which requires modification to all aspects of the production process of automobiles) and the development of the transistor, which has required the complete redesign of the modem electronic componentry if the full benefits afforded by this technology are to be obtained.

Systemic innovation generally favors integrated enterprises, while autonomous innovation can often be advanced rapidly by smaller autonomous structures, such as "virtual" firms, accomplishing necessary coordination through arm's-length arrangements in the open market. The former is because systemic innovation requires complex coordination amongst various subsystems, and this is often better accomplished under one "roof." The reason is that interfaces between subsystems are often poorly specified and in a state of great flux in a new product or design, thus confounding efforts to rely on (long-term) contracts to get the work done. In addition, simultaneous development of various subsystems requires that various development efforts be closely paced, to ensure that development goals are attained simultaneously. Given the uncertainties associated with innovation, close managerial monitoring and involvement will be needed to obtain such objectives—holding constant the relative capabilities of inside and outside developers.

Indeed, it ought be evident that one cannot realistically assume that the capabilities of entities outside and inside the firm are at all the same. Thus, in reality, organizational choices are made not just on the basis of the relative efficiency of the governance modes, but also on the basis of the organizational locus of the requisite talent. In some instances, where the capabilities do not exist externally, one must in fact engage in entrepreneurship—external or internal—to stimulate suppliers for the products/components that one might wish to procure.

An interesting conundrum along these lines currently faces Motorola as it continues to innovate in hand-held communication devices, including cellular phones. Future improvements on cellphone designs, and in particular weight reduction and extended operation, requires lighter and more long-lived batteries. Motorola is in a position to advance these technologies through its own internal R&D programs, which have historically been very productive. Because the older more established battery technologies like nickel cadmium have been widely diffused, Motorola can reasonably rely on outsourcing to access its requirements in the Ni-Cd domain. However, solid state and fuel cells are still in their infancy as technologies to support personal communication devices. Moreover, Motorola is as well placed as others to advance the development of such technologies. With reliance on unaffiliated parties leading to obvious contractual hazards (Teece 1988), internal development, or at minimum joint-venture development, is suggested for such technologies. As displayed in Figure 7.3, this suggests that desirable governance arrangements will migrate toward internal as the population of outsider vendors diminishes. It is likely to do so as one confronts more advanced technological options.

6. IMPLICATIONS AND CONCLUSIONS

If this analysis is correct, it has rather strong implications for theory building, for management and for public policy. With respect to theory building, it suggests that standard economic approaches that have market structure as the key if not the only element of organizational structure are inadequate, and consequently are likely to be poor guides to policy. At minimum, firm boundaries (the level of integration) and the formal and informal organizational structure must all be included. The problems associated with much contemporary modeling of innovation stem in part from inadequate attention to firm boundaries, and both types of structure. This paper has tried to suggest that firm organization (not just market structure) is an important determinant of firm and industry performance, a point made by Williamson (1975) but largely unheeded by industrial organization economists.

The framework developed here is designed to shift the market structure–innovation debate in industrial organization beyond the domain where Schumpeter (1942), Galbraith (1952), Mansfield (1968), Scherer (1980) and others have put it, and into a new domain where internal structure and interfirm agreements attain new significance. This also has obvious policy significance, as it suggests that agreements among firms that are aimed at the development and commercialization of new technology are likely to be very important to the production of new technology.[34]

The framework also has strong implications for business history. It suggests the possible viability of new hybrid organizational arrangements—such as complex forms of interfirm agreements linking firms with complementary capabilities and capacities—over both the integrated alternatives and the small firm alternatives. These organizational forms may well represent a new and dramatic organizational innovation in business history. In retrospect, the emergence and growth of these new forms, dating from about 1970, may turn out to be as significant an organizational innovation as the moving assembly line and the multidivisional firm.

NOTES

1. Of course there are governments, universities and professional societies in the system too, and certain activities that firms cannot be expected to do on their own because the returns are so low, are picked up by other institutions, or receive public monies, or both.
2. For a review, see Dosi *et al.* (1988).
3. The following statement by Little (1985: 14) is representative of accepted views: "Our work among innovative companies indicates that the management decision on how to organize for innovation is critical."
4. The approach rejects assumptions of temporal equilibrium. The framework does not assume that the selection process immediately weeds out all organizations that do not match the business environment at a particular point in time. While the organizational system is seen as gravitating toward an end point or equilibrium, it takes so long to reach it that the environment is likely to change again in the interim, leading to a state of perpetual disequilibrium.
5. Uncertainty also makes information a valuable commodity. Information about which outcomes will occur, or are more likely to occur, will obviously have great value. Information, of course, itself has very special characteristics. It is not only an indivisible commodity, in which case the classic problems of allocation in the presence of indivisibilities will be present, but it is also highly tacit, as discussed below. Often it cannot be readily articulated and codified in language. Combined with the absence of legal protection, these features make it difficult to trade.
6. Examples of paradigms include the internal combustion engine, biotechnology and tungsten filament lighting. Technological discontinuities occur when new paradigms emerge. Thus new technologies are more threatening to existing skills and capabilities if they embody a new paradigm. The emergence of microelectronics, which carried with it a new paradigm, was far more threatening to the skills of incumbents than the emergence of the facsimile, which fused the technology of the telephone and the copier.
7. Specific technological skills in one field (e.g. pharmaceuticals) may be applicable in closely-related fields (e.g. pesticides) but they are unlikely to be of use in distant fields (e.g. aircraft). See Teece (1988), and Teece, Dosi, Rumelt and Winter (1994).
8. If sailing ships ever replace propeller-driven ships, it will be with such a different sailing technology as to be almost unrecognizable from nineteenth-century counterparts. And if the prop-fan recaptures markets from the fan-jet, it will also be with a markedly different prop and engine.
9. That is, it is possible to receive a patent which is arguably too narrow or too in relation to the patent holder's contribution to economic welfare.
10. Schumpeter 1942: 105.
11. Relatedly, large firms are more innovative than small firms because there are economies of scale in R&D, because large firms are better able to exploit unforeseen innovations, and because indivisibilities in cost-reducing innovations make them more profitable for large firms.

12. See Kay, undated working paper.
13. Equity bears a residual claimant status, contracts for the duration of the life of the firm, and is protected through representation on the board of directors (Williamson 1988).
14. Indeed, there is evidence that individuals who make realistic forecasts are clinically depressed (Taylor and Brown 1980).
15. Hierarchical subdivision is not a characteristic that is peculiar to human organization. It is common to virtually all complex systems of which we have knowledge (Simon 1973: 202). The advantages of hierarchy are well understood. In particular, among systems of a given size and complexity, hierarchical systems require much less information transmission among their parts than do other types of systems.
16. Crozier (1964: 225) puts it this way: "People on top theoretically have a great deal of power and often much more power than they would have in other, more authoritarian societies. But these powers are not very useful, since people on top can act only in an impersonal way and can in no way interfere with the subordinate strata. They cannot, therefore, provide real leadership on a daily basis. If they want to introduce change, they must go through the long and difficult ordeal of a crisis. Thus, although they are all-powerful because they are at the apex of the whole centralized system, they are made so weak by the pattern of resistance of the different isolated strata that they can use their power only in truly exceptional circumstances."
17. Surrogate valuation indexes can sometimes be created based on the use of "yardstick" companies, but they typically do not convey liquidity.
18. This is discussed in Section 4.3.
19. Despite the fact that the ultimate objective of R&D programs is to produce innovations, not simply to dissipate resources on R&D activities, expenditure data can be viewed as a useful proxy for innovative performance in that it reveals the intensity of innovative activity. Furthermore, if the discount rate facing non-integrated firms is similar to that facing integrated firms and if similar risk preferences exist across the management of these firms, the higher productivity per dollar of research expenditure posited in vertically integrated firms implies that, *ceteris paribus*, such firms will devote more resources to R&D.
20. Technical aspects of interrelatedness do not seem to have held up the movement to more efficient size, either through making such a change uneconomic because of the enormity of the investment required or by adding amounts too great for any one firm to borrow. The sums involved were not large, and railway finance was rarely a limiting factor in the period up to 1914. Private ownership of the coal cars by the collieries, on the other hand, posed a type of interrelatedness that was institutional rather than technical.
21. The exception is the now discredited school of (old) institutional economists which recognized that "at least since mankind reached the human plane, the economic unit has been not a solitary hunter, but a community of some kind" (Veblen, 1972: 174).
22. Moreover, there is a tendency to squish such concepts into externalities, where it is not clear they belong. Thus Arrow (1974: 23) notes that: "Trust and similar values, loyalty or truth-telling, are examples of what the economist would call

'externalities.' They are good, they are commodities; they have real, practical economic value; they increase the efficiency of the system, enable you to produce more goods or more whatever values you hold in high esteem. But they are not commodities for which trade on the open market is technically possible or even meaningful."

23. Alchien and Demsetz (1972).

24. Ken-ichi Imai (1988: 2) notes that "corporate networks in a broad sense are the vital economic institution which has led the Japanese economic development. The long history of cooperation between firms may be a crucial factor to explain the special adaptability of the Japanese economy." Imai uses the term, as it is used in this paper, to indicate interfirm relationships in general, including *zaibatsu* and business groups.

25. Even setting aside protection issues, stand-alone R&D laboratories have problems in developing information channels to their sponsors to understand their sponsors' needs, and in transferring technology back to the sponsor if in fact useful technology is developed. Moreover, because of leakage problems, competitors are likely to be reluctant to use a common R&D laboratory.

26. Such as the one described in 6.3 below.

27. It is important to recognize, based on historical experience in the United States in the period up to 1980, that the acquisition of a (4.2) company by (4.3) company is often extremely difficult to achieve without destroying the creative and entrepreneurial capacity of the small companies. This is because the organizational controls of the large organization tend to destroy the innovative capacities of small firms, as discussed earlier.

28. Primary uncertainty can never be reduced, but organizations can adapt to it. Secondary uncertainty, due to ignorance of complementary investment plans, can obviously be much reduced through bilateral agreements which involve mutual commitments and the maintenance of reciprocity through the exchange of hostages (Williamson 1985).

29. It is perhaps in the realm of indivisibilities that bilateral exchange comes closest to the perfect solution of a market-failure problem. As discussed elsewhere (Teece 1980, 1982), interfirm agreements are a relatively straightforward way to access complementary assets, particularly if they are already in place, are in excess capacity and do not involve a high degree of asset specificity. Even when asset specificity is involved, the incentives for opportunistic recontracting can be attenuated by reputation effects, repeat contracting or exchange of hostages.

30. Inasmuch as firms can use bilateral contracts to access existing industry capacities so that new capacity does not have to be put in place de novo, product commercialization time can be reduced and lead time lengthened. Thus a major strategic advantage, lead time, can often be enhanced through the use of bilateral contracts. While the innovator may have to share part of the rent stream with the provider of complementary assets, investment risk for the innovator is typically reduced and imitators can be outpaced.

31. Bilateral contracts enable specialized assets to be protected. While the degree of protection may not be as great as is provided under vertical integration, it is likely to be significantly higher than under unilateral contracts. A "hostage," or its economic equivalent, including specific investments which are mutually dependent, can be used to help support exchange. Thus if a manufacturer installs

dedicated equipment to serve the developer, and the developer makes specialized investments which dovetail with the manufacturer, both can be assured that
transactions will have a better chance of continuing in the face of adversity or
superior opportunities.

32. Tacitness is less a problem if a bilateral relationship exists, particularly if it is
supported by equity. If repeated transactions are contemplated, spillovers and
costs associated with seconding technical staff are less severe as adjustments can
be made in subsequent transactions, as long as spillovers and costs are perceived
similarly by both parties.

33. There has been very little discussion of the relationship between the conglomerate and technological innovation. The arguments advanced by Williamson
(1975) that conglomerate firms possess miniature capital markets would suggest
that the conglomerate is an ideal form for identifying new investment opportunities, including process and product innovations, and funding them until they
become cash-flow positive. In the absence of market-for-venture capital, this
argument would seem to imply that the conglomerate form ought to be associated with a stream of new product and process launches.

34. For further elaboration, see Jorde and Teece (1989, 1990).

REFERENCES

Alchien, A. and Demsetz, H. (1972), "Production, Information Cost, and Economic
Organizations," *American Economic Review*, 62: 777–95.

Armour, H. and Teece, D. J. (1978), "Organizational Structure and Economic
Performance: A Test of the Multidivisional Hypothesis," *Bell Journal of Economics*, 9/2: 106–22.

Arrow, K. J. (1962), "Economic Welfare and the Allocation of Resources for
Invention," in *The Rate and Direction of Inventive Activity: Economic and Social
Factors* (NBER, Princeton: Princeton University Press), 609–25.

——(1974), *The Limits of Organization* (New York: Norton).

——(1983), "Innovation in Large and Small Firms," in Joshua Rosen (ed.),
Entrepreneurship (Lexington, Mass.: D. C. Heath).

Badaracco, J. L. (1991), *The Knowledge Link* (Cambridge, Mass.: Harvard Business
School Press).

Burgelman, R. A. (1984), "Designs for Corporate Entrepreneurship," *California
Management Review*, 26/3 (Spring), 154–66.

Coase, R. (1937), "The Nature of Firm," *Economica*, 4: 386–405.

Crozier, M. (1964), *The Bureaucratic Phenomenon* (Chicago: University of Chicago
Press).

Dasgupta, P. D. (1987), "The Economic Theory of Technology Policy: An Introduction," in P. Dasgupta and P. Stoneman, *Economic Policy and Technological
Performance* (Cambridge: Cambridge University Press).

——(1988), "The Welfare Economics of Knowledge Production," *Oxford Review of Economic Policy*, 4/4 (Winter).

——and Maskin, E. (1987), "The Simple Economics of Research Portfolios," *Economic Journal*, 97/387 (Sept.), 581–95.

——and Stiglitz, J. E. (1980*a*), "Industrial Structure and the Nature of Innovative Activity," *Economic Journal*, 90/358 (June), 266–93.

————(1980*b*), "Uncertainty, Industrial Structure and the Speed of R&D," *Bell Journal of Economics*, 11/1 (Spring), 1–28.

Deal, T. E. and Kennedy, A. (1982), *Corporate Culture* (Reading, Mass.: Addison-Wesley).

Dosi, G. (1982), "Technological Paradigms and Technological Trajectories: A Suggested Interpretation of the Determinants and Directions of Technical Change," *Research Policy*, 11/3 (June), 147–62.

——(1988), "Sources, Procedures, and Microeconomic Effects of Innovation," *Journal of Economic Literature*, 26 (Sept.), 1120–71.

——Freeman, C., Nelson, R., Silverberg, G. and Soete, L. (1988), *Technical Change and Economic Theory* (London: Pinter).

Downs, A. (1967), *Inside Bureaucracy* (Boston: Little, Brown).

Fama, E. (1970), "Efficient Capital Markets: A Review of Theory and Empirical Work," *American Economic Review*, 60: 163–74.

Frankel, M. (1955), "Obsolence and Technological Change in a Maturing Economy," *American Economic Review*, 45/3 (June), 296–319.

Freeman, C. (1974), *The Economics of Industrial Innovation* (Harmondsworth, UK: Penguin).

Galbraith, J. K. (1952), *American Capitalism* (Boston: Houghton Mifflin).

Imai, Ken-ichi, (1988), "Japan's Corporate Networks," unpub. Working Paper, Hitotsubashi University, Tokyo.

Jensen, C. (1989), "Eclipse of the Public Corporation," *Harvard Business Review*, 67/5 (Sept.–Oct.), 61–74.

Jorde, T. M. and Teece, D. J. (1989), "Innovation, Cooperation, and Antitrust," *High Technology Law Journal*, 4/1 (Spring), 1–112.

——and Teece, D. J. (1990), "Innovation and Cooperation: Implications for Competition and Antitrust," *Journal of Economic Perspectives*, 4/3 (Summer), 75–96.

Kahneman, D., and Lovallo, D. (1990), "Timid Decisions and Bold Forecasts: Cognitive Perspective on Risk Taking," paper prepared for Conference on "Fundamental Issues in Strategy," Napa, Calif., 29 Nov.–1 Dec. 1990.

Kamien, M. L. and Schwartz, N. L. (1982), *Market Structure and Innovation* (Cambridge: Cambridge University Press).

Kay, N., "Industrial Structure, Rivalry, and Innovation: Theory and Evidence," undated Working Paper, Department of Economics, Herriot-Watt University, Edinburgh.

Kindleberger, C. P. (1964), *Economic Growth in France and Britain, 1851–1950* (Cambridge, Mass.: Harvard University Press).

Kodama, F. (1986), "Japanese Innovation in Mechatronics Technology," *Science and Public Policy*, 13/1, 44–52.

Koopmans, T. C. (1957), *Three Essays in the State of Economic Science* (New York: McGraw-Hill).

Levin, R., Klevorick, A., Nelson, R. and Winter, S. (1987), "Appropriating the Returns from Industrial R&D," *Brookings Papers on Economic Activity*, no. 3: 783–831.

Little, A. D. (1985), *Management Perspectives on Innovation* (Cambridge, Mass.: Arthur D. Little).

Mansfield, E. (1968), *The Economics of Technical Change* (New York: Norton).

March, J. and Shapira, Z. (1987), "Managerial Perspectives on Risk and Risk Taking," *Management Science*, 33/11: 1404–18.

Marx, T. (1976), "Vertical Integration in the Diesel-Electric Locomotive Building Industry: A Study in Market Failures," *Nebraska Journal of Agricultural Economics*, 15/4 (Autumn), 37–51.

Nelson, R. R. (1981), "Assessing Private Enterprise," *Bell Journal of Economics*, 12/1 (Spring), 93–111.

——and Winter, S. G. (1977), "In Search of a Useful Theory of Innovations," *Research Policy*, 6/1.

————(1982), *An Evolutionary Theory of Economic Change* (Cambridge, Mass.: Harvard University Press).

O'Reilly, C. A. (1989), "Corporate Culture Considerations Based on an Empirical Study of High Growth Firms in Silicon Valley," *Economia Aziendale*, 3/3.

Orsenigo, L. (1989), *The Emergence of Biotechnology* (London: Pinter).

Pavitt, K., Robson, M. and Townsend, J. (1989), "Accumulation, Diversification and Organisation of Technological Activities in U.K. Companies, 1945–83," in M. Dodgson (ed.), *Technology Strategy and the Firm* (London: Longmans).

Peters, T. and Waterman, R. (1982), *In Search of Excellence* (New York: Harper & Row).

Pisano, G. P. and Teece, D. J. (1989), "Collaborative Arrangements and Global Technology Strategy," in R. A. Burgelman and R. S. Rosenbloom (eds.), *Research on Technological Innovation, Management and Policy* (Greenwich, Conn.: JAI Press), iv. 227–56.

Polanyi, M. (1962), *Personal Knowledge: Toward a Post Critical Philosophy* (New York: Harper & Row).

Richardson, G. B. H. (1990), *Information and Investment* (Oxford: Oxford University Press).

Scherer, F. M. (1980), *Industrial Market Structure and Economic Performance*, 2nd edn. (Chicago: Rand McNally).

Schumpeter, J. A. (1934), *The Theory of Economic Development* (Cambridge, Mass.: Harvard University Press).

——(1942), *Capitalism, Socialism and Democracy* (New York: McGraw-Hill).

Schwartz, H. and Davis, S. (1981), "Matching Corporate Culture and Business Strategy," *Organizational Dynamics*, 10/1: 30–48.

Simon, H. (1973), "Decision Making and Organizational Design," in D. S. Pugh (ed.), *Organizational Theory* (London: Penguin).

Taylor, S. E. and Brown, J. D. (1980), "Illusion and Well-Being: A Social Psychological Perspective on Mental Health," *Psychological Bulletin*, 103: 39–60.

Teece, D. J. (1977), "Technology Transfer by Multinational Firms: The Resource Cost of Transferring Technological Know-how," *Economic Journal*, 87/346 (June), 242–61.

——(1980), "Economics of Scope and the Scope of the Enterprise," *Journal of Economic Behavior and Organization*, 1/3: 223–47.

——(1982), "Toward an Economic Theory of the Multiproduct Firms," *Journal of Economic Behavior and Organization*, 3/1: 39–63.

——(1984), "Economic Analysis and Strategic Management," *California Management Review*, 26/3 (Spring), 87–110.

——(1986), "Profiting from Technological Innovation," *Research Policy*, 15/6: 285–306.

——(1988), "The Nature of the Firm and Technological Change," in Dosi *et al.* (eds.), *Technical Change and Economic Theory*.

——(1989), "Interorganizational Requirements of the Innovation Process," *Journal of Managerial and Decision Economics*, Special Issue (Spring), 35–42.

——(1990), "Innovation and Cooperation: Implications of Commercialization for Antitrust," *Journal of Economic Perspectives*, 4/3 (Summer), 75–96.

——Rumelt, R., Dosi, G. and Winter, S. (1994), "Understanding Corporate Coherence: Theory and Evidence," *Journal of Economic Behavior and Organization*, 23/1 (Jan.), 1–30.

Tirole, J. (1989), *The Theory of Industrial Organization* (Cambridge, Mass.: MIT Press).

Veblen, T. (1972), "Professor Clark's Economics," in E. K. Hunt and J. Schwartz, *A Critique of Economic Theory* (Harmondsworth, UK: Penguin).

Williamson, O. E. (1975), *Markets and Hierarchies* (New York: Free Press).

——(1980), "The Organization of Work: A Comparative Institutional Assessment," *Journal of Economic Behavior and Organization*, 1: 5–38.

——(1985), *The Economic Institutions of Capitalism* (New York: Free Press).

——(1988), "Corporate Finance and Corporate Governance," *Journal of Finance*, 43 (July), 567–91.

Winter, S. G. (1987), "Knowledge and Competence as Strategic Assets," in D. Teece (ed.), *The Competitive Challenge: Strategies for Industrial Innovation and Renewal* (Cambridge, Mass.: Ballinger).

8

A Three-Dimensional Model of Changing Internal Structure in the Firm*

PETER HAGSTRÖM AND GUNNAR HEDLUND

1. INTRODUCTION

There is a noticeable dissonance between the conceptualization of the firm in Economics and related disciplines, on the one hand, and the perspective on the firm from a management vantage point on the other. In the dominant strands of the former, the primary concern is to explain competitive efficiency today, sometimes taking into account how the firm got there—circumstances that imply constraints on the options available to the firm at present. Managers do share a concern for competitive efficiency, but, rather than past and present, that concern is one of present and future competitiveness. The claim here is not that the difference in emphasis makes either broad perspective illegitimate, but that an "inside view" of the firm can inform our understanding of the firm as a phenomenon.

At the risk of simplifying in order to drive home a point, academic inquiry vis-à-vis the firm can be characterized as "standing on the outside looking in," whereas practitioners "are on the inside looking out." We wish to exploit two particular aspects of this tension. First, is the appreciation of dynamics, where theory tends to end at the point where practice starts, that is the present. Second, there is a problem of language and the quest for generality. Theory commands the high ground with much of the dissemination—when it occurs—coming through the managerial literature in the form of "recipes" or through consultants. The return path is much less traveled, not least as a result of the relative paucity of high quality inductive research being carried out.

We bring dynamics and less restrictive language to the issue of internal organization of the firm. In line with a managerial perspective, the existence of the firm is taken as given. Dynamics translate into the imperative of the simultaneous needs for (flexible) efficiency today and for positioning for tomorrow for both exploitation and experimentation or creation strategies, respectively. The subsumption of all "internalized" governance structures in "hierarchy" is replaced by seeing internal structure as multidimensional.

* The paper benefited greatly from the discussions with the participants of The Prince Bertil Symposium on The Dynamic Firm in June 1994, in particular from the comments by Giovanni Dosi and Hiro Takeuchi.

In particular, three structural dimensions are suggested: position, action and knowledge. It is argued that the present competitive environment unmasks the hitherto unidimensional hierarchy as a special case of internal structure; a solution where the suggested three structural dimensions coincide perfectly.

The paper begins with a brief discussion of the restrictive assumptions of dominant theories of the firm and how they frame—and thus limit—the interpretation of internal structure. The second section turns to the pressures the traditional firm is experiencing; pressures that have led many firms to experiment with their internal structure. The subsequent conclusion that the internal structure has to be interpreted as being multidimensional is the subject of the third section.

2. THE "FETTERED" FIRM

The smallest common denominator in mainstream theory of the firm has firms to be the institutional extreme that relies on hierarchy in order to achieved control and coordination, whereas markets are found at the other extreme where the control and coordination function is performed by prices. In Economics the stress is very much on the role of hierarchy in ensuring control over behavior (as in neoclassical, agency, transaction cost and incomplete contracting approaches). In much of organization theory, efficient coordination of work takes the center stage (as in contingency and systems-based approaches). The unifying basic assumption still is that hierarchy as a design principle is the single most efficient way to simultaneously achieve the control and coordination that escapes organization by the market.

The case for hierarchy fundamentally appears to rest on one or more or both of two propositions; it is not the market, and it is a "natural" organizing principle. In both cases, hierarchy is an empirically observed phenomenon that is then "explained" in a number of ways. For instance, in their review of the theory of the firm, Holmström and Tirole (1989) look at internal structure as hierarchy and then identify seven categories of services that hierarchies provide: the function of an information system, a system for supervision, a structure for incentives, an internal labor market, a nexus of contracts, an authority structure and organizational form as essentially a measure of operational efficiency. As it stands, a single organizing principle hence delivers many functions. Only the perspectives on the firm as a nexus of (incomplete) contracts and as an organizational form can really be said to have dynamic elements. Incomplete contracting is compatible with evolutionary theories (cf. Nelson and Winter 1982), where organizational routines provide a stabilizing framework, but at the expense of imperfect adaptation to a changing environment. Regarding form, organizational innovation is explicitly seen as change to overcome external constraints to growth, but it is a change in form only, leaving the very principle of hierarchy intact (cf. Chandler 1962, and Williamson 1975). Williamson claims that whatever future organizational firms will emerge, after the M-form, they will be "essentially hierarchical."

Hierarchy as a "natural" principle has primarily taken hold in organization theory. Following Weber's postulate that bureaucratization—of which hierarchy is a part—follows from internal structural differentiation (Weber 1924/1947), Simon (1962) infers hierarchy as *the* organizing mode from the contention that it is the most efficient way to organize work flows.[1] Support also comes from prevalent hierarchical ordering in the natural sciences of natural phenomena and from systems approaches in the social science. The latter is strongly linked to the concept of complexity and the observation that not everything is tightly connected to everything else, wherefore there is scope for (hierarchical) reduction of apparent complexity (cf. Aldrich 1979, and Scott's 1987 discussion). In this vein, hierarchical decomposition is the only way we can understand large-scale systems[2] (see the overview by Gottinger 1983), and it is a foundation in much of modern decision theory and operational research (cf. Saaty 1980 and 1990).

Still, we know that managers cannot optimize objectively (March and Simon 1958). Behavioral constraints, and logics (in terms of problems with profit-maximization, see Alchian 1950) create a tension with optimization that, again, only hierarchy is argued to resolve (e.g. Williamson 1975). The limits to reductionist explanations and conceptualizations of the working of a firm's internal structure has over time come to prompt many adjunct theories and notions, particularly in organization theory. These developments have often been empirically driven and have reflected a perceived need to bridge a single organizational principle as dictated by Occam's razor, and the observed diversity of organizational mechanisms in place in firms. "Informal organization," "corporate culture," "project teams," "matrix organization," and a whole host of informal means of control and coordination have resulted in the literature. It seems that the proliferation of concepts has accelerated in the last couple of decades, a development that, we surmise, can be traced to the contemporary pressures the traditional firm is under at this juncture (a subject we will return to in the next section). An additional source for doubt concerning reductionist views of internal organization is the observed considerable variation across nations and cultures of chosen organizational forms (cf. the review by Caves 1980, and the discussion on Japanese firms by Aoki 1990).

If organizational survival is perceived as being very much in the balance at present, then what is the scope for change? In both Chandler's and in Nelson and Winter's worlds, organizational change is driven by technology, but it is also retarded and influenced by the organization's history. There is limited room for maneuver, in particular as firm structure and core capabilities are both costly and difficult to change (cf. Nelson 1991[3]). In the world of Simon, Cyert, and March, the firm is severely limited also in its search for alternatives. With this limited scope for change, firms also do exhibit some differences in internal structure.[4] The fundamental selection mechanism is external competitive pressure.

The rather circumscribed role for management and the reliance on hierarchy as the essence of internal organization tally less well with the perceptions of managers themselves. Taking this opportunity to reflect over our own contacts with managers in various research projects over several years, we are struck by how much effort is expended in attempts to articulate the problems and opportunities of the firm; it betraying both a growing need to do so and a lack of terms for an accurate description. Aggregate resource allocation is beset by the present/future tradeoff, and inherited internal structures are recognized as ill-equipped to deal effectively with that tradeoff, as well as to safeguard the maintenance and development of the firm's resources and capabilities. This is particularly the case in large, complex firms. There is no doubt that variations on the hierarchy has worked well for a long time, but the strains appear to show.[5] We will briefly review some of these in the next section.

3. THE UNDERMINING OF HIERARCHY IN THE MODERN FIRM

It is easy to enumerate problems arising from and being ignored in hierarchical organization in present-day firms. This has always been recognized. Galbraith (1973) suggests that an array of complementary control and coordination mechanisms are introduced to solve more intricate problems than those that can be dealt with by the simple division of tasks and power in a hierarchical structure. Williamson, in his early work, emphasizes "control losses" in hierarchies. The list could be made very long.

However, few—if any—of the leading theorists question the assumption that hierarchical decomposition is the primary control mechanism and a "natural," inherent part of internal organization. Task forces, information systems, etc., are subsidiary mechanisms for control and coordination but they are seen as compensation for "minor" shortcomings of the hierarchy and not as a replacement of the fundamental principle. We argue that the problems discussed below are so important that a more fundamental reassessment of hierarchy is going on in leading firms. Aspects such as informal organization, temporary teams and information systems then become the foundation of internal structure rather than embellishments on a hierarchical edifice.

We will proceed by briefly discussing how hierarchy constitutes an obstacle when dealing with some of the most pressing problems of large corporations today. For the moment, we will treat the definition of "hierarchy" in the same cavalier fashion as most other analysts, implying a treelike order of ranks (or rungs) of different levels, where responsibility and power increase as you go up the ladder.[6] In turn, we will consider how hierarchy squares with problems associated with the *size* of the firm, its *internationalization*, the generation and use of *new technology*, the compression of *time* through shorter product life-cycles and the general need to work faster, the impacts of *information technology* and with *motivational* issues.

4. SIZE

Hierarchy is often seen as the only way to deal with large size. Indeed, the beauty of hierarchical organization is that, through the power of exponential progression, a huge organization can be divided into a rather limited number of levels, given a certain control span. For example, with a control span of 10, a firm of over one million people (1,111,111 to be exact) can be harnessed in a 7-level structure. As anybody who has worked in an organization knows, however, that harness is far from perfect. The experience of conglomerates testifies to the difficulties of managing such constructions. The availability of the hierarchical form, therefore, could be seen to be as much of a snare as a salvation. Top managers running "portfolios" of companies through ever more abstract notions and remote systems have proved to be a menace to the economy (cf. the argument of Shleifer and Vishny 1991, that the M-form "spawned the monster of the conglomerate").

In line with this hypothesis, the economy of the industrialized nations seems to shift back towards reliance on smaller firms. The share of the US Fortune 500 in GNP seems to have peaked in the late 1980s and now appears to be declining.[7] Manufacturing technology is changing the rules of the game in terms of scale advantages with minimum efficient scale falling in many industries. Also in giant corporations, the virtues of small firms are commonly sought through various means, effectively subverting a clear hierarchy. The radical solution of "externalizing," i.e. spinning off units through separate stock market listing or management buyouts, has shown the efficiency gains possible by cutting loose from the internal hierarchy. The emergence of marketlike relations between units in a firm has similarly shown the limits of management by hierarchical fiat.[8] More pertinent to the effort to outline organizational (still internal, and "non-market") alternatives to the hierarchical principle, the differentiation of roles between classes of actors in the firm is changing in interesting ways. Top management is seen less as a monitor and resource allocator and more as a creator and upholder of a corporate ethos and clanlike relations between individuals (see Ouchi 1980), as an architect of a system allowing for maximum autonomy at a very detailed operational level, as ensuring that learning takes place, as a protector and initiator of novelty, as a symbolic carrier of basic corporate directions, etc. These may sound like woolly catch-phrases without much meaning, but it is a fact that they appear at top management meetings (a type of forum to which economists are rarely invited) and— perhaps more in line with expectations—in the applied management journals. The basic point is that it is no longer clear what happens at the apex of the hierarchy, or more generally, what is the basis for role differentiation between "levels."

5. INTERNALIZATION

In the MNC, the problems of hierarchy are accentuated in comparison with the large, national firm. There are three main reasons for this. First, the MNC encounters significantly more variation, which necessitates further and "stronger" (from the point of view of the national firm) specialization of tasks and multidimensional coordination. Today any large MNC wrestles with how to achieve coordination along at least product, geographical and functional lines simultaneously. Clear hierarchical ordering proves to be too inflexible, and three-dimensional matrices too unwieldy. Thus, there seem to be no good responses within the confines of thinking in terms of hierarchical organization.

Second, the MNC faces the problems and opportunities inherent in *globally distributed knowledge*. Thinking and acting parts of the corporation are both geographically diffused, and the scattered "brain" proves a significant obstacle to clear hierarchical structure. This has inspired the notion of the MNC as a *heterarchy* (Hedlund 1986). Many management scholars provide empirical support for the trend and suggest similar shifts in the character of the modern MNC (see Bartlett and Ghoshal 1989; White and Poynter 1990; Doz and Prahalad 1987).

Third, internationalization means a quantum jump in *uncertainty and change*. This makes a "freezing" of the structure more difficult. The MNC has to be able to shift the perspective between, for example, product, technological and geographical foci as the situation so requires. For example, the "simple" matter of exchange-rate changes affects optimal manufacturing location more than decades of rationalization efforts in many industries. This requires close collaboration between the financial function, product divisions, and country managers, with no clear super- or subordination (see Lessard and Nohria 1990).

For the reasons mentioned and others, the organizational structures of MNCs become immensely complicated. Several MNCs refuse to publish organization charts, reasoning that the chart is never correct for very long and, more importantly, tells rather little of what actually goes on. The classical model of separating units on geographical lines has long since given way to product-line forms in most MNCs, but this fashion is again challenged by notions of structuring according to a customer logic, or an internal competence one, etc. The very language needs to be changed. *Sub*sidiaries are becoming larger and smarter than the *parent* company. IBM Japan (a "subsidiary" of IBM Corporation) has four own "subsidiaries": one in Singapore, one in the United Kingdom, one on the US West coast, and one on the US East coast. Using the term "*auxiliaries*" is but one suggestion in order to capture this more complex and prominent role of many present-day "subsidiaries."[9]

6. NEW TECHNOLOGY

Traditional hierarchies are proving resistant to new technological impulses. Often, firms resort to creating special units, outside the normal structure, to develop new products and businesses (see Burgelman 1983). The power of committed small teams and project groups, "skunk camps," etc., is well known. The *original* idea of matrix organization—a kind of large project organization, where technical specialists collaborate on an urgent "mission"—is one version of the general idea of having to take people *away* from the hierarchy to get real work done.

Also within the more permanent life of the firm, it is found that the monitoring and development of internal competencies cut across lines drawn in the formal hierarchy. Particularly notorious is the M-form type of product logic, when sustainable competitiveness necessitates freeing resources from the narrow and bounded uses that the divisionalized structure puts them to (Prahalad and Hamel 1990).

7. SHORT LIFE-CYCLES AND TIME COMPETITION

More rapid replacement of products has consequences similar to those following from increased importance of new technology more generally: multifunctional teams pulled from "the line," initiative at "lower" levels, reliance on horizontal communication, etc. Time reduction also proves to require departure from the logic of hierarchical organization. Indeed, hierarchy assumes that goals are known and the environment is relatively stable (cf. Scott 1987). Tasks must be repetitive and broadly unchanged for the hierarchical division of labor to function. A hierarchy in constant flux is no hierarchy. Or the term loses its meaning, since the aim of reducing uncertainty to gain internal efficiency hinges on tasks being structured so that execution can be planned in advance.

Instead, projects are launched around processes spanning people and units horizontally, often cutting across and ignoring the formal hierarchy, and involving also external actors, mainly suppliers and customers. The alternative to "market" is thus neither hierarchical, nor internal. The closer you get to what takes place in, say, ABB—with its program to cut all cycle times by 50%—the less the accepted vernacular of organization theory and economics seems to fit. And it is *not* a matter of just degree of generality and abstraction, but of the basic categories allowing one to grasp reality or not.[10]

8. INFORMATION TECHNOLOGY

The derivation of hierarchy as a universal form is often posed in terms of information processing. Arrow (1974) briskly claims that since it is more efficient to send all information pertaining to a certain decision to a central point where the decision is made than to have the information floating around more freely (he is not very clear on what the alternative might be), thus hierarchy is a natural form of organization. Galbraith (1973) sees the "quantity [sic!] of information processing demands" as the determinant of structure, and as requiring hierarchy. The logic of the deduction, as in the case of Arrow, is implicit at best, and an alternative not really posed. It is significant that he speaks of "*vertical* information systems" (our emphasis) as a complementary coordination mechanism, far down the list of palliatives for the imperfections of hierarchy.

Clearly, modern information technology has changed the situation, and also allows us to see more clearly the gaps in the logic of the information–hierarchy link. Information can now be made accessible to virtually everybody in a firm, given proper training and incentives. Channeling of information can be, and is, organized horizontally as much as vertically. We can move decisions, together with the additional information needed, to key information points, rather than the other way around. Modern information technology allows a radical flattening of the hierarchy and substitutes for formal organizational structure.[11] Thus, information technology *allows* less hierarchical, vertical structures. They *can*, as much research shows, also be used to strengthen verticality and control. In particular, the widespread and effective use of information systems for control purposes basically removes one of the main reasons for having a hierarchy. It is further undermined by the proliferating, spontaneous use of information systems in organizations; a use that frequently short-circuits the hierarchy. Particularly salient examples of rendering the hierarchy obsolete are the cases of the observed emergence of firm *internal* markets (where none were planned or existed), and lateral sharing of operating information on a routine basis (which often circumvents the formal reporting hierarchy contrary to company policy). (See Hagström 1991 and 1992.)

At anyrate, the choice of basic form is less constrained than heretofore.

9. MOTIVATION

Most firms find that the extremes of hierarchy, in the sense of clear super-
and subordination and of rigorously defined areas of action and responsibility, are shunned by an increasing number of employees, and more so according to the amount of education they have. To some extent, this may be
a reflection of perceived inefficiencies of hierarchy and the associated arbi-
trariness of positions in it. However, there are probably also more cultural
and psychological factors at work. Competition for "human resources"
(a term rapidly losing credibility, the firm is seen as the resource for the
human investors, i.e. the employees!) is therefore adding to the pressures to
find alternatives to hierarchy. One indication that the hierarchy is creaking
is the emergence of dual (or more) career tracks. Increasingly, promotion is
not necessarily "upwards," but lateral, specialist careers are again respected
(a return to the U-form?), "managers" may be paid less than key technical
specialists.

10. THE DEFICIENCIES OF HIERARCHY AND DOMINANT THEORIES

Trying to make sense of the pressures on hierarchy discussed above in
terms of the received theories of organization forces a recognition of some
basic problems of the latter. Three weaknesses stand out: the lack of a
positive definition of hierarchy, which in its turn would allow a specification
of alternatives; the neglect of issues of *creation and innovation*; and the
associated shallowness in considering the complications of *knowledge*—its
distribution in space, over organizational boundaries and its change over
time.

Concerning *definition* little needs to be added to what has already been
said. The reliance on an intuitive understanding of the concept as a universal trait of organizational (or all) ordering masks a great diversity in actual
organizational forms, and a multifarious practical experimentation with
solutions to the coordination problems, broadly understood. On paper, two
direct competitors may appear to be "M-formed." However, when you look
at how they actually work, they may be very different, and the visible
structural aspects less important than other "control instruments."

The lack of precision and discrimination also means that alternatives are
conceived obscurely. Williamson (1975) sees the "peer group" as the real
alternative. In our view, this is to claim too much territory for "hierarchy,"
putting the alternatives on an infertile reservation where not much organization at all is possible. The relevant comparison is between ABB's radical
decentralization and "global matrix," and General Electric's "boundaryless
organization,"[12] not between any of these and a peer group. And, the

comparison cannot be reduced to one of U- vs. M-form, or geographical-vs. product-based organizations.

Another effect of the lack of definition is that explanation for the prevalence of hierarchy is imprecise or not seen as necessary. The most ambitious attempt is by Simon (1962). As argued in Hedlund (1993), Simon's contention for the omnipresence of hierarchy builds on assumptions of stability and prespecification of tasks and parts that are hard to reconcile with organizational life.

Innovation and the creation of novelty deserve more discussion. There are strong arguments for suggesting at least a hierarchical ordering of tasks or work processes, if the latter are well known and unchanging. Simon's clockmaker example is appropriate here. Thus, for *exploitation* of known advantages, strategies, transactions or resources, some form of hierarchy may well be optimal, at least if we disregard the motivational aspects. However, as much of the discussion of pressures on the hierarchy attempted to show, when it is a matter of *creation* of new advantages, strategies, resources or transactions, hierarchy fares much worse. The reason is simple. The optimal configuration, interaction and "ordering" of inputs is unlikely to be the same for a new as for an old task, and different new tasks require different constellations.

It is striking how much the basic theories of the firm, including the MNC, rely on assumptions of stability and see the task of the firm as the *exploitation of givens*. The information-processing view takes given information-processing demands (expressed as a unidimensional quantity) and analyzes the appropriate coordination and control mechanisms. Transaction-cost theory takes a given transaction and analyzes the optimal governance regime. Much of the theory of the MNC and foreign direct investment (FDI) takes a given firm-specific advantage and asks how it can best be exploited. Property rights approaches take a given problem of, for example, team production and ask how to prevent cheating and shirking. In all cases, it is seen as reasonable to posit some form of hierarchy as an adequate response. However, the solutions to the problems of optimal exploitation are often obstacles in addressing problems of optimal creation, or experimentation or exploration.[13]

The third basic problem with the theory/practice match has to do with the importance of *knowledge* and its structuring in the modern firm. Increasingly, knowledge is widely distributed in space and over organizational units, and formal position in the hierarchy tells less and less about the type and quality of knowledge residing there. Furthermore, knowledge changes much quicker than structure, and quicker than before, which makes the matching of *knowledge* and formal *position* even more problematic. In turn, this requires new forms and structures of *action*. Multifunctional teams, projects, ad hoc groups, process organization, etc., are, in our view, responses to the inadequacy of a traditional reliance on the "line organization" being the acting vehicle of a steering top management. The words *position, knowledge* and *action* hold the key to a richer conceptualization of internal structure.

11. A THREE-DIMENSIONAL MODEL OF THE INTERNAL STRUCTURE OF THE FIRM

Multidimensionality is often advocated. Our use of the term differs in two respects from most other treatments. First, we are speaking not of a multidimensional *hierarchy*, but of a multidimensional *internal structure*, defined by three separate structures or, rather, aspects: position, knowledge and action. Second, "hierarchy" is seen as one of many ways of structuring any or all of the three dimensions we propose. Hierarchy is thus an ordering principle, a way of structuring but not the thing structured. Briefly, this particular ordering principle entails stable and universal super- and subordination, in terms of command or status, classificatory inclusion or logical implication, causal primacy or initiative. For the positional structure, the relation is primarily a command and status one. For knowledge, inclusion, implication or causality is primary.[14] For action, causality and initiative are more important. Thus, hierarchy in the positional system is primarily a command structure, in the knowledge system a structure of more and less general knowledge or skills, and in the action system a structure where some action initiates or induces other actions.

Therefore, multidimensionality here has nothing to do with "matrix organization" or the multidimensionality of the MNC structure in Bartlett and Ghoshal (1989). In the first case, it is a matter of simultaneous hierarchical ordering of the command structure according to at least two principles, like product and geography. In the second, "multidimensionality" simply means that functional, geographical and product issues all have to be handled. In our view, matrix organization is probably mostly a grave mistake, and multidimensionality à la Bartlett and Ghoshal an expression of a wish rather than a specification of how to make it come true.[15]

Why then positions, knowledge and action? The test of the idea is in its application, and we will attempt to show that the distinctions cast light on the internal structure of modern firms. The diagnosis above of tensions in hierarchical organizations constitutes some ground for suggesting that the framework at least should be tried. In addition, we cannot refrain from adding that these three dimensions were constitutive of hierarchy in the first known use of the term. Dionysius the Areopagite invented the word hierarchy (literally, rule through the sacred) in the fifth century AD,[16] and defined it in two books on the celestial and ecclesiastical hierarchies, respectively. In the former, he claims that the "... divine hierarchy is a hierarchy *not only of beings, but also of knowledge and action*" (Dionysius (trans.) 1981

17, our emphasis). Replace "beings"—which for Dionysius covers everything from God to the lowest angels, strictly organized, in nine levels—with the more mundane and profane "positions," and we have our model.

The beauty of Dionysius' models is that *the three structures all coincide*. God is the highest being, so high indeed that he cannot be correctly understood by lesser beings. But he is also highest in terms of knowledge and all that is known at lower levels, and more. He is also highest in terms of action, takes the important initiatives and makes the rest of Creation move. The doctrines of God's omniscience and omnipotence flow directly as hypotheses from Dionysius' model.

A modern corporation is not heaven. Still, it is interesting to note the resemblance of the defense of hierarchy in various strands of economics and organization theory and Dionysius' arguments. There is a hierarchy because knowledge is greater, or at least more encompassing, higher up. Strategies (big action) emanate from the top and induce tactics (lesser action) further down. A structure of people with greater and/or more general knowledge, initiating big actions and therefore being entitled to top positions, emerges. We could call such a system, whereas in Dionysius the three dimensions coincide perfectly, a "Hierarchy," with a capital H. The humbler version, "hierarchy" is reserved for more limited application of the ordering principle. No modern organization is likely to be entirely free of hierarchy, but is even less likely to be close to a Hierarchy. The reason is that such coincidence is improbable and short-lived, because of the nature of the three systems.[17] We will consider them in turn.

12. THE POSITIONAL STRUCTURE

This denotes the ordering of individuals and organizational units in terms of formal status, location and authority—the "boxes and arrows" of the organization. It is usually, but not necessarily hierarchical in the sense of clear notions of levels and superiority. It is also relatively unambiguous, clearly delineating where things start and end, who belongs where, etc.

The relations between levels historically entail prerogatives of command and reflect status and perhaps seniority differences. In modern organizations, however, there is a "secularization" of the positional structure. Even if still hierarchical, relations become less of a matter of instruction and command and more of information, inspiration and—curiously— monitoring and control.[18] When action and knowledge meet in other constellations than those implied by the positional hierarchy, the role of the latter becomes in one sense more "old-fashioned." Seniority has much to do with it—the "know-how" and "know-what," and in monitoring them, albeit in a less direct way than in the "foreman model" and more substantially informed than in the "portfolio manager" model.

In the extreme, the positional hierarchy becomes an address list, facilitating the location of competence but involving little real action or decision. Some consulting organizations resemble this model. People work in projects temporarily molded to fit competence requirements. They do belong to an organizational unit, but this may mean very little except as an address and a psychological and logistical "home." Sometimes, the position is explicitly a reward, but does not entail any management responsibility "in the line." This happens, instead, in the action structure, typically in the form of temporary projects.

As the efficiency grounds for Hierarchy weaken, reward, monitoring, and status grounds for positional hierarchy are strengthened, relatively spoken. We see an almost ethical, symbolical, and mythical aspect of leadership emerging as important criteria for placement in the positional hierarchy. However, this applies primarily at very senior levels. For most organizations, *the positional hierarchy does, and in many cases probably should, reflect the prerequisites of exploitation.* Boxes and arrows can more easily be drawn for known things, and a "small coincidence" of position, knowledge and action may be possible for large parts of exploitation. The risk of course, is to reinforce the bias against creation. Therefore, insisting on the lack of coincidence and protecting the intensity of the knowledge and action systems become important, even if a rationale beyond rewards and corporate ethics can be given for the positional structure.[19]

13. THE KNOWLEDGE STRUCTURE

The humbler analogue of the omniscience idea in the secular realm has been the hope to establish a structure of knowledge with more "fundamental" or "basic" sciences at the top (in spite of fundaments usually being at the bottom), with the "queen of science" physics, at the most elevated position. All other knowledge should be derived from physical laws. Very few people today see things this way, even when it comes to the relation between, say, physics and chemistry. This is even more the case in industrial settings. A paper company harbors no illusions about the art of paper making being reducible to principles of forestry or vice versa. Thus, the knowledge structure of a firm is much more a matter of *combining* different elements "laterally" than of deriving one from the other. Knowledge is structured as an archipelago, where islands are distinct but reachable from each other, rather than as a mountain, where from the top, you can see all the rest.

The argument is strengthened when considering that "knowledge" is appropriately taken to imply both cognitive precepts and *skills*. The latter are even more "horizontally" related to each other than the former. They are probably also structured "flatter." Geometry can be expressed in a multilevel deductive system, but drawing is not easily described in terms of different distinct levels. The best way of learning a skill is to work directly with a master in the act. It is significant that the old master/young apprentice system is still the preferred route for transferring very complex skills, such as playing or building a violin. One can talk of a literal "embodiment" of these skills. With skills, we also observe a resistance to "decoupling" of levels. A master pianist cannot forget about technical details and concentrate only on interpretation and the large lines. Moreover, in knowledge-intensive organizations, it is common to require even the most recognized experts to be involved in seemingly menial activities. Professors have to teach undergraduates, take pride in performing experiments themselves, etc.

Another, related aspect of knowledge that makes it resistant to "hierarchization" is the need to keep in touch with the substance of knowledge. It is difficult to translate knowledge (and, in particular, skills) to higher, abstract principles. The more knowledge-intensive a firm, the more difficult it is to devise strategies and manage people through financial or other abstract criteria only. *Information* can of course be amassed on the financial consequences of the firm's action, and a crude feedback mechanism can be maintained, but the corrections are essentially blind and not likely to be very effective. Not least when it comes to recruitment and promotion, knowledge of substance is required, not only of consequences of prespecified actions.

It is obvious that relevant knowledge is widely and increasingly diffused in space, even within a single firm. If one considers the need to work closely with key customers and suppliers, this is even more so. In addition, knowledge and its location changes incessantly. Thus, even a simple list of competencies is an impermanent map, and much more so than any greater structured enumeration of a firm's knowledge. This is not to say that one cannot have ambitions to concentrate on some parts, only that their relative importance and interdependencies are hard to freeze for long, and that it may be ineffective to do so.

Thus, the knowledge structure is fleeting and everchanging. Knowledge is structured relatively *horizontally*, *flatly*, *temporarily* and *circularly*.[20] In comparison, the positional structure is more vertical, deep, permanent and sequential.

14. THE ACTION STRUCTURE

Action in the Hierarchy is structured in terms of big, inclusive versus small, derived, i.e. as strategy versus tactics, with strategy being the prerogative and responsibility of the positional top. Because knowledge is so diffused and concentrated further down in the positional structure, strategies in most firms today have to be initiated rather in the middle (cf. Nonaka 1988). Direction from the very top is suggestive and confined to judging the merits of substantive rival proposals from the middle. There is no doubt that it is an important task to confer much power on those who exercise it. However, the initiative and substantive design are in hands and brains further down.

Moreover, the main distinction may not be strategy and tactics. Competitive advantage seems to arise from many small things held together by historically inertial competencies and knowledge, rather than by premeditated strategic thrusts, such as in war. The integrity of action is achieved to a large extent by recruitment and other human-resource policies, and by the suggestive but open frameworks hinted at above. The role of the top is to inspire and provide the organizational framework allowing the experimentation ensuring a continuous development of old and creation of new ideas. Thus, the main distinction in the action structure is between the administration of the old and the generation of novelty, in our terms between exploitation and creation.

For reasons discussed under "knowledge structure" above, the optimal composition and leadership of units involved in innovation cannot be prespecified and are likely to involve much horizontal communication. *The archetypical action unit becomes the multiskilled, multiknowledgeable, and temporary project team.* As is known from research in product development, these need to be protected from the influence of "the line" (the positional hierarchy, as we hypothesize) and led by strong people. Indeed, here we find a flat and temporary—but very strong—mini-hierarchy. Words like discipline, leadership, and commitment figure prominently in analyses of the virtues of team-based organizations. Thus, the fleeting overall organization of the action structure *masks* a tough and sometimes rigid microstructure within single projects.

The difference between this archetypical action unit and the corresponding Hierarchical one (the department with a stable, given task) is very great: temporary instead of semipermanent; composed of people with widely varying competencies rather than similar ones; autonomy and protection from the line instead of always being subordinated to the next higher level; expected to handle uncertainty within its own activities instead of being buffered from it through sequencing and queuing; and so on. In practice, leadership furthermore often has to move as the project progresses, depending on the specific competencies needed. The consequences of this type of working for motivation are significant, and so are those for stress and for tolerance of uncertainty. Over time, there is also a rotation of roles, so that the same individual may be one person's superior in one project and his or her subordinate in the next one. This challenges the idea in the Hierarchy that the order is universal and eternal (for all issues and forever).

Clearly, this poses psychological problems for those raised in the logic of Hierarchy.

In the Weberian bureaucracy, positional structure exists almost by definition in conjunction with knowledge and action prerogatives. Even the language betrays the affinity to Dionysius' idea type. We speak of "areas of competence," simultaneously implying a task and the requisite knowledge to perform it.[21] The classical bureaucracy is a structure of impersonal *roles*, not of persons. The assumption is that there is a match between individual knowledge and domains of action, and that such a match can be upheld in a multilayered, hierarchical system. Our hypothesis is that such a match is increasingly impossible or constraining, and those firms that persist in trying to structure according to this principle will disappear through competition.

15. A DYNAMIC VIEW OF INTERNAL STRUCTURE

To recapitulate, we will summarize our view of the internal structure of a dynamic firm. We will assume that it is involved in knowledge-intensive business and is multinational in terms of sales, production and R&D.

The dynamic firm manages two sets of activities—for exploitation and creation, respectively. It consciously makes a distinction between the two and guards against a natural bias for exploitation to crowd out creation. Its internal structure is best understood as composed of three different systems—of positions, knowledge and action, respectively.

The *positional structure* is the most stable and the most "hierarchical." However, its importance is primarily as an address list, a psychological "home" for the employees of the firm, and a reward and status system. It has a more real, operational sense for exploitation than for creation. It is structured to match knowledge and action systems for exploitation as well as possible with positions.

However, the increasing importance of creation and continuous improvement also in exploitation undermines these efforts. The dynamic firm does not easily change its positional hierarchy, nor does it engage in matrix organization or other complex formal structures. Instead, it ensures flexibility by not investing the positional structure with tasks it is not equipped for. Thus, it is imperfect for action, but known to be so.

The *knowledge structure* is fleeting: diffused over geography and units, horizontal, flat, temporary, circular and rapidly changing. It is maintained to a large extent by recruitment, rotation and other human-resource policies. Its real core is in the middle rather than at the top of the positional hierarchy. It is managed[22] through creation of specialist careers, facilitating interaction between dissimilar fields of competence, by maintaining master/apprentice structures, by composing temporary teams, and by fostering close links with the outside world.

The *action structure* is by and large a mirror of the knowledge one. The archetypical unit of action is the temporary, multiskilled team with strong leadership and protected from encroachment by the line organizations.[23]

The dynamic firm does not dispose of hierarchy, but of Hierarchy, which in our terms becomes a special case where the three structures coincide and are all ordered in a one-way, non-recursive system of levels. There is still hierarchy in the dynamic firm, in the positional structures and typically in temporary projects.

16. DOES THE THREE-DIMENSIONAL STRUCTURE EXIST
IN REAL FIRMS?

The discussion so far has been conceptual, theoretical and speculative. We have relied on empirical research, primarily on the MNC and on product development, but on the whole the suggestions are derived on a priori grounds. The usefulness of the scheme needs to be tested on real firms. Does it help us understand the internal structure and dynamism of firms? Only thorough empirical research can provide answers. For example, *are* strategic initiatives being decoupled from the formal, positional hierarchy? *Is* the latter becoming flatter? *Do* companies work more in projects rather than departments? Arguably, the first recognizable firms were the *societas maris* (maritime firm) appearing in the ninth and tenth centuries in what is today Italy (Braudel 1979/1982). This was a partnership, typically for one voyage only, where one partner stayed on shore and the other went with the ship. The firm was clearly associated with a specific task and was dissolved upon completion.[24] In present-day terminology, the voyage was a project. Thus, there are historical precursors of the "projectified" firm.

It does seem that there are also important modern examples of firms on which our conceptual garment fits well. Particularly some consulting and professional service firms seem to describe themselves in terms very similar to ours; a structure of rewards and position with partnerships of varying seniority, a system for nurturing specialized skills and knowledge, and extreme reliance on temporary projects as the way of acting, for exploitation as well as for creation. Promotion in the positional hierarchy is dependent on performance in projects and concerning professional development. The CEO, or corresponding role, in such firms is not the most glamorous one, but rather a service function among many.

Perhaps an interesting parallel to our posited disjunction of positional and other realms is provided by Aoki (1990) in his analysis of the Japanese firm. Here, a vertical reward structure is combined with a horizontal information structure, which is very close to our notion of positional and knowledge structures, respectively.

Less of a parallel, but instead a sequel, to our proposed conceptualization is given by Nonaka and Takeuchi (1995). Their "hypertext" (see pp. 233 ff) organization is claimed to be more of an inductive model (Sharp and Kao being offered as companies that have come the furthest). Although Nonaka and Takeuchi (1995) preferred not to use our terminology, their proposed three dimensions of "hierarchy," "task force" and "knowledge base" map very closely on our positional, action and knowledge structures respectively.[25]

The control function of hierarchy in its traditional expression is intimately linked to a legalistic view of the firm. Our suspicion is that a strong cultural/institutional bias lurks here; a bias that in part explains the remarkable resilience of hierarchy as a model. Western countries in general, and Anglo-Saxon ones in particular, place a premium on (legal) accountability so that the structure (and associated controls) should be transparent also to external observers. In addition, this assumes a revealed—or at least latent—*adversarial* relationship between the parties involved, both outside and inside the firm. When this adversarial relationship is dissipated (as it often is in the modern firms) and/or is incongruent with the dominant values of a society (as in the Eastern world) the presumption of the hierarchical model as a valid generalization is called into question. Our explication of three dimensions of structure does away with the restrictive assumption of necessarily adversarial relationships. The positional dimension deals with people, and the action dimension with what is done. "Control and command" coupled with financial reward do not convey the different incentives that are associated with the three dimensions. Instead, they offer a much greater repertoire, which do not preclude that the interests of the firm and of the individual employees coincide.[26] Words like "trust," "common values," "commitment" are readily compatible with our view of the internal structure, and are often found to be remarkably effective for fostering motivation. Managers know this, while academics all too often reduce them to "self-interest," which is the only way they can be squeezed into the traditional hierarchical model.

Our treatment of the internal structure of the firm also has implications for how to view "boundary for the firm" issues. Such a discussion would lead too far, however. Suffice it to say that the "internal" structure also accommodates "external" parties. In particular, action and knowledge are not confined to any legal boundaries of the firm. Moreover, it is not unlikely that the increasing dissonance between the formal, legal structure of many complex firms and the de facto structure of how they function is a practical indication of the untenability of a single dimensional hierarchy as mirrored in the firm's legal structure.

17. THREE DIMENSIONS: AN ILLUSTRATION

The management literature is presently full of advocacy for temporary and multifunctional teams, and for nonhierarchical organizations (although exactly what this means is rarely clarified). An example is Peters (1993), where both knowledge management and project organization are extensively discussed and documented. For example, the structures of EDS and McKinsey as described by Peters are not too dissimilar from our prescriptions for the dynamic firm. Our contribution may thus be a modest attempt to provide a conceptual scheme and framework for hypothesis formulation, making sense of the intensive experimentation with new organizational forms.

However, this type of evidence is indirect, at best. Employing the notion of *trying out theory*,[27] we investigated one firm that purportedly exhibited many of the traits of dynamism in the internal structure that has been discussed above. Trying out theory does not amount to any testing of our hypotheses, but is rather a confrontation of theory with a real-life setting which allows for an initial test for plausibility and consistency.

Oticon A/S is a $100 million hearing-aid producer domiciled in Denmark. The company employs some 1,000 people worldwide and sells more than 90% of its production outside Denmark through its own subsidiaries or agents in more than 100 countries. Oticon has gone through a process of forceful organizational transformation, having fallen on hard times at the end of the 1980s after a long history of success. The most radical change to date concerns the white-collar workers and management in Denmark, making up a total of 150–200 people. As of 8:00 a.m., 8 August 1991, this is what the company calls a "spaghetti organization."

Every employee is perceived as belonging to one pool of resources. At any given time, a person is tied to a *project* (or—more likely—several projects), to a *specialty* or profession, and to a *"people" dimension*. Projects are most important as they come closest to constituting the operations of Oticon. Specialities represent the vestiges of a functional organization by providing mechanisms for the maintenance of distinctive, often functional, skills and expertise. "People" refers to a personal development. Whereas an individual's boss could be virtually anybody in a project, the other two dimensions each have 10 to 12 people appointed as supervisors (with considerable overlap of individuals in the two groups). Assignment along any one dimension is voluntary and varies over time. The "spaghetti" of the organization is seen to illustrate *the* disorderly links *resulting, but deceptively so, in an appearance of chaos*. Looking down into a pot of boiling spaghetti, there is no apparent order. However, we can easily pull out a single strand of spaghetti and follow it from beginning to end. The individual strands are the projects in Oticon. Perhaps needless to say, there is no formal organization chart for the company.

It is important that none of the three dimensions implies any direct, formal managerial control. Project leaders have responsibility for their projects, but Oticon relies on personal interest (in the true sense of the word) and peer pressure to ensure performance. There is no control of working hours. "People" is a supportive activity with a mentor, who informally discusses personal goals and development with an individual: discussions that recur on an ad hoc basis but at a minimum are held twice in a year. Specialities are similar in that they largely boil down to meeting as a group, e.g. marketing or mechanical development, on Friday afternoons listening to an invited speaker or exchanging views on a specific, common topic.

At any given time some 90 projects are running at Oticon. They can be anything from acquiring a new financial software package to improving production support for local customization of hearing-aids. Traditional job specifications do not exist any more. Everybody has several "jobs"; some permanent, some temporary. Instead of selecting people for fixed positions, the idea is one of fitting jobs to people. That way, Oticon can reduce training costs and benefit from people's multiple skills. The basis idea is that people have long been recognized as multidimensional in their everyday lives; that they play different roles at different times. Why should they not do so when in organizations?

Departments have not disappeared totally. The Accounting "Department" has 12 people, but they do the accounts for all the Danish units, which comprise some 200 salaried staff and 500 workers in total. Two people manage the reception. The Information Systems Group amounts to six persons. These "Departments" are seen as more or less permanent projects. The "executive management" for all of Oticon, including the foreign subsidiaries, consists of two managers, two assistants and two secretaries. However, all these people also have other tasks. This includes the CEO, who lately has been working on rewriting the instruction booklets for hearing-aids in order to improve their readability.

Projects rely on physical co-location of team members. The instability of projects in terms of size and duration means that people will move around a lot. To the greatest extent possible, places of work are standardized, and furniture, plants and equipment easy to shift. What remains of the personal "office" is a small (filing) cabinet on wheels,[28] since real mobility precludes tugging around masses of documentation. However, not all paper has been eliminated. On the top floor, there is a "paper room" where incoming mail is sorted into pigeonholes. The mail is read, whatever is to be kept is scanned into the computer archive system, and the paper is then shredded. Paper confetti then floats gently down a plexiglass chute for all to see. Some mail has to be kept as originals, primarily for legal reasons, amounting to about ten items a day. After scanning, they are literally stacked in the basement. If a hard copy of an electronically stored document is needed, it is simply printed out, worked on, and then either sent from the head office or shredded at the end of the day.

Electronic storage not only permits access from any desktop computer, it also improves the general availability of information. The insistence of face-to-face oral communication whenever and wherever at all possible is an article of faith at Oticon, since it is seen as the most effective way of coordinating work and of inducing creative new ideas. The main activity of the "spaghetti organization" is product development, in a broad sense.

Basically, only information on salaries and reviews, as well as on performance and cost of products under development, are protected. Project leaders determine who has access to what information about projects. The general rule is that all

Strategy/Organization

information is open unless a good case can be made for keeping it restricted, and then one has to spend a considerable time on specifying access rules. For example, if any employee wants to see last month's report from the Dutch subsidiary, it is possible to do so.

In terms of short-term performance, the experiment is a success. After losses that threatened Oticon's very survival, profits have returned and reached DKK 86 million (pretax) on sales of DKK 661 million in 1993, and DKK 134 million on sales of DKK 750 million the following year. In addition, R&D spending has grown to almost 7% of turnover; a very high figure for a hearing-aid manufacturer. However, the jury is obviously still out on the question of the long-term viability of Oticon's "spaghetti" organization.

Although the three structural dimensions arguably are present in all firms, they are neatly demonstrated in the case of Oticon. Action and Oticon's projects, as well as knowledge and Oticon's "specialties," map well onto each other. The "people" dimension at Oticon and our positional structure are less well aligned, however. One reason could be the relatively small size (cf. the discussion above) of Oticon and there being no need to identify the positional structure explicitly (cf. the groups of supervisors). The Oticon illustration also has a clear bias towards creation over exploitation and is this far an experiment on a rather small scale. Still, there is a remarkable congruence between our scheme and with the operationalization of structure at Oticon.

The resulting complexity of the internal organization is only a "problem" for the external observer who tries to draw the organization chart. Internally, the complexity disappears as each employee knows his/her role in the organization and is never required to provide a rationale in traditional terms for how the whole organization functions. The degree of complexity perceived depends on one's vantage point.

Moreover, the Oticon experience shows that people's function and position along the three structural dimensions can change over time: a recognition that firms are less stable than Dionysius' celestial Hierarchy.

NOTES

1. For an extensive critique of Simon's assumptions, and particularly his famous clockmaker example, see Hedlund (1993), and for a theoretical assessment that hierarchical design of a production process does not necessarily imply hierarchical management, see Radner (1992).
2. Hedlund (1986) discusses the possibility, implied by Koestler (1978) that hierarchy is a perceptual and cognitive interpretation scheme rather than an attribute

of the "real world," i.e., that hierarchy is in the eye of the beholder rather than existing within the organization.

3. Rumelt (1984) provides an extreme account of why firms find it difficult to change. For an overview of the evolutionary approach, see Teece, Pisano and Schuen (1990).

4. In Economics, firms are naturally basically the same, either minimizing production costs or transaction costs. There is, however, a recent surge in interest in the role of management in formal theoretical Economics (in particular as exemplified by Radner (1992); see also Milgrom and Roberts (1992, esp. ch. 4)).

5. Wary of being too sweeping, we can still acknowledge support for our view from Radner: "Students of management are well aware that many interactions in a typical firm are not organized hierarchically, even if the formal organization chart looks that way. Nevertheless, it is an important principle of organization, both in its prevalence and in the prevalence of attempts to circumvent it." (1992: 1383)

6. The definition may seem impressionistic, and indeed is so. Simon (1962) uses much the same words, so we are in good company. Most people do not bother to define the concept at all, treating it as intuitively clear. We will get to a more precise definition below. See also Hedlund (1993), where a slightly more formal treatment is attempted.

7. See further Hedlund and Ridderstråle (1992).

8. For an analysis in the case of the multinational corporation (MNC), see Hennart (1982).

9. See Hagström (1991 and 1992).

10. In Swedish and German the word "concept" literally and etymologically has to do with the grasp (*grepp*, *Griff*, respectively) of the hand, a characteristically empirical position. "Concept" and its Latin origins have to do with being conceived from something, created either out of the womb or, more commonly, the imagination of an intellect. Hierarchy seems to be more of a concept than a *begrepp/Begriff*.

11. For a discussion and empirical evidence in the context of MNCs, see Hagström (1991 and 1992).

12. An interesting side-issue is the coining of descriptions in firms themselves, of their own organization. This contributes to a Tower-of-Babel situation, where the same term means different things to different people, and different terms stand for the same thing. Combined with the Tower-of-Babble erected by organizational consultants trying to push their wares and the Tower-of-Abstraction inhabited by many scholars, both in Economics and organization theory, there is little wonder that intelligent and constructive discussion is rare.

13. See March (1991) for some reasons why exploitation crowds out exploration.

14. Logics surely does not *command* mathematics, but *may* imply or contain it. It is worthy of note that Simon's defense of hierarchy partly relies on allowing *physical composition* to define hierarchy. Elementary particles constitute atoms, which constitute molecules, which form tissue, and so on to organs, individuals (thus exactly nonindivisible; that is, divisible . . .), groups, societies, etc.

15. Bartlett and Ghoshal (1989) explicitly warn against taking their view as support for a formal matrix structure. Instead, they emphasize a number of subtler managerial levers.

16. See Hedlund (1988) and (1993) for a fuller discussion of this remarkable source.
17. We will use "system" and "structure" interchangeably and in a nontechnical sense.
18. Control in a wide sense; it is directed to people, to individuals rather than to operations. Traditionally, people and their actions were not seen as separable.
19. We do not discuss the possibility of nonhierarchical positional structures here, although for sure they exist. In the MNC, the status and power structures are often very complex and are not easily—even in terms of boxes and arrows—collapsed into a hierarchical structure. Parallel positional hierarchies coexist, and the historical track record for such seemingly unwieldy structures is rather impressive. The European model of MNC organization (see Franko 1976) entailed such personalized, nonformal, elements and still survives beneath the surface of cleaner boxes and arrows in many firms. Also, higher position in terms of formal management responsibility may not mean highest status, as in universities and professional firms.
20. Circular in the sense that different levels and items imply and require each other reciprocally, as in the case of the pianist above. Also, the importance of learning through feedback for knowledge development makes for circularity. Such recursiveness was central in McCulloch's (1965) original suggestion that the brain was organized heterarchically.
21. In Swedish, there is a saying comforting those who may feel they are not up to the requirements of a high position: "To those God gives a position, he also gives the wisdom to manage it."
22. It should be remembered that "manage" is not really the right word here, if anywhere in the dynamic firm. The word comes from French "*manège*" and other similar Latin words, indicating the usually circular course on which horses are trained. To liken the manager to the horse trainer with the whip in the middle of the *manège* is amusing, but in itself suggests that other concepts are needed.
23. It should be noted that projects are increasingly used also for exploitation. *Kai-zen*, process management, reengineering, time competition and other popular approaches to operational improvement all rely to a large extent on temporary teams.
24. The word "firm" comes from the Portuguese *firma* signature. In some languages, e.g., Swedish, the word "firm" (*företag*) has two distinct meanings: firms and tasks.
25. Nonaka and Takeuchi (1995), however, build their discussion more closely around knowledge. "Hierarchy" concerns the "exploitation of knowledge," "the task force" deals with the "creation of new knowledge", and "the knowledge base" refers to the "recategorizing" and "recontextualizing of knowledge" (see pp. 233 ff).
26. Whereas we see it to be likely that interests coincide and the structural dimensions do not, the opposite holds for traditional conceptions of hierarchy.
27. For an introduction and elaboration of the concept, see Hagström (1991). One can think of *trying out* theory as an initial field test of a prototype.
28. The contents of the cabinet is left up to individual choice. Apart from "necessary" papers, brochures, pictures, office supplies and the like, they tend to be used for personal belongings.

REFERENCES

Alchian, A. A. (1950), "Uncertainty, Evolution and Economic Theory," *Journal of Political Economy*, 58/2: 211–22.

Aldrich, H. E. (1979), *Organizations and Environments* (Englewood Cliffs, NJ: Prentice-Hall).

Aoki, M. (1990), "Toward an Economic Model of the Japanese Firm," *Journal of Economic Literature*, 28/1: 1–27.

Arrow, K. (1974), *The Limits of Organization* (New York: W. W. Norton).

Bartlett, C. A. and Ghoshal, S. (1989), *Managing Across Borders: The Transnational Solution* (Cambridge, Mass.: Harvard Business School Press).

Braudel, F. (1979/1982), *Civilizations and Capitalism 15th–18th Century, ii. The Wheels of Commerce* (New York: Harper & Row) (originally pub. in French, 1979).

Burgelman, R. A. (1983), "A Process Model of Internal Corporate Venturing in the Diversified Major Firm," *Administrative Science Quarterly*, 28/2: 223–44.

Caves, R. E. (1980), "Industrial Organization, Corporate Strategy and Structure," *Journal of Economic Literature*, 28/1: 64–92.

Chandler, A. D., Jr. (1962), *Strategy and Structure: Chapters in the History of the American Industrial Enterprise* (Cambridge, Mass.: MIT Press).

Cohen, M. D., March, J. G. and Olsen, J. P. (1972), "A Garbage Can Model of Organizational Choice," *Administrative Science Quarterly*, 17/1: 1–25.

Cyert, R. M. and March, J. G. (1963), *A Behavioral Theory of the Firm* (Englewood Cliffs, NJ: Prentice-Hall).

Dionysius, The Pseudo-Areopagite (1981 edn.), *The Ecclesiastical Hierarchy*, trans. and annotated by Thomas L. Campbell (Lanham, Md.: University Press of America).

Doz, Y. L. and Prahalad, C. K. (1987), "A Process Model of Strategic Redirection in Large Complex Firms: The Case of Multinational Corporations," in A. Pettigrew (ed.), *The Management of Strategic Change* (Oxford: Blackwell) 63–83.

Franko, L. G. (1976), *The European Multinationals* (Greenwich, Conn.: Greylock Press).

Galbraith, J. R. (1973), *Designing Complex Organizations* (Reading, Mass: Addison-Wesley).

Gottinger, H. W. (1983), *Coping with Complexity: Perspectives for Economics, Management and Social Sciences* (Dordrecht, Neth.: D. Riedel).

Hagström, P. (1991), *The "Wired" MNC: The Role of Information Systems for Structural Change in Complex Organizations* (Stockholm: Institute of International Business).

——(1992), "Inside the 'Wired' MNC," in C. Antonelli (ed.), *The Economics of Information Networks* (Amsterdam: Elsevier Science Publishers).

Hedlund, G. (1986), "The Hypermodern MNC—A Heterarchy?", *Human Resource Management*, 25/1: 9–35.

——(1988), "The First Theory of Hierarchy: Contemplation on Its Pervasiveness in Modern Business Life." Research Paper 88/16, Institute of International Business, Stockholm.

Hedlund, G. (1993), "Assumptions of Hierarchy and Heterarchy," in S. Ghoshal and D. E. Westney (eds.), *Organization Theory and the Multinational Corporation* (New York: St. Martin's Press), 211–36.

—— and Ridderstråle, J. (1992), "Toward the N-form Corporation: Exploitation and Creation in the MNC," in B. Toyne and D. Nigh (eds.), *Perspectives on International Business: Theory, Research and Institutional Arrangements* (Columbia, SC: University of South Carolina Press), forthcoming.

—— and Rolander, D. (1991), "Action in Heterarchies: New Approaches to Managing the MNC," in C. A. Bartlett, Y. L. Doz and G. Hedlund (eds.), *Managing the Global Firm* (London: Routledge).

Hennart, J. F. (1982), *A Theory of Multinational Enterprise* (Ann Arbor, Mich.: University of Michigan Press).

Holmström, B. R. and Tirole, J. (1989), "The Theory of the Firm," in R. Schmalensee and R. D. Willig (eds.), *Handbook of Industrial Organization*, (Amsterdam: Elsevier Science Publishers), i. 61–133.

Koestler, A. (1978), *Janus—A Summing Up* (New York: Random House).

Lessard, D. R. and Nohria, N. (1990), "Rediscovering Functions in the MNC: The Role of Expertise in Firms' Responses to Shifting Exchange Rates," in Bartlett, Doz, and Hedlund (eds.), *Managing the Global Firm*.

McCulloch, W. (1965), *Embodiments of Mind* (Cambridge, Mass.).

March, J. G. (1991), "Exploitation and Exploration in Organizational Learning," *Organization Science*, 2/1: 71–87.

—— and Simon, H. (1958), *Organizations* (New York: John Wiley).

Milgrom, P. and Roberts, J. (1992), *Economics, Organizations and Management* (Englewood Cliffs, NJ: Prentice-Hall).

Nelson, R. R. (1991), "Why Do Firms Differ, and How Does It Matter?" *Strategic Management Journal*, 12 Special Issue: 61–74.

—— and Winter, S. G. (1982), *An Evolutionary Theory of Economic Change* (Cambridge, Mass.: Harvard University Press).

Nonaka, I. (1988), "Toward Middle-Up-Down Management: Accelerating Information Creation," *Sloan Management Review*, 29/3 (spring), 9–18.

—— and Takeuchi, H. (1995), *The Knowledge-Creating Company: How Japanese Companies Create the Dynamics of Innovation* (New York: Oxford University Press).

Ouchi, W. (1980), "Markets, Bureaucracies, and Clans," *Administrative Science Quarterly*, 25: 129–40.

Paine, L. (1972), *The Hierarchy of Hell* (London: Robert Hale).

Penrose, E. (1959), *The Theory of the Growth of the Firm* (London: Blackwell).

Prahalad, C. K. and Hamel, G. (1990), "The Core Competence of the Corporation," *Harvard Business Review*, 68/3 (May/June), 79–91.

Radner, R. (1992), "Hierarchy: The Economics of Managing," *Journal of Economic Literature*, 30/3: 1382–415.

Rumelt, R. P. (1984), "Towards a Strategic Theory of the Firm," in R. B. Lamb (ed.), *Competitive Strategy Management* (Englewood Cliffs, NJ: Prentice-Hall), 556–70.

Saaty, T. L. (1980), *The Analytic Hierarchy Process: Planning, Priority Setting, Resource Allocation* (New York: McGraw-Hill).

—— (1990), "How to Make a Decision: The Analytic Hierarchy Process," *European Journal of Operational Research*, 48/1: 9–26.

Scott, W. R. (1987), *Organizations: Rational, Natural, and Open Systems*, 2nd edn. (Englewood Cliffs, NJ: Prentice-Hall).

Shleifer, A. and Vishny, R. W. (1991), "Takeovers in the '60s and the '80s: Evidence and Implications," *Strategic Management Journal*, 12, Special Issue (Winter), 51–9.

Simon, H. (1962), "The Architecture of Complexity," *Proceedings of the American Philosophical Society*, 106: 467–82.

Teece, F., Pisano, G. and Schuen, A. (1990), "Firm Capabilities, Resources, and the Concept of Strategy," CCC Working Paper 90–8, CRM, U. C. Berkeley, Calif.

Weber, M. (1924/1947), *The Theory of Social and Economic Organization* (New York: Oxford University Press) (orig. publ. in German, 1924).

White, R. E. and Poynter, T. A. (1990), "Organizing for a World-Wide Advantage," in C. A. Bartlett, Y. L. Doz and G. Hedlund (eds.), *Managing the Global Firm* (London: Routledge).

Williamson, O. E. (1975), *Markets and Hierarchies: Analysis and Antitrust Implications* (New York: Free Press).

9

The Wide (and Increasing) Spread of Technological Competencies in the World's Largest Firms: A Challenge to Conventional Wisdom*

PARI PATEL AND KEITH PAVITT

1. INTRODUCTION

The purpose of this paper is to throw light on the nature and determinants of the technological competencies of the world's largest firms, and on their implications for corporate strategy. The subject of firm-specific competencies is of increasing interest to practitioners, and to theorists, who are seeking to explain why firms provide different ranges of goods and services, why they change at different rates and in different directions over time, and what makes them competitive (Rumelt 1974; Prahalad and Hamel 1990; Dosi *et al.* 1992; Carlsson and Eliasson 1991; Teece *et al.* 1990). Our main data source is systematic information of US patenting by more than 400 of the world's largest technologically active firms, broken down by each firm's headquarters country and principal product group, and by the technical field and country of the inventor of each patent.[1]

1.1 Coping with Complexity

Our theoretical framework is based on the pioneering work of Nelson and Winter (1982) that combines the insights of Schumpeter on the central importance of innovation in the dynamics of competition, and of Simon and his colleagues on the satisficing behavior of business firms. Technological artifacts, and the organizational and economic worlds in which they are embedded, are complex: they each comprise so many variables and interactions that it is impossible fully to model, predict and control their behavior through explicit and codified theories and guidelines. Certainty about the future, probabilistic risk and optimization are therefore impossible. Management solves problems and makes improvements through step-by-step

* This paper is based on research at the Centre for Science, Technology and Energy and Environment Policy (STEEP), funded by the Economic and Social Research Council (ESRC) within the Science Policy Research Unit.

experimentation. In addition to codified knowledge, experience and tacit knowledge improve the effectiveness of experimentation. Essentially the same approach underlies Lindblom's prescriptions in public policy (1959), Quinn's in corporate strategy (1980), and Kline's in engineering design and development (1990). It helps explain the characteristics of the technological competencies that we observe in our large firms.

1.2 Multi-technology Firms

We show in Section 2 that the technological competencies of large firms are diversified (or "multitechnology"), reflecting the complex and multivariate nature of their specific products and methods of production, and requiring the combination and application of advances in many fields of specialized knowledge. Over time, they are accumulating competencies in an increasing number of technological fields. Our results are consistent with the research by Granstrand and his colleagues,[2] who conclude that the number of technological fields that large firms must master is increasing, with widening range of technological opportunities emerging from information and other technologies.

1.3 Stability and Differentiation

However, complexity constrains firms to search and experiment in and around what they already know. As a consequence, we find in Section 3 that each firm's technology "mix" (or *profile*) is very stable over time, and strongly differentiated from most other firms, except those in the same industry. They confirm the hypothesis of Dosi, Teece and Winter (1992) that differentiated and firm-specific technological competencies are a central feature of corporate coherence.

1.4 Constraints on Managerial Choice

The rate and direction of a firm's search is also influenced by the available technological opportunities and the incentives and capacities that it has to respond to them. These depend on its competitive environment and its own accumulated competencies. In this context, we show in Section 4 that:

• the firm's home country influences its rate of technological accumulation, thereby confirming the importance of the nationally based supply- and demand-side inducement mechanisms described by Porter (1990). These are likely to remain strong since large firms continue to perform an overwhelming proportion of their R&D activities (~90%) in their home countries (Patel and Pavitt 1991; Patel 1995);

• the firm's product range influences its rate and direction of technological accumulation, given that the firm's competencies and directions of search are determined in large part by what it produces, and that techno-logical opportunities are unequal across fields (Malerba 1992);

• there remains considerable unexplained variance in firms' levels and rates of increase in technological activities, reflecting the different bets made by different managements in the face of complexity and uncertainty (Nelson and Winter 1982).

1.5 Data Sources and Limitations

The data set has been compiled from information, provided by the US Patent Office, on the name of the company, the technical sector and the country of origin, of each patent granted in the USA from 1969 to 1990.[3] We have also included in our data set the following information on each firm: country of origin, sales, employment and (where possible) R&D expendi-tures. Given the requirements of our statistical analysis, we have excluded firms with 50 or fewer patents in the period 1981–90. The distribution of our firms according to product groups is shown in Table 9.1. The distribution according to nationality shows that 47% are of US origin, 29% from Europe and 25% from Japan. Our earlier analysis shows that these firms account for more than 40% of total patents granted in the USA, with considerably higher shares in the chemicals, electrical-electronic and transport sectors (Patel and Pavitt 1991).

This approach has three limitations:

1. It measures only technological competence, and thereby neglects others that are important.[4]

2. It measures technological competencies only imperfectly through pat-ent data.[5] In particular, patenting does not fully measure competencies in software technology, since copyright law has been an important means of protection against imitation (see Barton 1993; Samuelson 1993). We have nonetheless been able to identify the growing importance in firms' compe-tencies in information technology.

3. It does not assess how differences in the rate and direction of techno-logical accumulation affect firms' economic and competitive performance. Suffice to say that a growing number of studies confirm the economic importance of technological competencies at the level of the firm,[6] which should in principle heighten interest in studies like ours that attempt to describe and explain how they are acquired.

2. THE PREVALENCE OF THE "MULTI-TECHNOLOGY" FIRM

2.1 The Extent of Technological Diversity

The most striking feature of the technological competencies of large firms is the *diversity* of technological fields in which they are active. This is shown in

Table 9.1, which shows the distribution of US patenting of our large firms, in each of the sixteen principal product groups, across four major techno-logical families: chemical, electrical-electronic, non-electrical machinery and transport.[7] Firms have substantial technological competencies outside what would appear to be their core areas. Thus, both electrical and chemical firms have about two-thirds of their competencies in their obvious core areas, but each has 15% or more in non-electrical machinery. Only firms principally in pharmaceuticals have less than 10% on average of their

TABLE 9.1. The distribution of large firms' technological activities in five broad technological fields, according to their principal product group, 1981–1990

Principal product group (PPG)	Percentage share of the PPG's patents in technology field					
	Chemical	Non-electrical machinery	Electrical	Transport	Other	Total
Chemicals (66)	71.0	16.9	8.9	0.6	2.6	100.0
Pharmaceuticals (25)	80.2	8.0	2.1	0.0	9.7	100.0
Mining and petroleum (31)	57.1	34.2	6.7	0.9	1.1	100.0
Textiles, etc. (10)	52.9	31.7	9.5	0.6	5.3	100.0
Rubber and plastics (9)	43.2	29.3	4.7	20.1	2.7	100.0
Paper and wood (18)	25.4	47.1	12.4	0.4	14.6	100.0
Food (14)	70.6	21.9	3.0	0.1	4.3	100.0
Drink and tobacco (8)	40.8	50.3	4.6	0.3	3.9	100.0
Building materials (16)	30.5	51.3	10.0	0.9	7.3	100.0
Metals (38)	26.8	54.9	13.9	2.1	2.2	100.0
Machinery (58)	7.6	64.9	13.9	10.2	3.3	100.0
Electrical (56)	7.6	21.2	67.0	1.3	2.8	100.0
Computers (17)	5.2	16.3	77.3	0.2	1.0	100.0
Instruments (21)	14.3	18.3	64.2	0.1	3.0	100.0
Motor vehicles (35)	3.8	44.8	20.7	28.8	1.9	100.0
Aircraft (18)	8.1	48.5	31.2	8.3	3.9	100.0
All 440 large firms	28.8	27.9	35.7	4.4	3.1	100.0

Note: Number of firms in each product group in parentheses.

Source: Calculated from data supplied to SPRU by the US Patent and Trademark Office.

technological competencies in non-electrical machinery. Both automobile and aircraft firms have a small proportion of their patenting in their core fields.

Another measure of technological diversity is the number of technical fields—out of the total of thirty-four used in our analysis[8]—in which our firms have been granted a patent and are therefore technically competent. Only 4% of our firms were active sometime in the 1980s in 10 or fewer of these technical fields, whilst 52% were active in between 10 and 20, and 44% in more than 20—hence the term "multi-technology" firm (See Archibugi 1988; and Granstrand and Sjolander 1990). More detailed statistical analysis[9] shows that firms' technological diversity increases with their size and technological intensity (patents per unit sales), and that there are some industry effects: in particular, food firms are significantly less diverse than the average, and aircraft and chemical firms significantly more so. On the other hand, a firm's home country has no significant effects.

2.2 The Evolving Knowledge Base over Time

The above cross-sectional analysis does not capture the effects of changing technological opportunities, reflecting the evolution of the knowledge base over time. This is done in Table 9.2, which shows the total number of large firms that have been active in each of our thirty-four technical fields in 1969–74 and 1985–90. The technological fields are sorted according to the last column, namely, the change in the number of active firms between the two periods. From this it emerges that:

- the most widespread competencies in our firms were in instrumentation and control, production machinery and chemical processes, in all of which an overwhelming majority of our firms were technologically active;
- the least widespread competencies were in aircraft, nuclear energy and textiles, the last two of which had the steepest decline over the period;
- the fields in which the number of firms with competencies increased most rapidly were computing, drugs and bioengineering, and materials—confirming them as the sectors in which technical managers have identified the richest potential of new opportunities;
- firms' *technological* diversity is much greater than their *production* diversity. Thus, around 250 of our firms were technologically active in computing in the 1980s, when certainly not more than ninety-four (the combined number of firms in the computer, electrical-electronic and instrument sectors) were actually making computers. The case holds even more strongly in production equipment of various kinds.

TABLE 9.2. Number of firms that are active in thirty-four technical fields, 1969–1974 to 1985–1990 (sorted by total change)

	1969–74	1985–90	Change
Calculators and computers, etc.	215	285	70
Drugs and bioengineering	159	204	45
Materials (incl. glass and ceramics)	321	362	41
Plastic and rubber products	251	287	36
General electrical industrial apparatus	331	367	36
Instruments and controls	373	407	34
Metallurgical and metal treatment processes	238	270	32
Dentistry and surgery	143	173	30
Miscellaneous metal products	351	380	29
Other (ammunitions and weapons, etc.)	314	337	23
Image and sound equipment	209	231	22
Chemical processes	392	413	21
Mining and wells: machinery and processes	117	137	20
Hydrocarbons, mineral oils, fuels, etc.	135	152	17
General non-electrical industrial equipment	363	377	14
Agricultural chemicals	96	108	12
Semiconductors	154	166	12
Photography and photocopying	137	147	10
Apparatus for chemicals, food, glass, etc.	384	393	9
Assembling and material handling apparatus	310	319	9
Road vehicles and engines	134	142	8
Electrical devices and systems	259	267	8
Organic chemicals	281	284	3
Non-electrical specialized industrial equipment	391	394	3
Power plants	135	138	3
Inorganic chemicals	181	183	2
Aircraft	71	73	2
Metallurgical and metal-working equipment	366	366	0
Telecommunications	253	252	−1
Bleaching, dyeing and disinfecting	113	110	−3
Other transport equipment (excl. aircraft)	211	206	−5
Food and tobacco (processes and production)	127	119	−8
Induced nuclear reactions	48	30	−18
Textile, clothing, leather, wood products	119	94	−25

3. STABILITY AND DIFFERENTIATION

3.1 Defining and Measuring Firms' Technological Profiles

Given these results, it is difficult to define a firm's technological competencies in terms of a few fields of excellence.[10] It is probably more useful to think in terms of *profiles* of competencies, with varying levels of commitment and competitive advantage in a range of technological fields. With our data, these profiles can have two dimensions:

1. The shares of a firm's total patenting in each of the thirty-four technological fields shown in Table 9.2: in other words, the relative importance for the firm of competencies in each of these technological fields.
We call this the Patent Share (PS) profile.
2. The shares of the firm in total patenting in each of the 34 technological
fields, divided by the firm's aggregate share in all the fields: in other
words, the relative importance of the firm to each field of technological competence, after taking account of the firm's total volume of
competencies. We call this the Revealed Technology Advantage
(RTA) profile.[11]

3.2 High Stability

Evolutionary theory tells us that, under conditions of complexity and
change, firms' technological and other competencies will develop cumulatively through localized search. By accident or design, firms accumulate
a portfolio—or profile—of technological competencies to cope with what
they make and sell today, and what they hope to make and sell in future. As
a consequence, we would expect their technological profiles to be both
stable and differentiated, with the shape of the profiles determined by the
problems they must solve (i.e. the products that they make). Our data
confirm that this is the case.

For each firm, we correlated both the patent shares and the RTAs in each
of the 34 fields for the periods 1969–74 and 1985–90.[12] According to both
measures, an overwhelming majority (more than 90%) of firms have profiles of technological competence that are statistically similar between
1969–74 and 1985–90, at the 1% level of significance. Large firms clearly do
not shift around rapidly in their fields of technological competence. This
turns out to be the case, even when acquisitions and divestments over the
period are taken into account. We have examined in further detail their
effects on the technological competencies of 41 of the larger firms in our
population. From this, it emerges that:

• stability in firms' technological profiles remains very high. Table 9.3
shows that, for the periods 1979–84 and 1987–92, the correlation coefficient
was greater than 0.90 in 28 out of 41 cases for each firm's patent share , and
in 27 out of 41 cases for each firm's revealed technology advantage. In only
one case the correlation was not significant at the 5% level;

• in only very few of the cases involving substantial technological activities were the technological profiles of the acquired firm different from the
acquiring firm, either before or after acquisition. All these cases involved
US-owned firms (Black and Decker's purchase of Emhart, General Motors
of Hughes, General Electric of RCA, and Kodak of Sterling Drug). In
contrast, ATT and the European firms (ABB, Alcatel, Philips, Thomson

TABLE 9.3. Stability of firms' technological profiles including acquisitions and divestments: Correlation coefficients*

Firm	RTA	Shares	Firm	RTA	Shares
Rolls-Royce	1.00	0.97	Canon	0.92	0.81
Bosch	0.99	0.95	MAN	0.92	0.97
Kodak	0.99	0.91	Thomson	0.92	0.94
Merck	0.99	0.99	Zeiss	0.92	0.97
NEC	0.99	0.97	Texas Instruments	0.91	0.87
Sony	0.99	1.00	Takeda Chemical	0.90	0.96
Xerox	0.99	0.99	Dow Chemical	0.89	0.99
Ciba-Geigy	0.98	0.99	United Technologies	0.89	0.93
Fujitsu	0.98	0.97	Caterpillar	0.88	0.86
Hitachi	0.98	0.91	Komatsu	0.87	0.82
IBM	0.98	0.98	Gould	0.86	0.91
Nissan	0.98	0.94	Alcatel	0.84	0.85
Philips	0.98	0.99	Bayer	0.84	0.99
ABB	0.97	0.84	ICI	0.82	0.96
Du Pont	0.97	0.98	Mitsubishi Denki	0.77	0.66
Olivetti	0.97	0.94	NTT	0.76	0.81
Sumitomo Chemical	0.97	1.00	General Motors	0.71	0.74
Nippondenso	0.96	0.92	General Electric	0.70	0.81
ATT	0.95	0.94	Black and Decker	0.51	0.61
Fanuc	0.94	0.95	Nokia	0.00	0.07
Siemens	0.94	0.96			

*Correlations between patents granted in 1979–84 to company as it existed in 1984, and patents granted in 1987–92 to company as it existed in 1992.

Notes: Shares = Percentage share of total company patenting in each of the 34 technological fields specified in Table 9.2. RTA = Company patent share in each of the 34 technological fields, divided by the share of total patenting in the same field.

and Olivetti) reinforced their existing profiles through their acquisitions, as did Hitachi and Fujitsu.

3.3 Strong Differentiation

In addition to being very stable, our data also show that large firms' technological profiles are highly differentiated. To begin with, profiles of technological competence of each of the 16 industries (i.e. aggregated sectoral data based on our firms) are in general very different. We systematically correlated each industry's technological profile, in terms of patent shares in each of the thirty-four technical fields, against all others and found that only 23% of the cross-industry correlations are positive and significant at the 5% level: in other words, there are no similarities amongst industries in their technological competencies in about three-quarters of all cases. We then did the same correlations in terms of RTAs, and found that the share of industries that are technologically similar is reduced to 5% (see Table 9.4).

In both cases, there are essentially three clusters of industries with significant similarities:

- the chemicals, pharmaceuticals, and mining and petroleum sectors;
- machinery and vehicles;
- electrical and computers.

There is also one significantly negative correlation that is important: between the RTAs of firms in chemicals and in electrical products. Although both are often lumped together as "high technology" or "sciencebased" firms, they are clearly based on significantly different profiles of technological competence.

One drawback in this analysis is its neglect of diversity in profiles of technological competencies of firms *within* each industrial sector. For this reason, we systematically correlated each firm's profile of patent shares against that of all other firms, and did the same for their RTAs.[13] The results confirmed what has been shown in Table 9.4.

- Firms have significantly different profiles of technological competence to most others: in aggregate around 28% are similar in patent shares and 15% in RTAs.
- In all sectors, firms have a higher probability of finding others with similar technological profiles *within* their sector than *outside* their sector: from twice as high for machinery firms, to more than ten times as high for pharmaceutical firms.
- The frequency of technological proximity between firms in different sectors is not evenly spread or random, but reveals distinct groupings, many of which have been anticipated in Table 9.4: in particular, those with competencies in chemistry, in electronics and in production machinery.
- These sectoral similarities and differences amongst firms in the sources and directions of technological accumulation are broadly consistent with a sectoral taxonomy of technical change proposed earlier by one of us (Pavitt 1984):
    - (i) two distinct science-based sectors centred on organic chemistry (chemicals, pharmaceuticals, petrochemicals), and on physics-based technology (electrical, computers);
    - (ii) machinery suppliers with areas of specialization influenced by major users;
    - (iii) a range of scale intensive sectors with production technologies dependent on improvements in chemical processes, instrumentation and production machinery.

TABLE 9.4. Correlations of average RTAs across sixteen principal product groups, 1981–1990

	1	2	3	4	5	6	7	8	9	10	11	12	13	14	15	16
1. Chemicals																
2. Pharmaceuticals	0.53*															
3. Mining and petroleum	0.16	-0.05														
4. Textiles, etc.	0.51*	0.20	-0.06													
5. Rubber and plastics	0.14	-0.02	0.02	0.20												
6. Paper and wood	0.01	-0.03	-0.12	0.30	0.30											
7. Food	0.09	0.15	-0.07	0.08	-0.05	0.23										
8. Drink and tobacco	-0.03	0.05	-0.07	0.00	-0.04	0.24	0.99*									
9. Building materials	0.20	-0.07	-0.01	0.34	0.27	0.55*	0.01	0.01								
10. Metals	0.04	-0.13	0.11	0.01	0.01	-0.08	-0.08	-0.07	0.20							
11. Machinery	-0.39*	-0.35*	0.06	-0.24	-0.04	-0.10	-0.20	-0.15	0.01	0.16						
12. Electrical	-0.36*	-0.29	-0.25	-0.24	-0.13	-0.35*	-0.20	-0.16	-0.17	-0.08	-0.06					
13. Computers	-0.25	-0.18	-0.17	-0.17	-0.11	-0.20	-0.12	-0.10	-0.14	-0.13	-0.20	0.65*				
14. Instruments	-0.01	-0.08	-0.12	-0.03	-0.07	0.13	-0.09	-0.07	-0.03	-0.12	-0.21	0.06	0.14			
15. Motor vehicles	-0.27	-0.20	-0.17	-0.18	-0.07	-0.26	-0.13	-0.11	-0.14	-0.05	0.52*	-0.04	-0.06	-0.14		
16. Aircraft	-0.20	-0.18	0.00	-0.13	0.02	-0.25	-0.11	-0.09	-0.10	0.01	0.04	-0.03	-0.05	-0.14	0.10	

* Denotes correlation coefficient significantly different from zero at the 5% level.

Strategy/Organization

4. CONSTRAINTS ON MANAGERIAL CHOICE

One implication of the high stability and differentiation of large firms' technological competencies is the severe constraint it puts on managerial choice and discretion. We shall now show more specifically that:

- each firm's *direction* of technological search (and accumulation of competence) is strongly constrained by its prior competencies;
- each firm's *rate* of search is significantly influenced by its home country and the products that it makes.

4.1 Constrained Directions of Search

The stability over time that we have observed in firms' technological profiles is defined by relatively broad technological fields, and does not reflect the more localized processes of search that firms undertake within these fields. For this reason, we have identified in US patenting activities the 1,000 (out of a total of around 100,000) technological subclasses of the highest technological opportunity, as measured by their absolute increase in patenting from the 1960s to the late 1980s. In aggregate, their share increased steeply from 3% to 18% of total US patenting. A relatively high proportion of fast growing fields are to be found in electronics and chemical technologies, but cases can be identified in all technological fields. They reflect the areas of greatest technological opportunity.

Nonetheless, we show in Table 9.5, that firms are in fact heavily constrained by their prior competencies in the *directions* in which they exploit opportunities in these fast-growing fields. Their shares of total fast-growing

TABLE 9.5. Correlations of past (1969–1984) shares of total patenting with shares of patenting in fast-growing areas in 1985–1990

	Shares of patenting in fast-growing areas in 1985–90				
	Chemicals	Non-electrical Machinery	Electrical	Transport	Other
Share of total chemicals 1969–84	0.91*	−0.41	−0.61	−0.26	0.00
Share of total mechanical 1969–84	−0.41	0.68*	−0.10	0.14*	0.09
Share of total electrial 1969–84	−0.58	−0.12	0.87*	−0.17	−0.17
Share of total transport 1969–84	−0.34	0.18*	−0.13	0.85*	−0.04
Share of total other 1969–84	0.06	−0.12	−0.18	−0.07	0.55*

* Denotes a coefficient that is significant and positive at the 5% level.

patenting in 1985–90 within the five broad fields of technology used in Table 9.1—chemicals, non-electrical machinery, electrical-electronic machinery, transport and "other"—are strongly and positively correlated with their prior shares of total patenting in these same fields over the period 1969–84, but not with their shares in any other of the fields. Hence, firms' capacities to exploit specific fields of high technological opportunity are strongly constrained by the fields of their prior competencies.

4.2 Constrained Rates of Search

In other words, a firm's existing product mix and associated competencies strongly constrain the *directions* in which it seeks to exploit technological opportunities and acquire competence. We shall now explore the determinants of the *rate* of the firm's technological search activities. We have suggested in Section 1.4 that three factors will influence the rate of search: home country, product mix and managerial discretion.

In Table 9.6, we present the results of our analysis of the effects of home-country conditions and of product mix (both measured through the appropriate aggregate indicators from our large firm database) on three measures of the rate of accumulation of technological competencies in firms. From this it emerges that:

- both home country and product mix have a statistically significant influence on the rate of technological accumulation, whether measured in terms of patents per unit of sales, growth in patent share or share of total patenting in fast-growing fields;[14]
- the unexplained variance amongst firms nonetheless remains considerable—between 56% and 80% of the total, which suggests that company-specific factors—and particularly managerial choice—

TABLE 9.6. Factors influencing firms' rate of technological accumulation

Dependent variable	Patent intensity, 1985–90		Change in patent share, 1969–74 to 1985–90		Share of patents in fast-growing fields, 1985–90	
	Coeff.	Std. error	Coeff.	Std. error	Coeff.	Std. error
Constant	−32.08*	10.90	0.83	0.52	−6.71*	1.69
Industry average	1.03*	0.07	1.88*	0.42	0.82*	0.05
Country average	0.62*	0.16	0.68*	0.07	0.38*	0.07
R Sq. (adj.)	0.33		0.20		0.44	
F	113.3*		57.1*		172.7*	
N	462		462		447	

*Denotes coefficient significantly different from zero at the 5% level.

remain important in the volume of resources allocated to technological accumulation.

5. CHALLENGES TO CONVENTIONAL MANAGEMENT WISDOM

We conclude by identifying where we think our results challenge current conventional wisdom about technology and strategy in large firms.

5.1 The Strong Constraints on Managerial Choice

We have identified a number of important constraints on the strategies for technological competence-building that managements can follow in large firms.

- Their technological strategies can only rarely be "focused," since the products they develop and make require the integration of knowledge from a wide range of technological fields (see also Freeman 1982).
- Their capacity to modify their profiles of technological competence is limited, and takes a long time (see also Rosenbloom and Cusumano 1987).
- In addition to these constraints on the *directions* of technological accumulation, both home-country and industry characteristics have a significant influence on the firm's *rate* of competence accumulation.
- However, the unexplained variance suggests considerable scope for managerial discretion in fixing the rate of competence accumulation. Given uncertainties, different managements make different bets, based on different "rules of thumb" or "routines," which may be influenced by their professional backgrounds and associated loyalties. For example, Scherer and Huh (1992) have shown in the USA, and Bosworth and Wilson (1992) in the UK, that the volume of resources allocated by firms to technological activities is positively associated with the presence of graduate scientists and engineers in top management.

5.2 Alliances as Complements (not Substitutes) for In-House Competencies

The technological fields where firms have been acquiring in-house capabilities most vigorously since the early 1970s—computers, biotechnology and pharmaceuticals, and materials (see Table 9.2)—are also those where firms have increased most vigorously their external alliances for technological exchanges and joint developments (see Mowery 1988; Hagedoorn and Schakenraad 1992). This suggests—as Granstrand *et al* (1992) have observed in case-studies—that external alliances are complements to internal learning, and not substitutes: both are necessary if firms are to master the increasing range of technologies necessary to make competitive products.

5.3 Competence-Augmenting rather than Competence-Destroying Innovations

Our finding that large firms have competencies in a large number of fields suggests that dramatic "competence-destroying" innovations are unlikely in large firms with diversified competencies and R&D programs (Tushman and Anderson 1987; Utterback and Suarez 1993). Although radical breakthroughs may destroy one part of such a firm's competence, it is unlikely to destroy them all. An example is the new biotechnology, where—in spite of a slow start—established chemical and pharmaceutical firms have succeeded in combining the radical breakthroughs with their established fields of competence (Arora and Gambardella 1992; Galimberti 1993). More generally, the observed rapid spread amongst firms of competencies in computing and other fast-moving technologies suggests that radical breakthroughs can better be described as "competence augmenting" than as "competence destroying."

5.4 "Distinctive Core" Competencies are not Enough

However, probably the most important of our findings for practitioners probably emerges from the "multi-technology" nature of large firms. This confirms the requirement in all firms for an organizational competence, namely, the capacity to develop, orchestrate and integrate the wide variety of technological competencies—including new competencies in promising and fast-moving technological fields—necessary for competitive innovations (see Kodama 1986; Prahalad and Hamel 1990).

At the same time, our findings suggest that policy prescriptions like "focus on your distinctive technological competencies" (in particular, Prahalad and Hamel 1990) are not being followed by the majority of our large firms that are technically active in between ten and twenty out of our thirty-four technical fields. As we shall now see, such prescriptions neglect the importance of technological competencies that provide an interface to outside sources of technological competence, especially amongst suppliers of production equipment, materials and components.

For this purpose, we begin by distinguishing—as shown in Figure 9.1— the two dimensions of any large firms' technological competencies, already defined in Section 3.1 above:

- on the Y-axis, the percentage share of each of our 34 technical fields in total patenting (Patent Share), reflecting the relative importance of each field in the firm's total technological portfolio;

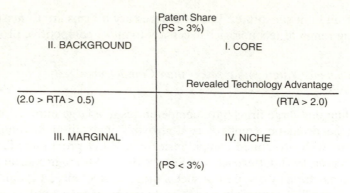

FIG. 9.1. A classification for firms' technological profiles

- on the X-axis, the firm's Revealed Technology Advantage (RTA) in each of the 34 technical fields, reflecting the relative importance of the firm for the field.

On this basis, the "distinctive" technical competencies of the firms are those in which the RTA is relatively high: namely, in the first quadrant, which defines and describes the core of its competencies, and in the fourth quadrant, where it may have niche advantages in a relatively small technological field. Many analysts would argue that most of the firm's technological resources should be concentrated in these two quadrants, rather than in *background* or *marginal competencies*, where it does not have a distinctive advantage. In fact, this is often *not* the case.

This is illustrated in Figures 9.2a, b and c, which describe the technological profiles of three large and well-known firms in the period 1981–90: Bayer in chemicals, Hitachi in electrical and electronic products, and Ford in motor vehicles. As we would expect from our analysis, all three firms have competencies in a substantial number of fields: Bayer in eleven (out of thirty-four), Hitachi in eighteen, and Ford in twenty. In addition, all three have very different *core* competencies. But the relative importance of *core*—as compared to *background*—competencies varies widely amongst the three firms, as is shown in Table 9.7.

The relatively high share of total patenting in *background*—rather than *core*—competencies in Hitachi and Ford cannot be explained away as exceptions. Our data show similar patterns in many firms, who typically devote considerable technical resources to fields where they do *not* have a distinctive advantage, but which are central to their production (e.g. machinery, instrumentation and chemical processes), and to their supply chain of components and materials.

The reasons have little to do with notions of transaction costs or bilateral bargains, and all to do with technical interdependence between the complex

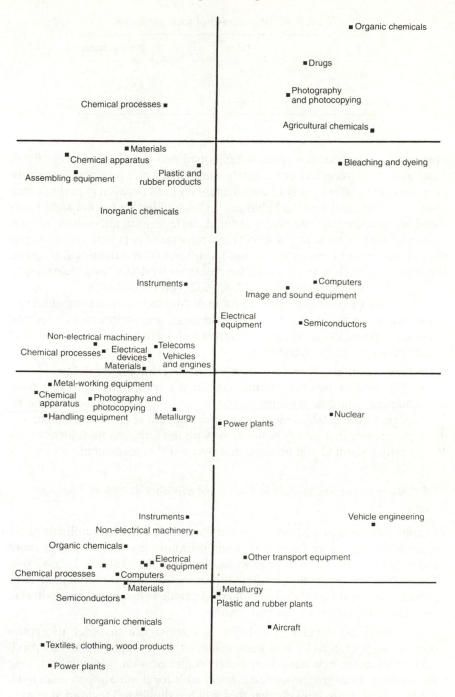

FIG. 9.2. (a) Technological profile of a chemical company: Bayer
(b) Technological profile of an electrical company: Hitachi
(c) Technological profile of an automobile company: Ford

TABLE 9.7. Percentage of total patenting

	Core	Background
Bayer	75	7
Hitachi	37	47
Ford	18	64

products and production systems developed and produced by large firms, and what their suppliers of materials components and production machinery are able to offer by way of complementary (and necessary) performance improvements and technical changes.[15] Case-studies show that such background competencies are essential for the effective identification, integration and adaptation to firm-specific requirements of pervasive technologies, where no one firm can expect to have a distinctive and dominant position. In other words, they are essential for "learning by doing" and "learning by using" (Arrow 1962; Rosenberg 1976, 1982; von Hippel 1988).

We therefore conclude that the notion of "distinctive core competencies" does not describe adequately how technology contributes to firm-specific competitive advantage. We would suggest instead the notion of "distributed competencies," in the sense that:

- they are spread across a wide number of technological fields;
- they serve a number of functions in the competitive process, from helping establish effective networks with outside sources of knowledge, to the establishment of unique and firm-specific advantage;
- they reside in a variety of locations with the firm, and therefore are not easily identified and manipulated by central management.

5.5 "More Focus in Production" does not translate as "More Focus in Technology"

Finally, our findings cast doubt on the commonly (if often implicitly) held assumption that more focus and specialization in production means more focus and specialization in production. In particular, Table 9.2 shows that firms are more diversified in their technological competencies than their product mix, and that their technological profile is becoming more diverse over time. This results from two trends:

1. Firms must develop new fields of competence in order to exploit opportunities created by new knowledge, either to improve existing products, or to create new ones. In the early stages of what is inevitably a long and uncertain learning process, it is impossible for these competencies to be distinctive. It is also unlikely that they will be (should be) focused at least at the early stages.[16]

2. Even when firms buy rather than make their inputs of machinery, materials and components, they require (as we have seen in Section 6.4 above) at least some background competence of their own, either to improve their own purchasing and production activities, or to cope, during innovation and change, with systemic interdependence between what they make and what they buy.

NOTES

1. Similar data has been used by Hall and her colleagues (1986) to measure lags between R&D and patenting at the firm level; by Narin and his colleagues (1987) for corporate and competitor analysis; by Jaffe (1989) to identify and measure technological "spillovers"; and by Cantwell (1991) to explain patterns of international production.
2. See, in particular, Granstrand and Sjolander (1990); Granstrand *et al.* (1992); Oskarsson (1993); Jacobsson and Oskarsson (1995).
3. One weakness with this source is that many patents are granted to large firms under the names of subsidiaries and divisions that are different from those of their parent companies. Consolidating patenting under the names of parent companies can only be done manually, on the basis of publication like "Who Owns Whom." Our consolidation shows that some firms have considerably more patents in our consolidated classification than in the original compilations of the US Patent Office (see Patel and Pavitt 1991).
4. Dosi and Teece (1993) have distinguished organizational-economic competencies from technical competencies: "Organizational/economic competence involves: (1) allocative competence—deciding what to produce and how to price it; (2) transactional competence—deciding whether to make or buy, and whether to do so alone or in partnership; and (3) administrative competence—how to design organizational structures and policies to enable efficient performance. Technical competence, on the other hand, includes the ability to develop and design products and processes, and to operate facilities effectively."
5. The uses and abuses of patent data have been extensively discussed elsewhere, See, for example, Basberg (1987); Pavitt (1988); Grilliches (1990); Patel and Pavitt (1995).
6. See, for example, Cantwell (1989), Franko (1989), Geroski *et al.* (1993), Oskarsson (1993).
7. The method for distributing firms' technological activities amongst four technological families is described more fully in Patel and Pavitt (1994*a*). Briefly stated we reclassified the US Patent Classes and Subclasses into thirty-four technical fields, and ninety-one subfields. On the basis of the ninety-one subfields, we recombined patenting into the four technological families shown in Table 9.1.

The "Other" category includes traditional manufacturing (e.g. textiles) and non-manufacturing (e.g. construction, medicine, agriculture).

8. See Table 9.2 for the name of each of the technical fields.
9. See Patel and Pavitt (1994*b*).
10. For example, "Few companies are likely to build world leadership in more than five or six fundamental competencies. A company that compiles a list of 20 to 30 capabilities has probably not produced a list of core competencies" (Prahalad and Hamel 1990).
11. The firm's RTA in each of the 34 technological fields is similar to the Revealed Comparative Advantage (RCA) measure used to assess the export performance of countries. The higher the RTA, the greater the relative strength of a firm in a technological field.
12. For more details see Patel and Pavitt (1994*b*).
13. For more details see Patel and Pavitt (1994*b*).
14. Since all three dependent variables are based on patenting, part of the unexplained variance may reflect interfirm differences in the propensity to patent the results of R&D and related technological activities. However, this is less likely to operate in shares of total patenting in fast-growing fields.
15. For example, a large automobile firm may not make either the window glass or the tyres that it uses, but it will need (at the very least) to have its own technical capacity in these fields to judge whether its suppliers can be expected to provide (say) more streamlined glass shapes and higher quality tyres, as complements to its own development of more powerful internal combustion engines.
16. In recent study, Miyazaki (1994) used bibliometric techniques and interviews to trace over time how a number of major companies assimilated opto-electronics technology. She found cumulative paths of learning: directions of search were influenced by previously accumulated competencies, and over time search processes became more focused and applied.

REFERENCES

Archibugi, D. (1988), "In Search of a Useful Measure of Technological Innovation," *Technological Forecasting and Social Change*, 34/3 (Nov.), 253–77.

Arora, A. and Gambardella, A. (1992), "New Trends in Technological Change: The Use of General and Abstract Knowledge in Industrial Research," *Rivista Internazionale di Scienze Sociali*, 3 (July–Sept.), 259–77.

Arrow, K. (1962), "The Economic Implications of Learning by Doing," *Review of Economic Studies,* 29: 155–73.

Barton, J. (1993), "Adapting the Intellectual Property System to New Technologies," in Wallerstein, Mogee and Schoen (eds.), *Global Dimensions of Intellectual Property Rights*.

Basberg, B. (1987), "Patents and the Measurement of Technological Change: A Survey of the Literature," *Research Policy*, 16/2–4 (Aug.), 131–41.

Bosworth, D. and Wilson, R. (1992), *Technological Change: The Role of Scientists and Engineers* (Aldershot: Avebury).

Cantwell, J. (1989), *Technological Innovation and Multinational Corporations*, (Oxford: Blackwell).

——(1991), "The Theory of Technological Competence and its Application to International Production," in D. McFetridge (ed.), *Foreign Investment, Technology and Economic Growth* (Calgary: University of Calgary Press).

Carlsson, B. and Eliasson, G. (1991), "The Nature and Importance of Economic Competence," Working Paper, Swedish Board of Technical Development, Stockholm.

Dosi, G. and Teece, D. (1993), " Competencies and the Boundaries of the Firm," CCC Working Paper No. 93-11, CRM, Graduate Business School, U. C., Berkeley, Calif.

——and Winter, S. (1992), "Towards a Theory of Corporate Coherence: Preliminary Remarks," in G. Dosi, R. Giannetti and P. A. Toninelli (eds.), *Technology and Enterprise in a Historical Perspective* (Oxford: Clarendon Press).

Franko, L. (1989), "Global Corporate Competition: Who's Winning, Who's Losing, and the R&D Factor as One Reason Why," *Strategic Management Journal*, 10/5 (Sept./Oct.), 449–74.

Freeman, C. (1982), *The Economics of Industrial Innovation* (London: Pinter).

Galimberti, I. (1993), "Large Chemical Firms in Biotechnology: Case Studies of Learning in Radically New Technology," D. Phil. thesis, University of Sussex.

Geroski, P., Machin, S. and van Reenen, J. (1993), "The Profitability of Innovating Firms," *RAND Journal of Economics*, 24/2 (Summer), 198–211.

Granstrand, O. and Sjolander, S. (1990), "Managing Innovation in Multitechnology Corporations," *Research Policy*, 19/1 (Feb.), 35–60.

——Bohlin, E., Oskarsson, C. and Sjorberg, N. (1992), "External Technology Acquisition in Large Multitechnology Corporations," *R&D Management*, 22/2 (Apr.), 111–33.

Griliches, Z. (1984) (ed.), *Patents, R&D and Productivity* (Chicago: University of Chicago Press).

Hagedoorn, J. and Schakenraad, J. (1992), "Leading Companies in Networks of Strategic Alliances in Information Technologies," *Research Policy*, 21/2 (Apr.), 163–90.

Hall, B., Griliches, Z. and Hausman, J. (1986), "Patents and R&D: Is there a Lag?" *International Economic Review*, 27/2 (June), 265–83.

Hughes, T. and Pinch, T. (1987) (eds.), *The Social Construction of Technological Systems* (Cambridge, Mass.: MIT Press).

Jacobsson, S. and Oskarsson, C. (1995), "Educational Statistics as an Indicator of Technological Activity," *Research Policy*, 24: 127–36.

Jaffe, A. (1989), "Characterizing the 'Technological Position' of Firms, with Application to Quantifying Technological Opportunity and Research Spillovers," *Research Policy*, 18: 87–97.

Kline, S. (1990), "A Numerical Measure for the Complexity of Systems: The Concept and Some Implications," Report INN-5, Dept. of Mechanical Engineering, Stanford University.

Kodama, F. (1986), "Japanese Innovation in Mechatronics Technology," *Science and Public Policy*, 13/1: 44–51.

Lindblom, C. E. (1959), "The Science of Muddling Through," *Public Administration Review*, 19: 78–88.

Malerba, F. (1992), "Learning by Firms and Incremental Technical Change," *Economic Journal*, 102/413 (July), 845–59.

Miyazaki, K. (1994), *"Building Competencies in the Firm: Lessons from European and Japanese Opt-electronics* (Basingstoke: Macmillan).

Mowery, D. (1988) (ed.), *International Collaborative Ventures in US Manufacturing* (Cambridge, Mass: Ballinger).

Narin, F., Noma, E. and Perry, R. (1987), "Patents as Indicators of Corporate Technological Strength," *Research Policy*, 16/2–4 (Aug.), 143–55.

Nelson, R. and Winter, S. (1982), *An Evolutionary Theory of Economic Change*, (Cambridge, Mass: Belknap, Harvard University Press).

Oskarsson, C. (1993), "Diversification and Growth in US, Japanese and European Multi-Technology Corporations," Dept. of Industrial Management and Economics, Chalmers University of Technology, Gothenburg (mimeo).

Patel, P. (1995), "Localised Production of Technology for Global Markets," *Cambridge Journal of Economics*, 19: 141–53.

——and Pavitt, K. (1991), "Large Firms in the Production of the World's Technology: An Important Case of 'Non-Globalisation'," *Journal of International Business Studies*, 22: 1–21.

————(1994*a*), "The Continuing, Widespread (and Neglected) Importance of Improvements in Mechanical Technologies," *Research Policy*, 232: 533–46.

————(1994*b*) "Technological Competencies in the World's Largest Firms: Characteristics, Constraints and Scope for Managerial Choice," Discussion Paper no. 13, ESRC Centre on Science, Technology, Energy and Environment Policy, Science Policy Research Unit, Sussex University.

————(1995), "Patterns of Technological Activity: Their Measurement and Interpretation," in P. Stoneman (ed.), *Handbook of the Economics of Innovation and Technical Change* (Oxford: Blackwell).

Pavitt, K. (1984), "Sectoral Patterns of Technical Change: Towards a Taxonomy and a Theory," *Research Policy*, 13: 343–73.

——(1988), "Uses and Abuses of Patent Statistics," in van Raan, *Handbook of Quantitative Studies*.

Porter, M. (1990), *The Competitive Advantage of Nations* (London: Macmillan).

Prahalad, C. K. and Hamel, G. (1990), "The Core Competence of the Corporation," *Harvard Business Review* (May–June), 79–91.

Quinn, J. (1980), *Strategies for Change: Logical Incrementalism* (Homewood, Ill: Irwin).

Rosenberg, N. (1982), "Learning by Using," in *Inside the Black Box: Technology and Economics* (Cambridge, University Press: Cambridge).

Rosenbloom, R. and Cusumano, M. (1987), "Technological Pioneering and Competitive Advantage: The Birth of the VCR Industry," *California Management Review*, 29.

Rumelt, R. (1974), *Strategy, Structure and Economic Performance*, (Cambridge, Mass: Harvard University Press).

Samuelson, P. (1993), "A Case-Study on Computer Programs," in Wallerstein, Mogee and Schoen (eds.), *Global Dimensions*.

Scherer, F. and Huh, K. (1992), "Top Management Education and R&D Investment," *Research Policy*, 21.

Teece, D., Pisano, G. and Schuen, A. (1990), "Firm Capabilities, Resources, and the
Concept of Strategy," CCC Working Paper no. 90–8, Centre for Research in
Management, Berkeley, Calif.

Tushman, M. and Anderson, P. (1987), "Technological Discontinuities and Organization Environments," in A. Pettigrew (ed.), *The Management of Strategic
Change* (Oxford: Blackwell).

van Raan, A. (1988) (ed.), *Handbook of Quantitative Studies of Science and
Technology* (Amsterdam: North Holland).

von Hippel, E. (1988), *The Sources of Innovation*, (New York: Oxford University
Press).

Utterback, J. and Suarez, F. (1993), "Innovation, Competition and Industrial
Structure," *Research Policy*, 22/1 (Feb.), 1–21.

Wallerstein, M., Mogee, M. and Schoen, R. (1993) (eds.), *Global Dimensions of
Intellectual Property Rights in Science and Technology* (Washington, DC.:
National Academy Press).

10

A Theory of the Firm's Knowledge-Creation Dynamics

IKUJIRO NONAKA AND
HIROTAKA TAKEUCHI

1. INTRODUCTION

Japanese companies remain an enigma to most Westerners. They are not terribly efficient, entrepreneurial or liberated. Yet, slowly but surely, they have advanced their position in international competition.

Why have Japanese companies become successful? In this paper, we offer a new explanation. We argue that Japanese companies have been successful because of their skills and expertise at "organizational knowledge creation." By organizational knowledge creation, we mean the capability of a company as a whole to create new knowledge, disseminate it throughout the organization, and embody it into products, services and systems. Organizational knowledge creation is the key to the distinctive ways that Japanese companies innovate. They are especially good at bringing about innovation continuously, incrementally and spirally.

2. THE DISTINCTIVE JAPANESE APPROACH TO KNOWLEDGE CREATION

The focus of this paper is on knowledge *creation*, not on knowledge *per se*. But before we can embark on the task of trying to master an understanding of the Japanese techniques of knowledge creation, a close examination of knowledge itself is in order.

A keen interest has been developing in the West on the subject of knowledge. Many observers of business and society have recently highlighted the central role of knowledge to competitive success. In his recent book *Post-Capitalist Society*, for example, Peter Drucker argues that knowledge is not only one resource among many but "the only meaningful resource" in business today. In *Powershift*, Alvin Toffler sees knowledge as the ultimate source of power in the world economy, which, according to Toffler, helps explain why the battle for control of knowledge and the means of communication is heating up all over the world. And in

Intelligent Enterprise, James Quinn argues that a company's competitive advantage increasingly depends on "knowledge-based intangibles" such as technological know-how, product design and deep understanding of the customer.

The realization that knowledge is the new competitive resource has hit the West like lightning. But all this talk about the importance of knowledge for both companies and countries does little to help us understand how knowledge gets created. Despite all the attention devoted by the leading observers of business and society, none of them has really examined the mechanisms and processes by which knowledge is created. This distinction is what separates our approach from theirs. More importantly, it is precisely for this reason that the Japanese experience is especially interesting and useful.

There is a reason why Western observers tend not to address the issue of organizational knowledge creation. They take for granted a view of the organization as a machine for "information processing." This view is deeply ingrained in the traditions of Western management, from Frederick Taylor to Herbert Simon. And it has a view of knowledge as necessarily "explicit"—something formal and systematic. Explicit knowledge can be expressed in words and numbers, and easily communicated and shared in the form of hard data, scientific formulae, codified procedures or universal principles. Thus, knowledge is viewed synonymously with a computer code, a chemical formula or a set of general rules. When Drucker (1993: 38) observes that "within a few years after Taylor began to apply knowledge to work, productivity began to rise at a rate of 3.5 and 4 per cent compound a year," he is actually referring to the application of quantifiable data to work. Similarly, Toffler (1990) uses the words "data," "information," and "knowledge" interchangeably throughout his book "to avoid tedious repetition."

Japanese companies, however, have a very different understanding of knowledge. They recognize that the knowledge expressed in words and numbers only represents the tip of the iceberg. They view knowledge as being primarily "tacit"—something not easily visible and expressible. Tacit knowledge is highly personal and hard to formalize, making it difficult to communicate to others or share with others. Subjective insights, intuitions and hunches fall into this category of knowledge. Furthermore, tacit knowledge is deeply rooted in an individual's action and experience, as well as in the ideals, values or emotions he or she embraces.

To be more precise, tacit knowledge can be segmented into two dimensions. The first is the technical dimension, which encompasses the kind of informal and hard-to-pin-down skills or crafts captured in the term "know-how." A master craftsman, for example, develops a wealth of expertise "at his fingertips" after years of experience. But he is often unable to articulate the scientific or technical principles behind what he knows.

At the same time, tacit knowledge contains an important cognitive dimension. It consists of schemata, mental models, beliefs and perceptions so ingrained that we take them for granted. The cognitive dimension of tacit knowledge reflects our image of reality (what is) and our vision for the future (what ought to be). Though they cannot be articulated very easily, these implicit models profoundly shape how we perceive the world around us.

The distinction between explicit knowledge and tacit knowledge is the key to understanding the differences between the Western approach to knowledge and the Japanese approach to knowledge. Explicit knowledge can easily be "processed" by a computer, transmitted electronically or stored in data bases. But the subjective and intuitive nature of tacit knowledge makes it difficult to process or transmit the acquired knowledge in any systematic or logical manner. For tacit knowledge to be communicated and shared within the organization, it has to be converted into words or numbers that anyone can understand. It is precisely during the time this conversion takes place—from explicit to tacit, and, as we shall see later, back again into explicit—when organizational knowledge is created.

Although Western managers have been more accustomed to dealing with explicit knowledge, the recognition of tacit knowledge and its importance has a number of crucially relevant implications. First, it gives birth to a whole different view of the organization—not as a machine for processing information but as a living organism. Within this context, sharing an understanding of what the company stands for, where it is going, what kind of a world it wants to live in, and how to make that world a reality becomes much more crucial than processing objective information. Highly subjective insights, intuitions and hunches are an integral part of knowledge. Knowledge also embraces ideals, values and emotion as well as images and symbols. These soft and qualitative elements are crucial to an understanding of the Japanese view of knowledge.

The second implication follows naturally from the first. Once the importance of tacit knowledge is realized, then one begins to think about innovation in a whole new way. It is not just about putting together disembodied bits of data and information. It is a highly personal process of personal and organizational self-renewal. The personal commitment of the employees and their identity with the company and its mission become indispensable. In this respect, the creation of new knowledge is as much about ideals as it is about ideas. And that fact fuels innovation. The essence of innovation is to re-create the world according to a particular ideal or vision. To create new knowledge means quite literally to re-create the company and everyone in it in a nonstop process of personal and organizational self-renewal. It is not the responsibility of the selected few—a specialist in R&D, strategic planning or marketing—but that of everyone in the organization.

Creating new knowledge is also not simply a matter of learning from others or acquiring knowledge from the outside. It has to be built on its own, frequently requiring intensive and laborious interaction among members of the organization. New product-development team members at Canon, for example, held "camp sessions" at a local hotel over the weekend to brainstorm through a critical problem or issue. In this respect, the Japanese approach is at variance with the "best practices" and "benchmarking" practices carried out at companies like GE, AT&T, Xerox and Milliken who are bent on learning from others. The Japanese approach also runs counter to the basic premise of the "modular" or "virtual" corporation, which uses the knowledge of outside partners—suppliers, customers, rivals and outside specialists—in lieu of its own. Companies in Japan believe that new and proprietary knowledge cannot be created without an intensive outside–inside interaction. To create knowledge, the learning that takes place from others and the skills shared with others need to be internalized—that is, reformed, enriched and translated to fit the company's self-image and identity.

Third, another important implication that can be drawn from the above discussion is the fact that Western managers need to "unlearn" their old view of knowledge and grasp the importance of the Japanese view. They need to get out of the old mold of thinking that knowledge can be acquired, taught and trained through manuals, books or lectures. Instead, they need to pay more attention to the less formal and systematic side of knowledge and start focusing on highly subjective insights, intuitions and hunches that are gained through the use of metaphors, pictures or experiences. Doing so will enable Western managers to understand what successful Japanese companies are doing right. And indeed, our theory will help them do just that.

3. NEW THEORY OF ORGANIZATIONAL KNOWLEDGE CREATION

To explain innovation, we need a new theory of organizational knowledge-creation. Like any approach to knowledge, it will have its own "epistemology" (the theory of knowledge), although substantially different from the traditional Western approach. The cornerstone of our epistemology is the distinction between tacit and explicit knowledge. As we have emphasized, the key to knowledge creation lies in the mobilization and conversion of tacit knowledge. And because we are concerned with organizational knowledge creation, as opposed to individual knowledge creation, it will also have its own distinctive "ontology," which is concerned with the levels of knowledge-creating entities (individual, group, organizational and interorganizational). In this paper, we present our theory of knowledge creation, keeping in mind the two dimensions—epistemological and on-tological—of knowledge creation.

We present the four modes of knowledge conversion, which are created when tacit and explicit knowledge interact with each other. These four modes—which we refer to as socialization, externalization, combination and internalization—constitute the "engine" of the entire knowledge-creation process. These modes are what the individual experiences. They are also the mechanisms by which individual knowledge gets articulated and "amplified" into and through the organization. After laying out these four modes and illustrating them with examples, we will describe five conditions that enable or promote this spiral model of organizational knowledge creation. We also present a five-phase process through which knowledge is created over time within the organization.

3.1 Two Dimensions of Knowledge Creation

To understand how knowledge, which is defined as "justified true belief," is created, we first turn to two dimensions of knowledge—epistemological and ontological. Let us start with the ontological dimension. In a strict sense, knowledge is created only by individuals. An organization cannot create knowledge without individuals. The organization supports crea-tive individuals or provides contexts for them to create knowledge. Organizational knowledge creation, therefore, should be understood as a process that "organizationally" amplifies the knowledge created by individuals and crystallizes it as a part of the knowledge network of the organization. This process takes place within an expanding "community of interaction," which crosses intra- and interorganizational levels and boundaries.[1]

As for the epistemological dimension, we draw on Michael Polanyi's distinction between *tacit knowledge* and *explicit knowledge*. As mentioned earlier, tacit knowledge is personal, context-specific, and therefore hard to formalize and communicate. "Explicit" or "codified" knowledge, on the other hand, refers to knowledge that is transmittable in formal, systematic language. Polanyi's argument on the importance of tacit knowledge in human cognition may correspond to the central argument of Gestalt psychology, which has asserted that perception is determined in terms of the way it is integrated into the overall pattern or *Gestalt*. However, while Gestalt psychology stresses that all images are intrinsically integrated, Polanyi contends that human beings acquire knowledge by actively creating and organizing their own experiences. Thus, knowledge that can be ex-pressed in words and numbers represents only the tip of the iceberg of the entire body of knowledge. As Polanyi (1966) puts it, "We can know more than we can tell" (p. 4).[2]

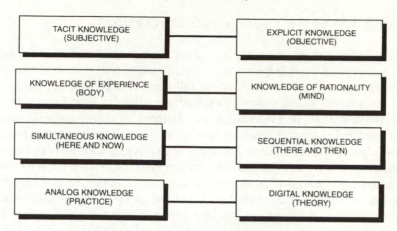

FIG. 10.1. Two types of knowledge

Some distinctions between tacit and explicit knowledge are shown in Figure 10.1. Features generally associated with the more tacit aspects of knowledge are listed on the left, while the corresponding qualities related to explicit knowledge are shown on the right-hand side. For example, knowledge of experience tends to be tacit, physical and subjective, while knowledge of rationality tends to be explicit, metaphysical and objective. Tacit knowledge is created "here and now" in a specific, practical context and entails what Bateson (1973) referred to as "analog" quality. Sharing tacit knowledge between individuals through communication is an analog process. This requires a kind of "simultaneous processing" of the complexities of issues shared by the individuals. On the other hand, explicit knowledge is about past events or objects "there and then" and is oriented toward a context-free theory. It is sequentially created by what Bateson (1973) calls "digital" activity.

3.2 Knowledge Conversion: Interaction Between Tacit and Explicit Knowledge

The history of Western epistemology can be seen as a continuous controversy about which type of knowledge is more truthful. In our view, however, tacit knowledge and explicit knowledge are not totally separate but mutually complementary entities. They interact with and interchange into each other in the creative activities of human beings. Our dynamic model of knowledge creation is anchored to a critical assumption that human knowledge is created and expanded through social interaction between tacit knowledge and explicit knowledge. We call this interaction "knowledge conversion."

4. FOUR MODES OF KNOWLEDGE CONVERSION

The assumption that knowledge is created through the interaction between tacit and explicit knowledge allows us to postulate four different "modes" of knowledge conversion. They are as follows: (1) from tacit knowledge to tacit knowledge, which we call socialization; (2) from tacit knowledge to explicit knowledge, or externalization; (3) from explicit knowledge to explicit knowledge, or combination; and (4) from explicit knowledge to tacit knowledge, or internalization. Three of the four types of knowledge conversion, i.e. socialization, combination and internalization have been partially discussed from various perspectives in organizational theory. For example, socialization is connected with the theories of group processes and organizational culture; combination has its roots in information-processing; and internalization is closely related to organizational learning. However, externalization has been somewhat neglected.[3] Each of these four modes of knowledge conversion will be discussed in detail below along with actual examples.

4.1 Socialization: From Tacit to Tacit

Socialization is a process of sharing experiences and thereby creating tacit knowledge such as shared mental models and technical skills.[4] An individual can acquire tacit knowledge directly from others without using language. Apprentices work with their masters and learn craftsmanship not through language but through observation, imitation and practice. In the business setting, on-the-job training uses basically the same principle. The key to acquiring tacit knowledge is experience. Without some form of shared experience, it is extremely difficult for one person to project himself into another individual's thinking process. The mere transfer of information will often make little sense, if it is abstracted from associated emotions and specific contexts in which shared experiences are embedded. The following example illustrate how socialization is employed by Japanese companies within the product development context.

The example of socialization, which shows how a tacit technical skill was socialized, comes from the Matsushita Electric Industrial Company. A major problem at the Osaka-based company in developing an automatic home bread-making machine in the late 1980s centered on how to mechanize the dough-kneading process, which is essentially tacit knowledge possessed by master bakers. Dough kneaded by a master baker and by a machine were X-rayed and compared; but no meaningful insights were obtained. Ikuko Tanaka, head of software development, knew that the area's best bread came from the Osaka International Hotel. To capture the tacit knowledge of kneading skill, she and several engineers volunteered to apprentice themselves to the hotel's head baker. Making the same delicious bread as the head baker's was not easy. No one could explain why. One day, however, she noticed that the baker was not only stretching but also "twisting" the dough, which turned out to be the knack for making tasty bread. Thus, she socialized the head baker's tacit knowledge through observation, imitation and practice.

4.2 Externalization: From Tacit to Explicit

Externalization is a process of articulating tacit knowledge into explicit concepts. It is a quintessential knowledge-creation process in that tacit knowledge becomes explicit, taking the shapes of metaphors, analogies, concepts or models. When we attempt to conceptualize our image, we express its essence mostly in language—writing is an act of converting tacit knowledge into articulable knowledge (Emig 1983). Yet, expressions are often inadequate, inconsistent and insufficient. Such discrepancies and gaps between images and expressions, however, help promote "reflection" and interaction between individuals.

The externalization mode of knowledge conversion is typically seen in the process of concept creation and is triggered by dialogue or collective reflection.[5] When we cannot find an adequate expression for our image through analytical methods of deduction or induction, we have to use a nonanalytical method. Externalization is, therefore, often driven by metaphor and/or analogy. Using an attractive metaphor and/or analogy is highly effective in fostering direct commitment to the creative process. In developing the Honda City, Hiroo Watanabe and his team used a metaphor of "automobile evolution." His team viewed the automobile as an organism and sought its ultimate form. In essence, Watanabe was asking, "What will the automobile eventually evolve into?"

I insisted on allocating the minimum space for mechanics and the maximum space for passengers. This seemed to be the ideal car, into which the automobile should evolve. . . . The first step toward this goal was to challenge the 'reasoning of Detroit', which had sacrificed comfort for appearance. Our choice was a short but tall car . . . spherical, therefore lighter, less expensive, more comfortable, and solid.[6]

The concept of a tall and short car, "Tall Boy", emerged through an analogy between the concept of "man maximum, machine minimum" and an image of a sphere that contains the maximum volume within the minimum area of surface, which ultimately resulted in the Honda City.

This example within Honda clearly shows how the use of metaphor and analogy is effective in creating and elaborating a concept. As Honda's Watanabe commented, "We are more than halfway there, once a product concept has been created." In this sense, the leaders' wealth of figurative language and imagination is an essential factor in eliciting tacit knowledge from his project members.

4.3 Combination: From Explicit to Explicit

Combination is a process of systematizing concepts into a knowledge system. This mode of knowledge conversion involves combining different bodies of explicit knowledge. Individuals exchange and combine knowledge through such media as documents, meetings, telephone conversations or computerized communication networks. Reconfiguration of existing information through sorting, adding, combining and categorizing of explicit knowledge (as conducted in computer databases) can lead to new knowledge. Knowledge creation carried out in formal education and training at schools mostly takes this form. An MBA education is one of the best examples of this kind.

In the business context, the combination mode of knowledge conversion is most often seen when middle managers break down and operationalize corporate visions, business concepts or product concepts. Middle management plays a critical role in creating new concepts through networking of codified information and knowledge. Creative uses of computerized communication networks and large-scale databases facilitate this mode of knowledge conversion.[7]

At the top management level of the organization, the combination mode is realized when mid-range concepts (such as product concepts) are combined with and integrated into grand concepts (such as a corporate vision) to generate new meanings of the latter. Introducing a new corporate image in 1986, for example, Asahi Breweries adopted a grand concept dubbed "live Asahi for live people." The concept stood for the message that "Asahi will provide natural and authentic products and services for those who seek active minds and active lives." Asahi inquired into the essence of what makes beer appealing along with this grand concept, and developed Asahi Super Dry beer based on the new product concept of "richness and sharpness." The new product concept is a mid-range concept that made the grand concept of Asahi more explicitly recognizable, which in turn altered the company's product-development system. The taste of beer was hitherto decided by engineers in the production department without any participation of the sales department. The "richness and sharpness" concept was realized through cooperative product development by both departments.

4.4 Internalization: From Explicit to Tacit

Internalization is a process of embodying explicit knowledge into tacit knowledge. It is closely related to "learning by doing." When experiences throughout socialization, externalization and combination are internalized into individuals' tacit knowledge bases in the form of shared mental models or technical know-how, they become valuable assets. All the members of the Honda City Project team, for example, internalized their experiences that took place in the late 1970s and are now making use of that know-how and leading R&D projects in the company. For organizational knowledge creation to take place, however, the tacit knowledge accumulated at the individual level needs to be socialized with other organizational members, thereby starting a new spiral of knowledge creation.

For explicit knowledge to become tacit, it helps to have knowledge become verbalized or diagrammed into documents, manuals or oral stories. Documentation helps individuals internalize what they experienced, thus enriching their tacit knowledge. In addition, documents or manuals facilitate the transfer of explicit knowledge to other people, thereby helping them experience their experiences indirectly (i.e. "re-experience" them).

Internalization can also occur even without having to really "re-experience" other people's experiences. For example, if reading or listening to a success story makes some members of the organization feel the realism and essence of the story, the experience that took place in the past may change into a tacit mental model. When such a mental model is shared by most members of the organization, tacit knowledge becomes part of the organizational culture. This practice is prevalent in Japan, where books and articles on companies or their leaders abound. Free-lance writers or ex-employees publish them, sometimes at the request of the companies. One can find about two dozen books on Honda or Soichiro Honda in a major bookstore today, all of which help instill a strong corporate culture for Honda.

4.5 Knowledge Spiral

As already explained, socialization aims at the sharing of tacit knowledge. On its own, however, it is a limited form of knowledge creation. Unless shared knowledge becomes explicit, it cannot be easily leveraged by the organization as a whole. Also, a mere combination of discrete pieces of explicit information into a new whole—e.g. a comptroller of a company collects information from throughout the company and puts it together in a financial report—does not really extend the organization's existing knowledge base. But when tacit and explicit knowledge interact, as in the Matsushita example, an innovation emerges. Organizational knowledge creation is a continuous and dynamic interaction between tacit and explicit knowledge. This interaction is shaped by shifts between different modes of knowledge conversion, which are in turn induced by several triggers (see Figure 10.2).

First, the socialization mode usually starts with building a "field" of interaction. This field facilitates the sharing of members' experiences and mental models. Second, the externalization mode is triggered by meaningful "dialogue or collective reflection," in which using appropriate metaphor or analogy helps team members to articulate their hidden tacit knowledge

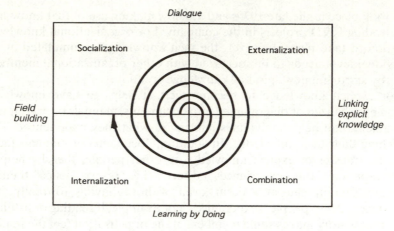

FIG. 10.2. Knowledge spiral

that is otherwise hard to communicate. Third, the combination mode is triggered by "networking" newly created knowledge and existing knowledge from other sections of the organization, thereby crystallizing them into a new product, service or managerial system. Finally, "learning by doing" triggers internalization.

So far, we have mainly discussed the epistemological dimension of organizational knowledge creation. As noted before, however, an organization cannot create knowledge by itself. Tacit knowledge of individuals is the basis of organizational knowledge creation. The organization has to mobilize tacit knowledge created and accumulated at the individual level. The mobilized tacit knowledge is "organizationally" amplified through four modes of knowledge conversion and crystallized at higher ontological levels. We call this the "knowledge spiral," in which the interaction between tacit knowledge and explicit knowledge will become larger in scale as it moves up the ontological levels. Thus, organizational knowledge creation is a spiral process, starting at the individual level and moving up through expanding communities of interaction, which crosses sectional, departmental, divisional, and organizational boundaries (see Figure 10.3).

This process is exemplified by product development. Creating a product concept involves a community of interacting individuals with different backgrounds and mental models. While the members from the R&D department focus on the technological potential, those from the production and marketing departments are interested in other issues. Only part of those different experiences, mental models, motivations, and intentions can be expressed in explicit language. Thus, the socialization process of sharing tacit knowledge is required. Moreover, both socialization and externalization are necessary for linking individuals' tacit and explicit knowledge.

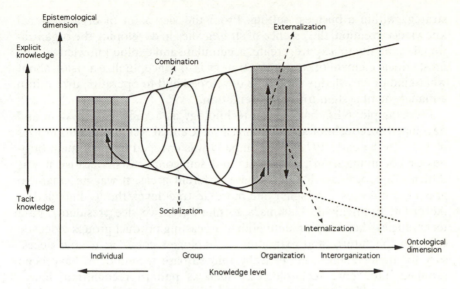

FIG. 10.3. Spiral of organizational knowledge creation

Many Japanese companies have adopted brainstorming camps as a tool for that purpose.

The product created by this collective and cooperative process will then be reviewed for its coherence with mid-range and grand concepts. Even if the newly created product has superior quality, it may conflict with the whole divisional or organizational goals expressed by the mid-range and grand concepts. What is required is another process at a higher level to maintain the whole integrity, which will lead to another cycle of knowledge creation in a larger context.

5. ENABLING CONDITIONS FOR ORGANIZATIONAL KNOWLEDGE CREATION

The role of the organization in the organizational knowledge creation process is to provide the proper context that facilitates group activities as well as the creation and accumulation of knowledge at the individual level. In this section, we will discuss five conditions required at the organizational level to promote the "knowledge spiral."

5.1 *Intention*

The knowledge spiral is driven by organizational intention, which is defined as an organization's aspiration to its goals.[8] It usually takes the form of strategy within a business setting. From the viewpoint of organizational knowledge creation, the essence of strategy lies in developing the organizational capability to acquire, create, accumulate and exploit knowledge. The most critical element of corporate strategy is to conceptualize a vision about what kind of knowledge should be developed and to operationalize it into a management system for implementation.

For example, NEC has viewed technology as a knowledge system and developed core technology programs at its Central Research Laboratories in 1975. In the early 1970s, the company was engaged in three main businesses: communications, computers and semiconductors. Because it was difficult to coordinate R&D of these different areas, it was necessary to grasp technologies at a higher and more abstract level, that is, knowledge. According to Michiyuki Uenohara, former executive vice president, "base technologies" have been identified by forecasting product groups a decade out into the future, and extracting technologies common to and necessary for them. Then, synergistically related base technologies have been grouped into "core technologies," such as pattern recognition, image processing, and VLSI were identified. Since 1975, NEC expanded its core-technology programs using autonomous teams. Today, it has 36 core-technology programs in action.

In addition, NEC devised a concept called the "strategic technology domain" (STD) in order to match core technologies with business activities. An STD links several core technologies to create a concept for product development. Thus, an STD represents not only a product domain but also a knowledge domain. At present, there are six STDs: (1) functional materials/devices; (2) semiconductor; (3) materials/devices functional machinery; (4) communications systems; (5) knowledge information systems; and (6) software. Those STDs interact with core technology programs in a matrix. By combining core-technology programs and the STDs, the knowledge bases at NEC are linked horizontally and vertically. Through this endeavor, NEC has attempted to develop a corporate strategic intention of knowledge creation at every organizational level.

Also, organizational intention or the knowledge vision provides the most important criterion for judging the truthfulness of a given piece of knowledge. If not for intention, it would be impossible to judge the value of information or knowledge perceived or created. At the organizational level, intention is often expressed by organizational standards or visions which can be used to evaluate and justify the created knowledge. It is necessarily value-laden.

To create knowledge, business organizations should foster their employees' commitment by making an "organizational" intention and proposing it to them. Top or middle managers can draw organizational attention to the importance of commitment to fundamental values by addressing such fundamental questions as "What is truth?", "What is a human being?" or

"What is life?" This activity is more organizational than individual. Instead of relying solely on individuals' own thinking and behavior, the organization can reorient and promote them through collective commitment. As Polanyi (1958) notes, commitment underlies the human knowledge-creating activity.

5.2 Autonomy

The second condition for promoting the knowledge spiral is autonomy. At the individual level, all members of an organization should be allowed to act autonomously as far as circumstances permit. By allowing them to act autonomously, the organization may increase the chance of introducing unexpected opportunities. Also, autonomy increases the possibility that individuals will motivate themselves to create new knowledge. Moreover, autonomous individuals function like a part of the holographic structure, in which the whole and each part shares the same information. Original ideas emanate from autonomous individuals, diffuse within the team, and then become organizational ideas. In this respect, the self-organizing individual assumes a position that may be seen as analogous to the core of a series of nested Russian dolls called "Petrouchka." From the viewpoint of knowledge creation, such an organization is more likely to maintain greater flexibility in acquiring, interpreting and relating information.

Autonomous individuals and groups in knowledge-creating organizations set their task boundaries by themselves to pursue the ultimate goal expressed in the higher intention of the organization. In the business organization, a powerful tool for creating circumstances where individuals can act autonomously is provided by the self-organizing team.[9] Such a team should be cross-functional, involving members from a broad cross-section of different organizational activities. Project teams with cross-functional diversity are often used by Japanese firms at every phase of innovation. Most innovation project teams consisted of 10 to 30 members with diverse functional backgrounds, such as R&D, planning, production, quality control, sales and marketing, and customer service. In most companies, there are four to five core members, each of whom has had a multifunctional career. For example, the core members who developed Fuji Xerox's FX-3500 have had at least three functional shifts, even though they were in their thirties at that time.

Moreover, the autonomous team can perform many functions, thereby amplifying and sublimating individual perspectives to higher levels. Honda, for example, organized a cross-functional project team to develop the City model, which comprised people from the sales, development and production departments. This system was called the "SED system," reflecting the sales, engineering and development functions. Its initial goal was to manage development activities more systematically by integrating knowledge and wisdom of "ordinary people" instead of relying on a few heroes. Its operation was very flexible. The three functional areas were nominal and there was a built-in learning process that encouraged invasion into other areas. The members jointly performed the following functions:

- procuring personnel, facilities, and budget for the production plant;
- analyzing the automobile market and competition;
- setting a market target;
- determining a price and a production volume.

The actual work flow required team members to collaborate with their colleagues. Hiroo Watanabe, the team leader, commented:

I am always telling the team members that our work is not a relay race in which my work starts here and yours there. Everyone should run all the way from start to finish. Like rugby, all of us should run together, pass the ball left and right, and reach the goal as a united body.[10]

5.3 Fluctuation and Creative Chaos

The third organizational condition for promoting the knowledge spiral is fluctuation and creative chaos, which stimulate the interaction between the organization and the external environment.[11] Fluctuation is different from complete disorder and characterized by "order without recursiveness." It is an order whose pattern is hard to predict at the beginning (Gleick 1987). If organizations adopt an open attitude toward environmental signals, they can exploit those signals' ambiguity, redundancy, or noise in order to improve their own knowledge system.

When fluctuation is introduced into an organization, its members face a "breakdown" of routines, habits or cognitive frameworks. A breakdown refers to the interrupted moment of our habitual, comfortable "state of being." When we face such a breakdown, we have an opportunity to reconsider our fundamental thinking and perspective. In other words, we begin to question the validity of our basic attitudes toward the world. Such a process requires a deep personal commitment on the part of the individual. A breakdown demands that we turn our attention to dialogue as a means of social interaction, thus helping us to create new concepts.[12] This "continuous" process of questioning and reconsidering existing premises by individual members of the organization fosters organizational knowledge creation. An environmental fluctuation often triggers a breakdown within the organization, out of which new knowledge can be created. Some have called this phenomenon creating "order out of noise" or "order out of chaos."[13]

Chaos is generated naturally when the organization faces a real "crisis," such as a rapid decline of performance due to changes in market needs or significant growth of competitors. It can also be generated intentionally when the organization's leaders try to evoke a "sense of crisis" among organizational members by proposing challenging goals. Ryuzaburo Kaku, chairman of Canon, often says, "the role of top management is to give employees a sense of crisis as well as a lofty ideal" (Nonaka 1985: 142). This latter intentional chaos, which is referred to as "creative chaos," increases tension within the organization and focuses the attention of organizational members to define the problem and resolve the crisis situation. This approach is in sharp contrast to the information-processing paradigm, in which a problem is simply given and a solution is found through a process of combining relevant information based upon a preset algorithm. Such a process ignores the importance of defining the problem to be solved. To do so, problems must be constructed from the knowledge available at a certain point in time and context.

Japanese companies often resort to the purposeful use of ambiguity and "creative chaos." Top management often employs ambiguous visions (or so-called "strategic equivocality") and intentionally creates a fluctuation within the organization. Nissan's CEO, Yutaka Kume, for example, coined the catch phrase "Let's change the flow," by which he tried to promote creativity through an active investigation of alternatives to established procedures. When the philosophy or vision of top management is ambiguous, that ambiguity leads to "interpretative equivocality" at the level of the implementing staff.

It should be noted that the benefits of "creative chaos" can only be realized when organizational members have the ability to reflect upon their actions. Without reflection, fluctuation tends to lead to "destructive" chaos. Schön (1983) captures this key point as follows: "When someone reflects while in action, he becomes a researcher in the practice context. He is not dependent on the categories of established theory and technique, but constructs a new theory of the unique case" (p. 68). The knowledge-creating organization is required to institutionalize this "reflection-in-action" in its process to make chaos truly "creative."

5.4 Redundancy

Redundancy is the fourth condition that enables the knowledge spiral to take place organizationally. To Western managers who are preoccupied with the idea of efficient information processing or uncertainty reduction (Galbraith 1973), the term "redundancy" may sound pernicious due to its connotations of unnecessary duplication, waste or information overload. What we mean here by redundancy is the existence of information that goes beyond the immediate operational requirements of organizational members. In business organizations, redundancy refers to intentional overlapping of information about business activities, management responsibilities and the company as a whole.

For organizational knowledge creation to take place, a concept created by an individual or group needs to be shared by other individuals who may not need the concept immediately. Sharing redundant information promotes the sharing of tacit knowledge, because individuals can sense what others are trying to articulate. In this sense, redundancy of information speeds up the knowledge-creation process. Redundancy is especially important in the concept-development stage, when it is critical to articulate images rooted in tacit knowledge. At this stage, redundant information enables individuals to invade each other's functional boundaries and offer advice or provide new information from different perspectives. In short, redundancy of information brings about *"learning by intrusion"* into each individual's sphere of perception.

There are several ways to build redundancy into the organization. One is to adopt an overlapping approach as illustrated by Japanese companies' "rugby-style" product development in which different functional divisions work together in a "fuzzy" division of labor (Takeuchi and Nonaka 1986). Some companies divide the product development team further into competing groups that develop different approaches to the same project and then argue over advantages and disadvantages of their proposals. This "internal competition" encourages the team to look at a project from a variety of perspectives. Under the guidance of a team leader, the team eventually develops a common understanding of the "best" approach.

Another way to build redundancy into the organization is through a "strategic rotation" of personnel, especially between vastly different areas of technology or functions such as R&D and marketing. Such rotation helps organizational members understand its business from multiple perspectives, thereby making organizational knowledge more "fluid" and easier to put into practice. It also enables each employee to diversify his or her skills and information sources. The extra information held by individuals across different functions helps the organization expand its knowledge-creation capacity.

One of the most notable characteristics of Japanese organizations compared with their Western counterparts is the value placed on redundant information. Leading Japanese firms have institutionalized redundancy within themselves to develop new products and services swiftly in response to fast-changing markets and technologies. Japanese firms have also developed many other organizational devices that increase and maintain redundancy. Among them are frequent meetings on both regular and irregular bases (e.g. Honda's brainstorming camp or *tama dashi kai*) and formal and informal communication networks (e.g. *nommunication* or drinking sessions after working hours). These devices facilitate the sharing of both tacit and explicit knowledge.

Redundancy of information, however, increases the amount of information to be processed and can lead to the problem of information overload. It also increases the cost of knowledge creation at least in the short run (e.g. decreased operational efficiency). Therefore, the balancing between creation and processing of information is another important issue. One way to deal with the possible downside of redundancy is to make clear where information can be located and knowledge is stored within the organization.

5.5 Requisite Variety

The fifth condition that helps to advance the knowledge spiral is requisite variety. According to Ashby (1956), an organization's internal diversity must match the variety and complexity of the environment to deal with challenges posed by the environment. Organizational members can cope with many contingencies if they possess requisite variety, which can be enhanced by combining information differently, flexibly and quickly and by giving equal access to information throughout the organization. To maximize variety, everyone in the organization, therefore, should be assured of the fastest access to the broadest variety of necessary information, going through the fewest steps.

When information differentials exist within the organization, organizational members cannot interact on equal terms, which hinders the search for different interpretations of new information. Kao Corp., Japan's leading maker of household products such as detergents, believes that all employees should have equal access to corporate information. Kao has developed a computerized information network for this purpose. It has become the basis for opinion exchanges among various organizational units with different viewpoints.

Developing a flat and flexible organizational structure in which the different units are interlinked with an information network is one way to deal with the complexity of the environment. Another way to react quickly to unexpected fluctuations in the environment and maintain internal diversity is to change organizational structure frequently. Matsushita, for example, restructured its divisional system three times in the past decade. In addition, frequent rotation of personnel enables employees to acquire multifunctional knowledge, which helps them to cope with multifaceted problems and unexpected environmental fluctuations. Such a fast-cycle rotation of personnel can be seen at the Ministry of International Trade and Industry (MITI), where the bureaucrats rotate from one job to the next every two years.

6. FIVE-PHASE MODEL OF THE ORGANIZATIONAL KNOWLEDGE-CREATION PROCESS

Thus far, we have looked at each of the four modes of knowledge conversion and the five enabling conditions that promote organizational knowledge creation. In this section, we present an integrated, five-phase model of the organizational knowledge-creation process, using the basic constructs developed within the theoretical framework and incorporating the time dimension to our theory. The model, which should be interpreted as an ideal type of the process, consists of five phases: (1) sharing tacit knowledge; (2) creating concepts; (3) justifying concepts; (4) building an archetype; and (5) cross-leveling knowledge (see Figure 10.4).

The organizational knowledge-creation process starts with the sharing of tacit knowledge, which corresponds roughly to socialization, since the rich and untapped knowledge that resides in individuals must first be amplified within the organization. In the second phase, tacit knowledge shared by, say, a self-organizing team is converted to explicit knowledge in the form of a new concept, a process similar to externalization. The created concept has to be justified in the third phase, in which the organization determines if the new concept is truly worthwhile to pursue. Receiving the go-ahead, the concepts are converted in the fourth phase into an archetype, which can take the form of a prototype in the case of "hard" product development or an operating mechanism in the case of "soft" innovations, such as a new corporate value, a novel managerial system, or an innovative organizational structure. The last phase extends the knowledge created in, say, a division to others in the division, across to other division, or even to outside constituents in what we termed cross-leveling of knowledge. These outside constituents include consumers, affiliated companies, universities, and distributors, to name a few. As such, a knowledge-creating company does not

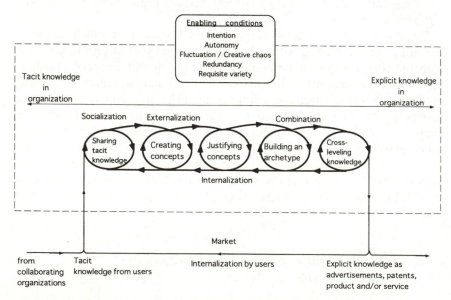

FIG. 10.4. Five-phase model of the organizational knowledge creation process

operate itself in a closed system but in an open system where knowledge is constantly exchanged with the outside environment. We shall describe each of the five phases in more detail below.

6.1 The First Phase: Sharing Tacit Knowledge

As we mentioned repeatedly, an organization cannot create knowledge by itself. Since tacit knowledge held by individuals is the basis of organizational knowledge creation, it seems natural to start the process by focusing on tacit knowledge, which is the rich, untapped source of new knowledge. But tacit knowledge cannot be communicated or passed on to others easily, since it is acquired primarily through experience and not expressible in words. Thus, the sharing of tacit knowledge among multiple individuals with different backgrounds, perspectives and motivations becomes the critical step for organizational knowledge creation to take place. Their emotions, feelings and mental models have to be shared to build mutual trust.

To do so, we need a "field" where individuals can interact with each other through face-to-face dialogues. It is here that they share experiences and synchronize their bodily and mental rhythms. The typical field of interaction is a self-organizing team, in which members from various functional departments work together to achieve a common goal. Examples of a self-organizing team include Matsushita's Home Bakery team and the Honda City team. At Matsushita, team members apprenticed themselves to the head baker at the Osaka International Hotel to capture the essence of kneading skill through bodily experience. At Honda, team members shared their mental models and technical skills in discussing what an ideal car should evolve into, often over *sake* and away from the office. These examples show that the first phase of the organizational knowledge-creation process corresponds to socialization.

A self-organizing team facilitates organizational knowledge creation through the requisite variety of the team members, who experience redundancy of information and share their interpretation of organizational intention. Management injects creative chaos by setting challenging goals and endowing team members with a high degree of autonomy. An autonomous team starts to set its own task boundaries, and as a "boundary spanning unit," begins to interact with the external environment, accumulating both tacit and explicit knowledge.

6.2 The Second Phase: Creating Concepts

The most intensive interaction between tacit and explicit knowledge occurs in the second phase. Once a shared mental model is formed in the field of interaction, the self-organizing team then articulates it through further continuous dialogue, i.e. collective reflection. The shared tacit mental model is verbalized into words and phrases, and finally crystallized into explicit concepts. In this sense, this phase corresponds to externalization.

This process of converting tacit knowledge into explicit knowledge is facilitated by the use of multiple reasoning methods, such as deduction, induction and abduction. Particularly useful for this phase is abduction, which employs figurative language such as metaphors and analogies. In developing City, for example, the Honda development team made ample use of figurative language such as "automobile evolution," "man maximum, machine minimum," and "Tall Boy." The quality of dialogue among team members can also be raised through the use of dialectics, which instills a creative way of thinking of the organization. It is an iterative and spiral process in which contradictions and paradoxes are utilized to synthesize new knowledge.

Concepts are created cooperatively in this phase through dialogue. Autonomy helps team members to diverge their thinking freely, with intention serving as a tool to converge their thinking into one direction. To create concepts, team members have to fundamentally rethink their existing premises. Requisite variety helps the team in this regard by providing different angles or perspectives to look at a problem. Fluctuation and chaos, either from the outside or inside, also helps members to change their way of thinking fundamentally. Redundancy of information enables team members to understand figurative language better and to crystallize their shared mental model.

6.3 The Third Phase: Justifying Concepts

In our theory of organizational knowledge creation, knowledge is defined as "justified" true belief. Therefore, new concepts that individuals or the team create need to be justified somewhere in the process. Justification involves the process of determining if the newly created concepts are truly worthwhile for the organization and society. It is similar to a screening process. Individuals seem to be justifying or screening information, concepts or knowledge continuously and unconsciously throughout the entire process. The organization, however, must conduct this justification in a more explicit way to check if the organizational intention is still intact and to ascertain if the concepts being generated meet the needs of society at large. The most appropriate time for the organization to conduct this screening process is right after the concepts have been created.[14]

For business organizations, the normal justification criteria include cost, profit margin and the degree to which a product can contribute to the firm's growth. But, justification criteria can be both quantitative and qualitative. For example, in the Honda City case, the "Tall Boy" concept had to be justified against the vision that top management set, namely to come up with a product concept fundamentally different from anything the company had done before and to make a car that was inexpensive but not cheap. It also had to be justified against the product-line concept articulated by middle management namely to make the car "man maximum, machine minimum." More abstract criteria may include value premises such as adventure, romanticism and aesthetics. Thus, justification criteria need not be strictly objective and factual; it can also be judgmental and value-laden.

In a knowledge-creating company, it is primarily the role of top management to formulate the justification criteria in the form of organizational intention, which is expressed in terms of strategy or vision. Middle management can also formulate the justification criteria in the form of mid-range concepts. Although the key justification criteria are set by top management, and to some extent, by middle management, this does not preclude other organizational units from having some autonomy in deciding their own sub-criteria. To avoid any misunderstanding about the company's intention, redundancy of information helps facilitate the justification process.

6.4 The Fourth Phase: Building an Archetype

In this fourth phase, the justified concept is converted into something tangible or concrete, namely an archetype. An archetype can be thought of as a "prototype" in the case of a new product-development process. In the case of service or organizational innovation, an archetype could be thought of as a "model" operating mechanism. In either case, it is built by combining newly created explicit knowledge with existing explicit knowledge. In building a prototype, for example, the explicit knowledge to be combined could take the form of technologies or components. Because justified concepts, which are explicit, are converted into archetypes, which are also explicit, this phase is akin to combination.

Just as an architect builds a mockup before starting the actual construction, organizational members engage themselves in building a prototype of the real product or a model of the actual system. To build a prototype, they pull together people with different expertise (e.g. R&D, production, marketing, quality control, etc.), develop specifications that meet everyone's approval, and actually manufacture the first full-scale form of a newly created product concept. To build a model, say, of a new organizational structure, people from the affected sections within the organization as well as experts in different fields (e.g. human-resources management, legal, strategic planning, etc.) are assembled to draw up a new organizational chart, job description, reporting system or operating procedures. In a way, their role is similar to that of an architect—they are responsible for developing the blueprint as well as actually building the new form of an organizational concept. Attention to details is the key to managing this complex process.

Because this phase is complex, a dynamic cooperation of various departments within the organization is indispensable. Both requisite variety and redundancy of information facilitate this process. Organizational intention also serves as a useful tool for converging the various know-how and technologies that reside within the organization as well as promoting interpersonal and interdepartmental cooperation.

6.5 The Fifth Phase: Cross-leveling of Knowledge

Organizational knowledge creation is a never-ending process that upgrades itself continuously. It does not end once an archetype has been developed. The new concept, which has been created, justified and modeled, moves on to a new cycle of knowledge creation at a different ontological level. This interactive and spiral process, which we call "cross-leveling of knowledge," takes place both intraorganizationally and interorganizationally.

Intraorganizationally, knowledge that is made real or takes form as an archetype can trigger a new cycle of knowledge creation, expanding horizontally and vertically across the organization. An example of a horizontal cross-fertilization can be seen within Matsushita, when Home Bakery induced the creation of other "Easy and Rich" product concepts, such as a fully automatic coffee-maker within the same division and a new generation of large-screen TV sets from another division. In these cases, cross-fertilization took place across different sections within the division as well as across different divisions. An example of vertical cross-fertilization also comes from Matsushita. The development of Home Bakery inspired Matsushita to adopt "Human Electronics" as the umbrella concept at the corporate level. This umbrella concept opened up a series of soul-searching activities within the company on what kind of a company Matsushita should be in the twenty-first century and how "human" Matsushita employees can be. These activities culminated in the development of MIT'93 (Mind and Management Innovation Toward '93), which was instrumental in reducing the number of annual working hours at the front line to 1,800 hours, thereby freeing up time for people at the front line. In this case, knowledge created in one division led to the adoption of an umbrella concept at the corporate level, which in turn, affected the lives of employees at the front line.

Interorganizationally, knowledge created by the organization can mobilize knowledge of affiliated companies, customers, suppliers, competitors, and others outside the company through dynamic interaction. For example, an innovative new approach to budgetary control developed by one company could bring about changes in an affiliated company's financial control system, which, in turn, may trigger a new round of innovation. Or, a customer's reaction or feedback to a new product concept may initiate a new cycle of product development.

For this phase to function effectively, it is essential that each organizational unit have the autonomy to take the knowledge developed somewhere else and apply it freely across different levels and boundaries. Internal fluctuation, such as the frequent rotation of personnel, will facilitate knowledge transfer. So will redundancy of information and requisite variety. And intraorganizational cross-leveling, organizational intention will act as a control mechanism on whether or not knowledge should be cross-fertilized within the company.

Explicit knowledge as products and/or services will go into the market, where users internalize the new knowledge and create more knowledge such as unexpected uses of the products and suggestions for improving them. Also, there exist a variety of unsatisfied needs in the market. Therefore, we can view the market as a repository of knowledge.[15] According to Hayek (1945, 1978), furthermore, the market can be seen as the process through which dispersed knowledge in society is mobilized and the place where competitors learn and improve upon each other's goods (i.e. benchmarking) or gain hints for further innovations, thereby creating new knowledge.[16]

7. SUMMARY

We presented a new explanation on why Japanese companies have become successful in the past. The key to understanding the new explanation lies in the creation of organizational knowledge. We have described the distinctive approach to knowledge creation among Japanese companies along two dimensions—epistemological and ontological. The epistemological dimension, which is graphically represented on the vertical axis, is where knowledge conversion takes place between tacit knowledge and explicit knowledge. Four modes of this conversion—socialization, externalization, combination and internalization—were discussed. These modes are not independent of each other, but their interactions produce a spiral when time is introduced as the third dimension. We introduced five organizational conditions—intention, fluctuation/chaos, autonomy, redundancy and requisite variety—that enable (thus the term "enabling conditions") the four modes to be transformed into a knowledge spiral.

The ontological dimension, which is represented in the horizontal axis, is where knowledge created by individuals is transformed into knowledge at the group and organizational levels. Again, these levels are not independent of each other but interact with each other iteratively and continuously. We introduced time as the third dimension here again to develop the five-phase process of organizational knowledge creation—sharing tacit knowledge, creating concepts, justifying concepts, building an archetype and cross-leveling knowledge. Another spiral takes place at the ontological dimension, when knowledge developed at, say, the project-team level is transformed into knowledge at the divisional level, and eventually to the corporate or interorganizational levels. The five enabling conditions promote the entire process and facilitate the spiral.

The transformation of that process within these two knowledge spirals is the key to understanding our theory. If we had a three-dimensional chart, we could show that the knowledge spiral at the epistemological level rises upward, whereas the knowledge spiral at the ontological level moves from left to right and back again to the left in a cyclical motion. And, of course, the truly dynamic nature of our theory can be depicted as the interaction of the two knowledge spirals over time. Innovation emerges out of these spirals.

NOTES

1. Brown and Duguid's (1991) work on "evolving communities of practice" show how individuals' actual ways of working and learning might be very different from relatively rigid, official practices specified by the organization. In reality, informal groups evolve among individuals seeking to solve a particular problem or pursuing other commonly held objectives. Membership of these groups is decided by individuals' abilities to trade practically valuable information. Also, Orr (1990) argues that members exchange ideas and share narratives or "war stories," thereby building a shared understanding out of conflicting and confusing information. Thus, knowledge creation includes not only innovation but also learning that can shape and develop approaches to daily work.
2. For example, we recognize our neighbor's face without being able to explain how to do so in words. Moreover, we sense others' feelings from their facial expressions, but explaining them in words is more difficult. Put another way, while it is virtually impossible to articulate the feelings we get from our neighbor's face, we are still aware of the overall impression. For further discussion on tacit knowledge, see Polanyi (1958) and Gelwick (1977).
3. For a limited analysis of externalization from a viewpoint of information creation, see Nonaka (1987).
4. Cannon-Bowers, Salas and Converse (1993) define "shared mental models" as "knowledge structures held by members of a team that enable them to form accurate explanations and expectations for the task, and in turn, to coordinate their actions and adapt their behavior to demands of the task and other team members" (p. 228) based upon their extensive review of the literature on the shared mental model and for their research on team decision-making. To understand how a shared mental model is created, the German philosopher Hans-

Georg Gadamer's concept of "*fusion of horizons*" is helpful. The concept was developed for philosophical hermeneutics or the study of methodology for interpreting historical texts. Gadamer (1989) argues that a true understanding of a text is a "fusion" of the interpreter's and the author's horizons. He defines the horizon as "the range of vision that includes everything that can be seen from a particular vantage point"(p. 302). Applying this concept to our context, we can argue that socialization is a "fusion" of participants' tacit knowledge into a shared mental model.

5. Graumann (1990) views dialogue as multiperspective cognition. As noted before, language is inherently related to action, as suggested by the term "speech act" (Austin 1962; Searle 1969). Dialogue, therefore, may be seen as a collective action. Moreover, according to Kant, the world is created by language and creating concepts is creating the world.

6. Interviewed on 25 January 1984.

7. Information and communications technologies used for this purpose include VAN (Value-Added Network), LAN (Local Area Network), E-Mail (Electronic Mail), POS (Point-Of-Sales) system, "Groupware" for CSCW (Computer Supported Cooperative Work), and CAD/CAM (Computer-Aided Design/Manufacturing).

8. Neisser (1976) argues that cognition as knowing and understanding occurs only in the context of purposeful activity. From an organization theory perspective, moreover, Weick (1979) contends that an organization's interpretation of environmental information has an element of a self-fulfilling prophecy, because the organization has a strong will to self-actualize what it wants to become. He calls this phenomenon the "enactment" of environment.

9. The team should be established in due consideration of the principles of self-organization such as learning to learn, requisite variety, minimum critical specification, and redundancy of functions (Morgan 1986). Requisite variety will be discussed later.

10. In our 1986 *Harvard Business Review* article entitled "The New New Product Development Game" (Jan.–Feb. 1986), we argued that in today's fast-paced and fiercely competitive world, this overlapping, rugby-style approach has tremendous merit in terms of speed and flexibility.

11. Gibson (1979) hypothesizes that knowledge lies in the environment itself, contrary to the traditional epistemological view that it exists inside the human brain. Also, Norman (1988) argues that knowledge exists not only inside the brain but also in the external world in the forms of things, others, and situations, etc.

12. Piaget (1974) notes the importance of the role of contradiction in the interaction between the subject and the environment. The root of contradiction, he argued, lies in the coordination between the positive and negative sides of specific perception or behavior, which in turn is indispensable for creating new concepts.

13. According to the principle of "order out of noise" proposed by von Foerster (1984), the self-organizing system can increase its ability to survive by purposefully introducing such noise into itself. Order in the natural world includes not only the static and crystalized order in which entropy is zero but also the "unstable" order in which new structures are formed by the working of matter

and energy. The latter is what Prigogine and Stengers (1984) call "order out of chaos" in their theory of dissipative structure. In an evolutionary planning perspective, moreover, Jantsch (1980) argues: "In contrast to widely held belief, planning is an evolutionary spirit and therefore does not result in the reduction of uncertainty and complexity, but in their increases. Uncertainty increases because the spectrum of options is deliberately widened; imagination comes into play" (p. 267). Researchers who have developed the chaos theory have found the creative nature of chaos. See, for example, Gleick (1987) and Waldrop (1992).

14. The final justification of created concepts and their realized forms, i.e. products and/or services, occurs in the marketplace.

15. It should be noted that Nelson and Winter (1977, 1982) viewed the firm as a repository for a quite specific range of knowledge. Such specific knowledge is stored as "regular and predictable behavioral patterns" of business firms. They called such knowledge "routines" which are regarded as the tacit knowledge accumulated in organizations.

16. Hayek also posited that the function of the price mechanism is to communicate information and was a pioneer in drawing attention to the importance of implicit, context-specific knowledge.

REFERENCES

Ashby, W. R. (1956), *An Introduction to Cybernetics* (London: Chapman & Hall).

Austin, J. L. (1962), *How to Do Things with Words* (Oxford: Oxford University Press).

Bateson, G. (1973), *Steps to an Ecology of Mind* (London: Paladin).

Brown, J. S. and Duguid, P. (1991), "Organizational Learning and Communities-of-Practice: Toward a Unified View of Working, Learning, and Innovation", *Organization Science*, 2/1: 40–57.

Cannon-Bowers, J. A., Salas, E. and Converse, S. (1993), "Shared Mental Models in Expert Team Decision Making," in N. J. Castellan, Jr. (ed.), *Individual and Group Decision Making* (Hillsdale, NJ: Lawrence Erlbaum Associates).

Drucker, P. (1993), *The New Society: The Anatomy of Industrial Order* (New Brunswick, NJ: Transaction; orig. pub. 1950, New York: Harper).

Emig, J. (1983), *The Web of Meaning*, (Upper Monteclair, NJ: Boynton/Cook).

Gadamer, H. (1989), *Truth and Method* (2nd edn. trans. J. Weinsheimer and D. G. Marshall (New York: Crossroad).

Galbraith, J. (1973), *Designing Complex Organizations* (Reading, Mass.: Addison-Wesley).

Gelwick, R. (1977), *The Way of Discovery: An Introduction to the Thought of Michael Polanyi* (Oxford: Oxford University Press).

Gibson, J.J. (1979), *The Ecological Approach to Visual Perception* (Boston, Mass.: Houghton Mifflin).

Gleick, J. (1987), *Chaos* (New York: Viking Press).

Graumann, C. F. (1990), "Perspectival Structure and Dynamics in Dialogues," in I. Markova and K. Foppa (eds.), *The Dynamics of Dialogue*, (New York: Harvester Wheatsheaf).

Hayek, F. A. (1945), "The Use of Knowledge in Society," *American Economic Review*, 35/4.

——(1978), "Competition as a Discovery Procedure," in *New Studies in Philosophy, Politics, and the History of Ideas* (Chicago: University of Chicago Press).

Jantsch, E. (1980), *The Self-Organizing Universe* (Oxford: Pergamon Press).

Morgan, G. (1986), *Images of Organization* (Beverly Hills, Calif.: Sage).

Neisser, U. (1976), *Cognition and Reality* (San Francisco: W. H. Freeman).

Nelson, R. R. and Winter, S. G. (1977), "In Search of a Useful Theory of Innovation," *Research Policy*, 6/1: 36–77.

————(1982), *An Evolutionary Theory of Economic Change* (Cambridge, Mass.: Harvard University Press).

Nonaka, I. (1985), *Kigyo Shinka-ron* (Corporate Evolution: Managing Organizational Information Creation) (Tokyo: Nihon Keizai Shimbun-sha) (in Japanese).

——(1987), "Managing the Firms as Information Creation Process," Working Paper, Jan. (pub. in J. Meindl (1991) (ed.)), *Advances in Information Processing in Organizations*, iv (Greenwich, Conn.: JAI Press).

Norman, D. A. (1988), *The Psychology of Everyday Things* (New York: Basic Books).

Orr, J. E. (1990), "Sharing Knowledge, Celebrating Identity: Community Memory in a Service Culture," in D. Middleton and D. Edwards (eds.), *Collective Remembering* (Newbury Park, Calif.: Sage).

Piaget, J. (1974), *Recherches sur la Contradiction* (Paris: Presses Universitaires de France).

Polanyi, M. (1958), *Personal Knowledge* (Chicago: University of Chicago Press).

——(1966), *The Tacit Dimension* (London: Routledge & Kegan Paul).

Prigogine, I. and Stengers, I. (1984), *Order out of Chaos: Man's New Dialogue with Nature* (New York: Bantam Books).

Schön, D. A. (1983), *The Reflective Practitioner* (New York: Basic Books).

Searle, J. R. (1969), *Speech Acts: An Essay in the Philosophy of Language* (Cambridge: Cambridge University Press).

Takeuchi, H. and Nonaka, I. (1986), "The New New Product Development Game," *Harvard Business Review* (Jan.–Feb.), 137–46.

Toffler, A. (1990), *Powershift: Knowledge, Wealth, and Violence at the Edge of the 21st Century* (Alvin, NY: Bantam Books).

von Foerster, H. (1984), "Principles of Self-organization in a Socio-Managerial Context," in H. Ulrich and G. J. B. Probst, *Self-Organization and Management of Social Systems*, (Berlin: Springer-Verlag).

Waldrop, M. M. (1992), *Complexity: Life at the Edge of Chaos* (New York: Simon & Schuster).

Weick, Karl E. (1979), *The Social Psychology of Organizing*, 2nd edn. (Reading, Mass.: Addison-Wesley).

11

Dynamics of Overlapping Networks and Strategic Actions by the International Firm

LARS-GUNNAR MATTSSON

1. INTRODUCTION

Over time both firms and markets change along internationalization dimensions. As both firms *and* markets become increasingly internationalized, the interdependencies between the individual firm's strategic actions and its dynamic international market context become more important to understand. To understand contemporary international business we need analytical frameworks that explicitly consider the dynamic interaction between the micro aspects of the individual firm and the macro aspects of the market.

In this chapter I will pursue some ideas based on the "markets-as-networks" approach, specifically the notion of "overlapping networks." In Figure 11.1(a) some actors in network A are related to actors in network B. This actor-based overlap influences strategic actions and network processes in both A and B. Actor-based *overlapping* is a network process by which, due to strategic actions, the overlap increases (Figure 1 (b)). A complementary definition of overlap(ping) is based on the number of relationships in A and B for which the counterpart is an actor in B and A respectively. While the actor-based definition means that an actor in A has at least one relationship to one actor in B, the relationship-based definition also considers the number of relationships in B that the actor in A has. Both actor-based and relationship-based definitions will be used in the following.

First, I will present such basic characteristics of a markets-as-networks approach that are necessary for my arguments. Second, I suggest that contemporary developments in international business increase the validity of this theoretical framework. Third, I will use the framework to analyze some types of firm behavior, i.e. foreign market entry, defense of the home market and international integration of production systems. Fourth, I will discuss some issues at the macro level and finally comment on the potential use of more formal sociological network analysis.

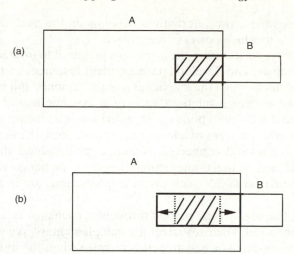

F<small>IG</small>. 11.1. Overlap and overlapping between networks. (a) Overlap between A and B; (b) Overlapping between A and B as an extension of the overlap

2. MARKETS-AS-NETWORKS

2.1 The general framework

In the "markets-as-networks" research tradition, initially developed by researchers specializing in industrial and international marketing research, individual firms are connected to other firms in networks of *exchange relationships* between firms. (See Johanson and Mattsson 1994, for an overview of this research tradition as it has developed in Sweden.) The generic governance structure for production systems is networks of multidimensional exchange relationships between actors who control heterogeneous, interdependent resources and carry out interlinked activities for production, distribution and consumption. The production system concept, as it is used here thus includes also distribution and consumption. The network concept includes both the notion of "market" and the notion of "industry." The conceptual framework presented here builds on Johanson and Mattsson 1992.

A network is *not* viewed as an intermediate, unstable governance structure "between market and hierarchy." Markets (and industries) are network structures according to the view presented here. The basic coordinating mechanism in a market is interaction within and between connected exchange relationships between actors. In contrast to most research on intermediate governance structures, be it in the transaction cost or relational contracting approaches, network research is not "dyadic." The firm is treated as a hierarchy or as a network connecting several actors. The choice between these two alternatives depends on the analytical purpose and the degree to which power is centralized.

In an exchange relationship the actors are prepared to interact with each other to coordinate and develop interdependent resources and interlinked activities in order to reach the individual actor's efficiency and effectiveness objectives. An exchange relationship is of a dynamic nature. It changes over time and it influences both actors' activities and resources. Exchange relationships inherently are of a long-term nature. Since the network structure consists of several connected exchange relationships, there are dynamic, direct and indirect interactions between exchange relationships (Cook and Emerson 1978). Such dynamic interactions are in focus in this chapter.

Two firms that are directly related through an exchange relationship are positively connected. Their resources are complementary. An indirect connection can be positive or negative. It is positive when the interconnected activities and the interdependent resources are complementary. It is negative due to substitutability, such as when two sellers compete for the limited purchasing capacity of a buyer. The sign of the connection might change or become less distinctly positive or negative. Two competitors might, for example, merge or begin to cooperate regarding some activities in a strategic alliance, a supplier might be acquired by the buyer's competitor and no longer be available for joint technical development with this specific buyer.

Over time new relationships are established and existing ones maintained, developed and sometimes disrupted. The network structure thus shows both important changes and a considerable stability.

Within a network there are sets of positively connected relationships that have closer interdependencies within the set than with relationships outside the specific set. Such a "cluster" within a network is called a *net*.

Each actor has a *position* in a specified network that can be described by its relationships to other actors and by the actor's functional and quantitative roles in the production system. Each actor's position in the network can similarly be described in terms of its relationships and roles. The position of an actor in a network can be more or less central.

Strategic objectives can be defined in terms of network positions. A firm aspires to sustain and develop its network positions to get such control over interdependencies between its own resources and activities and those of other firms that the firm can be efficient and effective. The network position both describes the base upon which strategic actions might be implemented and the objective for such strategic actions. The actor's *strategic actions* are aimed at influencing exchange relationships in networks, i.e. influencing actor positions. Strategic actions by others might facilitate or hinder the fulfillment of such aims by a focal actor. Strategic actions are thus constrained by history and by current network structure and concurrent change processes. Over time, the accumulated effects of strategic actions by individual firms will likely lead to substantial structural changes in the network, thereby also influencing future developments, for instance, the possibilities to establish specific new relationships.

2.2 Network boundaries and network overlap(ping)

For analytical and action purposes it is necessary to distinguish between different networks. However, networks are inherently open, and connected to some other networks through one or more exchange relationships. Network boundaries can be set according to objective criteria or subjective perceptions of interdependencies between exchange relationships, with reference to analytical purposes and to the theoretical foundations on which an analysis is performed. This makes boundary setting a non-trivial, creative act by the actor and/or the analyst. Since I here will use traditional spatial market and industry classifications, the subjective aspects of network boundaries mostly refer to the definition of subgroups in the network.

Overlap is a static, structural measure and implies interdependence between two or more networks. If both actor and relationship overlaps are high, two networks are very interdependent and might by actors and analysts be regarded more validly as one network instead of two. Through strategic actions an overlap changes over time. This process is called *overlapping*. Overlapping may increase, decrease and/or change the composition of the overlap. Overlapping changes the network structure and thus also actors' positions and the conditions for network coordination. Overlapping will therefore initiate further strategic actions by firms, thus making overlapping a continuous network process.

2.3 Different types of network boundaries

Four types of network boundaries are discussed in this chapter.

First, a firm's *focal net* consists of the other firms that the focal firm has direct exchange relationships with and also firms with such indirect, complementary relations that are used for coordination with the focal firm's resources. Examples of such indirect relations in the focal net of a manufacturer are those between the end users of the product and the distributors and between the subsuppliers and the suppliers. When the firm is a multiunit firm, separated into several actors, such as divisions and subsidiaries, we will distinguish between the *internal* and *external* parts of the focal net. A focal net is an extension of the concept "organization set" (Aldrich 1979) because important indirect relations are also included. Strategic actions are aimed at influencing the focal net for the focal firm's benefit, e.g. in terms of adding and dropping suppliers and customers, changing the role of intermediaries, increasing technical cooperation with complementary firms or with competitors. Since all the firms have focal nets, all focal nets overlap with several other focal nets.

Second, as mentioned above, a *net* without specification of a focal firm, contains positively connected actors with closer interdependencies within the net than outside the net.

Third, a network may be delimited due to geographical, *spatial boundaries* such as nations, regions within nations and regions consisting of several nations. Spatial boundaries are of course a foundation for the study of international markets and international business. Internationalization processes imply overlapping between spatially bounded networks. Further internationalization of already highly internationalized markets is a matter of overlapping in highly overlapped spatial networks.

Fourth, a network may be delimited due to *technological interdependencies* in the production system. This is an identification, in network terms, of different "industries." Delimitation criteria focusing on complementarity will result in different network boundaries than those that refer to substitutability. Overlap between technically defined networks always exists, especially when network boundaries are primarily based on substitutability. Overlapping is of special importance during technological change processes.

Overlap and overlapping between the three types of networks, i.e. the focal net, the spatial network and the technological network are also meaningful to consider. A focal net may, due to internationalization, overlap with several spatial networks. Overlapping due to changes in the focal net represents a micro behavior which is thus influencing the macro structure. At the macro level, international diffusion of an innovation might be interpreted as a technological network overlapping with several spatial networks.

The perceived network structure and expected future changes in that structure might differ between the analyst and the actor and also between actors. Such differences are in themselves interesting since they influence the validity of the research approach and the explanations for strategic actions. The latter might be interpreted as differences in the actors' *network theories* (Johanson and Mattsson 1992).

2.4 Dynamic aspects of overlaps and overlapping

Network openness has a dynamic effect, i.e. overlaps stimulate strategic actions and strategic actions affect overlapping. Such dynamic effects are due to both positive and negative connections between actors. I will first discuss the implications of overlap and then of overlapping.

Overlap *Positive connections* through overlaps introduce variation and complementarities in the network. This stimulates innovation and increases opportunities to coordinate extended production systems for increased efficiency. Positive connections through overlaps also increase information exchange between networks, not only through the direct exchange relationships but also indirectly to more distant actors and relationships. Overlaps open opportunities for "weak ties" to convey new information between networks (Granovetter 1973).

Negative connections due to overlap signify that competitors from other networks exist. This could imply threats to actor positions but also stimuli to improve present exchange relationships and to establish new ones, perhaps in the other network as a competitive reaction. This can be interpreted as overlapping, thereby further increasing the overlap. Negative connections might cause two competitors to merge, to cooperate or to specialize on dissimilar activities to avoid competition due to the overlap.

Both negative and positive connections through overlaps increase the interdependency between actors and between exchange relationships in the overlapped networks. Examples of high degrees of both actor and relationship overlap are highly internationalized markets, industries characterized by a large number of strategic alliances and industries characterized by multidisciplinary technologies. These three attributes might even coincide, for example in the automotive industry and in telecommunications.

Overlapping   Overlapping is in itself a dynamic network process. Three major forces drive overlapping.

First, *reduction of barriers to overlapping* due to formal and informal institutional rules, such as restrictions for foreign trade or foreign investments.

Second, *an individual actor's overlapping strategy* will influence the strategic actions by others. International expansion, multidisciplinary innovation, internationalization of specific functions in the firm are examples of this.

Third, several actors belonging to different networks might *jointly act to restructure the networks* through an overlapping process, for instance they merge or develop a strategic alliance. This will initiate strategic reactions from other network actors. Such actions might also be proactive, that is an actor might act due to expected actions by others.

Markets for food and telecommunications show examples of the three driving forces. Deregulation lowers the barriers to overlapping, but differently so in different countries; individual actors internationalize, which is followed by similar moves by competitors; several actors in different constellations, over time develop strategic alliances, thus forming clusters in the network.

Overlapping introduces both positive and negative connections to a network and thereby affects the opportunities and restrictions for future overlapping. Overlapping changes the network structure and the opportunities for future change in production systems. Overlapping is a process comprising consecutive strategic actions in overlapped networks.

Barriers to overlapping must also be considered. They are related to the reversal of the driving forces. First, formal and informal institutions, as mentioned above, might act as barriers. Second, also quite obvious, the already established individual relationships in the overlap might act as barriers to further overlapping. Third, and not so obvious, overlapping might be hindered by created interdependencies within the established nets. Overlapping, e.g. finding a new customer or increasing the number of customers in another network, is not then just an issue of overcoming institutional barriers or changing individual direct relationships in one other network. Instead several relationships, and thereby also several actors, are affected by efforts to establish one new relationship.

3. SOME CONTEMPORARY CONDITIONS FOR INTERNATIONAL BUSINESS DEVELOPMENT

Against the general empirical background given below, the dimensions of which seem to be generally acknowledged in the literature (Dunning 1993) I argue that contemporary developments in terms of interdependencies within governance structures and technological interdependencies in the production systems make a focus on the dynamics of overlapping networks increasingly valid for analyses of micro/macro interaction. Also some major changes in the institutional setting for international business point in the same direction.

First, the internationalization processes for major firms in many industries have brought these firms to quite advanced stages of internationalization. Their activities are already extended to most major markets, they already have significantly penetrated those markets and therefore a third dimension of internationalization, i.e. international integration across nations to utilize and create advantages of being international, is an increasingly important aspect of organizational and strategic change.

Second, restructuring of industries through mergers and acquisitions to an increasing extent is now international and not national in nature and not primarily aimed at serving national markets, but part of strategies to establish international production systems and thus closely linked to issues of increased international integration.

Third, there is a proliferation in most industries of strategic alliances, to a large extent international in scope, that formally and positively connect individual firms for purposes like market access, manufacturing rationalization, development of new products and joint marketing.

Fourth, technological changes are often of an interdisciplinary nature and require development of hardware and software components and systems from several different industries. The technological development is in many respects quite costly and there is in many industries a growing need to speed up the product- and process-development process.

Fifth, technological changes in information handling, in transportation of people and goods and in manufacturing have increased the ability to efficiently integrate international production systems. This has thus led to reduced lead times, customized products, reduced inventories, "lean manufacturing."

Sixth, large firms have reorganized to allow for decentralized actions and accountability within organizational structures designed according to strategic business areas and product and application interdependencies, rather than functional and geographic area delimitations.

Seventh, corporate strategies have emphasized specialization. "Back to basics," "customer orientation," "out-sourcing" are some of the symbolic expressions for this development. This specialization means that the firm recognizes an increased dependency on external complementary resources.

Eighth, markets where internationalization has been limited by regulations and other institutional barriers are now in many cases deregulated or reregulated, thereby opening up those markets for international competition and international cooperation, e.g. in telecommunications, for financial services, for some food-product categories, for public-sector services and public works. The transformation of centrally planned economies into market economies and the efforts to increase economic integration among nations within regions also belong in this category of institutional change.

Taken together these developments, that have characterized many industries and markets during the last decade, have three major implications for the international firm.

First, it makes the individual firm more dependent on coordination with *specific* other firms through exchange relationships. Coordination through arm's-length, separate transactions seems to be less and less feasible, due to interdependencies in network structures and production systems. Coordination through sets of interconnected exchange relationships, i.e. through *nets* within networks, seems to offer an increasingly more valid description of the mechanism used.

Second, due to the increased interdependency between actors, including the overlap between focal nets, structural changes in such nets might be problematic. How and by whom then can such nets be "constructed"? To what extent can the focal nets of competitors overlap without disturbing the focal firm's coordination requirements? What happens if one of our competitors acquires one of the suppliers with whom we cooperate closely in product development? Can this supplier still continue in its role or do we need to search for a replacement? Is it possible to find a replacement who is not already linked to another, competing firm or net?

Third, overlaps and overlapping of networks are of increasing importance. Competition is also increasingly international and competitors come
from different industries. Deregulations of various kinds open up for new
entrants who may be viewed as potential competitors, potential partners, or
both. Coordination and competition between firms increasingly involve
activities in more than two nations and activities carried out by more than
two actors in more than one industry.

4. STRATEGIC ACTIONS INTERPRETED AS OVERLAPPING PROCESSES

I will discuss three categories of internationalization of the firm in highly
internationalized markets: foreign market entry, defense of home market
and integration in international production systems.

4.1 Foreign market entry

The traditional textbook view of foreign market entry is to focus on two
decisions by an individual, selling firm with a defined home market. The
first is the selection of a specific foreign market, among several potential
ones. The second is the selection of a specific mode of entry.

According to a network view foreign market entry may be seen as an
overlapping process by which exchange relationships are established and
developed over time. The firm establishes a position in a network defined as
a specific foreign market. That position is related to its positions in other
markets, including its home market. A highly internationalized firm's focal
net overlaps in several spatial networks. An additional entry might originate in other markets than the home market. (Cf. the concept of "secondary
degree of internationalization": Forsgren 1989.) It might even be difficult to
define a specific network as the home market. An additional entry might
also, due to the high degree of overlap between networks, be initiated
through already existing relationships in other networks. For a firm with a
low degree of internationalization, this means that its relationships in the
highly internationalized home market are more likely to initiate a foreign
market entry than self-initiated actions to develop new relationships to
firms in the foreign market.

When the overlaps between spatial networks are high, the strategic
actions by individual actors are highly constrained by international
interdependencies. An entrant must therefore either fit into such interdependencies, for example be able to deliver products that fit in internationally integrated production systems, or be powerful enough to influence
several relationships and thus get the network to adapt to the entrant. The

existing overlaps might thus be a barrier to self-initiated foreign market entry by firms with a low degree of internationalization.

This leads to the observation that an entry should be analyzed as a strategic action in a dynamic context. Timing of the entry is important. The structure of positive and negative connectedness in the overlapping networks change over time, e.g. through mergers, divestments, alliance developments, competitive entries. Therefore a specific entrant will find that the availability and identity of suitable network connections in a foreign market vary over time.

For highly internationalized firms, an entry on a new foreign market is likely to be a rather marginal addition to the focal net. The objective of the entry should be regarded in the total international context and not primarily as an entry in a specific market to exploit sales or procurement opportunities in that market (Johanson and Mattsson 1988). However, entries can in this case also be major ones, e.g. if important, formerly closed, markets become deregulated and opened to spatial overlapping. Entries into the Russian or Chinese markets can be of this nature. The timing of such entries is important, since entry is often restricted and sometimes dependent on connection to specific local firms. An entry is also dependent on the activities and resources controlled in the firm's focal net and therefore can be regarded as an international overlapping involving several spatial networks. Firms like ABB and Ericsson draw on their world-wide resources in their entries into what for them are new markets. They also develop their focal nets in the new market. For example, in China ABB's overlap becomes substantially larger when it enters the market for service and maintenance of local electrical and industrial equipment instead of restricting itself to major infrastructural projects. The entry of firms in China, just to perform offshore production for other markets, obviously implies a much lesser overlapping in the Chinese network than if Chinese customers are sought.

In a network view foreign market entry is a much less distinct event than in the traditional foreign entry literature. Entries can be "channeled" through indirect routes. They can be preceded by entries in overlaps between several networks. An entry is treated as a process rather than as an event.

4.2 Defense of the home market

When network overlapping, due to the entry of foreign competition into a firm's home market, threatens the network positions of incumbent firms there is an obvious need for strategic action by the latter. Since this chapter deals with highly internationalized markets the process that is relevant to discuss here is when barriers to overlapping are removed through radical institutional changes. Examples of such cases are found in service industries such as telecoms, financial services and transportation, but also in the food sector.

One type of action is to compensate for the weakening position on the home market by increasing the firm's own internationalization. We are then again approaching the foreign-market entry issue but now with the objective to strengthen the home-market position. When the production system is internationalized it will be difficult to internationalize for home-market defense without mergers or alliances. The development of regional and even global alliances among telecoms operators (Ioannidis 1998) and among passenger airlines serve to improve the ability to defend relationships with domestic customers for international services by making these services more effective.

Also for less internationalized production systems, overlapping that turns potentially negative connections to positive ones are possible. The firm can merge with competitors or enter into an agreement about market sharing. A firm can invite a competitor to enter the market under the control of the incumbent firm. Cooperation in distribution or manufacturing gives a foreign brand market access, that is controlled by an incumbent actor (Ulfsdotter 1996). A foreign, branded product can, for instance, be manufactured under license rather than imported. A foreign retail concept can be acquired and used by a domestic retail firm rather than be the base for a foreign direct investment.

Some international strategic alliances are mostly directed towards strengthening the positions on the home market of the partners. A large number of retail alliances in the food sector, such as AMS, are overlapping initiatives with such purposes. An international retail alliance also influences overlapping at the supplier level since the alliance strives to increase the number of common suppliers to the retail members in the different countries. However, the strength of present relationships in the focal nets of each retail member might act as barriers to such overlapping processes (Kjellberg and Ulfsdotter 1994).

If both the actor and relationship overlapping continues, some actors may begin to perceive the overlapped networks as one network. The "home market" becomes enlarged. The positions of actors in the enlarged network will be quite different than when the networks were perceived as separate ones. A firm with a dominating position in the old home market might therefore take strategic actions, overlapping into neighboring markets to avoid being marginalized in the emerging regional home market (Mattsson 1995*b*).

4.3 *Integration of international production systems*

These strategic situations are characteristic of an international firm in the later stages of internationalization. Such a firm has positions in many net-

works and its strategic actions are much influenced by this situation
(Johanson and Mattsson 1988). Its focal net overlaps in a large number of
spatial networks. The external parts of such focal nets also comprise firms
with low internationalization. Such firms will also be involved in overlapping processes that are initiated due to increased international integration
by the focal firm.

Two, in some respects related, aspects are integration of logistic processes and of innovation processes. I will comment on both.

Integration of logistic processes   International standardization and adaptation between several consecutive stages in a value-added chain serve to
increase logistic efficiency. When standardization increases there are more
opportunities to specialize and concentrate production to fewer networks.
Efforts to increase logistic efficiency in internationalized markets require
internationally extended focal nets within which actors are adapted to each
other. Overlapping is then a process by which such nets can be developed.
Such overlapping might however be difficult due to the structure of positive
and negative connections. In other words, as interdependencies between
actors increase, the sensitivity to changes in network structures also
increases.

Such a high sensitivity is described in a study of the internationalization
of Swedish freight forwarders (Hertz 1993). Suppose that firm A uses firm
B as an agent for its *b*-destinations and B uses A for its *a*-destinations. The
two firms are positively connected and their focal nets overlap. Firm C, a
competitor to A, acquires B. Then A's positive connection to B changes
to a negative one. A must search for another firm who can handle the
b-destinations or A must make a greenfield investment. If the overlap
between several focal nets is high, and if interdependencies within and
between focal nets are high, then changes in one relationship will lead to a
series of consecutive relationship changes. Hertz showed that the internationalization process for freight forwarders during the 1980s and the increasing need to integrate international production systems (including the
transportation systems) led to such increased network interdependencies.
She described how a strategic action by one firm in the early 1990s, that
changed the overlap structure, was followed by a series of changes in
network connections. That would hardly have been the case 10–15 years
earlier. She labeled these changes "domino effects," i.e. indirect effects
causing consecutive changes over time in the network structure.

The development towards higher international integration has effects on
the external actors in focal nets. This is especially so after international
mergers or alliances. One of the network consequences of the formation of
Saab Automobile as an alliance between Saab and GM is that common
suppliers are used to an increasing extent. Thus an overlapping at the
supplier level has been initiated by an earlier overlapping at the buyer level

(Lilliecreutz, 1996). It is however often problematic to implement such changes in the network structures due to the nature of the actors' existing relationships (Nyberg 1994). This is true also for the focal nets of subsidiaries to international firms.

Integration for innovative processes   Interdependencies of a complementary nature are of course the major attribute of all "value chains." Overlaps between technological networks are necessary in most innovative processes. Håkansson (1987) has in a couple of studies clearly demonstrated this. Thus in a study of process development in the sawmilling industry he showed how overlaps with the construction, carpentry, mechanical engineering, steel, tool and electronic industries were influential. From a dynamic point of view it is obvious that the roles of suppliers to an industry and users of the industry's products are important and that integration of resources from different industries are needed for innovative effectiveness. A more problematic issue is to what extent overlapping, i.e. changes in overlaps, is important. The sawmill case describes change within a rather stable overlap structure.

A study of technological change concerning development of computerized-image processing (Lundgren 1995) describes a quite different network process. It required many rather complicated overlapping processes such as between networks defined according to different scientific disciplines, different industrial applications and the different industries where the developing technology was eventually adopted. The use situation was much less defined and more diverse than in the sawmill case. The creation of new actors and new relationships was a more important aspect.

Even if both Håkansson's and Lundgren's empirical studies are restricted to Swedish networks they can be used to illustrate also international contexts. If complementary resources for innovation are internationally spread they have to be coordinated through focal nets allowing overlaps with both spatial and technological delimited networks. Such overlaps might have been created by earlier overlapping as firms have internationalized their activities, perhaps also including R&D, both as regards the internal and external parts of their focal nets. Some such situations might be similar to the sawmill case in the sense that the network structures are relatively stable, allowing also for international standardization as an aspect of international integration. Other situations however, might be more like the computerized-image processing case, requiring more complicated overlapping of an evolutionary nature and with no specific firm's focal net dominating the process.

The international diffusion of an innovation is dependent on effective international logistic integration. New products and processes cannot be adopted within a relatively short time span without internationally extended focal nets. To create, through overlapping, effective and efficient combinations of net structures for logistics and for innovation is an important strategic and organizational issue for the international firm. In a study of a firm that over the years had undergone many changes in the structure of its international focal net, through acquisitions, divestments, changes in customer categories, internal reorganizations, etc. Andersson (1996) shows how the ability to implement current strategic actions is dependent on other concurrent strategic actions and on more long-term change processes.

5. MACRO ISSUES

In this section I will touch upon two macro issues: the nature of the market concept and the competitiveness of a nation.

5.1 The market concept

The idea that transactions on a market do and should take place at arm's-length and that a market consists of many independent competing suppliers and buyers is an increasingly unrealistic view. This does not imply that competition is absent. A more realistic view is that competition takes place between more or less clearly delineated nets of firms, sometimes dominated by a few actors, sometimes related to each other in less hierarchial forms. Competition also takes place between actors for the development of exchange relationships, i.e. for the formation of nets. Thus, cooperation within exchange relationships is needed to compete effectively and competition to develop such relationships is needed to cooperate effectively.

During the last decade there has been an increasing belief in the effectiveness of "market solutions." Through various institutional changes opportunities for increased competition have been created. In this context I will offer two propositions:

Proposition 1: Changes in the institutional structure aiming at creating more "market-like" governance structures, when there is a high degree of potential interdependence between nations and between technologies, will not serve to make arm's-length transactions a dominating form for coordination of production systems. Instead such institutional changes will initiate strategic actions by firms that create more integrated international nets within the network structures (Mansell 1993; Johanson and Mattsson 1991).

Proposition 2: Effective transformation from centrally planned national economies to market economies includes institutional changes that stimulate higher intensities of cooperation between firms as well as competition between firms.

Adoption of the idea of arm's-length transactions as typical of a well-functioning market economy is dysfunctional for the transformation process and for the contribution of international firms to this process. For example, the lack of institutional norms for effective cooperation between firms in Russia will act as an important barrier to the transition from a centrally planned to a well-functioning market economy. Overlapping between Russian and West European networks may over time help to transfer such norms (Mattsson 1995*a*).

5.2 The competitiveness of a nation

When markets are highly internationalized and firms are highly internationalized, then the further internationalization processes are not driven by the same forces as when internationalization in both respects is low. In this chapter I have tried to demonstrate some of the probable effects at the firm level. What about the national level? Let us consider Sweden, a small industrial nation with highly internationalized firms. I will again offer two propositions:

Proposition 3: Imports to and exports from a country to an increasing extent are composed of goods and services used in international production systems, controlled by exchange relationships within international nets. Therefore the positions of a nation's actors in such nets will strongly influence its international trading patterns.

Proposition 4: Overlapping changes the positions of actors within the international nets and thereby also the connections between actors located in a national network. This means that the structure of positive and negative connections within such a national network will change substantially over time as overlapping continues.

Sweden is very dependent on international trade. A substantial proportion of her exports already consists of transfers within integrated production systems (cf. Andersson *et al.* 1994). What will be the position in the future for the Swedish actors as both firms and markets continue to internationalize?

What kind of production resources will be located in Sweden? How will these be influenced by the increased importance of international integration in Europe and the further extension of focal nets to development of positions in distant and more rapidly growing Asian markets?

The industrial structure in Sweden has historically shown a high degree of complementarity between major industries. Such "development blocs" (Dahmén 1988) or "industrial clusters"(Sölvell *et al.* 1991; Porter 1990) have had a very important positive influence on the international competitiveness of both Swedish industrial firms and of Sweden as an industrial nation.

Contemporary internationalization changes those conditions. Swedish firms are now, to an increasing extent, being acquired by foreign firms.

Some modern technological networks are weakly represented in Sweden. Some long-term cooperative relationships for innovation between large public buyers and Swedish industry are weakened when the home market is opened up for competition. One example is that the scope and intensity of the longstanding cooperation between the Swedish national Public Telephone Operator, Telia, and the Swedish telecom equipment manufacturer, Ericsson, diminished and Telia developed international alliances with a number of other telephone operators as Telia adapted to the deregulation of the Swedish domestic market (Ioannidis 1998 forthcoming).

Local suppliers and customers become less important for highly international Swedish firms when manufacturing and also increasingly when R&D activities are located outside of Sweden.

A precondition for an effective public policy to preserve the competitiveness of a country as an industrial nation is to understand how interdependencies in highly internationalized network structures and in highly internationalized production systems influence the strategic actions of highly internationalized firms. It seems to me that there is still much research on the dynamic firm in a dynamic context to be done. A yet mostly unexplored approach is to use more formal network analytical concepts and methods. I will therefore make a few comments on this.

6. A NOTE ON POTENTIAL USE OF FORMAL NETWORK ANALYSIS

I have argued that a markets-as-networks approach is increasingly valid for analyses of dynamic interaction between the international firm and the international markets and industries. However, the conceptual complexity and the lack of readily available network data present difficult methodological research problems. The structural/positional network approach analyzes how actors in bounded networks are related (Burt 1980). It is possible to describe individual actor positions, overall network structure and to identify subgroups in the network. It is also possible to describe how different networks are related to each other. Thus an actor can have a more or less central position, be a bridging point connecting two networks, be a member of a subgroup, etc. The overall network structure can be described in terms of measures of size, density, degree of hierarchy, etc. There are several concepts that describe subgroups in the network such as components, cliques, structural equivalence. How these measures can be interpreted in a markets-as-networks sense is discussed in Kjellberg (1994). The outcome of his analysis is that even if many concepts can be reinterpreted as aspects of market structure, the theoretical validity is not clear. It is especially problematic when we are interested in studying change processes.

The notion of overlap between networks makes it possible to open a bounded network to interaction with interconnected actors outside the network. Overlapping introduces changes in the structure. The structures and the changes in the structure can, in principle, be described. I believe that even such quite limited descriptions would be of value for two reasons. First, quantitative, formal descriptions of "markets-as-networks" is an important step in scientific progress. Second, it is a useful exercise to give theoretical interpretation to sequences of changes in network structure and to base further research on such studies.

The growing sociological network literature in "economic sociology" and "interorganizational studies" is only partially related to formal network analysis and only partially related to a "markets-as-networks" approach (See Nohria and Eccles 1992).

It is thus a real challenge to make efforts to move from the conceptual foundations discussed in this chapter to more systematic formal descriptions.

REFERENCES

Aldrich, H. A. (1979), *Organisations and Environments* (Englewood Cliffs, NJ: Prentice-Hall).

Andersson, P. (1996), *Concurrence, Transitions and Evolution: Perspectives of Industrial Marketing Change Processes* (Stockholm: Economic Research Institute, Stockholm School of Economics).

Andersson, T., Fredriksson, T. and Svensson, R. (1994), "Förändrade utlandsinvesteringar under 1980-talet," *Ekonomisk Debatt*, 3, Årgång 22: 261–74.

Burt, R. S. (1980), "Models of Network Structure," *Annual Review of Sociology*, 6: 79–141.

Cook, K. S. and Emerson, R. M. (1978), "Power, Equity and Commitment in Exchange Networks," *American Sociological Review*, 43: 712–39.

Dahmén, E. (1988), "Development Blocks in Industrial Economics," *Scandinavian Economic Review*, 1: 3–14.

Dunning, J. H. (1993), *Multinational Enterprises and the Global Economy* (Wokingham, UK Addison-Wesley).

Forsgren, M. (1989), *Managing the Internationalisation Process: The Swedish Case* (London: Routledge).

Granovetter, M. S. (1973), "The Strength of Weak Ties," *American Journal of Sociology*, 78/6: 1360–80.

Håkansson, H. (1987) (ed.), *Industrial Technological Development: A Network Approach* (London: Croom Helm).

Hertz, S. (1993), *The Internationalization Process of Freight Transport Companies* (Stockholm: Economic Research Institute).
Ioannidis, D. (1998), *I nationens häust? Strategisk handling i politisk miljö. En nationell teleoperatörs internationlisering och strategier för interorganisatorisk interaletion.* (Stockholm: Economic Research Institute) (forthcoming).
Johanson, J. and Mattsson, L. G. (1988), "Internationalisation in Industrial Systems: A Network Approach," in N. Hood and J. E. Vahlne (eds.), *Strategies in Global Competition* (London: Croom Helm).
———(1991), "Strategic Adaptation of Firms to the European Single Market: A Network Approach," in L. G. Mattsson and B. Stymne (eds.), *Corporate and Industry Strategy for Europe* (Amsterdam: North-Holland).
———(1992), "Network Positions and Strategic Action: An Analytical Framework," in B. Axelsson and G. Easton (eds.), *Industrial Networks: A New View of Reality* (London: Routledge).
———(1994), "The Markets-as-Networks Research Tradition in Sweden," in G. Laurent, G. Lilien and B. Pras (eds.), *Research Traditions in Marketing* (Boston: Kluwer Press).
Kjellberg, H. (1994), "Formal Network Analysis of Markets and Industries," Lic. thesis, Stockholm School of Economics.
——and Ulfsdotter, F. (1994), "Internationalisering för hemmaförsvar-förändringar inom nordisk livsmedelsproduktion och -distribution," (Internationalization for Home Market Defense Within Nordic Food Production and Distribution), in L. G. Mattsson and S. Hultén (eds.), *Företag och marknader i förändring-dynamik i nätverk* (Stockholm: Nerenius & Santérus).
Lilliecreutz, J. (1996), *En leverantörs strategi fraî lager-hill system leverantör—en studie civ Köpare—och leverantörsrelationer inom svensk personbilsindustri*, Linköping Studies in Management and Economics. Dissertations No. 32 (Linköping: Linköping University).
Lundgren, A. (1995), *Technological Innovation and Network Evolution: The Emergence of Industrial Networks* (London: Routledge).
Mansell, R. (1993), *The New Telecommunications* (London: Sage Publications).
Mattsson, L. G. (1995a), "Firms, 'Megaorganizations' and Markets-as-Network View," *Journal of Institutional and Theoretical Economics* (JITE), 151/4: 760–6.
——(1995b), "The Nordic Countries as a Home Market?", in *Essays in Marketing and Management: A Festschrift in Honour of Kjell Grönhaug* (Bergen, Norway: Fagboksforlaget), 257–66.
Nohria, N. and Eccles, R. G. (1992) (eds.), *Networks and Organizations* (Boston: Harvard Business School Press).
Nyberg, A. (1994), "Distribution System Consequences of Mergers Between Manufacturers," Lic. thesis, Stockholm School of Economics.
Porter, M. E. (1990), *The Competitive Advantage of Nations* (New York: Free Press).
Sölvell, Ö., Zander, I. and Porter, M. E. (1991), *Advantage Sweden* (Stockholm: Norstedts Juridikförlag).
Ulfsdotter, F. (1996), *Internationalisering för expansion eller hemmamarknadsförsvar: De nordiska marknaderna för fruktyoghurt 1982–1994* (Internationalization for Expansion or for Home Market Defense: The Nordic Markets for Fruit Yoghurt 1982–1994) (Stockholm: Economic Research Institute).

PART III

REGIONS

12

The Globalization of Technology: What Remains of the Product Cycle Model?*

JOHN CANTWELL

1. INTRODUCTION

This paper reexamines two hypotheses associated with earlier versions of the product cycle model (Vernon 1966), using new historical evidence on the international dispersion of corporate technological activity by large American and European industrial firms, based on patents granted to these companies at the US Patent Office since the turn of the century. The first hypothesis states that innovations are almost always located in the home country of the parent company, and usually close to the site of the corporate technological headquarters. The second hypothesis is that international investment is led by technology leaders, as a means by which they increase their share of world markets and world production. If the first hypothesis does not necessarily hold, then the second can be interpreted more specifically to state that the internationalization of technological development is led by firms with the strongest records in innovation.

Contrary to the first hypothesis, a new literature on the recent internationalization of industrial research (for example, Ronstadt 1977; Lall 1979; Pearce and Singh 1991; Granstrand, Håkanson and Sjölander 1992) has suggested that innovations may be geographically dispersed within multinational corporations (MNCs). US-owned MNCs have recently witnessed an increase in the degree of internationalization of their research, from low levels in the 1960s. It is perhaps no accident that empirical support for the product cycle hypothesis and subsequent criticism of it was largely derived from data on US MNCs. The new trend towards the internationalization of research and development (R&D) in US MNCs became evident by the 1970s (see, for example, Mansfield, Teece and Romeo 1979).

Three kinds of theoretical justification were provided for the first product cycle hypothesis. First, there are economies of scale in the R&D function, and if they are strong enough R&D will be concentrated in a single center.

* University of Reading. I am grateful to the referees for helpful comments on an earlier draft, and to the Economic and Social Research Council (ESRC) for their support under research grant R000232250. I wish to thank also Pilar Barrera who worked on related aspects of the project, Jane Myers and Jim Hirabayashi of the US Patent and Trademark Office for their invaluable assistance, and Cathy Jones and her many fellow students for their tremendous efforts during the data collection.

Second, there are locational economies of integration and agglomeration in innovation. In new product development a close interaction is normally required between research and production facilities and users, while if several firms are engaged in the development of related new products (or processes) geographical proximity will encourage a greater volume of beneficial spillovers between them. Third, the original product cycle model viewed innovation as a demand-led process (see Schmookler 1966, for another contemporary account), and thus for US MNCs innovation would be located in the more conducive environment of their home country, stimulated by the particular characteristics of the demand of high-income consumers and skill-intensive downstream production facilities.

However, more recent evidence has demonstrated that the internationalization of technological activity in large MNCs is not simply the outcome of a new trend (Cantwell and Hodson 1991; Patel and Pavitt 1991). As early as the 1960s many European MNCs (especially those originating from the UK, the Netherlands, Belgium and Switzerland) had already been quite highly internationalized in their technological activity. In Europe, the largest French and German industrial MNCs come closest to the US pattern, recently increasing the extent of internationalization of their R&D from comparatively low levels in the 1960s. By contrast, large Japanese firms owned few research facilities outside Japan in the 1960s. Although their international R&D has been expanding, research in Japan itself has been growing at least as quickly, so the degree of internationalization of research in Japanese-owned MNCs has remained low.

Here, it is argued that the first product cycle hypothesis should be rejected, not so much as a result of recent trends, as on the basis of historical evidence. In particular, the leading US electrical equipment companies and European chemical firms enjoyed a significant international dispersal of their technological activity in the interwar period. The source of evidence for this view is the US patenting of the largest US and European industrial companies over time, which identifies the location of technological activity at the corporate level, and thus provides a measure of the geographical dispersion of corporate invention. It is this same source of evidence that has been used often in other similar international comparisons that relate to the recent period, and which has helped to create the reevaluation of trends in the international R&D of MNCs just described. What is new about the data in this study is the extension of records of corporate patenting back in time: here they are considered back to 1920.

The second early product cycle hypothesis states that international investment (and here, the international dispersion of technological activity) is led by technology leaders. The theoretical justification for this hypothesis is that the most technologically competent companies enjoy lower operating costs than their competitors and provide higher product quality, which generate higher profits and rising international market shares. In their turn, different degrees of technological competence across companies are a consequence of the firm-specific and path-dependent characteristics of technological change (Cantwell 1991*b*, 1994; Nelson 1991; 1992; Dosi, Teece and Winter 1992; Pavitt 1992; Teece, Pisano and Shuen 1990). The greater capability of the most competent or technologically leading firms (or their greater capability to release able management resources and team expertise to plan for and organize growth, as argued by Penrose (1959)), enables them to better expand their activity in new fields or environments, and higher profits provide them with the financial wherewithal to offset the costs of doing so. An ancillary argument is especially important in the case of early internationalization and is featured in the contemporary explanation of the product cycle hypothesis; that is, a technologically leading group of firms from a particular location may—past some point—find that the continued increase in its penetration of foreign markets is challenged by protectionist barriers, and by the gradual learning of local competitors in those markets. This raises the incentive to produce locally, and insofar as indigenous companies develop their own lines of related technological development there is also a greater incentive to internationalize innovation (in addition to the need to adapt products to the distinctive features of host country demand).

This hypothesis appears to be consistent with the historical evidence, except perhaps during phases of technological hegemony when innovative development is concentrated in the home country. However, the explanatory power of this hypothesis has been eroded by recent trends; the composition of firms involved in the internationalization of technological activity has now been broadened, extending to cover a much wider range of companies. Therefore, an alternative version of the second hypothesis is proposed to fit the current situation. It is suggested that technology leaders are now ahead instead in the globalization of technology—that is, in the development of international intrafirm networks to exploit the locationally differentiated potential of foreign centers of excellence. These networks are internal to the firm in order to build upon or extend its core technological competence through an internally coordinated learning process, but they are complementary to external interfirm networks whose role is the exchange of knowledge and occasionally cooperation in learning through technology-based joint ventures (Cantwell 1991*b*, 1994; Cantwell and Barrera 1995).

The data employed are described further in Section 2, while Sections 3 and 4 relate to the reassessment of the first and second product cycle hypotheses respectively. Section 3 examines the historical importance of the international dispersion of technological development in the leading American and European firms. Particular attention is paid to firms in the chemical and electrical equipment industries broadly defined, as these are the industries which are most reliant on science-based technologies.

Historically, US firms were strongest in the electrical equipment industry, while European (and especially German) firms were stronger in chemicals (Chandler 1990; Cantwell and Barrera 1993). Among leading companies such as these, technological activity is not always much more widely geographically dispersed today than it was in the interwar or early postwar periods. However, Section 4 considers what has changed recently for these firms, and terms this a new trend towards the globalization of technology— that is, the emergence of internationally integrated structures for technological development. It is suggested that globalization in this sense is a modern characteristic of corporate technology leaders. Some conclusions are set out in Section 5.

2. THE DATA

Patenting is a measure of invention, and so corporate patenting is more a measure of wider technological activity (changes in production methods) in firms, and not just R&D as such. For large firms like those covered here, R&D is the most important source of new knowledge and skills, and so for them the internationalization of technological activity revolves around the internationalization of research. However, production engineering is often an important complementary source of new inventions that are incorporated into technology. It should also be noted that the location of basic R&D that feeds into the development of productive applications at some other site may not itself be picked up separately in the patent statistics. For these reasons the title of the paper refers to the internationalization of technological activity (the development of new methods of production), and not to the internationalization of R&D as such.

Two types of information have been collected manually from the *US Index of Patents* and the *US Patent Office Gazette*. First, all patents were recorded that were assigned to a selection of large US-owned and European-owned firms between 1890 and 1968. From 1969 onwards equivalent information has been computerized by the US Patent Office. The firms selected for the historical patent search were identified in one of three ways. The first group consisted of those firms which have accounted for the highest levels of US patenting after 1969; the second group comprised other US, German or British firms which were historically among the largest 200 industrial corporations in each of these countries (derived from lists in Chandler 1990); and the third group was made up of other companies which featured prominently in the US patent records of earlier years (a method that proved most significant for a number of French firms that had not been identified from other sources).

In each case, patents were counted as belonging to a common corporate group where they were assigned to affiliates of a parent company. Affiliate names were normally taken from individual company histories. In all, the US patenting of 857 companies or affiliates was traced historically; together these comprise 284 corporate groups. Owing to historical changes in ownership, 17 of the affiliates were allocated to more than one corporate group over the period as a whole. No significance has been attached to the location of the particular affiliate to which each patent is assigned, since this may be different from the location of the inventive activity that gave rise to the patent. However, the location of the parent company is an important dimension in the analysis, as this is treated as the home country or the country of origin of the corporate group. By consolidating patents attributable to international corporate groups, it is then feasible to examine the geographical distribution of technological activity within groups, and the possible formation of internal intragroup international networks (as opposed to external interfirm networks, which are not the subject of this paper). Each corporate group is also allocated to an industry on the basis of its primary field of production; occasionally, firms have moved between industries historically, sometimes associated with changes in ownership, and this has been allowed for.

The company to which a patent has been assigned (if any), and the name and location of residence of the inventor responsible for the underlying invention, are both recorded separately in the US Patent Office data, including the earliest data. Where patents have been assigned to firms, the inventor is normally an employee of the company or is directly associated with it in some other way, but occasionally independent individual inventors do choose to assign their patents to firms (Schmookler 1966). Assignments by independent individuals were more common in the nineteenth century but, at least from the interwar years onwards, the typical assignor was a prominent member of a corporate research laboratory, or some other similar in-house company facility. Although it is normally difficult to trace these named individuals in secondary sources on the firms concerned (as they are not usually also senior managers), the location of assignors can be checked against business history sources on the international location of activity in particular firms. Such checks on a selection of large firms have confirmed that whenever a location has been responsible for significant numbers of patents being assigned to a company, that firm did indeed have some in-house facility in the location in question at the relevant time. Companies checked in this fashion include various US firms active abroad and European companies in the USA (Stocking and Watkins 1946; Beaton 1957; Wilkins 1974, 1989; Chandler 1990), Courtaulds and British Celanese (Coleman 1969), Du Pont and ICI (Hounshell and Smith 1988), and General Electric and GEC (Reich 1986; Jones and Marriot 1971).

Second, using once again the *US Index of Patents* and the *US Patent Office Gazette*, for every patent granted in years between 1890 and 1962 the country of residence of the inventor has been recorded. From 1963 this information has already been computerized by the US Patent Office. Where patents are assigned to companies, these data on the country of origin of invention indicate the location of the R&D facilities (or other sources of technological improvement) that gave rise to each patent. As this information on the location of invention relates to individually numbered patents, it can be combined with a sectoral classification of the technological activity with which the patent is associated. This employs the system of patent classes used by the Patent Office; fortunately, as these classes change the Office reclassifies all earlier patents accordingly, so the classification is historically consistent. Although patents may be assigned to several fields, the primary classification was used in all cases. Various broad categories of technological activity were derived by allocating classes or subclasses to common groups of activity.

Two distinctions between different aspects of these classifications of the data are worth reemphasising. First, the sectoral classification of patents, in terms of the type of technological activity with which each patent is associated, is distinguished from the main industrial output or markets of the companies to which patents may be assigned, both of which have been recorded separately. Most large companies have engaged in at least some development in most of the general spheres of technological activity (for instance, chemical firms develop many mechanical technologies, including chemical machinery and equipment), irrespective of the industry in which they operate.

Second, the country of location of the invention, which for large firms typically represents or is allied to the location of corporate R&D, is distinguished from the location of the firm to which a patent is assigned, and from the location of the parent company which owns this firm. While no significance is attached to the location of the assignee, the location of research and the location of ultimate ownership (the parent company) are critical. The extent to which these locations differ over the total patenting of each corporate group is the measure of the degree of internationalization of that group's technological activity. These distinctions are crucial to understanding that the measurement of the degree of internationalization of technological activity in what follows is not to be mistaken for a measure of the international spread of patents taken out by firms (the patents counted were all those—and only those—granted by the US Patent Office), nor should it be mistaken for a measure of the international dispersion of the legal departments or agents responsible for making patent applications on behalf of the group (the actual assignee is ignored once it has been linked to a parent company of a large group in the dataset). Instead, what is measured is the internationalization of the underlying technological activity that gave rise to the knowledge which subsequently led to a patent being granted to the group.

3. THE HISTORICAL ROLE OF THE INTERNATIONALIZATION OF
TECHNOLOGICAL ACTIVITY

As just described, the degree of internationalization of corporate technological activity is measured by the share of patenting that is attributable to
research (or other sources of invention) located outside the home country
of the corporate group or groups in question. The broad changes in internationalization of technological activity between 1920 and 1990 measured in
this way are set out in Table 12.1, organized by national groups of firms
according to the location of ultimate ownership. The share of foreign research in the total corporate technological activity of the largest US and
European industrial firms considered together averaged about 8% in 1920–
39 and 1940–68, before rising significantly to roughly 14.5% in 1969–90.
However, this recent average trend increase in the internationalization of
activity as measured by corporate patenting reflects primarily the rising
share of US patenting accounted for by European firms (which are more
internationalized) vis-à-vis their US counterparts.

There appear to be three categories of national groups of firms. In the
first, German- and French-owned firms come closest to the standard view,
in the sense that the degree of internationalization of their technological
activity was very low historically, but has been on a slowly rising trend, and
has increased significantly recently. The second category comprises the
historically more multinational British, Swiss and Dutch companies, whose

TABLE 12.1. Shares of US patenting of the largest US-
owned industrial firms due to research located abroad,
1920–1939, 1940–1968, and 1969–1990 (%)

	1920–39	1940–68	1969–90
USA	6.81	3.57	6.82
Europe	12.03	26.65	27.13
UK	27.71	41.95	43.17
Germany	4.03	8.68	13.72
Italy	29.03	24.76	14.24
France	3.35	8.19	9.55
Netherlands	15.57	29.51	52.97
Belgium	95.00	53.90	60.60
Switzerland	5.67	28.33	43.76
Sweden	31.04	13.18	25.51
TOTAL	7.91	8.08	14.52

Sources: US patent data compiled at the University of
Reading, with assistance from the US Patent and Trademark Office, US Department of Commerce.

TABLE 12.2. Shares of US patenting of the largest US-owned industrial firms
due to research located abroad: detailed periodization (%)

	USA	Europe	UK	Germany	France	Switzerland	Sweden	Totals
1920–4	3.32	8.45	7.61	2.89	3.02	4.00	39.77	4.03
1925–9	6.61	8.19	14.26	5.42	2.67	3.73	29.88	6.87
1930–4	8.17	10.83	25.88	4.79	4.12	6.38	27.08	8.80
1935–9	6.94	15.11	34.63	2.83	3.33	6.04	30.23	8.86
1940–59	3.79	27.10	40.84	9.46	8.90	22.24	11.98	7.67
1960–4	2.85	24.22	39.52	8.26	7.46	27.28	13.24	7.62
1965–8	3.69	28.02	46.44	8.21	7.76	39.56	15.22	9.42
1969–72	5.22	28.21	42.66	12.65	7.71	45.86	18.14	12.21
1973–7	5.98	25.42	40.09	11.03	6.44	44.67	21.15	13.18
1978–82	6.65	24.60	39.17	12.14	6.66	43.68	27.25	13.82
1983–6	8.51	27.13	45.32	14.83	9.20	41.02	29.84	15.92
1987–90	8.95	30.86	50.55	17.76	18.26	42.74	31.49	18.56

Sources: As for Table 12.1.

technological activity became substantially internationalized after World
War II, achieving an early increase in international scope that is reflected in
the picture for large European firms as a whole. The third category is very
different from the others. The technological activity of the largest US and
Swedish firms was as highly internationalized historically as it is today; and,
of course, for some individual companies (such as the American General
Electric) the extent of internationalization was much higher in the interwar
period than it has been recently. The largest American and Swedish firms
retreated from their international research operations after World War II,
and they have only recently regained the position they held before that
time.

A more detailed periodization of the records of each of these three
groups of large firms can be gleaned from Table 12.2. For French and
German companies this shows that the upward trend in the internationalization of technological activity is not as gradual as might have been supposed from Table 12.1, but in fact is based on some discrete jumps. As for
other European firms, there was an increase in internationalization immediately after World War II, following the nationalist retreat of the late
1930s, and the expropriations of German-owned firms abroad in the 1940s.
There was then a further rise in the early 1970s in German firms, and in the
late 1980s for German companies again, but more especially for French
firms (Cantwell and Kotecha 1994). British and Swiss firms increased to
much higher rates of internationalization of technological activity after the
war than did French or German companies. In the British case the origins
of the process can be traced to a trend increase throughout the interwar
period, which was consolidated after the war, rising close to a peak by the

late 1960s, before recovering again in the 1980s. The degree of internationalization of Swiss firms reached a peak in the early 1970s, which has not
quite been matched since.

For the largest US firms the internationalization of technological activity
peaked in the early 1930s (at a level they have only very recently equalled),
while Swedish firms began in the early 1920s from a high point that they
have not yet since recaptured. The internationalization of research in both
the US and Swedish groups fell sharply after the war, but picked up again
from the late 1960s onwards. It is this latter trend that has been quite widely
commented upon, perhaps not surprisingly, especially by American and
Swedish scholars (such as Ronstadt 1977; Mansfield, Teece and Romeo
1979; or Granstrand, Håkanson and Sjölander 1992). However, this contrasts with the more general European experience. The internationalization
of technological activity in large European firms considered as a whole
increased after World War II (as did all the constituent European national
groups except the Swedish), and again from the mid-1980s (again this
applies to all groups except the Swiss).

Besides their national groups, firms may also be allocated to industrial
groups. The broad industrial classification adopted here groups industries in
accordance with the prevailing type of technological activity in the sector in
question. Thus, firms in the chemical, pharmaceutical and coal and petro-
leum-products industries all rely mainly on chemical and related technologies; firms in the electrical equipment and office equipment or computer
industries base themselves principally on electrical technologies; and firms
in the motor vehicle, aircraft, and rubber and plastic products industries are
concerned with the major transport technologies (engines and tyres). For
ease of exposition these are each referred to collectively as the chemical,
electrical equipment and transport industries. Firms in all other industries
rely mainly on more traditional mechanical technologies, so the mechanical
group is a much more heterogeneous mixture.

As shown in Table 12.3, the US electrical equipment firms were much
more internationalized in their research than were European firms in the
equivalent industry in the interwar period, despite the much higher overall
rate of internationalization of technological activity in the European group.
In Britain, Germany and France large chemical firms were more internationalized historically than those in the electrical equipment sector; although in Switzerland the electrical companies featured more strongly, and
in Sweden it was mechanically based firms that were responsible for the
very high overall internationalization of research in the largest nationally
owned firms at that time. The mechanical group was also highly internationalized in the UK (notably the textile companies British Celanese and
Courtaulds), and British and French transport firms (particularly the tyre
companies Dunlop and Michelin) appear more prominently than the other
members of that group.

TABLE 12.3. Shares of US patenting of the largest US-owned industrial firms due to research located abroad, grouped by industry, 1920–1939, 1940–1968, and 1969–1990 (%)

	USA	Europe	UK	Germany	France	Switzerland	Sweden	Totals
1920–39								
Chemical	2.75	12.42	41.48	4.88	4.64	5.02	4.44	6.88
Electrical	10.13	3.21	1.98	2.58	0.63	8.02	8.89	9.42
Mechanical	5.15	20.18	29.27	3.56	2.93	1.94	36.45	9.17
Transport	1.61	4.95	8.02	2.76	4.89	n.a.	0.00	2.01
TOTAL	6.81	12.03	27.71	4.03	3.35	5.67	31.04	7.91
1940–68								
Chemical	2.24	39.91	66.42	12.51	15.65	31.65	12.40	11.74
Electrical	6.03	14.15	8.81	6.01	5.16	14.31	8.40	7.26
Mechanical	3.27	23.54	37.94	4.15	12.72	17.12	15.70	7.85
Transport	1.41	4.26	5.52	2.36	2.22	n.a.	5.50	1.77
TOTAL	3.57	26.65	41.95	8.68	8.19	28.33	13.18	8.08
1969–90								
Chemical	5.65	32.65	55.33	18.08	9.03	46.84	14.52	17.91
Electrical	9.09	27.32	27.11	11.01	8.43	34.22	29.32	14.65
Mechanical	6.51	23.94	50.31	7.67	16.83	33.23	27.75	13.58
Transport	4.95	10.16	10.55	8.47	4.98	n.a.	12.36	6.53
TOTAL	6.82	27.13	43.17	13.72	9.55	43.76	25.51	14.52

n. a. = not applicable.

Sources: As for Table 12.1.

A similar discrepancy between the relative extent of internationalization of research in chemical and electrical equipment firms in the USA and Europe still existed in recent years, but the difference is less marked than it was. Among European companies the stronger internationalization of chemical than electrical firms also holds now for Switzerland, but not for Sweden. For Swedish firms the mechanical group does not dominate international research as it once did, but in the UK and France the mechanical group is relatively more prominent than it used to be. What this reflects in each case is a broadening of the range of firms engaged in the internationalization of technological activity across a wider spectrum; for example, while the mechanical engineering firm Alfa-Laval accounted for the bulk of the foreign research of Swedish companies historically, its share has steadily declined as other firms have begun to engage in technological development abroad (Zander 1994).

For US and European firms as a whole a more detailed periodization for the major industrial groups can be found in Tables 12.4 and 12.5. Table 12.4 shows that US-owned electrical equipment firms in the 1930s had a higher degree of internationalization of technological activity than they have had at any time since, including the 1980s. About 12% of their research was located abroad in the 1930s, compared to roughly 11% in the 1980s. Two

TABLE 12.4. Shares of US patenting of the largest US-owned industrial firms due to research located abroad, grouped by industry: detailed periodization (%)

Firms	1920–4	1925–9	1930–4	1935–9	1940–59	1960–4	1965–8	1969–72	1973–7	1978–82	1983–6	1987–90
Chemical	0.96	1.90	4.03	2.36	1.87	2.12	3.08	4.37	5.21	5.33	6.36	7.71
Electrical	4.14	8.50	12.27	11.99	7.01	3.81	5.23	7.29	7.94	9.00	11.60	10.90
Mechanical	3.31	5.72	5.83	5.06	2.87	4.00	3.58	4.61	5.39	6.71	9.36	9.34
Transport	0.12	1.37	1.94	1.73	0.90	1.69	2.36	3.45	4.21	4.51	5.81	7.59
TOTAL	3.32	6.61	8.17	6.94	3.79	2.85	3.69	5.22	5.98	6.65	8.51	8.95

Sources: As for Table 12.1.

Table 12.5. Shares of US patenting of the largest European-owned industrial firms due to research located abroad, grouped by industry (%)

Firms	1920–4	1925–9	1930–4	1935–9	1940–59	1960–4	1965–8	1969–72	1973–7	1978–82	1983–6	1987–90
Chemical	7.07	7.52	8.15	18.22	42.55	37.17	38.46	35.40	31.25	30.51	32.30	34.77
Electrical	4.12	2.81	5.14	1.73	11.01	13.87	19.96	26.90	24.51	21.44	28.17	34.10
Mechanical	10.84	12.91	23.00	24.74	25.73	18.73	23.31	25.45	22.25	23.98	23.87	24.59
Transport	3.75	9.15	4.69	3.04	4.77	3.34	4.45	7.12	7.40	7.69	12.76	16.19
TOTAL	8.45	8.19	10.83	15.11	27.10	24.22	28.02	28.21	25.42	24.60	27.13	30.86

Sources: As for Table 12.1.

American-owned companies that contributed especially heavily to European-located research and production in the interwar years were General Electric and RCA. The degree of internationalization of technological activity in General Electric was 18.3% in 1920–39 but only 2.4% in 1968–90, while in RCA the equivalent proportions were 20.4% and 5.4%.

In contrast, the largest European firms sustained a sizeable increase in the extent of the internationalization of their research between the early 1930s and the 1950s. This increase was led by companies in the science-based sectors, and especially those in chemicals. The share of foreign research in the leading European chemical firms rose from 8.2% in 1930–4 to 42.6% in 1940–59, while for electrical equipment companies it increased from 5.1% to 11.0% (see Table 12.5). For the largest European chemical firms the immediate postwar rate of internationalization proved to be a peak that has not since been surpassed (for them the foreign share stood at 34.8% in 1987–90), but in the postwar period the major European electrical equipment companies steadily increased their international research, to a point where the foreign share is now similar to that in chemicals.

The European story partly reflects the British experience, which is described in Table 12.6. For UK-owned companies the increase in the internationalization of technological activity between the early 1930s and the 1950s (from 25.9% to 40.8%) was also largely associated with a very strong internationalization of research in the chemical industry (from 23.3% to 66.7%). The prominent contribution of the chemical companies is consistent with the view that, historically, internationalization was linked to technological competence. European firms were technologically strongest in the chemical fields, in which areas they internationalized their research early; while American firms were relatively stronger in the development of electrical technologies, and in this field they led the early internationalization of technological activity.

Thus, at least for technology leaders, the internationalization of technological activity is not a new phenomenon. Of course, the first product cycle hypothesis might be rescued by a restatement to the effect that as a general rule the home country centre has been and remains the single most important site for the technological development of MNCs. Given that, as reported in Tables 12.1 to 12.6, the foreign share of technological activity has rarely been greater than two-thirds and is usually much less. MNCs are not "stateless corporations" (Patel and Pavitt 1991). The national originals of MNCs have been and continue to be critical in determining the geographical and sectoral composition of their technological activity, based on their path-dependent evolution from nationally differentiated expertises (Kogut 1987, 1990). While globalization has been defined here as the international integration of MNC networks, some authors have used the term to mean the loss of national identity by companies, and when defined in this unhelpful way, globalization has not taken place.

Regions

TABLE 12.6. Shares of US patenting of the largest UK-owned industrial firms due to research located abroad, grouped by industry (%)

Firms	1920–4	1925–9	1930–4	1935–9	1940–59	1960–4	1965–8	1969–72	1973–7	1978–82	1983–6	1987–90
Chemical	22.22	19.44	23.27	52.12	66.66	64.19	67.90	57.79	49.61	50.03	58.82	62.50
Electrical	7.14	4.67	0.55	0.67	5.61	6.94	17.37	27.09	33.56	24.85	19.53	26.53
Mechanical	6.55	16.34	36.51	32.13	35.57	38.53	44.70	50.05	48.10	45.57	51.14	59.88
Transport	5.45	14.46	8.13	5.68	5.75	4.37	6.03	7.75	7.65	7.77	13.29	20.31
TOTAL	7.61	14.26	25.88	34.63	40.84	39.52	46.44	42.66	40.09	39.17	45.32	50.55

Sources: As for Table 12.1.

It is also clear that from the perspective of the MNC as a whole, or from that of its home country, the internationalization of research is generally less than the internationalization of production (Patel and Pavitt 1991). One possible way of thinking about this is that most MNCs constitute an internal locational hierarchy of activity (Hymer 1975). To simplify matters for the sake of exposition, suppose that the production of each firm is divided into the technologically sophisticated and the simple or assembly type. Then, technologically sophisticated production tends to become geographically concentrated in certain locations, and assembly-type production tends to agglomerate in others (Cantwell 1987). The home country operations of the MNC stand at the pinnacle of its hierarchy, as a base for technologically sophisticated production, as hinted at by both Vernon and Hymer. Since the siting of research facilities is normally linked to the local support of technologically sophisticated production while little or no research accompanies assembly-type production, it follows that production in total is more widely geographically dispersed than research. So, while the home country is the single most important site for innovation, it does not necessarily follow that production in the home centre is more research-intensive than in the other advanced centres in which the MNC establishes technologically sophisticated production.

This argument suggests that, of the original theoretical underpinnings of the first product-cycle hypothesis, locational economies of integration and agglomeration play a greater role than do economies of scale in the R&D function. Previous criticisms of the first product-cycle hypothesis had shown that, while there is a minimum efficient scale for R&D facilities, the effect of firm size on the degree of internationalization of R&D is ambiguous (Mansfield, Teece and Romeo 1979). By contrast, a good deal of evidence has been gathered in support of the importance of economies of agglomeration or local clustering in the location of production (Krugman 1991; Porter 1990; Dahmén 1970; Sölvell, Zander and Porter 1991), and especially in the geographical location of innovation (Jaffe 1989; Jaffe, Trajtenberg and Henderson 1993; Feldman 1993; Cantwell 1991a) and in the location of the technologically sophisticated production of MNCs (Cantwell 1987). The lesson seems to be that economies of locational agglomeration are important, but that for MNCs they may occur in various centres and not exclusively in the home country, although the home base is the most significant single such centre.

4. THE NEW GLOBALIZATION OF TECHNOLOGY BY CORPORATE LEADERS

It has been shown that technological activity in some US MNCs was more widely dispersed internationally in the interwar period than it is today, while many European MNCs were already geared up to technology creation abroad by the 1950s. The companies that achieved the greatest internationalization of activity historically were generally technology leaders. This is what is suggested by the second product cycle hypothesis as formulated above, although there is a qualification to an acceptance of the hypothesis. This is, that where technology leaders are in a very strong or hegemonic position through rapid innovation at home, the home centre may exercise such a strong attraction for further research that the internationalization of technological activity is weak—a situation that seems to have applied to US companies in the early postwar years, and to Japanese firms today. Yet despite the historical significance of the geographical dispersion of innovation by MNCs, it is only relatively recently that the literature on MNCs has devoted much attention to the international creation of technology, as opposed to international technology transfer (Cantwell 1994).

The more recent broadening of the internationalization of technological development to a wider range of firms is partly responsible for finally drawing attention to this issue. The reduction in the industrial focus of internationalization mentioned previously offers some indirect evidence consistent with the broadening of internationalization across firms, but Table 12.7 provides direct evidence of this process within industrial groups. This shows that the extent of variation across firms in the degree of internationalization of their technological activity has been generally on a downward trend. A wider range of companies has now engaged in foreign technological development, in what was once mainly the province of a smaller number of leading firms. However, there are occasional exceptions to this trend. In the US electrical equipment group, ITT has remained highly international, and Sperry (prior to the formation of Unisys) also became strongly committed to foreign research, leaving others in their wake. In the Swiss electrical equipment group it was Brown Boveri (prior to the formation of ABB) that pulled ahead of the pack in its foreign operations, and in the German transport group the motor vehicle component producer Robert Bosch played this role, in each case sustaining the extent of cross-firm variation in the degree of internationalization. Elsewhere, lower transport and communication costs contributed to a general expansion across large firms in the internationalization of technological activity.

The other recent change which has often been discussed in other contexts is that formerly local market-oriented affiliates have been increasingly integrated into international networks within their respective MNCs, such networks coming to resemble "heterarchies" more than hierarchies (Hedlund 1986; Doz 1986; Porter 1986; Bartlett and Ghoshal 1989; Dunning 1992). In technological activity, too, the location-specific capabilities of internationally dispersed MNC affiliates may have become more closely integrated than in the past, linked to a strategy for technology creation in the MNC as

TABLE 12.7. The cross-firm coefficient of variation (expressed as a percentage) of the share of patenting due to research located abroad

	USA	UK	Germany	France	Switzerland	Sweden
Chemical industry group						
1920–39	217.5	135.1	177.3	89.0	88.6	190.9
1969–90	112.1	84.6	47.4	90.4	25.1	21.1
Electrical equipment industry group						
1920–39	144.7	232.5	165.6	223.6	38.9	141.4
1969–90	148.5	31.7	95.9	74.7	86.1	73.5
Mechanical industry group						
1920–39	289.2	181.3	193.6	189.3	141.4	219.7
1969–90	106.0	63.3	119.8	118.3	36.1	115.3
Transport industry group						
1920–39	202.4	219.4	117.4	264.6	n.a.	n.a.
1969–90	101.0	157.1	126.2	207.1	n.a.	99.1

n. a. = not applicable.

Sources: As for Table 12.1.

a whole, and not only with separate reference to each of the geographical parts of the company's business. This can be termed a new globalization of technological innovation.

The theoretical rationale for the recent international integration of productive activity is that the economic benefits attributable to a more refined locational division of labor within the MNC have often come to outweigh the costs of being less nationally responsive in each market, costs associated with adverse political repercussions and the continued national differentiation of demand (Doz 1986). In an integrated MNC network each affiliate specializes in accordance with the specific characteristics of local production conditions, technological capabilities and user requirements. The network benefits from economies of scale through the local concentration of particular lines of activity (increasing returns from local research in a specialized field as opposed to research in general), economies of locational agglomeration through an interchange with others operating in the same vicinity in technologically allied fields as suggested earlier, and economies of scope through the international intrafirm coordination of related but geographically separated activities. The experience acquired in a specialized activity in one location creates technological spillovers that can be passed on to other parts of the MNC network elsewhere. It has been shown that since the 1970s, in industries in which such net advantages to multinational integration were available, multinationality has been a source of competitive success and faster growth (Cantwell and Sanna-Randaccio 1993).

The transformation of the MNC, from a mainly multidomestic structure of separate affiliates each serving their local markets, to an integrated internal network structure, has relevance to other aspects of the product-cycle model apart from the hypotheses mentioned earlier. The wider product uct cycle model extended beyond the two hypotheses discussed here, to various other hypotheses and assumptions, such as that foreign direct investment can be treated as essentially local market-oriented, and that firms can be thought of as akin to single-product producers. It can be argued that this wider model broke down largely because of globalization in the sense just described, entailing the international integration of MNC networks. A global scanning for (new sources of) innovation and greater international linkages between production facilities imply an interactive flow of products and technological knowledge between countries (Vernon 1979). This contrasts strongly with the original product cycle perspective of innovation and technological knowledge essentially flowing outwards from a single major centre, namely the home country.

The new globalization of the responsibilities of affiliates to the MNC as a whole can be illustrated with reference to the shift that has occurred in the pattern of technological specialization of foreign-owned research facilities. To examine this issue the patent data were used to construct a measure of the distribution of technological specialization across various types of activity, for different groups of firms within their industry. It is also possible to distinguish between the pattern of specialization in domestic technological activity and in research abroad, with reference to a corporate group or groups. The index of technological specialization across different fields of activity that has been calculated is often termed an index of revealed technological advantage (RTA). The RTA value of a selected group of firms in a particular sector of technological activity is given by its share of US patents in that sector granted to companies in the same industry, relative to that group's overall share of all US patents assigned to firms in the industry in question. Denoting as P_{ij} the number of US patents granted in the field of technological activity i (defined with reference to the patent class system, as described earlier) to the selected group of firms j in a particular industry, then the RTA index is defined as follows:

$$RTA_{ij} = \left(P_{ij}/\Sigma_j P_{ij}\right) \Big/ \left(\Sigma_i P_{ij}/\Sigma_{ij} P_{ij}\right)$$

The index varies around unity, such that values greater than one suggest that a group of firms is comparatively specialized in the activity in question relative to other firms in the same industry, while values less than one are indicative of a lack of specialization by the standards of the industry (see Cantwell 1993, for further discussion). For the purposes of historical comparison attention is focused on the two groups of corporate technology leaders most prominent historically, each originating from major centres of

TABLE 12.8. The RTA values in selected sectors of technological activity of US-owned firms in the electrical equipment industry, and German-owned firms in the chemical industry

Firms	1920–68		1969–90	
	At home	Abroad	At home	Abroad
US-owned firms in the electrical equipment industry				
Lighting and wiring	0.96	1.30	0.94	0.77
General industrial equipment	1.07	0.67	0.97	1.96
German-owned firms in the chemical industry				
Bleaching and dyeing processes	2.43	1.43	1.91	0.71
Organic chemicals (dyestuffs)	1.46	1.47	1.33	0.97
Pharmaceuticals	1.22	3.16	1.22	2.04

Sources: As for Table 12.1.

innovation in their respective industries—that is, US-owned firms in the electrical equipment industry, and German-owned companies in the chemical industry. For each group the RTA index is separately calculated for activity located in its home research and its foreign research facilities, and for each of the two broad periods 1920–68 and 1969–90. In order to avoid the problems associated with low numbers of patents, the analysis is restricted to sectors of technological activity in which all large firms in the industry in question were granted 900 US patents or more in 1920–68. This involved 19 sectors in the electrical equipment industry, and 20 in the case of chemicals. The values of the RTA index calculated for a few selected sectors are shown in Table 12.8.

The European-located research of US-owned electrical equipment firms was not historically (1920–68) geared to local European strengths, but instead represented the local development of fields related to the core technologies that had been pioneered at home (in telecommunications and general electrical systems, including lighting). For these purposes the pattern of technological specialization of countries and broader regions such as Europe relative to one another was observed using an analogous RTA measure for countries rather than national groups of firms, grouping all patents (and not just those assigned to the largest firms) by the location of invention—indeed, it was in this country-specific (as opposed to firm-specific) form that the RTA index was originally proposed (Soete 1987; Cantwell 1989). In more recent years (1969–90), while the domestic activity of US-owned firms in this sector has continued to concentrate on general electrical equipment, the focus of their foreign research has shifted to specialized machinery and general industrial equipment, both of which are areas of European advantage. Thus, the technological activity of US-owned foreign affiliates (which is still mainly conducted in Europe) has shifted towards an attempt to exploit the technological potential of the location in which it is carried out.

Similarly, the largest German chemical firms were strongly specialized historically (between 1920 and 1968) in the same fields in developing technology both at home and abroad—namely, in bleaching and dyeing processes, in organic chemicals including dyestuffs, and to a lesser extent in pharmaceuticals. Thus, these large German companies quite directly exploited their major strengths abroad, further developing these new products and techniques for local industries and markets in other countries. In foreign research today (since 1969) these firms are no longer specialized in their corporate strengths of dyes and dyeing, but they retain a stronger focus on pharmaceuticals in which they are not quite so strong at home. Rather like the American electrical companies, the German chemical firms have shifted their international research strategies away from the pure exploitation of their own strength adapted to the needs of each particular local market, and towards an attempt to tap into foreign centres of expertise, in their case mainly in the development of pharmaceuticals in the US, Britain and Switzerland.

Other recent evidence also suggests that this type of internationally integrated or globalized strategy for innovation characterizes corporate technology leaders today. The extent to which the affiliates of MNCs specialize within their industry across national boundaries in accordance with the comparative advantage of local expertise seems to depend upon the pattern of locational hierarchy that exists between alternative centres. In the European chemical industry Germany is the dominant centre, the UK is a second-order centre, and Italy is of the third order. In this sector, German MNCs (the leaders) are technologically specialized in the other European centres in line with host country strengths, and the same is true of British chemical MNCs in Italy (Cantwell and Sanna-Randaccio 1992).

However, when operating in Germany, British chemical companies follow a pattern of technological specialization that accords with their own comparative advantages in the industry and those of their home centre, the UK. They do not appear to be especially prone to try and tap into the areas in which German expertise is relatively greatest, but rather treat Germany as a general reservoir of skills that can be used principally to extend those lines of operation on which they are already focused in their home base. Technology leaders originating from higher-order centres tend to establish a more extensive locationally specialized network of technological activity in support of an international innovation strategy than has been developed as yet by firms that originate from lower-order centres.

It is true that this result depends upon an analysis of cross-border technological specialization conducted at a fairly broad level of aggregation—across 20 or 30 sectors of technological activity, as described earlier. It may well be that when companies from a lower-order centre locate research in a higher-order one to engage in the same broad lines of activity in which they are specialized at home, there is still some geographical specialization at the more detailed level of particular products or processes, and at the more finely disaggregated patent class level (Zander 1994). In this event the distinction between corporate technology leaders and other firms would be more a matter of the degree of locational specialization that they have managed to achieve in technological development, rather than the existence of such a strategy of specialization across centres.

The globalization of technological innovation in MNCs, in the sense here of an international integration of geographically dispersed and locally specialized activities, tends to reinforce and not to dismantle nationally distinctive patterns of development or national systems of innovation (Nelson 1993). Contrary to what is sometimes alleged, globalization and national specialization are complementary parts of a common process, and not conflicting trends (see Archibugi and Michie 1993, for further discussion). The incentive to organize affiliate specialization is the desire to tap into the locally specific and differentiated stream of innovation in each centre, but by specializing in accordance with these local strengths the latter are reinforced. The creation of tacit capability is localized and embedded in social organizations (Nelson and Winter 1982), and this organizational distinctiveness has a location-specific as well as a firm-specific dimension. The particular path of innovation followed in each country or region has historical origins (Rosenberg 1976, 1982). In the period of globalization since the late 1960s the general tendency has been for MNCs to become more technologically diversified as they establish newly integrated technological systems, while countries or locations have become more specialized in their technological activity (Cantwell 1993).

5. CONCLUSIONS

One aspect of the product cycle is now rather discredited, namely the idea that demand-led innovation (together with economies of scale in R&D) in the home country dictates the geographical restriction of corporate research and the most technologically sophisticated production to the site of the parent company. For one thing, the demand-led view of innovation that was prevalent in the 1960s is now more widely acknowledged to be onesided and potentially misleading (Mowery and Rosenberg 1979). Innovations generally rely on a firm-specific learning process that interacts with both the growth of demand and the creation of new scientific and technological knowledge. In a region or country that enjoys technological leadership, high incomes and demand are as much a consequence of that leadership (high technological capability and thus high productivity) as they are a cause of it. For another thing, the peculiarities of foreign production conditions and demand have required leading MNCs historically to develop innovations abroad, related to those that had been pioneered at home.

For this latter reason, another aspect of the model can be extended to provide a further historical application that remains relevant. That is, the product cycle view that outward industrial investment is most widely associated with technology leaders, generally in conjunction with their holding a strong export position; so, too, the earliest internationalization of technological development was largely due to such leaders. Historically, some highly competent US electrical equipment firms were considerably more international in their technology creation then than they are now. In Europe large chemical firms were relatively technologically stronger, and it was they that led the historical internationalization of corporate research facilities.

In more recent times technology leaders have altered the nature of international technology creation by pioneering the international integration of MNC facilities into regional or global networks. Globalization in this sense involves the establishment of new international structures for technology creation. In the past, foreign technological activity exploited domestic strengths abroad, it was located in response to local demand conditions, it assisted in the growth of other high-income areas, and its role ranged from the adaptation of products to suit local tastes through to the establishment of new local industries. At that time the capacity to develop internationally dispersed innovations derived from a position of technological strength in the firm's home-country base, and led to similar lines of technological development being established abroad. By contrast, today, for companies of the leading centres, foreign technological activity now increasingly aims to tap into local fields of expertise, and to provide a further source of new technology that can be utilized internationally in the other operations of the MNC. In this respect, innovation in the leading MNCs is now more genuinely international or, in the terminology used here, it has become "globalized".

There are two similarities in the theoretical rationale provided for the product cycle model (which applied best to the USA and to US-owned MNCs in the early postwar period) and that suggested for the current globalization of technological activity in MNCs. Both explanations rely on the role of the economies of locational agglomeration, and on the leadership exercised by the most technologically competent firms. The essential difference is that in the product cycle model just one preeminent center for innovation was recognized, whereas in the globalization story there are multiple locations for innovation, and even lower-order or less-developed centers can still be sources of innovation. Hence, the theoretical concepts also used in the product cycle approach apply differently in the account of globalization; locational agglomeration occurs in the clusters of distinctive innovations that occur in many centers and not only in one unique center, while the greater capability of the most competent firms manifests itself not just in the wider geographical dispersion of their investments (a more important consideration historically), but in the broader degree of cross-border specialization that they are able to manage.

The product cycle view of the MNC as a locational hierarchy also remains relevant, although this too needs extending. It is still true that the home country is generally the single most important site for corporate technological development. More interestingly, the form of locational hierarchy in the leading firms of the most advanced centres is now much more complex than it used to be, and more complex than is the equivalent hierarchy of other MNCs. The affiliates of the leading companies in other major centres may be thought of as constituting an interactive network. Cross-investments between the major centres in the most technologically dynamic industries (Dunning 1988; Cantwell 1989; Cantwell and Sanna-Randaccio 1992) have probably helped to reinforce the existing pattern of geographical specialization, and the importance of these centres as locations for innovation. Having been the first to establish an international spread of technological activity, MNCs from the leading centers in a given industry now exploit locational diversity in paths of innovation to a greater extent than do other firms.

REFERENCES

Archibugi, D. and Michie, J. (1993), "The Globalization of Technology: Myths and Realities," *University of Cambridge Research Papers in Management Studies*, no. 18, May.

Bartlett, C. A. and Ghoshal, S. (1989), *Managing Across Borders: The Transnational Solution* (Boston: Harvard Business School Press).

Beaton, K. (1957), *Enterprise in Oil: A History of Shell in the United States* (New York: Appleton-Century-Crofts).

Cantwell, J. A. (1987), "The Reorganisation of European Industries after Integration," *Journal of Common Market Studies*, 26: 127–51.

——(1989), *Technological Innovation and Multinational Corporations* (Oxford: Basil Blackwell).

——(1991a), "The International Agglomeration of R&D," in M. C. Casson (ed.), *Global Research Strategy and International Competitiveness* (Oxford: Basil Blackwell).

——(1991b), "The Theory of Technological Competence and its Application to International Production," in D. G. McFetridge (ed.), *Foreign Investment, Technology and Economic Growth* (Calgary: University of Calgary Press).

Cantwell, J. A. (1993), "Corporate Technological Specialisation in International Industries," in M. C. Casson and J. Creedy (eds.), *Industrial Concentration and Economic Inequality* (Aldershot: Edward Elgar).

——(1994), "Introduction", in J. A. Cantwell (ed.), *Transnational Corporations and Innovatory Activities* (London: Routledge).

——and Barrera, M. P. (1993), "The Rise of Corporate R&D and the Technological Performance of the Largest European Firms from the Interwar Years Onwards," *University of Reading Discussion Papers in Economics*, no. 271, Sept.

——————(1995), "Inter-company Agreements for Technological Development: Lessons from International Cartels," *International Studies in Management and Organisation* (forthcoming).

——and Hodson, C. (1991), "Global R&D and UK Competitiveness," in Casson (ed.), *Global Research Strategy and International Competitiveness*.

——and Kotecha, U. (1994), "L'internationalization des activités technologiques: Le cas français en perspective," in F. Sachwald (ed.), *Les Défis de la Mondialisation: Innovation et Concurrence* (Paris: Masson).

——and Sanna-Randaccio, F. (1992), "Intra-industry Direct Investment in the European Community: Oligopolistic Rivalry and Technological Competition," in J. A. Cantwell (ed.), *Multinational Investment in Modern Europe* (Aldershot: Edward Elgar).

——————(1993), "Multinationality and Firm Growth," *Weltwirtschaftliches Archiv*, 129: 275–99.

Chandler, A. D. (1990), *Scale and Scope: The Dynamics of Industrial Capitalism* (Cambridge, Mass.: Harvard University Press).

Coleman, D. C. (1969), *Courtaulds: An Economic and Social History*, ii. *Rayon*, (Oxford: Oxford University Press).

Dahmén, E. (1970), *Entrepreneurial Activity and the Development of Swedish Industry, 1919–1939* (Homewood, Ill.: American Economic Association Translation Series).

Dosi, G., Teece, D. J. and Winter, S. G. (1992), "Towards a Theory of Corporate Coherence: Preliminary Remarks," in G. Dosi, R. Giannetti and P. A. Toninelli (eds.), *Technology and Enterprise in a Historical Perspective* (Oxford: Oxford University Press).

Doz, Y. (1986), *Strategic Management in Multinational Companies* (Oxford: Pergamon).

Dunning, J. H. (1988), *Multinationals, Technology and Competitiveness* (London: Unwin Hyman).

——(1992), *Multinational Enterprises and the Global Economy* (Wokingham, UK: Addison-Wesley).

Feldman, M. P. (1993), "An Examination of the Geography of Innovation," *Industrial and Corporate Change*, 2: 451–70.

Granstrand, O., Håkansson, L. and Sjölander, S. (1992) (eds.), *Technology Management and International Business: Internationalisation of R&D and Technology* (Chichester: John Wiley).

Hedlund, G. (1986), "The Hypermodern MNC: A Heterarchy?" *Human Resource Management*, 25: 9–25.

Hounshell, D. A. and Smith, J. K. (1988), *Science and Corporate Strategy: Du Pont*

R&D, 1902–1980 (Cambridge: Cambridge University Press).

Hymer, S. (1975), "The Multinational Corporation and the Law of Uneven Development," in H. Radice (ed.), *International Firms and Modern Imperialism* (Harmondsworth, UK: Penguin).

Jaffe, A. B. (1989), "Real Effects of Academic Research," *American Economic Review*, 79: 957–70.

——Trajtenberg, M. and Henderson, R. (1993), "Geographical Localization of Knowledge Spillovers as Evidenced by Patent Citations," *Quarterly Journal of Economics*, 108: 577–98.

Jones, R. and Marriot, O. (1971), *Anatomy of a Merger: A History of GEC, AEI and English Electric* (London: Cape).

Kogut, B. (1987), "Country Patterns in International Competition: Appropriability and Oligopolistic Agreement," in N. Hood and J. E. Vahlne (eds.), *Strategies in Global Competition* (London: Croom Helm).

——(1990), "The Permeability of Borders and the Speed of Learning Among Countries," in J. H. Dunning, B. Kogut and M. Blomström, *Globalisation of Firms and the Competitiveness of Nations* (Lund, Sweden: Lund University Press).

Krugman, P. R. (1991), *Geography and Trade* (Cambridge, Mass.: MIT Press).

Lall, S. (1979), "The International Allocation of Research Activity by US Multinationals," *Oxford Bulletin of Economics and Statistics*, 41: 313–31.

Mansfield, E., Teece, D. J. and Romeo, A. (1979), "Overseas Research and Development by US-based Firms," *Economica*, 46: 187–96.

Mowery, D. C. and Rosenberg, N. (1979), "The Influence of Market Demand Upon Innovation: A Critical Review of Some Recent Empirical Studies," *Research Policy*, 8: 103–53.

Nelson, R. R. (1991), "Why do Firms Differ and How Does it Matter?" *Strategic Management Journal*, 12: 61–74.

——(1992), "The Role of Firms in Technical Advance," in Dosi, Giannetti and Toninelli (eds.), *Technology and Enterprise in a Historical Perspective*.

——(1993) (ed.), *National Innovation Systems* (Oxford: Oxford University Press).

——and Winter, S. G. (1982), *An Evolutionary Theory of Economic Change* (Cambridge, Mass.: Harvard University Press).

Patel, P. and Pavitt, K. L. R. (1991), "Large Firms in the Production of the World's Technology: An Important Case of 'Non-Globalisation'," *Journal of International Business Studies*, 22: 1–21.

Pavitt, K. L. R. (1992), "Some Foundations for a Theory of the Large Innovating Firm," in Dosi, Gianetti and Toninelli (eds.), *Technology and Enterprise in a Historical Perspective*.

Pearce, R. D. and Singh, S. (1991), *Globalising Research and Development* (London: Macmillan).

Penrose, E. T. (1959), *The Theory of the Growth of the Firm* (Oxford: Basil Blackwell).

Porter, M. E. (1986), "Competition in Global Industries: A Conceptual Framework," in M. E. Porter (ed.), *Competition in Global Industries* (Boston: Harvard Business School Press).

——(1990), *The Competitive Advantage of Nations* (New York: Free Press).

Reich, L. S. (1986), *The Making of American Industrial Research: Science and*

Business at GE and Bell, 1876–1926 (Cambridge: Cambridge University Press).

Ronstadt, R. C. (1977), *Research and Development Abroad by US Multinationals* (New York: Praeger).

Rosenberg, N. (1976), *Perspectives on Technology* (Cambridge: Cambridge University Press).

——(1982), *Inside the Black Box: Technology and Economics* (Cambridge: Cambridge University Press).

Schmookler, J. (1966), *Invention and Economic Growth* (Cambridge, Mass.: Harvard University Press).

Soete, L. L. G. (1987), "The Impact of Technological Innovation on International Trade Patterns: The Evidence Reconsidered," *Research Policy*, 16: 101–30.

Stocking, G. W. and Watkins, M. W. (1946), *Cartels in Action* (New York: Twentieth Century Fund).

Sölvell, Ö., Zander, I. and Porter, M. E. (1991), *Advantage Sweden* (Stockholm: Norstedts).

Teece, D. J., Pisano, G. and Shuen, A. (1990), "Firm Capabilities, Resources and the Concept of Strategy," U.C., Berkeley, Consortium on Competitiveness and Cooperation Working Papers, nos. 90–8.

Vernon, R. (1966), "International Investment and International Trade in the Product Cycle," *Quarterly Journal of Economics*, 80: 190–207.

——(1979), "The Product Cycle Hypothesis in a New International Environment," *Oxford Bulletin of Economics and Statistics*, 41: 255–67.

Wilkins, M. (1974), *The Maturing of Multinational Enterprise* (Cambridge, Mass.: Harvard University Press).

——(1989), *The History of Foreign Investment in the United States to 1914* (Cambridge, Mass.: Harvard University Press).

Zander, I. (1994), *The Tortoise Evolution of the Multinational Corporation* (Stockholm: Institute of International Business, Stockholm School of Economics).

13

Globalization, Technological Change and the Spatial Organization of Economic Activity

JOHN H. DUNNING

1. INTRODUCTION

One of the most distinctive features of the globalizing economy of the early 1990s is the extent to which the cross-border movement of created assets—and particularly technological and organizational capability—is internalized either within multinational hierarchies or between two or more separately owned, but interrelated, firms[1] located in different countries. It is the contention of this presentation that the resulting international division of labor, and the nature of the competitive advantages of both firms and countries, is fundamentally different from that determined solely by the disposition of locationally immobile assets and the transactions between independent buyers and sellers.

For most of the past century, most of the explanations for the international specialization of value-added activity have been based upon the uneven spatial distribution of natural resources. But, today, the competitive and comparative advantages of countries are increasingly determined by the ability of governments and firms to create and organize the deployment of created assets, and from the trade in foreign direct investment (FDI) arising from these assets. At the same time, the significance of intrafirm or interalliance trade is also increasing.

The metamorphosis in the organization of natural and created assets, and of international transactions, is having critical implications for both the ownership and location of economic activity. This is most conspicuously shown by the increasing role of multinational enterprises (MNEs) in global production and trade (UNCTAD 1994). It is true that new organizational systems are favoring the participation of small firms, but there are strong suggestions that those involved in the most dynamic sectors of the international economy are most likely to be part of a business district or cross-border network of activities, in which the pivotal role is played by large multiactivity and multilocational corporations (Harrison 1994).

2. EXPLAINING CHANGES IN THE SPATIAL ALLOCATION OF ECONOMIC ACTIVITY

Under classical and neoclassical theories of trade, the international division of labor was determined entirely by the geographical disposition of natural resources and the stock of capital. Changes in economic activity were presumed only to occur as a result of the increase or depletion of such resources. Trade in capital and intermediate products, like that of finished goods and services was assumed to be arm's-length; otherwise assets were perceived to be completely location-bound. There was no reason for foreign direct investment (FDI) to exist, as there were no incentives for firms to internalize cross-border markets. Neither was there any reason for firms to engage in cross-border alliances or networks.[2]

The treatment of technology in neoclassical theory was ambiguous. Either it was ignored altogether or it was assumed to be freely available to all firms, and instantaneously transferable across national boundaries. The transborder locational consequences of technological change were rarely considered in the literature, although, in part, this deficiency was partly remedied by the neotechnology theories of trade of the 1950s.[3]

A central feature of received trade theory was the complete disregard of the firm, or interfirm alliances, as institutional entities and of the costs of organizing economic activity. The competitiveness of a country was judged by the ability of its economic system to allocate resources in a way which maximized their comparative advantage. It is, perhaps, worth emphasizing that *international economics*—as a distinctive discipline—originated because of the presumed differences in the determinants and outcomes of the allocation of resources *within* a nation as compared to those *between* nations. In turn, these were postulated to arise because, beyond the jurisdictional boundaries of nations, all resources were perceived to be completely immobile. It was also assumed that each country processed a distinctive pattern of resource endowments.

In the neoclassical tradition, trade economists gave little attention to the distribution of international economic activity *within* countries. This lacuna was taken up by locational economists. However, their focus of interest was rather different. Rather than asking the question "What determines the optimum mix of activities for a subnational location?" they asked the question "What determines the optimum location for a particular mix of activities?" Partly, this lack of concern with issues central to international economics is reflected in the fact that resources were assumed to be fully mobile within countries. Consequently, the dominant paradigm of locational economics became the principle of *absolute* competitive advantage, rather than that of *comparative* competitive advantage.

In contrast to trade theory, the unit of analysis in locational economics was the firm, and most of the neoclassical models constructed, e.g. by Von Thunen (1876), Weber (1929), Hotelling (1929), Losch (1940) and Hoover (1948) were extensions of the profit-maximizing theory of the firm. Given a particular market, the optimum location was that which minimized production plus transport costs. In imperfect markets, firms had to balance the spatial implications for maximizing revenue with those of minimizing costs. No such spatial choice was allowed firms between a domestic and foreign location.

For the most part, the dichotomy between intra- and intercountry spatial economics remains. One notable exception is the work of Bertin Ohlin, who, perhaps, more than any other economist, tried to bridge the gap[4] between the two intellectual strands. In 1976, he organized a symposium in Stockholm to which he invited some leading economists, geographers and regional scientists to share their thoughts on the determinants of the international allocation of economic activity. However, for the most part, the papers presented, and the ensuing discussion (later published in book form by Ohlin, Hesselborn and Wijkman 1977), proceeded on parallel lines with few interdisciplinary bridges being built. Trade economists stuck to their last and apart from my own contribution, which gave birth to the eclectic paradigm of international production, there was no attempt to take on board either organizational issues or the implications of the growing mobility of intangible assets.[5]

It is, I think, no accident that the emphasis of this particular symposium is on *firm* rather than *country* specific considerations. Quite apart from the interests of the organizers, I believe that the main advances in our intellectual apparatus in explaining the international allocation of value-added activity over the last two decades has not come from extant international economics—but from a juxtaposition of organizational theory, institutional and technological economics and business strategy.

As yet, however, most of the work of scholars from these disciplines has not generally embraced an international dimension and, as a result, our understanding of the way resources are organized and distributed across national boundaries has been constricted.[6] But, I believe that the globalization of economic activity is forcing scholars, working both in traditional trade and locational economics, and in a variety of business-oriented disciplines, to search for a more common paradigmatic approach.

What then might be the intellectual components of any future explanation of the spatial organization of economic activity? For the rest of this contribution, I propose to examine a number of features of the globalizing economy and how they are affecting the extant paradigms and theories of the disciplines represented at this symposium; and also to speculate a little on the future direction of both uni- and interdisciplinary research in the later 1990s.

3. THE ROLE OF CREATED ASSETS IN TRADITIONAL THINKING

As countries move along their development paths, the role of *created*, relative to *natural*, assets, as the main generators of future income increases. As their name implies, created assets embrace all forms of wealth produced from natural resources. More particularly, they include accumulated knowledge, skills, learning and experience, and organizational competence, which are embodied in human beings, proprietary rights, institutions and physical capacity. Some scholars may add to these, other "softer" assets, such as an entrepreneurial spirit, an ability to benefit from cooperative alliances and networking, and a mentality which favors wealth creation and a continual upgrading in quality and efficiency of existing assets. Unlike natural resources—notably land, power sources and climate—many, but not all, created assets are transportable over space; although, the precise way in which they are packaged may not be.[7] Unlike natural assets too, most created assets are likely to be the privileged possession of particular private or public institutions. These two characteristics of created assets—namely their mobility and their ownership specificity—cut right across the assumptions of neoclassical international economics,[8] and are forcing scholars to reappraise their explanations of spatial activity.

For the most part, organizational scholars have paid only limited attention to the underlying characteristics of created assets. Two notable exceptions are Alfred Chandler and David Teece, who in their various writings,[9] have distinguished between the competitive advantages of firms arising from their possession of a "core" asset, e.g. a patent, brand name or the exclusive access to a market, and those which arise from the efficient coordination of these assets with complementary assets owned by other firms. In Chandler's view, it is the access to and efficient deployment of the latter kind of competence, which has been one of the key components of corporate success over the past century, and, by inference, that of nations as well. However, while examining some of the country specific features which might lead to the creation of coordinating assets, neither Chandler nor Teece has given much attention to the spatial implications of the governance of interrelated assets; except, perhaps, to suggest that these might aid, rather than inhibit, industrial clustering and the concentration of economic activity.[10]

In contrast to organizational scholars, scholars in the Schumpeterian tradition have placed rather more emphasis on the possession and accumulation of technological assets as a firm-specific advantage; and of the role of innovatory systems as a country-specific advantage. More recently, as attention has become focused on the learning experiences, technological trajectories and innovatory strategies of firms, the interests of the neo-Schumpterians, such as Antonelli, Chesnais, Dosi, Freeman and Pavitt, and those of the organizational and business strategists such as Teece, Hedlund,

Bartlett and Ghoshal, have begun to converge. Both approaches have paid some attention to the spatial implications of technological innovation. In particular, building on the work of Ray Vernon (1970) and Gary Hufbauer (1965, 1970), Dosi, Pavitt and Soete (1990) have incorporated this variable, at a *country* level, into extant trade theory. Several Italian scholars, notably Cainarca, Colombo and Mariotti (1988), Antonelli (1991) and Archibugi and Pianta (1993) have examined the international and intraregional diffusion of technological activity; while Bartlett and Ghoshal (1989) have argued that MNEs which have most successfully coordinated and integrated their technological strategies are those which have recorded the most creditable performances as international direct investors.

For their part, international economists have treated assets as a country-, rather than a firm-specific competitive advantage. Using such indices as R&D expenditure as a proxy for created assets, and patents or technology-intensive products as the output of such assets, they have sought to incorporate this variable into H-O type models—and to undertake some evaluation of its importance.[11] In his explanation of Japanese direct investment abroad, Kojima (1978, 1990) argued that *countries* which had a comparative advantage in the *creation* of technological assets, but not in their *use*, should export technology as an intermediate product, and import those products which required other created, or natural, assets in which they were comparatively disadvantaged. Only in his more recent writings, e.g. Kojima (1992), has Kojima considered the mode by which technology is exported as a factor influencing the spatial distribution of economic activity.[12]

Until the 1970s, relatively little attention was given to the competitive advantages of firms by microeconomists. In the heritage of Edward Chamberlin (1933), Joan Robinson (1933) and Joe Bain (1956), any advantage one firm was supposed to have over another was presumed to reflect the form and degree of its monopoly power. Only in the last twenty years or so has the emphasis on firm-specific advantages switched to its ability to create or acquire assets which yield competitive enhancing results. The work of Michael Porter (1980, 1985), following in the tradition of industrial economics, and that of Barney (1986), Dierickx and Cool (1989) and Rumelt (1984), which has helped refocus attention on the resource-based theory of the firm (Penrose 1959), are examples of two schools of thought which specifically address the question of why some firms are more successful than others.

To what extent is it possible—or indeed desirable—to integrate these various approaches? My own preference is to first accept that, at any given moment of time, each firm possesses a unique portfolio of accumulated assets—including those which may be located outside its national boundaries; and that the way these assets are organized is determined by the trajectory chosen by the management of the firm to advance its time-related objectives and its position on that path. These assets, which elsewhere (e.g.

Dunning 1977 and subsequent writings) we have called ownership-specific (O) assets as, in the last resort, it is ownership which determines the jurisdictional boundaries of a firm. In turn, however, the fecundity of assets may be influenced by the extent and type of activity in which a firm engages, the region or country in which it operates and the characteristics of the firm, other than its ownership.

I have suggested that, in its explanation of the international allocation of economic activity, received trade theory treats firms as "black boxes", and only locationally bound country-specific assets are assumed to determine the trading patterns of nations. Both the asset portfolios and the products supplied by competing firms are assumed to be homogeneous, and all firms are presumed to engage in only a single activity, and to be price-takers. Even the concept of dynamic comparative advantage pays little attention to the growth of the firm. However, in practice, we know that the propensity of firms, within a particular sector and of a particular nationality, to engage in intra- and international activity varies a great deal; and this is because of their distinctive asset portfolios and/or the way in which they organize and manage such assets.

Now, if it were possible to identify a "best practice" asset structure and a "best practice" usage of a dynamic firm, normalizing for such variables as its nationality, size and product range, one could presumably incorporate these ownership-specific characteristics into any macromodel of spatial activity. The problem—at least as I see it—is to define what is the "best practice" firm, when each firm is moving along a different trajectory of innovatory activity, product specialization or spatial diversification.[13] In an uncertain world, only with hindsight can the optimum behavior of a firm be identified and, most certainly, yesterday's "best practice" firm is not necessarily a guide to tomorrow's "best practice" firm. This makes the incorporation of firm-specific behavior into any *normative* theory of the spatial allocation of economic activity a very difficult thing to do.[14] Indeed, it may be questionable how productive such an effort might be!

Yet, in explaining the spatial activity of resources, as it *is*, as opposed to how it *ought* to be—it is surely incumbent on scholars to at least identify, if not to evaluate—the way in which the O specific asset portfolios of firms affect both their ability to compete in spatial markets, and their preference for siting their value-added activities in different locations. But, for the most part, this has not been done. For example, while it is generally acknowledged that patent protection may confer an O advantage on the patenting firm, without a knowledge of the asset portfolios, production functions, interfirm relationships and strategies of that firm and those of its competitors, it is impossible to gauge the consequences of that patent protection for either the industry of that firm or the country in which it is domiciled. Thus, for example, the impact of patent protection on the competitiveness of an auto firm engaging in scale production may be very

different from that on one pursuing a more flexible manufacturing strategy. On the other hand, it may be reasonable to hypothesize that, in the
absence of patent protection, there would be less incentive to engage in
research and development in the first place, and, if and when, countries
differ in their national innovatory systems, this could have considerable
spatial consequences.

It is possible to analyze the spatial consequences of other O-specific
advantages in a similar way. However, it may be conceptually useful to
distinguish between those advantages which arise from the privileged access to specific assets and those which stem from the way in which such
assets, and those which are more generally available, are organized. We
shall consider the spatial implications of these latter assets in our next
section.

We would, however, make one further point about firm-specific assets.
Much of received spatial economics rests on the assumptions that the sole
objective of firms is to maximize profits and that there is minimal market
failure. In practice, neither assumption is legitimate. However, where competitive pressures exist, then, as the theory suggests, firms are forced to look
more closely at ways and means of lowering production costs and/or increasing revenues, and of organizing their assets in a way which minimizes
transaction costs. A similar argument applies to reaping economies of scale.
To overcome the costs of market failure, it may be inevitable that some
concentration of competitive advantages among firms arises. So long as the
privileged firms are not protected, i.e. markets are contestable, this may be
an optimum solution and the most analogous to the perfect market model
so favoured by received theory.

So far in my analysis of the spatial implications of firm-specific advantages, I have been concerned with those which, independently, arise directly
from a firm's *own* asset portfolio and management. But, sometimes, these
advantages may, themselves, be influenced by its participation in interfirm
networks and its locational choices. The gains to be derived from the
geographical concentration, agglomeration or clustering of related activities have been well acknowledged by industrial and locational economists,
at least since the time of Alfred Marshall.[15] By contrast, until recently they
had been relatively neglected by trade economists, mainly, I suspect, because of the latter's narrow interpretation of the boundaries of a firm and
their reluctance to embrace endemic market failure (in this case arising
from externalities) into their models or theories.

However, over the last decade, a systemic approach to the dynamics of
the firm, and its interaction with related firms located in close proximity to
each other, has gained increasing attention by scholars from economics,
organization theory, business strategy, geography and sociology.[16] Due to
the increased ease with which products, assets and people can move across
national boundaries, the traditional paradigms of the microorganization of

business activity, and their spatial implications, are becoming increasingly inappropriate. In particular, as flexible and network-related production systems tend to replace Fordist type hierarchies as the dominant system of value-added activity, the concept of "neo-Marshallian" subnational spatial areas, e.g. the business or industrial district as a critical unit of economic organization, is gaining ground. I have already alluded to the main feature of the globalizing economy as the replacement of an "arm's-length" international division of labor by one largely characterized by trading and production relationships between related parties.[17] It is also evident that this leads both to some clustering of value-added activities by foreign direct investors in particular countries—very much on the lines earlier observed by Knickerbocker (1973),[18] and to an increasing spatial concentration of such activities—and particularly innovatory activities—between countries.

The renaissance of the Marshallian agglomerative economies has been acknowledged by several scholars, including Michael Porter (1990) and Paul Krugman (1991), both of whom assign it considerable importance in affecting the competitive advantages both of the participating firms, and of the regions and countries of which they are a part. The point at issue here is the extent to which firms with O specific assets, critical to their global competitiveness, need to be in close proximity to other firms supplying complementary assets in order to minimize their transaction and coordination costs.

It is not difficult to find historical or contemporary examples of the way in which agglomerative economies have added to the O advantages of the participating firms, and also to the competitiveness of the regions and countries. Among the best known are the square mile (= City) of London, Silicon Valley in California, the Geneva watch, the Solingen cutlery, and the Portuguese Cork industries.[19] However, there are strong suggestions that, in spite of (or perhaps it is because of) advances in transportation and communication technologies, the value of agglomerative economies is increasing.[20] This is especially so in the more dynamic and service-intensive industrial sectors, in which there is usually an above-average representation of smaller and entrepreneurial firms, which are likely to gain particular benefit from networking with other firms, and the near presence of diverse, yet, complementary assets.[21] It also reflects the increasing need of firms producing or using complementary assets at the top end of the value chain to keep in close touch with each other,[22] and is encouraged by various facets of innovatory-led production, including the desire of firms to keep inventories to the minimum. One of the fastest growing sectors of economic activity is that of industrial and science parks. Here, too, there is a good deal of intraindustry FDI in research and development activity, as the major MNEs seek to acquire, as well as to exploit, already existing knowledge.[23]

It is difficult, if not impossible to define an optimum space of a regional cluster, as this will critically depend on the composition of the activities making up the cluster. But, one noticeable result of European integration is the realignment of the geography of agglomeration, which, *inter alia*, is leading to the emergence of new cross-border networks. Examples include, those parts of the Low Countries and Germany adjacent to the Ruhr Valley, and along the borders of Northern Italy and France. It is most conspicuous in sectors no longer encumbered by nontariff barriers; in those which gain most benefit from labor pooling and the common availability of specialized inputs and services; in those which comprise activities which are technologically or organizationally synergistic to each other, and in those which are faced with relatively insignificant transport and communications costs.

Trade liberalization has also affected the location of economic activity in other regions of the world. In his study of the Mexican economy, for example, Hanson (1994) found that the introduction of more market-oriented policies of the Mexican government has led to a relocation of the geographical clustering of manufacturing activity from Mexico City to the US border region. Trade liberalization has also tended to compress regional wage differentials.

4. THE GROWING SIGNIFICANCE OF THE COORDINATING AND TRANSACTION FUNCTIONS OF THE FIRM

I have already observed that neoclassical economists regarded the firm solely as a production unit, and markets to be the optimal modality for the exchange of inputs and outputs relevant to that production. Prior to Knight (1921) and Schumpeter (1947) and Penrose (1959), the coordinating role of the entrepreneur was given little attention, except that it was generally accepted by microeconomists that, in conditions of perfect competition, the eventual limit to the size of firms were the rising costs of coordination.

Yet, as several scholars from a wide range of disciplines have demonstrated, the relative significance of the transaction and coordinating costs (compared, for example, to production costs) of economic activity tends to increase with economic development.[24] This is essentially because, as the division of labor becomes more specialized, the likelihood of learning constraints, information asymmetries and opportunism between independent transacting parties increases. Where it is perceived these costs are higher than those of internal, or quasi internal,[25] organizational mechanisms, then individual hierarchies, or groups of related firms, will replace the market as an organizational mode. Hence, the growth of multiactivity firms and networks is directly correlated with the growth of market-related transaction and coordination costs, and also with advances in organizational and communications technology.

The geographical specialization of economic activities across space is likely to lead to additional transport and coordinating costs, both of the market and of firms. Sometimes—as in the case of some service-intensive activities, e.g. R&D and merchant banking, where face-to-face contact between producers and users is imperative—such costs are infinite. Initially, economists measured distance costs entirely by the direct costs of traversing space. But again, due to technological advances and a more complex division of labor, these costs, relative to market-related transaction and coordinating costs, have fallen. Increasingly, the locational preferences of firms are being set by their ability to organize spatially dispersed or spatially concentrated activities.

Although international economists have largely ignored them, international business scholars have long recognized that the distinction between cross-border and domestic value-added activities lies in the presence of transnational market failures. These include not only the most obvious coordinating costs and learning and information constraints firms have to incur when they commence production in a less familiar, and perhaps riskier, economic and political environment, but those to do with establishing and fostering relationships between individuals and institutions in countries with different historical and institutional backgrounds, legal systems, life-styles, political and religious ideologies and business customs.

Historically, cultural distance[26] has been one of the key variables determining the geographical pattern of economic activity, notably between metropolitan countries and their colonies, and between countries with comparable legal systems and commercial practices. Almost certainly, the globalizing economy is eroding some types of cultural distance and causing a realignment of spatial preferences among firms. On the other hand where, to acquire the intermediate products or complementary assets necessary to protect or advance their own competitive advantages, firms perceive a need to be part of a subnational network, this could add to their spatial specific coordination and transaction costs. Whether the resulting spatial realignment is predominantly centripetal or centrifugal will obviously reflect a balance between the production, transaction and coordinating costs of clustering particular kinds of economic activities, and those of decentralizing such activities.

While scholars have long since recognized that the gains to be derived from agglomerative economies are activity-specific, rather less attention has been paid to the role of subnational or country-specific variables in determining such clusters. To some extent, Michael Porter (1990) rectifies this deficiency, and correctly points to the growing importance of subnational clusters as a variable influencing the competitiveness of firms and countries. Building on Porter's analysis, I would like to suggest that the capability of countries to develop and sustain efficient clusters rests first, on the macroeconomic and organizational policies of governments; second, on the innovating and marketing strategies of the participating firms; third, on the willingness and ability of those firms to capture the benefits and minimize the costs of clustering; and fourth, on the availability and quality of complementary assets—notably R&D, transport and communication infrastructure and a flexible labor market. Such a capability may well become one of the most important location-bound and country-specific characteristics determining the competitive advantages of particular activities and the composition of a country's economic activities in the emerging age of alliance capitalism.[27]

To what extent, then, have scholars embraced the spatial consequences of the inability of arm's-length markets to maximize the net benefits of the coordinating and transaction functions of a market economy? As far as much of extant international trade theory is concerned, the answer is very little,[28] although there have been some brave attempts to integrate theories of trade and international production.[29] As far as international direct investment theory, the record is much better. Indeed, perhaps the critical contribution of international business scholars over the past two decades, has been to develop a firm-level theory of international direct investment, by explaining the situations in which firms will internalize cross-border intermediate product markets—the so-called internalization (I) paradigm,[30] and also why firms should opt to undertake the value-added activities arising from such internalization from one location rather than another.

At the same time, IB scholars have paid much less attention to the ways in which the intracountry allocation of economic activity might affect the competitive advantages of firms or nations, or indeed to the significance of agglomerative economies in explaining the intracountry distribution of FDI.[31] This deficiency is in the process of being partially corrected by economic geographers,[32] and by economists interested in the spatial distribution of technological innovation.[33] I say "partially" for although this group of scholars has sought to identify the reasons why particular activities tend to agglomerate together, there has been little rigorous effort to evaluate either the origins or the significance of systemic market failure leading to the clusters, or to how these failures may differ between industrial sectors.[34] And, although organizational scholars have considerably advanced our knowledge about the nature and determinants of networks or related activities,[35] and of the management of innovatory systems,[36] they, too, have been slow to embrace the spatial dimension in their models.

Business analysts, notably Chandler (1977, 1990) and Porter (1990) have, in general, confined their attention to examining the attributes of industrial clusters of activities within a country, although, in his work, Porter has made some attempt to relate the location-bound characteristics of countries to the kind of subnational clusters they generate. Porter, however, does not draw much on the market failure paradigm for his explanation of why a group of firms with synergistic O assets may wish to be clustered in one region or country rather than another, nor how this clustering may vary, according to country-specific characteristics, and to the asset management strategy of the participating firms.

What, then, can one glean from these rather diffuse disciplinary perspectives? To what extent is it possible to evaluate the role of organizational structures as they affect the competitiveness of firms and countries and the location of economic activity? I would suggest a three-pronged approach. The first, drawing mainly on organizational theory and industrial economics, is to identify which kinds of coordination and transaction costs are most likely to be space-related, and how far these costs are likely to vary between different types of activities and/or countries. The second, which combines the work of scholars on the dynamics of the firm, technological accumulation and business strategy, is to look more closely at the determinants of the asset portfolios of firms, and the strategic management of these portfolios, so as to identify the critical firm-specific characteristics influencing the location of activity.

The third prong is to relate the findings of the first two prongs to the received theories of trade and location, and to see whether country- and firm-specific coordinating and transaction costs can be incorporated into these theories. This, like the inclusion of created assets—and particularly firm-specific mobile assets—into existing explanations of the spatial allocation of resources is a tall order!

5. THE ROLE OF GOVERNMENTS IN AFFECTING THE SPATIAL ORGANIZATION OF ACTIVITY

I now turn to consider the consequences of globalization for the actions of national and subnational governments,[37] and of supranational institutions and regimes, insofar as they affect the locational choices of the dynamic firm—or groups of firms. Again, historically, international economics—and neoclassical economics in particular—has ignored the macroorganizational (as opposed to the macroeconomic[38]) role of government. This is mainly because in a Pareto optimal world, markets are assumed not to fail, and only where structural distortions occur is any government intervention considered necessary.[39]

More recently, this analytical lacuna has, at least partly, been overcome by the work of two groups of scholars. The first, typified by the writings of Paul Krugman (1986, 1994), has injected new life into international trade theory by extending the tools of industrial economics to explain how strategic trade policy by governments might affect the location of economic activity. The second is the ongoing research of a group of mainly US scholars, notably Ray Vernon, Fred Bergsten, Gary Hufbauer and Monty Graham, on the changing interface between trade, FDI and global business activity, and its implications for a whole range of domestic economic and other issues. Nevertheless, neither group of scholars has given much attention to the ways in which governments might interact with firms and markets to lessen or circumvent the endemic failure of different organizational forms of economic activity, and how these, in turn, might affect the international and intranational disposition of national and created assets.

Turning to locational economics and geography—including that part of it concerned with the extranational activities of firms—we see a much greater willingness of scholars to tackle head-on the role of government-related variables, notably fiscal penalties and incentives. Indeed, in recent work on the determinants of the locational preferences of MNEs,[40] the role of host governments, and particularly their ability to affect the coordinating and transaction costs[41] of economic activity—has been shown to be a critical one. Much of this latter research has been undertaken by economic geographers, regional scientists, urban economists and international business specialists; but it is, perhaps, the international marketing scholars[42] who have gone furthest in their attempts to embrace psychic distance (which includes noneconomic spatial market failures, many of which are government-influenced) into their thinking. Economists interested in the interaction between MNE activity and the pattern and path of technological accumulation are increasingly acknowledging the decisive role of national innovatory systems as a competitive enhancing instrument of governments (Chesnais 1993, Nelson 1993).

By contrast, organization theory has generally neglected government-related and other exogenous variables in its examination of the decision-making practices of firms. The same charge may also be leveled at much of the strategic management literature,[43] notwithstanding a copious volume of research which has sought to analyze the ways in which business strategy may be affected by a firm's external environment. Since, in the past, both organization and management theory has been geared towards explaining the internal functioning of firms operating largely within their national boundaries, this neglect is, perhaps, understandable. But in today's globalizing economy, where governments exercise so much influence on the extent and pattern of cross-border market failure,[44] this neglect—even at the most micro level of analysis—is quite unacceptable.

It is difficult to conclude from the above paragraphs that the role of government as an organizer and coordinator of economic activity has, in the past, been given the attention it deserves.[45] There are signs that this is changing and this, I believe, is primarily due to the effect the globalizing economy is having on the costs and benefits of alternative organizational modes—and particularly on the role of governments as facilitators of efficient markets.

The concept of government as a superintendent of the organization of economic activity, and the instruments which government may use

to facilitate an efficient market system are now being much more
closely examined by political scientists, economists, organizational scholars and business strategists alike.[46] This, as we have already said, is because the kinds of coordination and transaction costs most influenced
by the actions of governments are exercising a more important part
in the locational decision process of firms and networks than once they
did. This, in turn, reflects the convergence of many kinds of production
costs across national boundaries—particularly among advanced industrialized countries, and the increasing role of created assets in the production
process.

The macro-organizational actions of government—and elsewhere (Dunning 1994*b*) we have explored the situations in which government action to
reduce market failure is likely to be the most cost-effective[47]—are clearly
likely to be discriminatory in their impact, both between firms and types of
economic activity. Of the former, those most likely to be affected are those
whose competitiveness rests on continuous product innovation and improvement; new ventures, especially in relatively high-risk sectors; those
whose assets are most spatially mobile; and those most dependent on the
kind of complementary assets, which are critically influenced by government actions. Viewed from a functional or strategic perspective, the influence of government is most likely to affect the decisions of firms about
expenditure on R&D and training, the extent of vertical integration or
horizontal diversification and the locational configuration of high value-
added activities.

The subject matter of this conference embraces several of these areas and
the ways in which they interact with each other. To tackle these effectively,
government action must be more explicitly considered as a critical explanatory variable; and much more rigorous work needs to be done on the
consequences of collective and specific macroorganizational strategies on
the ownership, organization and competitiveness of firms, and on the location of different types of economic activity.

6. CONCLUDING REMARKS

The key message of this chapter is that globalization—or more particularly
the forces driving it and its consequences—is affecting the costs and benefits
of the four main modalities of organizing economic activity in capitalist
economies, namely markets, hierarchies, interfirm alliances and governments. It is further argued that, while in the past, these modalities have
largely been viewed as alternatives to one another, the growing economic
interdependence of domestic and cross-border activities and the increasing significance of cooperative ventures, both between firms and between
firms and governments, are requiring scholars to search for a more macro-
systemic approach to the organization of resources and capabilities in which

markets, hierarchies, networks and governments each have complementary roles to play.

Such a macro-systemic approach is especially relevant when considering the interaction between the dynamic firm and its external environment, and especially between the former and firms supplying goods and services, the price and quality of which influence its own competitiveness. The chapter further suggested that the introduction of flexible production systems and alliance capitalism is causing firms to reorganize their asset portfolios, *inter alia* by externalizing some of their internal markets, but, at the same time, reinternalizing them among a network of related firms. Finally, it argued that both the intra- and international locations of economic activity are being increasingly guided by the desire of firms to reduce the costs of market failure and/or to capture the synergies offered by business districts and other spatially related networks of firms, and by the actions of governments designed to promote the competitiveness of their location-bound assets and that of their own MNEs.

None of the traditional disciplines analyzing the behavior of firms has yet fully embraced the features and consequences of the globalization in their paradigms and theories. In particular, the significance of firm-specific competencies and management strategies, not to mention the growing cross-border mobility of assets, has still not engaged the attention of mainstream economists. On the other hand, the need for a more systemic approach in addressing issues relating to the growth of firms and groups of firms, the role of governments and the organization and management of a complex bundle of created assets, is forcing a reassessment of our ideas about the very nature of economic activity, and the relationships between the major institutional entities.

While it seems probable that, barring catastrophes, the forces currently driving globalization will continue in the foreseeable future, it is less certain how these will affect the organization of created assets between and within firms, the dynamics of technological accumulation and the location of economic activity. As far as the leading global players are concerned, there are suggestions of a flattening of organizational structures and a divestment of activities which do not directly enhance their core competences. At the same time, firms are becoming increasingly aware of the need to balance the advantages of a centralized control of financial assets, intellectual capital and markets, with those of the decentralization of entrepreneurial initiative and managerial competence, and the need to adapt asset usage to local needs and customs.

While lean and flexible organizational structures are likely to follow—and sometimes lead—the technoeconomic system of flexible production and the socioinstitutional system of alliance capitalism, and some of the advantages of hierarchical capitalism may disappear, I think it is premature to suggest that today's successful large corporations will become tomorrow's dinosaurs. At the same time, as well as studying the production and coordinating functions of individual firms, economists should give more attention to the concept of a systemic group or network of firms as a unit of analysis,[48] and of the positioning of individual firms in that grouping or network. It is, indeed, quite possible that some of the economies of scope and coordination enjoyed by independent firms will be transferred to the "flagship" or lead firms in a network while, concurrently, some of the erstwhile functions of large firms be contracted out to medium and small-size firms in the network.

The impact of future technological and organizational advances on the location of economic activity is also unclear. While there is some indication that the leading MNEs are decentralizing some of their production and innovatory activities, this is largely taking place in the same countries or regions from which other MNEs, namely Japan, the USA and the EU, are decentralizing their activities. Moreover, as we have seen, despite advances in telematics, the need for close, if not face-to-face, contact between the managers, administrators, scientists and technologists of interrelated firms—particularly at the top end of the value-added chain and between the factory and the research laboratory—is encouraging centripetal tendencies. Across countries and regions, too, there are suggestions that the principle of comparative advantage may be applied to explaining different clusters or networks of activities,[49] the willingness and ability of firms to embrace alliance capitalism, and the macroorganizational policies of national and regional governments come into play.

There are also suggestions that the forces affecting the geography of innovatory activities are also encouraging similar networks or firms producing at different stages of the same value-added chain. There is nothing particularly new in this phenomenon. What, perhaps, is new is the extent to which the composition and character of such clusters has been affected by inward and outward direct investment. Indeed, one especially interesting feature of networks in the auto and electronics sectors, as for example fashioned by Japanese MNE activity in the EU and the USA, is the extent to which horizontal cross-border linkages have been formed between particular component manufacturers in the host countries and their opposite numbers in Japan.

What of the role of the developing economies in the emerging global economy? This could easily be a subject for a separate conference; and I have touched upon some of the relevant issues in another paper (Dunning, 1994c). But, just as the presence of created complementary assets— and particularly in those which are government induced, and a market-facilitating environment—are becoming increasingly important determinants of both domestic and inbound investment in developed countries; so these location-bound characteristics are also the prerequisites for the upgrading of economic activity in most developing countries—and especially in those which compete with each other. But, as Porter (1990) and others have shown, because of the limited size of their domestic markets, it is much more difficult for the poorer nations to create the educational system and infrastructures needed to participate in global trade and investment. While the examples of Singapore and Hong Kong are salutary, I find it difficult to perceive how the smaller developing nations, especially in sub-Saharan Africa and Latin America, can expect to experience the benefits of their counterparts in Europe, either by forging networks with foreign firms or by participating in regional integration schemes.

Finally, I cannot escape the conclusion that it is only by intellectual foraging which is prepared to cross disciplinary boundaries that scholars can hope to make much sense of either the macro- or microorganizational and management issues now being researched. In this respect, borrowing David Teece's distinction between the core and complementary assets of firms, while each scholar should have a core expertise in his own discipline in order to make the best use of that asset, he has to draw on the complementary assets of other disciplines. Indeed, it may be that it is the way in which scholars package, i.e. organize, their own portfolio of intellectual assets which will determine their own contribution to this fascinating "salad bowl" of studies in the 1990s.

NOTES

1. Interrelated in the sense that the participating firms incur certain costs and enjoy certain benefits which are internal to the relationship, e.g. a strategic alliance or network, but external to their own activities.
2. Although the presence of intranational networks has long been acknowledged for example, by Alfred Marshall (1919).
3. For a review of these and other trade theories of the time, see Hufbauer (1970) and Stern (1975).
4. See especially his classic volume on interregional and international trade (Ohlin 1933).
5. Although, in his paper, Hla Myint (1977) did discuss the role of institutional factors in economic development.
6. There are, of course, notable exceptions, including the work of Mark Casson and Peter Buckley, Bruce Kogut, David Teece, Gunnar Hedlund, Yves Doz, Sumantra Ghoshal and Christopher Bartlett.
7. One example of a package of assets which is not transportable is the macroorganizational strategies of domestic governments.
8. Although not necessarily of the predictions of international economics. See Dunning (1994*a*).
9. See, for example, Chandler (1962, 1977, 1990) and Teece (1986, 1992*a*).
10. Teece, however, has written on the implications of cross-border transfer of

technology to the competitive advantages of the transferring firms (Teece 1977).

11. See, for example, Vernon (1966) Keesing (1966) and Gruber, Mehta and Vernon (1970).

12. See also the next section of this chapter.

13. The problem is composed when the unit of analysis is extended to an alliance or network of firms.

14. There are other areas of imperfect competition and the appropriate behavior of strategic oligopolists which cloud the issue even further!

15. See especially Marshall (1919).

16. See, for example Piore and Sabel (1984), Best (1990), Casson (1991), Gerlach (1992), Patel and Pavitt (1992), Cantwell (1992), Archibugi and Pianta (1993), Harrison, Kelley and Appold (1993), Harrison (1994), and various contributions to an edited volume by Grabher (1993).

17. The relationship might be by nonequity ownership, or by some form of cooperative agreement.

18. More recent examples include the "follow my leader" behavior by Japanese consumer electronics and auto MNEs into the USA and Europe.

19. Other examples are given by Enright (Ch. 14, present vol.).

20. Venables (1994) has demonstrated that the forces of agglomeration in vertically linked industries are likely to be most pronounced at intermediate levels of transport costs. He suggests that beyond a certain point, lower transport costs will cause industries to operate in multiple locations, which will lead to a spatial convergence, rather than a concentration, of economic activity.

21. In a study on employment growth of industrial sectors in major US cities and countries, Henderson (1994) found that employment gains from dynamic externalities were most marked in cities and counties which offered the most diversified range of complementary assets to their core activities.

22. The kind of face-to-face contact, which has always characterized transactions in the City of London (which, in its square mile, probably comprises the most intimate network of firms in the world), seems now to be increasingly valued by firms in the dynamic manufacturing sectors, and particularly those whose technologies and organizational competences are complementary to each other. In a recent paper, dealing with intra-US geographical clustering and using employment data for three two-digit industrial sectors and four US cities, Hagen and Hammond (1994) found that asset-sharing produces significant localization economies, while the economies of labor-pooling tend to be most significant in rapidly growing labor markets.

23. Archibugi and Michie (1993) refer to technological acquirers as "polyp" firms which "acquire from each country its excellence in research rather than to decentralize their brains."

24. Notably, Emile Durkheim (1964 edn.) from sociology, Douglass North (1990) from economic history, Alfred Chandler (1990) from business strategy, Oliver Williamson (1975, 1990) from organizational theory and Ronald Coase (1937, 1960), Edith Penrose (1959) and Kenneth Arrow (1969, 1974) from economics. An interesting collection of cross-disciplinary essays on the nature of the firm is contained in Gustafsson and Williamson (1990) and Williamson and Winter (1991).

25. Quasi-internal embraces relationships between related parties other than those

arising from the ownership of one party by the other. These include nonequity cooperative agreements and networks.

26. The concept of business-related cultural distance is broadly similar to that of psychic differences between countries.

27. This theme is explored in more detail in Dunning (1994c).

28. This is not to say trade economists, notably Paul Krugman, have not concerned themselves with market imperfections and the strategic behavior of firms, but to the best of my knowledge, they have not embraced transaction and coordination costs in their analyses.

29. Notably by Ethier (1986), Horstman and Markusen (1987) and Gray (1992).

30. See especially the various writings of Peter Buckley and Mark Casson, of Alan Rugman and of Jean Francois Hennart, as set out in Dunning (1993).

31. There are some exceptions, noticeably Teece (1992b), in his study of FDI in California and Wilkins (1979) in a study of FDI in Florida.

32. See for example, the various contributions of Alan Scott, including his paper to this Conference, and that of Malecki (1985), Thwaites and Oakey (1985), Hall, Breheny, McQuaid and Hart (1987), Howells (1990) and Feldman (1993). See also several of the contributions to Krugman and Venables (1994) and especially those of Audretsch and Feldman, Hagen and Hammond, Henderson, and Venables.

33. See especially references set out in Section 3, and in OECD (1992) and Kenney and Florida (1994). In their contribution to the Krugman and Venables volume, David Audretsch and Maryann Feldman (1994) found that the propensity of innovatory activity to spatially cluster was greater in industries in which the creation of knowledge spillovers are important; and in which university researchers provide important inputs for such knowledge.

34. The concept of hierarchical failure is rarely discussed in the literature. Yet, it seems to me that the existence of networks rests on the failure of both markets and industrial hierarchies to generate the relational or agglomerative economies which networks provide. The more significant these benefits are to protecting or advancing the core competencies of firms, and the greater the costs of engaging in vertical or horizontal integration, the more networks and/or bilateral alliances are likely to replace or supplement hierarchies and markets as an organizational form.

35. See especially the work of the Uppsala scholars (e.g. Johanson and Mattson 1987).

36. See, for example, Bartlett and Ghoshal (1990).

37. We are using action of governments as a proxy for all actions affecting the allocations which are not taken by the constituents of a market system.

38. The macroeconomic role is concerned with the level of economic activity, unemployment, prices, exchange rates; the macroorganizational (sometimes called microeconomic) role is concerned with the allocation of economic activity via industrial, trade, innovation, education, transport, fiscal, environment, etc. policies; and the response of such activity to changes in demand and supply conditions. For a contemporary examination of the macro-organizational role of government see Dunning (1992 and 1994b), Stopford (1994) and Stopford and Strange (1991).

39. In other words, governments act to correct market imperfections rather than to prevent market imperfections.

40. As, for example, described in Dunning (1993) and Loree and Guisinger (1995).
41. Or what I have elsewhere described as the "hassle" costs of doing business (Dunning 1992).
42. See e.g. Johanson and Vahlne (1977, 1990), Nordström (1991), Reid (1984), Welch and Luostarinen (1988) and Vahlne and Nordström (1992).
43. Although, in some recent thinking (e.g. Teece 1986) more stress is being given to the ways in which governments may affect the provision of complementary assets necessary to the efficient exploitation of the O advantages of firms. A recent paper by Kobrin (1993) also tackles the interface between networks and government behavior.
44. Illustrations include the strategic trade policies of individual governments; the formation of regional economic blocs; and the role of GATT in setting the rules of the game for international commerce.
45. This may seem a strange statement, as governments have always acted as regulatory agencies, as well as initiating and monitoring the economic system, which is responsible for the allocation of scarce resources. But, rarely, as I see it, have governments attempted to optimally coordinate the alternative modes of organization of economic activity. Perhaps this is an impossible dream!
46. See, for example, Krueger (1990), Stopford and Strange (1991), Audretsch (1989), McKenzie and Lee (1991), Wolf (1988) and Osborne and Gaebler (1992).
47. The costs of government intervention have been extensively discussed in the literature. See especially Wolf (1988), Audretsch (1989) and Krueger (1990). For a more in-depth analysis of the comparative advantage of governments as organizing mechanisms, cf. unaided markets and hierarchies, see Wade (1988), World Bank (1993) and Hämäläinen (1994).
48. Of course, there have been various attempts by economists in the past to classify firms into groups, and for various reasons. Yet such terms as "industry," "strategic groups" and "clusters" do not encompass the idea that firms become part of a larger entity in order to capture the external economies which are internal to the entity; and that they perceive this to be a preferable way to advance their competitiveness than by engaging in vertical or horizontal integration. Marshall's concept of "agglomerative economies" and the Japanese "keiretsu" system of relational enterprises come closest to what we have in mind.
49. To this extent, we do not agree with Porter (1990) that his analysis negates the validity of the concept of comparative advantage, but rather that it suggests that the components and determinants of that advantage have changed.

REFERENCES

Antonelli, C. (1991), *The Diffusion of Advanced Telecommunications in Developing Countries* (Paris: OECD Development Centre).
Archibugi, D. and Michie, J. (1993), *The Globalization of Technology: Myths and Realities* (Cambridge: Judge Institute of Management Studies).

——and Pianta, M. (1993), "Patterns of Technological Specialization and Growth of Innovatory Activities in Advanced Countries," in K. Hughes (ed.), *European Competitiveness* (Cambridge: Cambridge University Press).

Arrow, K. J. (1969), *The Organization of Economic Activity: Issues Pertinent to the Choice of Market versus Non-market Allocation*, testimony presented to the Joint Economic Committee, 31st Congress, 1st Session, "The analysis and evolution of public expenditures: the PPB system," (Washington, DC: US Government Printing Office).

——(1974), *The Limits of Organization* (New York: W. W. Norton).

Audretsch, D. B. (1989), *The State and the Market* (New York: Harvester Wheatsheaf).

——and Feldman, M. P. (1994), "External Economies and Spatial Clustering," in P. Krugman and A. Venables (eds.), *The Location of Economic Activity: New Theories and Evidence*.

Bain, J. (1956), *Barriers to Competition* (Cambridge, Mass.: Harvard University Press).

Barney, J. B. (1986), "Strategic Factor Markets: Expectations, Luck and Business Strategy," *Management Science*, 32: 1232–41.

Bartlett, C. G. and Ghoshal, S. (1989), *Managing Across Borders: The Transnational Solution* (Boston: Harvard Business School Press).

——(1990), "Managing Innovation in the Transnational Corporation," in C. A. Bartlett, Y. Doz and G. Hedlund (eds.), *Managing the Global Firm* (London: Routledge).

Best, M. (1990), *The New Competition: Institutions of Restructuring* (Cambridge, Mass.: Harvard University Press).

Cainarca, G. C., Colombo, M. G. and Mariotti, S. (1988), *Cooperative Agreements in the Information and Communication Industrial System* (Milan: Politecnico de Milano).

Cantwell, J. A. (1992), "The Internationalization of Technological Activity and its Implications for Competitiveness," in O. Granstrand, L. Hakanson and S. Sjölander (eds.), *Technology, Management and International Business: Internationalization of R&D and Technology* (Chichester: John Wiley).

Casson, M. (1991), "Internalization Theory and Beyond," in P. J. Buckley (ed.), *Recent Research on the Multinational Enterprise* (Cheltenham: Edward Elgar).

Chamberlin, E. (1933), *The Theory of Monopolistic Competition* (Cambridge, Mass.: MIT Press).

Chandler, A. D., Jr. (1962), *Strategy and Structure: The History of American Industrial Enterprise* (Cambridge, Mass.: MIT Press).

——(1977), *The Invisible Hand: The Managerial Revolution in American Business* (Cambridge, Mass.: Harvard University Press).

——(1990), *Scale and Scope: The Dynamics of Industrial Capitalism* (Cambridge, Mass.: Harvard University Press).

Chesnais, F. (1993), "National Systems of Innovation, Foreign Direct Investment and the Operations of Multinational Enterprises," mimeo.

Coase, R. H. (1937), "The Nature of the Firm," *Economica*, (NS) 4 (Nov.), 386–405.

——(1960), "The Problem of Social Cost," *Journal of Law and Economics*, 3: 1–10.

Dierickx, I. and Cool, K. (1989), "Assets, Stock Accumulation and Sustainability of Competitive Advantage," *Management Science* 35: 1504–11.

Dosi, G., Pavitt, K. and Soete, L. (1990), *Technical Change and International Trade* (New York: Harvester Wheatsheaf).

Dunning, J. H. (1977), "Trade, Location of Economic Activity and the MNE: A Search for an Eclectic Approach," in B. Ohlin, P. O. Hesselborn and P. M. Wijkman (eds.), *The International Allocation of Economic Activity*. 395–418.

——(1992), "The Global Economy, Domestic Governance, Strategies and Transnational Corporations, Interactions and Policy Recommendations," *Transnational Corporations*, 1 (Dec.), 7–45.

——(1993), *Multinational Enterprises and the Global Economy* (Wokingham, UK: Addison Wesley).

——(1994a), "What's Wrong—and Right—with Trade Theory?" *International Trade Journal*, 9/2: 153–202.

——(1994b), *Globalization: The Challenge for National Economic Regimes* (Dublin: Economic and Social Research Council).

——(1994c), *Globalization, Economic Restructuring and Development* (Geneva: UNCTAD), the 6th Prebisch Lecture.

Durkheim, E. (1964 edn.), *The Division of Labor in Society* (New York: Free Press) (originally pub. in German in 1893).

Enright, M. J. (1997), *Regional Clusters and Firm Strategy*, Ch. 14 present volume.

Ethier, W. J. (1986), "The Multinational Firm," *Quarterly Journal of Economics*, 101: 806–33.

Feldman, M. P. (1993), "An Examination of the Geography of Innovation," *Industrial and Corporate Change*, 2: 451–70.

Gerlach, M. L. (1992), *Alliance Capitalism: The Social Organization of Japanese Business* (Oxford: Oxford University Press).

Grabher, G. (1993) (ed.), *The Embedded Firm* (London: Routledge).

Gray, H. P. (1992), "The Interface Between the Theories of Trade and Production," in P. J. Buckley and M. Casson (eds.), *Multinational Enterprises in the World Economy* (Vermont: Aldershot and Brookfield).

Gruber, W., Mehta, D. and Vernon, R. (1970), "The R&D Factor in International Trade and International Investment of US industries," in R. Vernon (ed.), *The Technology Factor in International Trade*.

Gustafsson, B. and Williamson, O. E. (1990), *The Firm as a Nexus of Treaties* (London: Sage Publications).

Hagen, Jürgen von and Hammond, G. (1994), "An Empirical Test of the Marshall/Krugman Hypothesis," in P. Krugman and A. Venables (eds.), *The Location of Economic Activity: New Theories and Evidence*.

Hall, B., Breheny, M., McQuaid, R. and Hart, D. (1987), *Western Sunrise* (Hemel Hempstead, UK: Allen & Unwin).

Hämäläinen, T. (1994), "The Evolving Role of Government in Economic Organization," (Newark, NJ: Rutgers University), mimeo.

Hanson, G. H. (1994), "Increasing Returns and Regional Structure of Wages," in P. Krugman and A. Venables (eds.), *The Location of Economic Activity: New Theories and Evidence*.

Harrison, B. (1994), *Lean and Mean: The Changing Landscape of Power in the Age of Flexibility* (New York: Basic Books).

——Kelley, M. and Appold, S. J. (1993), "Spatially Distributed and Proximate Inter-organizational Networks, Agglomeration and Technological Performance in US Manufacturing," Heinz School of Public Policy and Management Congress, Pittsburgh, Mellon University Working Paper 93–120.

Henderson, V. (1994), "Externalities and Industrial Development" in P. Krugman and A. Venables (eds.), *The Location of Economic Activity: New Theories and Evidence.*

Hoover, E. M. (1948), *The Location of Economic Activity* (New York: McGraw Hill).

Horstman, I. and Markusen, J. R. (1987), "Strategic Investments and the Development of Multinationals," *International Economic Review*, 28: 109–21.

Hotelling, H. (1929), "Stability in competition," *Economic Journal*, 29: 41–57.

Howells, J. (1990), "The Location and Organization of Research and Development: New horizons," *Research Policy*, 19: 133–46.

Hufbauer, G. (1965), *Synthetic Materials and International Trade* (London: Duckworth).

——(1970), "The Impact of National Characteristics and Technology on the Commodity Composition of Trade in Manufactured Goods," in R. Vernon (ed.), *The Technology Factor in International Trade.*

Johanson, J. and Mattsson, L. G. (1987), "Internationalization in Industrial Systems: A Network Approach," in N. Hood and J. E. Vahlne (eds.), *Strategies in Global Competition* (Chichester: John Wiley).

——and Vahlne, J. E. (1977), "The Internationalization Process of the Firm: A Model for Knowledge Development and Increasing Market Commitments," *Journal of International Business Studies*, 8: 23–32.

————(1990), "Management of Foreign Market Entry," *Scandinavian International Business Review*, 1/3: 9–27.

Keesing, D. B. (1966), "Labor Skills and Comparative Advantage," *American Economic Review*, Papers and Proceedings 1965, Annual Meeting.

Kenney, M. and Florida, R. (1994), "The Organization and Geography of Japanese R&D: Results from a Survey of Japanese Electronics and Biotechnology Firms," *Research Policy*, 23/3 (May), 305–23.

Knickerbocker, F. T. (1973), *Oligopolistic Reaction and the Multinational Enterprise* (Cambridge, Mass.: Harvard University Press).

Knight, F. (1921), *Risk, Uncertainty and Profit* (Chicago: University of Chicago Press).

Kobrin, S. J. (1993), "Beyond Geography: Inter-Firm Networks and the Structural Integration of the Global Economy", William H. Wurston Center for International Management Studies, Philadelphia, Wharton School Working Paper 93–10.

Kojima, K. (1978), *Direct Foreign Investment: A Japanese Model of Multinational Business Operations* (London: Croom Helm).

——(1990), *Japanese Direct Investment Abroad* (Tokyo: International Christian University, Social Science Research Institute), Monograph Series 1.

——(1992), "Internalization vs International Business Approach to Foreign Direct Investment," *Hitosubashi Journal of Economics*, 23: 630–40.

Krueger, A. (1990), "Economists' Changing Perception of Government," *Weltwirtschaftliches Archiv*, 126/3: 417–31.

Krugman, P. (1986) (ed.), *Strategic Trade Policy and the New International Economics* (Cambridge, Mass.: MIT Press).

—— (1991), *Geography and Trade* (Cambridge, Mass.: MIT Press).

—— (1994), "Competitiveness a Dangerous Obsession," *Foreign Affairs*, 73/2, (March/April), 28–44.

—— and Venables, A. (1994) (eds.), *The Location of Economic Activity: New Theories and Evidence* (London: Centre of Economic Policy Research (CPER)).

Loree, D. W. and Guisinger, S. E. (1995), "Policy and Non-policy Determinants of US Equity Foreign Direct Investment," *Journal of International Business Studies*, 26/2, 281–300.

Losch, A. (1940), *Die Raeumliche Ordnung der Wirtchaft*; trans. (1954), *The Economics of Location* (New Haven: Yale University Press).

McKenzie, R. B. and Lee, D. R. (1991), *Quicksilver Capital* (New York: Free Press).

Malecki, E. J. (1985), "Industrial Location and Corporate Organization in High Technology Industries," *Economic Geography*, 61/4 (Oct.), 345–69.

Marshall, A. (1919), *Industry and Trade* (London: Macmillan).

Myint, H. (1977), "The Place of Institutional Change in International Trade Theory in the Setting of the Underdeveloped Economies," in B. Ohlin, P. O. Hesselborn and P. M. Wijkman (eds.), *The International Allocation of Economic Activity*, 367–86.

Nelson, R. R. (1993) (ed.), *National Innovation Systems* (New York: Oxford University Press).

Nordström, K. A. (1991), *The Internationalization Process of the Firm: Search for New Patterns and Explanations* (Stockholm: Stockholm School of Business, IIB). publ. Doctoral diss.

North, D. (1990), *Institutions, International Change and Economic Performance* (Cambridge: Cambridge University Press).

OECD (1992), *Technology and the Economy* (Paris: OECD).

Ohlin, B. (1933), *Inter-regional and International Trade* (Cambridge, Mass.: Harvard University Press, rev. ed. 1967).

—— Hesselborn, P. O. and Wijkman, P. M (1977) (eds.), *The International Allocation of Economic Activity* (London: Macmillan).

Osborne, D. and Gaebler, T. (1992), *Reinventing Government* (Reading, Mass.: Addison Wesley).

Patel, P. and Pavitt, K. (1992), "The Innovatory Performance of the World's Largest Firms: Some New Evidence," *Economic Innovation and New Technology*, 2: 91–102.

Penrose, E. (1959), *The Theory of the Growth of the Firm* (Oxford: Basil Blackwell).

Piore, M. and Sabel, C. (1984), *The Second Industrial Divide: Possibilities for Prosperity* (New York: BasicBooks).

Porter, M. (1980), *Competitive Behavior* (New York: Free Press).

—— (1985), *Competitive Advantage* (New York: Free Press).

—— (1990), *The Competitive Advantage of Nations* (New York: Free Press).

Reid, S. D. (1984), "Market Expansion and Firm Internationalization," in E. Kaynak (ed.), *International Marketing Management* (New York: Praeger), 197–206.

Robinson, J. (1933), *The Economics of Imperfect Competition* (London: Macmillan).

Rumelt, R. P. (1984), "Towards a Strategic Theory of the Firm," in R. B. Lamb (ed.), *Competitive Strategic Management* (Englewood Cliffs, NJ: Prentice Hall), 556–70.

Schumpeter, J. A. (1947), *Capitalism, Socialism and Democracy* (New York: Harper and Row).

Stern, R. M. (1975), "Testing Trade Theories," in P. B. Kenen (ed.), *International Trade and Finance* (Cambridge: Cambridge University Press).

Stopford, J. (1994), "The Growing Interdependence Between Transnational Corporations and Governments," *Transnational Corporations*, 3/1: 53–76.

——and Strange, S. (1991), *Rival States, Rival Firms: Competition for World Market Shares* (Cambridge: Cambridge University Press).

Teece, D. J. (1977), *The Multinational Corporation and the Resource Cost of International Technology Transfer* (Cambridge, Mass.: Ballinger).

——(1986), "Profiting from Technological Innovation," *Research Policy*, 15/6: 286–305.

——(1992a), "Competition, Cooperation and Innovation," *Journal of Economic Behavior and Organization*, 18: 1–25.

——(1992b), "Foreign Investment and Technological Development in Silicon Valley," *California Management Review* (Winter), 88–106.

Thwaites, A. T. and Oakey, R. P. (1985) (eds.), *The Regional Economic Impact of Technological Change* (New York: St Martin Press).

UNCTAD (1994), *World Investment Report, 1994: Employment and Human Resources Management* (Geneva: UNCTAD).

Vahlne, J. E. and Nordström, K. A. (1992), "Is the Globe Shrinking?: Psychic Distance and the Establishment of Swedish Sales Subsidiaries During the Last 100 Years," Stockholm, mimeo.

Venables, A. (1994), "Equilibrium Locations of Vertically Linked Industries," in P. Krugman and A. Venables (eds.), *The Location of Economic Activity: New Theories and Evidence*.

Vernon, R. (1966), "International Investment and International Trade in the Product Cycle," *Quarterly Journal of Economics*, 80: 190–207.

——(1970) (ed.), *The Technology Factor in International Trade* (New York: Columbia University Press).

Von Thunen, J. H. (1876), *Der Isolierte Stoat*, trans. in P. Hall (ed.), *Von Tulden's Isolated State* (Oxford: Oxford University Press).

Wade, R. (1988), "The Role of Government in Overcoming Market Failure in Taiwan, Republic of Korea and Japan," in H. Hughes (ed.), *Achieving Industrialization in East Asia* (Cambridge: Cambridge University Press).

Weber, A. (1929), *Ueber den Standort der Industrien*, trans. by C. Friedrich as *The Theory of the Location of Industries* (Chicago: University of Chicago Press).

Welch, L. S. and Luostarinen, R. (1988), "Internationalization: Evolution of a Concept," *Journal of General Management*, 14/2 (Winter), 34–55.

Wilkins, M. (1979), *Foreign Enterprise in Florida* (Gainesville, Fla.: University of Florida Press).

Williamson, O. E. (1975), *Markets and Hierarchies, Analysis and Antitrust Implications* (New York: Free Press).

——(1990), *Organization Theory* (New York: Free Press).

Williamson, O. E. and Winter, S. G. (1991) (eds.), *The Nature of the Firm* (Oxford: Oxford University Press).

Wolf, C. (1988), *Markets or Governments* (Cambridge, Mass.: MIT Press).

World Bank (1993), *The East Asian Miracle* (Oxford: Oxford University Press).

14

Regional Clusters and Firm Strategy

MICHAEL J. ENRIGHT

1. INTRODUCTION

Interest in regional (subnational) clusters[1] and their role in economic development has grown substantially over the last several years, particularly among academics and economic development professionals. The main reason has been the increased importance of interregional and international competition in the world economy. At the same time, difficulties faced by large firms in North America, Europe and Japan and the examples of successful regional clusters of small and medium-sized firms have highlighted alternatives to development via large, managerial firms.[2] Academics have investigated the development of particular regional clusters as well as the organization and coordination of activities within clusters. Economic development authorities have placed promotion of regional clusters at the heart of development policies at the local and national levels.[3]

Much of the literature on regional clusters is descriptive, often consisting of rich case-studies of individual clusters or a small set of clusters, such as high-technology clusters or the Italian industrial districts. Much of the prescriptive work is aimed at policy-makers that wish to develop or support such clusters in their jurisdictions. Relatively few researchers have attempted to link the literature on regional clusters to the firm-strategy literature, or explored the implications of the existence of regional clusters for firm strategy. The main purpose of this paper is to explicitly link the two literatures, explore the implications of the existence of regional clusters for firm strategy, and highlight topics that require more detailed investigation.

The paper concludes that much can be learned by linking the study of regional clusters with that of firm strategy. This is particularly true when discussing the sources of advantage of regions and firms. The paper also concludes that there are three principal features of regional clusters that influence firm strategy. The first is that the resources and capabilities vital for firms to succeed in interregional and international competition can often be found inside a region, rather than within any single firm. The second is that regional clusters often involve activities that are shared across firms within the cluster. Thus both the resource-based and activity-based views of the firm can be extended to help explain the implications of regional clusters for firm strategy. The third realization is that firm-strategy choices can be influenced by the strategic interdependence, rapid information flows and unique mix of competition and cooperation often found in regional clusters.

The rest of the paper is divided into five sections. Section 2 provides an introduction to the regional clustering phenomenon. Section 3 examines the links between regional clusters and the resource-based and activity-based views of the firm current in the strategy literature. Section 4 describes the structure of firms and industries in regional clusters. Section 5 explores the implications of the existence of regional clusters for specific strategic and organizational choices. Section 6 describes the paper's conclusions and suggests avenues for further research.

2. REGIONAL CLUSTERS

Regional or local clusters feature prominently in the economies of most nations. "Hollywood," "Wall Street," "Madison Avenue," "Detroit," "Silicon Valley," and "Route 128" immediately evoke thoughts of specific industries in the United States. In Switzerland, Geneva and Biel are centers of the watch industry, Basel is the home of the dye, pharmaceutical and freight-forwarding industries, and Zurich is the center for banking, trading and other financial services. Some of the most striking examples of regional clusters are found in Italy. Prato and Biella account for approximately 80 per cent of the nation's wool textile output. Arezzo and Valenza Po account for nearly $2 billion in precious metal jewelry exports each year. The Bologna area is the home of nearly 200 packaging machinery firms. These, and numerous other examples from these and other countries, show that the geographic clustering of firms in the same industry or related industries is an important fact of economic life.

2.1 Economic Rationales

The economic rationales for the existence of regional clusters, and localized industries in general, have been explored by several authors dating back to Weber (1929) and Marshall (1920, 1923). More recent reviews include Lloyd and Dicken (1977), Enright (1990), Krugman (1991) and Harrison (1992). The explanations identified in this literature include the presence of unique natural resources, economies of scale in production or purchasing, the development of specialized labor markets, the development of local equipment suppliers, shared infrastructure and other localized externalities.

Though this literature provides us with a wealth of explanations for the development of regional clusters, it generally does not tell us why specific clusters arise in specific locations. It might be clear why some clusters have developed near natural resources, but it is less clear why industries with limited dependence on such resources have located in particular places. The framework developed by Porter (1990) to help explain why nations succeed in some industries and not in others is useful in this regard. According to Porter, the success of firms from a particular nation in a given industry is influenced by the factor conditions; demand conditions; related and supporting industries; and firm strategy, structure and rivalry present in the local environment.

This framework can also be used to characterize the influences that can cause a cluster to locate in a particular region. Enright (1990), for example, shows that many regional clusters had their origins in some specific local factor condition, local demand or related industry. Specific natural conditions figured in the early development of the Solingen (Germany) cutlery industry (local sources of iron ore, wood for furnaces and water power), the Carrara (Italy) stoneworking industry (marble deposits), the silk industry of western Japan (proximity to China, consistent and moist climate), and the Hollywood motion-picture industry (sunny climate, cheap land, and proximity to varied outdoor locations). Pools of specific expertise figured prominently in the establishment of the electronics and biotechnology industries around the San Francisco Bay Area and Boston, and the optics industries of Rochester and Wetzlar (Germany). Specific local demand led to the establishment of the Bologna packaging-machinery industry, the textile-machinery industry of eastern Switzerland, the factory automation equipment industry around Turin, Basel's freight-forwarding industry, and the silk industry of western Japan. Location near market cities aided the initial development of the Prato textile industry and the Solingen cutlery industry. Other industries, such as the Basel pharmaceutical industry and Japan's synthetic-weave industry, grew out of related industries (dyes and silk respectively).

The forces that have fostered the subsequent growth of regional clusters have not necessarily been those that gave the location its initial advantage. The creation of industry-specific knowledge, development of supplier and buyer networks, and local competitive pressures that have forced firms to innovate and improve have fostered the subsequent growth of many regional clusters, even after the cluster's initial advantages have been superseded. Solingen's natural advantages eroded as electricity replaced water power, coal replaced wood in the forges, and high-quality steel became generally available. By the latter portion of the twentieth century, the expertise of the Solingen work force and the area's focus on the cutlery industry was far more important to the local industry's success than natural advantages. Carrara originally exported indigenous marble, but now has a thriving industry in which stone from all over the world is imported, cut and then reexported. The specialized expertise of the Carrara stonecutters more than compensates for the expense of importing and reexporting heavy slabs of stone. The capabilities of Basel's scientists and technicians is far more of an advantage to the local pharmaceutical industry today than proximity to the local dye industry. Although natural features have become less advantageous in the motion-picture industry (given indoor filming and high land prices), Hollywood continues to prosper, benefiting from the presence of artistic and technical talent from all over the world, as well as an unequalled network of specialized suppliers.

2.2 Innovative Performance in Regional Clusters

Enright (1990) concludes that the growth and persistence of regional clusters results from the development of pressures, incentives and capabilities to innovate provided by the local environment. It is these pressures, incentives and capabilities that allow certain regional clusters to compete successfully against dispersed competitors. Although the innovative performance of high-technology clusters, such as Silicon Valley and Route 128 have received disproportionate attention, this has been true of regional clusters in what might be considered low-technology industries as well as high-technology industries.

There is a vast literature on industrial innovation, a literature that will not be reviewed here.[4] Generally, this literature concludes that innovative performance is a function of innovative investment, technological opportunities, and the effectiveness, direction and degree of focus of innovative activity. Investment in innovative activity, in turn, depends on the incentives to innovate and the appropriability of gains associated with innovation, both of which depend on the nature of rivalry and market structure found in the industry. The effectiveness of innovative activity is a function of the skills and knowledge of researchers and managers, the information that is available to them, and the firm's ability to bring innovations to the marketplace. The direction and focus of innovative activity is affected by the opportunities and problems perceived within an industry.

The frequent interaction and rapid information flow found in most regional clusters tends to enhance the innovative performance of such clusters. Utterback (1974) indicates that informal and oral information sources provide the majority of the key communications about market needs and technological possibilities that lead to innovation. According to Utterback, it is the unanticipated, or unplanned encounter that often proves the most valuable. It should be noted that it is precisely this type of interaction in which a geographically concentrated industry configuration has a substantial advantage over a dispersed configuration. Goddard (1978) points out that specialist, or industry-specific, information is subject to steep distance decay and that a geographically concentrated configuration allows for more interchange and exchange of such information. More recent studies by Saxenian (1990) and Grefsheim et al. (1991) have emphasized the importance of networking and face-to-face interaction in the innovation process. Even in the age of rapid communication and advanced information systems, it appears that important forms of information are still best transmitted when the parties are in close geographic proximity.

Regional clusters often become repositories for industry-specific skills. Over time, knowledge cumulates, skills are handed down from person to person, and industry-specific knowledge becomes common knowledge within the cluster. Marshall (1920) pointed out that people in such communities discuss new developments in the industry, improve upon them, and combine them with other ideas. There are numerous examples of industries that have persisted for decades or even centuries in which this phenomenon occurs. The Prato wool-textile industry has a tradition that goes back more than eight hundred years. The silk industry in western Japan has persisted since the Middle Ages. The Solingen cutlery industry relies on a centuries-old craft tradition. The Genevan luxury-watch industry has been unrivalled for three hundred years. Regional clusters can also attract ideas and individuals from outside the cluster. The pharmaceutical industries of Basel and the New York, New Jersey, Pennsylvania areas attract scientists and researchers. Wall Street, London, Zurich, and Tokyo attract those with an interest in finance. Hollywood has attracted actors, writers, directors and producers from around the world.

Regional clusters often provide the stimulus for public and private investments. Local industry associations provide commercial research on foreign markets. Local governments often make contributions to industry-specific infrastructure. Local universities often provide industry-specific research and specialized training. Localized skills, information sources and investments can provide a fertile base that firms within the cluster can use to leverage their own investments in innovative activities. Regional clusters that dominate local economies also provide a focus for the innovative efforts of local communities. In such communities, the problems of the industry are of critical importance to all local citizens. Talented people with an engineering bent work on engineering problems in the industry. Those with a marketing bent work on the marketing problems of the industry and so on. This focus provides clear direction for innovative activity.

The geographic concentration of firms, suppliers and buyers found in many regional clusters provide firms within the cluster with short feedback loops for ideas and innovations. This is particularly important for products and services that emerge through an iterative process between producer and customer (as in Clark 1985), or in industries in which suppliers or buyers are important sources of new products or services (as in von Hippel 1988). Russo (1985) emphasizes the interrelationships between Sassuolo ceramic-tile firms and their local suppliers as a major force leading to the generation of new techniques. Oakey (1985) found that proximity to specialist local suppliers is a major contributor to the innovative performance of small firms in Silicon Valley. Regional clusters often attract sophisticated buyers from outside the region that can provide additional insights into advanced market demands. Buyers from around the world, for example, go to the textile, apparel and shoe clusters of northern Italy.

The development of spinoff firms within regional clusters highlights the ability of such clusters to foster new companies and to enhance innovation. Miller and Côte (1987) emphasize the role of the local business environment in supplying needed expertise and capital for high-technology spinoffs. Regional clusters can provide the suppliers, information and role models that create a favorable environment for innovative spinoffs. Many regional clusters, in fact, have developed largely through the formation of spinoffs. Many of the packaging-machinery companies in the Bologna area can be traced to a single firm, ACMA. Several Wetzlar optical firms were founded by the colleagues and employees of Charles Kellner. Several Piacenza area factory-automation firms trace their origins to a single firm. The Minnesota supercomputer cluster can be traced back to ERA, a company founded by former members of the World War II naval communications group. According to Saxenian (1985), virtually every semiconductor firm in Silicon Valley can trace its roots back to Fairchild, itself a spinoff from Shockley Transistor.

3. RESOURCES, ACTIVITIES, AND REGIONAL CLUSTERS

Our understanding of regional clusters can be enhanced by linking the analysis of regional clusters to the strategy literature. In particular, we can learn by linking two views of the firm current in the strategy literature, the resource-based and activity-based views of the firm, to the regional cluster phenomenon.

3.1 Regional Clusters and the Resource-Based View of the Firm

Recently, there has been a resurgence of interest in the resource-based view of the firm in its academic (Wernerfelt 1984) and managerial (Prahalad and Hamel 1990) incarnations. The resource-based view portrays the firm as a bundle of resources and capabilities (see also Barney 1986, 1991; Collis 1991; and Peteraf 1993). Resources are construed quite broadly to include "anything which can be thought of as a strength or weakness of a given firm." (Wernerfelt 1984: 172). In this view, firms achieve a competitive advantage if they can acquire or develop superior individual resources or a superior mix of resources. Thus the goal of firm strategy is to obtain and deploy resources that are superior to those of competitors.

The resource-based view of the firm has a long history in the literature on the nature of the firm (see Penrose 1959, for example) and strategic management (Andrews 1971; Learned *et al.* 1969). In the former, the resources of the firm allow it to grow by using firm resources more intensively and extensively. In the latter, firm strategy is viewed in the context of the strengths (or "distinctive competencies") and weaknesses of the firm. The resurgence of the resource-based view of the firm has focused attention on the internal resources and capabilities of the firm, as opposed to its external environment and product positioning, as determinants of firm performance.

In general, resources can be obtained through internal development or purchased on factor markets. They can be heterogeneous and immobile across firms. In fact, some resources must be heterogeneous and relatively immobile if they are to be sources of competitive advantage. Barney (1991) states that a firm's resource position can lead to a sustainable competitive advantage if its resources are valuable (they must allow the firm to create value), rare (they cannot be in abundant supply), imperfectly imitated (other firms cannot readily copy them), and if they are not subject to substitution (especially by other resources that are not rare or are easy to imitate). When these conditions are met, the firm earns Ricardian rents on its resources. Three of the four conditions, value, rareness and imperfect substitutability, have relatively straightforward interpretations. The fourth, imperfect imitation, is perhaps the most interesting condition. According to Dierickx and Cool (1989), firm resources are difficult to imitate if they depend on unique historical conditions, the link between resources and competitive advantage is causally ambiguous or the resources are socially complex. These three features, individually or in combination, can make it difficult for other firms to identify and duplicate a resource advantage.

Grant (1991: 115) outlines the implications of the resource-based view of the firm for strategic management in a five-stage framework involving: "analyzing the firm's resource-base; appraising the firm's capabilities; analyzing the profit-earning potential of the firm's resources and capabilities; selecting a strategy; and extending and upgrading the firm's pool of resources and capabilities." In this framework, firm resources and capabilities provide a firm with its identity (a firm is, in large part, the sum of its resources), a source of strategic direction (the strategy should fit with and extend existing resources), and a basis for corporate profitability (superior resources result in superior performance). Surprisingly, Grant does not include the *execution* of the selected strategy as part of his framework. This same absence is seen in the rest of the resource-based literature, in which firms are seen as *having things* (resources and capabilities), but they are generally not seen as *doing things*.

A resource-based analysis can be readily extended to regional clusters.[5] Whereas the resource-based view of the firm distinguishes between resources that are internal to the firm and resources that are generally available on markets, a resource-based view of regional clusters posits an additional category of resources that are internal to a region, but external to any single firm. In other words, there are spatial asymmetries in the presence of, and the market for, certain critical resources. Spatial asymmetries in resources, including natural resources, skilled labor, specialized inputs and industry-specific expertise, have been cornerstones of location theory since the days of Marshall (1920, 1923) and Weber (1929). More recently, the notion that industry-specific knowledge becomes cumulative and embedded in a particular region or area has figured in the work of Dosi (1988), Lundvall (1988) and Grossman and Helpman (1992).

The arguments cited above allow us to identify when region-specific resources will lead to sustained competitive advantages. Region-specific resources will lead to a sustainable advantage when they are valuable, rare, imperfectly imitable and imperfectly substitutable. Under these conditions, the region earns Ricardian rents on its resources. Presumably a regional cluster will falter if its resources lose their value, lose uniqueness, are imitated or are substituted. As with firms, the region's resources will be difficult to imitate if they depend on unique historical conditions, the link between resources and competitive advantage is causally ambiguous or the resources are socially complex. When these conditions hold within a regional cluster, information and knowledge become impacted within the region rather than inside a firm.

Unique historical conditions have played a role in many, if not most, regional clusters. The roles of Stanford University, Shockley Transistor, local entrepreneurs and local financiers in the growth of Silicon Valley have been well documented (Saxenian 1985; Hall and Markusen 1985; Preer 1992; and others). The luxury watch industry in Geneva got its start in the sixteenth century when Protestant watchmakers from France and the Low Countries sought refuge from religious persecution in French-speaking Geneva. Around the same time, John Calvin's edicts against displays of wealth and "useless jewelry" decimated the Geneva goldsmithing industry, which had been one of the continent's largest. Since watches served a "useful" function, they were exempt from the edicts. The refugees and goldsmiths soon combined their talents to make the Geneva area a center for luxury watches that is unrivalled even today. Switzerland still accounts for approximately 85 per cent of the world's output of luxury watches (Bumbacher 1992; Enright 1995). The Japanese continuous synthetic-weave industry, which produces fabrics that are synthetic substitutes for silk fabrics, is centered in the same three prefecture area where silk was first introduced to Japan nearly a thousand years ago. This area is near Kyoto, the major center of silk demand in Japan for centuries, and Osaka, where most of Japan's leading trading, textile machinery and synthetic-fiber companies were founded (Enright 1993*a*). In each case, historical circumstances have shaped the development of area-specific resources that are difficult or impossible to match.

Causal ambiguity arises when managers outside a given firm or area cannot ascertain the precise causes of the firm's or area's competitive advantage. Causal ambiguity can arise from the knowledge that is tacit, complex or specific (Reed and De Fillippi 1990). Tacit knowledge within regional clusters can arise through experience and practice. Complexity arises through multiple relationships with local suppliers, buyers and competitors. Enright and Tenti (1990), for example, liken the Italian ceramic-tile industry, with its hundreds of tile firms, suppliers, and related companies all located in the area in and around Sassuolo in north-central Italy, to an organism and conclude that it is the systemic nature of the local industry that is its most enduring advantage. The variety of interpretations of the success of the industrial districts described by Harrison (1992) shows that researchers often do not agree on the key sources of advantage within the districts. Presumably managers have a difficult time ascertaining the sources of advantage as well.

Social complexity is a hallmark of localized industries (see Brusco 1982; Piore and Sabel 1984; Scott 1986, 1988*a*, 1988*b*). Managers and workers in localized industries tend to live and work in a small geographic area. The result is a set of complex, varied and repeated interactions involving family relationships, ownership links, contacts through industry and employer associations, local union ties and social ties in addition to economic ties. Thus the economic activity of a regional cluster is often firmly "embedded" (as in Granovetter 1985) in the region's social fabric. Becattini (1989: 132) states, for example, that what holds the Italian industrial districts together "is a complex and tangled web of external economies and diseconomies, of joint and associated costs, of historical and cultural vestiges, which envelops both inter-firm and interpersonal relationships . . ." This has many consequences for firms. Regional clusters often develop a clear set of "rules of the game" within which competition takes place. Relationships with local suppliers and buyers are often governed by common local practice, usually sealed with a handshake or oral guarantee. Social, as well as economic, strictures are used to punish opportunistic behavior. Whereas it might be difficult to imitate the social complexity of a firm that gives rise to its sources of competitive advantage, it is virtually impossible to duplicate the social complexity of a regional cluster.

3.2 Regional Clusters and the Activity-Based View of the Firm

If the resource-based view of the firm focuses on what the firm *has*, the activity-based view of the firm (see Porter 1985, 1991) focuses on what the firm *does*. In this view, the firm is characterized by the bundle of activities it performs and the way in which it performs them. Porter (1985) characterizes inbound logistics, operations, marketing and sales, outbound logistics, and after-sales service as primary activities and firm infrastructure, human-resource management, technology development, and procurement as support activities. In the activity-based view, firms achieve advantage through superior execution of individual activities or superior coordination across activities that allows the firm to lower cost or create greater value for the buyer. The drivers of competitive advantage in an activity include scale, cumulative learning, pattern of capacity utilization, timing of investment, level of vertical integration, location of the activity, institutional factors that govern the activity, links between activities, the ability to share activities across business units and discretionary policies independent of other drivers. The activity and resource-based views of the firm are complementary. Resources are not valuable in and of themselves. They are valuable only if they can be used by the firm in its activities. Some of the most important firm activities are those that identify, acquire, develop and deploy resources (Porter 1991).

Porter (1986) and Hagström (1990) have highlighted the geographic implications of the activity-based view of the firm in the context of multinational firms. Porter states that a firm's international strategy is essentially an issue of geographic scope. The firm that competes in international (or interregional markets) must decide how to spread and manage its activities. In particular it must choose how to *configure* and *coordinate* its activities. Configuration refers to the pattern of location of firm activities. Coordination refers to both the level of autonomy of local operations and the means by which they are coordinated. Hagström states that the geography of the firm is best understood by thinking of the firm as a bundle of activities. The firm faces a location decision for each activity. Some activities might be located on the basis of lowest cost, but others can be located in accordance with the availability of localized information-based external economies. Linkages among activities and the firm's initial configuration place some limits on the set of locations the firm might consider for a given activity. Hagström emphasizes the firm increasingly has the ability to relocate activities. He also states that broad site and community-level location factors are losing relevance to location decisions, while very specific location advantages may still attract specialized activities.

There are several links between regional clusters and the activity-based view of the firm. Regional clusters will persist if localization allows the firms in the cluster to perform or coordinate activities in ways that create superior buyer value, or achieve lower cost. The effect of localization on scale, cumulative learning, comparative advantages and the ease of coordinating activities within and across firms seem to be the most promising advantages. There are a number of activities that can be more easily shared among firms within a regional cluster than among geographically dispersed firms. These include joint purchasing and warehousing, basic training of workers and region-specific promotion efforts (including branding by region). In addition, some activities, such as lobbying efforts and investments in environmental facilities, are often more effective when carried out by a group of firms in a single location. The basic result is that regional clusters often have a greater potential scope for sharing activities than geographically dispersed firms.

There are numerous examples of firms from regional clusters sharing activities. In recent years, wine-makers from the Marlborough region in New Zealand have banded together to promote their wines in foreign markets, just as firms from European wine regions have for decades or centuries. Textile firms from Biella and Prato run trade fairs in which buyers from around the world are invited to see the newest products of local firms. In Solingen, cutlery firms and the local government have set up training schools and materials-research centers. The Solingen name has been trademarked, as has "Scotch" whisky and the names of several French wine-producing areas. The industry associations of north-central Italy have engaged in a variety of activities including coordination of bulk purchasing, basic training, promotion in foreign markets and basic research within their industries. This ability to share activities has allowed several regional clusters to obtain the advantages of relatively small-scale production units, by allowing high-powered incentives (as in Williamson 1985) to permeate the cluster, while overcoming the disadvantages of limited scale.

4. THE STRUCTURE OF FIRMS AND INDUSTRIES IN REGIONAL CLUSTERS

There is a substantial literature on the optimal scope of the firm. Teece (1982), for example, focuses on specialized indivisible assets or organizational knowledge common to more than one product to explain the development of the multiproduct firm. Wernerfelt (1989) shows that the firm's corporate strategy is often a function of its resources. Porter (1987), on the other hand, cites activities that can be shared across business units as a rationale for the multiproduct firm. The recent emphasis on downsizing, outsourcing and forming business networks to improve company competitiveness highlights the importance of corporate scope issues. GE's Jack Welch has written of the "boundaryless" firm (General Electric 1991). Others write of the "value constellation" to focus on the idea that more and more firms are choosing to mix and match their activities with those of buyers and suppliers in order to deliver value to the customer (Normann and Ramirez, 1993).

4.1 The Scope of the Firm

Geographic proximity can influence the vertical structure of industries by increasing the size and extent of the local market and reducing the transaction costs faced by the industry. The net result is that geographic concentration allows for the development of vertically disintegrated structures by allowing each activity to be performed at its optimal scale, reducing the cost of negotiating and monitoring transactions, enhancing the interdependence of firms, and by supplying additional mechanisms that limit opportunistic behavior (Enright 1995). As a result, firms within a geographic cluster often exhibit lower levels of vertical integration than their dispersed counterparts. Bologna-area packaging-machinery companies, for example, subcontract out a far higher proportion of their production than competitors both inside and outside of Italy. The same is true of Sassuolo ceramic-tile companies. In Prato, there are no vertically integrated textile firms. Most of the thousands of firms in the local textile industry concentrate on a single stage in the production process. A single bolt of cloth can pass through five or six firms before it is finished. There are hundreds of small firms in Solingen each performing a single step in the cutlery-production process. A single product will often pass through many craft shops before it is finished.

The existence of regional clusters can influence the optimal scope of the firm in a number of ways. The notion that resources can be specific to a region rather than a firm lies at the heart of many of the major explanations for localization in industry. In regional clusters, tacit knowledge can be internal to an area without being internal to any specific firm. Such knowledge can be tradeable locally without being tradeable outside the regional cluster. In this context, spatial agglomeration becomes a substitute for both vertical integration and diversification (Goldstein and Gronberg 1984). Furthermore, the close coordination possible in regional clusters can create localized shareable inputs. All of these factors will tend to reduce the optimal scope of the firm. Firms within regional clusters can thus have a narrower scope than might be expected otherwise. Similarly, the diversification of a cluster will depend on the specific resources that are present, or can be developed, in the region and the critical activities that can be shared among local firms. Clusters, and firms within them, tend to diversify in patterns that exploit region-specific resources and locally shared activities.

4.2 *Interfirm Coordination*

Disintegrated structures create substantial cross-firm coordination requirements. Regional clusters have developed a variety of coordinating mechanisms and coordinating agents to meet these needs. Enright (1995) suggests a categorization of coordinating mechanisms, based on types of transactions, that distinguishes between coordination through spot markets, short-term coalitions, long-term relationships, and vertical integration (hierarchy). The corresponding coordinating agents are market-makers, organizers, partners and managers. In the Prato textile industry, for example, spot markets are used as coordinating mechanisms. *Impannatori*, entrepreneurs that take orders, subcontract production and arrange logistics, often without controlling any productive capacity directly themselves, have emerged as the main coordinating agents. In Hollywood, short-term coalitions have evolved as the major coordinating mechanisms for motion-picture production. A bewildering array of coordinating agents and organizers including producers, talent agents, lawyers, union representatives, business-affairs executives and completion-bond companies are involved in negotiating and monitoring the large number of contracts that are necessary for each major motion picture. In the Swiss watch industry, SMH has replaced coordination through a loose holding-company structure with co-ordination through a managerial hierarchy for much of the industry.

There is, of course, substantial variation in the industrial organization of regional clusters. Some clusters, the automotive cluster around Toyota City, for example, are built around a single firm. At the other extreme are localized industries that contain dozens, hundreds, or thousands of firms with no dominant entity. Storper and Harrison (1991) characterize production systems by the extent of the division of labor, the size of individual production units, the degree of connection among units, the territorial extent and the governance structures found in the system (power relationships among firms). The authors divide input–output systems into those populated by atomistic producers, process producers (scale-intensive, continuous-production processes), agglomerated networks mostly made up of small producers, agglomerated networks with some large units, dispersed networks with mostly small producers, and dispersed networks with some large units. They divide governance structures into all-ring, no-core (regional clusters with no hierarchy); core-ring, with coordinating firms (a cluster with a lead agent, but one that cannot operate alone); core-ring, with lead firm (a cluster in which the lead firm is substantially independent); and all-core (the vertically integrated firm). In this framework, regional clusters correspond to the two forms of agglomerated networks and some of the process producers. The upshot is that regional clusters are characterized by complex sets of relationships among constituent firms, with coordination governed by the nature of the transactions, economies and firm strategies found in the clusters.

4.3 Strategic Interdependence

The above discussions indicate that there is often substantial strategic interdependence among the firms in a regional cluster. The most straightforward interdependencies are among firms that are related through vertical production relationships (firms, their suppliers and their customers). Firms within regional clusters are also dependent on their direct competitors. Direct competitors can allow a firm's suppliers to achieve efficient scale in production, contribute to industry-specific infrastructure and other local-ized public goods, and provide information through informal trading of know-how (as in von Hippel 1987). All firms within the cluster contribute to the cluster's resource base, even if it is just by providing employment that keeps people with industry-specific knowledge and expertise up-to-date. As indicated above, firms within a regional cluster are often able to share activities that would be difficult for dispersed firms to share. Interdependence also extends to reputation that can be used to market products, attract buyers, and attract resources to a cluster. The strategic interdependence of firms within a cluster adds an additional layer of complexity to their relationships.

The Scotch whisky industry provides a good example of the strategic interdependence that often is present within regional clusters. Production of Scotch whisky is centered in northeastern Scotland near the River Spey. The typical blended Scotch contains whiskies from between twenty and fifty different distilleries. United Distillers, now part of Guinness, by far the largest firm in the industry, is also the most vertically integrated. Other firms are not so vertically integrated. Some firms distill whisky and sell it to blenders, whereas others firms do not do any distilling, but focus on blending. Other firms are partially integrated, supplying part of their own needs and sourcing the remainder externally. The whisky firms engage in a complex web of purchase and trade arrangements. The blendmasters from the different companies know each other and are familiar with each others' operations. They frequently discuss the availability of different types of whiskies and work out trades. One company will often supply another with the understanding that there would be reciprocity at a later date. The proximity of major industry participants and rapid information flows ensure that attempts at opportunistic behavior would be punished swiftly and surely. According to industry experts, the extent of these interactions is unique to the Scottish industry (Enright and Phillips 1987).

5. REGIONAL CLUSTERS AND FIRM STRATEGY

There are several implications of the existence of regional clusters for firm strategy. The presence of region-specific resources, the types of coordination and organization possible in regional clusters, and the ability to share activities within regional clusters can have a substantial influence on firm strategy.

5.1 Competitor and Self-Analysis

Perhaps the simplest implication of the existence of regional clusters involves self-analysis and competitor analysis. Analysis of the strengths and weaknesses of a firm and its competitors are important components of the strategy-formulation process (Grant 1991, for example). The above discussion indicates that an assessment of regional context or contexts within which the firm and its competitors operate should become part of an ongoing process of self- and competitor analysis. In particular, it is important to understand the region-specific resources available to the firm (and its competitors) as well as the activities that the firm (and its competitors) might share with other local firms. This type of analysis will allow the firm to fully exploit the advantages and overcome the disadvantages present in its local environment and to identify resources or the potential for shared activities that competitors might not have drawn upon to date, but which might prove advantageous in the future. The firm with multiple sites, or with multisite competitors, should undertake similar assessments for each major site.

Such analysis is particularly important if the firm is a member of, or competes with, a regional cluster with many members. In such cases, it is important to distinguish present strategies and firm-specific advantages from the strategies that firms from the cluster can potentially adopt and region-specific advantages. Competing with a regional cluster of firms is often like competing with a multiheaded hydra, with many different firms with different strategies all drawing from a common resource base. The cluster as a whole is often far more durable than any individual firm. If one firm is beaten, another often rises to take its place.

5.2 Regional Clusters, Firm Scope and Organizational Structures

Firms within regional clusters often have more freedom of action in choosing their competitive scope and organizational forms than firms outside the cluster. Firms within a cluster can often mix and match firm and region-specific resources and make use of local suppliers and third party firms to a greater extent than firms outside the cluster. In addition, knowledge that is not tradeable outside the cluster, which might cause the firm to expand its scope, might prove to be tradeable within the cluster due to local knowledge and reputation effects. Firms within the cluster might therefore choose a narrower scope than is feasible or optimal outside the cluster. The numerous fragmented industrial districts are perhaps the best examples in which individual firms have kept the scope of their activities narrow. Firms within regional clusters can also find it easier to expand or contract firm scope than other firms due to the presence of localized resources that can be readily internalized or externalized and activities that can be readily outsourced or brought in house.

It is not surprising that changes in the competitive environment and firm strategies have coincided with changes in organization and coordination in regional clusters. In the years immediately following World War II, the Prato area textile industry changed its focus from long runs of lesser quality wool cloth for developing nations to short runs of higher quality fabrics for fashion markets in industrialized nations. This shift was accompanied by a process of vertical disintegration in which the large vertically integrated companies that had dominated the local industry before the war gave way to hundreds and then thousands of small shops. The resurgence of the low- and medium-priced segments of the Swiss watch industry in the 1980s was due to the new production and marketing strategies developed by SMH. According to SMH management, the strategic changes could not have been accomplished without the installation of a vertically integrated corporate structure which replaced the more fragmented structure that had existed. The Hollywood motion-picture industry underwent a process of disintegration as it changed its focus from relatively low-budget formula films to high-budget blockbuster films. The implication for firms within a regional cluster is that strategic change within the cluster often involves a disruption of traditional organizational forms.

Multiple forms of organization and coordination often coexist within regional clusters. In Silicon Valley, vertically integrated semiconductor firms coexist with design houses, foundry operations, and other less integrated firms. In the Hollywood motion-picture industry, studio projects, studio-backed independent productions and negative pick-up films (films that are made independently and then sold to a studio) provide coordination through hierarchy, quasi-markets, and spot markets respectively. The Scotch whisky industry also exhibits multiple forms of organization and coordination. This further highlights the fluidity of organizational forms within regional clusters.

5.3 Location Decisions

Another natural intersection between regional clusters and firm strategy involves location decisions. As indicated earlier, the firm has a series of decisions to make concerning the location of business units and activities. The large literature on industrial location will not be reviewed here. Instead, the focus will be on some of the issues that arise in locating in regional clusters. As communication within firms improves, firms are increasingly able to separate specific activities and locate each for maximum advantage. One way to locate activities is to invest in regional clusters. There are several reasons that a firm from outside a regional cluster might wish to acquire or establish a presence within the cluster. One is to create a listening post that keeps track of the developments within the cluster as part of industry and competitor analysis. A second reason is to place a stand-alone operation, essentially a corporate portfolio investment, in the place that is most favorable for that particular business unit or activity. A third reason to expand into a regional cluster is to supply products and specific activities for an existing business unit. A fourth, and perhaps the most interesting, reason is to actively transfer skills and expertise from the cluster back to the rest of the company.

There are numerous examples of each type of investment. Several Swiss and German machinery firms have obtained electronics and software expertise from subsidiaries located in United States clusters. The investments by Sony and Matsushita in the Hollywood motion-picture industry were made to control stand-alone motion-picture operations and to exploit synergies between hardware and software businesses rather than to transfer motion-picture production expertise from Hollywood to Japan. The investments of several large pharmaceutical firms, both American and non-American, in American biotechnology clusters have generally involved efforts to supply new products for existing distribution networks and to transfer expertise back into the parent company. These examples, and others, show some of the variety of reasons firms choose to invest in regional clusters.

The different types of investments in a regional cluster require different levels of integration into the local environment. The stand-alone operation can be managed locally and will tend to have limited transmission of information to other units. In order to be effective, the listening post must have access to industry-specific news and information that can be passed back to the company. Actively passing skills and capabilities back to the company's other facilities requires a closer coordination with the facility located inside the cluster. The firm's ability to do this often depends on its ability to become an "insider" in the cluster and the type of information that is critical to the success of the cluster. Given the social, as well as economic, relations often found in regional clusters, it can be difficult to achieve "insider" status. It can be difficult, for example, for outsiders to become true insiders in regional clusters that involve relatively closed communities, such as several of the Italian industrial districts. The United States high-technology clusters, on the other hand, which are characterized by open social structures and relatively free flow of information, appear to be relatively easy to join.

5.4 Regional Clusters and Investments in Innovative Activities

One type of investment that deserves special attention is investment in innovative activities. The arguments above indicate that the innovative performance of regional clusters of firms is often superior to that of a group of similar, but dispersed, firms. Spillover of innovation from firm to firm is likely to be greater in regional clusters than among dispersed firms. Employees are more mobile among firms that are located in close proximity. Local suppliers, buyers, family members, friends and acquaintances can all become sources of industry and company-specific information. There are, however, other considerations that a firm must take into account when planning its investments in innovative activities. In particular, the enhanced information flows within regional clusters can make it more difficult to appropriate the gains from innovation.

In Solingen, hundreds of local cutlery firms constantly fight for orders and constantly seek to innovate to improve their position. The disintegrated nature of the industry and the close proximity of suppliers and equipment manufacturers ensures a rapid flow of information in the industry. New machines and equipment are quickly copied by competitors. Some firms have tried to protect their innovations by refusing to cooperate with local machinery manufacturers for fear of giving away trade secrets (van der Linde 1991). In the mid-1970s, Marazzi and equipment manufacturer SITI introduced the rapid single-firing method to the Sassuolo ceramic-tile industry. This innovation reduced cycle times from more than twenty-four hours to less than one hour. According to industry sources, the innovation was copied in a few months by local competitors. Since then, advantages over local competitors in production technology and design have been short-lived (Enright and Tenti 1990). Several observers have claimed that the free flow of information and people in Silicon Valley has become a disadvantage rather than an advantage for local firms. Local firms have taken increased precautions to try to protect intellectual property (see Preer 1992, for example). Thus the interests of the firm, which wishes to appropriate intellectual property, might run counter to the interests of the cluster, which might thrive on the free flow of information.

It appears that in practice the increase of effectiveness of innovative investments possible within regional clusters, and the competitive pressures within such clusters, frequently outweigh the potential loss of appropriability of innovations. Thus research and development activities tend to be localized (see Feldman 1993, for example). In any event, the firm must understand both the enhancement of the efficiency of innovative activities and the loss of appropriability that can occur in regional clusters. Researchers, in turn, who have tended to ignore the role of information flow on the incentives to invest in innovative behavior in regional clusters, must do likewise.

5.5 *Expansion Out of a Regional Cluster*

Firms from within a geographic cluster often try to expand their operations outside the cluster. The ability of a firm to expand beyond a regional cluster clearly depends on the nature of the firm and the cluster. Presumably Storper and Harrison's (1991) core firms, which are firms that are substantially independent, would have the easiest time expanding outside a regional cluster. Core firms are often relatively self-sufficient, or are able to attract suppliers and other supporting firms to locate near their new facilities. The experiences of the United States facilities of Japanese auto companies provide examples. An important question for core firms might be which local suppliers and related firms they wish to try to take with them into other regional or international markets.

Geographic expansion by a ring firm is another matter. By definition, such firms are either not fully self-sufficient, or have limited ability to influence the behavior of other firms. For a ring firm in a core-ring configuration, the most natural way to expand into other markets is to follow the expansion of a core firm. Another potential strategy is to enter other markets by trying to supply a core firm in the same industry, but in another location. For firms from regional clusters without large units, geographic expansion can be more problematic. The limited scope of the firm that is allowed by the presence of region-specific resources and the ability to have activities done by other firms may limit an individual firm's ability to expand into other locations. Such expansion might require the firm to perform more activities in its new location than it has to in its home location. In addition, it might not be able to draw upon the same resources that it can at home.

Marazzi, the Italian ceramic-tile firm, is the largest firm in a cluster that really has no large production units. In recent years, Marazzi has tried to expand its operations into overseas markets. Due to the absence of its local supplier base, the firm has found that it has to perform more activities for itself in its new locations than it has to at home. It has also found that the work force available in its new locations, even in other industrialized nations, lacks the appreciation and knowledge of the industry that is taken for granted in the Sassuolo area. Thus the firm has had to make greater investments in training than it has to at home. Although Marazzi finds operating in foreign locations in some ways more difficult than at home, it still is able to draw from the skills and capabilities that it has developed as part of the Italian tile cluster to compete successfully. The implication is that firms within clusters must carefully assess their ability to expand beyond the cluster and the activities and resources that may or may not be available in their new locations. The firm must find ways of substituting for the resources and activities available within its home cluster.

5.6 Competing and Cooperating

Several authors have noted the mix of competition and cooperation that appears characteristic of regional clusters (see Harrison 1992, for example). Paradoxically, regional clusters often appear to have both greater cooperation and greater competition than dispersed industries. Greater cooperation can come about due to the strategic interdependence of clustered firms as well as through the fact that there are simply more activities in which firms in close proximity can cooperate. Greater competition occurs because competitors in close proximity often focus on each other to a greater extent than firms at a distance. In addition, in many clusters, the owners and managers of the leading firms are also the leading citizens of the same towns. In such circumstances, competition among firms also becomes competition for positions in the local social hierarchy.

Firms within a regional cluster must decide in which activities they will cooperate with local firms and in which they will compete. In doing so, they must distinguish between cooperation with direct competitors and cooperation with suppliers and customers. This is an important distinction that some researchers fail to make. There is always at least some cooperation between a firm and its suppliers and customers. All market transactions must be beneficial to both parties or else the transaction would not take place. The arguments for cooperation with suppliers and customers are therefore straightforward. Even so, one question that arises is how much cooperation with suppliers and buyers is enough and how much is too much? Should a firm encourage its suppliers to sell in international markets? Encouraging suppliers to go international might help the suppliers improve their products and keep their edge over suppliers from other regions or nations. On the other hand, if localized knowledge can be embodied in equipment, encouraging suppliers to compete in international markets could accelerate the diffusion of industry-specific knowledge that might be difficult for foreign competitors to obtain otherwise. The closeness with which a firm works with its local suppliers should depend on what the suppliers bring to the table in terms of contribution to the creative process and the extent to which joint developments can be appropriated by the firm in question.

Foreign competitors were only able to copy the rapid single-firing process developed within the Sassuolo area ceramic-tile industry when Italian equipment manufacturers began to sell equipment abroad. There is a concern within the tile industry that local equipment manufacturers, which now export some 80 per cent of their output, are spreading knowledge and expertise to foreign competitors. The edge that Italian firms have had in terms of their preferential access to world-class suppliers appears to be declining. As indicated above, Solingen cutlery companies tend to buy relatively standardized equipment from local suppliers and then modify it in-house, even though several of these equipment suppliers are world leaders in their fields. The cutlery firms have generally refused to work with local equipment suppliers on an ongoing basis so they can keep their modifications of purchased equipment secret. Of course, this is not a new phenomenon. British textile-machinery firms were forbidden to export in the nineteenth century. This helped provide an impetus for the development of textile machinery in Germany, Switzerland and elsewhere.

Arguments for cooperating with direct competitors tend to focus on the creation of localized public goods, eliminating "wasteful" duplication, and combining complementary assets. For firms, cooperation with direct competitors involves the tradeoff between access to greater resources and the potential for loss of proprietary information or the creation of stronger competitors. Cooperating with local direct competitors can be beneficial if such cooperation helps the cluster compete against outside competitors. Successful regional clusters tend to have cooperation among direct competitors in some activities, such as lobbying, trying to create markets, participation in trade fairs, investing in industry-specific infrastructure, provision of specialized training, obtaining market intelligence, and generic promotion. Other activities, such as company-specific marketing, production, sales, new product development and process development tend to be carried out in a competitive fashion. The Zurich Gold Pool, for example, was created by the three large Swiss banks in order to foster a larger, more efficient market for gold-trading in the city. The banks then competed actively for business in that market. The Pool itself eventually dissolved. Firms from Prato and Biella cooperate to organize trade shows, but then compete fiercely for business within the shows. There are often sharp limits to cooperative behavior in regional clusters. The Italian Packaging Machinery Industry Association, for example, has been forbidden to compile information from the published annual reports of members. There has been little research that has focused on the optimal mixture of competition and cooperation in regional clusters.

5.7 Consolidating a Cluster

One of the most important strategic decisions that a firm within a relatively fragmented regional cluster can make is to try to consolidate the cluster. There are several reasons a firm might choose to try to consolidate a cluster. In some cases, firms move to consolidate a regional cluster in order to achieve scale or scope economies, to overcome coordination failures within the cluster, or to combine to make specific investments. There, of course, have been countless examples of clusters of firms that have eventually consolidated. There have also been a number of notable recent attempts to consolidate clusters.

Turin and Piacenza are two centers of the Italian factory-automation equipment industry. Comau, a subsidiary of Fiat, is by far the largest factory-automation company in the Turin area. During the early 1970s, a combination of falling demand and increasingly difficult labor relations forced Fiat, which dominated the economy in the Turin area, to rethink its manufacturing strategy. At the time, the firm owned a small factory-automation division in Modena, but purchased most of its equipment from outside suppliers. In 1976, under Fiat's urging, the twelve largest machine-tool and factory-automation firms in Turin created a consortium. Several smaller firms were merged into this consortium to form Comau. Fiat soon acquired a controlling stake in Comau (by 1986 Fiat owned 90 per cent of

Comau). Industry experts claimed that the large level of investment and coordination necessary to develop automatic-production systems for Fiat prompted the auto-maker to absorb Comau. It simply would have made no sense for an independent supplier to make the necessary investments to serve a single large customer. Mandelli, the largest factory-automation firm in the Piacenza area, has recently acquired several local companies in an attempt to consolidate the factory-automation equipment cluster in the area. The firm claims that it is trying to achieve the scale necessary to obtain a "critical mass." It is yet to be seen whether the firm will succeed in its efforts.

Much of the Swiss watch industry was consolidated under the auspices of SMH in the mid-1980s. Even though much of the industry had been nominally under the control of two holding companies, ASUAG and SSIH, in reality neither entity was able to ensure effective coordination in production or marketing. Designers refused to incorporate standardized parts, production schedules were not met, and brands were not well focused. Cartel arrangements and negotiations among several industry associations had frozen the structure of the industry for decades. Rationalization had proven nearly impossible. In 1926, for example, seventeen *ébauche* factories were joined into a trust, Ébauche SA. In 1985, there were still seventeen *ébauche* factories. Industry politics made it difficult to act against the old-line watch families, or "watch barons," who retained control of individual firms under the holding companies. Effective interfirm coordination in production and marketing had almost ceased to exist. The financial difficulties that the industry faced in the late 1970s and early 1980s allowed new management to take control of the two holding companies. The new management broke down organizational barriers, rationalized production and coordinated the positioning of brands on a worldwide basis. It also introduced new products, production technologies and marketing concepts.

A firm can try to consolidate a cluster in order to internalize the resources that were once external to any single firm. In this way, the firm can attempt to internalize the rents that otherwise would accrue to the resources of the area. Consolidating the cluster might be a good strategy for the firm, but it is not clear that it is the best for the cluster itself. This depends on the extent to which the success of the cluster comes from the existence of multiple firms. Consolidation can cause a cluster to lose its vibrancy if consolidation reduces the number of independent information sources and outlooks, or reduces competitive pressures that stimulate innovation. Consolidation of the cluster can also upset the balance between companies and their suppliers and buyers, thus reducing the information flow from these sources. The precise impact that consolidation will have on a cluster therefore involves a complex question of the impact of firm strategy on the structure and dynamism of the cluster.

6. CONCLUSIONS

The study of regional clusters can benefit by incorporating existing knowledge from the strategy field. The strategy field can benefit to an even greater extent by incorporating existing knowledge of regional clusters. These clusters provide fertile ground for examining the optimal scope of the firm, optimal levels of cooperation and competition, and sources of advantage external to any given firm. Improvements in logistics, communications and information systems are starting to allow firms operating farflung networks, or at a distance from each other, to do what regional clusters have been able to do all along: introduce new methods of combining activities and resources and continually reassess and reoptimize intra- and interfirm relationships. In a world that seems to be moving more and more toward "boundaryless" or "virtual" firms, regional clusters, in which such firms already exist, and in some cases have existed for centuries, provide important sources of information and concrete examples of how to organize, coordinate and manage within such structures.

There are also substantial research opportunities at the intersection of regional clusters and firm strategy. Although anecdotal evidence and economic theory might suggest that firms in regional clusters are less vertically integrated and diversified than other firms, these hypotheses have not been tested in large-sample, cross-sectional studies. There has also been relatively little work that explicitly examines optimal levels of cooperation and competition in regional clusters, or identifies the patterns of activities that tend to be carried out cooperatively and competitively in successful clusters. Another promising area for further research involves the motivations for investing in a regional cluster and the extent to which "outside" firms can transfer knowledge gained inside the cluster to their other facilities and operations. Advances in our knowledge on these and related questions will help firms formulate strategies to build and take advantage of regional clusters.

NOTES

1. Regional clusters are defined here as groups of firms in the same industry, or in closely related industries that are in close geographic proximity to each other. This definition is meant to include geographically concentrated industries, including so-called "industrial districts" (see Pyke, Becattini and Sengenberger 1990; Goodman, Bamford and Saynor 1989). Regional clusters differ from

business networks, which have also received considerable attention in recent years (see Bosworth and Rosenfeld 1993). Business networks involve communication and cooperation among firms that need not be located in close physical proximity.

2. Brusco (1982) and Piore and Sabel (1984) were among the first to bring the resurgence of study of regional clusters of firms to the attention of a wide audience. Porter (1990) further underlined the importance of regional clusters in international competition.

3. Examples include New Zealand, Ireland, Finland, several states in the United States, provinces in Italy, Canada, and Germany and so on (see Industrial Policy Review Group 1992; Crocombe, Enright and Porter 1991; Cortwright 1991; British Colombia 1992). There is also substantial literature on regional clusters in high-technology industries, including Preer (1992) and Hall and Markusen (1985).

4. Useful reviews of the economics of industrial innovation include Baldwin and Scott (1987), Freeman (1982), Rosenberg (1982) and Reinganum (1989). Roberts (1988) and the papers in Tushman and Moore (1988) review much of the managerial literature on industrial innovation. Reviews of the regional economics literature on innovation include Malecki (1983), Malecki and Varaiya (1986) and Feldman (1993).

5. Gabor (1991) in her description of the optical-equipment industry of Rochester, NY, begins to make this link.

REFERENCES

Andrews, K. (1971), *The Concept of Corporate Strategy* (Homewood, Ill.: Irwin).

Arthur, B. (1986), "Industry Location Patterns and the Importance of History," CEPR Technical Paper, no. 84, Stanford University.

Baldwin, W. and Scott, J. (1987), *Market Structure and Technical Change* (New York: Harwood Academic Publishers).

Barney, J. (1986), "Strategic Factor Markets: Expectation, Luck, and Business Strategy," *Management Science*, 32: 1231–41.

——(1991), "Firm Resources and Sustained Competitive Advantage," *Journal of Management*, 17: 99–120.

Becattini, G. (1989), "Sectors and/or Districts: Some Remarks on the Conceptual Foundations of Industrial Economics," in Goodman, Bamford and Saynor (eds.), *Small Firms and Industrial Districts in Italy*.

Bosworth, B. and Rosenfeld, S. (1993), *Significant Others: Exploring the Potential of Manufacturing Networks* (Chapel Hill, NC: Regional Technology Strategies).

British Columbia Trade Development Corporation (1992), "Flexible Networks in Theory and Practice: How and Why to Set Up Flexible Networks in British Columbia," Vancouver, BC.

Brusco, S. (1982), "The Emilian Model: Productive Decentralization and Social Integration," *Cambridge Journal of Economics*, 6: 167–84.

Bumbacher, U. (1992), "The Swiss Watch Industry," Harvard Business School, Case 9-792-046.

Casson, M. (1991) (ed.), *Global Research Strategy and International Competitiveness* (London: Basil Blackwell).

Caves, R. (1982), *Multinational Enterprise and Economic Analysis* (Cambridge: Cambridge University Press).

Clark, K. (1985), "The Interaction of Design Hierarchies and Market Concepts in Technological Evolution," *Research Policy*, 14: 235–51.

Collis, D. (1991), "A Resource-Based Analysis of Global Competition: The Case of the Bearings Industry," *Strategic Management Journal*, 12: 49–68.

Cortwright, J. (1991), *Third Wave Economic Development in Oregon* (Salem, Oreg.: Oregon Joint Legislative Committee on Trade & Economic Development).

Crocombe, G., Enright, M. and Porter, M. (1991), *Upgrading New Zealand's Competitive Advantage* (Auckland: Oxford University Press).

Dierickx, I. and Cool, K. (1989), "Asset Stock Accumulation and Sustainability of Competitive Advantage," *Management Science*, 35: 1504–11.

Dirven, E., Groenewegen, J. and van Hoof, S. (1993) (eds.), *Stuck in the Region?: Changing Scales for Regional Identity* (Utrecht: Netherlands Geographic Studies, 155).

Dosi, G. (1988), "Sources, Procedures and Microeconomic Effects of Innovation," *Journal of Economic Literature*, 36: 1120–71.

Enright, M. (1990), "Geographic Concentration and Industrial Organization," Ph.D. diss., Harvard University.

——(1993*a*), "The Geographic Scope of Competitive Advantage," in Dirven, Groenewegen and van Hoof, *Stuck in the Region?*

——(1993*b*), "The Determinants of Geographic Concentration in Industry," Harvard Business School, Working Paper 93-060.

——(1995), "Organization and Coordination in Geographically Concentrated Industries," in N. Lamoreaux and D. Raff (eds.), *Coordination and Information: Historical Perspectives on the Organization of Enterprise* (Chicago: Chicago University Press for the NBER).

——and Phillips, T. (1987), "The Scotch Whisky Industry," unpub. ms.

——and Tenti, P. (1990), "La Competitività della Ceramica Italiana," *Harvard Espansione* (Sept.), 28–41.

Feldman, M. (1993), "An Examination of the Geography of Innovation," *Industrial and Corporate Change*, 2: 451–70.

Freeman, C. (1982), *The Economics of Industrial Innovation* (Cambridge, Mass.: MIT Press).

Gabor, A. (1991), "Rochester Focuses: A Community's Core Competence," *Harvard Business Review* (July–Aug.), 116–26.

General Electric (1991), *Annual Report* (Cincinnati, OH: GEC).

Goddard, J. (1978), "The Location of Non-manufacturing Activities Within Manufacturing Industries," in Hamilton (ed.), *Contemporary Industrialization*.

Goldstein, G. and Gronberg, T. (1984), "Economies of Scale and Economies of Agglomeration," *Journal of Urban Economics*, 16: 91–104.

Goodman, E., Bamford, J. and Saynor, J. (1989) (eds.), *Small Firms and Industrial Districts in Italy* (London: Routledge).

Granovetter, M. (1985), "Economic Action and Social Structure: The Problem of Embeddedness," *American Journal of Sociology*, 91: 349–64.

Grant, R. (1991), "The Resource-Based Theory of Competitive Advantage: Implications for Strategy Formulation," *California Management Review* (Spring), 114–35.

Grefsheim, S., Franklin, J. and Cunningham, D. (1991), "Biotechnology Awareness Study, pt. 1: Where Scientists Get Their Information," *Bulletin of the Medical Library Association*, 79: 36–44.

Grossman, G. and Helpman, E. (1992), *Innovation and Growth in the Global Economy* (Cambridge, Mass.: MIT Press).

Hagström, P. (1990), "Unshackling Corporate Geography," *Geografiska Annaler, Series B, Human Geography*, 72B: 3–12.

Hall, P. and Markusen, A. (1985) (eds.), *Silicon Landscapes* (Boston: Allen & Unwin).

Hamilton, F. (1978) (ed.), *Contemporary Industrialization* (London: Longman).

Harrison, B. (1992), "Industrial Districts: Old Wine in New Bottles?" *Regional Studies*, 26: 469–83.

Industrial Policy Review Group (Ireland) (1992), *A Time for Change: Industrial Policy for the 1990s* (Dublin: Government Publications Sales Office).

Krugman, P. (1991), *Geography and Trade* (Cambridge, Mass.: MIT Press).

Learned, E., Christensen, C., Andrews, K. and Guth, W. (1969), *Business Policy* (Homewood, Ill.: Irwin).

Lloyd, P. and Dicken, P. (1977), *Location in Space* (London: Harper & Row).

Lundvall, A. (1988), "Innovation as an Interactive Process: User–Producer Relations," in G. Dosi, C. Freeman, R. Nelson, G. Silverberg and L. Soete (eds.), *Technical Change and Economic Theory* (London: Pinter).

Malecki, E. (1983), "Technology and Regional Development: A Survey," *International Regional Science Review*, 8: 89–125.

——and Varaiya, P. (1986), "Innovation and Changes in Regional Structure," in P. Nijkamp and E. Mills (eds.), *The Handbook of Urban and Regional Economics* (Amsterdam: North-Holland).

Marshall, A. (1920), *Principles of Economics*, 8th edn. (London: Macmillan).

——(1923), *Industry and Trade*, 3rd edn. (London: Macmillan).

Miller, R. and Côte, M. (1987), *Growing the Next Silicon Valley: A Guide for Successful Regional Planning* (Lexington, Mass.: Lexington Books).

Normann, R. and Ramirez, R. (1993), "From Value Chain to Value Constellation: Designing Interactive Strategy," *Harvard Business Review* (July–Aug.), 65–77.

Oakey, R. (1985), "High-Technology Industry and Agglomeration Economies," in Hall and Markusen (eds.), *Silicon Landscapes*.

Penrose, E. (1959), *The Theory of the Growth of the Firm* (London: Basil Blackwell).

Peteraf, M. (1993), "The Cornerstones of Competitive Advantage: A Resource-Based View," *Strategic Management Journal*, 14: 179–91.

Piore, M. and Sabel, C. (1984), *The Second Industrial Divide* (New York: Basic Books).

Porter, M. (1985), *Competitive Advantage* (New York: Free Press).

——(1986) (ed.), *Competition in Global Industries* (Boston: Harvard Business School Press).

——(1987), "From Competitive Advantage to Corporate Strategy," *Harvard Business Review* (May–June), 43–59.

——(1990), *The Competitive Advantage of Nations* (New York: Free Press).

——(1991), "Toward a Dynamic Theory of Strategy," *Strategic Management Journal*, 12: 95–117.

Prahalad, C. and Hamel, G. (1990), "The Core Competence of the Corporation," *Harvard Business Review* (May–June), 79–91.

Preer, R. (1992), *The Emergence of Technopolis* (New York: Praeger).

Pyke, F., Becattini, G. and Sengenberger, W. (1990), *Industrial Districts and Inter-Firm Cooperation in Italy* (Geneva: International Institute for Labour Studies).

Reed, R. and De Fillippi, R. (1990), "Causal Ambiguity, Barriers to Imitation, and Sustainable Competitive Advantage," *Academy of Management Review*, 15: 88–102.

Reinganum, J. (1989), "The Timing of Innovation: Research, Development, and Diffusion," in R. Schmalensee and R. Willig (eds.), *The Handbook of Industrial Organization* (Amsterdam: North-Holland).

Roberts, E. (1988), "What We've Learned: Managing Invention and Innovation," *Research-Technology Management*, 31: 11–29.

Robins, J. (1993), "Organization as Strategy: Restructuring Production in the Film Industry," *Strategic Management Journal*, 14: 103–18.

Rosenberg, N. (1982), *Inside the Black Box: Technology and Economics* (Cambridge: Cambridge University Press).

Russo, M. (1985), "Technical Change and the Industrial District: The Role of Interfirm Relations in the Growth and Transformation of Ceramic Tile Production in Italy," *Research Policy*, 14: 329–43.

Saxenian, A. (1985), "The Genesis of Silicon Valley," in Hall and Markusen (eds.), *Silicon Landscapes*.

——(1990), "The Origins and Dynamics of Production Networks in Silicon Valley," paper presented at the International Workshop on Networks of Innovators, Montreal.

Scherer, F., Beckenstein, A., Kaufer, E. and Bougeon-Maassen, F. (1975), *The Economics of Multiplant Operation* (Cambridge, Mass.: Harvard University Press).

Scott, A. (1987), "Industrial Organization and Location: Division of Labor, the Firm, and Spatial Process," *Economic Geography*, 63: 214–31.

——(1988a), *New Industrial Spaces* (London: Pion Limited).

——(1988b), *Metropolis* (Los Angeles: University of California Press).

Stalk, G., Evans, P. and Shulman, E. (1992), "Competing on Capabilities: The New Rules of Corporate Strategy," *Harvard Business Review* (May–June), 57–69.

Storper, M. and Harrison, B. (1991), "Flexibility, Hierarchy and Regional Development: The Changing Structure of Industrial Production Systems and their Forms of Governance in the 1990s," *Research Policy*, 20: 407–22.

Teece, D. (1982), "Towards an Economic Theory of the Multiproduct Firm," *Journal of Economic Behavior and Organization*, 3: 39–63.

Tushman, M. and Moore, W. (1988) (eds.), *Readings in the Management of Innovation* (Cambridge, Mass.: Ballinger).

Utterback, J. (1974), "Innovation in Industry and the Diffusion of Technology," *Science*, 183: 658–62.

van der Linde, C. (1991), "The Competitive Advantage of Germany," Ph.D. diss., St. Gallen University.

von Hippel, E. (1987), "Cooperation Between Rivals: Informal Know-how Trading," *Research Policy*, 16: 291–302.

——(1988), *Sources of Innovation* (Oxford: Oxford University Press).

Weber, A. (1929), *Theory of the Location of Industries* (trans. C. Friedrich) (Chicago: University of Chicago Press).

Wernerfelt, B. (1989), "From Critical Resources to Corporate Strategy," *Journal of General Management*, 14: 4–12.

——(1984), "A Resource-Based View of the Firm," *Strategic Management Journal*, 5: 171–80.

Williamson, O. (1985), *Markets and Hierarchies* (New York, Free Press).

15

Global Location Behavior and Organizational Dynamics of Japanese Electronics Firms and Their Impact on Regional Economies*

MASAHISA FUJITA AND RYOICHI ISHII

The single finite movement from a disturbance to a restoration of equilibrium is not enough if genesis is to be followed by growth. And, to convert the movement into a repetitive, recurrent rhythm, there must be an *elan vital* (to use Bergson's term) which carries the challenged party through equilibrium into an overbalance which exposes him to a fresh challenge and thereby inspires him to make a fresh response in the form of a further equilibrium ending in a further overbalance, and so on in a progression which is potentially infinite.   (Toynbee 1946: 187.)

The innovational process "incessantly revolutionizes the economic structure *from within*, incessantly destroying the old one, incessantly creating a new one. This process of Creative Destruction is the essential fact about capitalism."   (Schumpeter 1942: 83.)

We have to be willing to cannibalize what we're doing today in order to ensure our leadership in the future. It's counter to human nature, but you have to kill your business while it is still working.

  (Chairman Lewis Platt of Hewlett-Packard, the fastest growing electronics giant in the world today: *Fortune*, 2 May 1994, p. 90.)

Since its inception, Motorola has been managing on the concept of renewal, a willingness to renew our technologies and to renew the processes by which we run the institution.

  (President Christopher Galvin of Motorola, quoted as the best-managed company in the world today by *Fortune*, 18 April 1994, p. 70.)

1. INTRODUCTION

How can a civilization/nation/city/firm continue to grow over a sustained period of time? This is the most fascinating, and most challenging question that a scholar in any social science field can ask. Of course, the growth of a

* An earlier version of this paper was presented at The Prince Bertil Symposium on The Dynamic Firm, Stockholm, 13–14 June, 1994. The authors are grateful to Toni Horst, Ho-Yeon Kim, Michael E. Porter, and Tony E. Smith for their valuable comments, and to the International Centre for the Study of East Asian Development (Kitakyushu City, Japan) for the financial support in conducting this research.

civilization and that of a firm, for example, are fundamentally different phenomena. Nevertheless, there seems to exist some consensus among scholars that whatever an organization is, it can grow (or develop in the sense of Schumpeter) over a sustained period of time only when it continues to renew itself through a recurrent sequence of challenge-responses (Toynbee 1946) or creative destruction (Schumpeter).

Focusing on the main topic of this book, then, it is not surprising to observe that only a *relatively* very small number of firms have been able to grow (i.e. maintain competitive advantage) over a long period of time. For, as noted above by Chairman Lewis Platt of Hewlett-Packard, the preemptive self-destruction of today's successful business for tomorrow's leadership is counter to human nature. Such a heroic act could be practiced recurrently only by a small number of bold (and lucky) entrepreneurs under intense pressures or strong stimulation.

It is, then, equally surprising to observe that a significant number of firms (including Hewlett-Packard and Motorola mentioned above, and the nine Japanese electronics firms to be studied in this paper) have indeed grown over a sustained period of time. The question of how a particular firm has been able to maintain the spirit and energy, or *elan vital*, for incessant self-renewal may remain beyond the domain of science. An easier and more relevant question for us is: what has been the nature of the environments that have stimulated growth? Indeed, for the latter question, there seems to exist some consensus. Toynbee (1946) and Porter (1990), for example, agree that ease is inimical to growth. Both emphasize the stimulus of hard countries (or selective factor disadvantages) and the stimulus of pressures (or rivalry). Furthermore, again as both Toynbee and Porter agree, if genesis is to be followed by growth, positive feedbacks (to use the term employed by Arthur (1994)) must be created both within the firm and between the firm and its environment. In the long run, the environment itself will change due to both internal and external forces, and the firm needs to renew itself in order to sustain growth. Therefore, it is also important to ask: what are the types of feedback loops (internal and external to firms) which nurture (or hinder) the growth of firms, and how do they develop?

The central objective of this paper is to examine the role of location (or geographical space) in the growth of firms and to study the interactions between firms and regions. In the study of the growth or innovation process of firms, location is important for several reasons. First, according to Schumpeter (1934), innovations cover the following five types: (1) the introduction of a new good or a new quality of a good; (2) the introduction of a new method of production; (3) the opening of a new market; (4) the conquest of a new source of supply of raw materials or half-manufactured goods; and (5) the carrying out of the new organization of any industry. Among these five types of innovations, (3) and (4) directly relate to location if a new market or a new source is in a new location. As will be demonstrated below, the remaining three types of innovations also have close linkages with space (as illustrated by modern production methods such as JIT and TQC, and by the multinationalization of firms). In particular, given recent development of transportation and telecommunication technologies and liberalization of the world economy, almost every type of innovation would involve the spatial dimension. Therefore, location constitutes a vital element of corporate strategies. Second, location plays a major role in defining the environments of firms. In particular, as emphasized by Porter (1990), the home base of a firm significantly affects its competitive advantages. More generally, given that a typical large multinational firm today consists of hundreds of operational units scattered around the world, the firm's spatial organization greatly affects its efficiency or competitiveness. Finally, due to the endogenous forces of external economies or agglomeration economies, a location (e.g. a city or a region) creates its own dynamics, which in turn affect the long-run competitiveness of firms and regions.

In this paper, we focus on the nine largest Japanese electronics firms, and examine how they have been changing their global location and organizational behavior over the past several decades.[1] The firms considered are Hitachi, Matsushita Electric, Toshiba, NEC, Mitsubishi Electric, Fujitsu, Sony, Sanyo Electric and Sharp. We intend to illuminate the importance of the spatial dimension in the innovation strategies and growth processes of firms. We also demonstrate that the recent industrial and regional transformations in both developed and developing countries are closely linked to each other through the location and organizational behavior of modern multinational firms.

Our study of large electronics firms necessarily means a study of modern multinational firms (MNFs). To understand this point, we may adopt the OLI (ownership, location, internalization) model of MNFs developed by Dunning (1981, 1988).[2] In particular, following Markusen (1991), we assume that among ownership advantages (that assure the existence of a firm), knowledge-based (firm-specific) assets are the most fundamental for a firm to successfully become multinational. These are proprietary assets of the firm embodied in such corporate resources as the human capital of employees, patents or exclusive technological knowledge, copyrights or trademarks, and intangible assets such as management know-how, R&D capability and the reputation of the firm. These knowledge-based assets can be transferred relatively easily (within the corporate organization) across space at low cost. Furthermore, they have the characteristic of "jointness" or "public goods" in that they can be supplied to additional production facilities at very low cost. This joint input characteristic of knowledge-based assets generates scope economies or economies of multiplant production where a single two-plant firm has a cost advantage over two independent single-plant firms.[3] In addition, given that technical and other trade secrets passed to a subsidiary or a licensee can be easily lost, the existence of knowledge-based assets tends to rule out licensing or other arm's-length arrangements, reinforcing the correlation between these assets and multinationality. Given their knowledge-based firm-specific assets, MNFs will try to exploit most effectively the potential local advantages in different countries/regions in consideration of distance-related transport/coordination costs and scale economies at individual plants.[4] This basic principle will guide the location behavior and the spatial organization of MNFs (within each country and globally) under given specific environments at each time.

The OLI model of MNFs with an emphasis on knowledge-based assets fits very well with the fact that among manufacturing industries, the electronics industry has been one of the most active in overseas production during the past several decades.[5] Indeed, first, the electronics industry is perhaps the most knowledge/technology-driven industry among all manufacturing sectors. Second, as explained in the next section, a typical large Japanese electronics firm produces a very broad range of products located at different stages of their product cycles. Third, a typical electronics product (e.g. a television) consists of quite a large number of components which are often designed and produced based on firm-specific technology. Finally, the production of many of these components (e.g. semiconductors) itself consists of a long series of manufacturing processes based on proprietary technology. In short, a typical large electronics firm is engaged essentially in a huge assembly operation (as well as the design, development and marketing) of a large variety of products and components which have different requirements for production factors and different geographical focuses in marketing. Therefore, given on one hand intensive competition in both domestic and foreign markets, and given on the other hand recent development in transportation and telecommunication technologies, not surprisingly, these electronics firms have intensively globalized their operations to make them most efficient.

The plan of the rest of the paper is as follows. In Section 2, we introduce the nine Japanese electronics firms for our study, and describe their characteristics. In Section 3, we describe the global location and organizational behavior of a representative firm, NEC. In Section 4, we conduct the synthetic study of the global location and organizational behavior of the nine firms. Section 5 examines the interactions between firms and regions by considering two examples. Finally we conclude the paper by examining the major problems faced by Japanese electronics firms today.

2. CHARACTERISTICS OF THE NINE JAPANESE ELECTRONICS FIRMS STUDIED

Table 15.1 summarizes the basic information on the nine Japanese electronics firms in terms of the location of their HQs, year of establishment, total sales, world ranking in sales, share of capital investment in sales, share of R&D expenditure in sales, export share in sales and worldwide employment in 1990.[6] For the purpose of comparison, the table also includes those data on the two largest Korean firms (Samsung and Goldstar) and three US high-tech firms (IBM, Motorola and Texas Instruments) in the electronics industry. Next, Table 15.2 presents the major products which are currently produced by these fourteen firms. For the purpose of our study, we categorize electronics products as follows: (i) consumer electronics which include both consumer electric appliances (such as refrigerators and washing machines) and consumer electronics products (such as TVs and VCRs); (ii) information electronics (such as computers and copiers); (iii) communication electronics (such as telephone systems and facsimiles); (iv) industrial systems (such as motors and various industrial machines); and (v) electronics devices (such as condensers and semiconductors). For the details of products in each category, refer to Table 15.2.

Concerning the nine Japanese firms, although the origins and the strengths differ among them, all have grown up as general electronics enterprises, providing a broad range of products. This is in sharp contrast with the three US high-tech firms which specialize in a very narrow range of products. The two Korean firms are similar to the Japanese firms.[7]

Among the nine Japanese firms, Hitachi, Toshiba and Mitsubishi Electric produce (by themselves) almost all of the products listed in Table 15.2, which we call the general electronics firms. In contrast, the four consumer electronics firms (i.e. Matsushita Electric, Sony, Sanyo Electric and Sharp) focus on consumer products, although Matsushita produces a wider range of products. The two high-tech firms (i.e. NEC and Fujitsu) concentrate on information and communication electronics, although their subsidiaries produce consumer electronics products. We can see from Table 15.1 that in comparison with the rest of the firms, these two high-tech Japanese firms have extraordinarily high shares of R&D expenditure (16% for NEC and 12% for Fujitsu). The depth and width of overlapping products among Japanese firms in Table 15.2 indicate the intense rivalry in the Japanese electronics industry. This is even more true if we consider the great number of other smaller firms in the Japanese electronics industry (which has about 35,000 establishments today).

Figure 15.1 depicts the conceptual relationships among the five groups of electronics products and related industries in Japan. Actually, in Japan today all electronics subsectors are tightly clustered, centering around the electronics devices (such as semiconductors and electronics tubes), and the boundaries between subsectors often blur and change constantly because of the incessant introduction of new products such as personal computers (PCs), cellular telephones and video games. Furthermore, the electronics industry is closely tied to a number of specific industries (listed on the right side in Figure 15.1) through a vertical (buyer/supplier) relationship. This represents a typical example of the clustering of competitive industries in a

Regions

TABLE 15.1. Basic information on the fourteen electronics firms in 1990

Home country	Name	Location of HQ	Year of es.	Sales ($b)	Rank	Percentage share in sales of:			Worldwide employment (1,000s)
						Capital investment	R&D expenditure	Exports	
Japan	Hitachi	Tokyo	1910	44.8	9	4	6	23	274.5
	Matsushita	Osaka	1918	37.9	12	6	6	32	193.1
	Toshiba	Tokyo	1875	26.9	24	6	6	29	125.0
	NEC	Tokyo	1899	21.8	32	6	16	22	104.0
	Mitsubishi E.	Tokyo	1921	18.8	42	6	7	21	85.7
	Fujitsu	Tokyo	1935	16.1	49	12	12	20	104.5
	Sony	Tokyo	1946	12.1	57	11	6	60	78.9
	Sanyo E.	Osaka	1947	9.3	107	n.a.	n.a.	32	55.5
	Sharp	Osaka	1935	8.7	121	11	7	46	32.3
Korea	Samsung E.	Seoul	1969	6.3	—	n.a.	n.a.	59	43.0
	Goldstar	Seoul	1959	3.9	344	n.a.	6	50	33.0
USA	IBM	Armonk, NY	1914	63.4	5	n.a.	9	n.a.	383.2
	Motorola	Schaumburg, Il.	1928	9.6	128	12	9	n.a.	104.0
	TI	Dallas, Tex.	1930	6.6	197	n.a.	8	n.a.	73.9

TABLE 15.2. Products of the fourteen electronics firms

Product category and main products	General electronics firms			Consumer electronics firms				High-tech firms		Korean firms		US high-tech firms		
	Hitachi	Toshiba	Mitsubishi	Matsushita	Sony	Sanyo	Sharp	NEC	Fujitsu	Samsung	Goldstar	IBM	Motorola	TI
Consumer electric appliances:														
Refrigerators	O	O	O	O		O	O			O	O			
Washing machines	O	O	O	O		O	O	△	△	O	O			
Vacuum cleaners	O	O	O	O		O	O	△	△	O	O			
Microwave ovens	O	O	O	O		O	O	△	△	O	O			
Air conditioners	O	O	O	O		O	O	△	△	O	O			
Fans	O	O		O		O	O	△		O	O			
Lamps	O	△		△		O	O			O	O			
Consumer electronic products:														
TVs	O	O	O	O	O	O	O	△	△	O	O			
VTRs	O	O	O	O	O	O	O	△	△	O	O			
Radios	O	O	O	O	O	O	O			O	O			
Tape recorders	O	O	O	O	O	O	O			O	O			
Stereos	O	O	O	O	O	O	O	△		O	O			
Electronic devices:														
Resistors	O	O	O	△						△	△			
Electric condensers	O	O	O	△						△	△			
Transformers	O	O	O	△						△	△			
Electron tubes	O	O	O	△	O		O	O	O	△	△	O	O	O
Semiconductors	O	O	O	△	O	O	O	O	O	O	△	O	O	O
Information electronics:														
Computers	O	O	O	O	O	O	O	O	O	O	△	O	O	O
Copiers	O	O	O	O			O	O	O	O				
Communication electronics:														
Telephones	O	O	O	O	O	O	O	O	O	O	△		O	
Telephone switching	O	O	O	O				O	O	O	△			
Facsimiles (FAXs)	O	O		△			O	O	O	O	△			
Transmission terminals	O	O						O	O	O	△		O	
Radio communication	O	O	O		O	O		O	O	O	△		O	
Industrial systems:														
Industrial meters	O	O	O	△							△			
Generators	O	O	O	△							△			
Motors	O	O	O	△							△			
Electric tools	△	O	O	△							△			
Breakers	O	O	O	△							△			
Industrial systems	O	O	O	△							△			
Batteries	△		O	△	△	△	O	O	O	O	△		O	O

O = produced by the firm.

△ = produced by the firm's subsidiaries or affiliated firms.

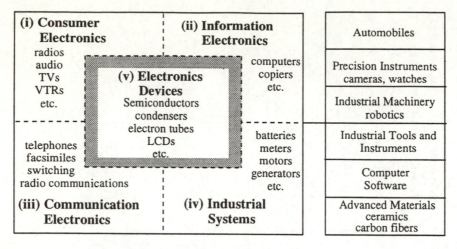

Fig. 15.1. Electronics products and related industries in Japan

country, which has been emphasized by Porter (1990) as an outcome of the systematic nature of positive feedbacks among the determinants of national competitive advantages. Since the dynamic process of the formation of this industrial clustering (centered around the electronics industry) in Japan has been described lucidly in Porter (1990: 383–421), in this paper we will concentrate on the geographical aspects of this industrial clustering in Japan and overseas.

Table 15.3 provides a grouping of the nine Japanese firms based on their product composition, the location of their HQs, and whether they were established before or after World War II. It is interesting to observe that all general electronics firms and high-tech electronics firms are based in Tokyo while, except for Sony, all consumer electronics firms are based in Osaka. (For the definition of the Osaka MA and Tokyo MA and other information of Japanese regions, refer to Figure 15.2.) This indicates that the Japanese electronics industry has two geographical centers of clustering with different origins. This is an outcome of Japanese modern history. When the Japanese capital moved from Kyoto (near Osaka) to Tokyo at the time of the Meiji Revolution in 1868, defense-related industries and then "high-tech industries" (including electric machinery, industrial systems, tele-communications and automobiles) were nurtured near Tokyo under the support of the national government, while Osaka (together with Kyoto) remained and flourished (independently of the national government) as the Japanese center of commerce and consumer-oriented light industries. The two cities have been intense rivals since then. To this "tale of two cities", we will return in Section 5.2. The position of firms in the matrix of Table 15.3

TABLE 15.3. Grouping of the nine Japanese firms

Home-base Product composition	Tokyo-based	Osaka-based
General electronics	Hitachi Toshiba Mitsubishi	
High-tech E. Information and communications	NEC Fujitsu	
Consumer electronics		Matsushita Sharp
after World War II		
	Sony	Sanyo

has important implications for their growth processes and innovation strategies.

3. LOCATION BEHAVIOR AND ORGANIZATIONAL DYNAMICS OF A REPRESENTATIVE FIRM, NEC

In this section, we describe the global location and organizational behavior of NEC which was selected as a representative high-tech firm in Japan.[8]

3.1 Evolution of the corporate organization

NEC was established in 1899 in Tokyo as the first international joint venture with Western Electric Inc. in the USA. Since then, it has grown as a leading maker of telecommunication equipment (including both radio and telephone transmissions) in close association with NTT (Nippon Telephone and Telegram). Although NEC had developed its own technologies in transistors and computers by the late 1950s (in connection with the development of advanced telecommunication equipment), it languished as a typical NTT-dependent (undistinguished) firm until the early 1960s. Its phenomenal growth as a leading high-tech Japanese firm started when Hiroji Kobayashi assumed the presidency of NEC in 1964. (According to Kanemori (1987), Kobayashi was the perfect example of a Schumpterian entrepreneur, endowed with superb creativity, charisma, far-sighted visions and strong leadership.) Based on the two innovative strategies below,

FIG. 15.2. Tokyo and Osaka MAs

Kobayashi achieved a radical transformation of NEC from an NTT-dependent firm to a global high-tech enterprise.

First, based on NEC's experiences during the 1950s, he developed a clear corporate vision that the key for the future development of the electronics industry is the integration of computers and communications through the development of semiconductors (i.e. in terms of Figure 15.1, a diagonal integration of (ii) and (iii) through (v)). Based on this famous "C & C" strategy, NEC kept investing heavily in the development of computers and semiconductors (by diverting initially the profits earned in its telecommunication sector). Furthermore, he reorganized NEC into a product division system centered around these three strategic sectors. As a consequence, by the mid-1980s, NEC became a leading world producer in each of the three sectors.

The other innovative strategy introduced by Kobayashi was prominently spatial. Like Matsushita, Kobayashi vigorously promoted the decentralization of management at NEC through a product division system. (Today, NEC has the following nine product divisions (called groups): (1) Home Electronics, (2) Semiconductors, (3) Electronic Components, (4) Switching, (5) Transmission, (6) Radio Communications, (7) Telecommunication Terminal, (8) Information (computers), (9) Industrial Systems.) Unlike Matsushita, however, the management of each product division itself is further decentralized through a regional system. That is, while each product division of NEC (proper) has only a small number of its own plants that are all located in the Tokyo MA, it has many manufacturing subsidiaries, called *local NECs*, which are systematically located to cover the non-metropolitan regions of Japan. (This regional system was later extended to overseas countries.) Each local NEC is wholly owned either by NEC (proper), NEC Home Electronics (an affiliated firm of NEC), or another local NEC. While the major corporate decision-making is conducted by NEC (proper), each local NEC is fully responsible for its manufacturing activity as an independent firm. It turns out that this decentralized regional system was quite effective in three ways: (1) in exploring and securing a relatively inexpensive and young labor force in peripheral regions; (2) in enhancing cost-consciousness and technological development of individual production units; and (3) in developing managerial capability of young managers (who are periodically rotated between NEC (proper) and local NECs). During the 1980s, a similar regional production system was created by NEC Software Inc. (an affiliated firm of NEC) for NEC's software development.

Today, the production system of NEC assumes a clear two-layer structure: 6 mother plants of NEC (proper) in the Tokyo MA engage in product development and trial production, while local NECs pursue mass-production. For example, in the Semiconductor Group today, as can be seen from Figure 15.3, the Tamagawa and Sagamihara plants engage in product development and trial production, while Yamagata, Kansai, Yamaguchi and Kyushu NECs engage in the integrated production of ICs, focusing on wafer fabrication. Furthermore, local NECs' subsidiaries (i.e. grandchild-plant for NEC (proper)) conduct assembly and testing operations of IC production. For example, Kyushu NEC has three subsidiaries, the Fukuoka, Kumamoto and Oita NECs, which conduct assembly and testing operations for Kyushu NEC. Overseas production is organized by each product group, and each product group has its foreign subsidiaries under a different name. For example, the Semiconductor Group has NEC Electronics Inc. in several foreign countries. Therefore, domestic plants and overseas plants within the same group have close ties in their production operations. For example, in the case of NEC Electronics (Singapore), 70% of IC wafers assembled there comes from Japanese plants, while one-third

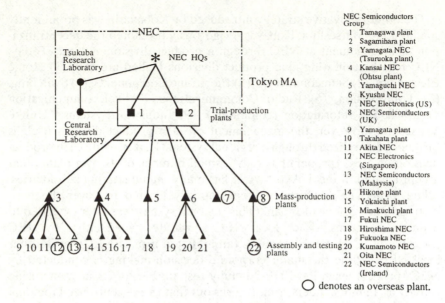

FIG. 15.3. The production system and its hierarchical structure in the semiconductor division at NEC

of them comes from US plants in the same group; 30% of assembled ICs are sent to Japan, the USA and Singapore respectively.

3.2 Business changes at NEC

As can be seen from Figure 15.4, in 1975, the share of communication equipment to the total sales was over 50%, and the export rate was 34%. At that time, the basic character of NEC was of an export-oriented communication equipment-maker. However, during the 1970s and 1980s, the firm invested heavily in semiconductors and computers. As a consequence, in 1993, the sales of information systems exceeded 50%, and the export rate has decreased to 19%. Due to the absence of industrial systems business, its growth rate over the last two decades has been extremely high. As can be seen from Figure 15.4, the total sales in 1993 were more than seven times those of 1975. Its strategy for autonomous local manufacturing subsidiaries (local NECs) has been very instrumental in sustaining this rapid growth. The number of employees in NEC (proper) has not increased despite this rapid expansion of sales. Local NECs have absorbed most necessary increases in employment, restraining the employment growth at NEC (proper). Today, NEC intends to develop a new industry which is an integration of software and hardware, promoting R&D in software. Further-

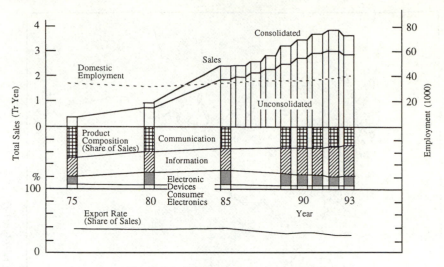

FIG. 15.4. Business changes at NEC

more, NEC plans to extend the C & C strategy to include also consumer electronics by focusing on multimedia. In terms of Figure 15.1, NEC intends to expand today's main business on the diagonal axis, (ii)–(v)–(iii), towards (i).

3.3 Location behavior and the evolution of spatial organization

The business changes at NEC described above were accompanied by a rapid expansion of its spatial activity-network globally.

(a) Up to 1975 (Figure 15.5) In 1975, NEC had its own 5 plants in the Tokyo MA, and 19 plants of local NECs. In several foreign countries, mostly in Latin America and East Asia, NEC established manufacturing subsidiaries for communication equipment production in order to adjust to local market conditions.

(b) From 1976 to 1985 (Figure 15.6) During this period, 19 plants of local NECs were established in response to the NECs' shift in product structure, while NEC plants gradually came to specialize in product development and trial-production. At the same time, 8 overseas manufacturing plants were added. One group of new overseas plants was for production of ICs, computers, facsimiles, and car phones in the USA and EC in order to avoid trade friction with these countries. The other group was for assembly and testing operations of semiconductors in East Asia by taking advantage of the low labor cost there.

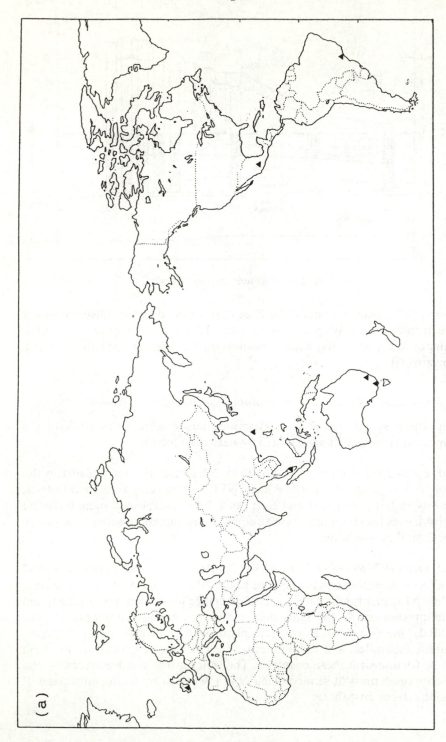

Fig. 15.5. Location of R&D facilities and plants of NEC in 1975

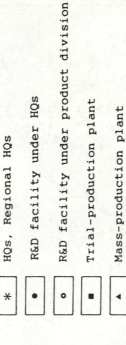

HQs, Regional HQs

R&D facility under HQs

R&D facility under product division

Trial-production plant

Mass-production plant

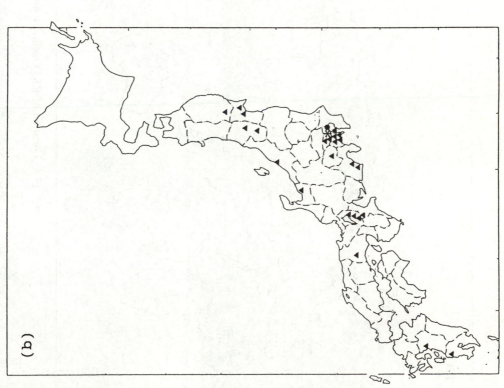

(b)

FIG. 15.5. *Continued*

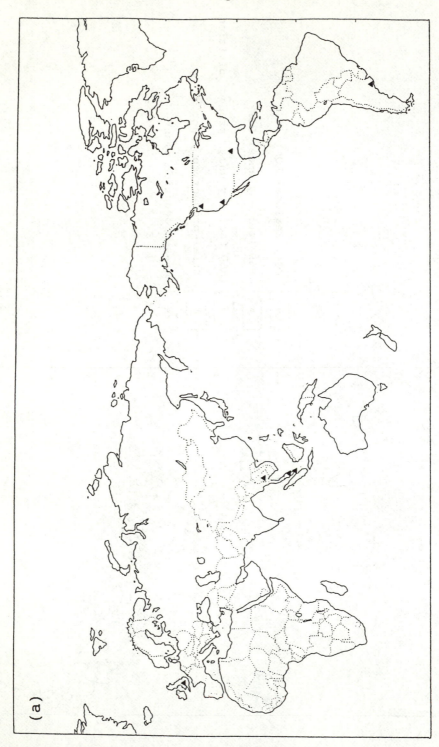

Fig. 15.6. Location of R&D facilities and plants of NEC in 1976–85

(a)

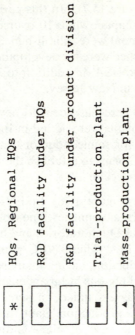

✳	HQs, Regional HQs
●	R&D facility under HQs
○	R&D facility under product division
■	Trial-production plant
◂	Mass-production plant

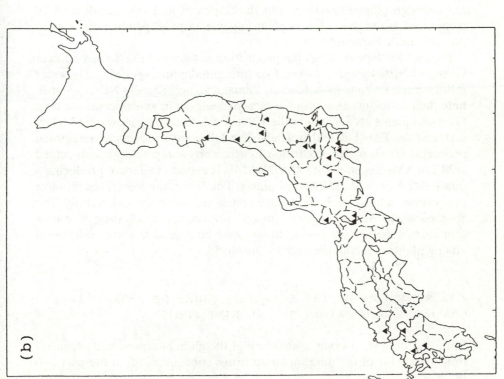

(b)

Fig. 15.6. *Continued*

(c) From 1986 to 1990 (Figure 15.7)   In this period, only 3 new domestic plants were established in Japan, while 10 overseas plants for computers and communication equipment were established. Six overseas plants established in East Asia and Mexico were for development of export bases to the USA, EC and Japan. In the USA, in addition to 3 plants, a basic research laboratory was established in New Jersey.

(d) From 1991 to 1993   There has been no new plant establishment in Japan since 1991, while 4 plants were added in Indonesia (communication equipment) and China (1 for semiconductors and 2 for communications equipment). In Japan, NEC plans to establish the Kansai Central Research Laboratory for human interface in 1995.

(e) Present position: 1994 (Figure 15.8) In 1994, NEC has 46 plants in Japan, and 29 plants in overseas countries. The world HQ of NEC is located in the Tokyo CBD. Two R&D laboratories and 6 plants of NEC (proper) are located in the Tokyo MA. These NEC plants specialize in product development and trial production, having many software engineers. Local NECs are dispersed in rural regions in Japan, engaging in mass production. As overseas production has expanded, in some overseas regions, trial-production plants and mass-production plants have been separated as in Japan. For example, in the case of NEC Industries in the USA, the Boxborough plant engages in the development and trial production of computers, while the Georgia plant engages in mass production of components and computers.

Figure 15.9 depicts the global production network in the Semiconductor Group of NEC today. In Japan, four integrated plants specialized in wafer fabrication (i.e. Yamagata, Kansai, Yamaguchi and Kyushu NECs) coordinate their subplants and subsidiaries which engage in assembly and testing. Overseas plants are located in the USA, East Asia (Singapore and Malaysia), and the EU (UK and Ireland). The US plant conducts an integrated production from wafer production to assembly, and produces high-valued 16M DRAMs together with 4M DRAMs. It exports to Japan, producing a quarter of NEC's 4M DRAM products. The UK plant specializes in wafer production, while the Irish plant engages in assembly and testing. The Singapore and Malaysia plants engage in assembly and testing of wafers sent from Japan. As a result, wafers and final products are transferred among plants and countries across the world.

4. A SYNTHESIS OF THE LOCATION BEHAVIOR AND SPATIAL ORGANIZATION OF THE NINE FIRMS

In this section, we present a summary of the global location and organizational behavior of the nine Japanese firms, concentrating on the past two decades.

As can be seen from Figure 15.10, over the 19-year period from 1975 to 1994, the number of worldwide manufacturing plants owned by the nine Japanese firms increased rapidly from 285 to 689. In particular, while the number of domestic plants increased about 70% (from 211 to 354), that of overseas plants jumped 4.5 times (from 74 to 335). As a consequence, today the nine firms have roughly the same number of plants in Japan and overseas. Their overseas plants are mostly concentrated in East Asia, North America and the EU. While the number of plants in East Asia quadrupled, those in North America and the EU increased nearly 10 times.

Figure 15.11 indicates that over the same 19-year period, the nine firms greatly expanded their R&D capacity in Japan (from 24 to 115 laboratories) and in the USA (from 1 to 18, mostly located in California State and the Northeast Coast). Several R&D laboratories were also established in the EU. The number of overseas R&D laboratories (of the nine firms) in East Asia is very small in comparison with that of their manufacturing plants there, which indicates the spatial division of labor among global regions being developed by the firms.

In the following, we describe in more detail the evolution of location behavior and spatial organization of the nine firms since the 1950s.

(a) Up to 1975 By approximately 1960, all nine firms became heavily multilocational, first by Tokyo-based (Osaka-based) firms adding their new plants in the Osaka MA (Tokyo MA) for regional-market penetration, and then by dispersing their labor intensive plants into the peripheral regions of Japan to save rising labor costs in the MAs. Up to this period, overseas markets were served mostly by exporting. By this time, most firms adopted a product-division system. Then, from about 1960 to 1975, two major changes occurred in their location behavior and business. First, their consumer electronics division started overseas assembly-production in East Asia and other developing countries to circumvent rising import restrictions there. At the same time, most firms started creating their export bases in NIEs. Their major overseas markets, the USA and EU, continued to be served mostly by exporting (from Japan or export bases in NIEs). Second, many firms started new businesses in high-tech products (e.g. semiconductors and computers), adding new product divisions. The assembly plants for these high-tech products were established in selected peripheral regions of Japan having an inexpensive young labor force and good transport access.

(b) From 1976 to 1985 Between 1975 and 1985, the nine firms established 60 new domestic plants (17 in the Tokyo and Osaka MAs and 44 in nonmetropolitan areas) and 92 overseas plants mostly in East Asia, the USA, and the EC. During the same period, they built 25 domestic R&D laboratories (21 in the Tokyo and Osaka MAs and 3 in nonmetropolitan regions) and 6 overseas laboratories. In Japan, mass-production plants

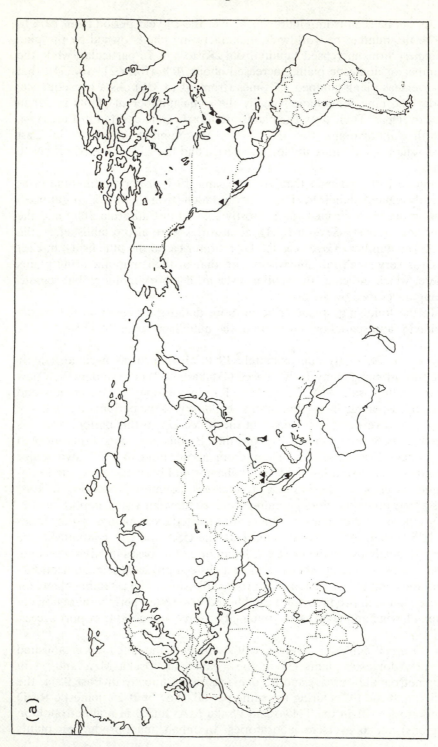

Fig. 15.7. Location of R&D facilities and plants of NEC in 1986–90

(b)

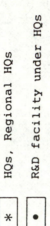

✳	HQs, Regional HQs
●	R&D facility under HQs
○	R&D facility under product division
■	Trial-production plant
◄	Mass-production plant

FIG. 15.7. *Continued*

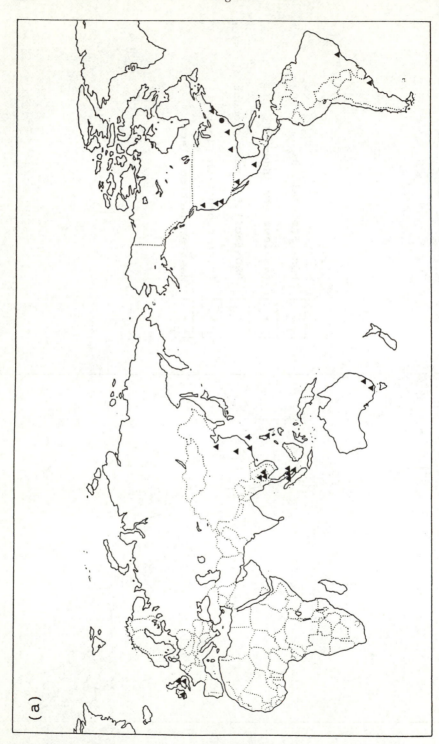

F*ig*. 15.8. Location of R&D facilities and plants of NEC in January 1994

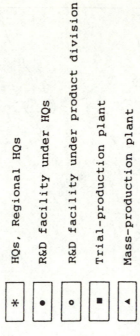

*	HQs, Regional HQs
●	R&D facility under HQs
○	R&D facility under product division
■	Trial-production plant
◄	Mass-production plant

(b)

Fig. 15.8. *Continued*

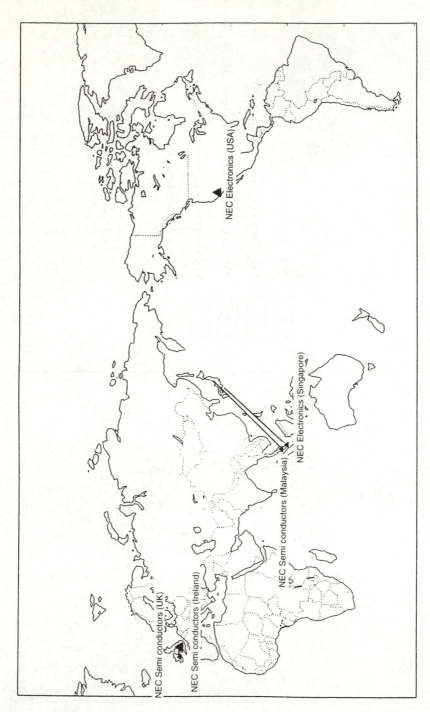

FIG. 15.9. Global production network of semiconductors at NEC

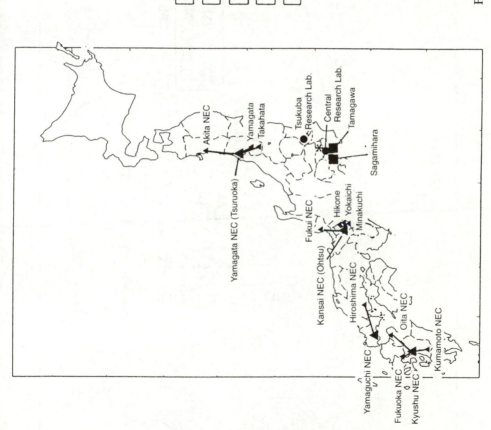

Fig. 15.9. *Continued*

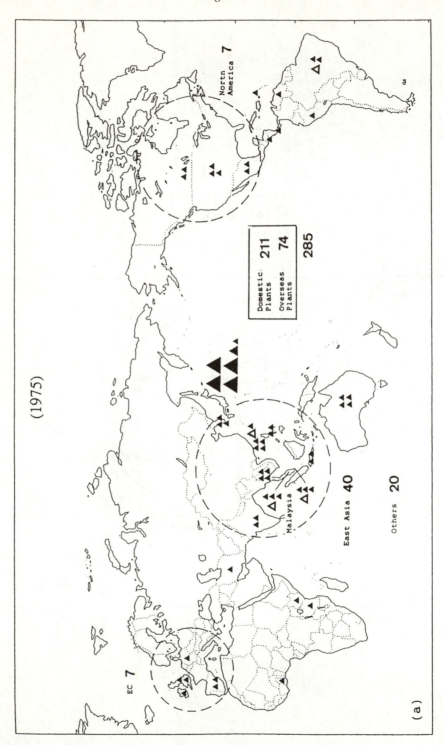

(1975)

North America 7

Domestic Plants 211
Overseas Plants 74
285

EC 7

Malaysia

East Asia 40

Others 20

(a)

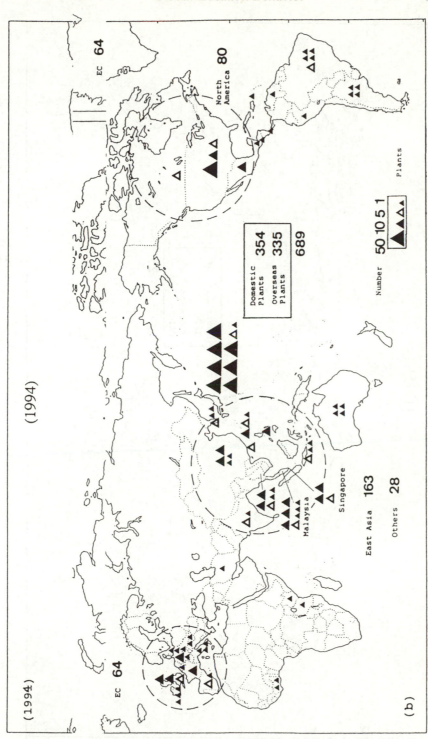

FIG. 15.10. Location of plants in 1975 and 1994 (Japanese nine firms)

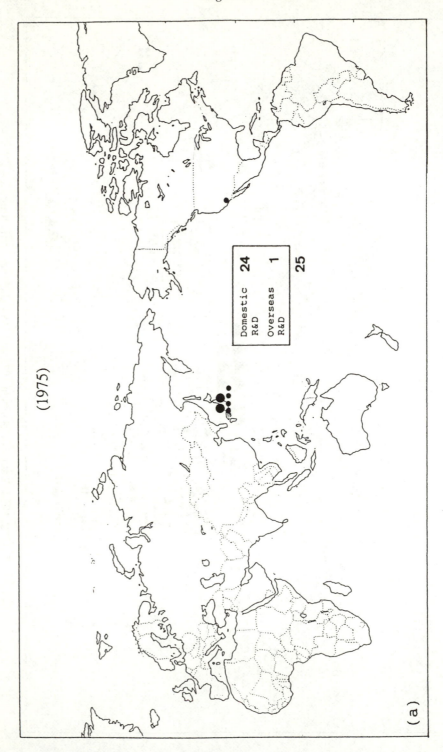

(1975)

Domestic R&D   24
Overseas R&D   1
                25

(a)

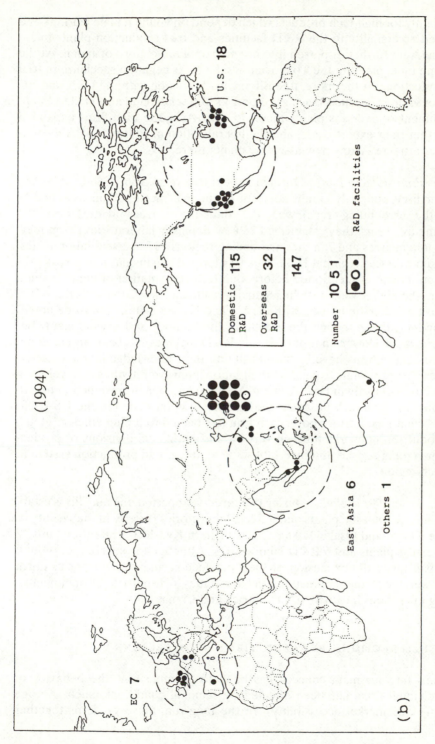

(1994)

Domestic 115
R&D

Overseas 32
R&D

147

Number 10 5 1

R&D facilities

U.S. 18

East Asia 6

Others 1

EC 7

(b)

FIG. 15.11. Location of R&D facilities in 1975 and 1994 (Japanese nine firms) (mainly for high-tech products which depend on young female workers and need accessibility to the R&D facilities and trial-production plants in Japan) were further dispersed into nonmetropolitan regions of Japan. At the same time, plants in the Tokyo and Osaka MAs began to specialize in trial production. Furthermore, intensifying trade friction with the USA and EC over various products (such as color-TVs and semiconductors) led to establishment of overseas plants there. In East Asia, the nine firms expanded further their export bases, and the liberalization of FDI in ASEAN countries attracted many new assembly plants there.

(c) From 1986 to 1990   During the next five years from 1986 to 1990, the nine firms built only 21 new domestic plants (6 in metropolitan areas and 15 in the surrounding areas), while they built 125 overseas plants. During the same five years, they established 28 new domestic laboratories (21 in metropolitan areas and 7 in the surrounding regions), 17 overseas laboratories, and 5 overseas regional HQs. This accelerated expansion of overseas production was, as mentioned before, due to a combination of higher valued yen, the higher wage rate in Japan, intensified competition with the NIEs, and further trade friction with the US and EC countries. It must be noted, however, that although the growth in the number of domestic plants became much slower, that of domestic R&D facilities has been accelerating. Thus, these firms have been intensifying their knowledge-intensive activities in Japan, while expanding their labor-intensive activities in developing countries (mostly in East Asia and Mexico) and specific production operations (for high-tech products and/or trade-friction items) in the USA and EC countries. Furthermore, each firm has been developing efficient global production networks through vertical and horizontal divisions of production among regions and by establishing an integrated production system in each region.

(d) From 1991 to 1993   During this three-year period, the nine firms established 13 domestic plants and 9 R&D laboratories (mostly in the vicinity of the Tokyo and Osaka MAs and in northern Kyushu), while they built 42 overseas plants and 6 R&D laboratories. Although the severe recession in Japan made the expansion of their production and R&D capacity much slower, the further appreciating yen continues to disperse their manufacturing operations into ASEAN countries and China.

5. INTERACTIONS BETWEEN FIRMS AND REGIONS

Thus far, our main concern has been to examine how the behavior of individual firms has been affected by regional conditions (such as wage rates and market accessibility). In the long run, however, firms together change regional conditions through positive feedback, which in turn will affect the behavior (and competitiveness) of each firm. In this section, we examine such interactions between firms and regions by taking two examples. The first example explores the interactions between the nine firms (together with millions of other Japanese firms) and the regional system of Japan. The second example studies the interactions between these Japanese electronics firms and a foreign city, Tijuana, Mexico.[9]

5.1 The Japanese regional system and the spatial organization of firms

As mentioned before, each of the nine firms has already developed a very advanced global network for its integrated operation of management, production, R&D, procurement, distribution, and sales worldwide. Figure 15.12 depicts the typical spatial organization of these firms. In fact, this corporate spatial organization structure is closely related to the Japanese urban/regional system. Figure 15.13 summarizes the locational tendencies of organizational units of the nine firms in 1994. As can be seen from the figure, each unit has a different locational tendency. (In these figures, MAs mean the Tokyo and Osaka MAs, while Non-MAs represent the rest of Japan.)

As shown in the top box in Figure 15.13, all HQs are located in the two primary MAs in Japan (i.e. 6 in the Tokyo MA and 3 in the Osaka MA), and are mostly in the CBDs. The figure also indicates that all their basic R&D

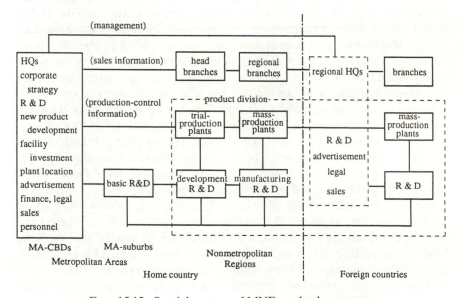

FIG. 15.12. Spatial system of MNFs and urban system

laboratories (R&D controlled by HQs) are located in the two MAs, where 95% of them are in their suburbs. Furthermore, 65% of development R&D laboratories are located in the suburbs of the two MAs and 30% of them in nonmetropolitan areas (mostly together with mother plants). The middle two boxes in Figure 15.13 indicate that trial-production plants, which are closely related to their HQs and R&D laboratories in terms of information exchange, are mostly located in the two MAs (24% of them in the CBDs and 67% in their suburbs). In contrast, domestic mass-production plants are much more dispersed: 40% of them are located in the suburbs of the two MAs, while 57% in nonmetropolitan areas of Japan. Next, as indicated in the bottom three boxes of Figure 15.13, overseas regional HQs are located either in North America (7 in the USA), the EU (3 in the UK and 1 in Germany), or East Asia (2 in Singapore). Fifty-six per cent of overseas R&D laboratories are located in the USA, while 22% of them are in the EU, and 12% in East Asia. Finally, overseas production plants are dispersed throughout the world: specifically, in North America (24%), the EU (19%), NIEs (16%), ASEAN together with China and India (33%), and the rest of the world (8%).

From Figure 15.13, we can conclude that the knowledge-intensive activities (such as HQs, R&D laboratories and trial-production plants) of the nine Japanese electronics firms are mostly concentrated in the Tokyo and Osaka MAs, while their mass-production plants are dispersed throughout Japan and overseas countries. In fact, this phenomenon is common for almost all MNFs based in Japan (regardless of their industrial types). It is interesting to note that this dual spatial trend (i.e. the increasing agglomeration of knowledge-intensive activities into the primary cities and the global dispersion of mass-production plants) emerged from the dual nature of recent developments in communications technologies and transportation networks. That is, the recent development of computer integrated manufacturing (CIM) methods enables the complex production technologies to be embodied in capital, and thus reduces the skill-requirements of workers in standard production operations. In addition, the development of telecommunication technologies is vastly improving the speed, reliability and capacity of communications; furthermore, the costs of such communications are less sensitive to distance. Therefore, by effectively combining CIM methods and modern telecommunication technologies, large firms (which have a sufficient capital and accumulation of know-how together with R&D capability) can rather freely choose the location of their mass-production plants. Thus, the location of mass-production plants follows basic local (non-agglomeration) factors such as availability of disciplined workers, basic infrastructure, low wage rates and low land prices. Therefore, new mass-production plants do not follow the urban hierarchy, but tend to disperse themselves to nonmetropolitan areas in Japan and even overseas. On the other hand, in general, the technological and managerial knowl-

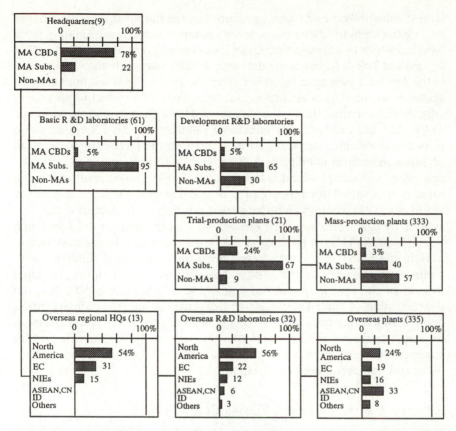

FIG. 15.13. Location tendencies of organizational units of the Japanese nine electronics firms (1994)

edge/information has the characteristic of *local public goods* which can be shared/exchanged among agents, most effectively through face-to-face communications. Therefore, these knowledge-intensive or information-oriented activities favor close clustering in the primary cities due partly to the convenience of face-to-face communications and more generally to enjoy the agglomeration economies which are generated by accumulated as well as newly created knowledge and information there.

In particular, the fact that the leading activities of the Japanese economies have recently been changing from material-production to information-oriented or knowledge-intensive activities has been bringing about a major transformation of the traditional *Tokyo–Osaka bipolar Japanese regional system* to a new system dominated by Tokyo, i.e. the *Tokyo-monopolar system*. That is, in the beginning of the rapid growth of the Japanese economy in the mid-1950s, Osaka (mainly based on light industries) was the largest industrial core of Japan (measured by the output share). Even in the late 1960s (when the Japanese economy completed its transformation from light industries to heavy industries), Osaka (dominating the western half of Japan) and Tokyo (dominating the eastern half) had nearly the same weight in the Japanese economy. However, from the mid-1970s when the Japanese economy initiated its other major shift from material-production to knowledge-based activities, the Osaka MA started losing its population, while the Tokyo MA has been steadily increasing population. This is because these information-oriented activities strongly favored the largest agglomeration of Japanese central management functions (both economic and political) and other knowledge-based activities in the Tokyo MA, resulting in the formation of the Tokyo-monopolar regional system. Today, as a major world city, Tokyo enjoys an unparalleled position in the Japanese regional system, by agglomerating, for example, 88% of the foreign firms in Japan and 65% of the HQs of the largest 2,000 firms in Japan. In contrast, beginning in the mid-1970s, Osaka-based firms have been at a relative disadvantage (in comparison with Tokyo-based firms). Furthermore, the dual aspects of the recent spatial reorganization of Japanese MNFs (i.e. the concentration of their knowledge-based activities into the primary cities, and the establishment of most of their new mass-production plants overseas by skipping the peripheral regions of Japan) partly explains the recent renewed trend in the increasing income differential between the core regions and peripheral regions of Japan.

5.2 Growth of the TV-capital, Tijuana City, Mexico

Figure 15.14 describes how dramatically the US import market of color-TVs changed over a two-year period from 1986 to 1988. We can see that Japan as the top exporter of TVs to the USA in the beginning of 1986 changed to a bottom exporter (among major exporters) in less than two years, while over the same two-year period, Mexico changed from a nearly bottom exporter to the top exporter. Furthermore, at the end of 1986, TV exports from Korea and Taiwan started decreasing sharply, and the exports from Malaysia also soon started declining. As explained below, this drastic change in the US import market of color-TVs coincided with the sudden emergence of Tijuana City (located in the northeast corner of Mexico, just across the border from San Diego in the USA) as the 'TV-capital' of North America.

Recall from Section 2 that to overcome the import restriction of TVs by the USA, nine Japanese electronics firms (all nine firms in our study except for Fujitsu plus JVC) established their TV-assembly plants in the USA during the 1970s. Given the high wage rates and extremely competitive environment of the TV market in the USA, these Japanese transnationals drastically rationalized their assembly operations through automation,

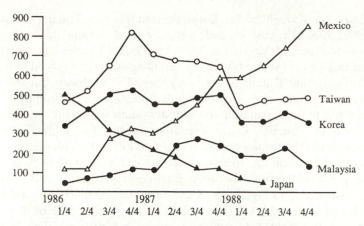

FIG. 15.14. US imports of color-TVs (units: 1,000 sets)
Source: Hattori 1990, p. 11.

which resulted in significant cost saving and quality enhancement. In contrast, US TV producers such as Zenith moved their assembly operations (to save costs) to the *maquiladora* (free trade zone) in northern Mexico, and applied manual assembly utilizing cheap labor (while avoiding costly automation). Then, given continuous improvement of productivity and quality of TV production by Japanese multinationals through further process and product innovations, most US TV producers soon lost competitiveness to Japanese producers and left the market (except for Zenith).[10]

In the early 1980s, while competition in the US TV market became more intensified because of challenges from Korea with low-priced products, some labor-intensive parts of the Japanese production line in the USA were transferred to Mexico. Matsushita started a small chassis subassembly operation in Tijuana. Sony began subcontracting production of deflection yokes there. By 1987, Mexico was more deeply integrated into Japanese TV firms' North American operation. Matsushita added final assembly to its Tijuana plant. Sony established an assembly plant in Tijuana using CRTs produced in San Diego. Sanyo also started new subassembly and some final operations in Tijuana. Hitachi established a new plant in Tijuana to produce cabinets and large televisions. Korean manufacturers such as Goldstar and Samsung soon followed suit (due to appreciating won and the increasing wage rate in Korea). As a consequence, as indicated in Figure 15.14, exports to the USA from Japan, Korea and Taiwan (by Japanese producers there) rapidly declined in a short time.

Most of these Japanese and Korean firms (i.e. Matsushita, Sony, Sanyo, Hitachi and Samsung) chose Tijuana for their TV-assembly plants in Mexico partly because it has excellent accessibility to the US market as well as because it is the most convenient location to import TV-components from East Asia through the San Diego port. In this way, Tijuana became the TV-capital of North America over a short period of time, producing most TVs exported from Mexico to the USA. Figure 15.15 depicts the electronics complex in Tijuana (and in bordering San Diego) today. It should be noted from the figure that Tijuana has not only these TV producers but also many consumer-electronics makers (other than TVs) such as Canon and Casio. Furthermore, many Japanese parts suppliers such as Mutsuki and Kyocera are located in Tijuana, which is another reason for agglomeration of many consumer-electronics producers there. Therefore, Tijuana represents a typical example of the formation of a local industrial agglomeration through positive feedback between final-good producers and part suppliers.[11] Notice also in Figure 15.15 that many plants in Tijuana are linked with sister plants on the US side. This is an interesting case of division of labor across the border, in which the *maquiladoras* specialize in labor-intensive products and US plants focus on high value-added products and/ or knowledge-intensive activities. This agglomeration of Japanese and Korean electronics producers has been providing much of the leverage behind the development of industrial parks in Tijuana, employing now more than 15 per cent of all *maquiladora* workers in Tijuana (the population of which is about 1.5 million today).[12]

6. CONCLUSION: "IN YOUR STRENGTH LIES YOUR WEAKNESS"[13]

During the rapid growth period of the Japanese economy (1955–70), the powerful steel industry used to boast that "iron is the state." After the first oil shock in 1973, however, the steel industry changed suddenly to a declining industry in Japan. In turn, the phenomenal growth of the electronics industry began at the same time. Indeed, during the past two decades, electronics *was* the state. In this paper, we have reviewed the growth of the Japanese electronics industry since World War II, focusing on global location and organizational behavior of the nine largest firms.

Although the astonishing growth of the Japanese electronics industry seemed unstoppable several years ago, its growth suddenly halted with the collapse of the Japanese "bubble" economy (like the steel industry after the first oil shock). It seems that now the Japanese electronics industry is facing not just a temporary recession but a major crisis caused by deep structural and cultural problems which have simultaneously affected many industries in Japan. The basic causes of such problems seem to be well summarized in the quotation above from T. J. Rodgers. In particular, these problems have arisen mostly from the lock-in effects of the past success of both the industry and the Japanese economy as a whole.[14] In general, these effects tend to provide powerful advantages at the beginning, but eventually become strong obstacles to change. In the following, we discuss some of the most

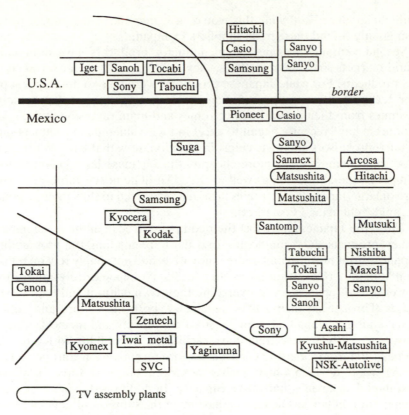

FIG. 15.15. Tijuana complex of consumer electronics

fundamental problems faced by both the electronics industry and the Japanese economy.

First, the now famous Japanese lifetime employment system (which was actually created during the past four decades of steady economic growth) has haunted Japanese firms. The system works well only when firms grow steadily at a substantial speed. In spite of the recent slow growth of the Japanese economy, however, no large firm dares to break this cherished social norm. As a result, Japanese firms are greatly constrained in their ability to restructure themselves by cutting unnecessary work force. This is one of the major reasons why Japanese electronics firms have recently lost some competitiveness relative to US electronics firms, that have drastically downsized their work force. As a way to solve this problem, some Japanese firms are now considering a revision of their global production system. That is, instead of conducting assembly operations abroad by using components (or parts) produced in Japan, they propose to assemble components in their home plants by importing components produced in their overseas plants with cheap labor. But while this would save manufacturing jobs, it would also greatly offend these parts suppliers in Japan.

Second, although Japanese semiconductor producers have dominated world markets since the mid-1980s, they have recently been overtaken by US producers. For while Japanese producers were able to develop a superior technology for mass-producing memory chips (supported by huge revenues from their consumer electronics and mainframe computers), US producers have recently begun to excel in high-value-added products such as microprocessors and logic chips. In addition, now that Korean firms are producing memory chips more cheaply, the Japanese have begun to lose competitiveness to Korea as well as the USA. The heavy corporate structure of large Japanese electronics firms has also acted to slow their response to rapidly changing PC markets.

Third, the Japanese have lost their competitive edge in the development of new products and technologies. In order to regain long-run profitability, Japanese firms must become more innovative, and not simply rely on refinements of imported technologies and ideas. To become truly innovative, however, the Japanese must overcome their own cultural and educational biases. Throughout their 2000-year history, both the culture and educational system of Japan have emphasized conformity and memorization of knowledge. While these traits have facilitated their ability to learn from abroad (first from India and China, and more recently from Europe and the USA) and to develop a high-quality, homogeneous work force, they have also impeded Japan's innovative capacity. In addition, Japan's restrictive immigration policy has acted as a barrier to the infusion of new ideas and knowledge.

Finally, Japan's political system has failed to keep pace with its rapid economic growth. While the perspective of Japanese firms has become truly global in nature, their political perspective has remained parochial. Indeed the politics of Japan may be their most serious problem today. Here the Japanese would do well to heed the lesson of the Hellenic civilization (Toynbee 1946: 275), where the failure of political reform to keep pace with economic growth led ultimately to its decline.

Can Japan rise to meet these new challenges? Only time will tell.

NOTES

1. Our original study summarized in Ishii (1992) includes not only these nine Japanese firms but also the two largest Korean electronics firms (Samsung Electronics and Goldstar) and three US high-tech firms (IBM, Motorola and

Texas Instruments). This paper is largely complementary to the seminal work of Chandler (1990) which examined the rise of managerial industrial enterprises in the USA, UK and Germany from the 1880s to 1940s that were permitted by the development of new transportation and communication technologies, i.e. the railway and telegraph systems. In contrast, this paper focuses on the growth of Japanese electronics enterprises since the early 1950s that were supported by the development of air transportation and telecommunication technologies. It is interesting to observe that the recent globalization of electronics firms has become technologically feasible by the usage of the modern telecommunication technologies that were developed by themselves.

2. The OLI model assumes that for a (parent) firm based in a home country to engage in offshore production (through foreign direct investment) in a host country, three conditions are necessary. First, the firm must have firm-specific *ownership advantages (O)* such as proprietary technology and management skills that allow it to compete successfully with other companies. This is a precondition for the existence of any firm. Second, the host country must have *location advantages (L)* such as low factor prices and transport/tariff barriers to imports that lead the firm to produce in that country rather than serve it by exports from the home country (or from an export base in a third country). Third, there must be *internalization advantages (I)* that lead the firm to buy or create a foreign subsidiary rather than engage in non-equity arrangements such as license or franchise production.

3. For further discussion of this point, see Markusen (1991). See also Chandler (1990) for the roles of scale and scope economies in the growth of modern industrial enterprises.

4. Here, *potential local advantages* include not only those local advantages easily accessible for any firms (e.g. existence of good infrastructure) but also, and more importantly, those advantages that can be fully exploited only by those firms having sufficient knowledge-based assets. For example, many developing countries have well-motivated and easily trainable workers, but indigenous entrepreneurs cannot fully utilize them because they are lacking in those knowledge-based assets that make MNFs internationally competitive.

5. For example, in 1990, among all Japanese manufacturing industries, the electronics industry had the highest share (43%) in FDI (vs. 15% by auto) and also the highest share (25%) in the number of foreign subsidiaries (vs. 12% by auto).

6. Data are from the Fortune World Ranking and corporate annual reports. Sales and employment include those of the subsidiaries of which the parent firm holds more than 50% of the shares. Since the original figures for Samsung were those for the whole Samsung Group, we present here the figure of Samsung Electronics.

7. In the framework of the "chain-link" model of R&D processes developed by Kline and Rosenberg (1986), Aoki (1988) provides an explanation for this difference in the product range between Japanese firms and US firms.

8. For similar descriptions of the rest of the 14 firms listed in Table 15.1, see Ishii (1992).

9. Given the space constraint, our illustrations here are brief. For a further discussion of the topic in Section 5.1, see Fujita and Tabuchi (1995); and for that in Section 5.2, see Fujita *et al.* (1994).

10. For the analysis of the US–Japanese competition in the TV industry, see, for example, Porter (1983, 1990) and Koido (1991).
11. For modeling industrial agglomeration through positive feedback, see, for example, Krugman (1991).
12. For this point, see Koido (1991).
13. T. J. Rodgers, CEO of Cypress Semiconductor, *Electronic Business Buyer*, April 1994, p. 53.
14. Krugman (1994) calls lock-in effects "QWERTY" which represents the rather arbitrary ordering of the keyboard of the first typewriters.

REFERENCES

Aoki, M. (1988), *Information, Incentives, and Bargaining in the Japanese Economy* (Cambridge: Cambridge University Press).
Arthur, W. B. (1994), *Increasing Returns and Path Dependence in the Economy* (Ann Arbor, Mich.: University of Michigan Press).
Chandler, A. D., Jr. (1990), *Scale and Scope* (Boston: Harvard University Press).
Dunning, J. H. (1981), *International Production and the Multinational Enterprise* (London: Allen and Unwin).
——(1988), *Explaining International Production* (London: Unwin Hyman).
Fujita, M. and Tabuchi, T. (1995), "Regional Growth of Postwar Japan," *Regional Science and Urban Economics* (forthcoming).
—— Abdel-Musik, G., Hamaguchi, N., Kim, H. Y. and Pelletiere, D. (1994), "North American Regional Integration and Multinational Firms," pt. 2 in K. Ohno and Y. Okamotot (eds.), *Regional Integration and Foreign Direct Investment: Implications for Developing Countries* (Tokyo: Institute of Developing Economies).
Hattori, T. (1990), "Technological Development in Hardwares and Softwares," *Gekkan Asia* (June).
Ishii, R. (1992), "Location Behavior and Spatial Organization of Multinational Firms and their Impact on Regional Transformation in East Asia: A Comparative Study of Japanese, Korean, and U.S. Electronic Firms", Ph.D. diss., University of Pennsylvania.
Kanemori, H. (1987), *Innovation and Industrial Structure*, Nihon Keizai Sinbun (in Japanese) Tokyo.
Kline, S. and Rosenberg, N. (1986), "An Overview of Innovation," in R. Landau and N. Rosenberg (eds.), *The Positive Sum Strategy* (Washington, DC: National Academic Press).
Koido, A. (1991), "The Color Television Industry: Japanese–U.S. Competition and Mexico's Maquiladoras," ch. 3 in G. Szeleky (ed.), *Manufacturing Across Borders and Oceans* (San Diego: Center for US–Mexican Studies, University of California).
Krugman, P. (1991), "Increasing Returns and Economic Geography," *Journal of Political Economy*, 99: 483–99.

——(1994), *Peddling Prosperity* (New York: W. W. Norton).

Markusen, J. (1991), "The Theory of the Multinational Enterprise: A Common Analytical Framework," in D. Ramstetter (ed.), *Direct Foreign Investment in Asia's Developing Economies and Structural Changes in the Asia-Pacific Region* (Boulder, Colo.: Westview Press).

Porter, M. E. (1983), *Cases in Competitive Strategy* (New York: Free Press).

——(1990), *The Competitive Advantage of Nations* (New York: Free Press).

Schumpeter, J. A. (1934), *The Theory of Economic Development* (London: Transaction).

——(1942), *Capitalism, Socialism, and Democracy* (New York: Harper & Brothers).

Toynbee, A. J. (1946), *A Study of History,* abr. of vols. i–vi by D. C. Somervell (Oxford: Oxford University Press).

16

*The Geographic Foundations of Industrial Performance**

ALLEN J. SCOTT

1. ECONOMIC GEOGRAPHY AND INDUSTRIAL PERFORMANCE

The logic and dynamics of industrial performance (or, in more specific terms, growth and productivity) have long constituted one of the central questions of economic theory. Numerous studies of this question have been carried out, dealing not only with industrial performance in the sense just given, but also with important adjunct issues such as innovation, adaptability, competitive advantage, employment effects, and so forth. These studies have looked exhaustively at the role that variables like technological research, capital investment, corporate organization, labor skills, macro-economic policy and many others, play in the determination of industrial performance, and a body of important insights has been accumulated in this manner. However, with the exception of recent work by economic geographers and a handful of economists and sociologists, the problem as to whether or not industrial performance might also somehow be grounded in geography has been largely overlooked. This problem, as it turns out, is of some significance, and the present paper represents an effort to explore its logic and limits and to offer a modest reassessment of its general import.

With this goal in mind, I seek to build a view of modern capitalism as being endemically subject to geographic expression in the form of an inter-connected system of discrete regional production complexes. I argue that this tendency is strongly developed precisely because it results in many positive performance (growth, productivity, etc.) outcomes. Accordingly, I attempt to demonstrate how regional economic systems develop on the basis of endogenously generated increasing returns effects and agglomeration economies, and how the momentum of regional growth over time tends to reinforce these localized benefits to producers. I then show how the theoretical problem of regional development and industrial performance is concretely expressed and reexpressed in different episodes of historical geography. I go on to describe present-day aspects of regional development in some detail, and I characterize these as reflecting a state of affairs in which the massive globalization of economic activity actually reinforces

* I am grateful to Professor Bennett Harrison for constructive criticism of an earlier draft of this paper.

industrial agglomeration and local economic specialization. I round out the discussion with some comments on the possibilities of enhancing regional economic performance through collective action and public policy.

2. THE SPACE-ECONOMY OF REGIONS

2.1 Industrial organization and economic space

There is a long tradition in economic analysis, ranging from von Böhm-Bawerck (1891) through Young (1928) and Leontief (1941) to Perroux (1961) and Isard (1960), in which the structure of production is described in terms of a social division of labor held functionally together by roundabout networks of input–output linkages. One of the conditions of existence for any structure of this kind is that it function as a repository of external economies in that individual producers must always be able to obtain at least some of their needed materials or equipment more cheaply by purchasing them from other producers in the (socially divided) system of production than they can by manufacturing them themselves.

Any such system can in the first instance be thought of as existing in a purely *economic space* defined as a matrix of transactional interrelationships between firms or sectors (Perroux 1961). For the present, all reference to *geographic space*, in the sense of an ensemble of definite locations and places, is held in abeyance. Economic space itself can assume many different forms, though two archetypes are of great relevance in the present context. One of these is represented by pyramidlike industrial complexes where large lead plants sit at the top of transactional hierarchies of smaller direct and indirect input suppliers. This organizational form, of course, typifies the car industry or the aerospace industry. The other involves finely grained transactional networks linking together many small producers without any strongly evident growth-pole effects, as exemplified by industries such as clothing, jewelry or furniture. No matter what their specific form, however, industrial systems in economic space are sites of intense exchange, not just of simple physical inputs and outputs, but also business information, know-how, technological expertise, and so on. This exchange occurs in both traded form (mediated by relations of sale and purchase) and untraded form (where producers obtain useful inputs in the guise of non-commercial transactions), and it occurs in sundry institutional environments ranging from simple spot markets to tightly knit collaborative organizations (such as Japanese *keiretsu*). Analysts like Patchell (1993), Russo (1985) and von Hippel (1988) have argued that economic spaces characterized by intense transactional exchange are often important loci of learning effects and of informal but active innovation. These spaces are also apt to function as the physical foundations of specialized cultures and conventions that partially evolve in response to the peculiar tasks and problems that interrelated groups of producers face at every turn (Salais and Storper, 1993). Thus, such specific sectoral settings as the clothing industry, the motion-picture industry, the semiconductor-*cum*-computer industry, or the financial-services industry constitute the material milieux for identifiable business-culture complexes. We might say that the idea of *industrial atmosphere* (i.e. a set of sociocultural norms and practices revolving around the production system) as proposed originally by Marshall (1920), relates in the first instance to an underlying, placeless structure of production, and only in the second instance to a place-specific economic geography. Even in a placeless world—if such a thing were possible—differentiated cultural expressions of particular articulations of economic activity are perfectly imaginable, though they would now presumably have only a sectoral as opposed to a spatial expression.

That said, the fact that a place-specific economic geography is a persistent—if not dominating—feature of the world we live in now calls urgently for attention.

2.2 From external economies to locational agglomeration

The classical theory of regional economic development and specialization was based on the proposition that natural endowments differ from place to place, and that interregional trade would then encourage producers to concentrate on their (given) absolute and comparative advantages. This theory is still a serviceable item in the toolkit of the economic geographer and the regional economist, though as is now widely recognized it also suffers from fatal weaknesses, and it never came fully to grips with the real complexities of development and trade in capitalism, even in the nineteenth century when natural endowments unquestionably shaped the pattern of world economic geography more forcefully than they do today. This theoretical deficiency in part derives from the observation that production and exchange are shot through with increasing returns effects that undermine the conventional approach to this issue, as the new trade and growth theorists such as Krugman (1990, 1991) and Romer (1986) have argued. More importantly for present purposes, it also derives from the circumstance that regional development is—and to an ever increasing degree—based on competitive advantages that are socially and politically created, and not simply given by nature (Scott 1988*b*, 1993). In contradistinction to the conventional approach, I propose to show that we can only start fully to decipher the locational logic of the industrial landscape when we approach it in terms of its origins as a pure social construct, and more specifically as a question about external economies and locational agglomeration. The argument is made in two stages. In a first stage, I deal largely with static spatial issues; and in a second stage, I broach a series of more complex dynamic and historical considerations.

We may begin with the rather simple notion that since the core elements of capitalist industrial systems are invariably organized as networks of producers bound together in dense crisscrossing relationships, there will always be a tendency for at least some of the individual producers tied together in this manner to converge locationally towards a common geographic center of gravity (Scott 1988*a*, 1988*b*). Another way of expressing the same idea is to say that in the absence of magic carpets (i.e. cost-free, instantaneous transportation and communication over any distance), transacting is often more efficiently and effectively accomplished where mutual proximity is assured—even in today's world where electronic communications technologies have become so pervasive a part of the business environment. In the present instance, I do not intend the notion of transacting to be restricted only to the case of commercial linkages, but equally importantly, to all of those additional kinds of social and cultural interaction that underpin business communities and whose operation is often much enhanced when they are resolved as place-specific phenomena. At the outset, then, industrial agglomeration gives rise to three primary kinds of benefits, namely:

(a) reductions in the costs of interindustrial exchange;
(b) an acceleration of the rate at which circulating capital and information flow through the industrial system; and
(c) reinforcement of transactionally based modes of social solidarity that in many subtle ways help to underpin the functioning of industrial complexes (e.g. by intensifying Marshallian atmosphere or by promoting cooperative relationships between producers).

Accordingly, there is in many industrial sectors an important analytical and empirical relation between nonspatial external economies on the one hand, and geographically determinate agglomeration effects on the other. The former, as we have seen, reside in the organizational/transactional characteristics of production systems in general. The latter come into existence because producers, in their efforts to avail themselves of external economies, frequently engage in locational strategies that lead to spatial clustering. At the same time, the tendency to agglomeration is yet further magnified by a variety of other forces and beneficial emergent effects. Thus, locational agglomeration with its attendant reduction of transactions costs makes it possible for a widening of the social division of labor to occur (i.e. vertical disintegration), leading to yet more pronounced external economies. In addition, multifaceted local labor markets, with workers' skills and habits attuned to agglomeration-specific needs take shape. Job search and recruitment become more efficient than would be the case if producers were located at widely dispersed locations. Educational and training progams responsive to local needs can be provided at relatively low unit cost, and these help to upgrade the quality of the labor force. Equally, where geographic concentration prevails, and thus where the bases of local social solidarity are strengthened, distinctive business cultures and industrial communities are prone to emerge. Hence, agglomeration frequently facilitates (though it does not inevitably result in) the social construction of localized politico-cultural assets such as mutual trust, tacit understandings, learning effects, specialized vocabularies, transactions-specific forms of knowledge, and performance-boosting governance structures as in the case of the Japanese *kanban* system (Harrison 1994). Lastly, the concentrated assemblage of numerous production activities and workers' residences in one place means that significant economies of scale can be achieved in the local provision of essential infrastructural artifacts and services.

Even in this simple static world, however, the pressures to locational convergence are not limitless. In principle and practice, there are always counterforces that threaten the increasing returns effects alluded to above and that impose heavy costs on producers. Such counterforces are associated, for example, with congestion, pollution or high land prices, and at certain levels of agglomeration they may seriously disrupt the functioning of the industrial system. Nor are the pressures to locational convergence constant over all industries. They will be very intense in those cases where interindustrial linkages tend to be small in scale, unstable, and unpredictable (hence subject to high unit costs), where speed and face-to-face mediation of linkages are critical to competitive advantage, and where the successful operation of the production system is especially dependent on Marshallian atmosphere and transactions-intensive forms of interindustrial cooperation; and a converse tendency to the deterritorialization of industrial complexes may prevail where the opposite kinds of characteristics are dominant (for producers will now be relatively free to search for locational advantages other than those that come from agglomeration). Even when industrial agglomerations do condense out on the economic landscape, they are not hermetically sealed off from the outside world, for we will almost always find many of the producers that they harbor engaged in extraregional trading activities. Indeed, the ability of these producers to compete on wider national and international markets is often possible only because they draw major benefits from their participation in a strong and multifaceted regional economic system (Porter 1990; Storper 1992).

In these ways, the logic of the production system and its social appendages, irrespective of the distribution of natural endowments, will tend to give rise to locational agglomeration and regional specialization. Notwithstanding the exceedingly schematic outlines of the discussion so far, it adduces the main synchronic elements, as it were, of the theory of regional development. But industrial regions are also subject to peculiar diachronic tendencies that greatly modify the operation of these synchronic elements and that further transform the outlines of the economic landscape. The next section provides a brief exposition of these issues.

3. THE DYNAMICS OF REGIONAL DEVELOPMENT

The first and most obvious point to be made with regard to regional dynamics is that the heavy fixed costs of agglomerated industrial development are reflected in the pervasive inertia of the economic landscape over time. The second is that regional clusters of industrial activity, as we have seen, are invariably the source of increasing returns to scale and scope (Verdoorn effects), so that their competitive advantages tend to intensify over time (cf. Kaldor 1970). As Romer (1986) has suggested, situations like this are characterized by a temporal logic in which growth leads constantly onward to yet more growth. Consequently, in any given regional cluster at any given moment of time, we are unlikely to observe anything even approaching static equilibrium. What we are much more liable to observe is a cross section through a developmental trajectory that can only be understood in terms of a path-dependent process of evolution and adjustment structured by the phenomenon of localized increasing returns (Arthur 1990; David 1985; Nelson and Winter 1982).

Each region, of course, has its own unique history. The total set of (observed and imaginable) histories of regional development in capitalism, however, can be partially characterized in a sort of archetypical story. I shall try to capture what appear to me to be the more significant elements of this story by means of a stylized description of the agglomerated growth of an industry from infancy to full-blown development. For the sake of argument, I shall suppose that as it begins to make its appearance on the economic landscape, this industry is locationally indifferent to the existing spatial distribution of natural endowments, and that it can effectively be carried on—intially at least—at a wide variety of locations. Hence, this imaginary industry in its infant stage is not too different from a number of familiar empirical cases such as cars in the 1890s, aircraft assembly in the early decades of the present century, or semiconductors in the 1950s.

At the outset, then, the locational structure of the industry will be largely indeterminate in economic terms; it can be seen simply as an "accident"— an effect, for instance, of where its founding figure(s) happened to be living, or a result of a peculiar constellation of political forces in certain places at certain times. Let us suppose that this structure comprises several different locales, no one of which has any particular pre-given advantage over the others. Even so, small chance events alone are likely to push one locale into a leading position, if only in the sense that it begins fortuitously to expand more rapidly than the others (Arthur 1990). In other cases, a particular locale may experience in the postinfant industry stage what we might refer to as a "breakthrough moment," namely, a decisive technological or commercial incident that pushes it to the leading edge of development (examples are Henry Ford's managerial and organizational experiments in Detroit, Donald Douglas' development of the DC-3 aircraft in Los Angeles, and, arguably, the formation of the Fairchild Semiconductor Company in Silicon Valley). Once this occurs, there is a good chance that the locale will start to consolidate and extend its lead, especially where increasing returns and dynamic learning effects come into play.

Provided that markets continue to grow, the leading locale is now likely to be subject to a many-sided process of developmental self-transformation in which the agglomeration effects described in the previous section will be greatly amplified. Thus, there is apt to be a deepening and widening of the social division of labor leading to economic diversification and increased industrial synergies in the local area. Concomitantly, new labor skills are likely to emerge, and the general rounding out of local labor markets will occur. The industrial atmosphere of the locale will tend to thicken, and the business community may well begin to take on identifiable cultural attributes marked by distinctive conventions and routines. Information exchanges and learning effects are liable to become increasingly densely textured, with a corresponding sharpening of the stimuli to technological and commercial innovation. The ramifying social division of labor will in turn offer more and more real opportunities for such innovation. And as these processes move forward, a complex regional economic system will start to materialize and—at least for a time—to evolve forward on the basis of a deepening stock of external economies of scale and scope.

There are always, of course, numerous hazards (including the onset of agglomeration diseconomies) scattered along this pathway of regional development, and things do not always work out in practice quite so unproblematically from the producer's point of view. Among other things, the very geographical factors that facilitate the consolidation of the business community also facilitate the political organization of workers. But in the simple world of this imaginary example, our region's small head start will steadily be extended into massive competitive superiority, and it will progressively follow a recursive developmental trajectory characterized by what David (1985) has called "lock in." In other words, many indurated and mutually reinforcing relationships within the regional economy will ensure that this trajectory acquires a marked dependence on its own past. This does not mean that the regional economic system will now be set inevitably on a course to one final historical destination. To the contrary, the notion of path-dependence also implies the existence of critical branching points, representing conjunctures where the regional economy may move in any one of a number of different possible directions (though once it has moved, its future is then to that degree committed). It may thus occasionally be important for regional policy-makers to nudge the system in certain auspicious directions and away from others that seem to be less promising over the long run.

Unless there are bounds to the continued appropriation of increasing returns by producers in the region, development will continue in this manner, and the region will eventually tend to become a leading-edge center of production in its specialized domain of economic activity. Thus, our infant industry, which began as a set of essentially footloose ventures will now have attained a stage of historical and geographical development where it can only be effectively carried on in an extremely limited number of locational contexts. This, in part, is how it comes to pass that at certain historical moments, places like Lancashire, Detroit, Silicon Valley, Hollywood or the City of London become virtually synonymous with a particular type of product. By the same token, regions that fail to make an early start in fostering the development of a particular industry, or that fall behind in some way, are susceptible to "lock-out" in the sense that they are liable to find it increasingly difficult to catch up to—much less overtake—the leading contenders.

Nevertheless, the onward march of development in economically successful regions is always in practice subject to eventual cessation or reversal, not only because there *are* usually limits to the continued appropriation of external economies, but also because radical shifts in markets, technologies, skills, and so on, can undermine any given regional configuration of production. Indeed, the very existence of lock-in effects means that regions, as they develop and grow, will eventually find it difficult to adapt to certain kinds of external shocks. At times like these we often observe dramatic shifts in the geographic bases of production, involving the demise of formerly growing industrial regions, and the rise of alternative growth centers unhampered by the weight of antecedent production routines, cultures and norms, and more able to take advantage of the changing economic climate. The recent study by Saxenian (1994) of the relocation of the dominant spatial nexus of the US computer industry over the 1980s from the rather rigid production complex that had developed along Route 128 to the more open and flexible Silicon Valley, provides a vivid illustration of this point. On a grander scale, the decline of the US Manufacturing Belt and the rise of the Sunbelt after the late 1960s can in significant degree be interpreted as a locational response to the crisis of Fordist mass production and the rapid growth of new kinds of flexible production systems that right from the outset were indifferent to (if not averse to) the specific kinds of agglomeration economies available in the large industrial cities of the Northeast (Scott 1988*b*).

These last remarks bring us at once to the question of historical geography.

4. A HISTORICAL-GEOGRAPHIC PERSPECTIVE

From the very historical beginnings of capitalism, regions have functioned in important ways as sites of agglomerated and specialized production activities. The conceptual generalizations of the previous two sections represent important stepping stones toward an understanding of this phenomenon, but we also need to pay close attention to substantive problems of historical geography. This is an especially significant issue because the complex relationships discussed above do not play themselves out in stable configurations of forces in all times and in all places. Quite apart from the specific effects of variables like scale, sector or nation on the way these relationships operate, they are subject to massive restructuring as a function of periodic shifts in the organization and modalities of accumulation in capitalism. Moreover, as the Manufacturing Belt/Sunbelt example cited above suggests, such restructuring sometimes has the effect of freeing production from dependence on the preexisting geographic pattern of agglomeration economies, thereby opening up *windows of locational opportunity* and making it possible for new industrial spaces and regions to come into being.

The nature of these temporal shifts in capitalist accumulation processes has recently been the subject of much debate (cf. Boyer and Durand 1993; Leborgne and Lipietz 1992; Jessop 1992) focused above all on the question as to whether or not we can identify particular "regimes of accumulation" with distinctive spatio-temporal traits at different times in the history of capitalism. I cannot possibly hope to address this debate in any meaningful way in the present context, and in any case, my purpose here is limited to the much more modest goal of indicating how regional development processes are subject to intermittent historical transformation. I shall thus sidestep many of the more contentious analytical issues that are at stake in the debate on regulationism, and instead I shall proceed simply on the basis of a theoretically subdued and extremely brief examination of three patently contrasting historical instances of regional development. I shall leave open the issue as to whether or not these instances typify distinctive regimes of accumulation in capitalism; for the purposes of the present discussion it does not matter whether they have some sort of paradigmatic value or whether they are simply special historical and geographical cases.

In the first place, then, the *workshop and factory system* that emerged so strongly in parts of England in the late eighteenth and early nineteenth centuries gave rise to a veritable revolution in patterns of regional development at that time. Considerable segments of the production apparatus were made up of small and vertically disintegrated firms forming dense transactional networks. The geography of production was accordingly and to a significant degree arranged in classical Marshallian industrial districts forming the basis of much of the peculiar pattern of urbanization that characterized the period. Familiar examples of this phenomenon are cottons in Lancashire, woolens in Yorkshire, cutlery in Sheffield, and the metal trades of Birmingham. Industrial labor supplies were in part assured by a massive drift of displaced agricultural workers from the countryside to the manufacturing towns.

In the second place, the system of *Fordist mass-production* that flourished in the Northeast of the United States from the 1920s to the 1960s, also brought about significant reorganization of the economic landscape. In this instance, the leading edges of production were to a great degree embodied in large lead plants in growth-pole industries, around which multitiered complexes of direct and indirect input suppliers congregated in both functional and spatial terms. Such complexes typically constituted the economic foundations of the overgrown industrial metropolitan regions of the twentieth century (Detroit, Chicago, Pittsburgh and so on). This was a moment in the historical geography of capitalism when distinctive relations of polarization and trickle-down were established between the principal industrial core regions and a dependent set of peripheral areas, culminating in the so-called "new international division of labor" of the 1970s and 1980s (Fröbel *et al.* 1980; Hirschman 1958; Myrdal 1957). The polarization/trickle-down relationship was epitomized above all by a tendency for core regions to evolve as agglomerations of high-wage economic activities and for peripheral regions to become depots for dispersed low-wage, blue-collar branch plants.

In the third and final place, a contemporary process of *flexible industrialization* is helping to create a series of new industrial spaces in selected regions of world capitalism (cf. Scott 1988*b*). This third case is distinguished by a proliferation of flexible production networks in industries as diverse as biotechnology and financial services, and concomitantly, by a resurgence of industrial districts and agglomerations in many different parts of the world (even in areas located in what was formerly widely viewed as a development-resistant periphery). In their turn, the regions that have most actively participated in this type of industrialization now also find themselves bound tightly together in worldwide webs of interdependence, with multinational firms playing a major role in mediating between the local and the global. As a corollary, and in contrast to the older centralized multinational corporations of High Fordism, these newer global firms are often extremely fragmented in terms of their command structure and functional organization (Hart 1994). The *loci classici* of this current model of industrialization and regional development are places like Silicon Valley, the Third Italy[1], Southern Germany, and the rapidly growing industrial regions of East and Southeast Asia.

This latest episode in the historical geography of capitalism is based on industrial systems with a high degree of decentralization and open-endedness, and yet which are also capable of efficient and diversified production at many different levels of scale (Piore and Sabel 1984; Coriat 1990). We might say—very schematically—that whereas nineteenth-century workshop and factory systems were able to produce variety of output but were limited in the total scale that they could achieve, and whereas Fordist mass production freed industry from quantitative restraint but at the expense of product variety, modern flexible production systems (with the aid of new electronic and information technologies) are able to achieve considerable variety of output while they can also often generate significant economies of scale. Further, because flexible production systems tend to be strongly externalized (hence transactions-intensive), regional agglomeration seems once more to be resurgent, in contrast to the steady breakup of many industrial regions that was occurring as Fordism approached its climacteric. Regions are once again emerging as important foci of production and as repositories of specialized know-how and technological capability, even as the globalization of economic relationships proceeds apace.

Despite the claims one sometimes hears to the effect that this trend to globalization represents a sort of universal deterritorialization/liquefaction of world capitalism, modern flexible production activities remain firmly anchored in durable regional clusters of capital and labor. As Storper (1992) has very aptly pointed out, there are limits to globalization in the sense that agglomerated production systems remain critical foundations of value-adding activity in production and of competitive advantages in trade. Indeed, globalization itself, by dramatically widening the opportunities for ever more subtle social divisions of labor, helps to accentuate economic regionalization by making it possible for increasingly finely grained patterns of regional specialization to emerge.

The region, in sum, is a critical and all-too-often neglected dimension in the analysis of economic activity within capitalism at large. To be sure, patterns of regional development vary greatly in their empirical expression at different times and different places, yet they appear consistently to have important productivity- and growth-enhancing effects. Despite the diversity of actual cases that can be observed, it is evident that all of them yield in significant ways to a common theoretical language. In this sense, historical geography (in all of its idiosyncrasy) and theoretical analysis (in all of its generalized abstraction) are important adjuncts to—not negations of—one another in any attempt to come to terms with the problem of industrial performance.

5. REGIONAL DEVELOPMENT POLICY

We have noted that regional clusters of industrial activity are generally endowed with latent growth effects. Not all regional clusters perform equally well, however. In this penultimate section of the paper, I propose to look at some of the ways in which regional industrial performance can falter and at how policy can help to ameliorate this state of affairs. More generally, I describe here the beneficial effects of certain kinds of nonmarket coordination on regional economic development, and the role of public action in the construction of localized competitive advantages.

I argued earlier that one of the essential characteristics of industrial regions is their status as *collectivities* of producers, i.e. as clusters of interdependent activities whose mutual proximity to one another engenders complex, dynamic flows of agglomeration economies. In part, such economies (e.g. cost reductions resulting from proximity to specialized firms, or improved efficiencies of job search due to the massing of many different employers in one place) are activated by and consumed through the operation of simple market mechanisms. In part, however, powerful agglomeration economies may also be engendered by institutional infrastructures that lie well outside of the sphere of market relations. Variations in these kinds of infrastructures from region to region can have important implications for differences in industrial performance, and because they are inherently in the domain of collective (as opposed to individual) decision-making and behavior, they represent important opportunities for policy intervention in the interests of local economic competitiveness. Here, I am concerned not so much with the conventional problem of policy as viewed by many neo-classical economists where the issues boil down to a tradeoff between (lower levels of) market-driven economic efficiency on the one hand and social goals on the other, but with the actual enhancement of efficiency itself by means of collective action.

In its simplest form, the imperative of regional economic policy grows directly out of the general need to patch up manifest market failures in the external milieu of regional production systems. Indeed, regional authorities commonly deal in practice with this need by engaging in activities such as the provision of urban equipment, the planning of industrial land use, or the mitigation of pollution problems. But the imperative also goes far beyond this initial point of departure. It also grows out of the circumstance that economic competitiveness and growth can often be much improved by policies that take direct aim at the regional production system as such, and that seek to build on its many-sided spatial and temporal externalities as described above. It goes without saying that this is a tactic that is fraught with heavy risks, and much conventional ideology suggests that market-clearing mechanisms can always do the job more effectively than policy-makers. But quite apart from the possibility of market failures and dysfunctional competitive contests at the very heart of the regional production system itself, markets in any case can never (except in libertarian fantasies) occur in a pure form in capitalism. The very existence of markets is contingent on a framework of social norms and institutions—legal conventions, managerial ideologies and practices, structures of interfirm cooperation and collaboration, forms of worker socialization, traditions of craftsmanship, reputation effects, etc.—that at the same time profoundly shape the manner of their operation (North 1990). I want to argue that in the case of localized industrial complexes, significant augmentation of market capability by means of collective adjustment of the social bases of production can be achieved on at least three main fronts.

(a) *Critical inputs and services* supplied as public goods to producers represent an important extension of the more usual tasks of local government as noted above, and they can be decisive factors in stimulating regional growth. They are of special significance in cases (i) where private firms have a propensity to underinvest in the provision of essential needs, and (ii) where these needs also have an agglomeration-specific character. Two notable cases of this phenomenon are technological research and labor-training activities relevant to specialized regional requirements. However, many additional examples might be offered, ranging from the gathering of information about export opportunities to the advertising and marketing of regional products. The municipalities of the Third Italy have been in the vanguard of this sort of policy-making and planning (Bianchi 1992).

(b) *Cooperation* among firms in the tasks of production makes it possible to achieve more efficient transactional interactions, though its attainment is dependent on the willingness of firms to sacrifice some of their autonomy for the sake of higher aggregate levels of productivity. To achieve this goal, some sort of governance relation is needed to maintain order and continuity over time, and to minimize disruptive defections from the regional cohort of producers. Organized collaboration between firms also makes it more feasible for them to learn from one another and to pool critical technologies and labor skills in the interests of superior combinations of productive resources. Regional industrial consortia and private-public partnerships are one way of stimulating this sort of collaboration.

(c) *Forums for strategic choice and action* are also essential for regional economic success in the modern world. These may have quite limited scope and aims, as exemplified by agencies concerned with tasks like securing trademarks for regional products, or producers' associations that seek to head off short-term forms of wage or price gouging that might undermine the long-term viability of the regional production system as a whole. But they may also be much more ambitious in their objectives, as in the case of regional economic councils (in Germany, for example) that regularly bring together major local constituencies (e.g. employers, banks, workers' organizations and municipal government) to debate questions of long-term industrial order and that seek to forge viable strategies of regional management. Steering mechanisms like this are exceptionally significant given the tendency of regional economic systems to evolve through time on the basis of branching processes whose structure is such that there can be no assurances that the market will always select out the best long-run developmental options (David 1985; Lipsey 1994).

Observe that I refrain from intrusive pronouncement on the appropriate form of the agencies and organizations that might undertake the tasks enumerated above. Depending on local traditions, culture and dispositions, such tasks might be performed by local government bodies, associations of relevant civil parties such as employers and workers, or any number of different kinds of private-public consortia or partnerships. The point here is simply to aver that there is an important and positive role for agents of collective order to play in local industrial development. Quite apart from its significance in promoting agglomeration economies and regional competitive advantage, this role is critical to the maintenance of commitments by all major parties in the region to continued and creative participation (i.e. voice not exit), and thus to the reinforcement of the social cohesion of the entire regional economy (cf. Friedmann 1993).

This is a view of local economic development that diverges greatly from the standard approach based on direct and indirect fiscal incentives. In this standard approach, an arsenal of subsidies and tax-relief measures is typically deployed by state and municipal authorities in an effort to attract new industrial investments, often without proper scrutiny of the total social costs involved. By contrast, the kinds of development strategies suggested in the present paper involve system-wide (bottom-up) approaches and institutional reorganization—rather than large-scale financial commitments to narrowly defined objectives—and because of this, they are presumably quite cost-effective. They also have the desirable feature that they allow markets to eliminate firms that fail. The catch, of course, is that the approach outlined here is not a guaranteed passport to utopia. In particular, it does not seem to offer a great deal of hope to regions that have not already moved some distance down the pathway of development and that have not yet managed to acquire at least some sort of internal industrial synergy. To make matters even more difficult for the left-behinds, (and in view of the existence of first-mover advantages and dynamic lock-out effects, as argued earlier) any region that seeks to initiate a process of local economic development within its borders, needs to pay very close attention indeed to the task of identifying feasible production niches, i.e. forms of economic activity that have not yet been irreversibly dominated by more highly developed regions. As the experience of many actual local economic development efforts over the 1980s demonstrates, it is in general not advisable to attempt to become a Silicon Valley when Silicon Valley already exists elsewhere (that is, unless there are grounds for supposing that some decisive and hitherto unexploited local advantage can be brought into play).

If correct, this overall analysis suggests that we are likely to witness an efflorescence of region-based modes of economic regulation as modern flexible production begins to run its course and the imperative of localized coordination and cooperation becomes more pressing. The gales of intensified competition unleashed by economic globalization make this imperative all the more urgent, especially as much of the most intense competition comes precisely from regions (e.g. in Germany, Italy, Japan, Singapore and Taiwan) that have made substantial progress toward addressing problems of regional economic coordination and planning. Should the world's major industrial regions begin systematically to build strong collective political identities in this fashion, the result will almost surely be sharply intensified conflicts and collisions between them over the ways in which they seek individually to promote their economic interests.

The latter observation leads in turn to the prediction that in the new global mosaic of regional economies, we are also going to see novel forms of institution-building precisely for the purpose of regulating such friction, not just at the national level, but at the international level as well. This sort of institution building is already well under way in the European Union, and I believe that it is likely to become significantly evident in North America and Mexico as NAFTA begins to run its course. Interregional coordination will be necessary, too, to eliminate predatory poaching of any one region's industrial assets by others, to head off wasteful developmental races between different regions, and to promote beneficial interregional joint ventures. Such coordination will be even more essential if disputes between the world's succesful regions and the left-behinds should begin to escalate, and if there should be concomitant political pressures to achieve some form of interregional income redistribution. As we shift increasingly into the new global framework of regional production systems as described in this paper, many further tasks of political integration will predictably appear on the horizon, and many new and unforeseen challenges to democratic rules of order will no doubt need to be dealt with.

6. GEOGRAPHY AND ECONOMICS

In all of the above, I have attempted to provide a broad understanding of the ways in which economic geography and industrial performance are intertwined with one another. I have argued that the endemic tendency in capitalism for dense localized clusters of productive activity to appear at different locations on the landscape has major implications for economic growth and productivity. These clusters are constituted as transactions-intensive regional economies which are in turn caught up in structures of interdependency stretching across the entire globe. As such, they also represent important foundations of much contemporary international trade. I have shown that these clusters can be effectively scrutinized in terms of three main analytical maneuvers involving the study of:

(a) the synchronic formation of external economies in transactions-intensive production systems, and (in a world that is still without benefit of magic carpets) the associated tendency to agglomeration;

(b) the dynamics of path-dependent development within complex localized economic systems; and

(c) the periodic restructuring of these relationships, and their differential regional manifestation (including the cultures and habits that help to sustain them) in varying historical-geographical contexts.

In the light of these basic axes of analysis, I have also tentatively proposed a generic policy agenda for dealing with those tasks of regional development that will in all probability become urgent as we move more decisively into an era of international flexible capitalism. No doubt, if and when these tasks are more clearly formalized in practice, various kinds of intraregional as well as interregional political cleavages will start to take shape around them.

In sum, I have set forth a story about processes and patterns of regional development that is an amalgam of various theoretical influences, ranging from modern economic geography on the one side to institutionalist/evolutionary economics on the other, with gestures to the new trade and growth theory along the way. It is a story that breaks decisively with neoclassical regional science, and that sees structural relations, discontinuities, and increasing returns where the latter remains fixated on the assumptions of perfect competition and the quest for static equilibrium descriptions of the space-economy. Perhaps even more strikingly, this story also goes resolutely against the grain of those recent and numerous commentaries that describe the modern world as a sort of placeless expanse caught up in a universal structure of flows. It is true, of course, that the extraordinary efficiency of modern transportation and communication technologies makes possible many new and farflung spatial configurations of the world economy. This possibility is realized, however, not through the elimination of the effects of geography, but in the concrete appearance of ever more finely grained patterns of locational differentiation and specialization and interregional trade. In the world we inhabit today, space has not become less important as a factor in the structuring of economic processes; on the contrary, it has become considerably more important.

NOTES

1. In the Third Italy, Benetton is an outstanding example of some of the new forms of multinational corporate organization that have emerged as flexible production has begun to run its course.

REFERENCES

Arthur, W. B. (1990), "Silicon Valley Locational Clusters: When do Increasing Returns Imply Monopoly?" *Mathematical Social Sciences*, 19: 235–51.

Bianchi, P. (1992), "Levels of Policy and the Nature of post-Fordist Competition," in M. Storper and A. J. Scott (eds.), *Pathways to Industrialization and Regional Development* (London: Routledge), 303–15.

Boyer, R. and Durand, J.-P. (1993), *L'Après-Fordisme* (Paris: Syros).

Coriat, B. (1990), *L'Atelier et le Robot* (Paris: Christian Bourgois).

David, P. A. (1985), "Clio and the Economics of QWERTY," *American Economic Review*, 75: 332–7.

Friedmann, D. (1993), "Getting Industry to Stick: Enhancing High Value-Added Production in California," Working Paper No. 4, Lewis Center for Regional Policy Studies in A. J. Scott (ed.), *Policy Options for Southern California* (Los Angeles: University of California Press), 135–77.

Fröbel, F., Heinrichs, J. and Kreye, O. (1980), *The New International Division of Labour* (Cambridge: Cambridge University Press).

Harrison, B. (1994), *Lean and Mean: The Changing Landscape of Corporate Power in the Age of Flexibility* (New York: Basic Books).

Hart, M. (1994), *What's Next: Canada, the Global Economy and the New Trade Policy* (Ottawa: Carleton University, Centre for Trade Policy and Law).

Hirschman, A. (1958), *The Strategy of Economic Development* (New Haven: Yale University Press).

Isard, W. (1960), *Methods of Regional Analysis* (Cambridge, Mass.: MIT Press).

Jessop, B. (1992), "Fordism and Post-Fordism: A Critical Reformulation," in Storper and Scott (eds.), *Pathways to Industrialization and Regional Development*, 46–69.

Kaldor, N. (1970), "The Case for Regional Policies," *Scottish Journal of Political Economy*, 17: 337–47.

Krugman, P. (1990), *Rethinking International Trade* (Cambridge, Mass.: MIT Press).
——(1991), *Geography and Trade* (Leuven: Leuven University Press).

Leborgne, D. and Lipietz, A. (1992), "Conceptual Fallacies and Open Questions on Post-Fordism," in Storper and Scott (eds.), *Pathways to Industrialization and Regional Development*, 332–48.

Leontief, W. (1941), *The Structure of the American Economy* (Cambridge, Mass.: Harvard University Press).

Lipsey, R. G. (1994), "Markets, Technological Change, and Economic Growth," paper presented to the 10th Annual General Meeting of the Pakistan Society of Development Economics.

Marshall, A. (1920), *Principles of Economics* (London: Macmillan).

Myrdal, G. (1957), *Rich Lands and Poor* (New York: Harper and Row).

Nelson, R. R. and Winter, S. G. (1982), *An Evolutionary Theory of Economic Change* (Cambridge, Mass.: Belknap Press).

North, D. C. (1990), *Institutions, Institutional Change, and Economic Performance* (Cambridge: Cambridge University Press).

Patchell, J. (1993), "From Production Systems to Learning Systems: Lessons from Japan," *Environment and Planning, A*, 25: 797–815.

Perroux, F. (1961), *L'Economie du XXe Siècle* (Paris: Presses Universitaires de France).

Piore, M. J. and Sabel, C. F. (1984), *The Second Industrial Divide: Possibilities for Prosperity* (New York: Basic Books).

Porter, M. E. (1990), *The Competitive Advantage of Nations* (New York: Free Press).

Romer, P. M. (1986), "Increasing Returns and Long-Run Growth," *Journal of Political Economy*, 94: 1002–37.

Russo, M. (1985), "Technical Change and the Industrial District: the Role of Interfirm Relations in the Growth and Transformation of Ceramic Tile Production in Italy," *Research Policy*, 14: 329–43.

Salais, R. and Storper, M. (1993), *Les Mondes de Production: Enquête sur l'identité economique de la France* (Editions de l'Ecole des Hautes Etudes en Sciences Sociales).

Saxenian, A. (1994), *Regional Advantage: Culture and Competition in Silicon Valley and Route 128* (Cambridge, Mass.: Harvard University Press).

Scott, A. J. (1988a), *Metropolis: From the Division of Labor to Urban Form* (Berkeley and Los Angeles: University of California Press).

——(1988b), *New Industrial Spaces: Flexible Production Organization and Regional Development in North America and Western Europe* (London: Pion).

——(1993), *Technopolis: High-Technology Industry and Regional Development in Southern California* (Berkeley and Los Angeles: University of California Press).

Storper, M. (1992), "The Limits to Globalization: Technology Districts and International Trade," *Economic Geography*, 68: 60–93.

Young, A. (1928), "Increasing Returns and Economic Progress," *Economic Journal*, 38: 527–42.

von Böhm-Bawerck, E. (1891), *The Positive Theory of Capital* (New York: G. E. Stechert).

von Hippel, E. (1988), *The Sources of Innovation* (New York: Oxford University Press).

17

International Diffusion of Knowledge:
Isolating Mechanisms and
the Role of the MNE

ÖRJAN SÖLVELL AND IVO ZANDER

1. INTRODUCTION

The long-term competitiveness of nations and firms is a central topic in international business research. A major issue concerns the mechanisms of innovation and research has produced several models emphasizing the local process by which new knowledge is created. The sustainability of local innovation systems has been linked to institutional settings and research policies (Nelson 1993), first-mover advantages and clusters of related industries (Porter 1990), spillover effects from agglomeration (Marshall 1890/1916; Krugman 1991), technological lock-in or trajectories (Pavitt 1988; Cantwell 1989, 1991; Archibugi and Pianta 1992), and retarded international diffusion of knowledge (Kogut 1993). Somewhat paradoxically, in an increasingly global world the sustainable competitive advantage of international firms becomes intimately linked to the dynamism of local systems of innovation, tied to nations, regions or even cities.

Despite general support for the notion of technological specialization and trajectories, both at the national and firm level, the mechanisms behind retarded international diffusion of knowledge have received relatively limited attention in the literature. In this chapter, we explore the mechanisms that isolate local innovation systems in a world of increasing international competition. Our first ambition is to outline these isolating mechanisms and propose which type of knowledge is the least diffusible in an international context. Second, we address the issue of whether the multinational enterprise, MNE, is an effective boundary-spanning vehicle for overcoming these isolating mechanisms.

In contrast to some established literature on innovation in the MNE, we suggest that this type of firm is not particularly well equipped to continuously transfer technological knowledge across national borders and that its contribution to the international diffusion of knowledge has been overestimated. The argument rests on two observations which have received little attention in previous writings: the fundamental nature of the innovation process and the organizational changes that follow from increasing presence in foreign markets. The nature of the innovation process suggests that all international innovation projects, whether between individual firms or within the coordinated MNE, are associated with increasing costs and lengthened development times, which is a significant disadvantage in innovation-based competition. Moreover, as the MNE becomes more firmly established in foreign innovation systems, this "insiderization" process is accompanied by a process by which large, well-established subsidiaries become less prone to share and diffuse their core capabilities. As subsidiaries develop their own unique resources and capabilities, the formation of global product mandates is promoted at the expense of knowledge exchange across geographically dispersed subsidiaries. In the conclusions, we speculate that smaller scanning units within the MNE or migration, licensing and other non-hierarchical forms of organization are as important to the international diffusion of knowledge as is the well-established MNE.

2. ISOLATING MECHANISMS[1]

In spite of an increasingly integrated world economy, there remain persistent differences in technological capabilities, productivity growth, and the accumulation of economic wealth across nations. Even regions within nations exhibit large differences in technological capabilities without tendencies of convergence. Examples include the various German states and the northern and southern parts of Italy, which in spite of continuous efforts to diffuse knowledge and industrial activity still do not converge.

While the world is becoming increasingly integrated through trade of goods and services, migration, foreign direct investment and technology transfer, local innovation systems could thus be described as poorly functioning communicating vessels (Figure 17.1).

In order to understand why these local innovation systems work as poorly functioning communicating vessels and to assess the speed of international knowledge diffusion, we make a distinction between the mobility of knowledge embedded in physical, human and social capital (Malmberg, Sölvell and Zander, 1996). With reduced trade barriers in the postwar period, knowledge embedded in standard materials, components, products and machinery has become increasingly mobile. However, not even this type of knowledge is always easily transferable across national borders. For example, machinery as such can be transferred, but unless it is properly understood, or used, much of the value of the embedded knowledge is not utilized. This is a typical problem in the transfer of technology between developed and developing countries, but also between developed countries. While modern flexible machinery is being adopted at a high rate in most industrialized nations, empirical studies indicate that firms experience considerable difficulties in implementing this type of technology effectively.

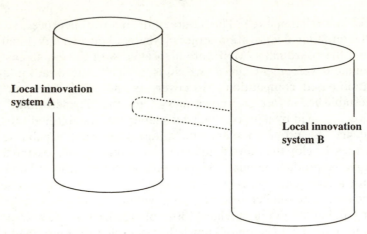

FIG. 17.1. Local innovation systems

The problems are aggravated when the buying firms are distant—physically and culturally—from the industrial environment where such new process technologies are developed and produced (Gertler 1995).

Furthermore, incentives to export advanced materials, cutting-edge components and products can be relatively weak, as they are often fundamental to competitive advantage and the profits that can be derived from temporary monopolies in innovation-based competition. Sometimes, diffusion is temporarily restricted by contracts between local suppliers and buyers stipulating that jointly developed technologies are not to be sold to other parties until after a certain period of time.

While some knowledge is embedded in materials, components, products and machinery, other knowledge is embedded in human capital, part of which is tacit. As a result of improved air transportation an increasing proportion of skilled human capital, such as top management and experts, has become internationally mobile. However, an important part of human capital is embedded in intrafirm relationships and therefore cannot be taken out of context without losing much of its value. These relationships include both formal and informal networks in the local innovation system. Furthermore, the large groups of middle and lower level managers and workers, who play an important role for the informal and formal knowledge exchange across firms, are typically much less mobile than are top management and experts.

The formal and informal networks between people in a common location, which have often been developed through long-term interaction, and the resulting evolution of institutions and business practices, form part of the social capital that surrounds local innovation systems (Coleman 1990; Putnam *et al.* 1993). Social capital differs across geographical locations, and it does not provide equal conditions for the development of all types of industrial activity (Saxenian 1991; Lazerson 1995). Whereas some knowledge embedded in physical and human capital to an increasing extent travels the world through trade, investment and migration, knowledge embedded in social capital does not, as it involves a large number of actors within a local environment and is historically bound to local circumstances, involving unique bonds, business practices and routines for the diffusion of knowledge between firms.

In summary, the diffusion of knowledge within the local innovation system is rapid, whereas it is typically slow from one innovation system to another. With reference to Hägerstrand's (1967) model of diffusion, expansion diffusion would be smooth and involve learning between firms in the local system, whereas hierarchical or sideways diffusion would be retarded. As a result of the isolating mechanisms that prevent the international diffusion of knowledge, locally embedded knowledge will remain scarce, nonimitable and nonsubstitutable on an international scale. From the firm's point of view, insider status in the relevant innovation system is critical for sustaining competitive advantage in innovation-based competition.

3. THE ROLE OF THE MNE—A SKILLED "PIPE ENGINEER"?

The international diffusion of knowledge is facilitated by the international trade of products and technologies, the migration of individuals (experts and entrepreneurs), the development of supranational organizations, and also the foreign expansion of MNEs. There is ample evidence that MNEs are becoming superior in exploiting technology on a global scale, involving elaborate systems of intrafirm trade, specialization and international technology transfer (Dunning 1993). In recent literature, it is often argued that MNEs controlling assets and developing insider status in many local innovation systems are also developing a capacity to coordinate and recombine technologies on an international scale, thereby acting as a superior form of "pipe engineer" (Figure 17.2). Some of the models developed around this theme include the multifocal firm (Doz 1986), the transnational firm (Bartlett 1986; Bartlett and Ghoshal 1989, 1990), the heterarchical MNE (Hedlund 1986; Hedlund and Rolander 1990), the diversified MNC, DMNC (Prahalad and Doz 1987), and the "wired" MNE (Hagström 1991).

These organizational frameworks suggest increasing interaction between geographically dispersed units in the innovation process, and emphasize that organizational structure is secondary to the management of decision-making and actual operations within the multinational firm (Perlmutter 1969; Bartlett 1981, 1983, 1986; Hedlund 1986; Ghoshal and Westney 1993). Accordingly, it is suggested that the broadening of management perspectives, the careful organization of information flows and the development

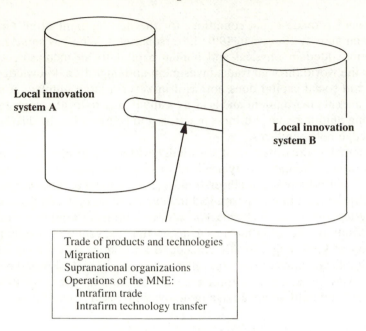

FIG. 17.2. Facilitators of international knowledge diffusion

of organizational norms and culture supportive of international coordination will significantly improve the pipe engineering capability of the
MNE. In particular, access to and integration of internationally dispersed
technological capabilities is believed to result in significantly new and superior technology.

It is evident that the MNE has become more firmly established in foreign
markets, sometimes relocating responsibility for technological activity in
certain fields to foreign units (Pearce 1989; Forsgren Holm and Johanson
1992; Cantwell 1992, 1995; Sölvell Zander and Porter 1993; Dunning 1994;
Birkinshaw 1995). However, the general preconditions for international
knowledge exchange within the MNE have only recently come to the fore
in international business literature, and very little is known about the
extent to which firms actually exchange technological knowledge across
geographically dispersed units.[2]

The well-established MNE represents a unique organizational capital
and could a priori be expected to increase the international fluidity of
knowledge within its boundaries. However, organizational frameworks that
suggest increasing interaction between geographically dispersed units in the
innovation process have emphasized the gains from cross-fertilization and
only to a lesser extent addressed the fundamental nature of the innovation
process. In particular, the disadvantages in terms of increasing costs and

lengthened development times associated with international innovation projects have not been extensively discussed.

Also, the cooperative capabilities that accompany increasing commitment to foreign markets have typically been overestimated. Literature on the management and organization of international operations acknowledges the possibility of organizational power struggles, not-invented-here syndromes, and communication barriers due to differences in national cultures, but it generally emphasizes refined management and information systems as a solution to these problems. This view, we argue, has underestimated how increasing commitments to foreign markets lead to difficulties in controlling operations outside the country of origin. As will be argued in the sections that follow, the process of becoming an insider in local innovation systems is likely to be accompanied by a process by which the large, well-established subsidiaries have less incentive to share and diffuse their core capabilities. Consequently, they tend to become outsiders within their own organizations. As a result, a pattern emerges whereby these semi-independent units take on the role of global product mandates, de-emphasizing continuous knowledge exchange with headquarters and other subsidiary units.

Costs and Time Associated with International Innovation Processes

MNEs which have created a unique organizational capital and become firmly established in many local innovation systems still face the problems of innovating across geographical distances. These problems originate in the fundamental nature of the innovation process, and are accentuated when operations are spread over an increasing number of locations. Research on the innovation process has identified three interrelated characteristics which are particularly important for understanding the costs and lengthened development times associated with carrying out international innovation projects (Freeman 1982, 1991):

- the need for incremental reduction of uncertainty through trial-and-error problem-solving;
- the need for face-to-face contact in the exchange and creation of new knowledge; and
- the need for interaction with other firms.

It has generally been recognized that the innovative process is uncertain in terms of technical feasibility and market acceptance. There is evidence that only one in ten research projects achieves commercial success, and that many patented inventions never find any direct commercial applications (see e.g. Schmookler 1966; Basberg 1987; Pavitt 1991). Although the level of uncertainty varies with the type of invention (incremental inventions are usually associated with a relatively low degree of uncertainty, whereas the potential of revolutionary inventions is more difficult to assess), the technical aspects are commonly reduced by means of trial-and-error testing and modification. While the initial inventive idea might not have required large amounts of capital investment, the trial-and-error process is usually associated with more significant capital expenditure.

In spite of increasingly sophisticated means of electronic communication, the need for personal, face-to-face contact in the exchange of information and technological knowledge has been emphasized by a large number of authors (for a summary, see Brown and Eisenhardt 1995). Moreover, it has been suggested that the probability of interpersonal communication through face-to-face contact declines with increasing distance between individuals (Hägerstrand 1967; Clark 1971). Face-to-face contact appears to be of particular value for the exchange of tacit knowledge, or when the exchange of knowledge involves the observation of products or production processes in use. This type of knowledge rarely resides in blueprints and formulae, but is based on personal skills and operational procedures which only lend themselves to be presented through on-site instruction.

In the study of innovative activity, it is common to assign a major role to the inventor or the technical department responsible for the inventions and technological improvements. However, a narrow focus on the inventor or innovating technical department obscures the fact that both the origin of inventions and their subsequent development generally involve external actors. One particular aspect of innovation is that ideas frequently originate outside the firm which carries out the actual development or manufacturing work (Rothwell and Robertson 1973; Pavitt 1984). The importance of customers as sources of innovation has been observed by several authors (von Hippel 1976; Håkansson 1989; Laage-Hellman 1989), while additional evidence suggests that the introduction of functionally useful innovations is sometimes dependent on suppliers (von Hippel 1988).[3]

The technological influences from other firms can take many forms, ranging from the one-time transfer of information to more extensive interaction and reciprocal knowledge exchange. However, repeated interaction and exchange of knowledge between firms appears to be common and necessary in the innovation process, such as in the context of long-term producer and buyer relationships (Rothwell 1977; Lundvall 1988). This exchange sometimes involves sensitive information, which might be harmful if used opportunistically by the firms involved. Linkages between the scientific community and firms engaged in technological improvements have also been illustrated. For example, it is noted that in the development of the chemical industry, university scientists or inventors worked closely as consultants with corporate research and development departments of industrial firms (Freeman 1982).

Cumulative Dependency on the Local Innovation System

Together, uncertainty and trial-and-error problem-solving, the need to exchange knowledge through face-to-face contact, and repeated interaction with other firms provide an interrelated set of factors which favors locally confined innovation processes. In particular, the costs of external knowledge exchange, involving suppliers, customers and other firms, as well as development times will be reduced if the development work takes place within the local innovation system. These two aspects are important determinants of success in innovation-based competition, as lowered costs and in particular shortened development times will increase the size and length of the temporary monopolies which firms can achieve.

The costs and time associated with local knowledge exchange are further reduced over time by the evolution of a common code of communication, particularly when knowledge is difficult or costly to codify. To a large extent, a common geographical location will offer language similarities which improve the ease of communication. The development of fluid communication also involves a cumulative element, which has been captured in the concepts of communicative and social learning (Lundvall 1993). While firms often start their activities in the local business community, the exchange of information and knowledge over time becomes supported by shared codes of communication and learning about whom to contact in other organizations in order to solve specific technological problems.

Moreover, the local business community offers an environment for the evolution of institutions, norms and values, i.e. a social capital that adds to the process of accumulated learning. Within the local innovation system, these institutions, norms and values become increasingly specialized and unique, adding to the fluidity of knowledge exchange in the local environment and preventing diffusion to the outside. Whereas physical and human capital to an increasing extent travel the world, social capital does not as it involves a large number of actors and is historically bound to local circumstances.

Consequently, a penalty will be associated with carrying out innovation across geographical distances and institutional settings, and the existence of MNEs will not make it possible to circumvent this penalty. When the development of new technology requires trial-and-error problem-solving and frequent interaction with other firms, development costs will be enhanced whether the exchange of knowledge takes place by telephone, mail or other means of communicating codified information. In particular, the need for face-to-face knowledge exchange will lead to increased traveling costs as well as significant costs in terms of the time which could otherwise be spent on on-site innovative efforts.

The costs of maintaining a sufficient degree of interaction across geographical distances would be particularly accentuated should the innovation process require the exchange of tacit rather than codified knowledge. The development of information technology, which in part drives globalization, has had little impact on the innovation process and has yet to show that it can be a substitute for face-to-face interaction as a means of transferring tacit knowledge (Howells 1990; Nohria and Eccles 1992). Also, should the exchange of knowledge require the observation of products or production processes in use, communication by means of blueprints, data sets or telephone conversations would prove inadequate.

Increasing geographical distances are also associated with greater variance in language and more pronounced differences in work organization. While none of these influences is lacking even within the local context (for example, there might be organizational differences between firms in a common location or even between units of the same firm), they become more accentuated in an international context (as suggested by Granstrand and Sjölander 1990). Differences will tend to be de-emphasized with an increasing number of international contacts, but because of the cumulative element they will typically remain more pronounced than in the local context (Håkansson and Henders 1992). Furthermore, differences in institutional frameworks and social capital appear to persist over time, sustaining the difference between the local and international innovation process.

Power Struggles Within the MNE

In addition to the extra costs and lengthened development times associated with international innovation, the international exchange of knowledge is affected by the inherent conflicts in headquarter–subsidiary relationships. Typical problems include maintaining a balance between efficient operations and responsiveness to local demands, the bargaining over internal technical standards (e.g. CAD systems), the not-invented-here syndrome, and frequently a lack of trust and cooperation between headquarters and foreign units. Typically, headquarter ambitions to control foreign operations, and subsidiary efforts to gain independence and take advantage of local business opportunities are a constant cause of conflict in headquarter–subsidiary relationships.

While these difficulties are recognized although underestimated in current literature on the management and organization of international operations, they are very much emphasized in other streams of research. In a formulation of headquarter–subsidiary relationships based on the network approach, it has been observed that clear differences exist in local network contexts of foreign subsidiaries. It is also suggested that headquarters' limited knowledge about these contexts is an important determinant of the degree of control that can be exercised (Holm Johanson and Thilenius 1995; also, see Grabher 1993; Johanson and Mattsson

1994). As the foreign unit accumulates in-depth and unique knowledge of the local network context, it gains access to resources and capabilities which makes it independent and more difficult to control from headquarters.

If a link does exist between headquarters' knowledge of the local environment and the amount of control that can be exercised, this opens up an intriguing perspective on the boundary-spanning properties of the MNE. As foreign units over time become more firmly established in their local innovation systems, they gain to an increasing extent unique and insider access to local knowledge exchange. This unique access to the local innovation system will create independence and simultaneously make the foreign unit more difficult to control from headquarters. Thus, while increasing commitments to operations in foreign countries provide the MNE with one of the prerequisites for assimilating knowledge on an international scale, integrating activities and exercising boundary-spanning activities becomes more difficult. Put somewhat differently, as the MNE becomes an insider in local innovation systems, it will at the same time become an outsider within itself.

Although this paradoxical development does not preclude knowledge exchange between geographically dispersed units, the implications are intriguing as it offers no best way of taking advantage of internationally dispersed knowledge. Development of global scanning units will not allow the MNE to gain inside access to local innovation systems and the local exchange of tacit knowledge, but provides more extensive opportunities for the internal transfer of information and knowledge unaffected by adverse relationships between home and foreign units. On the other hand, the mature MNE with firmly established operations in many locations might have gained direct access to the local exchange of tacit knowledge, but it will have a much more difficult time in integrating operations internally.

4. CONCLUSIONS

This article has outlined the mechanisms which tend to isolate local innovation systems in a world of increasing international competition, focusing on the varying degree of mobility of knowledge embedded in physical, human and social capital. It has been suggested that these isolating mechanisms have important implications for the ability of firms to be dynamic, as they remain dependent upon certain local environments for the upgrading of competitive advantage.

We have suggested that the MNE's ability to act as a boundary-spanning vehicle has been overemphasized in the literature. In particular, we have highlighted the costs and lengthened development times associated with international innovation, and also to a paradoxical development of reduced interaction across highly capable subsidiary units within the maturing MNE. The very fact that insider positions have been established through long-term investments or large-scale acquisitions and mergers, we hypothesize, has worked against the intrafirm diffusion of knowledge. Specifically, headquarter units of the MNE become outsiders in the international network of subsidiaries, and foreign units will acquire resources, capabilities, and more of a stand-alone nature with international technological responsibilities. With this evolution, MNEs would tend to draw upon and reinforce the strength of a local innovation system rather than promote the diffusion of unique local strengths.

Finally, we would hypothesize that the MNE with limited scanning operations will play as important a role in diffusing knowledge out of local innovation systems as the MNE with well-established subsidiary units. Diffusion of knowledge through a scanning unit is not constrained by the need for continuous interaction in the innovation process, nor is it subject to the power struggles that are associated with the development of large semiautonomous subsidiary units. As an example, Japanese firms have been able to successfully tap the American technological base by sending out people from headquarters on temporary missions and by establishing scanning units such as laboratories close to American universities.

NOTES

1. The term "isolating mechanisms" is borrowed from the resource-based framework in business policy literature, where it has been used to explain the sustainability of firm rents and interfirm differences in performance (Rumelt 1984).
2. Some case-study evidence is found in Bartlett and Ghoshal (1990), Hedlund and Ridderstråle (1995), Ridderstråle (1997) and Lindqvist, Sölvell and Zander (1996).
3. Accordingly, it has been noted that the use of innovations extends outside the boundaries of the individual firm. Sometimes, the firm's productivity or product offerings are improved through innovation among its suppliers; sometimes the firm itself might improve productivity or performance among its buyers. At other times, several firms might be involved in joint development work, where each firm supplies a limited component of the innovation that is to be used by others. Only a small proportion of all innovations has been found to be directed towards use within the inventing firm(s) and for improving internal processes (Scherer 1984).

REFERENCES

Archibugi, D. and Pianta, M. (1992), "Specialization and Size of Technological Activities in Industrial Countries: The Analysis of Patent Data," *Research Policy*, 21/1: 79–93.

Bartlett, C. A. (1981), "Multinational Structural Change: Evolution versus Reorganization," in: L. Otterbeck (ed.), *The Management of Headquarter-Subsidiary Relationships in Multinational Corporations* (Aldershot: Gower).

——(1983), "MNCs: Get off the Reorganization Merry-Go-Round," *Harvard Business Review*, 26: 138–46.

——(1986), "Building and Managing the Multinational," in M. E. Porter (ed.), *Competition in Global Industries* (Boston, Mass.: Harvard Business School Press).

——and Ghoshal, S. (1989), *Managing Across Borders—The Transnational Solution* (Boston, Mass.: Harvard Business School Press).

————(1990), "Managing Innovation in the Transnational Corporation," in C. A. Bartlett, Y. Doz and G. Hedlund (eds.), *Managing the Global Firm* (London: Routledge).

Basberg, B. L. (1987), "Patents and the Measurement of Technological Change: A Survey of the Literature", *Research Policy*, 16: 131–41.

Birkinshaw, J. (1995), *Entrepreneurship in Multinational Corporations: The Initiative Process in Foreign Subsidiaries*, Doctoral diss., University of Western Ontario.

Brown, S. L. and Eisenhardt, K. M. (1995), "Product Development: Past Research, Present Findings, and Future Directions", *Academy of Management Review*, 20/2: 343–78.

Cantwell, J. (1989), *Technological Innovation and Multinational Corporations* (Oxford: Basil Blackwell).

——(1991), "Historical Trends in International Patterns of Technological Innovation," in J. Foreman-Peck (ed.), *New Perspectives on the Late Victorian Economy: Essays in Quantitative Economic History 1860–1914* (Cambridge: Cambridge University Press).

——(1992), "The Internationalization of Technological Activity and Its Implications for Competitiveness," in O. Granstrand, L. Håkanson and S. Sjölander (eds.), *Technology Management and International Business: Internationalization of R&D and Technology* (Chichester: John Wiley).

——(1995), "The Globalization of Technology: What Remains of the Product Cycle Model?" *Cambridge Journal of Economics*, 19: 155–74.

Clark, N. G. (1971), "Science, Technology and Regional Economic Development," *Research Policy*, 1: 296–319.

Coleman, J. S. (1990), *Foundations of Social Theory* (Cambridge, Mass.: The Belknap Press of Harvard University Press).

Doz, Y. (1986), *Strategic Management in Multinational Companies* (Oxford: Pergamon Press).

Dunning, J. H. (1993), *Multinational Enterprises and the World Economy* (Wokingham, UK: Addison-Wesley).

Dunning, J. H. (1994), "Multinational Enterprises and the Globalization of Innovatory Capacity," *Research Policy*, 23: 67–88.

Forsgren, M., Holm, U. and Johanson, J. (1992), "Internationalization of the Second Degree: The Emergence of European-Based Centres in Swedish Firms," in S. Young and J. Hamill (eds.), *Europe and the Multinationals: Issues and Responses for the 1990s* (London: Edward Elgar).

Freeman, C. (1982), *The Economics of Industrial Innovation*, 2nd edn. (London: Pinter).

——(1991), "Networks of Innovators: A Synthesis of Research Issues", *Research Policy*, 20: 499–514.

Gertler, M. S. (1995), "'Being There': Proximity, Organization, and Culture in the Development and Adoption of Advanced Manufacturing Technologies," *Economic Geography*, 71: 1–26.

Ghoshal, S. and Westney, E. D. (1993) (eds.), *Organization Theory and the Multinational Corporation* (New York: St Martin's Press).

Grabher, G. (1993) (ed.), *The Embedded Firm: On the Socioeconomics of Industrial Networks* (London: Routledge).

Granstrand, O. and Sjölander, S. (1990), "Managing Innovation in Multi-Technology Corporations", *Research Policy*, 19: 35–60.

Hägerstrand, T. (1967), *Innovation Diffusion as a Spatial Process* (Chicago: University of Chicago).

Hagström, P. (1991), *The "Wired" MNC: The Role of Information Systems for Structural Change in Complex Organizations*, pub. doctoral diss., Stockholm School of Economics, Institute of International Business (Stockholm: IIB).

Håkansson, H. (1989), *Corporate Technological Behavior: Cooperation and Networks* (London: Routledge).

——and Henders, B. (1992), "International Co-operative Relationships in Technological Development," in M. Forsgren and J. Johanson (eds.), *Managing Networks in International Business* (Philadelphia: Gordon and Breach).

Hedlund, G. (1986), "The Hypermodern MNC: A Heterarchy?" *Human Resource Management*, 25/1: 9–35.

Hedlund, G. and Ridderstråle, J. (1995), "International Development Projects: Key to Competitiveness, Impossible, or Mismanaged?" *International Studies of Management and Organization*, 25/1–2: 158–84.

——and Rolander, D. (1990), "Action in Heterarchies: New Approaches to Managing the MNC," in Bartlett, Doz and Hedlund (eds.), *Managing the Global Firm*.

Holm, U., Johanson, J. and Thilenius, P. (1995), "Headquarters' Knowledge of Subsidiary Network Contexts in the Multinational Corporation," *International Studies of Management and Organization*, 25/1–2: 97–119.

Howells, J. (1990), "The Location and Organization of Research and Development," *Research Policy*, 19: 133–46.

Johanson, J. and Mattsson, L.-G. (1994), "The Markets-as-Networks Tradition in Sweden," in G. Laurent, G. L. Lilien and B. Pras (eds.), *Research Traditions in Marketing* (Boston: Kluwer Academic Publishers).

Kogut, B. (1993) (ed.), *Country Competitiveness: Technology and Organizing of Work* (Oxford: Oxford University Press).

Krugman, P. (1991), *Economic Geography and Trade* (Cambridge, Mass.: MIT Press).

Laage-Hellman, J. (1989), *Technological Development in Industrial Networks*, Doctoral diss., Uppsala University, Department of Business Studies.

Lazerson, M. (1995), "A New Phoenix? Modern Putting-Out in the Modena Knitwear Industry," *Academic Science Quarterly*, 40: 34–59.

Lindqvist, M., Sölvell, Ö. and Zander, I. (1996), "Local and Global Perspectives on the Innovation Process: Knowledge Exchange in International Firms," paper presented at the EMOT Workshop, European Science Foundation, University of Durham, 27–29 June 1996.

Lundvall, B.-Å. (1988), "Innovation as an Interactive Process: From User–Producer Interaction to the National System of Innovation," in G. Dosi *et al.* (eds.), *Technical Change and Economic Theory* (London: Pinter).

——(1993), "Explaining Interfirm Cooperation and Innovation: Limits of the Transaction-Cost Approach." in G. Grabher (ed.), *The Embedded Firm: On the Socioeconomics of Industrial Networks* (London: Routledge).

Malmberg, A., Sölvell, Ö. and Zander, I. (1996), "Spatial Clustering, Local Accumulation of Knowledge and Firm Competitiveness," *Geografiska Annaler*, 78B/2: 85–97.

Marshall, A. (1890/1916), *Principles of Economics: An Introductory Volume*, 7th edn. (London: Macmillan).

Nelson, R. R. (1993) (ed.), *National Innovation Systems: A Comparative Analysis* (Oxford: Oxford University Press).

Nohria, N. and Eccles, R. G. (1992), "Face-to-Face: Making Network Organizations Work," in N. Nohria and R. G. Eccles (eds.), *Networks and Organizations: Structure, Form, and Action* (Boston, Mass.: Harvard Business School Press).

Pavitt, K. (1984), "Sectoral Patterns of Technical Change: Towards a Taxonomy and a Theory," *Research Policy*, 13: 343–73.

——(1988), "International Patterns of Technological Accumulation," in N. Hood and J.-E. Vahlne (eds.), *Strategies in Global Competition* (London: Croom Helm).

——(1991), "Key Characteristics of the Large Innovating Firm," *British Journal of Management*, 2: 41–50.

Pearce, R. D. (1989), *The Internationalization of Research and Development by Multinational Enterprises* (Basingstoke: Macmillan).

Perlmutter, H. (1969), "The Tortuous Evolution of the Multinational Corporation," *Columbia Journal of World Business* (Jan.–Feb.), 9–18.

Porter, M. E. (1990), *The Competitive Advantage of Nations* (New York: Free Press).

Prahalad, C. K. and Doz, Y. (1987), *The Multinational Mission: Balancing Local Demands and Global Vision* (New York: Free Press).

Putnam, R. D., with Leonardi, R. and Nanetti, R. Y. (1993), *Making Democracy Work: Civic Traditions in Modern Italy* (Princeton: Princeton University Press).

Ridderstråle, J. (1997), *Global Innovation: Managing International Innovation Projects at ABB and Electrolux*, pub. Doctoral diss., Stockholm School of Economics, Institute of International Business (Stockholm: IIB).

Rothwell, R. (1977), "The Characteristics of Successful Innovators and Technically Progressive Firms," *R&D Management*, 7/3: 191–206.

——and Robertson, A. B. (1973), "The Role of Communications in Technological Innovation," *Research Policy*, 2: 204–25.

Rumelt, R. P. (1984), "Toward a Strategic Theory of the Firm," in R. Lamb (ed.), *Competitive Strategic Management* (Englewood Cliffs, NJ: Prentice- Hall).

Saxenian, A. (1991), "The Origin and Dynamics of Production Networks in Silicon Valley," *Research Policy*, 20: 423–37.

Scherer, F. M. (1984), *Innovation and Growth: Schumpeterian Perspectives* (Cambridge, Mass.: MIT Press).

Schmookler, J. (1966), *Inventions and Economic Growth* (Cambridge, Mass.: Harvard University Press).

Sölvell, Ö., Zander, I. and Porter, M. E. (1993), *Advantage Sweden*, 2nd edn (Stockholm: Norstedts).

von Hippel, E. (1976), "The Dominant Role of Users in the Scientific Instrument Innovation Process," *Research Policy*, 8: 212–39.

——(1988), *The Sources of Innovation* (New York: Oxford University Press).

18

The Geographies of Strategic Competence: Borrowing from Social and Educational Psychology to Sketch an Activity and Knowledge-Based Theory of the Firm

J.-C. SPENDER

1. INTRODUCTION

In recent years organizational theorists have been much influenced by "new institutional" economics (e.g. Williamson 1975; Porter 1980; Barney and Ouchi 1986; Aoki, Gustaffson and Williamson 1990; Best 1990; Furubotn and Richter 1991; Williamson and Winter 1991). Industrial organization economics, transaction cost analysis, and the resource-based approach, have revived older concerns about the nature and sources of scarce resources, rents, property rights, and competitive advantage. Though industrial organization's influence has been considerable, it has not yet reshaped organizational analysis into a subfield of economics, as some have argued. On the contrary, industrial organization economists have attempted to enter the "black box" of the firm to reach its managers and activities, only to find themselves confronting the limits of microeconomic analysis. In response they have developed new concepts, such as organizational routines, technological paradigms, coherence and relatedness, mobility barriers, integration and segmentation mechanisms, networking, appropriability regimes, relational contracting and institutional isomorphism, to help explain what seemingly cannot be explained within the more traditional economic discourse. These developments are evident in contemporary analyses of the growth and boundary changes of the enterprise, or of the economy, or the impact of technological or institutional change (Nelson and Winter 1982; Dosi, Gianetti and Toninelli 1992). It is also evident in the analyses of the changing geography of economic activity (Aydalot and Keeble 1988; Best 1990; Porter 1990; Saxenian 1994). The common feature is the great attention paid to knowledge as the key dimension of the enterprise.

This chapter continues this line of inquiry. Industrial location and localization used to attract more theoretical interest (Marshall 1969: 22; Florence 1961: 37) than it does presently (Krugman 1993), in spite of a revolution in the theories of human and economic geography since Marshall's time. Most explanations of the vitality around Route 128, or the Cambridge "phenomenon" in the UK, assume geographical proximity is crucial. This paper explores some reasons why. It is speculative, merely suggesting a research program, though there is considerable evidence that empirical research could be fruitful. The classical approach to industrial geography, based on the location of supply and demand, economies of scale, and the costs of transportation leaves knowledge, especially the collective knowledge that is "in the air," beyond the analysis. We argue that the organization's knowledge and learning activities must be brought to the center of this analysis rather than remaining on its periphery. We need a geography of organizational knowledge, and of its generation and application, rather than a geography of transport costs.

To move towards this we have to deal with the nature of organizational knowledge before dealing with its geography. In the first section we develop a framework of several different types of organizational knowledge. This becomes the preamble to arguing that each type of knowledge implies a different geography of its generation and application. We explain why a plurality of knowledge-types is necessary for a knowledge-based theory of the firm. We presume that the pursuit of the rents arising from knowledge differences, rather than efficiency differences, is the best method of achieving competitive advantage. Thus in the second section we reconsider economic rents and the ways in which different types of knowledge might be associated with different types of rent. In the third section we borrow theories of learning from developmental psychology to explain how these different types of knowledge might be generated. Only in the fourth section do we begin to touch on the geographical dimensions of the relationships between the knowledge and learning. This leads us to a knowledge-based interpretation of the "industrial districts," such as Emilia Romagna in Northern Italy, Silicon Valley in the USA, Tyne and Wear in the UK, and the Jura region in Switzerland, which are now attracting the "new competition" theorists. In the concluding section we offer some suggestions about how a knowledge-based approach might add to our understanding of organizations, management, cooperation and competition, and economic and technological growth. In particular we suggest a contingency theory relating different knowledge management strategies to different environmental conditions.

2. TYPES OF ORGANIZATIONAL KNOWLEDGE

The first topic is the plurality of types of knowledge. Since the time of the ancient Greeks, it has been suggested that there are different types of knowledge (Detienne and Vernant 1978; Spender 1993). In our own times

James (1950: i. 221) distinguished "knowledge about" from "knowledge of acquaintance," and Ryle (1949) between "knowing what" and "knowing how." Many contemporary authors, such as Nelson and Winter (Nelson and Winter 1982: Winter 1987), Kogut and Zander (1992), Brown and Duguid (1991), Hedlund (1992) and Nonaka (Hedlund and Nonaka 1991; Nonaka 1994; Nonaka and Takeuchi 1995), have adopted a knowledge typology based on the work of Michael Polanyi (1962). Polanyi distinguished "objective" from "tacit" knowledge, the former being abstract, communicable and conveyed by symbols and language, the latter being incommunicable and embedded in practice. Penrose (1959: 53) also suggested that the knowledge which could be learned through words differed from that which could be learned only through experience, and this distinction is crucial to her theory of the growth of the firm. It would follow that an organization cannot be understood solely in terms of the explicit or objective aspects of its knowledge or resource base. We must also consider its practices and the tacit knowledge it articulates. Practice is a distinct form of knowledge that is learned only by doing (Arrow 1962).

The separation of the explicit and implicit forms of knowledge cuts across an equally venerable debate about whether social entities, such as societies, institutions or organizations, are evidence of social or collective forms of knowledge distinguishable from individual forms of knowledge. The modern notion of collective knowledge derives from Durkheim (1964), who argued for a *conscience collective* or communal consciousness. Durkheim's arguments precipitated a continuing dispute about the ontological status of organizations, whether they exist independently or only in the minds of those whose activities manifest the coherence and intentionality we take as the defining characteristics of organization. Much of today's literature presumes that only individuals think and take decisions, denying the possibility of organizational mind or knowledge.

The relationship between the individual and the social is more complex. Each depends on the other, neither has priority, either ontological or epistemological. Halbwachs (1992), following Durkheim, argued that the individual's memory is fundamentally collective, stabilized and renewed through social practice. Connerton (1989) argued that social memory, such as an institution's culture, is largely collective, implicit, articulated, conveyed in and reconstituted through its social practices. These authors come from within sociology, but others, such as Jung, have proposed collective knowledge from within psychology. Social psychology, of course, takes collective forms of knowledge as a given. Weick and Roberts (1993) have illustrated ways in which the concept of "collective mind" can be applied without reifying the organization or suggesting a Jungian collective unconscious. Collective knowledge is embodied in the organization's practices or in the organizational members' "heedful interrelating."

The intersection of these two analytic distinctions suggests a four-fold

	Individual	Social
Explicit	Conscious	Objectified
Implicit	Automatic	Collective

FIG. 18.1. The different types of knowledge in organizational analysis
Source: Spender 1993: 39.

typology of organizational knowledge (Figure 18.1). There are similarities to the knowledge matrix offered in Hedlund and Nonaka (1991: 4), Hedlund (1992: 4), Kogut and Zander (1992: 388), Nonaka (1994: 16), and Nonaka and Takeuchi (1995). Hedlund and Nonaka proposed several levels of the "social" within a two by four (individual, group, organization and interorganizational domain) matrix rather than the basic two by two matrix shown in Figure 18.1. There is an even closer similarity to the matrix used by Seely Brown (in Bollier, 1993: 7) which proposed four types of "knowing in action": concepts, stories, skills and tools. Concepts and skills being individual, stories and tools social.

We suggest four types of knowledge: objectified, conscious, collective and automatic. Objectified knowledge is explicit, captured and communicated in language and symbols. It is abstract and detached from context and experience. It is validated by public (social) acceptance and its inclusion within the context of loosely shared meanings that make communication possible. Its archetype is positivistic scientific knowledge, its meaning established and stabilized independent of the social. Conscious knowledge is that which individuals can possess, articulate and manipulate purposively but which has yet to be made public. While individuals know a great deal of what is already public, they also create new knowledge. For instance, they generate testable hypotheses which are both conscious and still "private." The scientific method is one of several methods of controlling the public adoption of such private conscious knowledge. Patents, citations, copyrights and contracts are some of the many public or institutional mechanisms designed to protect the interests of individuals who make their private knowledge public.

As we move to the implicit parts of the matrix, explanation gets more difficult. The possibilities of saying anything are constrained by the power of the methods used to surface the taken-for-grantedness of everyday organizational life (Schutz 1967, 1972). Automatic knowledge is that which the individual knows but cannot make explicit and in this narrow sense does not know what he/she knows. Such knowledge can be demonstrated and communicated through practice showing it is known in this alternative sense. Rorschach tests and semiotic analysis reveal the taken-for-granted. Unfortunately the examples Polanyi (1962: 49) used to illustrate the tacit dimensions of everyday knowledge are kinetic—swimming and bike-riding. This conveys well the point about the embeddedness of tacit knowledge in practice, but it blinds us to the non-kinetic types of automatic knowledge which are equally important in our lives.

Polanyi used the term "subsidiary awareness" to suggest that a different type of intellectual processing takes place automatically outside our conscious or "focal awareness." Thus we are scarcely aware of the frame of the window as we look out at the park beyond. If we reverse our focus, and look at the frame, the trees and greenery outside drop into subsidiary awareness. Psychologists such as Bargh (1989) have explored the varieties of human automaticity and suggested that the issues which automaticity raises— awareness, intention, efficiency and control—are relatively independent and may or may not occur together. Thus we are often unaware of what we know. The efficiency aspect of this knowledge has been made popular through the notion of "flow" (Csikszentmihalyi 1988) wherein we seem to act without effort or an awareness of time whenever we are totally focused. Perhaps the most important type of automaticity is recognition, the "aha!" experience. Experimental psychological evidence increasingly suggests that recognition processes are automatic rather than conscious (Lewicki 1986).

The collective forms of knowledge are those social facts, such as culture, which confront us as constraints over our individual choices while we nonetheless remain largely unaware of them. The other side to collective knowledge, as Halbwachs suggested, is that collective knowledge is the public tool which individuals use to solve private problems, just as we use other types of public goods such as culture or religion, to deal with many of the uncertainties of everyday existence. Professional cultures (Abbott 1988) are bodies of collective knowledge that help individual professionals, such as surgeons (Cassell 1991), engineers (Ferguson 1992) or accountants, deal with the uncertainties of applying explicit and well-formed knowledge to a real messy world. Professionals absorb and use this body of collective knowledge to recognize and so diagnose ill-formed reality in ways that accord with the views of their professional peers. Collective knowledge is built up within "communities of practice" (Lave and Wenger 1992; Lave 1988; Rogoff and Lave, 1984) such as the group of technicians servicing photocopiers (Orr 1990; Brown and Duguid 1991). Spender (1989) has argued that managers operating under conditions of strategic uncertainty tacitly adopt an "industry recipe," the body of implicit knowledge held collectively by the industry members. On an even broader scale, North (1990, 1991) has argued that social institutions, such as the stock market or marine insurance, are evidence of social knowledge developed to deal with the uncertainties of socioeconomic life.

In this section we have argued that an organization's knowledge-base comprises four different types of knowledge. Most analysts, especially those trying to build expert systems, emphasize the explicit. Polanyi's work has helped us become more aware of the implicit. We add a distinction between the individual and social levels, recognizing collective knowledge which is socially contextualized or situated (Suchman 1987). Collective knowledge also provides us with a different answer to Coase's (1937) question about why firms exist. These knowledge categories are "ideal types," for every real organization articulates all four types of knowledge synthesized into a loosely focused or coupled set of activities (Starbuck 1983). In the next section we make links between the different types of rents and knowledge.

3. RENTS, INDIVIDUAL AND ORGANIZATIONAL

As industrial organization economics has shifted our attention onto firm-specific resources, and the rents and competitive advantage they engender, it has become customary to distinguish different types of rent. Thus Rumelt (1987: 142) saw three types of rent: Ricardian, Pareto and entrepreneurial. Mahoney and Pandian (1992: 364) saw four types: Ricardian, monopoly, entrepreneurial and quasi-rents. Amit and Schoemaker (1993: 34n) also saw four types: Ricardian, Pareto, monopoly and quasi-rents. Like Peteraf (1993: 184), these authors adopt Klein, Crawford and Alchian's (1978) definition of quasi-rents as Pareto rents that are transient and appropriable. However, inasmuch as these writers refer to factors which are not in fixed supply, all these rents are quasi-rents. Since entrepreneurial success draws other entrepreneurs into business, entrepreneurial rents are also quasi-rents.

Marshall (1964: 52) defined rent as the income deriving from the owner-ship of land and the other free gifts of Nature. He coined the term "quasi-rent" and defined it as the net income derived from the appliances of production already made (1964: 426). Even though these appliances are man-made and are not the free gifts of Nature, they still command a premium because supply cannot respond rapidly to increased demand. Alchian and Allen (1969: 117) similarly defined rent as that portion of the price that does not influence the amount of that good in existence in the short term. In her "digression on rent" Robinson (1969: 102) made a similar point defining rent as the surplus earned by a factor of production over and above the minimum earnings necessary to induce it to do its work. The minimum payment for a factor is not that which causes it to exist, but that which will attract it to that enterprise rather than to some other (Robinson 1969: 104). She also argued that the traditional treatment of rent is overly connected to the notion of Nature's free gifts, such as land and its fertility, whose characteristic is that they do not owe their origin to human effort. Rents due to human innovation, entrepreneurship, technology or team production are different. These factors are not in fixed supply and presuppose an expandable "internal" or artificial source of rent rather than the fixed natural source "external" to the enterprise.

Economists sometimes presume an initial similarity between firms, as if all firms start with similar endowments. The problem is then to find how heterogeneity is achieved and sustained. In practice, initial endowments are always different, thus rents are also evidence of the uniqueness of the firm's history. They may also be reminders of the ways economies worked before the emergence of the market economy. Commons (1957: 219), in his analysis of the "rent bargain," saw rent as a facet of the property rights granted to holders of productive factors by those, such as kings, local lords or governments, who previously owned everything and granted such property rights reluctantly. In the mercantile age superior political entities created "patents" to monopolize essential productive factors and these patents were sold to raise state revenue (Ekelund and Tollison 1981). Much of court intrigue revolved around discovering and bidding for these patents. As Demsetz (1968) has pointed out, were the bid competition perfectly efficient it would not be necessary for a superior political entity to regulate the monopolies. In practice, whenever the granter is able to discover the value of the monopoly to prospective purchasers, greater revenue can be raised (Ekelund and Tollison 1981: 132 n). The passing of the mercantile age led to the displacement of rents by taxes as the principal means of raising revenue. Monopoly rents sometimes persist as the result of government's direct involvement in the economy, sometimes where suppliers are able to acquire market power and restrain output. But monopoly typically depends on the widely known social institutions that protect the monopolist's ownership rights, and this, in turn reflects the political world outside the organization. So monopoly rent-seeking should be analyzed within political rather than economic theory. Tullock (1993) and others (Buchanan 1980; Ekelund and Tollison 1981; Oster 1990: 51; Milgrom and Roberts 1992: 270) have argued that the pursuit of politically sustained rents, through lobbying and other political practices, may be costly and socially wasteful.

While monopoly rents are reflections of what everybody knows about their society, and can be associated with social knowledge, Pareto and Ricardian rents are reflections of private ownership and knowledge. These derive either from the unpriced element of a past exchange of assets (Arrow in Ledyard 1989)—another way of referring to information asymmetry—or because some firm-specific knowledge has been created. If we regard the first as an inappropriate basis for a theory, because it depends on market failure, attention shifts to firm-specific knowledge. Inasmuch as this is conscious and potentially objective, there are agency issues around its acquisition and management, and appropriability issues around its sustainability. Teece (1987: 193) has noted that these depend on the social institutional context, and differ for different products and technologies. For those who believe all organizational knowledge is explicit and appropriable, the theory of the firm becomes a theory of managing the agency and appropriability issues. Our argument is that the implicit types of knowledge are at least equally important and that every organization therefore implies the coordinated interaction of all four types of knowledge.

Rumelt (1987: 143) defined entrepreneurial rents as the unanticipated difference between the *ex ante* cost of the resources that are combined in the enterprise and their *ex post* value. This points towards entrepreneurial knowledge which is not available to the market and thus to Pareto rents. As the enterprise demonstrates the value of the entrepreneur's insights, others understand and attempt to appropriate the knowledge by imitation. The entrepreneur makes his/her knowledge public through the activities of the enterprise and is proving out hunches and pursuing an economic legitimation of his/her private knowledge. It does not matter whether the entrepreneur's hunch is entirely in the conscious domain and easily explained or whether it is more of an automatic "Midas touch."

Turning to collective knowledge, we must emphasize that we do not mean individual knowledge that is shared. It is unfortunate that so many organizational analysts define culture so loosely as shared beliefs, norms and values (e.g. Schein 1985). Sharing is within a dialectical matrix that also allows sustained differences (Allaire and Firsirotu 1984; Goodenough 1971). Those socialized into the culture take both aspects of this matrix for granted. To the extent that culture is explicit, it is a body of shared knowledge that no one member is able to report or even comprehend. To the extent that it is implicit, it is a set of practices that no one member is able to demonstrate or interpret. Thus a culture, as a typical example of collective knowledge, emerges and becomes visible both as a set of coordinating practices and a system of beliefs.

The notion of emergent collective knowledge lies at the heart of Penrose's (1959: 78; 1971: 43) theory of the growth of the firm. She interposed managerial coordination between the firm and its inputs remarking that "it is never resources themselves that are the inputs to the production process, but only the services that the resources can render" (1959: 25). Such attention to coordination would be a distinction without a difference if the resulting organizational capability could be traded like any other resource. But the capability is implicit and embedded in the organization's practices. It is firm- and context-specific so that it cannot be acquired in this manner. Not only must it be evolved internally, its quality and value can only be measured *ex post* and, by definition, is limited elsewhere. Penrose argued that the firm's ability to generate this knowledge through learning by doing, and to apply the surplus developed as each project reaches fruition, provides the impulse to expand. The corresponding imperative to reinvest the accumulated tangible profits is the impulse to expand in Chandler's (1962: 383) theory of the enterprise. The difference is that Chandler's enterprise can choose to distribute its tangible surplus. Penrose's theory offers no such option, for the surplus is valueless to others. A firm could remove its managerial cadre but, unlike the sports team selling its key players, at no great profit to itself.

Alchian and Demsetz's (1972) concept of "team production" also dealt with collective knowledge focusing on the resources produced by joint activity. They defined team production as that in which several different types of resources were used, the collective product being greater than the output of each separately. Their subsequent debate with Williamson (1985) about whether the firm was an appropriate contractual structure for managing joint activity did not diminish the value of their suggestion that the firm is a special context for managing, monitoring and capturing collective activity, even though the relationship between the inputs and the outputs is uncertain *ex ante*.

Nelson and Winter (1982: 134) also focused on collective action with their notion of the organizational routines learned by doing and embedded in the organization's practices. The locus of the organizational memory and operational knowledge is the routinization of activity (1982: 104). These routines, as Halbwachs or Connerton might have noted, are refreshed and sustained by being exercised. Without this they erode. Nelson and Winter (1982: 104) do not offer a detailed analysis of how the organization's collective knowledge differs from the individual knowledge of members, save that the individuals' knowledge is contextualized in collective activity. But they argued that organizational routines are changed only with difficulty and as a result of considerable trial and error experimentation as new situations are confronted (1982: 131). Routines develop in part because they are under the direction of managers with specific goals in mind (1982: 112), in part stochastically as organization members cast about for new possibilities.

In this section we have argued that the rents due to collective knowledge are different from the monopoly rents due to social knowledge or individual knowledge (Pareto rents). We label the returns to collective knowledge Penrose rents and they will be central to our theory of the firm. In later sections we shall examine how collective knowledge is generated, thereby sketching a theory of the Penrosian firm. To the extent that collective knowledge is purely emergent and unintended, we have no theory. But a theory of directed collective learning can be used as a basis of a theory and our attempt to show that geography plays a considerable role in collective learning. We cannot credit collective knowledge with such a central position in our theory without being more specific about how it is generated, stored and controlled. If collective knowledge lies at the core of the firm, then implicit learning and forgetting become the basis of our theory. Up to this point we have only vague notions of learning by doing and by extension, forgetting by not doing. We can only guess at the way external changes obsolete the organization's knowledge. Our theory of learning and forgetting must embrace both the internal states and processes of the organization, and the relationship with the wider context in which this knowledge is embedded. In the next section we look more closely at learning. We shall suggest crucial relationships between the different types of knowledge and the boundaries around the learning process.

4. COLLECTIVE LEARNING

In the sections above we have used two different metaphors for learning; learning by doing and learning by communicating. Learning by communicating is appropriate for the upper part of the matrix in Figure 18.1. Learning by doing belongs to the lower part. Others have also noted the possibility of two kinds of learning, e.g. the distinction between procedural and declarative knowledge (Singley and Anderson 1989; Cohen 1991). Learning takes place at many levels. Some argue that individuals, teams, organizations and societies can all learn (Hedlund and Nonaka 1991). They can acquire both explicit knowledge and the behaviors which indicate the presence of implicit knowledge. Learning is the acquisition of the means to deal with particular situations. Unfortunately this does not help us see the relationship between what is learned and what is known previously. We have ignored the base on which learning itself stands.

Matters get more complicated when, as Nelson and Winter's (1982: 128) modification of organizational routines illustrated, we see learning as a second-order effect, the process of changing previously acquired knowledge or behaviors. Weick (1991: 117) has pointed out that the traditional psychological definitions of learning are based on this more complex view. Stable routines, rules and hierarchical structures are evidence of non-learning. Weick argued that learning, as traditionally defined, is likely to be rare in organizations because they tend to remain unchanged while dealing with constantly changing situations. He argued for two intellectual strategies to deal with organizational learning. The first would have us focus on the behaviors that the organization adopts to reconstruct changing situations to fit known categories, so developing new behaviors and learning. The second focuses on perception and sense-making, and this changes the definition of organizational learning. Instead of developing new behaviors in the face of old situations, the organization now develops new perceptions of them. This kind of discussion denies the possibility of a simple relationship between either experience and knowledge or between knowledge and behavior. Learning is problematic and we need to know where it begins. Later we borrow from educational psychology, in particular from Vygotsky's (1962) learning theory, and sketch ideas that bring cognition, activity and contextuality together. Vygotsky's theory is psychological and focused on children, but we shall argue that it can be adapted for the organization and thereby made to cover both the explicit and implicit dimensions of its knowledge.

Few discussions of organizational learning show the base from which the learning process can operate. Our sensitivity to this issue is revealed by the frequent references to "absorptive capacity" (Cohen and Levinthal 1990). Vygotsky went to the heart of the matter and focused on the development of consciousness and identity, the achievement of the child's sense of self, of other, and of place. Clearly consciousness is the fundamental prerequisite for learning, and we cannot deal with organizational learning without first considering how organizations might achieve a type of consciousness that is appropriate to our concept of organizational knowledge. The notion of collective knowledge presupposes a collective consciousness and identity, and therefore of a boundary around the organization. Tharp and Gallimore (1988: 33) have provided a summary of Vygotsky's theory in which the Zone of Proximal Development (ZPD) is crucial. Broadly speaking this means the extent of what the child can achieve over and above his/her present performance with the assistance and collaboration of fully capable others. The ZPD is a domain of performance rather than simple cognition. Vygotskian theory deals with the extension of the ZPD and with the changes in its nature as the child develops. The development process is a cooperative venture between the child and the capable other. To the extent that it is externally or socially driven, the child's consciousness is socially constructed. This contrasts with Piagetian theory, which puts the emphasis on the internal source and evolution of consciousness. Vygotsky argued that the individual and the social form in dialectical tension with each other, and there are parallels to symbolic interactionism (Blumer 1969) and to the work of Mead (1962).

Tharp and Gallimore described four stages in the child's development. In Stage 1, the child is unaware of his/her interaction with the world and of the way in which this is guided by capable others. Responses to stimuli are behavioral, without a cognitive element. However Vygotsky presumed that children possess innate capabilities that eventually enable them to shape their activities as if they were the capable others, even though they are still without a sense of self. This is Stage 2. It is marked by the appearance of self-directed speech, when the child talks to itself. Stage 3 occurs as the child achieves an initial sense of self, consciously displacing the capable other as the guide to behavior. Progress through every stage is marked first by patterned behavior and then by internalization so Vygotskian theory is characterized as "activity theory" or "performance before competence." This reverses the conventional view that activity is the result of explicit cognitive processes. The child now internalizes the control exercised by the capable other. At this point children begin to shape their own activities. Instructions from others become an irritant. The sense of self is egocentric, incompletely contextualized. Stage 4 is the final achievement of a mature sense of self—embedded in an active social environment. Once here the child, and the adult, may recycle into the earlier stages after discovering that they were not able to sustain performance and a sense of competence. The challenge for the capable other is to draw the child forward through the ZPD as it changes its extent and character. Progress through the stages is made only with the active involvement of the child. Too rapid movement, given the child's present level of performance and inherent development capabilities, causes the relationship to collapse and progress stops.

Reber (1993: 7) took these same ideas, together with the experimental evidence surrounding them, and elaborated the distinction between the implicit and the explicit. Like Vygotsky, he argued that the abilities on which the progress towards consciousness stands are "basic," given genetically. But they are phylogenetically older, grounded in our evolutionary past and give us the ability to respond to external stimuli and to our internal biological drives, they cover hunger, flight, mating and so forth. These behaviors are more robust and resilient, less prone to disruption than the explicit "higher order" reasoning faculties which are grounded in consciousness. Thus reasoning stands on and emerges from this implicit base and provides empirical evidence to support Polanyi's intuition about the primacy of the implicit.

We can take this crude sketch of Vygotskian learning theory and apply it to the organization, noting that it is the collective activity-based knowledge that supports the objective rational reasoning. The organization's sense of identity grows out of the interactions between a body of implicit practices and its environment. This touches on some of the oldest concerns about the nature of leadership. On the one hand we see the organization as being created and given its identity by a leader. This conforms with bureaucratic theory, which presumes that all the necessary knowledge precedes the formation of the organization. On the other hand, theorists such as Barnard (1938: 172) argued that such leadership results only with the assent of the led. Provided there is activity, leadership focuses the attention of those involved so that they develop a sense of purpose and begin to internalize the leader's direction. Only then will the Penrose effect begin, leading to collective knowledge about how to deal with the situation. Objective knowledge arises as the organization interacts with the environment and seeks to develop an identity and awareness of itself and its situation. The key is to generate activity. Competence and comprehension follow provided the challenge is within the organization's ZPD or region of reasonably related development. The ZPD can be seen as a theory about how what can be learned is related to what is already known.

In this section we have suggested that the key to managing implicit learning lies in generating directed activity. Our notion of learning by doing is affected because we imply that there will only be implicit learning when the doing is directed. Random doing, unstructured exploration, will not lead to either consciousness or knowledge. An objective precedes the learning. In the same way, collective learning implies some objective. Social institutions might emerge from the social process, but only when there is some prior sense of purpose about their function. This requirement, often noted as the team's shared sense of objective, also implies careful management of the boundary around the activity (Spender and Kessler 1994). The team's collective knowledge develops as it achieves a sense of identity and the members sense the team as a psychological entity (Kidder 1982). Its boundaries are crucial to its identity, stability and process. Its process is intimate, involving personal interaction as each actors' intuitions and implicit knowledge evolves into their collective. Another way to approach these notions is to consider the media richness argument (Daft and Lengel 1984, 1986). As the knowledge becomes more explicit, so the communications can become abstract and symbolic. But when we are dealing with collective knowledge, the learning depends on face-to-face interaction (Nohria and Eccles 1992). The geography of collective knowledge is determined by the geography of personal interaction.

5. THE GEOGRAPHY OF COLLECTIVE LEARNING

Classical theories of industrial localization deal with explicit knowledge. They cover the rational aspects of the firm's spatial embeddedness. Marshall (1969: 222) dealt with the localization of industry in ways that are more suggestive. He was particularly intrigued by learning by doing and argued that "practice makes perfect" (1969: 208) and that the skills developed would sediment into the "semi-automatic" (1969: 209n). Thus firms would be unlikely to move once they were established. In an oft-quoted sentence he remarked that the skills would be passed unconsciously from generation to generation, "the mysteries of the trade would be no mysteries: but are as it were in the air" (1969: 225). The firms' initial locations were likely to be determined by the physical conditions surrounding the factors of production or, giving the presence of a court as an example, around the principal locations of consumption. Every cheapening of the means of communication and transportation would extend the firm's geographical reach and free it from these constraints. Absent such explanations it is less clear why the firms within a single industry would cluster together. Florence (1961: 40) called it "swarming." He noted that even when an industry was "footloose," and not tied by reason of the location of factors which were costly to transport, swarming was still common. His conclusions, like

Marshall's, were that while the initial location may be accidental, once established, the industry's internal dynamic, as skills and other kinds of implicit knowledge developed and were communicated, ensured that agglomeration and specialization would follow. Porter's (1990: 72) "diamond," and his view that sectoral clustering is the engine of industrial and national growth, requires us to look at these geographical phenomena anew. While the precise learning mechanisms remained unclear, Porter's argument was that increased interaction and competition within the domestic industry accelerates innovation and international competitiveness. Indeed he remarked that geographical proximity elevated the diamond's separate influences into a true system (1990: 157).

Krugman (1993) has argued that economic analysts pay insufficient attention to location. Returning to classical theory, Krugman argued that Marshall saw three reasons for localization. First, concentrating a number of firms in the same place leads to a pool of skilled workers which generates a portfolio of possibilities for both firms and workers. Second, the localization of the market for other non-tradable inputs provides potential economies of scale and promotes the development of an infrastructure offering greater variety and lower cost. Finally, the localization of the flow of information promotes technological spillovers and the development of new products and services. Krugman observed that the last knowledge-based reason was that most often given for the clustering in Silicon Valley or along Route 128. Clustering may be especially important for modern high-technology information-intensive industries. Krugman explained the happenstance that led to the development of the cluster of carpet manufacturers around Dalton, Georgia, and, by extension, that of many other industrial districts. He also marshaled statistical evidence to show that most nonservice industries, high- and low-technology alike, are heavily localized and thus confirmed Florence's (1961: 24) earlier findings. Thus a theory of localization needs to embrace all industries, not only those heavily involved with science. Krugman argued that the first two explanations, which deal with easily obtained data about economies of scale, specialization and transportation costs, are surprisingly powerful, and that the knowledge- and spillover-based explanations depend on data that are difficult to obtain and have no special merit.

Localization, and its relationship to technological innovation, has also been studied extensively in Europe (e.g. Aydalot and Keeble 1988). Aydalot (1988: 23) offered three basic models of regional innovation which reveal different reasons for localization. The first is the restructuring and modernizing of preexisting industrial districts. Sometimes, under extreme pressure from technological obsolescence or external competition, firms successfully renew themselves, though maybe with a significant reduction in numbers and market share. The collapse of the Swiss watch-making industry in the Jura region between 1975 and 1985, and its resurgence in the 1990s with Swatch, was an example of this type of local revitalization. It was based on continuity among the pool of workers and on their skills. While new management had to bring in new electronic technology and develop additional skills, many other aspects of the industry remained the same. The second kind of local development is when large enterprises relocate plants in order to be closer to their markets, or to take advantage of preferential tax or investment supports or pools of skilled labor. They bring in new equipment and capital, train the existing workers into new skills, and develop their own infrastructure. The highly successful Nissan plant in the Tyne and Wear region in the north of England (Keeble 1988: 69) was an example of this second mechanism. The difference is that the knowledge necessary for the new activity was, in this instance, developed externally and applied locally whereas in the Swatch example, much of the necessary knowledge was generated internally within the region. Finally, Aydalot (1988: 23) proposed a mechanism focusing on the transfer of knowledge from university and research settings into commerce. Examples here are the high-tech firms around Cambridge (Keeble 1988: 88) and the influence of MIT over the Boston region (Rosegrant and Lampe 1992). The region to the west of London, though not drawing directly on universities, contains a number of government and defense-related laboratories (Keeble 1988: 90).

Aydalot's categories do not bear directly on our hypothesis that geographically constrained collective knowledge figures largely in localization and so leads directly to rents, advantage and high performance. But they provide ways of analyzing regional economic phenomena that, like Krugman's arguments, should probably be considered before we resort to psychological approaches. Best (1990: 234) argued that several of the industrial districts he studied, such as the north London furniture industry, could be explained in terms of economies of scale and the development of specialized infrastructure. In contrast, the "Third Italy" or Emilia-Romagna region could not be so explained. The explanatory emphasis must be shifted from the issues of distribution and labor productivity to those of industrial organization, both internal and external to the individual firms. In particular the interfirm institutions must be studied historically. Crucial, Best (1990: 235) argued, was the industrial district's capacity to innovate collectively rather than hierarchically, the result of some process such as the government might set up (1990: 207). His studies showed how particular political and historical circumstances were influential in the region's recovery.

Saxenian (1994) explored the differences in the way the Route 128 and Silicon Valley regions recovered from recent downturns—given that both seem good examples of localized industrial districts. She argued that Route 128 was less responsive than Silicon Valley and concluded that geographical proximity to other firms and local access to high-powered universities were not the sole determinants of their innovative activity. Best argued that the political context of Emilia-Romagna was crucial. Regional politics mattered less in Silicon Valley and Route 128. However the interfirm institutions which are characteristic of the Californian region, the extensive professional networks among the engineers, the executives and the venture capitalists, the rapid movement of personnel between firms, but, most of all, the close collaboration and mutual dependence between the different firms, were crucial. Route 128, by comparison, was largely populated by firms whose culture restrained the development of such interfirm institutional structures. DEC, Wang, Apollo, Symbolics and Data General were all intent on vertical integration and secure boundaries around the firm. They promoted formality, secrecy and hostility to the other firms in the region. Hewlett-Packard, Fairchild, Intel, Tandem and Apple, among the larger firms in Silicon Valley, showed a remarkable commitment to openness, interaction and mutual dependence. The most extreme example, according to Saxenian, was Sun Microsystems. Maybe making a virtue of necessity, Sun deliberately chose to start out with an open technology which virtually denied them any possibility of proprietary technology (Saxenian 1994: 141). They focused on service rather than product and bet that their close relationships with their suppliers and customers, and their aggressive and committed employees, would enable them to bring new technology to their customers faster than any of their competitors. Sun became Saxenian's archetype of the dynamic collective approach as the boundaries around the activity system were opened up to customers and suppliers alike. The resulting learning was both contextualized and rapid.

The multi-stage history of these regions is also important and is illuminated by Aydalot's categories. Both districts began from the university research in the area, corresponding to Aydalot's third category. Later, during the Korean and Vietnam wars, both experienced massive infusions of defense-related funding, corresponding to his second category. Soon Route 128 was the world's minicomputer center, while Silicon Valley was the world's memory chip center. Both suffered major reversals due to technological advances which, on the one hand, eclipsed the minicomputer and, on the other, resulted in DRAM production going overseas. Saxenian's study focused on the regions' very different responses to these downturns. While interfirm institutional activity grew in Silicon Valley and reinforced an extraordinary pace of development in disc drives and custom ASIC and RISC chips, the relative lack of such interaction in the Boston area led to a lesser recovery. Saxenian noted the counterintuitively large flow of East Coast venture capital to the West Coast. The implication is that the Silicon Valley firms redrew their boundaries to encompass a more powerful learning and innovation system. It required the development of collective knowledge in the community, observable as new institutional fabric. Saxenian's story may be overtold, but the outlines seem compelling.

There is the alternative idea of the importance of a number of firms pursuing similar innovations at the same time (Nelson 1961; Nelson and Winter 1982: 387; Scherer 1992: 180). Scherer, who has analyzed the US response to international high-technology competition, has also argued the importance of "learning by doing" (1992: 19) and of directed interactions between firms, government and industry. Saxenian's analysis fits with the widespread belief in the importance of close interaction to the vitality of networks and alliances. Powell and Brantley (1992: 389), examining the same phenomena in a different industry, likewise argued that the vitality of new biotechnology is a result of the cooperative interaction between large numbers of organizations. It leads to a new "locus of innovation," broadly dispersed through the network, producing new collective knowledge.

6. CONCLUSIONS

In this paper we have followed the current inquiries into organizational knowledge as the source of rents and strategic competence. We have focused particularly on geographical phenomena, localization, swarming and industrial districts. The localization of industry is especially interesting to analysts of the "new competition" who have argued that openness, interdependency and networking portend a new type of organization. Our objective has been to sketch a knowledge-based theory of the firm in which geography matters. This requires us to develop a geography of organizational knowledge rather than the traditional geography of transportation costs.

We began by proposing a matrix of four types of organizational knowledge. The upper part of the matrix, containing the individual and social objective types, deals with explicit knowledge. The lower part, containing the individual automatic and the collective types, deals with implicit knowledge. The upper is abstract, the knowledge is conveyed in symbols, leading to learning by communication. The information revolution would seem to make geography less important. But in the matrix's lower part, the knowledge is embedded in practice and is often defined as incommunicable and learning is by doing, especially by interacting. Here geographical proximity is crucial and communications technology less relevant. Inasmuch as this kind of knowledge, especially collective knowledge, is strategically important, geography continues to matter.

We argued that real organizations contain all four types of knowledge, thus combining knowledge with action in a purposive pattern of activity, but that each type of knowledge can, in principle, be associated with a different kind of rent and competitive advantage. Thus objective knowledge can be associated with monopoly rents, individual knowledge with Pareto quasi-rents. The collective knowledge which develops as the key players interact under conditions of uncertainty leads to Penrose rents, so labeled because such activity-based learning lies at the core of her theory of the growth of the firm. We argue that these rents are the principal reason for the existence of firms. Here we follow Alchian and Demsetz's view that the firm is a mechanism for monitoring and assigning property rights to the results of team production, but add that it is even more so a mechanism for creating collective knowledge and thus absorbing the uncertainties of the context in which it is embedded. Drawing on Vygotsky's theory of learning, we sketched how collective knowledge develops from directed practice, so providing a theoretical basis for the oft-used but still vague notions of learning by doing. This contrasts with learning by the communication of explicit knowledge. Effective organizations, containing all four types of knowledge, clearly need to achieve both kinds of learning, but the geographical implications of each are clearly different.

This framework suggests a contingency theory of systematic approaches to the pursuit of rents. Where the rents available to the industry result from government intervention, then the firms must engage in political activity and energetic rent-seeking. Where the rents available are the result of scientific research and the development of explicit knowledge, then management must focus on establishing intellectual property rights, and resisting their appropriation. However, there are many situations in which Penrose rents can be generated from collective knowledge and these are not readily appropriable. They are highly contextualized, embedded in the firm's activity and have little value elsewhere. We argued that managing learning by doing requires close attention to the boundaries around the innovation system.

Considering some of the new industrial districts such as Emilia Romagna, Silicon Valley and Route 128, we argued that they could not be explained solely in terms of pooling of labor and economies of scale in the provision of nontradable factors. They were operating as autonomous interorganizational innovation systems generating Penrose rents. Understanding their geography is crucial. But, as Saxenian has shown, proximity is only a necessary condition. The attitudes, policies and strategies of the firms comprising the innovation system also matter. Without an organization-level commitment to openness and interdependency the industrial district's collective knowledge will not develop.

REFERENCES

Abbott, Andrew (1988), *The System of Professions: An Essay on the Division of Expert Labor* (Chicago: University of Chicago Press).
Alchian, Armen A. and Allen, William R. (1969), *Exchange and Production: Theory in Use* (Belmont, Calif.: Wadsworth).

——and Demsetz Harold (1972), "Production, Information Costs, and Economic Organization," *American Economic Review*, 62: 777–95.

Allaire, Yvan and Firsirotu, Michaela E. (1984), "Theories of Organizational Culture," *Organization Studies*, 5: 193–226.

Amit, Raphael and Schoemaker, Paul J. (1993), "Strategic Assets and Organizational Rent," *Strategic Management Journal*, 14: 33–46.

Aoki, Masahiko, Gustafson, Bo. and Williamson, Oliver E. (1990) (eds.), *The Firm as a Nexus of Treaties* (Newbury Park, Calif.: Sage Publications).

Arrow, Kenneth (1962), "The Economic Implications of Learning by Doing," *Review of Economic Studies*, 29: 155–73.

Aydalot, Philippe (1988), "Technological Trajectories and Regional Innovation in Europe," in Philippe Aydalot and David Keeble (eds.), *High Technology Industry and Innovative Environments: The European Experience* (London: Routledge), 22–47.

Bargh, John A. (1989), "Conditional Automaticity: Varieties of Automatic Influence in Social Perception and Cognition," in James S. Uleman and John A. Bargh (eds.), *Unintended Thought* (New York: Guilford Press), 3–51.

Barney, J. B. and Ouchi, W. B. (1986) (eds.), *Organizational Economics* (San Francisco and London: Jossey-Bass), pp. xix, 495.

Barnard, Chester I. (1938), *The Functions of the Executive* (Cambridge, Mass.: Harvard University Press).

Best, Michael H. (1990), *The New Competition: Institutions of Industrial Restructuring* (Cambridge, Mass.: Harvard University Press).

Blumer, Herbert (1969), *Symbolic Interactionism: Perspective and Method* (Englewood Cliffs NJ: Prentice-Hall).

Bollier, David (1993), *The Promise and Perils of Emerging Information Technologies* (Queenstown, Md.: Aspen Institute).

Brown, John S. and Duguid, Paul (1991), "Organizational Learning and Communities-of-Practice: Towards a Unified View of Working, Learning, and Innovation," *Organization Science*, 2: 40–57.

Buchanan, James M. (1980), "Rent Seeking and Profit Seeking." in J. M. Buchanan, R. D. Tollison and G. Tullock (eds.), *Toward a Theory of the Rent-Seeking Society* (College Station, Tex.: Texas A & M University Press), 3–15.

Cassell, Joan (1991), *Expected Miracles: Surgeons at Work* (Philadelphia, Pa.: Temple University Press).

Chandler, Alfred D. (1962), *Strategy and Structure: Chapters in the History of the American Industrial Enterprise* (Cambridge, Mass.: MIT Press).

Coase, Ronald H. (1937), "The Nature of the Firm," *Economica*, NS, 4: 386–405.

Cohen, Michael D. (1991), "Individual Learning and Organizational Routine: Emerging Connections," *Organization Science*, 2/1: 135–9.

Cohen, Wesley M. and Levinthal, Daniel A. (1990), "Absorptive Capacity: A New Perspective on Learning and Innovation," *Administrative Science Quarterly*, 35: 128–52.

Commons, John R. (1957), *Legal Foundations of Capitalism* (Madison, Wisc.: University of Wisconsin Press).

Connerton, Paul (1989), *How Societies Remember* (Cambridge: Cambridge University Press).

Csikszentmihalyi, M. (1988), "The Flow Experience and its Significance for Human

Regions

Psychology," in M. Csikszentmihalyi and I. S. Csikszentmihalyi (eds.), *Optimal Experience: Psychological Studies of Flow in Consciousness* (Cambridge: Cambridge University Press), 15–35.

Daft, Richard and Lengel, Robert H. (1984), "Information Richness: A New Approach to Managerial Behavior and Organization Design," *Research in Organization Behavior*, 6: 191–233.

———— (1986), "Organizational Information Requirements, Media Richness, and Structural Design," *Management Science*, 32: 554–71.

Demsetz, Harold (1968), "Why Regulate Utilities?" *Journal of Law and Economics*, 11: 55–65.

Detienne, Marcel and Vernant, Jean-Pierre (1978), *Cunning Intelligence in Greek Culture and Society* (Hassocks, Sussex: Harvester).

Dosi, Giovanni, Gianetti, Renato and Toninelli, Pier A. (1992) (eds.), *Technology and Enterprise in a Historical Perspective* (Oxford: Clarendon Press).

Durkheim, Emile (1964), *The Division of Labor in Society* (New York: Free Press).

Ekelund, Robert B. and Tollison, Robert D. (1981), *Mercantilism as a Rent-Seeking Society: Economic Regulation in Historical Perspective* (College Station, Tex.: Texas A & M University Press).

Ferguson, Eugene S. (1992), *Engineering and the Mind's Eye* (Cambridge, Mass.: MIT Press).

Florence, P. Sargant (1961), *The Logic of British and American Industry*, rev. edn. (London: Routledge & Kegan Paul).

Furubotn, Eirik G. and Richter, Rudolf (1991) (eds.), *The New Institutional Economics: A Collection of Articles from the Journal of Institutional and Theoretical Economics* (College Station, Tex.: Texas A & M University Press).

Goodenough, W. H. (1971), *Culture, Language and Society: McCaleb Module in Anthropology* (Reading, Mass.: Addison-Wesley).

Halbwachs, Maurice (1992), *On Collective Memory* (Chicago: University of Chicago Press).

Hedlund, Gunnar (1992), "A Model of Knowledge Management and the Global N-form Corporation," Working Paper RP 92/10, Institute of International Business, Stockholm School of Economics.

———— and Ikujiro Nonaka. (1991), "Models of Knowledge Management in the West and in Japan." Working Paper RP 91/9, Institute of International Business, Stockholm School of Economics.

James, William (1950), *The Principles of Psychology*, i and ii (New York: Dover).

Keeble, David (1988), "High-technology Industry and Local Environments in the United Kingdom," in Aydalot and Keeble (eds.), *High Technology Industry and Innovative Environments*, 65–98.

Kidder, Tracy (1982), *The Soul of a New Machine* (New York: Avon Books).

Klein, Benjamin, Crawford, Robert G. and Alchian, Armen (1978), "Vertical Integration, Appropriable Rents and the Competitive Contracting Process," *Journal of Law and Economics*, 21: 297–326.

Kogut, Bruce and Udo Zander (1992), "Knowledge of the Firm, Combinative Capabilities, and the Replication of Technology," *Organization Science*, 3: 383–97.

Krugman, Paul R. (1993), *Geography and Trade* (Cambridge, Mass.: MIT Press).

Larson, Carl E. and LaFasto, Frank M. J. (1989), *Teamwork: What Must Go Right/ What Can Go Wrong* (Newbury Park, Calif.: Sage Publications).

Lave, Jean (1988), *Cognition in Practice: Mind, Mathematics and Culture in Everyday Life* (Cambridge: Cambridge University Press).

——and Wenger, Etienne (1992), *Situated Learning: Legitimate Peripheral Participation* (New York: Cambridge University Press).

Ledyard, John O. (1989), "Market Failure," in J. Eatwell, M. Milgate and P. Newman (eds.), *The New Palgrave: Allocation, Information, and Markets* (New York: W. W. Norton), 185–90.

Lewicki, P. (1986), *Nonconscious Social Information Processing* (New York: Academic Press).

Mahoney, Joseph T. and Pandian, J. Rajendran (1992), "The Resource-Based View Within the Conversation of Strategic Management," *Strategic Management Journal*, 13: 363–80.

Marshall, Alfred (1964), *Elements of the Economics of Industry* (London: Macmillan).

——(1969), *Principles of Economics: An Introductory Volume*, 8th edn. (London: Macmillan).

Mead, George H. (1962), *Mind, Self and Society* (Chicago: University of Chicago Press).

Milgrom, Paul and Roberts, John (1992), *Economics, Organization and Management* (Englewood Cliffs, NJ: Prentice-Hall).

Nelson, Richard R. (1961), "Uncertainty, Learning and the Economics of Parallel Research and Development Efforts," *Review of Economics and Statistics*, 43 (Nov.), 351–68.

——and Winter, Sidney G. (1982), *An Evolutionary Theory of Economic Change* (Cambridge, Mass.: Belknap Press).

Nohria, Nitin and Eccles, Robert G. (1992) (eds.), *Networks and Organizations: Structure, Form and Action* (Boston, Mass.: Harvard Business School Press).

Nonaka, Ikujiro (1994), "A Dynamic Theory of Organizational Knowledge Creation," *Organization Science*, 5/1 (Feb.), 14.

——and Takeuchi, H. (1995), *The Knowledge-Creating Company* (London: Oxford University Press).

North, Douglass C. (1990), *Institutions, Institutional Change and Economic Performance* (Cambridge: Cambridge University Press).

——(1991), "Institutions," *Journal of Economic Perspectives*, 5/1: 97–112.

Orr, Julian E. (1990), "Sharing Knowledge, Celebrating Identity: Community Memory in a Service Culture," in David S. Middleton and Derek Edwards (eds.), *Collective Remembering*: (Newbury Park, Calif.: Sage Publications), 169–89.

Oster, Sharon (1990), *Modern Competitive Analysis* (New York: Oxford University Press).

Penrose, Edith T. (1959), *The Theory of the Growth of the Firm* (New York: John Wiley).

——(1971), *The Growth of Firms, Middle East Oil and Other Essays* (London: Frank Cass).

Peteraf, Margaret A. (1993), "The Cornerstones of Competitive Advantage: A Resource-Base View," *Strategic Management Journal*, 14: 179–91.

Polanyi, Michael (1962), *Personal Knowledge: Towards a Post-critical Philosophy*, corr. edn. (Chicago: University of Chicago Press).

Porter, Michael E. (1980), *Competitive Strategy: Techniques for Analyzing Industries and Competitors* (New York: Free Press).

—— (1990), *The Competitive Advantage of Nations* (New York: Free Press).

Powell, Walter W. and Brantley, Peter (1992), "Competitive Cooperation in Biotechnology: Learning Through Networks?" in N. Nohria and R. G. Eccles (eds.), *Networks and Organizations* (Boston, Mass.: Harvard Business School Press), 366–94.

Reber, Arthur S. (1993), *Implicit Learning and Tacit Knowledge: An Essay on the Cognitive Unconscious* (New York: Oxford University Press).

Robinson, Joan (1969), *The Economics of Imperfect Competition*, 2nd edn. (Basingstoke: Macmillan).

Rogoff, Barbara and Lave, Jean (1984) (eds.), *Everyday Cognition: Its Development in Social Context* (Cambridge, Mass.: Harvard University Press).

Rosegrant, Susan and Lampe, David R. (1992), *Route 128: Lessons from Boston's High-tech Community* (New York: Basic Books).

Rumelt, Richard P. (1987), "Theory, Strategy, and Entrepreneurship," in Teece (ed.), *The Competitive Challenge*, 137–58.

Ryle, Gilbert (1949), *The Concept of Mind* (London: Hutchinson).

Saxenian, AnnaLee (1994), *Regional Advantage: Culture and Competition in the Silicon Valley and Route 128* (Cambridge, Mass.: Harvard University Press).

Schein, Edwin H. (1985), *Organizational Culture* (San Francisco: Jossey-Bass).

Scherer, F. M. (1980), *Industrial Market Structure and Economic Performance*, 2nd edn. (Chicago: Rand McNally).

—— (1992), *International High-Technology Competition* (Cambridge, Mass.: Harvard University Press).

Schutz, Alfred (1967), *Collected Papers: The Problem of Social Reality* (Amsterdam: Martinus Nijhoff).

—— (1972), *The Phenomenology of the Social World* (London: Heinemann).

Singley, Mark K. and Anderson, John R. (1989), *The Transfer of Cognitive Skill* (Cambridge, Mass.: Harvard University Press).

Spender, J.-C. (1989), *Industry Recipes: The Nature and Sources of Managerial Judgement* (Oxford: Blackwell).

—— (1993), "Competitive Advantage from Tacit Knowledge? Unpacking the Concept and its Strategic Implications," Academy of Management Best Paper Proceedings, 37–41.

—— and Kessler, Eric (1994), "Managing the Uncertainties of Innovation: Extending Thompson (1967)," *Human Relations* (forthcoming).

Starbuck, William H. (1983), "Organizations as Action Generators," *American Sociological Review*, 48: 91–102.

Suchman, Lucy (1987), *Plans and Situated Actions: The Problems of Human–Machine Communication* (Cambridge: Cambridge University Press).

Teece, D. (1987) (ed.), *The Competitive Challenge: Strategies for Industrial Innovation and Renewal* (Cambridge, Mass.: Ballinger).

Tharp, Roland G. and Gallimore, Ronald (1988), *Rousing Minds to Life: Teaching, Learning, and Schooling in Social Context* (Cambridge: Cambridge University Press).

Tullock, Gordon (1993), *Rent Seeking* (Aldershot, UK: Edward Elgar).

Vygotsky, Lev S. (1962), *Thought and Language* (Cambridge, Mass.: MIT Press).

Weick, Karl E. (1991), "The Nontraditional Quality of Organizational Learning," *Organization Science*, 2: 116–24.

—— and Roberts, Karlene H. (1993), "Collective Mind in Organizations: Heedful Interrelating on Flight Decks," *Administrative Science Quarterly*, 38: 357–81.

Williamson, Oliver E. (1975), *Markets and Hierarchies: Analysis and Antitrust Implications. A Study in the Economics of Internal Organization* (New York: Free Press).

—— (1985), *The Economic Institutions of Capitalism: Firms, Markets, Relational Contracting* (New York: Free Press).

—— and Winter, Sidney G. (1991) (eds.), *The Nature of the Firm: Origins, Evolution, and Development* (New York: Oxford University Press).

Winter, S. (1987), "Knowledge and Competences as Strategic Assets," Teece (ed.), *The Competitive Challenge*.

19

The Role of Geography in the Process of Innovation and the Sustainable Competitive Advantage of Firms*

MICHAEL E. PORTER AND ÖRJAN SÖLVELL

1. INTRODUCTION

In order to advance our understanding of how firms build and sustain competitive advantage over time, this book has suggested a new avenue of research involving the intersection of three fields; technology, strategy/organization and economic geography. The Competitive Advantage of Nations project (Porter 1990) was an early step in exploring this intersection. The Dynamic Firm Symposium, held in Stockholm in 1994, sought to bring together leading thinkers in these three fields and propose a long-term research agenda. In this chapter we will highlight some ways in which our understanding of innovation and competitive advantage can be enhanced by introducing the role of location. As time has passed since the symposium, there is an unmistakable trend towards work that brings these fields together.

2. ECONOMIC GEOGRAPHY

In the literature on economic geography there have been two important observations related to location and firm performance. First, economic, entrepreneurial and technological activities tend to agglomerate at certain places, leading to patterns of national and regional specialization. In fact, the persistent differences in economic performance of nations, and of states, regions and cities within nations, are striking. Second, the growth and performance of firms seems to a considerable extent to be influenced by the conditions that prevail in its environment. Conditions in the immediate proximity—in the local cluster—seem to be particularly important (Porter 1996; Malmberg, Sölvell and Zander 1996).

* We would like to thank Anders Malmberg and Ivo Zander for bringing our attention to some of the evolving bridges between the three areas of research which is the focus of this book. We would also like to thank them for valuable comments in preparing this concluding chapter.

Agglomeration

Agglomeration theory has evolved in response to three sets of empirical observations. First, a large proportion of total world output of particular goods is produced in a limited number of highly concentrated regions. Second, firms in particular industries, or firms which are technologically or otherwise related, tend to colocate and form spatial clusters. Third, both these phenomena tend to be persistent over time. Once in place, the agglomerative process tends to be cumulative as Myrdal (1957), Hirschman (1958), Ullman (1958) and Pred (1977) noted already several decades ago. This observation is consistent with the literature on technological trajectories.

The three sets of observations—regional concentration, spatial clustering and path dependence—have been described and analyzed by writers ranging from the early work by Marshall (1890/1916) and Weber (1909/1929), through such important building blocks as Hoover (1948) and Lloyd and Dicken (1977), to the new treatments by Porter (1990), Krugman (1991) and Enright (1997), to mention but a few.

A distinction should be made between two broad types of agglomeration economies. One type relates to general economies of regional and urban concentration that apply to all firms and industries in a single location. Such external economies lead to the emergence of manufacturing belts or metropolitan regions. A second type are the specific economies that relate to firms engaged in similar or interlinked activities, leading to the emergence of industry clusters, industrial districts, and innovative milieux. These two sets of forces have been referred to as urbanization economies and localization economies, respectively (Lloyd and Dicken 1977).

In both cases, agglomeration economies have their roots in processes whereby links between firms, institutions and infrastructures within a geographic area give rise to economies of scale and scope: the development of general labour markets and pools of skills; enhanced interaction between local suppliers and customers; shared infrastructure; and other localized externalities (Hoover 1948). Agglomeration economies are believed to arise when such links either lower the costs or increase the revenues, or both, of the firms taking part in the local exchange. Presence in an agglomeration then, can be seen as improving performance by reducing the costs of transactions for both tangibles and intangibles (Appold 1995). Some treatments attribute agglomeration to the minimization of the distance between a firm and its trading partners, as well as to the rapidity with which communication can take place between customers and suppliers. In Scott's (1983, 1988) formulation, regionalized industrial systems will be particularly likely where linkages tend to be small-scale, unstable and unpredictable, and hence subject to high unit cost.

Both generalized agglomeration of economic activity and spatial cluster-

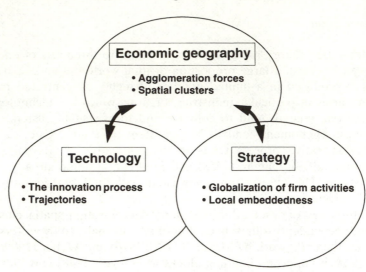

FIG. 19.1. Technology and strategy bridging to economic geography

ing of related firms and industries have traditionally been seen as driven by efficiency considerations. In particular, explanatory models are based on economies of scale in transportation and transaction costs. A more recent line of research has built models around the notion of flexible production systems in a more fast-moving world (Piore and Sabel 1984), but we would argue that the corresponding agglomeration model, i.e. industrial districts, is still oriented towards efficiency considerations. However, the industrial district model is interesting in that it highlights the special dynamism associated with firms using highly skilled proximate outside supply sources (flexible specialization) rather than the vertically integrated firm based on static efficiency.

Dynamic Accounts

Recent research approaches recognize the effects of clusters on efficiency but also emphasize dynamic effects. The focus is on the importance of localized information flows, technological spillover, and the creation of specialized pools of knowledge and skill when trying to explain the emergence and sustainability of spatial clusters of related firms. In this view, emphasized by Porter (1990), industry clusters are made up not only of physical flows of inputs and outputs, but also by intense exchange of business information, insight into customer needs, know-how, and technological expertise. Such knowledge comes in traded and untraded form (Scott 1995). In addition to reductions in the costs of interfirm and interindustry exchange and improved circulation of information and capital, increasing emphasis is now being placed on the role that spatial clustering may lead to reinforcement of transaction-based modes of social solidarity in a "Marshallian atmosphere." The latter point is of course far from new, since Marshall more than a century ago made a point of this "social effect" of localization when it comes to the stimulation of upgrading:

When an industry has thus chosen a locality for itself, it is likely to stay there long: so great are the advantages which people following the same skilled trade get from near neighbourhood to one another. The mysteries of the trade become no mysteries; but are as it were in the air, and children learn many of them unconsciously. Good work is rightly appreciated, inventions and improvements in machinery, in processes and the general organization of the business have their merits promptly discussed: if one man starts a new idea, it is taken up by others and combined with suggestions of their own; and thus it becomes the source of new ideas. And presently subsidiary trades grow up in the neighbourhood, supplying it with implements and materials . . . (Marshall 1890/1916: 271)

While Marshall's main concern was the existence and reproduction of spatial clusters of related firms, there are corresponding attempts to analyze the "learning abilities" of regional and urban agglomerations of the general type (Andersson 1985). Instead of specialization and spatial clustering of related industries, emphasis is here placed on the presence of a regional variety of skills and competencies, where the—often unplanned—interaction between different actors will lead to new—often unexpected—ideas or synergies (Malecki 1991; Johannisson 1987). In practice, however, such synergies seem to occur at the intersections among clusters rather than among collections of isolated disparate firms.

Recent work emphasizes that the benefits of agglomeration are subtle and combine social as well as purely economic influences, and suggest that the key to understanding both agglomeration in general and industry clusters lies in the superior ability of such spatial configurations to enhance learning, creativity and innovation, defined in a broad sense (Porter 1990; Saxenian 1994). Some basic characteristics of clusters may be identified. They contain multiple actors (firms, institutions) that are relatively autonomous in terms of decision making and strategy formulation. The interaction between these actors contains an element of both cooperation and rivalry. Furthermore, clusters are characterized by a specific set of tangible (firms, infrastructure), intangible (knowledge, know-how) and institutional (authorities, legal framework) elements. These elements make up a complex web of relations that tie firms, customers, research institutions, schools and local authorities to each other. The interaction between economic, sociocultural, political and institutional actors in a given location triggers learning and enhances the ability of actors to modify their behavior and find new solutions in response to competitive changes.

In the local cluster, it is argued, the fluidity of knowledge will be improved by the development of common codes of communication and interaction, particularly valuable when knowledge is difficult or costly to codify, and by the buildup of trust between interacting parties. To a large extent, a common location will offer language and cultural similarities which improve the ease of communication. The local cluster thus offers an environment for the evolution of a common language, social bonds, norms, values and institutions, i.e. a social capital (Putnam 1993; Enright, 1994) which adds to the process of accumulated learning. Within a local cluster, these institutional arrangements become increasingly specialized and unique, adding to the fluidity of knowledge exchange. This view of clusters has an affinity with the "innovative milieu approach" that has been developed predominantly in the French-speaking literature (Aydalot 1986; Maillat 1994).

3. THE BRIDGE BETWEEN TECHNOLOGY AND GEOGRAPHY

By bringing in theory from economic geography we can enrich research on the process of innovation and the strategic and organizational processes involved in creating sustainable competitive positions in world markets.

A central focus of the technology literature has been the innovation process, including incremental improvements in the product, architectural innovation putting together standard parts in unique ways, process innovation, and major breakthroughs. While the external environment in the form of buyers, suppliers and research organizations is treated in studies of innovation, issues related to geography are rarely addressed. Empirical studies of innovation networks are often nationally bound.

A subdiscipline within the technology field has built a new empirical tradition based on patent data. Here, a strong case for historically bound patterns or trajectories locking in firms and nations over substantial periods of time is developing (Pavitt 1988; Cantwell 1991a; Archibugi and Pianta 1992). Evolutionary-based theories have emphasized limited search routines, cumulative learning and learning-by-doing, suggesting that location and proximity are critical variables in the innovation process (for an overview, see Zander 1994).

Research on the innovation process has identified at least three important interrelated characteristics. First, the need for incremental reduction of technical and economic uncertainty over time. Second, the need for interaction with outside parties. Third, the need for face-to-face contacts in order to improve communication in the exchange and creation of new knowledge. The first characteristic derives from the fact that innovative processes are fundamentally uncertain in terms of technical feasibility and market acceptance (Freeman 1982, 1991; Pearson 1991). There is evidence that only one out of ten research projects turns out a commercial success, and that many patented inventions never find any direct commercial applications (Pavitt 1991; Schmookler 1966; Basberg 1987). Although the level of uncertainty varies with the type of innovation, the technical aspects are commonly worked out by means of trial-and-error testing and modification. Incrementalism and trial-and-error problem-solving in turn lead to a need for continuous interaction, both in informal networks and formal cooperative agreements.

The second feature of the innovation process is that ideas frequently originate outside the firm that carries out the actual development or manufacturing work (Pavitt 1984). In fact, only a small proportion of all innovations has been found to be directed towards use within the innovating organization (Scherer 1984). The importance of customers as sources of innovation has been verified in several studies (Håkansson 1989; Laage-Hellman 1989), while others have added evidence that the development of functionally useful innovations is sometimes dominated by the suppliers (von Hippel 1988). In yet other cases, several firms might be involved in joint development work, by which each of the participants supplies a limited component of the resulting innovation. This makes the innovation process highly interactive—between firms and the basic scientific infrastructure, between producers and users at the interfirm level and between firms and their wider institutional setting (Lundvall 1988; Nelson 1993; Morgan 1995).

Influences on technological innovation take on many forms, ranging from the one-time transfer of information to more extensive interaction between individual firms. However, there are reasons to believe that repeated interaction and lasting arrangements for the exchange of knowledge between firms, or technical learning, is very common in the innovation process. The importance of long-term producer and buyer relationships for the exchange and creation of new knowledge has been stressed by several authors (Lundvall 1988, 1993; Håkansson and Eriksson 1993; Hallén, Johanson and Seyed-Mohamed 1993). This exchange frequently involves sensitive information, which might cause damage if used opportunistically by the firms involved, and therefore requires a high level of trust between the parties. Similar linkages between the scientific community and firms engaged in technological improvements have also been illustrated (Freeman 1982).

The third characteristic of the innovation process is the employment of informal mechanisms for knowledge exchange. In spite of increasingly sophisticated means of communication, the need for personal, face-to-face contacts in the exchange of information has far from disappeared (Törnqvist 1970; Fredriksson and Lindmark 1979; Nohria and Eccles 1992). Also, personal contacts have been identified as important sources of technological information and improvements in the innovation process (Leonard-Barton 1982; de Meyer 1991, 1992). Moreover, traditional wisdom suggests that there is "friction of distance," implying that the probability of effective interpersonal communication through face-to-face contacts declines with increasing distance between individuals (Hägerstrand 1967; Pred 1977).

Face-to-face contacts appear to be of particular value for exchanging tacit knowledge, or when the exchange of knowledge involves direct observation of products or production processes in use. This type of knowledge typically does not reside in blueprints and formulae, but is based on personal skills and operational procedures which do not lend themselves to be presented and defined in either language or writing (Polanyi 1962; Winter 1987). Some studies indicate that informal and oral information sources are the key to discovering market opportunities and technological possibilities that lead to innovation. According to Utterback (1974), the unanticipated, or unplanned personal encounter often turns out to be most valuable. It is in this context that the geographically concentrated industrial configuration has substantial advantage over a dispersed configuration (Enright 1991, 1997).

The Local and Global Nature of the Innovation Process

The very nature of the innovation process as described above suggests strong links to geography. The nature of local customers and suppliers, the presence of nearby research institutions, and the intensity of local competition stressed by Porter (1990) become fundamental. The characteristics of innovation tend to make important aspects of technological activity locally confined (Malmberg, Sölvell and Zander 1996), while other technological activities are more global in character (e.g. basic scientific research, scientific publication, patents). In order to distinguish between the more local aspects and the more global aspects of the innovation process, a central issue is inertia and various barriers to diffusion of knowledge.

Inertia has always had a central place in the geographic literature, emphasizing the place-based firm. However, it is also central to the question of how easily knowledge embedded in one local cluster can be imitated by outside actors. If diffusion is indeed rapid and can be accomplished at low cost, globalization forces would override earlier locally confined innovation processes. If, on the other hand, diffusion in effect is sluggish, costly and involves long lead times, then localized innovation processes will remain essential. This distinction, in turn, has important implications for strategy and organization of firms, particularly the multinational firm with operations in many locations.

In order to understand the speed of international diffusion we must distinguish between the degree of mobility of knowledge embedded in physical, human and social capital. With reduced barriers to trade in the postwar period, knowledge embedded in physical capital such as standard materials, components, products and machinery moves relatively easily and at low cost. Even so, empirical studies have indicated that firms in one industrialized country experience considerable difficulty in deploying machinery developed in another industrialized country (Gertler 1995).

While some knowledge is embedded in materials, components, products and machinery, other knowledge is embedded in human capital, part of which is tacit. As a result of improved air transportation, an increasing proportion of skilled human capital, such as top management and scientific expertise, has become internationally mobile. However, highly specialized knowledge relating to applied technology appears to be far less mobile and difficult to decouple from the location. Moreover, an important part of human capital is embedded in a multitude of interfirm relationships and therefore cannot be taken out of context without losing much of its value. Applying that knowledge efficiently also depends on similar relationships (Porter 1994). These relationships include both formal and informal networks in the local cluster and have often been built over long time periods. Furthermore, the large groups of middle and lower level managers and workers, who are an important part of the formal and informal knowledge base and set of relationships between firms, are typically much less mobile than top management and experts. Finally, knowledge is continuously being created. Decoupling knowledge from the location where it is developed, then, increases lags that impact competitive advantage.

The formal and informal networks between people in a common location, which have often been developed through long-term interaction, and the resulting evolution of institutions form part of the social capital (Putnam 1993) surrounding local innovation processes. Whereas some knowledge embedded in physical and human capital travels the world through trade, investment, traveling and migration, knowledge embedded in social capital does not, as it involves a large number of actors within a local cluster and is path-dependent due to local circumstances, unique relationships and accumulated routines. Empirical evidence of the transfer of different principles of organizing work shows great difficulties and the need for extensive local adaptation as these principles are transferred (Kogut 1993). As the Swedish economist Johan Westerman wrote in 1768 "the new machines from England are important but they are of little use if there are not workers who understand how to use them and, if there is a lack of skill on how to organize production around them" (author' translation into English; Westerman 1768). In Figure 19.2 we can get an idea of increasing embeddedness as we move down from physical to social capital.

4. THE BRIDGE BETWEEN STRATEGY/ORGANIZATION AND GEOGRAPHY

Proximity and localization might seem paradoxical as a future research avenue in strategy and organization in an era of rapid globalization. As

International mobility Type of knowledge	High	Low
Knowledge embedded in physical capital	Materials Standard components and products Standard machinery Data in databases Blueprints CAD/CAM systems Published research	Certain newly launched components and machinery
Knowledge embedded in human capital	Top management Expertise	Middle management Personal networks
Knowledge embedded in social capital	Legal frameworks	History-bound routines Business practices Unique institutions Many linked actors

FIG. 19.2. International mobility of different types of knowledge

flows of people, products, information and capital are becoming increasingly extended in space, the question is whether there remains a role to be played by the local environment. Early observers came to the first-order conclusion that the role of the nation or region is rapidly diminishing with the emergence of global markets and firms. Others have begun to emphasize that globalization has neutralized many traditional competitive advantages and that the new methods of production in the "post-Fordist" era and new modes of transaction-based competition are a rejuvenating force for localization (Piore and Sabel 1984; Porter 1990; Amin and Malmberg 1992; Storper 1995).

Business scholars focusing on the multinational corporation (MNC), in particular, have raised doubts about the local environment as having an important role to play in how global firms formulate their strategies and build competitive advantage (Dunning 1993; Prahalad and Doz 1987; Bartlett and Ghoshal 1990). Yet a "counterreaction" has been set in motion which argues that the local environment, or what we call the home base, plays a continued or possibly increasingly important role for the global firm in particular businesses (Porter 1990; Sölvell and Zander 1995).

With the basis for competitive advantage rapidly shifting from static advantages of scale and low input prices to relentless innovation and upgrading of competitive advantage, the role of location is enhanced. Whereas firms can access global markets for most inputs, critical activities related to innovation such as strategic decision-making, R&D and core manufacturing and design, are, for each business segment, typically more embedded in one cluster or home base. In the home base the firm enjoys insider access to specialized inputs such as skill, applied technology and tailored infrastructure and a core of advanced customers and suppliers with which the firm can interact and create new knowledge. A dynamic cluster also offers stimulating rivalry shoulder-to-shoulder, with important informational and incentive benefits (Porter 1994).

Evolution of the Multinational Corporation

International business scholars have focused much attention on the emergence of large MNCs during the past century. Large MNCs have come to lead many industrial sectors, though we can also discern a pattern of small and medium-sized firms becoming multinational at a very early stage.

MNCs have begun to establish major operations outside their home countries as a result of long-term investment abroad, but more often through foreign mergers, acquisitions and strategic alliances (Dunning 1993). MNCs have typically built up international operations to access markets for final products and to a lesser extent factors of production. Whereas access to markets has been critical, access to technologies has come much later and on a smaller scale. In order to enhance its worldwide commercialization of products, MNCs have farflung networks of subsidiaries involving sales, service, local assembly and packaging and development functions. Typically, core manufacturing facilities, R&D laboratories and headquarters' functions are much less dispersed (see Figure 19.3).

However, leading MNCs have now established far more international organizations including a dispersion of core manufacturing and R&D facilities. Leading Dutch, British, Swiss and Swedish MNCs now have close to half or more of their R&D activity outside their home base (Papanastassiou and Pearce 1994; Håkanson and Nobel 1993; Zander 1994). Part of this R&D capacity has been built up over extended periods, but more often through mergers and acquisitions.

The establishment of foreign R&D centers has been driven by several factors. Traditional motivations include the need to efficiently transfer technology to subsidiaries (Dunning 1958), sometimes referred to as transfer technology units (Ronstadt 1977), the need for adaptation to fit local demands, direct pressures from host country governments, and sourcing of low-cost personnel (Terpstra 1977). A recent study of Swedish MNCs showed that 66% of all R&D centers were motivated by market proximity and political reasons. Hence the establishment of these R&D centers is driven by a concern for enhanced commercialization of core technologies created in the home base, i.e. of the home-base exploiting type (Kuemmerle 1996). Sometimes the development of foreign R&D capacity has been initiated from subsidiaries with growing ambitions (Birkinshaw 1995), drawing upon their local expertise and the local cluster (Andersson 1997). If these units are embedded in a leading cluster they may gain an international mandate over time as they become more and more important to the overall group. Such centers of excellence or global technology units (Ronstadt 1977) often form the basis for a new home base within a particular line of business.

In other cases the parent company, in its search for new strategic assets, decides to set up an R&D center close to a leading university or a dynamic cluster in order to tap into local expertise and to gain new ideas (Dunning and Narula 1995). This home-base augmenting strategy (Wesson 1993) is common in industries like electronics, computers, biotechnology, pharmaceuticals and chemicals. Whereas foreign monitoring units seem to be common among Japanese MNCs (Kuemmerle 1996) they are very rare among Swedish MNCs (Nobel 1996).

Even with the emergence of truly global firms with increased dispersion of production and R&D it does not follow that the innovation process has become a global phenomenon where spread-out units are tightly linked. For example, within the automobile industry there have been several attempts at integrating dispersed units in order to create a world-car concept—so far with little success (Jones 1989). Indeed, as recent research has shown, R&D centers tend to specialize, and duplication is kept to a minimum (Cantwell 1991*b*; Zander 1994). Sometimes a sequential pattern of specialization can be discerned where each unit is responsible for a part of the development process (Sölvell and Bresman 1997; Ridderstråle 1997).

Increasingly, divisional headquarters and all development activities for certain product or service areas are concentrated in home bases outside the home country (Wesson 1993; Dunning 1994; Zander 1994; Cantwell 1995). In these cases, diversified MNCs have created something of a "multi home-base" structure (Porter 1990; Forsgren, Holm and Johanson 1991; Sölvell, Zander and Porter 1991; Sölvell and Zander 1995), involving several distinct bases for innovation, often referred to as product mandates, centers of competence or centers of excellence (Birkinshaw 1996).

Where the leading MNCs are actually heading—global integration or multilocal specialization—is an empirical question, and there is some evidence for both cases. One set of studies emphasizes the integration of innovative activities across geographically dispersed units (Prahalad and

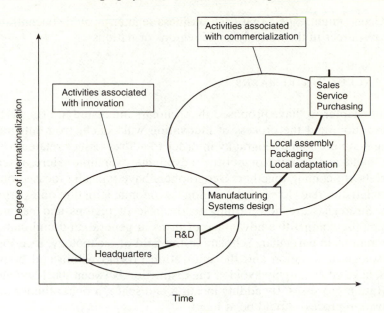

FIG. 19.3. Internationalization of innovation and commercialization activities of the firm

Doz 1987; Bartlett and Ghoshal 1990; Hedlund and Rolander 1990; Ridderstråle 1997). Implicitly, the authors stress the development of an "organizational capital" within the MNC organization, by which a common set of norms, values and routines makes it possible to overcome differences in social capital across regions (Hedlund 1986). In well-established MNCs, the geographically dispersed network of subsidiaries becomes a means for rapid knowledge exchange, leading to the development of unique advantages from the integration of the global corporate system.

However, there is also strong empirical evidence that MNCs are tied in with certain home bases (Porter 1990; Sölvell, Zander and Porter 1991; Wesson 1993; Zander 1994; Kuemmerle 1996). The emergence of specialized bases and centers of excellence would mainly be explained by the increasing costs and lengthened development times associated with innovation across geographical distances, which will be a significant disadvantage in global competition. Several authors have emphasized the difficulties involved in creating a set of common norms, values and working routines in the MNC that are necessary for cross-border innovation to take place (Kilduff 1992; Håkanson 1995; Holm, Johanson and Thilenius 1995). If, indeed, MNCs face inefficiencies resulting from internationally coordinated innovation processes, they would probably retain their character of local innovators and remain global commercializers. In the case of the diversified

MNC, one might expect that each business segment would concentrate its core resources in the most dynamic regions or nations.

5. CONCLUDING REMARKS

In this chapter we have proposed that scholars interested in firm strategy, organization, and the process of innovation will benefit from integrating research on economic geography in order to address issues related to how firms build and sustain competitive advantage over time. Here, research interests are coming together. Geographers have typically focused on the characteristics that determine a region's economic structure and performance. Strategists are now turning to the role of regions and nations in shaping the competitive advantage of firms in general, and multinational corporations in particular. Scholars in the field of technology, focusing on technological evolution and the innovation process within and between firms, have so far largely avoided the distinction between local and global innovation processes. By adding location and space, a richer theory of the innovation process should be at hand.

Locked-in disciplinary research has often limited the scope for new ground-breaking research. Just as there is often room for arbitrage among locations in global competition, there should be room for academic arbitrage between the fields emphasized here.

REFERENCES

Amin, A. and Malmberg, A. (1992), "Competing Structural and Institutional Influences on the Geography of Production in Europe," *Environment and Planning*, A24: 401–16.

Andersson, Å. E. (1985), "Creativity and Regional Development," *Papers of the Regional Science Association*, 56: 5–20.

Andersson, U. (1997), "Subsidiary Network Embeddedness: Integration, Control and Influence in the Multinational Corporation," Doctoral thesis, Dept. of Business Studies, Uppsala University.

Appold, S. J. (1995), "Agglomeration, Interorganizational Networks, and Competitive Performance in the U.S. Metalworking Sector," *Economic Geography*, 71: 27–54.

Archibugi, D. and Pianta, M. (1992), "Specialization and Size of Technological Activities in Industrial Countries: the Analysis of Patent Data," *Research Policy*, 21/1: 79–93.

Aydalot, P. (1986), *Milieux innovateurs en Europe* (Paris: GREMI).

Bartlett, C. A. and Ghoshal, S. (1990), "Managing Innovation in the Transnational Corporation," in C. A. Bartlett, Y. Doz and G. Hedlund (eds.), *Managing the Global Firm* (London: Routledge).

Basberg, B. L. (1987), "Patents and the Measurement of Technological Change: A Survey of the Literature," *Research Policy*, 16: 131–41.

Behrman, J. N. and Fischer, W. A. (1985), "Transnational Corporations: Market Orientations and R&D Abroad," in H. V. Wortzel and L. H. Wortzel (eds.), *Strategic Management of Multinational Corporations: The Essentials* (New York: John Wiley).

Birkinshaw, J. (1995), "The Entrepreneurial Process in Multinational Subsidiaries," unpub. Ph.D. thesis, Western Business School, University of Western Ontario, London, Ontario.

——(1996), "How Multinational Subsidiary Mandates are Gained and Lost," *Journal of International Business Studies*, 27/3: 467–95.

Cantwell, J. (1991*a*), "Historical Trends in International Patterns of Technological Innovation," in J. Foreman-Peck (ed.), *New Perspectives on the Late Victorian Economy: Essays in Quantitative Economic History 1860–1914* (Cambridge: Cambridge University Press).

——(1991*b*), "The International Agglomeration of R&D," in M. Casson (ed.), *Global Research Strategy and International Competitiveness* (Oxford: Blackwell).

——(1995), "The Globalization of Technology: What Remains of the Product Cycle Model?" *Cambridge Journal of Economics*, 19: 155–74.

de Meyer, A. (1991), "Tech Talk: How Managers are Stimulating Global R&D Communication," *Sloan Management Review* (Spring), 49–58.

——(1992), "Management of International R&D Operations," in O. Granstrand, L. Håkanson and S. Sjölander (eds.), *Technology Management and International Business* (Chichester: John Wiley).

Dunning, J. H. (1958), *American Investment in British Manufacturing Industry* (London: Allen and Unwin).

——(1993), *Multinational Enterprise and the Global Economy* (Wokingham, UK: Addison-Wesley).

——(1994), "Multinational Enterprises and the Globalization of Innovatory Capacity," *Research Policy*, 23: 67–88.

——and Narula, R. (1995), "The R&D Activities of Foreign Firms in the United States," *International Studies of Management and Organization*, 25/1–2: 39–73.

Enright, M. J. (1991), "Geographic Concentration and Industrial Organization," unpub. Ph.D. thesis, Department of Economics and Graduate School of Business Administration, Harvard University, Cambridge, Mass.

——(1997), "Regional Clusters and Firm Strategy," Ch. 14 this volume.

Estall, R. C. and Buchanan, R. O. (1961), *Industrial Activity and Economic Geography* (London: Hutchinson).

Forsgren, M., Holm, U. and Johanson, J. (1991), "Internationalisering av andra graden," in R. Andersson *et al.* (eds.), *Internationalisering, företagen och det lokala samhället* (Stockholm: SNS Förlag).

Fredriksson, C. and Lindmark, L. (1979), "From Firms to Systems of Firms: A Study of Interregional Dependence in a Dynamic Society," in F. E. I. Hamilton and G. J. R. Linge (eds.), *Spatial Analysis, Industry and the Industrial Environment: Progress in Research and Applications*, i *Industrial Systems* (Chichester: Wiley).

Freeman, C. (1982), *The Economics of Industrial Innovation.* 2nd edn. (London: Pinter).

——(1991), "Networks of Innovators: A Synthesis of Research Issues," *Research Policy*, 20: 499–514.

Gertler, M. S. (1995), "'Being there': Proximity, Organization, and Culture in the Development and Adoption of Advanced Manufacturing Technologies," *Economic Geography*, 71: 1–26.

Hägerstrand, T. (1967), *Innovation Diffusion as a Spatial Process* (Chicago: University of Chicago Press).

Hallén, L., Johanson, J. and Seyed-Mohamed, N. (1993), "Dyadic Business Relationships and Customer Technologies," *Journal of Business-to-Business Marketing*, 1: 63–90.

Håkansson, H. (1989), *Corporate Technological Behavior: Co-operation and Networks* (London: Routledge).

——and Eriksson, A.-K. (1993), "Getting Innovations Out of Supplier Networks," *Journal of Business-to-Business Marketing*, 1: 3–34.

Håkanson, L. (1995), "Learning Through Acquisitions: Management and Integration of Foreign R&D Laboratories," *International Studies of Management and Organization*, 25/1–2: 121–57.

——and Nobel, R. (1993), "Foreign Research and Development in Swedish Multinationals," *Research Policy*, 22/5, 6 (Nov.), 373–96.

Hedlund, G. (1986), "The Hypermodern MNC: A Heterarchy?" *Human Resource Management*, 25/1: 9–35.

——and Rolander, D. (1990), "Action in Heterarchies: New Approaches to Managing the MNC," in C. A. Bartlett, Y. Doz and G. Hedlund (eds.), *Managing the Global Firm.*

Hirschman, A. O. (1958), *The Strategy of Economy Development* (New Haven: Yale University Press).

Holm, U., Johanson, J. and Thilenius, P. (1995), "Headquarters' Knowledge of Subsidiary Network Contexts in the Multinational Corporation," *International Studies of Management and Organization*, 25/1–2: 97–119.

Hoover, E. M. (1948), *The Location of Economic Activity* (New York: McGraw-Hill).

Johannisson, B. (1987), "Toward a Theory of Local Entrepreneurship," in R. G. Wyckman, L. N. Merredith and G. R. Bush (eds.), *The Spirit of Entrepreneurship* (Vancouver, BC: Simon Fraser University).

Jones, D. T. (1989), "Corporate Strategy and Technology in the World Automobile Industry," in M. Dodgson (ed.), *Technology Strategy and the Firm: Management and Public Policy* (Harlow, Essex: Longman).

Kilduff, M. (1992), "Performance and Interaction Routines in Multinational Corporations," *Journal of International Business Studies,* 23: 133–45.

Kogut, B. (1993) (ed.), *Country Competitiveness: Technology and Organizing of Work* (Oxford: Oxford University Press).

Krugman, P. (1991), *Geography and Trade* (Cambridge, Mass.: MIT Press).

Kuemmerle, W. (1996), "Home Base and Foreign Direct Investment in Research and Development: An Investigation into the International Allocation of Research Activity by Multinational Enterprises," unpub. Doctoral diss., Graduate School of Business Administration, Harvard University.

Laage-Hellman, J. (1989), "Technological Development in Industrial Networks," *Acta Universitatis Upsaliensis*, 16 (Faculty of Social Sciences, Uppsala University, Uppsala).

Leonard-Barton, D. (1982), *Swedish Entrepreneurs in Manufacturing and Their Sources of Information* (Boston: Center for Policy Applications, MIT).

Lloyd, P. E. and Dicken, P. (1977), *Location in Space: A Theoretical Approach to Economic Geography*, 2nd edn. (London: Harper and Row).

Lundvall, B.-Å. (1988), "Innovation as an Interactive Process: From User–Producer Interaction to the National System of Innovation," in G. Dosi *et al.* (eds.), *Technical Change and Economic Theory*, (London: Pinter).

——(1993), "Explaining Interfirm Cooperation and Innovation: Limits of the Transaction-Cost Approach", in G. Grabher, (ed.), *The Embedded Firm: On the Socioeconomics of Industrial Networks* (London: Routledge).

Maillat, D. (1994), "Comportements spatiaux et milieux innovateurs," in J. P. Auray *et al.* (eds.), *Dictionnaire d'analyse spatiale* (Paris: Economica).

Malecki, E. J. (1991), *Technology and Economic Development: The Dynamics of Local, Regional and National Change* (New York: Longman Scientific and Technical).

Malmberg, A., Sölvell, Ö and Zander, I. (1996), "Spatial Clustering, Local Accumulation of Knowledge and Firm Competitiveness," *Geografiska Annaler, Series B, Human Geography*, 78B/2.

Marshall, A. (1890/1916), *Principles of Economics: An Introductory Volume*, 7th edn. (London: Macmillan).

Myrdal, G. (1957), *Economic Theory and the Underdeveloped Regions* (London: Ducksworth).

Nelson, R. R. (1993) (ed.), *National Innovation Systems: A Comparative Analysis* (New York: Oxford University Press).

Nobel, R. (1996), "Foreign R&D Units in Swedish MNCs," unpub. licentiate thesis, Institute of International Business, Stockholm School of Economics.

Nohria, N. and Eccles, R. G. (1992), "Face-to-Face: Making Network Organizations Work," in N. Nohria, and R. G. Eccles (eds.), *Networks and Organizations: Structure, Form, and Action* (Boston: Harvard Business School Press).

Papanatassiou, M. and Pearce, R. (1994), "The Internationalization of Research and Development by Japanese Enterprises," *R&D Management*, 24/2: 155–65.

Pavitt, K. (1984), "Sectoral Patterns of Technical Change: Towards a Taxonomy and a Theory," *Research Policy*, 13: 343–73.

——(1988), "International Patterns of Technological Accumulation," in N. Hood and J.-E. Vahlne (eds.), *Strategies in Global Competition* (London: Croom Helm).

——(1991), "Key Characteristics of the Large Innovating Firm," *British Journal of Management*, 2: 41–50.

Pearson, A. W. (1991), "Managing Innovation: An Uncertainty Reduction Process," in J. Henry and D. Walker (eds.), *Managing Innovation* (London: Sage).

Piore, M. and Sabel, C. (1984), *The Second Industrial Divide* (New York: Basic Books).

Polanyi, K. (1962), *Personal Knowledge: Towards A Post-Critical Philosophy* (Chicago: Chicago University Press).

Porter, M. E. (1990), *The Competitive Advantage of Nations* (London: Macmillan).

Porter, M. E. (1994), "The Role of Location in Competition," *Journal of the Economics of Business*, 1/1: 35–9.

——(1996), "Competitive Advantage, Agglomeration Economics, and Regional Policy," *International Regional Science Review*, 19/1 and 2.

Prahalad, C. K. and Doz, Y. (1987), *The Multinational Mission: Balancing Local Demands and Global Vision* (New York: Free Press).

Pred, A. (1977), *City Systems in Advanced Economies: Past Growth, Present Processes and Future Development Options* (London: Hutchinson).

Putnam, R. D. with Leonardi, R. and Nanetti, R. Y. (1993), *Making Democracy Work: Civic Traditions in Modern Italy* (Princeton: Princeton University Press).

Ridderstråle, J. (1997), *Global Innovation: Managing International Innovation Projects in ABB and Electrolux*, pub. Doctoral diss. (Stockholm: Institute of International Business, Stockholm School of Economics).

Ronstadt, R. (1977), *Research and Development Abroad by US Multinationals* (New York: Praeger).

Saxenian, A. (1994), *Regional Advantage: Culture and Competition in Silicon Valley and Route 128* (Cambridge, Mass.: Harvard University Press).

Scherer, F. M. (1984), *Innovation and Growth: Schumpeterian Perspectives* (Cambridge, Mass.: MIT Press).

Schmookler, J. (1966), *Inventions and Economic Growth* (Cambridge, Mass.: Harvard University Press).

Scott, A. J. (1983), "Industrial Organisation and the Logic of Intra-Metropolitan Location: 1. Theoretical Considerations," *Economic Geography*, 59: 233–50.

——(1988), *New Industrial Spaces: Flexible Production Organisation and Regional Development in North America and Western Europe* (London: Pion).

——(1995), "The Geographic Foundations of Industrial Performance," *Competition and Change*, 1: 51–66.

Sölvell, Ö. and Bresman, H. (1997), *Local and Global Forces in the Innovation Process of the Multinational Enterprise: An Hour-glass Model* (Copenhagen: Nordisk Institut for Regionalpolitisk Forskning) (forthcoming).

——and Zander, I. (1995), "Organization of the Dynamic Multinational Enterprise: The Home-Based and the Heterarchical MNE," *International Studies of Management and Organization*, 25/1–2: 17–38.

——Zander, I. and Porter, M. E. (1991), *Advantage Sweden* (Stockholm: Norstedts).

Storper, M. (1995), "The Resurgence of Regional Economies, Ten Years Later: The Region as a Nexus of Untraded Interdependencies," *European Urban and Regional Studies*, 2: 191–221.

Terpstra, V. (1977), "International Product Policy: The Role of Foreign R&D," *The Columbia Journal of World Business* (Winter), 24–32.

Törnqvist, G. (1970), "Contact Systems and Regional Development," *Lund Studies in Geography*, Ser. B. 35, University of Lund, Sweden.

Ullman, E. L. (1958), "Regional Development and the Geography of Concentration," *Papers and Proceedings of the Regional Science Association*, 4: 179–98.

Utterback, J. (1974), "Innovation in Industry and the Diffusion of Technology," *Science*, 183: 658–62.

von Hippel, E. (1988), *The Sources of Innovation* (Oxford: Oxford University Press).

Weber, A. (1909/1929), *Theory of the Location of Industries* (Chicago: University of Chicago Press).

Wesson, T. J. (1993), "An Alternative Motivation for Foreign Direct Investment," unpub. Doctoral diss., Department of Economics and Graduate School of Business Administration, Harvard University, Boston.

Westerman, J. (1768), *Om de svenske naeringarnes undervigt gentemot de utländske dymedelst en trögare arbetsdrift* (Stockholm).

Winter, S. G. (1987), "Knowledge and Competence as Strategic Assets," in D. Teece (ed.), *The Competitive Challenge: Strategies for Industrial Innovation and Renewal* (Cambridge, Mass.: Ballinger).

Zander, I. (1994), *The Tortoise Evolution of the Multinational Corporation: Technological Activity in Swedish Multinational Firms 1890–1990*, pub. Doctoral diss. (Stockholm: Institute of International Business, Stockholm School of Economics).

INDEX